COST ESTIMATING

COST ESTIMATING

SECOND EDITION

PHILLIP F. OSTWALD

University of Colorado
Boulder, Colorado

Prentice-Hall, Inc., Englewood Cliffs, New Jersey 07632

Library of Congress Cataloging in Publication Data

Ostwald, Phillip F.,
   Cost estimating.

   Rev. ed. of: Cost estimating for engineering and management. 1974.
   Bibliography: p.
   Includes index.
   1. Engineering—Estimates. I. Ostwald, Phillip F., . Cost estimating for engineering
and management. II. Title.
TA183.083 1984   658.1'55   83-27033
ISBN 0-13-181157-6

Editorial/production supervision: Mary Carnis
Cover design: Ben Santora
Manufacturing buyer: Anthony Caruso

Printed in the United States of America

10 9 8 7 6 5

ISBN 0-13-181157-6 01

Prentice-Hall International (UK) Limited, *London*
Prentice-Hall of Australia Pty. Limited, *Sydney*
Prentice-Hall Canada Inc., *Toronto*
Prentice-Hall Hispanoamericana, S.A., *Mexico*
Prentice-Hall of India Private Limited, *New Delhi*
Prentice-Hall of Japan, Inc., *Tokyo*
Simon & Schuster Asia Pte. Ltd., *Signapore*
Editora Prentice-Hall do Brasil, Ltda., *Rio de Janeiro*

To Doris, Mark, Phil, Lynne

Contents

Preface

Cost estimating is introduced in this text. As the first unified treatment, the book covers the philosophy, principles, and practices of a field that is growing in interest, enthusiasm, and numbers. This specialization is concerned with the evaluation of technology in business terms. While designs certainly differ, the principles and practices used for their appraisement are remarkably similar. We state, without proof, that all technology undergoes a business appraisal. This book, then, covers those subjects that contribute positively to the successful economic attainment of the design.

Design is given a broad and liberal interpretation. Every design (1) is a new combination (2) of preexisting knowledge (3) which satisfies an economic want. This three-part definition includes virtually every product and project such as airplanes, bridges, buildings, cars, chemical plants, computers, highways, machine tools, mining development, production lines, rockets, semi-conductors, ships, systems of machines and people, and toys. With technology as the focal point, cost estimating is the body of theory and business practice that provides an economic value for the design.

The experienced cost estimator, who, after a few times "looking down the barrel" defending his or her estimate (management calls it probing for softness; the estimator calls it picking on his professionalism), misunderstands management's interest in this topic. The exposure of cost overruns for weapon systems and public work projects testifies to the serious embarrassment that cost estimating has faced and the importance of this specialization for management. Indeed, the well-being of firms and our country rests, in part, on cost estimating. Business firms have realized that computer management information systems, notwithstanding their unmatched ability to handle data, are helpless to overcome a lack of trust in the truth of estimated data in their cost-forecasting systems. International trade and foreign competition with our past and future trading partners present a challenge, and cost and cost estimating will be important. Productivity needs an index, and cost estimating plays a prominent role in its measurement. Technology's impact on changing times, employment, growth and development, pricing efficiency, income, gold and foreign trade, and the blessings of our kind of democratic society are topics of today.

Cost estimating discloses the strengths of a company, country, or trading group for executive management—it should never hide weakness from management. Decisions, both large and small, depend in part on estimates. "Looking down the barrel" need not be an embarrassment for the cost estimator if newer techniques, professional staffing, and a greater awareness are provided for the cost-estimating function.

Cost is a nebulous term which has no standardized definition. Used in some contexts, it implies a meaning that is clearly not cost. To appreciate these distinctions, one must be prepared to understand the particular context in which the word is used. Surprisingly, the word cost could mean price, bid, or effectiveness, and dollars are one dimension for these measures. For management and many engineers, dollars are more important than amperes, foot-pounds, or mass flow. Whether the manager, businessman, or engineer is principally involved with cost-finding, profit, cost reduction, or value analysis, subtle variations of the word cost are understood.

The number of firms which provide a product is well above 250,000. In construction it is assumed that over 700,000 units are active. Perhaps when we consider professional estimating activities there may be over one million units in the United States. The field is not small. Each of these units *must* use modern cost estimating practices. The days of "guesstimating" are past.

This book would be suitable for courses such as Operations Planning, Cost Engineering, Industrial Analysis, Manufacturing Estimating, Construction Estimating, and Technology Planning, to name a few. These courses cover practical and theoretical techniques of cost estimating for various kinds of designs. Instructors teaching Engineering Economy will find a kindred usefulness for this text. Traditionally, engineering economy texts devote attention upon time-value-of-money concepts. This book reduces those principles to one section and instead concentrates upon the broader matters of estimating costs, time, etc. that are crucial for the time-value-of-money equations. This book is suitable for engineering and technology students whenever they reach their first level of specialization because specific programs restrict early opportunity for experimentation and broadening, and design evaluation is deferred. Although a great diversity of occupational problems has been included, the instructor may want to supplement the problems and design studies using his or her own experiences. The text covers both manufacturing and construction, as the distinctions between cost estimating principles are non-existent.

MBA programs, operations or production management, and other programs in the colleges of business may see fit to use this book. It should not be surprising, but the profession of cost estimating is truly interdisciplinary. In recent years, the number of courses that study economic appraisal of technology has grown. The author, in rewriting the second edition, attempted to harmonize these backgrounds, so necessary in this type of work.

Many men and women rise to cost estimating from the practical ranks of industry, construction, business, and government. Often they find self-study necessary to supplement their intimate grasp of practice with an appreciation of academic topics. This book will give them a taste of the principles of a special kind of topic.

The Second Edition is substantially different from the first. New developments and practices have emerged that warrant their inclusion. The lessons of my consulting and discussion with many estimators have aided the revision process. Practices and principles are appearing for the first time in this text.

The arrangement of the chapters and topics allows for a variety of teaching and self-study approaches. Basically, the text is broken down into four areas: design and business environment, methods, estimating, and assurance. Design customarily precedes its cost calculation. No reference is made to any specific designing, as that is left to other books. But on the design base, practices of cost estimating are built. The estimating portion, which is the largest of the four, considers the kinds of information and estimates for four categories of design. Operation, product, project, and system design contexts are constructed. Then various techniques that are pertinent to each are associated with that kind of design. After various designs are cost estimated, the processes of assurance and contractual consideration are presented.

The book has more material than can be covered in a one-semester course. The instructor can make selections based on the needs and interests of the class. There is considerable material on construction and manufacturing. Those classes having a manufacturing bent should be sure to include Chapters 7 and 8. Construction estimating objectives may desire Chapters 9 and 11. But it is a feature of the book that these differences are harmonized, and cost estimating principles relevant to both can benefit student understanding.

The Charles Kettering Foundation, which funded a grant called The BUILD Program, a cooperative venture between the University of Colorado and the University of Illinois, tangibly supported many of the thoughts and underpinning of this text. In a great measure the relevance of this book has been enhanced by my association with many estimators in industry, government, clinics, and seminars for over twenty-five years. I hope this text does justice to their practice. Several classes of students have been patient and understanding of poor drafts. The names used in various problems are real students, professional estimators, and friends who were helpful.

And most of all, I wish to thank my wife Doris for her help and encouragement, without which this book would have never been completed. And, 'α γ α π ά ω

Phillip F. Ostwald
Boulder, Colorado

COST ESTIMATING

1

Introduction

1.1 PROFIT IS NECESSARY FOR BUSINESS SURVIVAL

The Winston Dictionary defines *profit* as the amount by which income exceeds expense in a given time. This notion about profit leads to unfortunate conclusions. First, profit is necessary for taxes, dividends, and capital reinvestment in the firm. Taxes, whether they are national, state, or local, are the inescapable reward for successful operation—a vital contribution to continue a democratic society. If dividends, the rent upon invested capital and money, were not paid, it would lessen the faith of investors and jeopardize a source of money for growth. Once taxes and dividends are removed from profit, a portion referred to as *plowback* is necessary for equipment or other modernization needs. Successful managements do not ignore debt repayment, research funding, maintenance cost, salaries, or other expenses, but it is surprising that profit is sometimes overlooked. Is profit less vital than anticipated costs? Consequently, it is important that profit become a planned expense.

A new approach can be suggested: Everything is going to be spent. Thus it becomes a question of partitioning income and expense. To use a simple illustration, assume that sales revenue is going to be $1000. You expect to realize a net profit of $50. Based on your calculation the "net profit dollars after taxes" is $50 and all other costs, including income taxes, must be found within the $950. It is common at this point to hear the excuse "You can't tell until afterwards." What about prediction of sales income? Can it be safely approximated? Sales forecasts are surprisingly accurate and provide a foundation for profit estimating. The planning recognizes that what counts are current costs, not those of the previous quarter. How successfully can expenses be held to 95%? In controlling performance versus target, experience indicates that management can react to unplanned costs. For long-term survival, the assurance of profit remains a primary goal.

1.2 STEWARDSHIP NECESSARY FOR ECONOMIC SURVIVAL

Business, whether large or small, is not alone in its quest for survival. The pursuit of this objective includes government and the governed. A democratic government with authority to impose economic laws upon its citizens is not a wealth producer and has no inexhaustible source of wealth. Governmental activities such as public works, welfare, the military establishment, and a host of legislative-directed projects use the resources of its nation. Despite the nobility of cause and honest-meaning goals, governments suffer from financial bankruptcy. Curtailment of welfare programs, deevaluation, and heavy tax loads are symptoms of failure. Politics does not shield against economic ruin as the accounting ledger between nations is a reminder for long-term fiscal sobriety.

Even churches, foundations, charitable organizations, and not-for-profit trusts must have positive balances between short- and long-term debt and income. Individuals need no economic reminders. Despite credit, or loans, bankruptcy or poverty is not uncommon. Unfortunately, there is no inviolate equation that will prevent financial failure. The notion that receipts and expenses must maintain a positive cash flow is an oversimplification. Benefit–cost ratios, whereby social goals are evaluated in monetary terms, provide a narrow solution. Legally imposed restrictions on credit and spending are imperfect. Knowing the profound nature of this problem, a general objective for any steward is to simply husband resources.

1.3 COMPETITION AND FAILURE

It has been generally assumed that competition of all kinds is increasing. This statement can be examined on pragmatic grounds. A monopolist's product must be indispensable and have no opportunity for substitution, competition, and control by the government. These conditions are practically impossible to find, although they are sometimes approximated. Pure competition, on the other hand, is present when many firms provide a standard product to numerous purchasers. No single supplier or purchaser is strong enough to affect the price significantly by his actions. Pure competition does not prevail either. Rather, a form of imperfect competition is the usual marketplace.

Evidence of financial failure as a consequence of increasing competition may be found by examining companies, products, governments and their programs, and individuals. The profit squeeze on companies may result in public disclosure of bankruptcy. Mergers or sales of assets of the company, changes in title, and interdivisional failures within a larger corporation disguise the more subtle company failures. There is a good deal of empirical evidence that products fail as well. New products that enter the market but are withdrawn within a short time is a case in point. Curtailment or complete abandonment of various governmental programs, although politically inspired, is asserted to be a result of increasing social competition. If poverty may be accepted as evidence of failure for the individual, the probability of that is well known.

Although evidence of all types of failure is clear, the factors causing it are not. With production exceeding public demand, particularly true in the Western world, a temperamental society cannot guarantee long-term stability in the marketplace. Shifting consumer preferences, pliable and elusive, illustrate the short- and long-term effects of increasing competition. The effect of control by governmental legislation is an obvious business factor; increasing costs of production, inflation or recession, rising policy costs, new inventions, and improving technology are candidates for the causes of business failure.

Inasmuch as we are concerned with cost estimating, our attention is naturally directed to the matters of invention and the pace of general technology. For our purpose invention and technology are classified into four distinct areas: operations, products, projects, and systems. The understanding and manipulation of these areas are a result of the employment of the engineering sciences, business, and mathematics. Thus we deal with inventions and technology as factors of increasing competition within the firm and government.

1.4 MOTIVATION FOR ESTIMATING

Motivation for professional cost estimating is a result of the necessity for profits, stewardship of resources, and competition. For the alternative to failure is clear: a rational cost-estimating practice is necessary that reflects the economic advantages of the firm or government or individual. It does not always follow that an individual titled "estimator" dominates these economic decisions, but the act of estimating does require knowledge of engineering, science, business, and mathematics. An estimator is found in organizations whose development has matured, especially those organizations where engineering and design are important. The person may be titled *estimator, cost engineer,* or *technology analyst*, and we use these titles interchangeably in this text.

There is no trail of historical evidence that is associated with any cost-estimating title. That much is known; however, as a consequence of specialization many engineers and business professionals practice cost estimating within a dozen or so basic fields. The importance of the cost-estimating specialty is now an accepted fact, and increasing activity in industry and education is foreseeable. It is an activity done for engineering and management. Many professional societies regularly present papers, hold meetings, and sponsor clinics devoted to the many ramifications of cost estimating. Some professional groups have gone so far as to sanctify the title "cost engineer" or "estimator."* These groups recognize that the engineer and business professional, unlike a scientist, has an economic interest in the success of the design. A scientist, on the other hand, is more concerned with the idea or principle and less interested in an economic justification for the principle.

1.5 DESIGN

At this point we shall define several terms. Cost estimating is concerned with cost determination and evaluation of engineering design. The term *cost estimating* could well be *profit engineering* as the "making sure" of profits is a higher priority for many. However, it is recognized that cost estimating is a general title and includes many who may or may not see themselves causing profits directly. The estimate is the result of cost-estimating work. When used as a noun the estimate implies an evaluation of a design expressed as cost, amount, or value. When employed in its verb form, estimating means to appraise or to determine. There are four types of estimates: operation, product, project, and system. Their ordering does not suggest any ranking of difficulty.

The word *design* is given the broadest possible definition. It does not mean "board work." It implies the activities of creative engineers and is defined as follows: *Every design (1) is a new combination (2) of preexisting knowledge (3) that satisfies an economic want.* The phrase "is a new combination" emphasizes novelty and suggests the unusual characteristics of the designer or design team and the circumstances. The designer must possess ability or be the recipient of serendipity and its fortunate concentration of forces. "Preexisting knowledge" relates to a design's (not designer now) intellectual past and to the industry on which it has been built. For the third part of the definition the engineering activity ultimately fulfills economic satisfaction.

The driving forces for design are past knowledge and wants as each alone is insufficient. Without wants no problems exist, and without knowledge, they could not be solved. This is the chicken–egg riddle. How can a want–knowledge milieu be created? Simple answers are not possible, and to avoid reader–author disputes let us assume that demand and intellectual curiosity or sheer happenstance spurs on the design.

A design procedure can take the shape shown in Figure 1.1. One should realize that a precise sequential process is not intended. The design format is actually a hodgepodge of simultaneous continuous actions. The elements are

1. Problem
2. Concepts
3. Engineering models

*American Association of Cost Engineers, National Estimating Society.

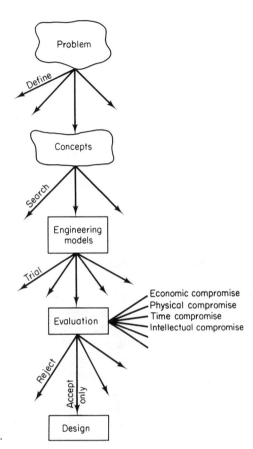

Figure 1.1.   Engineering design process.

4. Evaluation

5. Design

Problem.   The initial description of a problem is a vague representation satisfying some want. It is necessary to transform this into a more useful shape. By presuming the existence of a primitive problem, information (technical or nontechnical), costs, and other data are superficially gathered to give form to the problem. Suppliers, customers, competitors, standardization groups, safety and patent releases, and laboratories are sources for ideas. The reader may wonder why all the fuss over a simple problem statement. To give heed to a raw and imperfect problem is not unknown; students are not the only ones guilty. But a thoughtful and reasoned statement specifying the problem leads, perchance, to a more efficient result. Questions may guide the formation of a problem statement such as "Does this fit the company's needs, interests, and abilities? Are the people connected with the problem capable of carrying it to completion, or can suitable people be hired?"

Concept.   The stage is set for the concept search after a problem with subsidiary restrictions has been defined. The quest may start with idealism such as the perfect gas laws, frictionless rolling, or perpetual motion, for example. It is a searching, learning, and recognizing; it is not application, as that comes later. A timely and fortunate search may uncover unapplied principles. When one considers that a million scientific and technical articles, more or less, are published annually, it should be clear that a listing, ignoring study for the moment, of all information even within a narrow field is a hopeless cause. Here is a recognized defeat in the face of overwhelming odds. Nonetheless, the chance of finding the basic idea for a new development may be found through patent disclosures, new texts, or journals in the field. Instead of the unobtainable goal of completeness, there are other goals capable of being achieved in the search. Knowing where to start and when to stop are lessons of experience.

Engineering models.   The engineering model involves application of creditable concepts which were uncovered earlier. The formation of this model may range from a casual back-of-envelope model to a complicated physical shape. The formation of a model is an engineering trait and distinguishes the engineering pattern of thought. Models, whether they are experimental or rational, permit manipulation for theories or testing. Using physical mockups, laboratory testing is able to provide numerical answers. Data are obtained, results are noted, and conclusions are stated. An engineer will choose the cheapest of the methods to state and understand a model.

The word *model* has many meanings. We define it as a *representation* to explain some aspect. It is seldom that we are able to manipulate reality, as it may be either impossible or uneconomical. The market in a free economy is a illustration of the former, while an expensive nuclear reactor for electrical generation illustrates the latter. The prediction of reality through a form of mathematical abstraction is the cause for interest in models. Engineers apply these ideas as a means to scale larger problems. For example, many times the analyst is unable to comprehend the actual system, and with limited mental powers of perspective, a model is often a satisfactory substitute. Discovery of which variables are pertinent, rejection or confirmation of prototypes, and comparison to a standard give importance to modeling.

We segregate models according to physical, schematic, or mathematical notions. All three are important and are used in the design process. The scale of abstraction would proceed from the physical to the mathematical extreme.

Physical models principally involve change of scale. The globe looks like the earth, for instance.

When one set of properties is used to represent a second set of properties, a schematic model results. It may or may not have a look-alike appearance to the real-world situation it represents. Coding processes may be used, such as the chalkboard demonstration of a football play appearing as crosses ($\times$) and circles ($\bigcirc$). Hydraulic systems are of benefit in understanding electrical systems, and vice versa. Organization flow-process charts are other examples of schematic models. The schematic model captures the critical feature of the real thing and ignores the unimportant to reach a solution.

Mathematical models operate with numbers and symbols in their imitation of relationships. Although they are more difficult to comprehend, they are the most general.

In an approximate way mathematical models explain the real situation. It is customary to manipulate mathematical models according to the conventional rules of mathematics. Mathematical models are desirable in cost estimating not only because they are easy to manipulate but also because they yield more accurate results than do physical or schematic models. The *unit cost formula* is an example of a model found in operation estimating. Whenever an estimator uses a *recapitulation sheet,* where labor, material, and overhead are summed, we are employing a mathematical model in a procedural sense. The *discounted cash flow* model used to calculate a rate of return of an asset is the mathematical method for dealing with project estimates.

There are precautions in modeling. The rule of thumb is to use the fewest number. Models should be flexible to permit repeated applications. Mathematical manipulation should be simple. Arithmetic is preferred over algebra, algebra is preferred over calculus, calculus is preferred over vectors, and so forth. The model that is simple improves its saleability to management, and increased understanding and confidence result from its use.

Evaluation.   Ultimately, the engineering model reaches the evaluation point. A compromise forced on the engineer by economics, physical laws, social mores, ignorance, and the human fault of stupidity discolors our evaluation.

Even the moral questions may be debated. The wisest person alive cannot foresee all the future effects of the design, but it is bold to ask. Others may cooperate at this point: The stylist may abridge and direct the progress, the manager may foresee other problems, and the marketing person may be useful. But here is an appropriate place to stop, pause, and evaluate.

The cost estimator has a responsibility that parallels that of the design engineer. The cost-estimating process proceeds along lines similar to those which have been discussed. After the problem is wisely stated (couched in the design engineering model), estimating ideas are considered, a cost-estimating model is selected, evaluation trials are started (shortcomings with time, money, staff, programs, or information impede the model), and finally the cost estimate is completed.

Actually, the proper evaluation of engineering models is a continuous process. Experience says that it takes a long time to pass from the idea stage to the design stage. For instance, in the evaluation of new product ideas, one study uncovered the mortality of new products. Twenty companies with 540 possibilities in the idea stage distilled to only one that was placed into regular production.

There are questions that we ask in doing an evaluation: What will be the total cost of developing this design up to and including the sales promotion? What will be the profit of the total investment during the first few years of production and sales? How long will it take the initial investment to be returned? Does a new product coincide with the abilities and experience of our company? In considering these questions a number of factors should be noted. Experience, study, and a questioning attitude are required traits for evaluation.

Design.   Design is the execution of the plan into being and shape. In fulfilling functional requirements design involves computing, drafting, checking, specifying, and the like. It answers the question "How shall it be built?" rather than "How will it work?" By emphasizing the word *design* as a term in the *design process* we do not intend to overinflate its importance to the depreciation of other steps, as they are equally important; nonetheless, a greater proportion of the designers' time is tied to this work.

As a new combination of preexisting knowledge, design satisfies an economic want. Cost estimating attempts to measure this compliance. Despite the notion that cost estimating precedes design, cost estimating acts as a shadow and requires some sort of design even before a preliminary estimate is started. In view of this relationship, design is considered on the basis of an operation design, product design, project design, and system design. This artificial classification is tendered only to show compatibility with estimating. It only suggests a method for teaching of estimating. It does not describe a new classification for design.

1.6 CLASSIFICATION OF ESTIMATES

Initiation of cost-estimating work arises from design. Practical examples of designs include bridges, cars, chemical plants, highways, machine tools, radios, piece parts, service work, and systems of machines and people. With design as the focal point, cost estimating is the body of theory and practice that provides a measure of the economic want of the design. Notice that the cost-estimating activity is not involved with the "satisfaction" part of the design. Satisfaction is determined by the marketplace externally to the firm; or internally, the firm's management may stop an undesirable design. Politics may also approve or abrogate the satisfaction requirement of designs which deal with society. Thus the estimator finds an economic measure for the design.

From the operation, product, project, or system design, there are four kinds of estimates associated with these designs. Table 1.1 is a tabular description.

The process of producing a change in value or a way of working establishes the content of an *operation design*. An operation estimate is a forecast of labor and material required for an operation design. The design may be a toy or radio or building, and work, a worker, and a tool are involved. The tool may be simple or complicated. The definition of an operation estimate includes one worker with one tool, one worker with multiple machines, or crew work. The definition is appropriate for the factory, construction site, office, service station, maintenance yard, hospital,

Table 1.1.   A Classification of Design for Purposes of Cost Estimating

Design	Fundamental Characteristic	Symbolic Measure of Economic Want	Examples
Operation	Worker and tool	Cost	Assembler and hand tools, secretary in office, crew work, driver and transportation vehicle
Product	Quantity and replication	Price	Toys, radios, houses, typewriters, bridges, computer-controlled machine tools, transportation vehicles
Project	End item	Bid	Bridge, plant addition, refinery, 500-kV transmission line, capital tooling for product, right-of-way structure for transportation vehicles
System	Configuration	Public effectiveness	Weapon system, hospital, rapid transit system

or government. The worker can be skilled, unskilled, craft, apprentice, journeyman, or professional. Work is classified as direct if it can be clearly traceable to the function of the design; otherwise, it is indirect. The work that engineers do for a weapon system can be classified as direct or indirect. This is an optional management choice but an ordinary example is a turret lathe operator making parts that are identified clearly in a product or an electrician wiring a commercial building under construction. Methods used for operation estimating are different from those required for other types of estimates. Operation estimates may be input information for other kinds of estimates.

An entire product, rather than an operation, is estimated for a product design. In product estimating there is the fundamental characteristic of *replication*. We intend replication to mean a likeness or reproduction, not repetition or quantity. Replication is a *deliberate* change in a design. Model II is similar to model I, for instance. For many reasons these intentional design differences cause changes to the estimate, but the estimator would not estimate model II from scratch. Instead, by several methods, the estimator adds and subtracts for the replicated distinctions in design. Note that a product estimate does not depend on production quantity. Product quantity may be anywhere from a few to many. Traditionally, there is a mistaken belief that it is necessary to have large quantities of consumer goods for a product estimate, and that the production time should be reasonably brief in relationship to the quantity produced. We state that bridges, turbines, and airplanes, as well as toys, radios, and other consumer products, have the quality of replicated designs. Homes and apartments being constructed in a development have different facades, interiors, and so on, but there is similarity. The estimator in dealing with replicated product designs uses many similar methods whether the product estimate is for $2 toys or $200 million turbines. Methods used for product estimating are usually different from those required for other types of estimates.

A project design, whether it is a plan, plant, equipment, capital tooling for a product, or a prototype, is one of a thing. In a project design the emphasis is on the end item. The design is custom, perhaps, and there will be only one manufactured or constructed. Usually, the dollar amount is considered capital rather than expense. Examples include refinery, plant, turbine, bridge, prototype, and airplane. While some of these examples were listed in the product estimating category, project estimating is for singular rather than plural goods. Methods used in project estimating are essentially different from those used for other types of estimates; however, they may require operation and product estimates as input information. Project designs usually require a significant period of time for manufacture or construction.

Another distinction between product and project estimating is found in the buyer–seller viewpoint. For example, if a factory producing numerically controlled (NC) machine tools were manufacturing several or more units, the factory cost estimator would associate the problem with product design and use methods of product estimating. The estimator in evaluating the NC machine for purchase would approach the problem as a project design because of the single object and apply methods of project estimating.

A system design involves designs of operations, products, and projects in any arrangement. The fundamental characteristic term of a system is *configuration*. Thus we define system design especially for the purpose of cost estimating. A system design is complex and the elements of the system estimate include operation, product, and project estimates. In our terminology the system design deals in the public, government, or not-for-profit domain of enterprise. In these areas there are factors that are political, altruistic, and provide for general needs and goals of society. Profit is not determined explicitly for the system estimate. One example of a system design is a public rapid transit system and the estimator represents the public authority spending the money. This would involve, for example, initial nonrecurring costs such as securing right-of-way, constructing the road structure for the vehicles, and so on, and would involve project estimates. Transit vehicles, not all identical, would be necessary and product estimates are required. A driver and the vehicle, or the worker and tool, represent the grist for an operation estimate and become necessary information. Thus a system design is a configuration of operations, products, and projects and uses those estimates in arriving at a value for the measure of the economic want.

The task facing the estimator is to provide a fact or number that is representative of the economic want of the design. A want is a value exchanged between competing and self-interested parties. The price a buyer is willing to pay for a toy; a contractor–owner agreement on the bid value of a building project; or the fiscal-year budget value for a rapid transit system that the public authority proposes and elected representatives of public voters approve are typical examples of wants. Table 1.1 provides some symbolic measure of wants. While dollar cost is usual for operation estimates, so are man-hours or man-days. Price is the measure of want for products. In projects, we are interested in the value of the bid. In system designs, public effectiveness may imply a measure such as benefit–cost, or a budget fiscal-period total that sums cost streams throughout the system life cycle. However desirable various dimensions for the measurement of economic want may be, the estimator deals principally with money and dollars.

The dollar magnitude of an estimate varies with the design. A $0.10/unit price for a product and 10^8 bid for a project are not unknown. We assert that the intellectual requirements for either estimate are the same. The range of a minimum to maximum of 10^9 times underscores the variability of the estimating field.

1.7 INFORMATION

Before the estimator is able to determine the economic want of a design, it is necessary to have information of various kinds. There are two extremes in the amount of information. Visualize the case where virtually no information is available; then we presume that it is unlikely that an estimate can be made. At the other extreme, assume that all data are available, which implies that the money has been spent for the design and an estimate is unnecessary. Whenever the data are all available, the process of after-the-fact cost analysis is likely to be accounting, not estimating. The estimator works in a cost data and design environment where the information is not fully disclosed; thus the reason for estimating unknown information. We separate the accounting from estimating field on the principle that the accountant deals with cost quantities that have been spent and consistently recorded. The estimator reckons in cost quantities which have not been spent for a design. Cost accounting and cost estimating are specializations that work together and have much in common.

A major kind of cost data is *historical*. Data as typically characterized by accounting reports are historical in nature, as they emphasize the transactions recorded through cost-controlling accounts which may be kept in some ledger system. Money is expended, and materials, labor, services, and expenses (such as power, heat, and the like) are received. Specific accounting procedures must be provided for recording the acquisition and disposition of materials, for the recording and use of labor, and for their distribution. The internal function of cost accounting as it relates to our interest here is discussed in Chapter 3. Cost accountants are primarily responsible for this kind of information.

Measured data are another kind of information. Cost engineers may find that work measurement or the economist's methods of measurement give a form of information that is amenable to certain types of estimation, either in time or dollar dimensions. Sometimes these information forms may be measured or determined by the cost engineers. Material quantities calculated from drawings and specifications are another form of measured data.

The final kind of information is *policy* data and has the property of being *fixed* for cost estimating. Accepted as factual and often unchallengeable by the estimator the origins of policy data are varied. Union–management wage settlements or union-hall hiring of construction labor where predetermined policies dictate the wages and types of labor on equipment to be operated are commonplace. Budgets and legislative restrictions from municipal to national laws dictate certain codes of conduct and cost. The federal government requires a social security tax from the employer for the purpose of providing old-age benefits. An unemployment compensation tax, sometimes called Federal Unemployment Insurance Cost, is collected by the states for the purpose of providing funds to compensate workers during periods of unemployment. These data may emanate from internal departments within the organization, official government sources, international agencies, trade associations, trade unions, sampling organizations, or any office which gathers and divulges design and economic information. These sources may be *secondary*—that is, the source of data may be far removed from fundamental source—but what is more important is its reliability and timeliness.

In some situations we accept any available data and have little opportunity to be selective. Cost estimators may use their own measured data as an important source. While accounting is a major source of information, there are other departments internal to the organization that provide information. The personnel department charged with the handling of employees interprets the union contract (where unions exist), conducts labor contract negotiations, and keeps personnel records regarding wages and fringe costs.

Operating departments, whether in construction, manufacturing, or crafts, to name a few, are the producing organizations. They are concerned with doing. The foreman or department manager knows the operating details at that moment. Frequently, he is a direct source of information. The foreman may often assist in the collaboration of obtaining data on special forms that report extraordinary costs of process equipment, manning, efficiency, scrap, repairs, or downtime. Sometimes he is the oracle for a "guesstimate" on operations with which he is familiar.

In many organizations the purchasing department has the responsibility of spending money for materials. Some companies believe that purchasing is responsible for the outside manufacturer. Knowing about purchasing and shipping regulations, purchasing is frequently the source for this class of information.

Some companies require that only buyers contact vendors for trial quotes. A particular estimate may be so complicated that it requires several quotations. The magnitude of the quotation, the type of the organization, and particular policies dictate whether cost engineers are personally involved or whether buyers secure purchase information. The big steady-use item, big one-shot jobs, middle-sized orders, and small orders are factors in making this choice.

The contribution of sales and marketing is apparent in the pricing of products. Market demand, sales, consumer analysis, advertising, brand loyalty, and market testing are their fields of responsibility.

A great variety of basic economic facts and trends is available from the U.S. government. The Bureau of Labor Statistics (BLS) provides elements of cost on the prices of materials and labor.

Data may be found from manufacturers' agents and jobbers, who, although they promote special interests, are willing to release information given to them by their clients. Trade associations, which are subsidized by groups of businesses sharing a common need (i.e., machine tool builders, concrete, etc.), are typical organizations that publish data useful for cost engineering. Some firms and associations regularly publish different types of cost indexes.

1.8 UNITS AND MONEY

The student of cost estimating can no longer be uninformed about worldwide systems of units and money. Understanding in international trade and dimensional and monetary conversions is required. U.S. customary and metric units and the dollar, pound, deutsche mark, peso, and so on, are used throughout this book to provide this familiarity.

Le Système International d'Unités, known officially worldwide as "SI," is a modernized metric system and incorporates many advanced unit concepts. With SI it is possible to have a simplified, coherent, decimalized, and absolute system of measuring units. Because it will be many decades before the United States deals exclusively with SI units in engineering, we will use a mixture of SI and U.S. customary units. Sometimes the U.S. customary value is given first followed by SI units in parentheses, for example, 5.008 in. (127.20 mm). The SI system has seven base units (metre, kilogram, second, ampere, kelvin, candela, and mole), two supplementary units (radian, steradian), and additional derived units. The list of derived units within the SI system is extensive. Basic to SI is the definition: One newton is the force required to accelerate a mass of one kilogram at the rate of one metre per second squared; one joule is the energy involved when a force of one newton moves a distance one metre along its line of action; and one watt is the power that in one second gives rise to the energy of one joule. The SI units for force, energy, and power are the same regardless if the design is mechanical, electrical, hydraulic, or chemical. Confusion is often found in the U.S. customary system of using both pounds force and pounds mass, but this is avoided in SI. The SI system has a series of approved prefixes and symbols for decimal multiples and is shown in Table 1.2.

Table 1.2. SI PREFIXES

Multiplication Factor		Prefix	SI Symbol
1,000,000	= 10^6	mega	M
1,000	= 10^3	kilo	k
10	= 10^1	decka	da
0.1	= 10^{-1}	deci	d
0.01	= 10^{-2}	centi	c
0.001	= 10^{-3}	milli	m
0.000001	= 10^{-6}	micro	μ

One should be careful with capitalization of SI symbols to avoid confusion; for example, K is kelvin, whereas k means kilo. Furthermore, the U.S. practice of using commas to separate multiples of 1000 is followed rather than SI, which uses a space instead of a comma.

Data for units and money are from a variety of sources and have been recorded with varying degrees of refinement. Specific rules are observed when engineering and cost data are added, subtracted, multiplied, or divided. Consider the example of adding three numbers for engineering analysis, where the first is reported data in millions, the second in thousands, and the third in units, such as in (a):

	(a)	(b)
	163,000,000	163,000,000
	217,885,000	217,900,000
	96,432,768	96,400,000
	477,317,768	477,300,000

If these numbers were pure engineering data, the numbers should first be rounded to one significant digit farther to the right than that of the least accurate number and the sum given as in (b) and then rounded to 477,000,000. If the numbers are pure cost data, the overriding consideration depends on final disclosure of the information. The rule adopts (a) as preferred, but would accept (b) if an approximation is all that is required.

The rule for multiplication and division of engineering data is that the product or quotient must contain no more significant digits than are contained in the number with the fewest significant digits used in the multiplication or division. The difference between this rule for addition and subtraction should be noted. The last rule requires rounding digits that lie to the right of the last significant digit in the least accurate number.

Multiplication: $113.2 \times 1.43 = 161.876$ rounds to 162
Division: $113.2 \div 1.43 = 79.16$ rounds to 79.2
Addition: $113.2 + 1.43 = 114.63$ rounds to 114.6
Subtraction: $113.2 - 1.43 = 111.77$ rounds to 111.8

The product and quotient above are limited to three significant digits since 1.43 contains only three significant digits. The rounded answers in the addition and subtraction examples contain four significant digits.

Numbers that are exact counts are treated as though they consist of an infinite number of significant digits. When a count is used in computation with a measurement, the number of significant digits is the same as the number of significant digits in the measurement. If a count of 113 is multiplied by a value of 1.43, the product is $161.59. However, if 1.43 were a rough value accurate only to the nearest 10 and hence contained only two significant digits, the product would be 160. Rules for cost estimating are similar, although there are exceptions for dealing with the requirement of exaggerated precision, and these are given in later chapters. Essentially, the requirements for exaggerated precision come from large-quantity considerations.

Rules for rounding are the same as for cost estimating and engineering practice. If 3.46325 is rounded to four digits, it would be 3.463; if rounded to three digits, 3.46. Or if 8.37652 is rounded to four digits, it would be 8.377; if rounded to three digits, 8.38. If the digit discarded is exactly 5, the last digit retained should be rounded upward if it is odd, or not if it is an even number. For example, 4.365 when rounded to three digits becomes 4.36; 4.355 would round to 4.36 if rounded to three digits.

This book makes no exception to the practice of avoiding cents (¢) as a dimension. For instance, a unit of a product would be expressed as $1.43 and never as 143¢ because of potential confusion between the two dimensions.

Conversions from U.S. customary units to SI, and vice versa, are made using Table 1.3. Consider the following examples. Convert 12.52 ft to metres, 17.2 ft³ to cubic metres, 5.15 lbm to kilograms, 2.005 in. to millimetres, and 2.4637 in. to millimetres.

Table 1.3. APPROXIMATE CONVERSION FACTORS FOR U.S. CUSTOMARY UNITS TO SI

To convert from:	To:	Multiply by:
Area		
square foot	square metre (m²)	9.290×10^{-2}
square inch	square metre (m²)	6.451×10^{-4}
Energy		
Btu	joule (J)	1.055×10^{3}
kilowatt hour	joule (J)	3.600×10^{6}
Force		
pound-force	newton (N)	4.448
Length		
inch	millimetre (mm)	2.54×10^{1}
foot	metre (m)	3.048×10^{-1}
mile	kilometre (km)	1.609
Mass		
ounce	kilogram (kg)	2.834×10^{-2}
pound	kilogram (kg)	4.535×10^{-1}
ton (short, 2000 lbm)	kilogram (kg)	9.071×10^{2}
Power, horsepower (550 ft lb/sec)	watt (W)	7.456×10^{2}
Pressure, pound-force per square inch	pascal (Pa)	6.894×10^{3}
Temperature, degree Fahrenheit	degree Celsius (C)	$(t_f - 32)/1.8$
Velocity		
foot per second	metre per second (m/s)	3.048×10^{-1}
mile per hour	kilometre per hour (km/h)	1.609
Volume		
cubic foot	cubic metre (m³)	2.831×10^{-2}
cubic inch	cubic metre (m³)	1.638×10^{-5}
cubic yard	cubic metre (m³)	7.645×10^{-1}
board foot	cubic metre (m³)	2.359×10^{-3}
gallon	litre	3.785

$12.52 \times 3.048 \times 10^{-1} = 3.8161$, which using the rule of precision of the original measurements, becomes 3.82 m.

$17.2 \times 2.831 \times 10^{-2} = 0.48693$, which becomes 0.487 m^3.

$5.15 \times 4.53 \times 10^{-1} = 2.3350$, which becomes 2.34 kg.

$2.005 \times 2.54 \times 10^1 = 50.927$ and becomes 50.93 mm, because a two-place decimal for the millimetres has the same degree of accuracy as contained in the original inch measurement.

$2.4637 \times 2.54 \times 10^1 = 62.5780$, which when rounded to three decimal places becomes 62.578 mm because of similar degrees of accuracy implied by a measurement.

For many companies the opportunity to export is to spread risk among several countries and markets. But cross-frontier trade inevitably causes foreign exchange exposure for either one or both of the trading partners. Consider the example of a company that will purchase machinery from West Germany. We will assume that the purchaser is in the United States and has the choice of currency for buying and paying for the machine. Three options are available; the company may agree to buy in deutsche marks, dollars, or some third-country currency. If the purchase is in dollars, it may appear that the foreign exchange has avoided a problem, but do not forget that the problem exists for the seller of the machine. The seller will be in receipt of dollars and will wish to sell them for deutsche marks (DM). On the other hand, if the machine is invoiced in deutsche marks, the buyer will first have to buy deutsche marks before buying the machine. A foreign exchange transaction is involved for somebody either way. If the goods are invoiced in a third country, for instance British sterling, the U.S. buyer must arrange payment in British sterling to the German supplier, who in turn must sell the sterling and convert into deutsche marks. In this event we have two foreign exchange transactions, whereas previously it was only one. It is axiomatic that movement of goods or services across a frontier will cause a foreign transaction for somebody. In international trade the exporter and importer of any two countries think in terms of their own national currency.

The prevailing foreign exchange rates between any two countries are the prices at which *bills of exchange* on one of these countries will sell in the currency of the other and are of importance. The bills of exchange are expressed in terms of the price or rate at which the currency of one country is exchanged for that of another. Table 1.4 is a sample of foreign exchange rates. For instance, it takes $2.3665 U.S. to exchange 1£, or $0.5435 U.S. for 1 DM. But free and uncontrolled foreign exchange rates fluctuate almost daily. Low exchange (meaning a lower cost of purchasing foreign currencies) normally indicates a strong demand for foreign currency or a heavy offering of U.S. dollars. A distinction is also seen in Table 1.4 between spot and future exchange, perhaps 1 year from the date of the spot value. When an importer purchases spot exchange, he actually takes delivery for a definite amount of foreign exchange at the time of purchase for which he pays the rate then quoted for his particular bill of exchange. When he purchases a future exchange contract,

Table 1.4. TYPICAL EXCHANGE RATES IN U.S. DOLLARS

	West German Mark	Swiss Franc	Japanese Yen	Canadian Dollar	British Pound	Italian Lira	French Franc	Mexican Peso
Spot	0.5136	0.5862	0.004633	0.8378	2.3340	0.001085	0.2215	0.02231
One year	0.5435	0.6192	0.004874	0.8506	2.3665	0.001055	0.2262	0.02248

the importer agrees to purchase a given amount of exchange on a fixed date in the future, or within a fixed period to pay for it at the rate specified in the future contract. This future rate may be higher or lower than the spot rate. Consider the following examples.

A material is priced currently at $3.65/lb. Find the equivalent spot market in British pounds and SI.

$$\left(3.65\frac{\$}{\text{lbm}}\right)\left(\frac{1}{2.3340}\frac{\pounds}{\$}\right)\left(\frac{1}{0.4535}\frac{\text{lbm}}{\text{kg}}\right) = 3.4484\ \pounds/\text{kg}$$

German material is currently priced at 485 DM/m³. Determine equivalent values 1 year hence in U.S. dollars and customary dimensional units.

$$\left(485\frac{\text{DM}}{\text{m}^3}\right)\left(0.5435\frac{\$}{\text{DM}}\right)\left(0.02831\frac{\text{m}^3}{\text{ft}^3}\right) = \$7.4624/\text{ft}^3$$

Observe that the trailing decimals on the right-hand side of the equations are increased because of the exact nature of currency conversion.

1.9 A LOOK AT THE BOOK

This book provides the kinds of thinking that are found in cost-estimating work. The circular riddle—do problems provide the stimulus in finding solution methods, or do techniques heretofore unused discover and solve problems—is really never answered. An engineer would not seriously consider redesign of the wheel or feel any guilt in exploiting its theory and practice. An effort has been made to assimilate theories and practices that are broadly attractive to all business and engineering students, whether they are (or are to be) employed in research, development, design, production, sales, and management. While cost estimating practices vary among the several fields of technology, the principles do not. This becomes clearer by noting the organization of the book.

In the first chapter we couple engineering design to its business environment. In this text we assume that design neither leads nor lags its economic shadow. Vital to the design is the cost information on which decisions must be based. With the design and cost data at hand, the cost estimator builds a corresponding cost-design structure. In the past this consisted of columnar and recapitulation sheets. Now, however, the cost model is too involved for these simple maneuvers.

Chapters 2, 3, and 4 are concerned with labor, material, and accounting analysis. Labor and material costs items are the major contributions by the cost estimator for the design estimate. When accounting costs are considered, the cost is more complete. But before these costs can be estimated for a design, there must be analysis. Data are unfortunately out of date, demand is past history, and budgets need review; these are experiences that demonstrate the need for forecasting. In this book forecasting implies numerical analysis of information and Chapter 5 suggests several popular approaches. Methods are classed as preliminary or detail. Chapter 6 provides general methods suitable to various designs.

How might the act of estimating be classified? In cost estimating we follow the design in a logical manner to provide a scheme of estimating. We could concoct an estimate classification according to purpose, accuracy, time, type of commitment, or design. If one were to classify estimates based on purpose, as many are, we would find estimates for the *verification of a vendor quotation, appropriation, budgeting and funding,* and *evaluation studies* or *design feasibility* in addition to *cost* or *price.* If accuracy were the determining factor, one could imagine an estimate classification as *order of magnitude,* say ± 50%; as *ballpark,* say ± 20%; and as *accurate,* ± 5%. *Initial* and *final* are other possibilities. The classification scheme adopted in this book is associated with design. The designs, whether they are operation, product, project, or system, provide the identifying feature. Formats, procedures, and a host of ramifications vary for these types of designs. The methods of estimating do not. These design estimates are covered by operation (Chapter 7), product (Chapter 8), project (Chapter 9), and systems (Chapter 10).

The use of analysis, judgment, and experience will forever remain a vital factor in the cost estimating field. Certainly, without judgment chaos results; however, estimates will not be successful unless there are activities that ensure their success. This follow-through is called estimate assurance and is described in Chapter 11.

Contractual practices are presented in the final chapter. The thrust of the last chapter is dominated more by a discussion of goals than by rigid rules.

With a liberal interpretation, *cost* may mean cost, profit, income, expense, or any economical measure of want and is an important dimension. Many believe that a radio, car, or rocket design has economic value as the first and last requirement. The thought is this: Given a design (aerospace, agricultural, chemical, civil, electrical and electronic, industrial, manufacturing, marine, mechanical, metallurgical, mining, petroleum) physical and real-world restrictions are its companion. Engineering, production, marketing, sales, and finance conform to the engineering design, as the drawings and specifications are the authority for construction and operation. The salesperson sells the design; the service engineer maintains this design; the accountant classifies costing points about this design; the manager plans production schedules to build the design; and the construction engineer selects processes and equipment to construct the design. Used in its broadest context, *design* causes a long chain reaction. The engineering or business student who brings to his or her job an understanding of the economic consequence of design is valued in industry, business, and research. This person becomes a cost engineer, designer, a project engineer, a supervisor of engineering activities, or a businessperson who works closely with design, development, and the research team. For not only is cost estimating essential in order to thrive in our economy, it is also necessary for the survival of the economy.

QUESTIONS

1.1. Give an explanation of the following terms:

Profit	Administrative practices
Estimator	Operation estimate
Estimating	Product estimate
Design	Project estimate
Economic want	System estimate
Engineering model	SI
Historical information	Exchange transaction
Policy information	Spot exchange
Measured information	Bills of exchange

1.2. Prepare a list of career opportunities in estimating from the classified want ads of a newspaper and professional trade magazines.

1.3. How does competition and failure of the enterprise interact with principles of cost estimating? Discuss.

1.4. How would you define profit? Discuss fully. What are the consequences of negative profit (loss)? How can profit be made appealing to the individual?

1.5. List positive and negative benefits that may result whenever businesses fail. Should governments prevent business failure? Does company size and political power affect your answer?

1.6. How many not-for-profit organizations can you name? How do governments protect their interests?

1.7. Distinguish between product and technology competition. Which affects your life more?

1.8. What distinguishes the act of estimating? Will estimating become a science?

1.9. How do economic laws and physical laws differ? Are the well-ordered cause and effect relationships separable in business and engineering fields?

1.10. Describe how computers have improved on back-of-envelope techniques in estimating.

1.11. Relate the role of cost estimating to design engineering. Contrast this role.

1.12. Distinguish among an operation, product, project, and system estimate. Cover mutually exclusive descriptions applicable to these four estimates. How are they similar, and how are they different?

1.13. What do exchange rates between countries reflect? Why do they fluctuate?

1.14. Consider another rationale for the classification of the estimate. Would labor estimating, material estimating, and tools and machine estimating be complete?

1.15. Do you agree that the dimension dollar is as important as other engineering dimensions?

1.16. Do you agree with the statement: "Not only is cost estimating essential in order to thrive in our economy—it is also necessary for the survival of the economy"?

PROBLEMS

Convert the following 11 problems from U.S. customary units to the International System of units or from SI to U.S. units. Show correct abbreviations.

1.1. (a) 17 ft^2, 2.4 ft^2, 450 in.^{2}, 5000 ft^2 to metres^2 (m^2)
     (b) 0.15 in.^{2}, 0.035 in.^{2}, 20.61 to millimetres^2 (mm^2)

1.2. (a) 280,000 British thermal units (Btu) to joules (J)
     (b) 7,500,000 kilowatt hours (kWh) to J

1.3. (a) 18 pounds force (lbf) to newtons (N)
     (b) 180,000 lbf, 1.8 $\times$ 10^6 lbf to newtons with appropriate prefix

1.4. (a) 18 ft, 2.0 ft to metres (m)
     (b) 10 in., 0.01 in., 100 in., 0.00015 in. to millimetres (mm)

1.5. (a) 15 ounce mass (ozm) to kilograms (kg)
     (b) 25 ton to kilograms (kg)
     (c) 1400 kg to pounds (lb)

1.6. (a) 15 pounds-mass/foot^3 (lbm/ft^3 = density) to kilograms/metre^3 (kg/m^3)
     (b) 180 kg/m^3 to lbm/ft^3

1.7. (a) 2500 pounds-force/foot^2 (lbf/ft^2) to megapascals (MPa)
     (b) 180 pounds per in.^{2} (psi), 1750 psi to Pa
     (c) 17 MPa to psi

1.8. (a) 1500 C, 200 C, 1000 Celsius (C) to Fahrenheit (F)
     (b) 200°F, 1000°F to C

1.9. (a) 180 feet/minute (fpm), 500 fpm to metres/second (m/s)
     (b) 180 inches/second (in./s), 1855 to metres/min (m/min)

1.10. (a) 0.37 ft^3, 125 ft^3, 700 ft^3 to metres^3 (m^3)
     (b) 0.01 in.^{3}, 12 in.^{3}, 150 in.^{3} to millimetres^3 (mm^3)
     (c) 1000 yards^3 to m^3
     (d) 250 mm^3, 80 mm^3, 1500 mm^3 to in.^{3}

1.11. (a) 800 ft^3/min, 65 ft^3/sec to m^3/s
     (b) 1000 m^3/s, 75 m^3/s to ft^3/min

1.12. A casting costs $17.50 U.S. dollars per unit. What is the spot value of the casting (a) in German marks? (b) in Swiss francs? (c) in Canadian dollars?

1.13. If a catalyst is worth $85 per gallon in the United States, what is an equivalent value (a) in deutsche marks and metric units? (b) in Italian lire and SI?

1.14. International export opportunities may send materials from one country to another and back to the originating country because of labor cost or a technology advantage. An electronic product is transported to Japan and a value of 12,432 yen is added.
     (a) What is the U.S. value?
     (b) If a value of 58.65 U.S. dollars is estimated for equivalent U.S. work, what is the exchange rate that is indifferent to the decision?
     (c) For the work to remain in the United States, must the exchange rate increase or decrease relative to the indifference rate?

1.15. An American businesswoman travels from New York to four countries. She will start with U.S. currency and exchange her dollars in each country using that country's prevailing exchange rate. In each country she will buy the next airfare and will incur business expenses. Travel and expense budget expressed in the currency of the country are as follows:

U.S. to Canada	Canada to England	England to France	France to Germany	Germany to New York
$875 (U.S.)	$2200 (Canadian dollars)	£1600 (United Kingdom pound sterling)	12,000 F (French francs)	12,700 DM (deutsche marks)

What minimum amount of U.S. cash will she need in New York?

1.16. A U.S. contractor will design, fabricate, and erect a project in country X. Designing and fabricating are in the United States, while erection and assembly are in country X using the national labor of that country. The deal is agreed to at base time zero and will be adjusted for inflation within country X and exchange rate. The contract at time zero is as follows:

Time	U.S. Material	U.S. Cost for Erection in Country X
0	$6 million	$2 million

The estimator believes that the rate of inflation will be 10% and 25% annually in the United States and country X. The exchange rate of country X to the U.S. base is 1:1, 2:1, and 3:1 for years 1, 2, and 3. U.S. material cash flow is spread evenly over the first 2 years while erection will occur during year 3 in country X. The contract requires that the full lump sum is paid at year-end 3, adjusted for inflation and exchange rate. Assume that the inflation and exchange rates are independent.

  (a) If the U.S. material costs are spread uniformly over the first 2 years, what total amount will be roughly spent?

  (b) If the contractor will pay the national labor in that country's currency during year 3, how many country X value units are roughly expected? How many U.S. dollars?

  (c) What approximate sum of U.S. money is due to the contractor at year-end 3? What country X currency?

1.17. A reactor vessel can be built in Germany, England, or Italy and shipped to country Y for integration in a refinery. Quotes are received from contractors and ratioed to the U.S. estimate in terms of U.S. currency using Table 1.4 and spot exchange rates. According to the contract, payment is transacted between the two parties on the day the reactor reaches the port of entry of country Y. The exchange rate for the scheduled arrival is, however, different from that listed by the table and is shown as a relative change to the table.

	Germany	England	Italy
Ratio of subcontract bid to U.S. estimate	0.9992	1.0065	1.0062
Exchange rate on arrival compared to Table 1.4	+0.3%	−0.5%	+0.01%

The U.S. estimate for the reactor is $100 million.
(a) In which country should the vessel be built, and what is that cost in U.S. currency?
(b) What is the dollar penalty if the next-lowest country is selected?
(c) Where does nonnumerical judgment enter the decision process?

1.18. A small country is preparing for its anniversary and a politician wants 2500 busts of the president for distribution. Copper alloy will be used, but the weight of the bust depends on the copper alloy used. When the master of the bust was submerged in water, it displaced 0.00098 m^3 of water. An 80%–20% copper–zinc alloy required $2.50 per kilogram for copper and $2.07 per kilogram for zinc. The densities of copper and zinc are 8906 and 7144 kg/m^3. Your billing price is figured at seven times the metal cost. The country's currency is renolas, figured at a current exchange rate of 14.3 units to 1 U.S. dollar.
(a) Find the price for 2500 units in renolas and U.S. dollars.
(b) Convert the values to U.S. customary units and repeat part (a).

CASE STUDY:
THE VACUUM CHAMBER ENVIRONMENTAL TEST UNIT

A new vacuum chamber environmental test unit was required by an aerospace firm to supplement existing units because of an increased work load. The units were already scheduled to capacity during the contract time period. The test units are necessary as all components of a spacecraft require testing in a vacuum to simulate the altitude at which they will be operating in orbit. Existing vacuum units are a small 42-in.-diameter chamber with a high pumping capacity and fast vacuum pulldown time and a large 10-ft-diameter chamber for large-component testing. After a study of probable contract and component testing schedules and environmental requirements, it was decided that another unit was required. A satisfactory commercial system cannot be purchased, and a number of other solutions were proposed:

1. Repeat the existing design and construction of the small chamber, thereby saving the engineering design costs. This design sacrifices space (inside dimensions).
2. Design and build an intermediate-sized chamber with a larger 32-in. diffusion pump. This should relieve some of the load of the larger chamber.
3. Design and build an intermediate-sized chamber with the same pump stack as the small chamber, sacrificing some pumping capacity and pump time but saving the cost of the larger pump stack and its engineering.

4. Design and build an intermediate-sized chamber that is the same as described in solution 3 but add an additional port for another pump in the future, if required.

Although a solution to this case problem cannot be provided because pertinent information remains undisclosed, consider the initial design process facing the engineer. What steps of the (a) problem, (b) concepts, (c) engineering models, (d) evaluation, and (e) design are most significant here? Why? What kinds of information are necessary for estimating to accompany these plausible designs? What general elements of information would you classify as available or unavailable? Name typical measures of economic want that will allow selection of the preferred design. Prepare your answers in the form of a report.

2

Labor Analysis

Labor comprises one of the most important items of operation designs. Before one is able to estimate labor, there is an almost unquestioned dependence on an objective measurement or historical value of time. Methods to find labor time include time study, man-hour reports, and work sampling, and are provided in this chapter. Once time values are known for a design, they are multiplied by the wage or the wage and fringe costs. Sometimes labor time or cost are joint and must be examined to find unit cost. Thus analysis is required before labor estimating can begin.

2.1 LABOR

Labor has received intensive study, and many recording, measuring, and controlling schemes exist in an effort to manage labor. It can be classified a number of ways; for instance, direct–indirect, recurring–nonrecurring, designated–nondesignated, exempt–nonexempt, wage–salary, blue collar–management, and union–nonunion are choices. Social, political, educational, and type of work are other divisions that classify labor. Payment for wages may be based on attendance or performance. For cost estimating we select the *direct–indirect* classification as most appropriate.

For operation designs there is the simple qualitative formula

$$\text{labor cost} = \text{time} \times \text{wage} \tag{2.1}$$

The selection of *time* matches the requirements of the operation design. Time is expressed relative to a unit of measure and is denominated by terms such as piece, bag, bundle, container, 100 units, 1000 board feet (2.4 m^3), and so on. The unit of time may be second, minute, hour, man-day, man-week, month, or year. Thus we may use 15.025 hours per 100 units in manufacturing, or 14 man-hours per frame for building construction, or 15 man-months per tank for chemical processing construction. Neither the application nor the magnitude of the time affects the generality of Eq. (2.1). In early estimates the design may be only known roughly and larger chunks of time are used. But as the design becomes more detailed, so does refinement of time. In some situations the estimate of time may be a guesstimate and may be unrelated to any measured, referenced, or analyzed data. A *guesstimate* is based on the estimator's observational or rough experiences. There are circumstances where these personal judgmental values are unavoidable.

The second part of Eq. (2.1), *wage,* is defined in the context of the operation design. The design may be for one worker and one machine, or a crew with one machine, or a crew with several machines or processes. In the simplest case, one on one, the job description and job design are available to the estimator. The number used for the wage corresponds to the time period of work.

Units for the wage are dimensionally compatible to the time estimate. If the time as estimated is in hours per unit, the wage is expressed in dollars per hour. The wage may be the amount that the worker sees in the paycheck or it may include all or part of the fringe costs. The choice of what is included in the wage amount is coordinated with accounting analysis. Labor analysis is concerned with direct and not indirect labor. *Direct labor* is the time or cost of work that is directly related to the design. In manufacturing an example of direct labor is an assembler, while in construction the carpenter, mason, roofer, and so on, are typical. In some project designs engineers are classified as direct labor. Indirect labor in manufacturing is shop labor other than direct labor, such as stockroom clerks, foremen, and material handlers. In a construction project, indirect labor could be timekeepers or foremen. Said differently, direct labor "touches" the design, while indirect labor is supportive of that effort. Indirect labor and its costs are covered by overhead, a topic discussed in Chapter 4. Table 2.1 gives many of the definitions used in this chapter.

2.2 MEASURED TIME

There is a school of thought that asserts that "time is the measure of cost." Although the slogan is debatable, there is an element of truth when applied to the needs of detail cost estimating. For this activity there is an almost unquestioned dependence on an objective measure of time.

Historical facts may uncover costs about labor, supervision, methods, and a whole host of endeavors, but are subject to greater error. Measured time, on the other hand, is limited mostly to costs of direct labor. The two categories of work are direct and indirect. Most types of work can be segregated into one or the other category inasmuch as the direct–indirect category is determined by practice and definition. Discussed in this section are techniques of measuring labor. Time is measured, but it is the cost that is ultimately useful.

Although the cost estimator may not be concerned personally with the measurement of labor, he or she does depend on work measurement. The cost estimator is satisfied if such labor measurements are objective, as far as that is possible, and

Table 2.1. Definitions for Labor Analysis

Actual time	The time reported for work, which may include delays, idle time, and inefficiency as well as efficient effort
Allowance	An adjustment to the normal time providing for personal needs, fatigue, and special delays inherent in the work
Allowed time	Normal time increased by appropriate allowances (see Standard time); also, reported man-hours which are adjusted because of work differences or judgment
Avoidable delay	Interruption in the work that caused additional time which could have been avoided or minimized by the worker using better skill or judgment
Constant element	An element whose normal time is constant with respect to various independent effects on the element
Continuous timing	A method of time study where the total elapsed time from the start of the study is recorded at the end of each element
Cycle	The total time of elements from start to finish in a repetitive operation
Delay allowance	One part of the allowance included in the standard time for interruptions or delays beyond the operator's ability for prevention
Element	A subpart of an operation separated for timing and analysis; beginning and ending points are described, and the element is the smallest part of an operation observed by time study
Elemental breakdown	The description of the elements of an operation in a measurable sequence
Fatigue allowance	One part of the allowance caused by physiological reduction in ability to do work, sometimes included in the standard time
Foreign element	Unrelated to the operation and removed from the time study
Frequency of occurrence	The number of times an element occurs per operation or cycle
Idle time	A time interval in which the operator, equipment, or both are not performing useful work
Incentive	Financial methods motivating a worker to exceed a standard
Machine interference	Idle machine time occurring as a result of operator attention on another machine in multiple-machine work
Machine or process time	Time required by a machine or process
Man-hour	A unit of measure representing one person working for 1 hour
Normal time	An elemental or operation time which is found by multiplying the average observed time by a rating factor
Observed time	The time observed on the stopwatch/electronic clock and recorded on the time study sheet during the measurement process
Operation	Designated and described work subject to work measurement, estimating, and reporting

Table 2.1.   DEFINITIONS FOR LABOR ANALYSIS (continued)

Personal allowance	One part of the allowance included in the standard time for personal needs that occur throughout the working day
Rating factor	Involves comparing the performance of the operator under observation using experience or other bench marks; additionally, a numerical factor is noted for the elements or cycle; 100% is normal, and rating factors less than or greater than normal indicate slower or faster performance
Regular element	Elements that occur once in every cycle
Snap back	A method of timing that records the elemental time at the end point of the element
Snap observation	An observation made virtually instantaneous as to the state of the operation (i.e., idle, working, or the nature of the element)
Standard time	Sums of rated elements that have been increased for allowances
Variable element	An element whose normal time varies or depends upon one or more dependent effects

he or she is willing to use the information provided that plausible techniques were used in the determination of time. There are three methods for the measurement of time useful for estimating: time study, work sampling, and man-hour reports. Although one may argue in favor of a particular method, each is suitable and necessary for different occasions.

2.2.1 Fundamentals of Time Study

For our purpose it will not be necessary to delve into the historical background of time study. Suffice it to say that the founder of time and motion study was Frederick W. Taylor and that two of the leading pioneers were Frank and Lillian Gilbreth. Time study has many advantages, and it is useful in industry. With competition in any industry, it is necessary for management to know various cost factors and how much a proposed change decreases or increases cost. The determination of cost comparisons and analysis of this sort is made possible by time study, which is the backbone of many cost systems. Time study is the analysis of an operation to eliminate unnecessary elements and determine the better and cheaper method of doing the operation; to standardize methods, equipment, and conditions; and then, and only then, to determine by measurement the number of standard hours required for an average worker to do the job.

The stopwatch procedure goes something like this: (1) Conduct analysis of methods and improve if necessary; (2) record significant data; (3) separate the operation into elements; (4) record the time consumed by each element as it occurs each time; (5) rate the pace or tempo at which various elements of work are performed; (6) determine the allowances; and (7) convert rated elements into normal time, include allowances, and finally express the standard in common units of production.

Although this practice is criticized, its role in gathering time for production remains significant. Its greatest testimony lies in the fact that the majority of industrial enterprises in the United States depend on time study for a substantial amount of the data used in cost estimating.

The equipment for taking a time study is simple. A clipboard and an electronic timer or decimal minute or hour stopwatch is all that is required. The first and most important phase of taking a time study is its preparation. Is the job ready for timing? The time-study technician resolves this question by answering the following points: Is the proper tooling being used, and is it laid out correctly? Is the material laid out in an economical manner? Are proper machines or tools being used? Is the quality of the finished part or operation up to the inspection standards? Is the motion pattern employed the most economical that can be devised at this time? The second phase of the time study is to record the information on the time study form. After the title block information is recorded, the elements of work must be identified and written down in sequence. The technician keeps in mind when breaking down the operation that the elements should be as short as possible but long enough for timing accuracy. Wherever possible, manual operator time is separated from machine time. Wherever possible elements that are constant (or nearly so) are separated from variable elements. Elemental start and stop times should be easy to identify.

Consider the example of the assembly of a common electrical receptacle. A present method where assembly fixtures are not used is to be examined for possible improvements. The step to record significant information starts with a plan view sketch of the bench layout. Observe in Fig. 2.1 that only the barest of detail is shown, as certainly the precise location of the screwdriver or stackbins is not critical.

In Fig. 2.2 a sketch of the parts for assembly is given. Certainly, drawings are available if additional information becomes necessary. Notice that the title block lists other information which may be used for additional detail.

At this point the observer watches the details of the operation and separates the operation into elements. Trial and error is expected at this point because short-time elements having clearly defined start and stop points are important. Observe that element 1 is: "Right hand reaches for back plate at bin A and grasps." Bin A has been previously located on the layout sketch. In a similar way the other seven elements are described. There may be some experimental timing to get a feeling for the length of the time for the elements.

Observe Fig. 2.3, where the elements are abbreviated. Each line number is for a particular cycle. A cycle for the receptacle would be eight elements. Space on the form is available for foreign elements which are unrelated and a letter from A to I is used for coding if they occur unintentionally during a cycle. Foreign elements are removed from time studies later.

Actual timing is continuous or snap back. If the time study were continuous, the entry for line 1, element 1, would be 0830 (eight-thirty in the morning) under column R and each element would be registered consecutively. At the conclusion an approximate time of 0945 would be entered in line 15, element under column R. The "R" designates time-study *reading*. A snap-back method records the time for

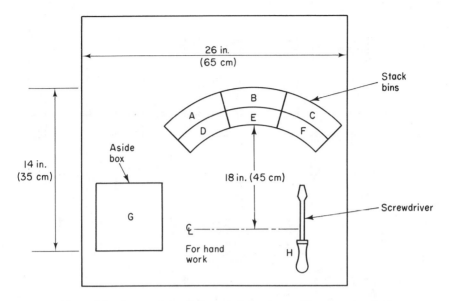

Figure 2.1.   Layout of electrical receptacle bench assembly—present method.

each element individually. On mechanical clocks, this involves depressing the crown, which resets the clock hands to zero. A similar "zeroing" button exists for electronic clocks. But observe that under element R, column 8, the times 0.60, . . . , 0.48, are the cycle times for the operations. Following the end of the cycle, the time is reset to zero, at which time the next line starts with zero. Thus the elements of this time study are continuously timed but have a cycle snap back.

Time studies for repetitive operations may be recorded in seconds, minutes, or hours. The time study of Fig. 2.3 is in decimal minutes. Once time recording is under way, the observer time-marks the end of each element for each line under the column R. The reading of a moving hand of a clock or electronic digital number and marking the value on the time-study form, which corresponds to the conclusion of the element, requires training. The number of readings necessary for a good average is a matter of judgment and depends on the consistency of the cycle time.

During the observation the observer has been judging the effort of the operator in performing the elements and operation. Called *rating,* the observer is watching the performance or speed as motions, elements, and operations are made and comparing this mentally to a 100% speed. This operator's effort, which is reflected in the rating factor, includes intangibles such as health, interest in work, and skill, as well as speed. If the operator's effort is considered in excess of normal, that being 100%, the rating factor is greater than 1. On the other hand, if the effort is considered less than 100%, the rating factor is less than 1. The rating factor is entered for each element in the row titled "Element rating factor." The rating factor for the elements and the operation are not necessarily equally weighted. This rating may be at the

Timed by R. Van Jones	Checked by Theo Davies	Workplace or mach. 0738	Mach. no. —
Operators name Gerald Jeffer	Clock No. 303 - 9109	Material See sketch	R.P.M. —
Time study no.	Dept. No. Electrical assembly	Lubricant —	Strokes per min. —
Special tools used None			Feed
Part name Electrical receptacle	Part No. 1050		Operation No. 40
Remarks			

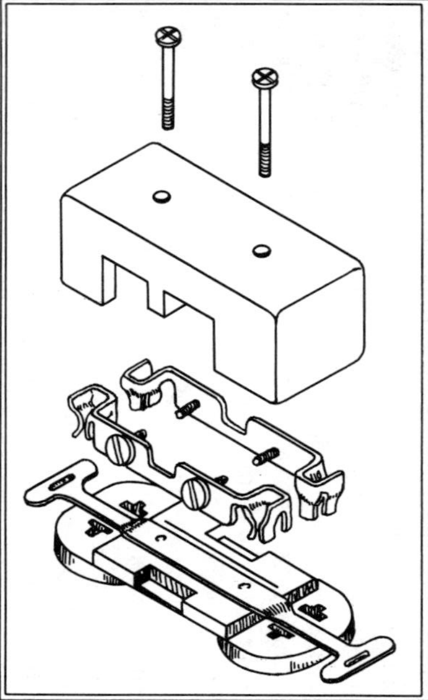

DETAILED DESCRIPTIONS OF ELEMENTS

1. Right hand reaches for back plate at bin A and grasps

2. Moves to left hand, reaches for mounting ear at B and grasps, mounting ear and inserts. Left hand holds.

3. Right hand reaches for contact and inserts (from C)

4. Right hand reaches for contact and inserts (from C)

5. Right hand reaches, grasps, transports, and places back plate over back plate. Left hand holds.

6. Reaches for A screw at F, grasps. Transports, positions with right hand. Left hand holds.

7. Same as 6.

8. Right hand reaches for screwdriver at H, grasps and transports to back plate, and tightens screw. Left hand aside assembly. Right hand returns screwdriver.

Figure 2.2

Time study observation

Date SEPT 23
Time start 8:30 AM
Time stop 9:45 AM
Elapsed time 1:15

Sheet no. 1
No. sheets 1

Elements
1. Pick up back plate
2. Mount ear to back plate
3. Gunbacks in back plate
4. Contacts in back plate
5. back plate, face plate
6. Place plate over back plate
7. Place screw in back plate
8. Tighten screw and assemble

Line	1 (T)	1 (F)	2 (R)	2 (T)	3 (R)	3 (T)	4 (R)	4 (T)	5 (R)	5 (T)	6 (R)	6 (T)	7 (R)	7 (T)	8 (R)	8 (T)
1	.03	.03	.06	.08	.08	.16	.05	.21	.05	.26	.09	.35	.04	.39	.21	.60
2	.03	.03	.03	.06	.05	.11	.03	.14	.06	.20	.04	.24	.05	.29	.17	.46
3	.02	.02	.04	.06	.04	.10	.04	.14	.08	.22	.04	.26	.05	.31	.16	.47
4	.02	.02	.04	.06	.04	.10	.04	.14	.06	.20	.04	.24	.05	.29	.16	.45
5	.02	.02	.06	.07	.05	.12	.03	.15	.05	.20	.04	.24	.05	.29	.15	.44
6	.02	.02	.03	.06	.05	.10	.04	.14	.04	.18	.06	.24	.04	.28	.16	.43
7	.02	.02	.03	.06	.06	.10	.05	.16	.06	.21	.04	.25	.06	.31	.16	.47
8	.04	.04	.03	.07	.05	.12	.06	.17	.04	.21	.06	.27	.05	.55	.14	.49
9	.02	.02	.04	.06	.06	.11	.04	.15	.05	.20	.04	.24	.08	.32	.15	.47
10	.04	.04	.08	.04	.04	.12	.04	.16	.05	.21	.06	.27	.05	.32	.16	.48
11	.02	.02	.05	.07	.07	.14	.07	.21	.05	.26	.04	.30	.09	.39	.14	.63
12	.03	.03	.04	.07	.08	.16	.07	.22	.05	.27	.04	.31	.04	.35	.21	.56
13	.02	.02	.03	.05	.06	.11	.03	.14	.08	.22	.06	.27	.05	.32	.15	.47
14	.03	.03	.04	.07	.02	.09	.06	.15	.12	.27	.06	.33	.05	.38	.18	.56
15	.03	.03	.02	.05	.06	.11	.03	.14	.08	.22	.06	.27	.06	.32	.16	.48
16																

Number / Notes

Summary

	1	2	3	4	5	6	7	8
Total time	.39	.52	.79	.67	.92	.75	.63	2.45
No. of readings	15	15	15	15	15	15	15	15
Average of readings	.026	.035	.053	.045	.061	.050	.055	.163
Frequency	One out	out	OP	One				
Average time	.026	.035	.053	.045	.061	.050	.055	.163
Element rating factor	1.05	1.00	1.00	.95	.90	1.00	1.00	1.05
Element normal time	.027	.035	.053	.043	.055	.060	.055	.171

SUM = 7.36

Sum = 0.489

Foreign elements

SYM	R	T	Description
A			
B			
C			
D			
E			
F			
G			
H			
I			

Av. cycle time $\frac{7.36}{15} = .491$
Cycle rating factor 1.05
Normal cycle time 0.515

Percent allowances

Pers.	Fat.	Delay	Total
5%	5%	5%	15%

Std. time per unit 0.606
Pieces per hour 99
Std hours per 100 1.010

Allowances in minutes

Pers.	Fat.	Delay	Total
.008	.008	.008	.024

Avail. prod. min. per hr.
Pieces per hour 1.05
Std hrs per 100

Figure 2.3

31

conclusion of the study. While the rating process is often criticized as arbitrary, observers can be trained. Despite the criticism, it will become evident later that rating is necessary for effective cost estimating. With the rating factor posted, the shop portion of the time study is concluded, and the observer returns to his or her desk to complete the analysis.

The next step is to analyze the time study. Subtractions are made for each element and posted under column T, which means *time*. For instance, line 1, element 4, has $0.21 - 0.16 = 0.05$, which is written under column T4. This subtraction is made for all T columns and cycles. If the timing had been snap back, the subtraction would not be required.

Next we total column T for each element and divide by the number of observations to obtain the average of the readings. In this time study, the elements are *regular*, as they occur once for each cycle. It is possible that an element may occur several times or fractionally for each element and be *irregular*. This fraction of the noncyclic elements is entered in the frequency row. Once the element is multiplied by the element rating factor, we have *normal time,* which is an average qualified workman working at a normal pace. This entry for each column T is made for the bottom row, "Element normal time," and the row sum $= 0.489$.

Observe the sum of 7.36 arising from the total under 8R. The average cycle time gives $7.36/15 = 0.491$, which is marked on the form. When multiplied by the 1.05 cycle rating factor the normal cycle time is 0.515 ($= 0.491 \times 1.05$), which compares to the 0.489. That these two values are not identical is not surprising because the rating factor is a trained but arbitrary value.

After determining the normal cycle time, we add for the job allowances. During a time study, all irregular elements or interruptions for personal and unavoidable delays are purged. Thus a time study is a picture of regular work elements only. But other legitimate needs are necessary for an operator to sustain work throughout the shift. Personal and functional body needs are added, and about 4 to 5% is the U.S. customary value.

Operator interruptions beyond his or her control required for tool breakage, out of parts, foreman instructions, and so on, are also considered, and the usual range is 2 to 8%. These are added to the allowances and are called *delays*.

Fatigue is another factor included within allowances. *Fatigue* is physiological body wear reducing the ability to do work—it is not "tiredness," as that is expected—and is not really subject to precise measurement. For instance, hot, heavy, dirty work such as forging of steel billets has a higher allowance than light assembly work in a controlled, air-conditioned factory. Some practitioners believe that fatigue does not really exist in most factory environments. But fatigue allowance percentages are determined by practice or union negotiation or common sense. Fatigue may vary from 0 to 25% depending on average weight handled, percent of time under load, repetitive or nonrepetitive work, sitting or standing, and cycle time.

These allowances—personal, fatigue, and delay—are sometimes referred to as *PF&D allowances*. A typical allowance is 15%, but it can vary from 8% to 35%. The allocation of the allowance in cost-estimating procedure is as a percentage of

480 minutes. As productive time in the workday is inversely proportional to the amount of PF&D allowance, the allowance should be expressed as a percentage of the total work day. The three portions of the allowance are added as a percent of the workday. Next we divide the total workday by the productive day expressed as a percent of the workday,

$$F_a = \frac{100\%}{100\% - PF\&D\%} \tag{2.2}$$

where F_a = allowance multiplier for PF&D

PF&D = personal, fatigue, and delay allowance expressed as a percentage

Assume that all allowances total 15%, which is 72 minutes of the 480-minute workday. Converting this allowance to a percentage of the 408-minute productive day results in a multiplier of

$$F_a = \frac{100\%}{100\% - 15\%} = 1.176$$

We apply the allowance by multiplying the normal time by the allowance factor. If the rated productive time is 408 minutes, the job standard would be 408 × 1.176 = 480 minutes.

The job standard is computed as*

$$T_s = T_n \times F_a \tag{2.3}$$

where T_s = standard time for a job per unit

T_n = normal cycle time per unit

Observe that for the electrical receptacle we have 0.515 × 1.176 = 0.606 standard minute per unit.

Equation (2.3) did not state whether the time was minutes, hours, or man-days; that depends on the dimension of the time measurement (i.e., hour, day, week, second, minute, etc.). While the basic approach is unaffected by the magnitude of the time, it is customary in production work to use minutes or hours. If minutes are the dimension of the measurement, they are converted to pieces or units of production per time period by a reciprocal relationship. If pieces per hour are desired, then

$$\text{pieces per hour} = 60/T_s \tag{2.4}$$

Various firms prefer expressions such as pieces per hour, units per minute, or packages per week. In some businesses it is common to express the rate per dozen or gross. However the expression may be written, the dimension *units per time* is not as preferred as *hour per unit or units* for cost-estimating work.

The conversion is handled by

$$H_s = T_s \times \frac{N}{60} \tag{2.5}$$

---

*An alternative common expression is $T_s = T_n(1 + PF\&D)$, where PF&D allowance is expressed as a decimal. It is not as accurate in definition, but is often used for simplicity.

where H_s = hours per quantity of units

T_s = standard minutes per unit

N = standard quantity of units, 1, 10, 100, 1000, or 10,000

The value N may be 1, 10, 100, 1000, or 10,000, depending on the nature of the production (i.e., one or several to large volume). When *hours* are used, a *standard* is always implied, meaning the rated time is adjusted by an allowance multiplier. As N may range from 1 to 10,000 (and even 10^6 quantities are common in cigarette manufacture), a principle called *exaggeration of precision* is stated for purposes of cost-estimating sensitivity. We recommend the following number of trailing decimals:

Standard Quantity	Required Trailing Decimals	Time-Study Example (Fig. 2.3)
1	.x	*
10	.xx	0.10/10 units
100	.xxx	1.010/100 units
1000	.xxxx	10.0979/1000 units
10,000	.xxxxx	100.97920/10,000 units

*Scientific notation (1.01×10^{-2}) is not used in cost-estimating work.

If H_s is expressed as "hours per 100 units," we would have for the time study (Fig. 2.3) $H_s = 1.010$ (= $0.606 \times 100/60$). Pieces per hour are 99 (= $60/0.606$). Industrial practice will round down and drop the fractional part. Pieces per hour is a rough shop value. The more accurate H_s is preferred for calculations. Once H_s is known for a job, we are ready to calculate operation labor cost after we have determined the wage.

Nonrepetitive time study. It should be understood what we examined previously dealt with repetitive work found in production industries. Frequently, we are unable to study more than one cycle. Nonrepetitive time study, although not as accurate and free from error as other methods, does provide information. Sometimes called production study or all-day time study, it has been found useful for construction operations, indirect labor, production setups for highly repetitive work, allowances for repetitive work, audits, and direct-labor long-cycle type of work. This class of work is called *undesignated*, as it is difficult to preplan. The nonrepetitive time study differs from the repetitive motion and time study in a number of ways. The job study is not as complete, rating is frequently ignored, the preliminary investigation may be less, and preknowledge of the elements is unknown. It uses continuous timing with a stop watch and the length of the elements is based on judgment. The types of work for which this is best suited are carpentry, railroad line work, material handling, maintenance, secretarial activities, and so forth.

Predetermined motion-time data.   These data systems are an organized body of information used in evaluation of manual work. The data are expressed in time units, such as hours or minutes, for human motions. The analysis involves breaking down the elements of an operation into motions and assigning a time value which has been previously determined and tabulated. These time values are published and generally available. Observe that the electrical receptacle time study for element 1 is described as: "Right hand *reaches* for back plate at bin A and *grasps*." Reach and grasp are typical motions that are too brief in terms of time to observe and record. These systems will provide time for these motions. Predetermined motion-time data systems require care in application and in the common form of tabular presentation are not significant in cost estimating, except in high-volume industries. For high-volume operations, time study is not required, which is one of the claimed advantages for these systems. Additional information may be studied by examining the References.

2.2.2 Man-Hour Reports

For certain types of work, such as construction, crew work, long-cycle production, job shops, or professional work, methods of obtaining time information for analysis and later estimating are different from those found within short-cycle production work. Man-hour reports are the usual way to deal with nonrepetitive work, which is difficult to measure. In some cases there may be company policies prohibiting the practice of time study.

The *man-hour, man-month,* or *man-year* is the measure of time eventually desired from these reports. The basic unit of measure represents one worker working for 1 hour. While the number of working days will vary in a month or year due to holidays, vacation, sick leave, and so on, for cost analysis the man-year is defined as work of 52 weeks with 40 hours in each week. A man-month is 173.3 hours per month. Man-minutes or man-weeks are uncommon units and are discouraged in cost estimating application. Some cost-estimating activities plan their calendar as 13 months of 4 weeks to avoid the unequal months. In practice, one can add qualifications such as the (1) time spent as actual clock hours or (2) adjustment of work effort to allowed time. In this first qualification the individual is assumed to have spent time in idleness, relaxation, or nonproductive effort, while in the second these conditions are removed and an allowance is contrived to give the standard requirement of the PF&D for the estimated work. Man-hours are used for estimating if they are relatively constant, preknown, and unaffected by changes in wage rates, overtime, bonuses, and so forth. Examples of man-hour units are as follows:

Number of man-hours per inch (2.54 cm) of weld

Number of man-hours to erect 100 ft^2 (9.3 m^2) of framework

Number of man-months per mile (1850 m) of road construction

Information for man-hour analysis is usually obtained from the job ticket or the foreman report. The worker usually completes his or her own job ticket, which is verified by a timekeeper or collected by the owner, foreman, or manager. The foreman's report, on the other hand, will have similar information and content, but is compiled by first-level functional management or a shop manager. In either situation the information can be computerized, but electronic reporting and analysis does not alter the fundamental approach. The job ticket or foreman's report is used initially to find the number of man hours. Later the same reporting document is used for cost and time control.

Consider an example in a small contract welding shop where job tickets are used. Observe from Table 2.2 that the items of interest are operation, elapsed time, and units completed. Note that this job ticket has no foreman's approval, time-keeper's mark, or any external verification. From the job tickets, and with the aid of other instruction sheets or engineering drawings, the cost estimator will examine the data for consistency, completeness, and accuracy. He or she may check back with the operator or foreman on questions that arise. In a contract job shop, there is little repetition of similar work, so the estimator may choose to purge or alter information. This reworking of data is risky, but in analyzing historical work data, the first step is to clean up the information as rationally as is possible. If raw data are used as received, other problems arise later.

Job tickets are collected for similar work and a *spread sheet* is devised to show the data of interest. There is no single best way to devise a spread sheet, but it brings together the facts and prepares the data for subsequent mathematical analysis. At this point judgment is necessary, as in our example, Triton Job Shop. The welding operations are varied and the cost estimator chooses to analyze the general operation *welding* rather than divide the process into one of the many welding methods. Observe in Table 2.3 that several thicknesses, welding methods, and two-part numbers have been posted on the spread sheet. The mixing of processes and handling time into one lump time value is not an immaterial detail. But the cost estimator in this small job shop may choose to reduce, leave as is, or increase the three job-ticket

Table 2.2 JOB TICKET USEFUL FOR MAN-HOUR ANALYSIS

TRITON JOB TICKET

Name _Michael Blakely_ Employee no. _505 30 9709_

Date _May 13_ Order no. _101_

Part no. _6682_ Part name _Bracket_

Time started _9:15_ Time stopped _11:43_ Quantity _3_

Operation _Weld 40 x 80 x 3/4 in. (100 x 200 x 1.9 cm)_

plate. Submerged arc weld. Butt weld two fillets, 240 in.

_(600 cm)_

Special instructions _Automatic weld_

Table 2.3. SPREAD-SHEET EXAMPLE OF A MAN-HOUR REPORT FOR WELDING

Part no.	Material	Thickness x length	Welding method	Job ticket actual man-hours	Remarks	Allowed time man-hours
6682 (3 units)	Steel	3/4 (1.9) x 240 in. (600 cm)	Submerged arc butt weld 2 fillets	2.47	Fillet 2 sides reduce by 1/2 for one side and 2 extra units	1.24
7216	Steel	1/2 (12.7) x 84 in. (213 cm)	Shielded metal arc, 1 fillet	1.06	No change	1.06
8313	Steel	3/16 (4.8), 1/4 (6.4), 1/2 (12.7), x 344 in. (874 cm)	Shielded metal arc	1.18	Increase by 1/4 for various thicknesses	1.48

times to give allowed time. The allowed times will later be considered for man-hour estimating data, but in this chapter our concern is measurement, collection, and data refinement.

In engineering construction a *cost code* is used for specifications, data filing, cost analysis, and estimate assurance. Labor, materials, equipment costs, subcontract payments, and all such expenditures are posted from original documents and recorded against a cost code number. This transfer of information is similar to accounting procedures. Posting may be handled by the cost estimator. For labor the man hours are removed from job tickets or foreman's reports and recorded against summaries arranged by a cost code suited to the needs of the contractor.

The structure of the cost code is a compromise. Overall, it cannot accommodate cost estimators exclusively. In a practical way, a cost-estimating department maintains its own library of information. The use of specific man-hour data is infrequent, but the requirements for diversified data are high. This results from the variety of work and implies that estimating-information preparation and retrieval is a large undertaking. A cost-estimating information system must serve many purposes. Can an information profile be developed, although not exclusively used by cost estimators, to provide data that will be germane to estimating? Fortunately, the content of the construction estimates is similar. The numbering of estimating cost codes should be arranged to allow consistent posting as well as retrieval of this information. Obviously, having fewer codes and subcodes reduces work, while many subcodes increase work. Inordinate detail tends to increase inaccuracies in cost distribution, while too few details limit cost control. Compromise and balance are necessary. Cost codes vary widely as arabic numerals, upper- and lowercase letters, and a sprinkling of periods, dashes, colons, and hyphens are found. A simple system using only arabic numerals in progressive order is satisfactory for general use. For example, a building construction cost code can be broadly divided into 16 divisions as shown in Table 2.4.

Each of these divisions can be expanded; for instance, Framing and Sheathing, can be indented into sections for further enlargement, as shown by Table 2.5. Not all numbers are assigned allowing opportunity for expansion. Observe in Table 2.4 that the first two digits indicate the division number, while the remaining three indicate a section number. Subordinate information may be further indexed by placing a decimal point at the end of the assigned number, and adding digits to the right

Table 2.4. INITIAL COST CODE FOR BUILDING CONSTRUCTION

1. General	9. Finishes
2. Site work	10. Specialties
3. Concrete	11. Equipment
4. Masonry	12. Furnishings
5. Metals	13. Special construction
6. Wood and plastic	14. Conveying system
7. Thermal and moisture protection	15. Mechanical
8. Doors and windows	16. Electrical

Table 2.5.   EXPANDED COST CODE FOR WOOD AND PLASTIC

06100 Rough carpentry
06110 Framing and sheathing
06111 Light wooden structure framing
06112 Preassembled components
06113 Sheathing
06114 Diaphragms
06130 Heavy timber construction
06150 Trestles
06170 Prefabricated structural wood
06200 Finish carpentry
06300 Wood treatment
06400 Architectural woodwork
06500 Prefabricated structural plastics
06600 Plastic fabrications

of the decimal point (i.e., 06111.10), such as rough framing a light wooden partition on the first floor of a two-story house.

Now we turn from the organization of construction information to labor analysis after its posting from job tickets or foreman's reports on cost code summaries. The reported man hours may be from a contractor who may or may not be familiar with the conditions at the project site; supervision can be adequate or inadequate. Climate and environment may range from harsh to favorable, and the workweek may be 40 hours or include overtime. A standard man hour, on the other hand, is one where the contractor is familiar with the site, the weather is favorable, supervision is adequate, and the workweek is 40 hours. The difference between favorable and unfavorable efficiency is a topic covered in Chapter 11.

If man-hour spread sheets are to be of value as a permanent measured record, their backup data must include a variety of information to permit the cost estimator to weigh deviations from the observations. In construction work, weather conditions, skill of the crews (experienced or green, native or imported) equipment, hazards, location of work, material condition, and type of construction are vital factors that need to be known. These remarks appear on the foreman's report and the cost estimator makes office adjustments for these effects. These adjustments lead to *allowed time,* which is an intermediate value from observed hours to standard manhours. The adjustments may be derived from engineering instructions, other information, or as a last resort be based on the estimator's experience or hunch. Sometimes the foreman's report lumps together elements of work which are unsuitable for this analysis.

Observe Table 2.6, in which the foreman reports the daily work associated with a residence, elapsed time, and weather conditions. At this point the estimator gathers other foreman's reports. After evolving a spread sheet, the work is matched against cost code 06111.10, "rough framing of partitions." Not all details are given in the foreman's report and the estimator will recapitulate the essence of the work to satisfy the requirements of the residence drawings. He or she may visit the job

Table 2.6. FOREMAN'S REPORT USEFUL FOR MAN-HOUR ANALYSIS

FOREMAN'S DAILY REPORT

Foreman _Jim Diekmann_ Date _Dec. 5_ Address _6682 Whaley_
Workman _Walter Meyer, Carpenter_
    Pete Weichmann, Laborer

Time start	Description
0800	Wall, wooden partition on wooden deck, westside.
	8 × 26 ft. (2.4 × 7.8 m)
	92 1/4 in. (2.34 m) studs, 16 in. (0.4 m) on
	Centers. Set windows. 2-3 × 4 ft.
16:30	(0.9 × 1.2 m). 4 Extra corner Studs.

Weather _Stormy, cold 40-50°F_
Other unusual conditions _None_

site from time to time and is informed about the skills of the carpenter and laborer who might be working on the job. In the remarks column the estimator will indicate the efficiency of the labor and provide a percentage of the work devoted to the major elements of the operation to construct a partition wall. Observe that in Table 2.7 the elapsed time of 8.0 hours × 2 crew = 16 total hours reduced by 80% for cold weather, which results in an allowed total of 12.8 hours. This is subdivided into work percentages required for window or door openings and extra corner studs. The man hours are matched to important units of output.

In summary, man-hour reports are derivative time values adjusted by the estimator from job tickets or foreman reports. That the data are nonhomogeneous is evident, and judgment and skill are inescapable to match the work to allowed man hours.

2.2.3 Work Sampling

Work sampling is another technique for gathering information about large segments of a work force population. It is a counting method for quantitative analysis in terms of time or percent of the activities of men, machines, or any observable state of an operation and is useful in analysis of undesignated or nonrepetitive work activities and allowances. Relatively inexpensive to obtain, and convenient to perform, it can be conducted without recourse to a stopwatch or the necessity for historical reports. A work-sampling study consists of a number of observations taken pertaining to the specific activities of the person(s) or machine(s) at random inter-

Table 2.7. SPREAD-SHEET EXAMPLE FOR MAN-HOUR REPORT OF ROUGH FRAMING

Cost code	Job description	Elapsed time	Crew size	Remarks	Allowed man-hours
06111.10	Frame west side of 2 story house	8.0	2	Cold, 80%	
	Standard 8 x 26 ft (2.4 x 7.8 m) partition			60%	7.68
	2 window openings 3 x 4 ft (0.9 x 1.2 m)			35%	4.48
	4 extra corner studs			5%	0.64
06111.10	Rough carpentry wall, first floor	5.55	2	Normal, 100%	
	Standard 8 x 31 ft (2.4 x 9.3 m) partition			40%	4.44
	1 window, 8 x 4 ft (2.4 x 1.2 m) opening			30%	3.33
	1 double door, 6 ft (1.8 m) wide, rough opening			14%	1.55
	8 extra studs			16%	1.78
06111.10	Rough frame side wall of house	9.0	3	Green labor, 60%	
	Standard 8 x 52 ft (2.4 x 15.6 m) partition			50%	7.9
	1 window 3 x 4 ft (0.9 x 1.2 m) opening			12%	2.0
	Glass door 6 ft wide (1.8 m) opening			10%	1.6
	1 window 6 x 4 ft (1.8 x 1.2 m) opening			15%	2.5
	10 extra studs			13%	2.2

41

vals. These observations are classified into predefined categories directly related to the work situation. During the course of the work-sampling study, tally marks are made by the technician, such as "work," "idle," or "absent." The key to the accuracy is the number of observations, which may vary according to the requirements. One survey may require very broad areas to be investigated, in which case relatively few observations will be necessary to obtain meaningful results. On the other hand, to establish production standards for use with construction costs, many thousands of observations may be needed. In determining the number of observations necessary, the technician predetermines the accuracy of his results. Four thousand observations will provide more reliable results than 400. However, if accuracy is unimportant, 400 observations may be ample.

As work sampling is a statistical technique, the laws of probability must be followed to obtain accuracy of the sampling estimate. In this type of observation, an event such as equipment working or idle is instantly tallied. For this selective choice mathematicians define a binomial expression where the mean of the binomial distribution is equal to Np_i, with N equaling the number of observations and p_i the probability or relative frequency of event i occurring. The variance of this binomial distribution is equal to $Np_i(1 - p_i)$. As N becomes large the binomial distribution approaches the normal distribution. As work-sampling studies involve large sample sizes, the normal distribution is considered an adequate approximation to the binomial. In work sampling we take a sample of size N observations in an attempt to estimate p_i or

$$p'_i = \frac{N_i}{N} \tag{2.6}$$

where p'_i = observed proportion of occurrence of an event i expressed as a decimal

N_i = number of instantaneous observations of event i

N = total number of random observations

Formula 2.6 is related to the binomial, and this random variable is called a *proportion*. As shown in textbooks on probability, the standard error of a sample proportion for a binomial distribution may be expressed by

$$\sigma_{p'} = \left[\frac{p'(1 - p')}{N} \right]^{1/2} \tag{2.7}$$

where $\sigma_{p'}$ is the standard deviation of the proportion of the binomial sampling distribution. In any sampling procedure, bias and errors may occur. This results in a deviation of p' and p *or the true value*. A tolerable maximum sampling error in terms of a confidence interval I commensurate with the nature and importance of the study can be preestablished. For instance, if $p' = 62\%$, and if a maximum interval of 4% is desired, then $I = 4\%$ for 60 to 64%, or 62% $\pm$ 2% where $I/2 = 2\%$. The relative accuracy is $0.02/0.62 \times 100 = 3.2\%$. This confidence and interval may be viewed by examining Fig. 2.4. The factor 1.645 is obtained from a table of probabilities for the normal distribution for a confidence of 90%, which is usual for work-sampling studies. The total area under a normal curve is 100% and the oppor-

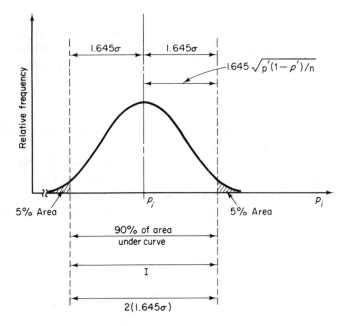

Figure 2.4. Analogous curve from "normal" relationships to binomial work-sampling practices.

tunity for a sampling value p' to fall within the tails is given by Appendix I, and is equal to $\pm Z = 2 \times$ probability from the table for a given Z. For instance, if Z ranges from -1.645 to $+1.645$, the probability that the true value p will be between the limits is $2 \times 0.45 = 0.90$, while the probability that the true value will be outside the limits is $1 - 0.90$ or 10%. The value 0.4500 is determined from Appendix I. Some values of Z corresponding to confidence areas are as follows:

Area between Limits (%)	$-Z$ to $+Z$	Area outside Limits (%)
68	±1.000	32
90	±1.645	10
95	±1.960	5
99	±2.576	1

The sampling interval is given by

$$I = 2Z \left[\frac{p'_i(1 - p'_i)}{N} \right]^{1/2} \tag{2.8}$$

where I = desired interval expressed as a decimal
      Z = factor from normal tables for a chosen confidence

We expect that the true value of p falls within the range $p' \pm 1.645\sigma_{p'}$ approximately 90% of the time. In other words, if p is the true percentage of work estimate, the estimate will fall outside $p' \pm 1.645\sigma_{p'}$ only about 10 times in 100 due to chance alone. Equation (2.9) may be solved for the sample size when the other factors are either assumed or known, as

$$N_i = \frac{4Z^2 p'_i(1\,(1 - p'_i)}{I^2} \qquad (2.9)$$

That value of N_i which is maximum from the events i is chosen as N for the work-sampling study. *Relative accuracy* is found as $I/2p'$.

As an example of work sampling in construction, assume a job where carpenter crews are forming layup walls on a dam. These concrete retaining walls are numerous and standard. In addition, the carpenters are doing other work, but their principal activity relates to the layup walls. Once the work is understood, we define the job elements as:

1. Form layup walls.
2. Inspection waits.
3. Set up for form work.
4. Crane waits.
5. Miscellaneous.

A preliminary study such as Table 2.8 will help to uncover problems before the major study is started. It will help to sell the idea, and importantly, a percentage of observations falling into each activity will give a useful, though rough, estimate of the universe percentages. Note in Table 2.8 that we might decide that inspection waits are not an important enough element to consider separately, especially if we have little control over them, so we decide to add inspection waits to the "miscellaneous" activity. But we found that material waits in miscellaneous deserved a separate category, and we may have some management control over these waits. Rearranging the data we would have (1) form layup walls, 62%; (2) set up for form work, 16%; (3) crane waits, 12%; (4) material waits, 4%; and (5) miscellaneous, 6%.

With the job elements now defined, the next step deals with calculating the number of observations. The number of observations for the study depends on the

Table 2.8. EXAMPLE OF STICK CHART FOR PRELIMINARY STUDY

Element	Observations	p'
1. Form layup walls	THL THL THL THL THL THL I	62 %
2. Inspections	III	6 %
3. Setup for form work	THL III	16 %
4. Crane waits	THL I	12 %
5. Miscellaneous	II	4 %
		100 %

percentage of observations in each element and the size of the desired confidence interval. For example, we might estimate that an element will occur somewhere close to 60 or 64%, and a 90% confidence interval on a plus-minus tolerance of 2% or less is desirable. Our first estimate of sample size in our example is based on preliminary percentages, and Table 2.9 indicates the appropriate tolerances. The largest sample size will control the study and in this case we need about 2858 observations. Notice that it is element 3, which is not the largest proportion. Our next step is to spread the observations equally among the days and then randomly within the working day, excluding break and lunch periods.

In retrospect it becomes possible to determine the magnitude of the sampling error after the test is underway or concluded. Assume that for element 2, and partially through the study where $N = 875$, a total of $N_2 = 184$ tally marks are indicated, and $p'_2 = 0.21$. This would give an interval of

$$I = 2(1.645)\left[\frac{0.21 \times 0.79}{875}\right]^{1/2} = 0.045$$

and we can say that the true value lies within 0.21 ± 0.023 with a probability of 90%. Observe that the lower value $0.187 (= 0.21 - 0.023)$ does not lie in the interval of element 2 $(0.145, 0.175)$ as given in Table 2.9. The student may want to explain this observation in terms of sampling errors, interval, and probability.

With work-sampling information about the event or job and a percentage fact for each, it is possible to compute labor cost. A model using these data is

$$H_s = \frac{(N_i/N)HR(1 + PF\&D)}{N_p} \tag{2.10}$$

where H_s = standard man-hours per job element i
N_i = number of event i observations
H = total man-hours worked during study
R = rating factor
PF&D = allowance decimal
N_p = work units accomplished during period of observing this event.

Table 2.9 FINDING SAMPLE SIZE FOR CONSTRUCTION STUDY
USING 90% CONFIDENCE INTERVAL

Element	Rough, p'	Desired Interval, I	N_i	Relative Accuracy, $\frac{I}{2p'} \times 100$ (%)	90% Confidence Interval
1	0.62	0.04	1594	± 3.2	0.60–0.64
2	0.16	0.03	1616	9.4	0.145–0.175
3	0.12	0.02	2858	8.3	0.11–0.13
4	0.04	0.02	1042	25	0.03–0.05
5	0.06	0.02	1527	17	0.05–0.07

Assume a construction job where carpenters form layup walls on a dam. The study runs for 3 weeks for 14 carpenters. During the course of random work sampling, ratings similar to time-study practices are made, and $R = 0.96$ is determined. A total of 17 frames are finished, and work sampling indicates that this event N_i/N = 62% of the total effort of the gang. For an allowance of 20% the time per frame may be found as

$$H_s = \frac{0.62(14 \times 3 \times 40) \times 0.96 \times 1.20}{17} = 70.6 \text{ man-hours per frame}$$

Work sampling is a tool that has broad ramifications for the cost estimator. It allows the work sampler to get the facts in an easy and fast way. In summary, the following considerations should be kept in mind for work sampling:

1. Explain and sell the work-sampling method before putting it to use.
2. Isolate individual studies to similar groups of machines, operations, or activities.
3. Use as large a sample size as is practical, economical, and timely.
4. Observe the data at random times.
5. Take the observations over reasonably long periods of time, for example, 2 weeks or more, although rigid rules must bend with the situation and design of the study.

2.3 WAGE AND FRINGE RATES

A *wage* is that money which is paid or received for work by the hour, day, or week, and once denominated by a period of time, it becomes a *wage rate*, for example, $12.75 per hour. A salaried employee is paid for a period of time, say a week, month, or year. Labor costs, which are dollars paid for wages or salaries for work performed, are a major ingredient of an estimate. In heavy construction, for example, labor costs constitute 40% or more of the bid on a building. Payrolls cover two classes of workers: first, management and general administrative employees who may or may not be on a salary basis and, second, hourly labor. General administrative employees may be management, engineers, foremen, inspectors, and clerk-typists. Hourly labor is sometimes classified as direct or indirect. The category direct refers to employees who can be associated with a product directly, such as milling machine operators or truck drivers. This classification presupposes that the work can be preplanned or *designated;* it is found in the manufacturing industries where the process sheet specifies the operations to follow in the manufacture of certain parts. The indirect hourly labor notion refers to workers that are generally performing undesignated work such as clerk-typists, janitors, industrial engineers, and superintendents. In an allocation sense of cost, their work and effort is usually for a variety of tasks, making it difficult to designate precisely what portion of their work contributes to the particular operation, product, project or system. In the main the indirect operator is not clearly identifiable to a particular task.

The principle is now established that one of the costs of labor is *fringe benefits*. In the past, estimators concluded that wages or salaries that were received directly constituted the total sum of labor costs. This is not so. Fringe benefits, which are related to wages and salaries, constitute as much as 30% of the actual cost incurred for labor.

There is variety in handling wages and fringes. But it should be understood that if a deduction occurs from the employee alone, then it is not explicitly identified for estimating, as it is included in the employee wage rate. There are labor costs not included in the wage rate which are known loosely as *fringes*, and it is necessary to understand their content and value.

With the design known the work is described and job descriptions of employees are matched to the work. These *job descriptions* indicate the skill, knowledge, and responsibility required of the worker. Each company will have occupational descriptions. Table 2.10 is an example of an assembler. The occupations are graded and a company will have a pay scale that increases from the very simple occupation to the most difficult. These job descriptions and their wage rates are policy information available to the estimator, especially for operation and product designs. Union halls or labor–management contracts may be the source of information for wages in construction, however. Wages and fringe effects are considered by one of two methods: (1) *wage only* and (2) *wage and fringe* combined, or the *gross hourly cost*. In the first method the fringe effects are collected in overhead, which will be described in Chapter 4.

2.3.1 Wage-Only Method

Wage payment can be classified into general groupings: those which pay for attendance and those which pay on performance. In time attendance wage plans, gross wages are figured easily. The time in attendance is multiplied by the rate. An executive who earns $54,000 per year earns $4500 per month. If he or she starts or leaves within the month, the pay is prorated to the number of calendar or working days, depending on company policy. The qualitative formula given by Eq. (2.1) can be more formally expressed as

$$C_{dl} = H_a \times R_h \tag{2.11}$$

where C_{dl} = time-rate cost

H_a = actual hours

R_h = rate per hour in dollars

Naturally, R_h can be found from annual, monthly, or weekly pay scales. For a $4500 monthly scale, the weekly scale is $4500 \times 12/52 = \$1038.46$. There are $173\frac{1}{3}$ hours per month ($= 52 \times 5 \times 8 \times 1/12$) and the hourly scale is $25.96. These calculations use the popular 40-hour week. In attendance-based plans, or as they are sometimes called *day work,* the worker is paid on the amount of time spent on the job.

Naturally, the worker is interested in as large a wage as possible. The employer, on the other hand, is interested in the reduction of labor costs. If the employer is

Table 2.10. JOB DESCRIPTION

Assembler
   (Bench assembler; floor assembler; jig assembler; line assembler; subassembler)

   Assembles and/or fits together parts to form complete units or subassemblies at a bench, conveyor line, or on the floor, depending on the size of the units and the organization of the production process. Work may include processing operations requiring the use of handtools in scraping, chipping, and filing of parts to obtain a desired fit as well as power tools and special equipment when punching, riveting, soldering, or welding of parts is necessary. *Workers who perform any of these processing operations exclusively as part of specialized assembling operations are excluded.*

   Class A.   Assembles parts into complete units or subassemblies that require fitting of parts and decisions regarding proper performance of any component part or the assembled unit. Work involves *any combination of the following:* Assembling from drawings, blueprints, or other written specifications; assembling units composed of a variety of parts and/or subassemblies; assembling large units requiring careful fitting and adjusting of parts to obtain specified clearances; using a variety of hand and powered tools and precision measuring instruments.

   Class B.   Assembles parts into units or subassemblies in accordance with standard and prescribed procedures. Work involves *any combination of the following:* Assembling a limited range of standard and familiar products composed of a number of small- or medium-sized parts requiring some fitting or adjusting; assembling large units that require little or no fitting of component parts; working under conditions where accurate performance and completion of work within set time limits are essential for subsequent assembling operations; using a limited variety of hand or powered tools.

   Class C.   Performs short-cycle, repetitive assembling operations. Work does not involve any fitting or making decisions regarding proper performance of the component parts or assembling procedures.

---

able to encourage increased output from the worker, the employer might be willing to pay higher wages. In these performance plans, the worker's earnings are related to productive output and are called *incentive* or *piece-rate plans*.

$$C_{dl} = N_p R_p \qquad (2.12)$$

where C_{dl} = piece rate cost for labor, dollars

   N_p = number of pieces produced

   R_p = standard rate per piece in dollars

If R_p = \$0.1466 per unit and N_p = 128 units, then C_{dl} = \$18.76 which is paid to the worker. Subsidy or bonus pay schemes have much in common with incentive plans, but will not be discussed.

   Most incentive plans do not pay additional wages until 100% standard is reached. Below that level a guaranteed wage or day work is pledged. A formula expressing this relationship is given as

$$C_{dl} = H_a R_h + R_h (H_s N_p - H_a) \qquad (2.13)$$

subject to

$$C_{dl} \geq H_a R_h$$

where C_{dl} = total cost per pay period for labor, dollars

H_s = standard hour per unit

Assume that H_a = 0.8 hour, R_h = 14.50, N_p = 128, and H_s = 1.011 hour per 100 units. Then

$$C_{dl} = 0.8 \times 14.50 + 14.50 \left(\frac{1.011}{100} \times 128 - 0.8 \right) = \$18.76$$

If only 70 units had been produced under the piece-rate plan during 0.8 hour, earnings would be \$10.26, while under the guaranteed 100% plan, earnings would be \$11.60 because $C_{dl} \geq H_a R_h$.

Earned hours are recorded for pay purposes when an incentive plan exists. Thus a job is set in standard hours and the worker may earn more dollars by producing the job in fewer actual or clock hours. The advantage of this approach is that the standard hour base is the same for each operation unit, whereas the actual hours for an operation unit vary with the worker's efficiency on that job. The ratio of the task amount of work, or hours standard to hours actually taken in performing the work, is

$$E = N_p \frac{H_s}{H_a} \times 100 \tag{2.14}$$

where E is the labor efficiency, percent. For the case where N_p = 128 units, E = $(128 \times 1.011/100)/0.8 \times 100 = 162\%$, and for 70 units E = 88%. Other measures of efficiency are discussed in Chapter 11.

2.3.2 Gross Hourly Cost

In some cases the fringe costs are not included in overhead and are determined explicitly for estimating. Combined wages and fringes are called *gross hourly cost* and may be determined for production or construction workers.

Federal and state laws regulate wages and salaries paid by employers. Two federal laws, the wage-hour law and the Walsh-Healy Act, are prominent. All manufacturers engaged in interstate commerce are covered by the wage-hour law. The Walsh-Healy Act covers only companies having federal contracts. Both laws require the payment of wages at time-and-a-half rates for more than 40 hours in one week; the Walsh-Healy Act adds the same requirement for more than 8 hours in one day. Some groups are exempted from the wage-hour law, such as management and engineers. A man with a 40-hour base rate of \$12 must be paid \$18 per hour for his overtime hours. The wage-hour law specifies a minimum per hour as the lowest paid wage. For example, the wage minimums as established by Congress constitute a floor for employed labor in most categories. There are other labor laws too numerous to mention here: Discrimination against minority races, women, or others; work hours for women and children; safety and sanitation laws; unemployment insurance, taxes, and social security taxes are typical.

Contractual agreements may specify additional requirements, such as number of holidays, time off, sick leave, and uniforms, for instance. In addition to wages earned by employees, the employer must pay the appropriate government agency or insurance carrier an additional amount.

A partial listing of fringe costs may include (1) legally required payments, such as payroll taxes and workmen's compensation; (2) voluntary or required payments, such as group insurance and pension plans; (3) sometimes, wash-up time, paid rest periods, and travel time; (4) payment for time not worked, holidays, vacations, and sick pay; and (5) profit-sharing payments, service awards, and payment to union stewards. Fringe costs depend on local situations and must be determined individually for each case.

In the Social Security Act the federal government requires that businesses pay a tax for old-age and medical benefits, called *social security tax,* or FICA (Federal Income Contribution Act). This amounts to a percentage of a fixed sum of gross earnings of an employee. The employee contributes an amount somewhat less than the employer. This rate and the base upon which it is levied are subject to change by Congress and have marched steadily upward since the first law back in 1935. Initially, the employee paid 1% of the first $3000 earned and the employer paid an equal amount. This matching amount is an employer cost and must be known for estimating.

Workmen's compensation is a levy against employers for continuation of income to employees in periods when they cannot work because of accidents occurring on the job. The payments may be made to the state compensation insurance fund or to state-approved carriers. Employees are grouped into work types, and rates based on experience of risk incidence are established for each type. In the event of injury or death, the insurance carrier provides financial assistance to the injured person or to the survivors in the event of death.

Another federal–state tax on wages is for *unemployment insurance.* This tax was established by the Social Security Act of 1935. The Act acknowledged the responsibility of government to help the unemployed. This legislation delegated the job of setting up the employment services to the states, which were to collect the major portion of the tax to operate their own unemployment offices. State legislation had to conform to the requirements of the federal Act. Built into the system was a merit-rating procedure to reward "good" employers (i.e., employers who so operated their labor pool as to prevent repetitive hirings and firings and who fired employees only for good economic reasons). When a business is established or enters the system, it pays the maximum state rate. If its employment record thereafter becomes stable, the rate drops until the minimum rate is reached. The employer is rewarded in monetary terms for good employment practices. Not all employees, such as farm workers, domestic help, and so on, are covered. If an employee is laid off, he or she is entitled to certain benefits for a limited period of time. The unemployment insurance pays for this involuntary employee termination.

Fringe benefits include expenditures, other than payroll taxes and workmen's compensation insurance, that benefit employees individually or as a group. Since these are not legally required, they may vary from employer to employer and be based on labor-market competitiveness, industry practice, management's attitude toward employees, management's social consciousness, or labor–management contract.

One such benefit is the portion of medical and dental insurance paid for by the employer. Supplemental medical insurance could cover the employee and family for all or part of ordinary illness, or could apply only to catastrophic illnesses. Usually, a schedule of payments by the employee and the employer is established, a percentage of present employees are required to initiate the plan, and all new personnel are included automatically. The company's portion of the premium needs to be considered for estimating.

Another supplemental benefit is *life insurance*. A schedule is established showing the employees' and employer's portion of the premium. In initiating this plan the personal histories of present employees are secured and a stated percentage of the work force must participate. All new personnel may be automatically included. The company's portion of the premium needs to be considered by estimating.

Vacation pay is also considered a fringe benefit. Vacation policy varies as to length of the vacation. When the employee becomes eligible to participate, the amount of vacation earned but yet unpaid is a company cost.

Sick pay is similar to vacation pay. It may not be formally set up on the accounting books as such, but is charged to overhead when taken. It can, however, be estimated on past experience.

Another fringe benefit is an *employee supplemental pension plan,* which provides retirement benefits in addition to social security. It may be self-funded, in which case the company agrees to invest contributions, or it may be funded by an outside agency such as an insurance company or a mutual fund company. In the latter case, the company makes the payments required under the plan. In a third arrangement, the plan may be fully funded by the company or partially by employees.

Another fringe benefit is the *stock-purchase* plan, by which the company encourages employees to become shareholders in the company, allowing them to purchase stock at less than market value. The immediate benefit the employee receives is the difference between market price and the price he or she pays.

Other miscellaneous fringe-benefit expenses include:

1. Cost of operating the cafeteria less receipts for sales made. The benefit to the employees is the difference between what they would pay in an outside cafeteria and their real cost.

2. Cost of equipping and operating the in-plant medical facilities.

3. Cost of equipping and operating sports teams and leagues, funding and supervising Christmas bonuses, and maintaining incidental employee conveniences.

4. Labor costs for foreign projects may include family living allowances, extra midday rest periods, severance pay, social taxes, and perfect attendance record bonuses.

Observe Table 2.11, where the effective gross hourly cost for a specific assembler is determined. A typical job description for an assembler is given by Table 2.10. Knowing the job title and employee, it is possible to know entitlement for vacation, shift differential, and so on. The expected nonchargeable hours of 5%, line 8, include wash-ups, which are not a part of overhead or not included in production allowances. Line 11, performance subsidy, may be used for award pay rates if provided by management policy. Thus an effective gross hourly cost of $20.16 is 28% greater than the basic wage. It is also possible to figure gross hourly

Table 2.11. CALCULATION OF GROSS HOURLY COST FOR INDUSTRIAL OCCUPATION
AND EMPLOYEE

Job title __Assembler__   Department __Mechanical__
Future effective period __Jan - July__   Wage __$14.50/hour__ Shift __1__
Name __Spencer Tucker__   Clock no. __10017__   Subsidy __10%__
Entitled vacation days __10__   Holidays __6__

Item	Annual hours	Annual cost	Annual excess cost
1. Regular paid clock hours	2080	$30,160	
2. Planned overtime hours	192	2784	
3. Overtime cost at 50% of 2	−	1392	$ 1392
4. Subtotal	2272	$34,336	
5. Holidays	48	696	696
6. Entitled vacation	80	1160	1160
7. Paid sick leave	−	−	
8. Expected nonchargeable hours, _5%_	104	1508	1508
9. Subtotal (5 + 6 + 7 + 8)	232	$ 3364	$ 3364
10. Chargeable (4 − 9)	2040	30972	
11. Expected performance subsidy _10%_ , X 10	204 −	3097	3097
12. Chargeable standard (10 − 11)	1936	$27875	
13. Non hourly costs			
FICA @ _0.068_ X 4			2335
Workmen's compensation, _3% x 15,000_			450
Unemployment insurance			300
Supplemental medical insurance			550
Supplemental pension			−
Supplemental life insurance			−
Union Welfare			−
Bonus, gifts			−
Uniforms, tools, etc.			50
Profit sharing			−
Other			−
14. Subtotal of 13			$ 3685
15. Excess costs (3 + 9 + 11 + 14)			$ 11538
16. Excess hourly rate (15/10)			5.66
17. Wage			14.50
18. Effective gross hourly cost (16 + 17)			$ 20.16
19. Increase in hourly base rate (16/18)			28%

costs for a class of employees, using averages for entitled vacation, overtime, holidays, and all of the items listed in Table 2.11. Construction gross hourly costs are figured differently from costs for industrial occupations, since in many cases unions are paid the money for health and welfare, pensions, vacations, and so on. The union reimburses the cost for these benefits, although they are paid by the contractor. An example of this method is shown by Table 2.12.

2.4 JOINT LABOR COST

Joint labor costs are those which are shared and act in common for an operation. The estimator "dejoints" or unitizes the cost. An operator simultaneously working on two or more parts, or an operator controlling the output of two or more machines, are joint cost examples. Joint costs include not only labor but material and overhead, which are studied later.

In a one-operator one-machine industrial operation, the worker may load two or more units onto the machine and process them simultaneously, or from one unit of original material, two or more units of output may be possible. Time-study or man-hour data can aid this analysis.

One of the production causes for joint costs is multiple-machine operation. In certain kinds of work it is possible for one operator to tend a number of machines—depending on the amount of attention that each machine requires. If a weaver is able

Table 2.12.   Calculation for Gross Hourly Cost for Construction Occupation

Job title: _Carpenter_____ Future effective period: _Jan-July1_ Wage: _$14.50/hour_

Item	Percentage	Hourly amount
1. Wage	—	$ 14.50
Mandatory contributions		
2. FICA	6.95	1.01
3. Workman's compensation insurance	4.40	0.64
4. Unemployment insurance	2.75	0.40
Union contract contributions		
5. Health and welfare	6.00	0.87
6. Pension fund	6.00	0.87
7. Vacation fund	2.00	0.29
8. Small tools	0.50	0.07
9. Show up time	0.50	0.07
Other		
10. Travel and subsistance allowance	0.50	0.07
11. Year-end bonus	—	—
12. Other	—	—
	Total	$ 18.79

to handle 8 looms, for example, then $\frac{1}{8}$ of the weaver's attention is required for changing shuttles, tying broken threads, and adjusting the machine. But when the weaver operates more than one loom and one of them stops while he or she is working on another, it must wait until the weaver can finish with the first loom. In fact, several machines may need attention at the same time. This waiting is called "machine interference" and is covered by queuing models. The problem arises, therefore, as to how many machines an operator should tend. Although queuing methods are more elegant and exact, at the moment of estimating simpler methods are preferred because this information is available. Machine interference exists whenever too many machines are assigned to one operator, but this may be less costly than operator idleness. Joint labor cost or time exists when an individual operator is involved with the following:

1. Similar machines each producing the same output
2. Similar machines each producing different output
3. Dissimilar machines each producing different output

Crew or team work is another example of joint labor cost. Crews are found frequently in construction and chemical manufacturing. For most construction situations crew time is estimated for a unit of output and is left as a joint cost. Examples of crew estimating are deferred to Chapter 7. In crew work, the interest is to balance the work load such that there is no idle time, or all idle time is equal. Usually, this is unlikely, and the entire crew time is subject to the longest time of one worker.

Dejointing of shared labor divides the time or labor cost. The point of division is called the *split point*. Labor up to the split point is joint, while afterward it is called unit. Splitting is handled by allocation or units of reference by which the joint costs are divided. Labor joint-cost splitting is usually handled by time or units or a combination of both.

A problem confronting a cost estimator is given as follows: Suppose that two camera brackets, left and right hand, are machined together. Loading and unloading are simultaneous. The left bracket requires special machining. Gross hourly costs are $20. A time study gives the following data.

Element	Bracket	Standard Minute/Element
1. Loading	Both	0.20
2. Position and drill hole	Both	0.15
3. Rotate and position	Left	0.05
4. Index collet	Left	0.08
5. Counterbore	Left	0.21
6. Eject parts	Both	0.15
7. Clean jig	Both	0.10
		0.94

A dejointing solution by time would be

Elements	Left	Right
1, 2, 6, 7	0.30	0.30
3, 4, 5	0.34	
	0.64	0.30

$$\text{cost for left bracket} = 0.64 \times \frac{1}{60} \times 20 = \$0.213/\text{unit}$$

$$\text{cost for right bracket} = 0.30 \times \frac{1}{60} \times 20 = \$0.100/\text{unit}$$

We can also use the two units of output to obtain $0.157 per unit ($= 0.94 \times \frac{1}{60} \times 20 \times \frac{1}{2}$).

Costs can be dejointed by market effects, which stipulate that cost be a function of price or number of units sold. Marketing strategy can affect allocation accuracy by falsely requiring that some products subsidize others. This policy says that selling price or market value is not proportional to processing costs and thus distorts the estimated cost. In the bracket example, suppose that the left bracket can be sold on a ratio of 4 to 3 units of dollar to the right bracket. We compute the cost as

$$\text{left bracket} = 0.94 \times \frac{1}{60} \times 20 \times \frac{4}{7} = \$0.179/\text{unit}$$

$$\text{right bracket} = 0.94 \times \frac{1}{60} \times 20 \times \frac{3}{7} = \$0.134/\text{unit}$$

SUMMARY

It is necessary to have measured, historical, and policy facts about labor before labor costs can be estimated. Often this information is provided to the estimator for his or her use, but it is after analysis that estimating begins. Whether internal or external agencies are the origin for these data, cost estimators go to others for it, and apply it to the design.

The usual ways to measure labor are time study, predetermined motion-time systems, work sampling, and man-hour reports. Job tickets, especially for smaller organizations, are analyzed and allocated to units of work. For instance, a job ticket may state "136 units turned of part number 8671" and lists "6 man-hours." Simple analysis would show 0.044 hour per unit. The estimator would use 0.044 hour the next time this part were run. Although hardly accurate because of the nature of historical work reports, man-hour reports are used because of their simplicity. Man-hour estimating data are popular in construction work.

While the cost estimator may not be directly involved with the measurement of labor, he or she does depend on work measurement. The estimator is satisfied if such labor measurements are objective, as far as that is possible, and he or she is willing to use the information provided that engineering techniques were used in the determination of time. Although the time measurements are of value, it is immensely more important that work measurement data be transformed into information that can be applied prior to the time of the operation design. This transformation of analyzed labor information is discussed in later chapters.

Although past wage and fringe data are useful for cost estimating, there is the caution that future circumstances will be different. Thus their manipulation for future use is a subject of later chapters.

QUESTIONS

2.1. Give an explanation of the following terms:

Direct labor	Job ticket
Indirect labor	Spread sheet
Measured time	Historical time
Time study	Foreman's report
Normal time	Cost code
Rating	Work sampling
Allowance	Interval
Standard	Job description
Pieces per hour	Gross hourly cost
Man-hour	Dejointing

2.2. Why do we separate labor into direct and indirect categories?

2.3. What is the purpose of rating? A job is time studied and rated greater than 100% and the standard is used for a second worker. What does the fact that the original rating was greater than 100% mean to the second worker?

2.4. What are allowances intended for?

2.5. Why is an operation divided into elements for the time study?

2.6. Why do we use man-hour reports? Name types of work that are appropriate.

2.7. Determine the current FICA rate and the base for the employee and employer. What are the political ramifications?

2.8. List mandatory and voluntary types of fringe costs. Is there a difference between manufacturing or construction? Union or nonunion?

2.9. Specify the nature of work which makes it joint. List allocators that dejoint work.

PROBLEMS

2.1. (a) A machine has a cycle time of $\frac{1}{2}$ second. What are the production pieces per hour at 100% and 75% efficiency?

(b) The floor-to-floor time (meaning a complete productive cycle) is 31 seconds. Find gross units per hour at 100% and 90% efficiency.

2.2. **(a)** If the hourly production is 11 units, find the hours per 1000 pieces.
   (b) The production is 29.5 units per hour. Find hours per 100, 1000, and 10,000 units.
   (c) Find pieces per hour and standard minutes per unit for 15.325 hours per 100 units.

2.3. A time study of an assembly operation is summarized below:

Element	Frequency	Element Minutes	Rating Factor
1. Part A to 5 in. (125 mm) dowel	1/1	0.037	1.10
2. Part B to 5 in. (125 mm) subassembly	2/1	0.064	1.15
3. Short piece to base	1/1	0.089	1.20
4. Long piece to base	1/1	0.129	1.10
5. Grab pieces from tote box	1/5	0.185	1.10
6. Place in conveyor	1/1	0.087	1.10

Allowances for this work are 9.5%. Find **(a)** the standard minutes per unit, **(b)** pieces per hour, and **(c)** hours per 100 units. **(d)** For a wage rate of $14.75 per hour, what is the labor cost per unit?

2.4. A mailroom prepares the company's advertising for mailing. A time study has been done on the job of enclosing material in envelopes. Develop the elemental normal time, cycle standard time, pieces per hour, and hours per 100 units, providing 15% for allowances based on the continuous watch data below. (Readings are in hundredths of minutes.)

Element	Cycle 1	2	3	4	5	6	7	Rating (%)
1. Get envelopes	11		55		105		151	105
2. Get and fold premium	22	41	65	83	116	134	160	115
3. Enclose premium in envelope and seal envelope	29	48	73	97	123	141	182	95

2.5. A method has been engineered and an individual has been time-studied. The method has produced an average overall time of 2.32 minutes by actual watch-timing. The overall pace rating applied to the job is 125%. This company, which uses an incentive system, adds extra time into the production rates to cover personal time, fatigue, and unavoidable delays. The total allowance is 15%.
   (a) Determine the rated time or normal minutes, the total allowed time or standard minutes, the standard hour rate for the job per unit and 100 units, and the pieces per hour.
   (b) The labor rate per hour is $15.30. What is the standard labor cost per unit?

2.6. Below are time-study observations. The elemental times are snapback.

Element	Reading	Rating (%)	Allowance (%)
1. Place bushing in jig	0.03 0.08 0.05 0.04 0.06	117	11
2. Drill hole	0.31 0.38 0.37 0.39 0.33	100	5
3. Remove bushing from jig and place on conveyor belt	0.07 0.08 0.09 0.12 0.11	93	13

(a) Find the average, normal, and standard times for each element.
(b) Calculate the production per hour and hour per 100 units.
(c) By an old method, 0.834 minute of standard time was required to complete this operation. Calculate the increase in output in percent and savings in time in percent.

2.7. A job is time-studied and a summary time sheet is given as follows:

Element Description	Frequency per Unit	Average Time	Rating Factor (%)
1. Get part off conveyor	1/1	0.040	100
2. Get incomplete part off	1/1	0.030	105
3. Connect length and joint	2/1	0.055	110
4. Connect 3	3/1	0.153	100
5. Assemble side	1/1	0.243	90
6. Mate two sides	1/1	0.183	90
7. Put on conveyor	1/1	0.032	100

(a) With an allowance factor of 15% to cover P (personal), F (fatigue), and D (delay), what are the normal minutes per piece, the standard minute per unit and the number of hours per 1000 units?
(b) If performance against incentive has averaged 20%, what is the incentive hourly rate if day work is paid at $15.75 per hour?

2.8. The following is a raw continuous-timing two-element time study of a punch press operation where the observations are minutes.

Element	Cycle				
	1	2	3	4	5
1. Handle part	0.01	0.04	0.08	0.11	0.14
2. Punch part	0.03	0.06	0.10	0.12	0.16

(a) What is the average time for elements 1 and 2? The ratings were +8% and −9% for elements 1 and 2. What is the normal time for elements 1 and 2? A man and machine allowance of 20% is used in this plant. What is the standard minute per piece for this operation? How many pieces per hour? How many hours per 100 units?

(b) If only a man allowance of 20% is used for element 1, what are the standard minutes per unit? How many hours per 100 units?

2.9. The fire department is concerned about the speed of the crews assigned to the all-purpose trucks. The chief wants to know the time required after receiving the alarm before starting to fight the blaze. To answer the chief's questions a time study of the activities of one crew on seven different alarms is conducted. On the observation sheet below, continuous (no reset) electronic watch readings in hundredths of minutes are recorded, indicating full minutes only when it changed.

	Alarm						
Crew Element	1	2	3	4	5	6	7
1. Start timing	0.00	.51	.33	.24	4.12	5.04	.91
2. Get dressed	0.12	.58	.43	.36	.25	.15	6.01
3. Board truck	0.29	.82	.60	.55	.41	.32	.19
4. Start engine	0.44	.94	.76	.70	.55	.48	.32
5. Drive to fire[a]							
6. Unload hoses	0.64	2.00	3.02	0.89	0.78	.63	.50
7. Connect hoses	0.89	.33	.24	4.12	5.04	.91	.75
8. Unload ladders	1.08						.95
9. Position ladders	.51						7.31
10. End timing for this alarm	.51	.33	.24	4.12	5.04	.91	7.31

[a]Watch stopped because of variable nature of distances.

(a) Determine the average time for the elements.

(b) If the crew is rated at 110% for all elements, find normal time in minute per occurrence.

(c) Determine the cycle-time standard for a 20% allowance.

2.10. A gang nonrepetitive time study was made of a construction crew, and the following is a tabulated summary. It is usually unrealistic to rate this kind of work and PF&D allowances are seldom a part of the calculation. Crosses in the table indicate that the job element was necessary for the worker.

(a) The work consisted of placing 180 yards of concrete by a pipeline. Determine the cost of the job and of placing a yard of concrete.

Pay time and a half for overtime for any assigned work in this job.

(b) Initially assume that when not assigned to this job the operator is doing something else profitable.

Assume that the union contract requires the entire crew (exclusive of concrete truck and driver) to be at the job site the entire time. What would this actual cost per yard be then? What is the cost of this nonproduction? Assume that element 1 starts a new workday.

| Element | Minutes | Crew and Equipment | | | | | | |
		Foreman	Pump Operator	Hopper Man	4 Laborers	2 Vibrator Crew	Truck, Driver	Pumps and Fittings Rental
1. Make ready	60	×			×			
2. Move to job site	15	×			×			
3. Pump machine to job	45	×	×	×	×			×
4. Set up machine	90	×	×	×	×			×
5. Inspect	30	×	×	×	×		×	×
6. Adjustment	30	×	×	×	×		×	×
7. Pump concrete to forms	360	×	×	×	×	×	×	×
8. Normal delay for set of concrete	80	×	×	×	×	×		×
9. Dismantle pump	45	×	×	×	×			×
10. Put tools away	15	×	×		×			×
11. Return pump	30	×	×		×			×
12. Clean up	10	×			×			
Cost per hour		14	16	16	12	16	70	50

2.11. Engineering aides prepare job tickets of their daily work, and after a sufficient period of data collection, classification of the information reveals the following:

Description of Work	Minutes per Occurrence	Frequency per Print
1. Post drawing numbers	7.0	1/1
2. Duplicate drawings	19.0	1/1
3. Correct computer cards	38.0	2/1
4. Phone calls	1.5	1/4
5. Update drawing changes	27.0	1/2

A personal allowance of 15% is used for this category of work.

(a) Determine the man-hour per engineering drawing.

(b) A new product design is anticipated and a separate staff will be collected. This product design will probably result in about 2500 prints over a 1-year period. How many aides will be required, and at $20 per hour, what amount would you estimate for this activity in a product expense budget?

2.12. A work-sampling survey of an operation, which was designated into 12 categories, has the following observations:

Item	Observations	Item	Observations
1	92	7	24
2	99	8	33
3	37	9	3
4	11	10	22
5	25	11	8
6	14	12	32
			400

If this sample covered a span of 25 days for 8 hours per day, what are the percents and expected hours per item of work?

2.13. The pediatrics department in a hospital was work-sampled for 608 hours.

Work Category	Observations	Work Category	Observations
1. Routine nursing	496	8. Other	79
2. Idle or wait	263	9. Feeding	52
3. Unit servicing	183	10. Bathing	22
4. Report	129	11. Elimination	11
5. Personal time	128	12. Transporting	8
6. Intervention	102	13. Housekeeping	7
7. Unable to sample	91	14. Ambulation	7

For the 1578 observations find the percent occurrence, percent cumulative occurrence, element hours, and cumulative hours for each work category.

2.14. A work-sampling study is taken of a department with the following information obtained: number of sampling days, 25; number of trips per day, 16; number of people observed per trip, 3; and number of items being sampled, 4. The four sample items are broken down as A, 80; B, 320; C, 1600; and D, 2800.

(a) How many man-days and observations were sampled?

(b) What are the percentage and equivalent hours for the activities?

(c) For a confidence level of 90%, what is the relative accuracy of each of the items?

2.15. Suppose that we want to determine the percentage of idle time of a machine shop by work sampling. Assume that a confidence level of 95% and a relative accuracy of $\pm 5\%$ are desired, where a rough estimate of 25% is suspected for idle time.

(a) How many observations are necessary?

(b) Assume that the relative accuracy is $\pm 2\frac{1}{2}\%$. How many observations are required now?

(c) What happens to the number as relative accuracy becomes less?

2.16. **(a)** To get a 0.10 interval on work observed by work sampling that is estimated to require 70% of the worker's time, how many random observations will be required at the 95% confidence level? Repeat for 90%.

(b) If the average handling activity during a 20-day study period is 85% and the number of daily observations is 45, what is the interval allowed on each day's percent activity? Use 90%. Repeat for 99%

(c) Work sampling is to be used to measure the not-working time of a utility crew. A preliminary study shows that not-working time is likely to be around 35%. For a 90% confidence level and a desired relative accuracy of 5%, what is the number of observations required for this study? Compare to 95% confidence level.

2.17. A shipping department that constructs wooden boxes for large switch gear has five direct-labor workers. A work-sampling study was undertaken, and the following observations of work elements were recorded over a 15-day, 8-hour period:

> Set up and dismantle   312
> Construct crates   264
> Load switch gear in crates   204
> Move materials   324
> Idle   96

A rating factor of 90% was found. The number of switch gear shipped during this period was 26. This firm uses an allowance value of 10% for work of this kind. Average labor cost $18.75 per hour.

(a) What are the elemental costs?

(b) What is the standard labor cost per box?

(c) What is the actual cost?

2.18. An eight-man drafting department concerned with size A, B, and C drawings is work-sampled by a management consultant over a standard 4-week period. A stick chart was summarized for the categories as follows:

Item	Count
Drafting and tracing	778
Calculating	458
Checking prints	110
Classroom	125
Professional time off	172
Personal time, idle	270

During this period 55 drawings ($A = 20$, $B = 25$, $C = 10$) were produced with a total payroll of $26,400. Let relative size $A = 1$, $B = 2A$, and $C = 2B$.

(a) If the policy is to accept professional and personal time as necessary to the drafting of prints, what is the man-hour factor?

(b) If personal time and idle time are prejudged at 10% only, what is the per print size factor?

2.19. Find the effective gross hourly cost for drill press operators paid an average wage of $11.00 per hour. No overtime is planned. Company policy allows six paid holidays and the average entitled vacation is 10 days. There is no nonchargeable time or performance subsidy. Sick leave is charged against vacation time. FICA is at current rate and workmen's compensation is at 2% of the first $20,000. The company pays $400 for unemployment insurance.

2.20. We are interested in finding the estimated direct-labor cost for the job description of industrial electrician. The year consists of 52 40-hour weeks, and overtime is seasonal for 12 weeks consisting of Saturday work of 8 hours. The contract allows for 9 paid holidays and 2 weeks of vacation at regular time. Four days of sick leave are paid. Expected nonchargeable hours are 5%. A subsidy for performance will be 15%. Nonhourly costs include FICA taxes at the current federal rate, workmen's compensation at 1% of regular wages up to $15,000, accident insurance sum of $200, major medical plans for $500, and Christmas gift of $50. The hourly base is $17.10.
(a) Find the effective gross hourly cost.
(b) What is the job cost for this electrician if a job requires 25 man-hours?
(c) What is the loss or gain if efficiency will be 85% or 115% for the job?

2.21. An industrial carpenter is paid $13.25 per hour. The work year consists of 52 40-hour weeks with overtime scheduled for 26 Saturdays. The company allows 8 paid holidays and 10 days of vacation. Four days of sick leave are budgeted and have historically been used. Expected nonchargeable hours are 2%. There is no subsidy for performance. Nonhourly costs include FICA taxes at current governmental rate, workmen's compensation at 2% of regular wages up to $15,000, accident insurance sum of $600, and a major supplemental medical plan for $300.
(a) Find the effective gross hourly cost.
(b) What is the job cost if a job will require 10 man-hours and a productivity of 90%?

2.22. Determine a company's base annual cost for a top-grade worker. The base hourly rate is $15.75. Use the current FICA costs of the base. State unemployment compensation runs 2%. Health insurance premiums cost $40 per month. The company carries term life insurance that costs $45,000 per year for all employees (there are 60 employees). In addition, the company profit-sharing plan usually pays 5% of the base wage.

2.23. One firm decides to find a typical hourly cost for direct labor. In this instance the average work week is 48 hours, of which the final 8 hours are premium at one and a half. The wage is $15.15 per hour. Each day a total of 20 minutes is permitted as a coffee break, the final 15 minutes are cleanup, there are 2 weeks of paid vacation on basis of 40 hours worked and five paid holidays, and there is FICA at the current rate, 1.2% workmen's compensation tax, $25 per month for company-paid medical and life insurance, and a $25 Christmas bonus, all considered pertinent to the calculation.

2.24. A man worked 8 hours on incentive and nonincentive jobs. While on incentive he completed 8 tasks, each with a 1-hour standard time. The nonincentive jobs took 2 actual hours. The incentive plan has a base rate of $13 per hour, while the man's wage rate for nonincentive tasks is $16 per hour. How much did the man earn?

2.25. **(a)** A worker produces 56 units on an incentive plan during the 40-hour week. His base hourly rate is $15 per hour, and the standard for one unit of accomplishment is 1.10. What are his weekly earnings?

(b) If FICA is $6\frac{3}{4}\%$, unemployment insurance costs the company 2.1%, the accident rate is 2.5%, 20 days of yearly vacation, and $40 per month for insurance, what is the actual wage and fringe cost per hour? Per unit?

2.26. A worker is paid the day-work rate if he or she earns less than 100% incentive premium. A standard is 75 units per hour and the operator completes 140 good parts in 1.4 hours. The rate is $12.50 per hour.
(a) Find the piece rate.
(b) What are the earnings and labor efficiency?

2.27. **(a)** A sheet metal operator is told that her standard is 1.875 hours per 100 units. If her wage is $16 per hour and she makes 800 units in 12 hours, what are her earnings?
(b) If the actual time is 16 hours, what is her guaranteed pay and efficiency for the 100% plan?

2.28. An estimator has efficiency information of 125% for an operation. The standard is 10 hours per unit, and the wage is $11.75 per hour. What is the expected cost for 210 units?

2.29. A molding operator tends two machines and plastic products A and B are produced. Machines A and B have a production rate of 400 and 250 strokes per hour. Molds A and B produce three or four buttons per stroke. Operator wage is $11.00 per hour. Dejoint these labor costs when allocation is based on: **(a)** number of machines, **(b)** product output of machines A and B, and **(c)** marketing believes that A to B value is 5:4.

2.30. A time study observed the operation of producing two parts, which are labeled "1" and "2." The elements and their standard minutes are given as follows:

Element	Part	Standard Minutes
1. Load part in vise	1	0.17
2. Load second part	2	0.08
3. Balance and tighten vise	1, 2	0.17
4. Start machine	1, 2	0.06
5. Machine	1, 2	1.17
6. Stop, unload	2	0.13
7. Start, retighten	1	0.15
8. Fine machining	1	0.83
9. Stop, unload	1	0.14
10. Clean vise	1, 2	0.16

The labor wage is $11.50 per hour. Dejoint cost using allocation methods of **(a)** number of parts, **(b)** time required by part, and **(c)** potential sales price ratio of 3:2.

2.31. One operator controls four automatic machines. After these machines are set up, they produce parts independent of the operator except for occasional inspection. A cam controls the unit time to make one piece and is 4 seconds at 100% efficiency. Ignore the setup time since it is very small.
(a) If the actual efficiency is 85%, the operator controls four machines, and the labor wage rate is $12.66 per hour, what is the dejointed labor cost per unit?

(b) Repeat (a) for hours per 100 units.

(c) Repeat (a) for dollars per 100 units.

2.32. A technician tests and repairs printed circuit boards. On the average printed circuit boards require 10 minutes for testing and 12 minutes for testing and repairing, if necessary.

(a) If during a man-hour study, 18 units tested OK and 5 failed requiring repair, what proportion of the labor wage is due to testing and repair?

(b) If the gross labor rate is $21.75 per hour, what is the labor charge per unit for testing and repair? Use proportional methods to dejoint cost.

CASE STUDY:
THE ENDICOTT IRON FOUNDRY

"We can't make any profit on that job; it has too much labor cost in it," said Dick Crawford, the foundry superintendent, to George Dobbins, cost estimator for the Endicott Iron Foundry. The Endicott Iron Foundry, like its competitors, has always estimated costs on a per pound (kilogram) basis for the delivered casting. Difficult castings were quoted at a higher price per pound (kilogram) than simple castings, but the difference in price (often based on the estimated cost) did not seem to be great enough to warrant the extra labor costs. Crawford suggested that the company was making little profit or loss on jobs that took considerable labor. What will happen if Endicott starts quoting higher prices for casting requiring extra labor? Should it recover the full cost? What ideas can you suggest at this time to improve the estimates? Should the cost estimator depend on the knowledge of Dick Crawford as final? What should constitute a loss or profit for the estimate?

3

Material Analysis

Material cost analysis can involve complicated bills of material, finishes, standard and nonstandard designs, and extensive inventories of direct and indirect materials. It is not surprising to find industrial and construction companies that have a material list of many millions. A vertically integrated company (i.e., copper ore to finished wire) has the problem of identifying the ore and intermediate cost values for their processed materials. A horizontally integrated company may often transfer materials between plants. Fluctuation of commodity prices adds to the apparent deorganization of material cost. Inflation or deflation of material cost is possible due to complex interactions. All of these factors produce the bewilderment facing the cost estimator in material analysis. The approach provided in this chapter is to identify the nature of materials, find their quantity, and pick a cost policy for a material. Only after material analysis is concluded can material estimating really begin.

3.1 MATERIAL

Before one considers the topic of materials, it should be realized that an understanding of physical materials associated with engineering design is required. The design may call for CA-610, AISI 1020, M type HSS, or A36 materials. While the terms are meaningless to the uninformed, materials are complicated in other respects. For instance, a casting has a variety of associated costs. There is the cost of melted metal, molding costs, core costs, cleaning costs, heat treatment costs, foundry tooling costs, and so forth. To estimate the cost for a casting, the estimator must be acquainted with the material and heat-treatment specifications, inspection requirements, and the design of the casting. Physical specifications such as tensile strength, yield strength, and elongation must be clarified as well as the chemical composition. The knowledge about engineering materials is so vast that we provide no information. Rather we consider the bill of materials and classifications of cost that relate to the needs of cost estimating.

Cost finding involved with material includes historical and measured information. In some cases, material costs are uncovered via company records, while for others the estimator must seek out the basic costs.

We define *materials* as the substance being altered or used in that alteration. This may involve iron ore, coke and limestone to a basic blast furnace industry for producing pig iron, steel ingots to a steel rolling mill for refining and rolling into strip and coil, tin sheet to a can producer manufacturing 6-ounce tins, and cases of 24 cans for a food processor for canning frozen orange juice. The scope of what constitutes materials depends on the situation. Materials have the property of having been purchased, not manufactured, by the plant to which they are materials. Thus sheet steel is a product from a rolling mill but a material to a sheet-metal forming plant.

For engineering design the documents of importance are the engineering bill of material and specifications in addition to the drawings. Engineers' bill of material or parts list accompany the blueprints and consist of an itemized list of the materials for a design. This list may be prepared on a separate sheet or may be lettered directly on the drawing. For example, a parts list contains the part numbers or symbols, a descriptive title of each part, the quantity, material, and other information such as casting pattern, number, stock size of the materials, weight of parts, or volume of materials. The parts are listed in general order of size or importance, or the special-design parts first and standard parts last. The list proceeds from the bottom upward on the drawings so that new items may be added later. In the case of a product that is to be constructed for the first time or in the case of the project where the contract must be executed, the materials must be purchased quickly to have them available when needed in the factory or on the job site. In some cases, the estimating department determines all the materials and job requirements. Inasmuch as they are conversant with the drawings and specifications and are already familiar with the details of the design and contract, they begin the job of *taking off* all material requirements. The quantity *takeoff* sheets must be made up in complete detail and include all descriptions necessary to obtain the materials as specified. Special forms are available for takeoffs.

Specifications are considered apart from the bill of material and engineering drawings. In construction, specifications are specific statements as to construction requirements, while in manufacturing, specifications relate to the performances, or materials, or special requirements. Basically these requirements are limited to the necessary technical details pertaining to the item itself. Specifications serve as a discussion of the proposed work so that bids may be compiled or quotations may be collected, to act as a guide or a book of rules during the construction and manufacturing time period, and finally they are legal documents to the construction industry and special requirements to manufacturing.

In addition to the type and character of the material, it is important that correct quantities such as units, weight, and volume are known. To have a correct cost such as 26 cents per pound of casting material and then improperly specify the number of pounds required for the casting is a serious flaw. In determining the quantities involved, the estimator would examine the plans and specifications and make the estimate, say, the number of cubic yards of 2800-psi concrete required by type of clean-and-sharp aggregate. In construction contractors would bid against a stated number of cubic yards and their price would be per cubic yard placed. In the product-oriented industries, the estimator determines the cost per unit of material after the count of materials has been established. In industry, as in construction, the estimate of materials involves extensive calculation to include allowances for waste, short ends, or losses. After these calculations are completed, often with the aid of data catalogs on weights, allowances, and the like, costs are determined.

Direct materials are subdivided into raw materials, standard commercial items, subcontract items, and interdivisional transfer items. *Raw materials* include fabricated, intermediate, or processed material in a form that will receive direct labor work in conversion to another design. For worked material, it is necessary to have designs, planning, and then to add direct labor.

Standard commercial materials are a class of materials normally not converted; rather they are accepted in a manufactured state, for instance, tires used by an automobile assembly plant. This category may be a significant proportion of total material cost, and it is considered separate from fabricated raw materials. Standard purchased parts and materials may carry a specific purchasing overhead rather than a larger general overhead rate, although the practice is not uniform. It may not be competitive to add a large markup on the same items that can be purchased by customers. Purchased parts and standard materials may be charged with out-of-pocket expenses for procurement, freight, receiving, handling, inspection, installation, and testing.

Standard commercial parts are costed either by estimating or purchasing. Estimating or engineering may provide a bill of material listing of the standard parts to purchasing, who will price them from catalogs or from quotations and return the information to estimating. Sometimes when a short lead time for sales prevails, estimating may compile the standard part costs. But with frequent price changes and negotiated price–volume breaks between the company's purchasing agents and seller, information from catalogs can be faulty. For some operations and products, the standard purchased parts such as nuts, bolts, and washers are estimated by a multiplying factor correlated to the direct materials. This happens whenever the standard purchased parts are insignificant.

Subcontract items are parts, components, assemblies, intermediate materials, or equipment produced by a supplier or vendor in accordance with designs, specifications, or directions that are applicable only to the design being estimated. *Interdivisional transfer materials* are materials sold or transferred between divisions, subsidiaries, or affiliates that have common ownership or control. These sales are ordinarily handled on a cost, no-profit, basis. On some occasions for items regularly manufactured and openly and widely sold, other arrangements may be made.

Materials can, alternatively, be classified into engineering, commodity, semi-engineering, and normative. *Engineering materials* are former commodities which have undergone substantial engineering processing, for example, iron ore to pig iron to hot rolled and pickled American Iron and Steel Institute (AISI) 1020, 40 × 120 in. (1.2 × 3 m) steel sheets. *Commodity* examples are foodstuffs, precious metals, timber, and extracted ores such as hematite (Fe_2O_3, iron ore) or chalcopyrite (Cu_2S, copper ore). *Semi-engineering materials,* insofar as cost value is concerned, behave as either an engineering or a commodity material. Copper is an example of a semi-engineering material, as occasionally its price is well behaved like an engineering material, while at other times it flip-flops and follows the roller coaster of commodity prices. *Normative materials* have price control or price fixing by various governments or cartels, such as oil or certain metals. In this book we are concerned only with the estimating of engineering materials which have reasonable price stability. Commodity prices are erratic and methods for accurate forecasting are beyond the needs of this elementary text. The direct materials that we estimate are engineering materials, as their cost fluctuation is moderated by the enormous processing requirements.

Indirect material costs cover those materials necessary for the conversion and are not traceable directly to the design. Nonassignable materials and perishable tooling expenses are prominent sources of expenses that are indirect. Some materials can be classified as either indirect or direct depending on convenience. Fuel, such as natural gas, is a bonafide raw material (e.g., cracking refinery gases for the production of ethylene or heat-treating furnaces). They can be treated as a direct raw material cost or an indirect utility expense. Operating supplies include such things as lubricating oil and brooms and are too diverse and unimportant to be directly considered by the estimator. Company records should be used for these indirect materials and overhead is the usual way to recover their costs.

3.2 SHAPE

The problem of estimating direct materials is broken down into three parts: (1) measurement of the shape, (2) finding the value of cost per unit shape, and (3) the value of any salvage. Qualitatively, the cost is found using

$$\text{cost of direct material} = \text{shape} \times \text{cost/unit shape} - \text{salvage value} \qquad (3.1)$$

Shape is a general word implying mass or area or length or count or one of the many engineering dimensional units. The cost per unit shape is in compatible dimensions. If shape is pounds (kilograms), then \$/lbm (\$/kg) is the appropriate cost rate. Salvage is a recovered material having a credit or debit applied against the direct material cost of the design.

During material takeoff the estimator determines the theoretical amount or count of the material as finally required by the design. The takeoff could be the bill of materials or it could be a separate listing indicating material specification, size, weight, length, shape, and so on. Sometimes this kind of takeoff is termed a *quantity survey,* and the estimator is called a *quantity surveyor.** To the exact shape, he or she adds for losses of scrap, waste, and shrinkage.

Scrap is faulty material because of human mistake. Mislocation of drill holes is a shop mistake, or it may have been caused by the designer's error, in which case the scrap is caused by engineering.

In manufacturing and construction work, the converting or changing of the properties or configuration causes *waste*. This loss is found in all durable-goods manufacturing. The width of the cutoff tool in a lathe cutting-off operation of a round bar becomes chips and is of no value to the design, except that it is necessary for part separation. The remaining stock, or skeleton-like structure remaining after parts have been blanked from sheet metal, is another example of waste. The overburden of castings, which is eventually removed as chips, is a well-known illustration. Another interesting term is *offal,* which originally meant the inedible parts of a butchered animal but is now sometimes used to mean waste. In construction, waste may be crop ends of boards. A great deal of engineering effort is concerned with the reduction or elimination of waste. Despite this activity, an amount of 1 to 12% is often appropriate as an allowance for waste.

Losses of materials because of theft or physical laws are termed *shrinkage*. Originally, shrinkage dealt with volumetric reduction of lumber due to drying, but nowadays we mean the economic effects due to deterioration of materials because of aging, oxidation, chemical reaction, natural spoilage, and so on, if reduction in quantity and quality will occur. A polymer raw material may have a limited shelf life, and if not molded and cured before the onset of deterioration, there is economic, not physical, shrinkage. Rusting of ferrous materials is a common form of shrinkage. Food commodities have serious problems with shrinkage losses, both economic and in the reduction of flavor or moisture.

These losses are determined by the estimator, usually as a percentage, and added to the theoretical amount; they are expressed as

$$S_a = S_t(1 + L_1 + L_2 + L_3) \tag{3.2}$$

where S_a = actual shape in units of area, length, mass, volume, count, etc.

S_t = theoretical shape required for design in units of area, length, etc.

L_1 = loss due to scrap, decimal

L_2 = loss due to waste, decimal

L_3 = loss due to shrinkage, decimal

If a piece is machined, the amount of stock removed by machining must be added to the final dimensions, and the volume is computed from these dimensions.

---

*This title is common in England.

Consider as a first example a $1\frac{7}{16}$-in. (36.5-mm)-OD (outside diameter) carbon steel bar that has a finish length of $1\frac{1}{8}$ in. (28.6 mm). Historical records indicate that scrap is 1% for this kind of operation. Waste is composed of a $\frac{1}{8}$-in. (3.2-mm) cutoff tool width, and a facing length of $\frac{1}{64}$ in. (0.4 mm) is required for accurate dimension. The machine selected for this turning is limited to a 6-ft. (1.8-m) bar length, but the lathe collet requires a gripping length which reduces the quantity produced from the bar stock by one. Each unit will require 1.266 in. ($= 1\frac{1}{8} + \frac{1}{8} + \frac{1}{64}$) (32.15 mm) of length and the exact number of pieces will be 72/1.266 $=$ 56.9. Reducing this to 55 units allows for last-part gripping. The percentage $= 55 \times 1.125/72 \times 100 = 85.9\%$, so the waste $=$ 14.1%. There is no shrinkage for this part, so

$$S_a = (1\tfrac{7}{16})^2 \frac{\pi}{4}(1\tfrac{1}{8})(1 + 0.01 + 0.141 + 0) = 2.116\,\text{in.}^3\,(34.7\,\text{cm}^3)$$

Waste in this example includes chips, short ends, cutoff, and facing material. We assumed a finished bar stock diameter equal to the original diameter. If there was chip removal on the circumference, our volume calculation will find the exact final amount plus these losses.

On rough carpentry, lumber is figured according to the board foot (metre³). Simply stated, a board foot (metre³) of lumber is equal to 144 in.³ (0.0024 m³) or 1 BF. If the lumber is 1 × 12 × 12 in. (25 × 300 × 300 mm), we have 1 BF (0.0024 m³). Similarly, a piece of wood 4 × 6 × 6 in. (100 × 150 × 150 mm) gives 1 BF. Suppose that we have a board 1 × 8 in. × 12 ft (25 × 200 mm × 3.6 m). The rule is to multiply thickness by width in inches (millimetres) by length in feet (metres) and divide the product by 12: for example,

$$S_a = \frac{1\,\text{in.} \times 8\,\text{in.} \times 12\,\text{ft}}{12} = 8\,\text{BF}\,(0.019\,\text{m}^3)$$

For another example, a 2 × 4 in. (50 × 100 mm) stud, 8 ft (2.4 m) long, contains the following board feet:

$$S_a = \frac{2\,\text{in.} \times 4\,\text{in.} \times 8\,\text{ft}}{12} = 5\tfrac{1}{3}\,\text{BF}\,(0.013\,\text{m}^3)$$

If the piece is irregular in shape, it is divided into simple subparts and the minor volumes are manipulated to give total volume. Stamping fabrication from coil stock or a blank and trim operation from sheets require slightly different shape calculations. Consider the workpiece in Fig. 3.1. In stamping fabrication the distance between blanks is restricted to a minimum 0.75 × thickness, while the margins between the edge of the strip and the blank are restricted to 0.90 × thickness for each side. The width of the strip is calculated as 1.3625 in. ($= 1.250 + 2 \times 0.9 \times 0.0625$) (34.61 mm). The part long-way dimension or length includes 75% of the stock thickness and the part dimension and in sheet metal manufacturing is called *advance*. The advance is 2.0469 (52.0 mm). If $L_1 = \frac{1}{4}\%$ and $L_3 = 0$,

$$S_a = (1.3625)(2.0469)(0.0625)(1 + \tfrac{1}{4}\%) = 0.175\,\text{in.}^3\,(2.86\,\text{cm}^3)$$

Observe that the corner radius and first operation slug have been ignored.

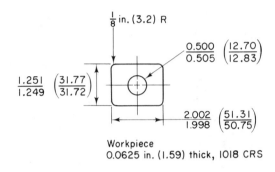

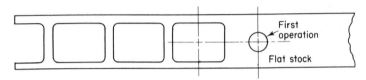

Figure 3.1.   Sheet metal component.

Other models for sheet metal estimating can be used depending on the engineering requirements, such as

$$\text{pieces per coil} = \frac{\text{coil length}}{\text{length of design}}$$

$$\text{weight of coil} = \text{gauge} \times \text{width} \times \text{length} \times \text{density} \qquad (3.3)$$

$$\text{weight per piece} = \frac{\text{weight of coil}}{\text{pieces per coil}}$$

Equation (3.3) is only typical of the many ways to calculate shape. Each design has its own mensuration, which is a field of mathematics that deals with finding length, area, and volume.

The estimator is required to compute the efficiency of conversion of raw materials such as

$$E_s = \frac{S_t}{S_a} \times 100 \qquad (3.4)$$

where E_s denotes the shape yield, percent. For the sheet metal component

$$E_s = \frac{2.2914}{1.3625 \times 2.0469} \times 100 = 82\%$$

where the four corner radii and the slug have been included in the calculation for the *shape yield*.

The final term in Eq. (3.1) deals with *salvage*. In many cases scrap and waste are sold to a junk dealer or the original processor, who credits the firm. In some cases the credit is significant enough to subtract the total unit cost, while in others, it is not worth the effort, as in the case of machine chips. Some waste and scrap may even add to the cost because of disposal problems.

Having discussed shape, cost per unit shape, and salvage, the usual cost estimating formula is given as

$$C_{dm} = S_a C_{ms} - V_s \qquad (3.5)$$

where C_{dm} = cost of direct material, dollars per unit

C_{ms} = cost of material, compatible to S_a units

V_s = salvage cost, dollars per unit

We presume that S_a and C_{ms} are in compatible units. If both sides are multiplied by N_p, the number of pieces produced, we have total or lot cost, depending on the nature of N_p.

The estimator is able to compute the efficiency of the economic conversion of raw materials, such as

$$E_m = \frac{N_p S_a C_{ms} - N_s V_s}{N_p S_a C_{ms}} \times 100 \qquad (3.6)$$

where E_m = material cost yield

N_s = number of salvage units

An example of material estimating is given by the 12-fluid-ounce (0.197-litre) beverage can, which is composed of the body, top, and pull ring. The container body is blanked from 3004-0 aluminum coils with the layout given by Fig. 3.2. An intermediate cup is formed without any significant change in thickness. The cup is drawn in a horizontal drawing machine and metal is squeezed to a side-wall thickness of 0.0055 in. (0.140 mm) while the bottom thickness remains unchanged. The can is trimmed to the final height to give an even edge for later rolling to the lid. The strip stock layout is called a "four-out" advance. For the 5.3176-in. (135.067-mm) advance in the die, four blanks are punched out simultaneously, and the coil is repeatedly punched in this manner, leaving a skeleton of waste. A summary of the calculations is given by Table 3.1. Line 1 of Table 3.1 provides the volume in a 12-oz can body, while line 2 indicates the strip volume of advance. Once divided by 4, we have the can body. Line 3 provides the shape yield of the can body to strip. The blank, 5.2476 in. (133.289 mm) OD, also has losses in drawing to the final can, and line 5 indicates a yield of 86.3%. Line 6 indicates the cost per pound (kilogram). The density of the material is 0.0982 lb/in.^{3} (2717 kg/m^3). Line 8 indicates the salvage value for the waste, and line 9 shows the recovery on a per can basis. Finally, the metal cost in the can body is calculated on line 11 as $0.0384 per can.

3.3 MATERIAL COST POLICIES

With the shape determined, material cost analysis proceeds to the second step of finding the cost per unit shape. This is not simple, as engineering classification, accounting systems, vendors, and professional, consulting, or association advice can add to the confusion of determining an accurate cost value.

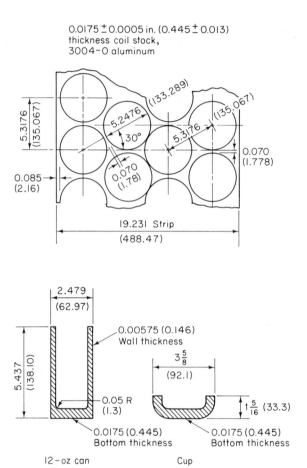

Figure 3.2.   Layout of strip for manufacture of the popular 12-oz beverage cans.

Manufacturing materials often have different technical specifications than those of construction materials (e.g., AISI 1035 versus A36). Furthermore, a manufacturing firm may build a product from a periodically replenished inventory, while a contracting firm or job shop may not order materials until the bid has been won. For cost-estimation purposes the differences in classification and material ordering policies are superficial. For example, a job-shop manufacturing firm or a contractor will not order materials until a particular bid is accepted. A manufacturing firm may order materials in building prototypes even though the equipment may be unsold at the time. The methods that follow suit the needs of both manufacturing and construction. The word "lot" as used subsequently is more commonplace in manufacturing than in construction. It implies a purchase order of a quantity of discrete items, perhaps as few as one.

Table 3.1. CALCULATION OF DIRECT MATERIAL COST FOR 12-OZ CAN BODY
GIVEN BY FIG. 3.2

---

1. Final metal volume in 12-oz can body = 0.3266 in.^{3} (5355 mm^3)
2. Strip volume per can body = 5.3176 × 19.231 × 0175/4 = 0.4474 in.^{3}
   (7328 mm^3)
3. Metal efficiency = 0.3266/0.4474 = 73.0%
4. Metal volume in 5.2746 (133.975) blank = 0.3785 in.^{3} $5 \cdot 2476$
5. Can body to blank efficiency = 0.3266/0.3785 = 86.3%
6. Cost of metal $1.0017/lb ($2.226/kg)
7. Cost of can body = 0.4474 × 0.0982 lb/in.^{3} × 1.0017 = $0.0441
8. Waste salvage value = $0.4830/lb ($1.073/kg)
9. Salvage of waste per can body = (19.231)(5.3176)(0.0175)(1 − 0.73)(0.00982)
   (0.4830) = $0.0057 (must $\div$ by 4)
10. Metal cost in can body = (0.3266)(0.0982)(1.0017) = $0.0321
11. Net cost per can body in strip = 0.0441 − 0.0057 = $0.0384
12. Economic yield = 0.0321/0.0384 × 100 = 83.6%

Within the company, one may state that direct material cost analysis is separated into *contractual* or *inventory* methods. The contractual methods, used for subcontract materials, imply that a buyer–vendor arrangement exists, and the company solicits a cost for a design. This excludes those materials which are informally purchased, or items that have wide usage and are produced by a number of individual manufacturers, as these materials have an ongoing market price. In this case, market competition has established reasonable prices. The estimator will use these market values as he or she picks a cost policy.

Complex and specialized items which have limited or special application and few suppliers are often subject to wide price variation. Greater care is required in estimating these values. The *quotation cost* method is the most widely used. The cost of the material is established by a vendor. The delivery price is considered fixed subject to the guarantees of the mutually-agreed-to contract. Quotations can be solicited orally if insufficient time is available or the purchases are relatively small in value. Written solicitations should generally be tendered where special specifications are involved, a large number of items is included in a single proposed procurement, or obtaining oral quotations is not considered economical or legal. Involved in the wording of the tendered quotation are statements about the design and specifications, terms or conditions, delivery date, and price. The obligation to contract at fair and reasonable prices does not diminish as one moves down the scale from multimillion-dollar contracts for system acquisition to the dime and quarter prices for nuts and bolts.

The *quote or price-in-effect* method is a collaborative legal agreement between the buyer and seller. As usually established, the contract allows for adjustment to the original price should the seller incur material costs in excess of those estimated.

If the seller's material cost falls below that which was estimated in the contract, the buyer agrees to the original price and adjustment is unnecessary. If at the time of delivery of the design, the seller can prove that the material costs incurred to the seller escalated above the original estimated value, the buyer will make up the difference via a formula. The quote or price-in-effect method may seemingly avoid the troublesome problem of making accurate material analysis and forecasts; however, competition and economy may not allow the luxury of this contract.

Most manufacturers carry inventories, and material costs are affected by the method used to evaluate inventory. Costs will vary depending on the method and market conditions. When materials are purchased specifically and are identifiable with a contract, the actual purchase cost is used as the estimate for the design, and contractual methods as described earlier are appropriate. However, when materials are issued from inventory, it is difficult to find the value as inventories are extensive. Often the raw materials are consolidated for many designs (e.g., a company may standardize on a special grade of steel for all shafts). Furthermore, purchases of material are done at different times and in various quantities. It is recognized that quantity discounts are normally offered as a business practice, and lower prices can be obtained when requirements can be consolidated into a single purchase order.

Before we discuss our methods for the evaluation of inventory cost, it is necessary to describe a specific example. The inventory to be considered for material estimating is given in Fig. 3.3. The horizontal axis is time. The time scale may represent days, weeks, months, or years and thus the model is general. The present is time 0 and is labeled *"E"* to designate it as the time of the estimate. Negative integers are past time periods and positive integers are future time periods. Point D is the delivery time for the product. The vertical axis represents units of quantity of the material.

The three functions designated by TS, TU, and JJ are defined as follows:

$TS(t)$ = total supply of the material, time t
$TU(t)$ = total usage of the material, time t
$JJ(t)$ = job J usage of the material, time t

These step functions will be used to obtain different estimates for the unit material cost for job J.

To the right of point 0 each of the functions represents inventory projections. The step sizes on each of the integers $t = 0, \pm 1, \pm 2, \ldots$ for the functions TU and JJ represent the material used in production during the period $(t - 1, t)$. The step sizes on each of the integers t for the function TS represent the quantity of material arriving at time t. Hence the inventory at time $t = 0, \pm 1, \pm 2, \ldots$ is the difference between the functions TS and TU during the period $(t, t + 1)$.

In this example it is assumed that the total usage curve, TU, is comprised of the job J curve, JJ, plus other curves. For example, at $t = 4$, job J uses 50% of the total for that period, and at $t = 5$, job J uses 100%. Material estimates are made assuming that job J is won because, as will be expanded shortly, quantity discounts are assumed to exist for material purchases.

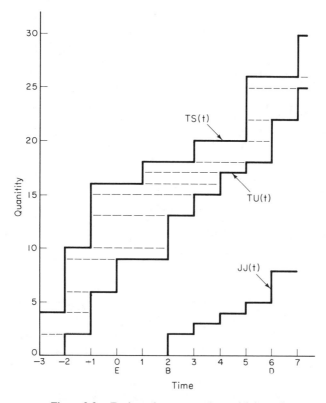

Figure 3.3. Total supply, usage, and material demand.

The inventory supply curve TS follows a general review and reorder discipline, such as MRP (material requirements planning). But this is unimportant to the objective of estimating the cost of the units withdrawn irregularly from inventory. A fixed lead time of one period is assumed for all orders. The JJ step function totals eight units with initial inventory withdrawal at period 2. Last inventory withdrawal occurs at period 6. During period 6 the units are delivered to the customer. When two units were issued for JJ at period 2, the total usage was four units. One, two, and one unit of the four were taken from inventory purchases made during periods -2, -1, and 1. The horizontal dashed lines indicate the units used between TS and TU.

Table 3.2 displays the historical and forecast unit costs the firm faces in purchasing the material. Price breaks are available for various quantity lots. For instance, if one or two units were purchased three periods back from the current time (period $= -3$) of the estimate (at $E = 0$), each unit costs \$10.70. If three or four units were purchased in a lot, the unit cost is \$8.60. If two periods in the future (at period $= 2$), and five or six units are to be purchased, each unit will cost \$9.10. It is seen that Table 3.2 reflects the period and the quantity purchased.

Now with the specific example given as Fig. 3.3 and Table 3.2, consider six methods of evaluating the material unit cost for a firm having inventory.

Table 3.2. HISTORICAL AND FORECAST UNIT COSTS

Period	Quantity			
	1–2	3–4	5–6	7–8
Historical				
−4	10.00	8.00	7.00	6.50
−3	10.70	8.60	7.50	7.00
−2	11.10	8.95	7.80	7.20
−1	11.25	9.00	7.90	7.30
0	12.00	9.65	8.40	7.85
Forecast				
1	12.95	10.01	8.73	8.12
2	12.97	10.44	9.10	8.46
3	13.52	10.89	9.49	8.83
4	14.10	11.36	9.89	9.20
5	14.69	11.84	10.32	9.60
6	15.31	12.35	10.75	10.01

1. The *original cost* method assumes that materials are used in the order they are received and establishes as a cost estimate the unit cost of the oldest material sustained in inventory. In Fig. 3.3 the oldest material in stock at time $E = 0$ came from a lot of six purchased at time -2. From Table 3.2 the unit cost is \$7.80. Commonly called FIFO (first in, first out), this method has been popularized by the accounting profession for inventory valuation purposes.

2. The *last-cost* method assumes that the latest materials purchased are the first to be used and establishes as a cost estimate the unit cost of the most recent material in inventory. In Fig. 3.3 the most recent material in stock at time E came from a lot of six purchases at time -1. From Table 3.2 the unit cost is \$7.90. This method, also called LIFO (last in, first out), is frequently used by the accounting profession.

3. A unit cost at period $E = 0$ is used in this method as the value of the estimate, and thus is time coincident to the preparation of the estimate. The method is known as *current cost*. If price breaks exist, a lot size must be determined before an estimate is arrived at. Remember, inventory need not be added every period. For example, if the purchase lot is assumed to be 6 at time 0 (even though no material purchases are made in Fig. 3.3) the estimate from Table 3.2 is \$8.40 per unit. Rules may be arbitrarily established, such as the entire requirement is purchased if no other quantity is known for that period.

4. The *lead-time replacement* concept adopts as an estimate the replacement cost of the first lot of the material at the time it arrives. This is commonly called the next in, first out method (NIFO), even though this label is an obvious anomaly. Given a lead-time requirement of one period, the order of two units arrived at time 1 and the unit cost estimate from Table 3.2 is \$12.95. This concept is used by estimators where material renewals are significant. For bidding situations there is a

delay from submission of the bid to knowing if the estimate wins. Once the estimate wins, material is ordered, and material specifically ordered for job J arrives.

5. The point in time when the production order is delivered to the customer establishes the policy for the *delivery cost* method. As in the methods above, if any quantity is to be purchased at time D, we use that. In the absence of a purchase, we assume a quantity, perhaps equal to the delivery, and use that as the value of the material estimate. In Fig. 3.3 the delivery time is point D and if we assume a lot size of eight, the unit cost is taken as $10.01. There were no scheduled purchases for inventory during period 6.

6. *Money-out-of-pocket* refers to a general class of techniques in which the overriding philosophy is to have the estimate reflect actual material expenditure. If the material is purchased in a single lot, the estimate would simply be the unit cost of the lot. If the material is taken from inventory, the estimate would be the original purchase cost of the material. If the material is to be purchased in the future, a forecast of the unit price would be used. Note Fig. 3.4, in which the material is from two purchases and the cost of total usage at period 2 is $31.50 ($= 7.80 + 3 \times 7.90$) and the weighted average is $7.88.

In the example of Fig. 3.3, the material for job J is actually taken from a number of past and future inventory purchases. The money-out-of-pocket method is a weighted method for forecasted usage of the material in as accurate a manner as possible. Suppose that at time t we have $n(t)$ lots of the material in inventory which were purchased at times $t_j; j = 1, 2, \ldots, n(t)$. At time t define

$f(t_j)$ = fraction of the material inventory coming from the time t_j lot

$p(t_j)$ = unit cost of the t_j lot

$d_j(t)$ = number of units of the material used for job J at time t

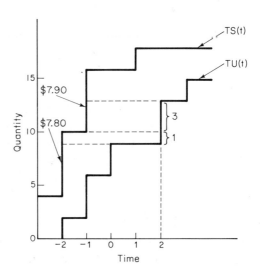

Figure 3.4.   Actual material expenditure of usage at period 2 is weighted average.

The estimated unit material cost is

$$C_{ms} = \frac{\sum_t \sum_{j=1}^{n(t)} p(t_j) f(t_j) d_J(t)}{\sum_t d_J(t)} \tag{3.7}$$

where C_{ms} is the cost of material shape, \$/unit shape.

To demonstrate the use of this formula, observe Fig. 3.3 and the data in Table 3.3. From Fig. 3.3 we see that of the four units total usage of period 2, one unit

Table 3.3.   VALUES USED FOR PROBLEM REMOVED FROM FIGURE 3.3 AND TABLE 3.2

Time	Units of Inventory Delivered	Unit Price of Inventory Delivered	Usage Units of Inventory of All Jobs	Units of Inventory for Job J
-2	6	$ 7.80	2	—
-1	6	7.90	4	—
0	0	—	3	—
1	2	12.95	0	—
2	0	—	4	2
3	2	13.52	2	1
4	0	—	2	1
5	6	10.32	1	1
6	0	—	4	$\frac{3}{8}$

can be considered as purchased at -2 time for \$7.78 per unit and three units as purchased at -1 time for \$7.90 per unit. The dashed horizontal lines of Fig. 3.3 relate the time of inventory purchase to time of usage. Under the out-of-pocket cost methods, the two units of job J usage for the second period would be costed as

$$(7.80 \times \tfrac{1}{4} + 7.90 \times \tfrac{3}{4}) \times 2 = \$15.75$$

The remaining periods of production for job J ($t = 3, 4, 5, 6$) are similarly costed as

$$(7.90) \times 1 + (7.90 \times \tfrac{1}{2} + 12.95 \times \tfrac{1}{2}) \times 1 + (12.95) \times 1 + (13.52 \times \tfrac{1}{2} + 10.32 \times \tfrac{1}{2}) \times 3 = \$67.04$$

Lot cost for job J is \$82.79 and for the lot quantity of 8, unit cost is \$10.35. Table 3.4 summarizes the estimated unit costs of raw material. The money-out-of-pocket cost method is, we contend, superior to other methods and is recommended for estimating.

3.4 JOINT MATERIAL COST

Joint labor costs were discussed in Chapter 2 and now our attention turns to joint material cost. While joint labor cost is exclusively labor, joint material is usually confronted with elements of material and labor costs. A common task for a cost

Table 3.4. Unit Cost Estimates for Inventory Material Depends on Method

Method	Candidate Value for Estimate, C_{ms}
Original	$ 7.80
Last	7.90
Current	8.40
Lead-time replacement	12.95
Delivery	10.01
Money-out-of-pocket	10.35

estimator is to prepare a detail cost analysis of a manufacturing process dejointing the cost of common material into finished product. Traditional approaches to joint costs of material involve concepts which serve accounting or marketing needs and do not reflect the true or actual costs of specific interest to the estimator.

Joint materials are those materials which begin with the processing of a singular raw material supply. Joint materials are intermingled up to the point at which the materials are divided into separable units. The point of division is called the ''split point.'' Material and labor costs up to the split point are referred to as joint costs, but afterwards are called unit cost.

The key element in this definition is the concept of the singular raw material which by virtue of a processing step becomes two or more discrete products. For example, the processing of raw milk into cream and skim milk illustrates the conversion of singular raw material into two discrete products which will be individually marketed. Another example is the rough log, which upon sawing and milling becomes first- and second-grade lumber and sawdust. A molded plastic part where the die has several cavities is a common production joint cost problem. Similar situations occur in a variety of industries, but especially in process-oriented industries such as chemical, petroleum, food, metallurgical, or timber. These industries include processes to make marketable products of what were essentially by-products of basic processing steps. The problem in processes that result in multiple products is the tracing of the cost contribution of raw material and labor to the individual final products. Often the choice of allocators is not clear, or product lines are not direct, or other factors appear to prevent cost traceability.

A distinction is necessary between distributing and converting types of joint costs. The *distributing* type of joint costs is illustrated by the multiple-cavity die problem as plastics pellets are intermingled prior to the molding operation. The characteristic of the plastic is not altered (in a joint cost sense) and cost traceability is valid albeit complicated. An example describes the analysis of the distributing type of joint cost shortly. In processing industries a quantity of raw material is transformed into a singular new product or material. A simple example is water + heat process = steam. Splitting of raw material requires that the essential cost nature of the material be changed, resulting in two or more discrete products or materials with differing characteristics and physical measures or values. Figure 3.5 describes this distinction between distributing and converting joint costs.

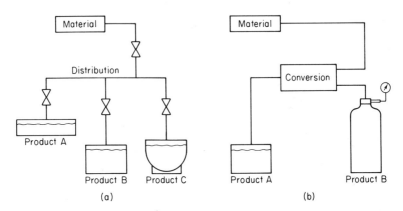

Figure 3.5. Two classes of joint cost: (a) material being "distributed"; (b) material being "converted" into two or more products.

Marketing practice can require that some products subsidize others. This policy recognizes that selling price or market value of a product is not necessarily proportional to processing costs. An accounting or marketing policy may distort true costs. The allocation of joint cost on the basis of quantity can result in invalid cost data. This arises when products are valued for inventory purposes at levels higher or lower than their actual production costs. A similar situation occurs when marketing policy dictates price levels which do not reflect manufacturing costs, but rather selling. Often the profitability of one product cannot be gauged by available data, whereas the profitability of a group of products may be properly represented due to schemes of cost accounting. The reverse may also be true. In the example of a rough log subject to a splitting process, the production of first-grade lumber and other lumber products are not independent actions, as the production of first-grade lumber is associated with the production of lesser-grade lumber and sawdust. The processing investment to finish and market secondary lumber products may be subsidized by profits (or operating costs) from first-grade lumber production. Profitability decisions on specific products cannot be made on the basis of accounting data, which may cover a group of products, and not reflect the true costs of an individual product. Herein arises the need for an exact cost estimate which examines joint product costs. We point out, however, that the traditional approaches are justified for their intended purpose.

Now consider allocators or those units of reference which are commonly used to prorate or allocate costs. To separate joint costs into unit cost, we select a unit of value per unit of reference. Commonly, this is a dollar value per unit of measure: $/ft^2 ($/m^2), $/lb ($/kg), $/kW, $/hr, $/product unit. Fundamental reference units which are readily measured are preferred. The simpler the measured unit, the clearer its use becomes and the more accurate are the conclusions drawn from the analysis. Allocators can be classified as follows:

1. Physical measure (geometry, weight, shape, etc.)
2. Energy (Btu, kW, etc.)

3. Time (second, year, man-hour, etc.)

4. Units of finished product, each, 100 units, etc.

For traceability of costs the unit of reference needs to be defined to avoid changing the unit through a process. For example, if pound (kilogram) is used in the material stage, pound (kilogram) is convenient as a finished product, rather than foot squared (metre^2). This becomes important with split converting where split products may be in different physical states. Unnecessary unit conversion should be avoided. For example, rather than defining the products of a petroleum cracking process as gallon (litre) and barrel (m^3), a common unit such as pound (kilogram) should be used throughout the process.

Now consider a manufacturing example for a distributing type of joint cost. A plastic material is blended, pigmented, and injection molded. Assume that a molded part is in a multiple-cavity mold and the die has runners that connect the pieces from a sprue. Furthermore, one operator tends two machines which are operating at different rates, and each machine produces a different part, designated A and B. Sets A and B are three- and four-cavity molds, respectively. The essential design features are given by Fig. 3.6.

Two machines are molding round preforms or buttons of a flour-like plastic. The material costs $2.50 per pound ($5.56 per kilogram) and has a density of 0.0275 lb/in.^{3} (760 kg/m^3). Machines A and B have a production rate of 400 and 300 sets per hour. A set is composed of three or four buttons having a sprue and runners. The runners and the sprue are considered waste and are eventually trimmed as only the button is used. The operator is paid $16.50 per hour. Four approaches are given in Table 3.5 and other methods are possible. Assume that the waste is lost and cannot be reground and used again. Usually, the waste degrades to lower quality in terms of specification, and thus has a reduction in real economic value. The student may

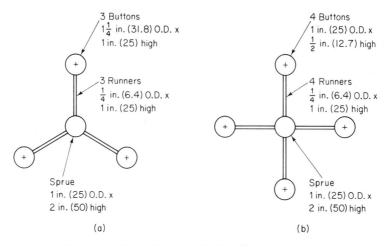

Figure 3.6.   Two designs for a distributed joint-cost problem.

Table 3.5. DISTRIBUTION TYPE OF JOINT COST ANALYSIS

Facts for the Designs

Design A: Volume = 3.6816 in.^{3} (60,305 mm^3) for 3 buttons
Weight = 0.1012 lb (0.046 kg) for 3 buttons
Sprue   = 1.5708 in.^{3} (25,730 mm^3), weight = 0.0432 lb (0.020 kg)
Runners = 0.1473 in.^{3} (2,413 mm^3), weight = 0.0041 lb (0.002 kg)

Design B: Volume = 1.5708 in.^{3} (25,730 mm^3) for 4 buttons
Weight = 0.0432 lb (0.020 kg) for 4 buttons
Sprue   = 1.5708 in.^{3} (25,730 mm^3), weight = 0.0432 lb (0.020 kg)
Runners = 0.1964 in.^{3} (3,217 mm^3), weight = 0.0054 lb (0.002 kg)

Set A	in.^{3}	mm^3	lb	kg	$
Waste	1.7181	28,140	0.0432	0.020	0.1080
Good product	3.6815	60,310	0.1012	0.047	0.2531
Total shot	5.3996	88,450	0.1485	0.067	0.3712

$$\text{Unit material cost for set } A = \frac{0.3712}{3} = \$0.1237/\text{unit}$$

$$\text{Material in good product for set } A = \frac{0.2531}{3} = \$0.0844/\text{unit}$$

Set B	in.^{3}	mm^3	lb	kg	$
Waste	1.7672	28,950	0.0486	0.022	0.1215
Good product	1.5708	25,725	0.0432	0.020	0.1080
Total shot	3.3380	54,675	0.0918	0.042	0.2295

$$\text{Unit material cost for set } B = \frac{0.2295}{4} = \$0.0574/\text{unit}$$

$$\text{Material in good product for set } B = \frac{0.1080}{4} = \$0.0270/\text{unit}$$

1. Labor apportioned on total lb/hr

   Set *A* output = 400 (0.1485) = 59.3960 lb/hr (26.942 kg/hr)
   Set *B* output = 300 (0.0918) = 27.5400 lb/hr (12.492 kg/hr)
   Total for machines *A* and *B* = 86.9360 lb/hr (39.434 kg/hr)

   $$\text{Unit labor cost for design } A = \frac{59.396}{86.936}(16.50)\left(\frac{1}{1200}\right) = \$0.0094$$

   $$\text{Unit labor cost for design } B = \frac{27.540}{86.936}(16.50)\left(\frac{1}{1200}\right) = \$0.0044$$

2. Labor apportioned on shots/hr and total shots = 700

   $$\text{Unit labor cost for design } A = \frac{400}{700}(16.50)\left(\frac{1}{1200}\right) = \$0.0079$$

Table 3.5.   *(cont.)*

Unit labor cost for design B $= \dfrac{300}{700}(16.50)\left(\dfrac{1}{1200}\right) = \$0.0059$

3. Labor apportioned on units/hr

$$\text{Machine } A \text{ units} = 1200 \text{ units/hr}$$
$$\text{Machine } B \text{ units} = 1200 \text{ units/hr}$$

Unit labor cost for design A $= \dfrac{1200}{2400}(16.50)\left(\dfrac{1}{1200}\right) = \$0.0069$

Unit labor cost for design B $= \dfrac{1200}{2400}(16.50)\left(\dfrac{1}{1200}\right) = \$0.0069$

4. Labor apportioned on lb/hr of final product produced

Total lb/hr for machine A $= \dfrac{1200}{3}(0.1012) = 40.48 \text{ lb/hr}$

Total lb/hr for machine B $= \dfrac{1200}{4}(0.0432) = 12.96 \text{ lb/hr}$

Unit labor cost for design A $= \dfrac{40.48}{53.44}(16.50)\left(\dfrac{1}{1200}\right) = \$0.0104$

Unit labor cost for design B $= \dfrac{12.96}{53.44}(16.50)\left(\dfrac{1}{1200}\right) = \$0.0033$

Solutions to Joint Cost Problem

Design	Basis for Apportioning of Labor Cost	Material	Labor	Unit Cost of Labor + Material
A	lb/hr input	$0.1237	$0.0094	$0.1331
A	shots/hr	$0.1237	$0.0079	$0.1316
A	units/hr	$0.1237	$0.0169	$0.1306
A	lb/hr output	$0.1237	$0.0104	$0.1341
B	lb/hr input	$0.0574	$0.0044	$0.0618
B	shots/hr	$0.0574	$0.0059	$0.0633
B	units/hr	$0.0574	$0.0069	$0.0643
B	lb/hr output	$0.0574	$0.0033	$0.0607

want to ponder the joint cost if the sprues and runners are reused at no loss in economic value.

In this example, the material cost is uniformly related to production values of output. Labor cost, however, can be apportioned on four basis. Arithmetically, these basis lead to different answers for the contribution of labor cost to joint cost. Four acceptable solutions are given in Table 3.5. Which of the four is best? The answer is a knotty one and we sidestep the question by saying that details outside the calculations will choose the "best" one. Traceability is the important element in this example, as the costs of the finished product can be calculated to the original material using a simple allocator and measure of quantity. This cost traceability is characteristic of simple distributing types of joint cost problems. However, in a converting type of joint cost the converting of a material creates two or more new products in a constant or variable ratio and with relative values and quantities disproportionate to original material values and quantities. The element of direct cost traceability becomes confused if the essential quantity measures vary or become meaningless. This is characteristic of converting processes. By following certain rules, these difficulties can be circumvented and a cost estimate can be calculated.

When the converting type of joint costs occur, the key to unscrambling the cost allocation is the selection of a primary product. With a selection made, unit costs for processed material can be established. The primary product is the product that forms the financial and physical justification for a company or process to exist. All other products are secondary products regardless of their value, and would not exist were it not for the production of the primary product. Where the primary product cannot be immediately identified, or can be changed by minor process changes, an economic profitability analysis should be performed. For example, in the dairy industry, raw milk can be processed into cream, skim milk, powdered milk, milk, cheese, and butter. All these products can be produced, yet the operation may be set up to optimize the production of only one product, say cheese. If concentrating on cheese production optimizes the profitability of the product line, then cheese is the primary product. The identification of a primary product allows the process to be presented schematically as a direct flow from material to finished product, with all secondary products branching off at their split points. The flow of material is an engineering decision, and once a design has been chosen, cost analysis can begin. Converting industries, unlike the manufacturing, fabrication, and the durable-goods industries, deal with this kind of joint cost problem.

SUMMARY

Direct materials include raw materials, standard commercial items, subcontract items, and interdivisional transfer items. Direct material cost is the cost of material used in the design. The cost should be significant enough to warrant the cost of estimating it. Some direct material, because of the difficulty of estimating, may be analyzed as indirect, although for accuracy direct costs are preferred to overhead. Paint material (such as enamels, laquers, etc) of irregular-shaped objects is an example of material that can be classified either way because of the difficulty of determining the shape (number of gallons or barrels).

The estimator begins by calculating the final exact quantity or shape required for a design. To this quantity he or she adds for losses of scrap, waste, and shrinkage. Once the cost of the material is referenced to a shape dimension, it is possible to find the direct material cost. Contractual arrangements and inventory schemes affect the method in which the material cost rate is found.

QUESTIONS

3.1. Give an explanation of the following terms:

Specification	Quantity survey
Bill of material	Offal
Takeoff sheets	Shrinkage
Direct materials	Quote or price in effect
Subcontract materials	Yield
Normative materials	Joint products
Shape	Out-of-pocket material cost

3.2. Discuss the complications of materials as they relate to the requirements of engineering design. Does the cost of materials affect their engineering selection?

3.3. What kinds of records would the estimator use in finding the cost?

3.4. Define material in terms of alteration.

3.5. Divide direct materials into categories. Discuss.

3.6. What makes commodity and semi-engineering materials difficult to estimate? Prepare a list of commodity and semi-engineering materials.

3.7. Give some typical engineering units for shape.

3.8. Indicate the similarities of manufacturing and construction in determining material cost policy. List some of the differences between manufacturing and construction.

3.9. What are the advantages of the money-out-of-pocket method over other inventory methods?

3.10. List allocators for joint material and labor costs.

PROBLEMS

3.1. Find the board feet (metre^3) of the following:
  (a) 20 pieces of 2 × 8 in. × 10 ft (50 × 200 mm × 3 m)
  (b) 60 pieces of 4 × 8 in. × 8 ft (100 × 200 mm × 2.4 m)
  (c) 30 pieces of 2 × 8 in. × 12 ft (50 × 200 mm × 3.6 m)
  (d) Find the number of pieces of 2 × 10 in. × 18 ft long (50 × 250 mm × 5.4 m) that will be delivered for an order of 2700 BF (6.37 m^3).

3.2. Find the board feet (metre^3) for 100 ft^2 (9.3 m^2) of partition shown by Fig. P3.2. Studs, plates, and firestops are 2 × 4 in. (50 × 100 mm). Assume 5% waste.

x	y	Firestops	Studs	Bottom Plates	Top Plate
(a) 8 ft 4 in. (2.5 m)	12 ft (3.6 m)	6	7	1	2
(b) 7 ft 2 in. (2.2 m)	14 ft (4.2 m)	5	16	1	2

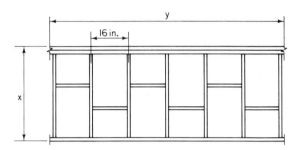

Figure P3.2

3.3. Find the board feet (metre^3) for the 8-ft (2.4-m) partition shown in Fig. P3.3, including the rough window opening. Include 5% waste. Work the problem only to the width of the king stud.

Window Size, A	Header Size
(a) 8/0 × 3/0 (2.4/0 × 0.9/0)	4 × 8 in. (100 × 200 mm)
(b) 8/0 × 5/0 (2.4/0 × 1.5/0)	4 × 8 in. (100 × 200 mm)
(c) 10/0 × 4/0 (3.0/0 × 1.2/0)	4 × 10 in. (100 × 250 mm)

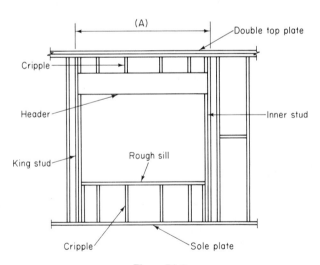

Figure P3.3

3.4. Find the cubic yards (metre^3) of material for the portland cement concrete steps shown as Fig. P3.4. Assume 5% waste for 10 risers for the width given as
(a) 4 ft (1.2 m)
(b) 4 ft 6 in. (1.4 m)
(c) 6 ft (1.8 m)

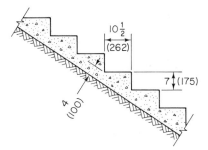

Figure P3.4

3.5. A round shaft, 6.5 in. (165 mm) O.D., has a drawing length of 31.675 in. (804.55 mm). The facing dimension necessary for a smooth end finish is 1/16 in. (1.6 mm). The width of the cutoff tool is 3/16 in. (4.76 mm). The length of the bar stock supplied to this turning machine is 12 ft (3.6 m). The collet requires 4 in. (100 m) of length for last-part gripping. Material will cost $0.95/lb ($2.11/kg) and density is 0.29 lb/in.^{3} (8024 kg/m^3).

  (a) What is the unit cost of the raw material?

  (b) What cost is lost to waste, given that waste is salvaged at 10% of original value?

  (c) Find the shape yield.

  (d) Repeat parts (a)–(c) for bar stock supplied in 16-ft lengths.

3.6. Examine the 2024-T4 aluminum shaft in Fig. P3.6. Raw material is purchased to match the outside dimensions. The bar stock for this part is supplied in 12-ft (3.6-m) lengths. The density is 0.0975 lb/in.^{3} (2700 kg/m^3) and the cost is $0.60/lb ($1.33/kg). Roughly scale for missing dimensions.

  (a) Estimate the cost of the raw material.

  (b) Find the approximate shape yield.

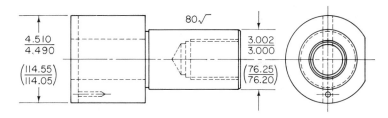

Figure P3.6

3.7. **(a)** Determine the theoretical and actual material required to produce the bayonet-clip half shown in Fig. P3.7. Raw stock is supplied in 0.875 in. (22.23 mm) diameter. A lathe cutoff tool width is 0.125 in. (3.18 mm). A 0.015 in. (0.38 mm) stock allowance is necessary for facing the spherical end. Allow 4% for shrinkage and bar end losses. The raw material weighs 2.05 lb/ft (3.05 kg/m).

  (b) Find the shape yield.

  (c) What is the unit cost for this hot-rolled steel stock, which costs $0.44/lb ($0.98/kg)?

  (d) Repeat (a)–(c) in metric units.

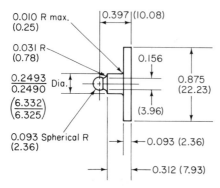
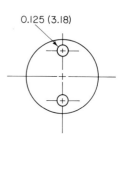

Figure P3.7

3.8. A part is machined as shown by Fig. P3.8. The original stock size of AISI 1045 material is 5 × 2.5 × 2 in. (125 × 63 × 50 mm).

    (a) If this material will cost $0.95/lb ($2.11/kg), what is the unit cost of the raw material?

    (b) What cost is lost to waste given that the waste is salvaged at 10% of original value?

    (c) Find the yield percentage and suggest ways for improvement. Density = 0.29 lb/in.³ (8024 kg/m³).

    (d) Find the approximate values for (a)–(c) in metric units.

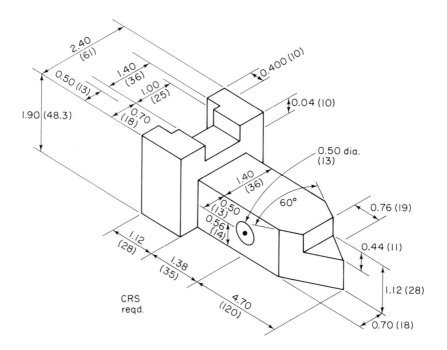

Figure P3.8

3.9. A foundry chooses to price its castings on the basis of delivered weight per 100 lb. Essentially, they price each new casting on past historical records of a similar design. A description of the procedure is as follows:

1. Poured metal cost per casting = (furnace labor and overhead + cost of metal charged) × casting poured weight.
2. Cost of metal in finished casting = poured metal cost per casting less amount of remelted metal × value of remelted metal.
3. Cost per pound of delivered metal is item (2) divided by finished weight. For our estimate the casting poured weight is (5 lb finished weight) 9 lb and the cost of charged metal is $0.60 per pound. Furnace labor and overhead is $0.10 per pound. The amount of remelted metal is expected to be 3.7 lb with a value of $0.30 per pound. Determine the resulting material cost per pound.

3.10. A V-block is manufactured of cast iron. Finish dimensions are shown in Fig. P3.10(a). A wood pattern is made using a shrink rule for the green sand casting. Recognizing that hot metal occupies a greater volume than cold, but upon cooling the shape is shown by Fig. P3.10(b). Extra material includes 3/32 in. (2.4 mm) finish stock on all surfaces and a $1\frac{1}{2}$% draft on four vertical sides for pattern withdrawal.

(a) Calculate the volume of the raw casting.

(b) Determine the shape yield.

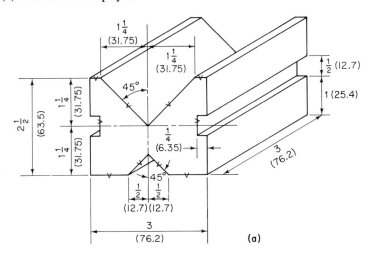

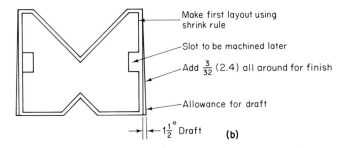

Figure P3.10

3.11. Find the part cost for the following casting. A foundry is to cast the motor cylinder shown in Fig. P3.11. Compute the volume and cost of casting based on volume and the following factors: the shop yield is 54.5% (from prior experience), the metal loss is 10% or 5.4% using shop yield, furnace labor and overhead are $0.03 per pound of poured metal, the cost of metal charged is $0.06 per pound, and the amount of re-melted metal is 40% and is valued at $0.04 per pound. For cast iron, the density is $0.2616/\text{in.}^3$. Allow $\frac{1}{8}$ in. of stock for all machined surfaces; the volume of cylinder is $\pi/4(\text{OD}^2 - \text{ID}^2) \times$ length. The pouring weight is finished weight per shop yield. The remelted metal weight is pouring weight $\times$ remelt factor. Consider what estimating factors are necessary. What items have been omitted in this estimate?

Material: Cast iron, 0.26 lb/in.^{3} (7194 kg/m^3)

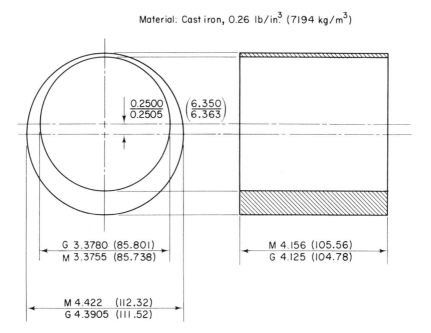

Figure P3.11

3.12. **(a)** Estimate the unit material cost for the two designs shown in Fig. P3.12. The cold-rolled steel material costs $0.57/lb ($1.27/kg).

(b) In addition to the blanking losses, add a 5% loss for overall waste. Find the losses for both designs.

(c) Density = 0.278 lb/in.^{3} (7692 kg/m^3). Salvage is recovered at 10% of original value. Find the economic yield.

3.13. The 12-fluid ounce (0.35-litre) beverage can is composed of the body, top, and ring. The container body is blanked from 3004-H19 aluminum coils with the layout given by Fig. P3.13. An intermediate cup is formed without any significant change in thick-ness. The cup is then drawn to a side-wall thickness of 0.0055 in. (0.146 mm) and the

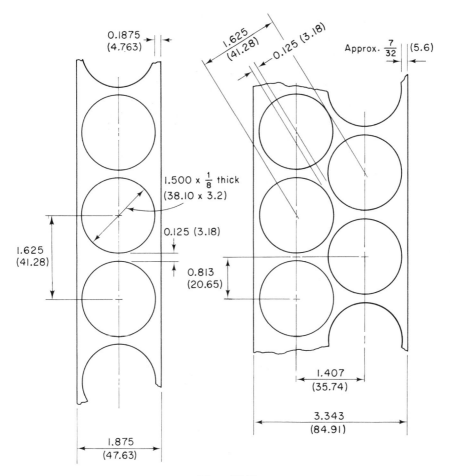

Figure P3.12

bottom thickness remains unchanged. The can is trimmed to a final height of 5.437 in. (138.10 mm) to give an even edge for later rolling to the lid. This coil stock costs $0.5364/lb ($1.183/kg) and the density is 0.0981 lb/in.³ (2715 kg/m³). Recovered waste is sold at $0.265/lb ($0.589/kg).

(a) What is the volume of metal in a trimmed can? (Ignore the 0.05-in. radius.)
(b) Find the strip metal per can body.
(c) Determine the shape yield.
(d) Find the yield of the can body to blank.
(e) What is the cost in trimmed can body?
(f) What is the cost of the can body in the strip?
(g) What is the prorated recovered value per can from waste?
(h) Estimate the net cost per can body.
(i) Repeat the above with metric units.

0.0135 ± 0.0005 in.(0.343 ± 0.013mm) thickness
coil stock, 3004 – HI9 aluminum

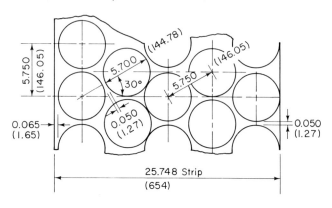

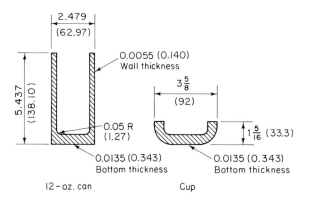

12 – oz. can   Cup

Figure P3.13

3.14. Reconsider Table 3.2 and Fig. 3.3. Find lead-time-replacement, delivery, and money-out-of-pocket unit material cost for the following step-size adjustment to the diagram:

Period	JJ(t)	TU(t)	TS(t)
2	1	2	2
3	2	3	0
4	0	1	2
5	1	3	4
6	4	4	8

(a) JJ(t) only; (b) TU(t) only; (c) TS(t) only; (d) parts (a), (b), and (c) together.

3.15. The inventory plan for a material is given by Fig. P3.15. Use Table 3.2 and find the following unit costs for six units of stock: (a) original, (b) last, (c) current, (d) lead-time replacement, (e) delivery, and (f) money-out-of-pocket.

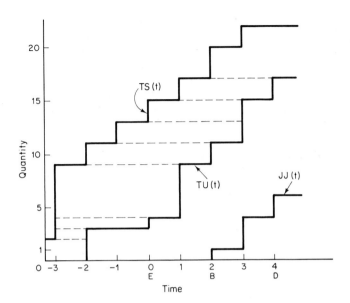

Figure P3.15

3.16. Repeat Problem 3.15 for a job L requirement of eight units using the inventory plan of Fig. P3.16.

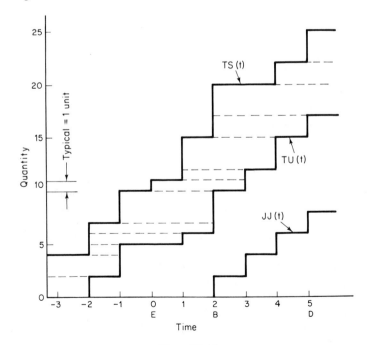

Figure P3.16

3.17. A flange is forged from C-1020 steel $1\frac{1}{2}$-in. (38-mm)-O.D. stock (Fig. P3.17). Each bar is $7\frac{9}{16}$ in. (190 mm) long, and will produce four flanges. The bar includes a 1-in. (25-mm) tong hold for all four flanges, which is later trimmed as waste. The material costs \$0.85/lb (\$1.89/kg) and has a density of 0.29 lb/in.^{3} (8025 kg/m^3). Waste and scrap is sold at 10% of original value. A labor crew consists of a hammerman (wage = \$21.75 per hour) and helper (\$19.65 per hour). Each member of the crew performs different elements of the operation, and their joint output is 0.540 hour per 100 units.
(a) Find material yield.
(b) Find the unit material cost adjusted for sold salvage material.
(c) On the basis of output of units, dejoint the cost of labor.
(d) Estimate the total unit cost.
(e) Repeat (a)–(d) with SI units.

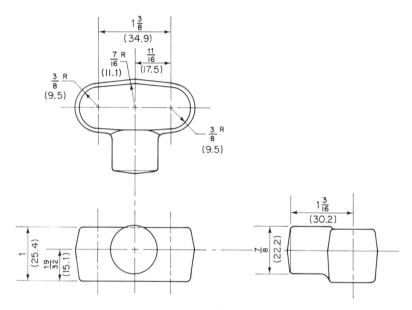

Figure P3.17

3.18. A back plate is used as a "snap-in" cover for a mating cassette case. Molded of polystyrene resin plastic, the back plate weighs 0.02 lb/unit (9 g/unit) and there is no waste. Each shot fills eight cavities or units. High-impact polystyrene costs \$1.10/lb (\$2.44/kg). Density = 0.0365 lb/in.^{3} (1009 kg/m^3). Production time is 8 seconds per shot or 0.028 hour per 100 units. The senior plastic press operator has a direct wage of \$14.40. The operator monitors three presses simultaneously. Nothing is known about production on the other two presses during a back plate run.
(a) Expressing the cost on a dollar per 100 unit basis, find direct material cost, direct labor cost, and total unit cost.
(b) Repeat in metric units.

3.19. A computer part is molded of clear polycarbonate plastic two at a time. A partially dimensioned sketch (Fig. P3.19) gives part size, sprue, and two runners.

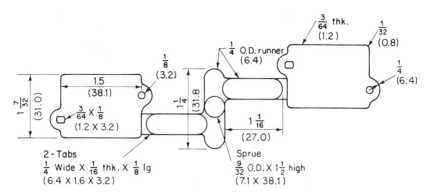

Figure P3.19

(a) Find the weight of one part and shot requirements for sprue, two runners, and two parts. Density = 0.0404 lb/in³ (1119 kg/m³).

(b) What is the yield of part material to total material?

(c) The cost of this material is $3.10/lb ($6.89/kg) and waste is recovered at 10% of the original value. Find the net cost per unit, including a fair share of waste.

(d) The cycle time for one operator and one injection molding machine is 45 seconds. Detab time is 10 seconds for both parts, which is done during molding cycle. For a labor rate of $16.50 per hour, find the labor cost per unit.

(e) What is the total cost per unit?

CASE STUDY:
DESIGN FOR RUNNER SYSTEM

Rich Hall, die designer for General Plastics, mutters to himself: "What counts in this problem is minimum plastic volume in the runner system." Rich knows that for this plastic mold design it will be impractical to reuse the scrap because the plastic part will be colored and the value of the scrap runners represents a small fraction of virgin material cost. The part to be molded is roughly 25 mm in diameter and 10 mm thick, similar to a preform except for the novelty impressions on the surface.

Rich, recently hired in his job, has learned that full-round runners are preferred; they have a minimum surface-to-volume ratio, thus reducing heat loss and pressure drop. Balance runner systems are preferred because they permit uniformity of mass flow from the sprue to the cavities, since the cavities are at an equal distance from the sprue. Main runners adjacent to the sprue are larger than secondary runners.

Rich has designed three configurations as in Fig. C3.1 and he will select the one that uses a minimum of runner material. The time factor is not critical, as the three arrangements provide identical number of parts per shot. The sprue volume for the three arrangements is equal. Die data are shown below. Determine which arrangement has a minimum of material for the runner system. If the plastic cost $0.60/kg and density is 1050 kg/m³, what is the prorated loss per unit? Determine the overall machine efficiency if

$$\text{shape efficiency} = \frac{\text{material in parts}}{\text{material in shot}}$$

Arrangement	Runner Section	Diameter (mm)	Section Length, (mm)
A	1	5	25
	2	6	25
B	3	5	12
	4	6	75
	5	8	25
C	6	5	8
	7	6	100
	8	10	175

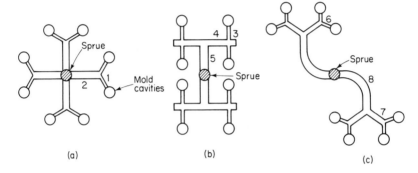

Figure C3.1.   Runner system configurations: (a) star pattern; (b) "H" pattern; (c) sweep pattern.

4

Accounting Analysis

Accounting is the means by which the money activities of an organization are recorded. Accountants are generally charged with the preparation of periodic balance sheets, statements of income, information to aid the control of cost, and essential data useful for the finding of overhead. Although cost-accounting data may have been wisely and carefully collected and arranged to suit primary purposes for accounting, raw data are usually incompatible with forecasting, product pricing, and the like. Accounting specialties are general, public, auditing, tax, government, and cost. Cost and tax accounting are more important to engineering and cost estimating. Cost accounting emphasizes accounting for costs, particularly the cost of manufacturing processes and construction. It deals with actual or historical costs using this base. Tax accounting, because of the myriad laws and practices, includes the preparation of tax returns and, importantly, the consideration of the tax consequences of proposed business transactions.

The relationship between estimating and accounting is an active one, for both deal with much of the same information. On the one hand, the cost estimator deals with costs and designs prior to the spending of money; on the other, cost accounting records the cash flow facts. Roughly, estimating looks ahead while accounting looks back, and both are necessary for any successful cost-estimating practice. However, before estimating can proceed, accounting analysis must be concluded.

4.1 BUSINESS TRANSACTIONS

A *transaction* is an exchange of wants. An operation, product, project, or system is received or given and a value, right, or service, collectively referred to as wants, is given or received. The transaction is composed of two elements which are reported in a financial record. This duality has led to *double-entry bookkeeping,* a practice several centuries old. Tested and found true, double-entry bookkeeping has changed little even though growth of industry and business have complicated the professional field of accounting. The essential practices show remarkable similarity to the earliest commercial records.

In double-entry bookkeeping, the results of business transactions are collected in records called accounts. The simplest form of the account is the *T-account* and the recording of a business transaction is an entry, as shown by Fig. 4.1(a). An entry on the left-hand side of the account is called a *debit (Dr.),* while an entry on the right-hand side is a *credit (Cr.).* The terms "debit" and "credit" when used for the bookkeeping of transactions have no other meaning than this. The T-account is an abbreviation and is used for textbook illustrations, but in practice a more complete account supplies columns for additional data, as shown in Fig. 4.1(b). The columns provide space for the date of each entry, description, folio (F), or cross-reference, to indicate the page in another record and amount. If the current status of the account is desired, it is only necessary to total the debit and credit and show the balance on the larger side. This summing and finding the larger amount is known as *footing.* This columnar arrangement, of course, can be rearranged to suit electronic data processing.

Vouchers, invoices, receipts, bills, sales tickets, checks, and the many documents relating to the transaction are used as supporting evidence of the entry. From this evidence, the original entry is made to a *journal* which contains the chronological record of the transactions. The information would be as summarized by Fig. 4.1(b). In practice, the journals may be files, punched cards, reels of computer tape, floppy disks, or other media. A single journal may suffice for entries for a small business. For the typical business, however, many types of journals exist, such as cash, sales, purchase, and general journals. This recording in journals is termed *journalizing.*

The transferring of journal entries to appropriate accounts in a ledger is the next step. The *ledger* is a group of accounts. Perhaps one page of the ledger is used for each account. *Posting* is the term applied to the process of transferring the debit and credit items from the journal ledger account. As each item is posted, the number

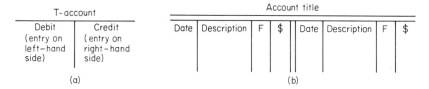

Figure 4.1   (a) Abbreviated T-account for instructional purposes; (b) regular account presentation.

of the ledger account is indicated in the journal folio. Similarly, the journal page number is placed in the folio column of the account of the ledger.

An *account* is established for the various business transactions. A total sales account may lead to a specific customer sales account, for instance. Every item of financial information on the balance sheet and income statement has an account.

The original recording of business transactions to the eventual development of the balance sheet and income statement is shown by Fig. 4.2. The accountant is required to adjust the accounting of the business to present the financial situation accurately.

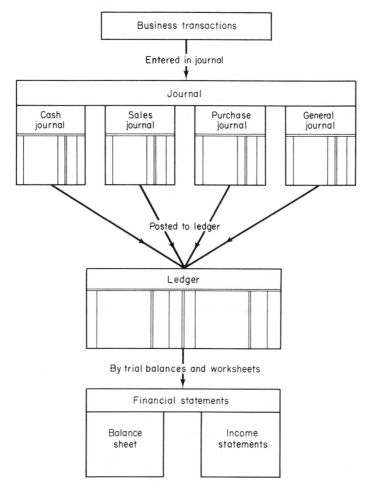

Figure 4.2 Diagram of accounting procedure.

4.2 FUNDAMENTALS

A *money-measurement* fundamental requires that business transactions be recorded only in terms of money. This practice allows for many different situations to be expressed in common units. A fabricating plant can be compared to a construction company. Moreover, designs expressed in number units, such as dollars, deutsche marks, francs, and pesos can be algebraically manipulated to plan the performance of the business. Because of the importance of the money-measurement fundamental, it must overlook technology know-how, engineering skill, prominence of design, and brand awareness.

A fundamental insists that business transactions be recorded in double-entry fashion as assets and equities, where the two must *equal or balance*. This leads to the important accounting equation, where assets equal equities, or expressed differently,

$$\text{assets} = \text{liabilities} + \text{owner's equities} = \text{liabilities} + \text{net worth} \qquad (4.1)$$

Both creditors and owners have claim to equities. The creditor has first rights, leaving remaining rights to owners. Owner's equities or net worth or proprietorship is the ownership interest in the business assets. Double-entry accounting is basic to balance sheet and income statement presentation.

A *conservatism* convention encourages the recording of financial data as the lower of possible choices. For example, in the evaluation of finished-goods inventory (merchandise held by the company for sale), we could value the inventory as either the cost to the business for production and materials or at market value. Conservatism will use the lower value. In public disclosure of audits, the statement may be made "the cost or market value, whichever is lower" to reflect this convention.

The *consistency* convention states that business transactions, if accounted for in one way, must be recorded and accounted that way in the future. Companies obtain discounts for prompt payments of materials. One firm may use the discounts to reduce the cost of the materials; another may take discounts and record them as income realized on prompt payment. The consistency convention adopts one of these two methods and persists in its use in succeeding accounting. This convention discourages a business from manipulating its figures to reflect favorable conditions on one occasion and, as convenient, changing approaches.

The *going-concern* fundamental implies that the business is operated in a prudent and rational way. This policy, it is assumed, will perpetuate the business over an extended period of time. A *business entity* fundamental is a simple notion that accounting transactions of a business are for the sake of the business rather than individuals. If an owner withdraws money from the cash account, the owner is richer, but the business has less. The accountant would record the effect of this transaction on the business and ignore the effect on the owner.

A *cost* fundamental recognizes that cost does not necessarily equal value. Stock shares of a company may have little relationship to the net value per share. While it is possible to list the assets in preparing a balance sheet, their value can be determined by several methods. Consider a car for sale. Early in the day a potential customer asks what you will sell it for. Later, a tax assessor asks the same question. While the answer might honestly differ, the point is that "value" is subjective. Even so, there are two other ways to evaluate business assets. *Market value* can be obtained, but this depends on the purchaser's needs. It is possible to find several evaluations of the worth of an asset, however, which returns the selection of value to subjective reasoning. We can value assets on their *replacement*. However, the cost of replacement depends on how and when it will be replaced. A replacement approach leads to a range rather than a single value. Market and replacement value lead to confusing choices, but it is possible to determine the value of the asset as given by original cost. The receipt for the payment of the asset is a document of record and can be used to demonstrate cost albeit not value necessarily. The primary appeal of the cost fundamental is objectivity and expediency. When coupled with the going-business principle, it is assumed that asset will be used to conduct business.

If a *cash* basis is used for accounting, income is recorded when the cash is received and expense is recognized when cash is paid out. The cash method is used by small businesses and individuals for personal and family records.

The *accrual* fundamental is concerned with the vast majority of business and is generally unfamiliar to us. In accrual, income is recorded when it is earned, whether it is received during the period or not. Expenses incurred in earning the income are recorded as expense, whether or not payment has been made during that period. The profit and loss statement includes incomes that were earned during the period covered by the statement and expenses concurrent to the same period. The time of collection of the income or payment of the expense is not a factor. Business transactions that affect income are measured by increases or decreases in net worth rather than increases or decreases in cash. When a business provides a design, goods, or services, the monies it receives increase net worth and are called *revenues,* while the costs that a business incurs to provide the design, goods, or services decrease net worth and are called *expenses*.

If a transaction is irrelevant to the financial results of the business, there is discretion as to how and when to record that event. If a piece of paper and pencil were consumed, theoretically it becomes an expense. However, this penny-watching is unwise, as average monthly office supply expenses are a commonsense way of handling this transaction. A convention of *relevance* permits the accountant to use judgment as to how these expenses can be handled.

4.3 STRUCTURE OF ACCOUNTS

An expanded accounting equation using income and expense accounts is given as

$$\underset{+\mid-}{\underline{\text{Assets}}} = \underset{-\mid+}{\underline{\text{Liabilities}}} + \underset{-\mid+}{\underline{\text{Net Worth}}} + \underset{-\mid+}{\underline{\text{Income}}} - \underset{+\mid-}{\underline{\text{Expenses}}} \qquad (4.2)$$

This equation is sometimes referred to as the financial and operating equation, since it has plus and minus signs for each class of T-accounts. The plus and minus signs show increases and decreases and are summarized as follows:

Debit indicates:	Credit indicates:
Asset increase	Asset decrease
Liability decrease	Liability increase
Net worth decrease	Net worth increase
Income decrease	Income increase
Expense increase	Expense decrease

Using the rules above for applying debit and credit, we can next record the transaction into a T-account. The numbers in parentheses in Table 4.1 relate to the transaction numbers shown by Table 4.2.

Because of the dual effect of a transaction, the record of the transaction must be equal, and for every debit there must be a credit. It is not necessary that there be the same number of debit and credit items in any T-account. Table 4.2 is a record of transactions that affect the amounts of assets, liabilities, net worth, income, and expenses of a business. On the basis of the increase or decrease effect, any business transaction may be selected into equal debit and credit elements. Purchases are considered an expense because they are an offsetting cost to income sales. That portion of purchases remaining unsold at the close of the period is termed inventory and is classed as an asset.

While these figures indicate movement within T-account debit and credits, a more comprehensive chart of accounts is necessary for a business. A chart or listing of accounts intended for a manufacturing company is provided by Table 4.3. Formal charts of accounts are grouped into six principal classes:

1. Assets accounts
2. Liability accounts
3. Net worth accounts
4. Summarizing accounts
5. Income accounts
6. Expenses accounts

A summarizing account, called an income and expenses summary, is used as a clearing account to which income and expense account balances are transferred at the end of the accounting period. The footing of their combined balances is then transferred to the net worth accounts. These principal accounts correspond to the statement sequence.

4.4 TRIAL BALANCE

An *open account* has either a debit or a credit balance. A *closed account* has the debit and credit of equal amount and, therefore, has no balance.

#1.	F. Baffett		**#310.**	Rent	
	$18,000	$12,000		$8000	$2000
		6,000			6000

Table 4.1.   T ACCOUNTS FOR TABLE 4.2

Cash					S. W. Specthrie		
(1)	$50,000	$ 1,500	(3)	(4)	$ 4,000	$10,000	(2)
(8)	2,000	4,000	(4)				
(10)	500	2,850	(6)				
		10,000	(7)				
		3,000	(9)				
		800	(12)				

Purchases				Sales			
(2)	$10,000			(11)	$ 4,000	$15,000	(5)

P. Hall				Equipment			
(5)	$15,000	$ 2,000	(8)	(9)	$ 3,000		
		4,000	(11)				

Rent				Salaries			
(3)	$ 1,500	$ 500	(10)	(6)	$ 2,850		

Capital Stock				Advertising			
(7)	$10,000	$50,000	(1)	(12)	$ 800		

Computer				Englewood & Co.			
(13)	$12,000					$12,000	(13)

#65.	Capital Stock		#350.	Building	
$2000	$9000		$7800	$ 800	

The F. Baffett and Rent accounts are closed accounts, while the other two are open. The sum of the debits ($35,800) is the same as the sum of the credits ($35,800), while the sum of the debit balances ($7000) equals the sum of the credit balances ($7000).

Each journal entry provides for equal debits and credits, which are posted to the ledger accounts. If the posting is accurate, the ledger must have equal debits and credits. Additionally, the sum of the debit ledger account balances must equal the sum of the credit ledger account balances. This equality is periodically tested by a *trial balance,* which is a list of the open ledger accounts as of a stated date. The trial balance shows the debit or credit balance of each account.

WESTBROOK AND COMPANY
Trial Balance—December 31, 19xx

Account No.	Account Name	Dr.	Cr.
65	Capital stock		$7000
350	Building	$7000	
		$7000	$7000

Table 4.2. Transaction Effects on a Business

Transaction	Accounts Affected	Type of Account	On Account	Is Recorded by a Debit of:	Credit of:
			Effect of Transaction		
1. Flying Magnetics Co. is founded and $50,000 paid for capital stock	Cash	Asset	Increase	$ 50,000	$ 50,000
	Capital stock	Net worth	Increase		
2. Business buys material from S. W. Specthrie on account, $10,000	Purchases	Expense	Increase	10,000	10,000
	S. W. Specthrie	Liability	Increase		
3. Pay monthly rent on plant, $1500	Rent	Expense	Increase	1,500	1,500
	Cash	Asset	Decrease		
4. Pay S. W. Specthrie on account, $4000	S. W. Specthrie	Liability	Decrease	4,000	4,000
	Cash	Asset	Decrease		
5. Sells to P. Hall on account all material	P. Hall	Asset	Increase	15,000	15,000
	Sales	Income	Increase		
6. Pay salaries for week, $2850	Salaries	Expense	Increase	2,850	2,850
	Cash	Asset	Decrease		
7. Retires for cash $10,000 of capital stock	Capital stock	Net worth	Decrease	10,000	10,000
	Cash	Asset	Decrease		
8. Collects $2000 from P. Hall	Cash	Asset	Increase	2,000	2,000
	P. Hall	Asset	Decrease		

Table 4.2. *(cont.)*

9. Buy computer for $3000 cash	Equipment	Asset	Increase	3,000	
	Cash	Asset	Decrease		3,000
10. Receives $500 rebate on month's rent	Cash	Asset	Increase	500	
	Rent	Expense	Decrease		500
11. P. Hall returns $4000 of material for credit	Sales	Income	Decrease	4,000	
	P. Hall	Asset	Decrease		4,000
12. Pays advertising bill for month, $800	Advertising	Expense	Increase	800	
	Cash	Asset	Decrease		800
13. Buys on credit for $12,000 a machine from Englewood & Co. for processing materials	Machine	Asset	Increase	12,000	
	Englewood	Liability	Increase		12,000
				$115,650	$115,650

Table 4.3.   MANUFACTURING COMPANY CHART OF ACCOUNTS

Current Assets	Summary
Cash in bank	Profit and loss account
Petty cash	Income
Notes receivable, customers	Sales
Accounts receivable, customers	Interest earned
Inventories	Dividends received
Prepaid insurance, taxes, interest	Sale of waste and scrap
Supplies	Manufacturing costs
Fixed assets	Purchases of materials
Land	Salaries and wages
Building, machinery	Heat, light, water
Reserve for depreciation	Telephone and telegraph
Furniture and fixtures	Depreciation
Current liabilities	Freight
Notes payable	Direct labor
Accrued wages payable	Indirect labor
Accrued interest payable	Factory insurance
Accrued taxes	Repairs and maintenance
Deferred rent income	Factory supplies used
Dividends payable	Taxes
Fixed liabilities	Selling Expenses
Mortgage payable	Salaries and commissions
Bonds payable	Advertising and samples
Capital stock	General and administrative expenses
Capital stock, preferred	Salaries
Capital stock, common	Traveling expenses
Surplus	Telephone, postage
Paid-in surplus	Supplies
Retained earnings	

The periodic trial balance of the ledger provides reasonable proof of the arithmetic accuracy of journalizing, posting, and ledger account balancing. It lists account balances from which the balance sheet and income statement are later prepared. In most business the trial balance is performed following the end of the month.

The account groups in the trial balance are broadly divided into those used to prepare the balance sheet and the income and expense statement. A few accounts contained both balance sheet and profit statement elements, and are called *mixed,* but these are separated into the two components during worksheet analysis.

Assets.   The assets of a manufacturing firm are those things of dollar value which it owns. These assets may be tangible as in the case of land, buildings, equipment, or inventory, or they may be intangible as in the case of trademarks, designs, and patents. For analysis, assets may be segregated into current assets, fixed assets, and intangible assets. Current assets may have three inventory accounts representing raw materials, in-process manufactured goods, and completed products.

Fixed assets include office equipment, factory equipment, and buildings, less accumulated depreciation reserves. Land is an asset that does not depreciate.

In the case of intangible assets, an engineering firm may design new products through its research and development and possibly obtain patents on them. The cost of research, engineering, and testing leading to the development of a new product may be significant and in theory could be treated as an asset in the same manner as other assets. As many research projects may be underfoot at the same time, cost can be incurred over a period of years. Some firms treat engineering costs as a part of current operating expenses.

Liabilities.   The liabilities of a firm are the debts it owes. The category of liabilities is frequently broken down into current and long-term debts. Some of the more common items of business liabilities are (1) accounts payable (for example, the debts of the firms to creditors for materials and services received), (2) bank loans (the amounts the firm owes to banks for money borrowed), and (3) mortgage payable (the debt to investors for money they loaned to the business on the security of its real estate or equipment).

Net worth.   The net worth of a business is the ownership interest in the firm's net assets. In certain accounting situations the use of proprietorship and capital are synonymous terms with net worth. In a simple case the net worth of a corporation consists of its capital stock and the surplus:

Net Worth

Capital stock	$40,000
Surplus (or retained earnings)	15,000
	$55,000

Broadly speaking, capital stock is the portion of the net worth paid in by the owners, while surplus or retained earnings is that portion of the net worth accumulated from the excess of profits earned over the dividends paid since the inception of the business. The corporation issues capital stock which is divided into units of ownership, termed shares, and the owners of the company are referred to as shareholders. The ownership of a shareholder in the net worth of the firm is related to the number of shares he owns. The surplus of a firm increases as the company earns profit and decreases as the company incurs losses or distributes the profits among the shareholders as dividends. If the losses and dividends of a corporation since inception exceed its profits, a negative profit or a deficit instead of a surplus results.

Income and expense in business.   Income represents the revenue from sales before the deduction of cost. Expenses represent costs of doing business. While income is received from the sale of merchandise or products, expenses include such common items as salaries, advertising, power and light, telephone, rent, insurance, and interest. The profit and loss statement of a firm is a summary of its incomes

Table 4.4. Flying Magnetics Company, Worksheet—December 31, 19xx

Account Title	Trial Balance Dr.	Trial Balance Cr.	Profit and Loss Dr.	Profit and Loss Cr.	Balance Sheet Dr.	Balance Sheet Cr.
Materials in process inventory	$ 6,000				$ 6,000	
Labor in process inventory	4,000				4,000	
Overhead in process inventory	5,000				5,000	
Finished products inventory	10,000				10,000	
Materials inventory	4,400				4,400	
Customers	18,000				16,100	
Reserve for bad debts		$ 1,900				
Cash	8,000				8,000	
Land	10,000				10,000	
Building	28,000				23,000	
Reserve for depreciation		5,000				
Prepaid insurance	1,000				1,000	
Prepaid advertising	600				600	
Accounts payable		8,000				$ 8,000
Bank loans		4,000				4,000
Accrued taxes		3,000				3,000
6% mortgage (due in 20 years)		5,000				5,000

Table 4.4. *(cont.)*

Capital stock		50,000				50,000
Surplus		12,000				12,000
Sales		104,000		$104,000		
Sales return	4,000		$ 4,000			
Cost of goods sold	54,000		54,000			
Lease	6,000		6,000			
Salaries	22,000		22,000			
Depreciation	800		800			
Promotion, advertising	6,400		6,400			
Bad debts	600		600			
Insurance	1,600		1,600			
Sales discounts	1,000		1,000			
Purchase discount		1,500		1,500		
Underabsorbed overhead	3,000		3,000			
	$194,400	$194,400	$ 99,400	$105,500	$88,100	$82,000
Net profit to retained earnings			6,100			6,100
			$105,500	$105,500	$88,100	$88,100

and expenses for a stated period of time. If the statement discloses a net profit or loss, the change represents an increment or decrement in the net worth during the period arising from business incomes and expenses and is carried to the net worth section of the balance sheet.

Most businesses use the accrual basis of accounting, where income is recorded when it is earned and expense is recorded when it is incurred. The time of collection of the income and payment of the expense is a secondary consideration. The accounts are adjusted for accrued expenses, accrued incomes, deferred expenses, depreciation, and bad debts. Once these adjusting entries are disposed, the next step concludes the trial balance using a worksheet. Observe in Table 4.4 that the first trial balance shows the effect of the ledger accounts. These in turn are separated and extended horizontally into profit and loss and balance sheet entries. The worksheet must balance; if it does not, an error of some kind is indicated, and it is necessary to find it.

4.5 BALANCE SHEET STATEMENT

The balance sheet is a tabular presentation of the important accounting Eq. (4.1). It is a summary of the assets, liabilities, and net worth as of a point in time. The data used to prepare the balance sheet are removed from the worksheet. A simple balance sheet is shown for XYZ Manufacturing Company and shows the accounting equation terms.

XYZ MANUFACTURING COMPANY

Balance Sheet—May 31, 19xx

Assets		= Liabilities	
Cash	$15,000	Bank Loan	$15,000
Inventory	10,000	Mortgage	15,000
Land	15,000		
Building and equipment	40,000		
		+ Net worth	
		Capital stock	45,000
		Retained earnings	5,000
	$80,000		$80,000

But this little table is too simple, and the Flying Magnetics balance sheet is given next (Table 4.5). Important points about the balance sheet are the length of time, handling of the depreciation reserves, and the asset and liability groups disclosed. Observe in Table 4.5 that the closing date is end of year, December 31. It does not provide any hint what the assets, liabilities, and net worth were for any date prior to or subsequent to December 31.

The balance sheet assets are not valued on the same basis. Cash, customer receivables, and inventories are valued at cost or cash-realizable value according to the conservatism convention. Land is valued at the amount originally paid for it,

Table 4.5. FLYING MAGNETICS COMPANY BALANCE SHEET—DECEMBER 31, 19xx

Assets

Current assets:			
Cash		$ 8,000	
Customers	$18,000		
Less reserve for bad debts	1,900	16,100	
Inventories:			
Material	4,400		
Material in process	6,000		
Labor in process	4,000		
Overhead in process	5,000		
Finished products	10,000	29,400	
Total current assets			$53,500
Deferred expenses:			
Insurance	1,000		
Advertising	600		1,600
Fixed assets:			
Land		10,000	
Building	28,000		
Less reserve for depreciation	5,000	23,000	33,000
Total assets			$88,100

Liabilities and Net Worth

Current liabilities:			
Accounts payable		8,000	
Bank loans		4,000	
Accrued taxes		3,000	
Total current liabilities			15,000
6% mortgage (due in 20 years)			5,000
Net worth:			
Capital stock		50,000	
Retained earnings:			
Balance—January 1, 19xx	12,000		
Net profit for 19xx	6,100	18,100	68,100
Total liabilities and net worth			$88,100

while depreciable fixed assets are valued at original cost less the reserve for depreciation. The liabilities are valued at the cash amount required to liquidate at the time of their maturity date. The net worth is a conglomerate value since it represents the difference between assets and total liabilities.

4.6 INCOME STATEMENT

The statement of earnings of the firm, known either as the *profit and loss* or *income* or *income and expense* statement, is a summary of its incomes and expenses for a stated period of time. The net profit or loss it discloses represents the net change in net worth during the reporting period arising from business incomes and expenses.

Definition of profit.   Profit represents the excess of revenue over cost and is an accounting approximation of the earnings of a manufacturing firm after taxes, cash and accrued expenses (representing costs of doing business), and certain tax-deductible noncash expenses such as depreciation are deducted. Loss represents the excess of cost over selling price, such as a product costing $8000 and selling for $6000 has a loss of $2000. The following example describes the effect on business net worth of profit and losses:

INVENTIONS, INC.

Balance sheet—May 31, 19xx

Assets		Liabilities	
Customers	$ 4,000	Bank loan	$ 1,000
Gadget A inventory	8,000	Accounts payable	2,000
Gadget B inventory	6,000		
		Net worth	
		Capital stock	15,000
	$18,000		$18,000

If Inventions, Inc. sold the asset gadget A for $10,000 cash, its balance sheet would change to

INVENTIONS, INC.

Balance sheet—June 30, 19xx

Assets		Liabilities	
Cash	$10,000	Bank loan	$ 1,000
Customers	4,000	Accounts payable	2,000
Gadget B inventory	6,000		
		Net worth	
		Capital stock	15,000
		Retained earnings	2,000
	$20,000		$20,000

Here it is found that net worth was increased $2000. If the business sold the asset gadget B inventory for $5,000 cash, its balance sheet would look like

INVENTIONS, INC.

Balance sheet—July 31, 19xx

Assets		Liabilities	
Cash	$15,000	Bank loan	$ 1,000
Customers	4,000	Accounts payable	2,000
		Net worth	
		Capital stock	15,000
		Retained earnings	1,000
	$19,000		$19,000

The $6000 gadget B inventory was replaced by $5000 cash, and the net assets and the net worth was decreased $1000. From the foregoing illustrations it is seen that profits increased the net worth because they increased the net assets and losses decreased the net worth because they decreased the net assets.

An example of a profit and loss statement for a nonproduction operation and the relationship it bears to the balance sheet follows:

SCIENCE COMMODITIES

Profit and Loss Statement—Month Ended June 30, 19xx

Income		
Fees for engineering services	$37,000	
Royalties on patents owned	3,400	
Product sales, subcontracted service	4,000	
Interest on securities	100	
		$44,500
Expenses		
Salaries	$32,600	
Rent of office	3,000	
Leasing of equipment	4,000	
Traveling	2,000	
Utilities	200	
Office supplies	500	
		$42,300
Net profit (to retained earnings)		$ 2,200

SCIENCE COMMODITIES

Balance Sheet—June 30, 19xx

Assets		Liabilities		
Cash	$ 5,700	Accounts payable		$ 2,500
Receivables	8,500			
Bonds	12,000	Net worth		
Equipment	2,500	Capital stock		25,000
Patents	11,000	Retained earnings		
		Balance June 1	$10,000	
		Profit June 30	2,200	12,200
	$39,700			$39,700

The profit and loss statement is related to the balance sheet, in that it details the profit and loss elements which caused a June 1 retained earnings of $10,000 to become a June 30 surplus of $12,200. It should be apparent that the profit amount is needed for completing the balance sheet since it is necessary to prepare the profit and loss statement first.

Continuing on with the worksheet and balance sheet, as developed previously for the Flying Magnetics Company, its profits and loss statement is given by Table 4.6.

Table 4.6. FLYING MAGNETICS COMPANY PROFIT AND LOSS STATEMENT
(YEAR ENDED DECEMBER 31, 19xx)

Net sales		$100,000
Cost of goods sold		54,000
Gross profit on sales		$ 46,000
Operating expense:		
Lease	$ 6,000	
Salaries	22,000	
Depreciation	800	
Advertising	6,400	
Bad debts	600	
Insurance	1,600	$ 37,400
Net profit from operations		$ 8,600
Miscellaneous income and expense		
Purchase discount	1,500	
Sales discount	1,000	500
Net profit before special charges		$ 9,100
Underabsorbed overhead		3,000
Net profit to retained earnings		$ 6,100

These P & L statements should be studied for their heading, income and expense groupings, and length of time and dates covered. Certainly, profits depend on the time of earnings. Observe that net sales measure the net revenue from sales, while allowances for sales returns, freight out, and sales discounts are deducted from gross sales. *Cost of goods sold* covers the expense of the products sold to the customer. If the cost of goods sold is a gross value, freight in and purchase discounts may reduce the value. Operating expenses list recurring usual and necessary costs for conducting the business. Miscellaneous income and expense arise from interest and discounts and other small items of revenue and expense which are unrelated to the major business thrust. Except for depreciation, the income statement items result from current-period transactions. Depreciation is an allowable noncash tax expense, reducing total income. Administrative expenses are found in almost all firms and cover the cost of managing the organization, and additionally may include heat, power, rent, insurance, accounting, engineering, legal, and so on, as they relate to administration. Income taxes, or the provision for income taxes, is an item reducing business income and is identified separately.

4.7 BUDGETING

Budgeting is a frequent cost-estimating task. A budget is a written plan covering the activities for a definite future time, and dimensions are in monetary terms for a specific period, such as a quarter or year. Budgets deal with information based on data derived from cost-estimating and accounting records and conjectures of future activities. The budgeted cost center should be the smallest unit to which a cost can be clearly traced, provided there is a balance between excessive and too little detail, consistent with the cost of preparing the budget. For example, if all cost centers within the engineering department are physically located together, heat and light should be charged to the entire department as a practical expedient.

Appropriation, fixed, and variable budgets are common classifications. An *appropriation budget* may be directed toward proposed expenditures for a machine tool. A *fixed budget* may be directed toward an operation with only one level of activity for a definite time period. This budget may not be adjusted to actual levels; this may be satisfactory if the company activities can be predetermined accurately. Budgets may be prepared for one level of activity, or for a number of levels of activity. This last one is *variable* or flexible budgeting. A variable budget requires greater knowledge of cost behavior.

Regardless of the level of productive activity, some costs are almost completely fixed per time period; others are constant within certain ranges of activity; some change as the activity fluctuates. Depreciation of a building is an example of the first class, superintendence of the second, while consumption of factory supplies qualifies as the third.

The cost-accounting cycle is framed about the skeleton of the manufacturing process or the physical arrangement or the service for jobs. Since cost accounts are an expansion of general accounts they should, as a basic accounting procedure, be related to them. Figure 4.3 shows the relationship between general accounts and cost accounts. The bigger an organization is, the greater its span of accounting records. To illustrate: A materials account controls hundreds of different material items, the payroll account controls departmental labor costs and payroll records for each employee, and the factory overhead account controls indirect labor, supplies, rent, insurance, repairs, and many other factory expenses.

As shown in Fig. 4.3, the direct material, payroll (or direct labor), and expenses are transferred to in-process work, to inventory, and eventually to cost of goods sold. *In-process work* describes material which is incompletely processed. This material is usually on the factory floor. An inventory account as shown in Fig. 4.3, if it is finished, has completed processing and is ready for shipment to a customer.

All of the foregoing discussion indicates that the process of budgeting draws from many sources of information, and as a detailed plan, the budget is the first step in finding overhead. The chart of accounts or the engineering cost codes are used for budget preparation.

Observe Table 4.7, which is a budget for production centers. It includes the planned number of machines, floor space, and other pertinent data determined for these cost centers. It is necessary to recognize that the January–December period must be further identified as 49 weeks and two-shift operation. A second closely identified budget is given by Table 4.8. This table connects the direct-labor man-power for operation to the identical production centers. The wage and fringe rates are matched to the same annual period. The gross hourly cost, as typically found by Table 2.11, would be entered for the appropriate production center. The table

Accounts

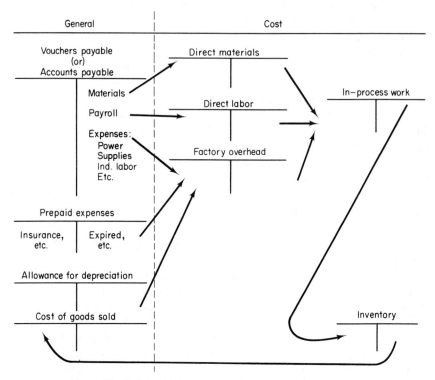

Figure 4.3 Relationship between general accounts and cost accounts.

shows the budgeted direct-labor hours and cost. The budgeted direct-labor hours are
15% greater than machine hours, as shown by Table 4.7.

Notice in Table 4.9 that factory, engineering, and general management expenses
are planned. Each item of the factory overhead is further stipulated as fixed or
variable. For instance, the rent of $180,000 is fixed because of contractual require-
ments. Electrical power has been broken into fixed and variable components. Analysis, historical information, and judgment will lead to this separation. The fixed
portion would be for engineering and general management needs. Variable power
would be identified with production power, which is affected by output. All three
tables will be used for various overhead rate determination.

4.8 DEPRECIATION

The purpose of a discussion about depreciation is to present the generalized mechanics of depreciation calculations and some of the thinking in cost estimating. A great
deal of ambiguity exists about depreciation. Forces of politics enter into the picture

Table 4.7. PRODUCTION CENTER BUDGET FOR JANUARY–DECEMBER PERIOD

Machine Center	Number of Machines	Floor Space ft²	Floor Space m²	Budgeted Hours[a]	Machine Horsepower Hours	Depreciation Charges	Tooling Expenses
Light machining	20	2800	260	49,300	443,000	$ 52,500	$200,000
Heavy machining	2	3000	279	6,800	748,000	95,000	80,000
Assembly	15	900	(84)	17,000	24,000	—	10,000
Finishing	8	1600	(149)	13,600	68,000	22,500	65,000
		8300	(772)	86,700	1,283,000	$170,000	$355,000

[a]Budgeted hours are reduced by 15% for nonproductive hours (two-shift operation, 49 weeks).

Table 4.8. BUDGETED MANPOWER FOR PRODUCTION CENTERS FOR JANUARY–DECEMBER PERIOD

Machine Center	Number of Direct-Labor Employees	Average Direct Hourly Wage Rate	Average Direct Fringe Hour Rate	Gross Hourly Wage Rate	Budgeted Direct-Labor Hours	Total Direct-Labor Cost
Light machining	29	$16.40	$4.92	$21.32	58,000	$1,236,560
Heavy machining	4	19.75	5.93	25.68	8,000	205,440
Assembly	10	15.65	4.70	20.35	20,000	407,000
Finishing	8	17.05	5.12	22.17	16,000	354,720
					102,000	$2,203,720

Table 4.9. FACTORY, ENGINEERING, AND GENERAL MANAGEMENT
BUDGET FOR JANUARY-DECEMBER PERIOD

A. Factory overhead	
Space	
Rent (Fixed)	$180,000
Repairs to factory (Fixed)	60,000
Heat (Fixed)	16,000
	$256,000
Power	
Electricity (Fixed)	$ 50,000
Electricity (Variable)	139,625
Other utilities (Fixed)	15,000
Other utilities (Variable)	35,000
	$239,625
Indirect labor	
Material handling (Variable)	$ 64,000
Inspectors (Variable)	48,000
Supervisor (Fixed)	30,000
Supervisors (Variable)	60,000
Clerical personnel (Variable)	27,000
	$229,000
Equipment, tooling, services	
Depreciation (Fixed)	$170,000
Repairs and maintenance (Variable)	30,000
Perishable supplies (Variable)	38,000
Tooling (nonperishable) (Variable)	355,000
Repairs on tools (Variable)	28,000
Outside services (Variable)	18,600
	$639,600
B. Engineering and development	
Professional budgeted labor	$105,000
Clerical support labor	67,000
Rent	42,000
Utilities	18,000
Depreciation	15,000
	$247,000
C. General management	
Professional budgeted labor	$280,000
Clerical support labor	125,000
Rent	67,000
Utilities	18,000
Depreciation	15,000
	$505,000

of depreciation. Surtax, credits, accelerated write-off, inflation or recession, obsolescence, and new technology obscure thinking about this matter. Even various accounting terms such as reserves for depreciation, allowances for depreciation, and amortization and retirement enlarge the ambiguity.

Depreciation is an accounting charge that provides for recovery of the capital that purchased the physical assets. It is the process of allocating an amount of money over the recovery life of a tangible capital asset in a systematic manner. It is cost, as of a certain time, not value, that changes with time and that is allocated and recovered. There are no interest charges or any recognition of a changing dollar value. The depreciation charge is not a cash outlay. The actual cash outlay takes place at the time that the asset is acquired. Depreciation charges are the assignments of that initial cost over the recovery life of the asset and do not involve a periodic disbursement of cash. When the rate at which the asset is depreciated increases, it does not increase the outflow of cash. In fact, it has the opposite reaction, as the depreciation charges reduce taxable income and the outflow of cash for taxes. The initial investment is a prepaid operating cost that is expensed or allocated to an operating expense account. Examples of typical fixed assets are given by Table 4.10.

Initial costs are undertaken to acquire assets that contribute to the production of revenue over long periods of time. The cost of a factory building or a machine, for example, will remain a positive factor in generating revenue provided that the building and equipment are used in the manufacture of a sellable product. As federal

Table 4.10.   Typical Fixed-Asset Items

A. *Production and process equipment*
      Bins and tanks for inventory and storage of raw materials
      Turret lathes
      Milling machines
      Equipment for manufacturing basic materials into finished products
      Automatic transfer equipment
      Converting-type equipment
      Piping, material-handling trucks, and other moving devices
      Industrial pumps and compressors
      Instruments and controls
      Trucks

B. *Construction equipment*
      Bulldozers
      Trench excavators
      Backhoe
      Crane
      Mobile bituminous plant
      Dragline
      Trucks

C. *Service or nonprocess facilities*
      Power generation and distribution
      Furniture
      Business machines
      Motor vehicles
      First aid and safety installations

D. *Buildings and land*
      Factory buildings, land
      Warehousing
      Roadways, parking areas
      Shops, maintenance garages

---

laws require income measurement, it is necessary that an appropriate portion of the cost of the building or equipment be charged to or matched with each dollar of revenue resulting from the sale of products produced within its walls and machines. The amount of such cost, matched with revenue, during any one period is the estimated amount of the cost that expires during the period. Thus, a fixed asset, which will not last forever, has its useful value exhausted over a period of time. In the mineral industries and forestry, depletion, somewhat analogous to depreciation, is a noncash expense representing the portion of a limited natural resource such as oil, shale, and minerals utilized in a product which is sold.

The factors contributing to the decline in utility are considered in the categories of (1) physical wear and tear resulting from ordinary usage or exposure to weather, (2) functional factors such as inadequacy and obsolescence, and (3) governmental actions. Physical factors are commonplace such as the wear and tear on buildings and corrosion that impairs efficiency and safety. Due to technological progress, obsolescence is a frequent situation where the fixed asset is retired not because it is worn out but because it is outmoded. The superior efficiency of an asset of a later design is one reason compelling new product designs for the market. Sometimes alterations of the design through research and development techniques make for immediate obsolescence. There is the instance of inadequacy where the asset, although neither worn out nor obsolete, is unable to meet the demands on it. An electric power company installs a hydroelectric generator and in the course of several years finds that the demands of an expanding community placed on it exceed the ability of the water and hydroelectric power to meet peak loads. Governmental or other forces may prevent operation (e.g., loss of raw material source or a new law prohibiting waste disposal are possibilities).

The government alters the tax laws and affects the depreciation directly. Changes in the laws governing income taxes and codes are enacted periodically. In recent years* the federal government coined the term "accelerated cost recovery system." Useful life, recovery period, and salvage value are terms that are carefully defined. These laws have various motives to encourage economic growth, redistribute income, or provide for social needs.

For consideration of new projects, engineering estimates would be required for the asset, erection, and operating capital and costs. There are in every project certain costs that can be tax expensed immediately, such as expenditures for non-physical assets, some physical assets of extremely short life, and certain installation and startup expenses.

The question of life is an important matter. Some firms are concerned about economic life with little regard for physical life, while others, public utilities, for example, are restricted to earning a specified amount on capital invested, and *life* takes on another ramification. The *economic life* estimate is affected by tax laws and the actions of Congress. *Book value* is ordinarily taken to mean the original cost

*Economic Recovery Tax Act of 1981, Aug. 13, 1981.

of the asset less any amounts that have been charged as depreciation. It should not be confused with salvage.

Before one can calculate depreciation, it is necessary to understand property or asset classification. A *depreciable property* is used in the business or held for the obtaining of income, and has a useful life longer than 1 year. The property will wear out, decay, become obsolete, or lose value from natural causes. Depreciable property may be tangible or intangible, personal or real. Tangible property is seen or touched, such as buildings and equipment. Designs, patents, and copyrights are examples of intangible property. Intangible property can be depreciated if its useful life can be found. Real property is land and generally anything attached to, growing on, or erected on the land. Land, which has an indeterminant life, cannot be depreciated. Personal property, which does not include real estate, is machinery or vehicles, for example. Cost estimating deals with tangible personal property and tangible real property.

Recovery property is subject to the allowance for depreciation. A recovery period, a prescribed length of time, is designated for recovery property.

1. Three-year property has a life of 4 years or less and is used in connection with research and experimentation, autos, light trucks, and production tooling.
2. Five-year property that is not 3-, 10-, or 15-year public utility property. Examples include machinery and equipment not used in research and development.
3. Ten-year property is public utility property with a class life of more than 18 years but less than 25 years. Another example could be railroad tank cars.
4. Fifteen-year property would include buildings not otherwise designated as 5- or 10-year property.

A method called *accelerated cost recovery* is defined as follows:

$$D_j = P(j) \times P \tag{4.3}$$

where D_j = depreciation in jth year for specified property class

$P(j)$ = percentage for year j for specified property class

P = cost of asset, dollars

Typical values of $P(j)$ are given below for years 3, 5, 10, and 15. Note that the sum of each column is 100%, and values are not constant year to year. If percentage values were equal (i.e., 33 1/3% for the 3-year property class), the depreciation is straight line. The method of Eq. (4.3) disregards any expected salvage value.

A variety of laws are connected with this table. For instance, if an asset is commissioned any time during the first year of a 3-year recovery period, the entire first-year depreciation is not permitted the year the asset is removed from service. If the property is held for a period at least as long as the associated recovery period, the asset value will be entirely depreciated. If, on the other hand, the asset is disposed of prior to the period, the asset will not be entirely depreciated. If the asset is held

Recovery Year	Percentage Depreciation			
	3-Year	5-Year	10-Year	15-Year Public Utility
1	33	20	10	7
2	45	32	18	12
3	22	24	16	12
4		16	14	11
5		8	12	10
6			10	9
7			8	8
8			6	7
9			4	6
10			2	5
11				4
12				3
13				3
14				2
15				1

for the recovery period or longer, it is possible for the book value to be less than the anticipated salvage value.

Consider a 3-year recovery property having a cost of $100,000. The property will be sold at the end of the fourth year.

Year	Cost	Percentage Depreciation, $P(j)$	Book Value at Year Beginning	Yearly Depreciation, D_j
0	$100,000		$100,000	
1		33	100,000	$33,000
2		45	67,000	45,000
3		22	22,000	22,000

A firm may choose an alternative method to determine depreciation by using a longer recovery period.

Recovery Period	Optional Recovery Period, $N(K)$
3	3, 5, or 12
5	5, 12, or 25
10	10, 25, or 35
15	15, 35, or 45

The percentage for each and every year is

$$P(j) = \frac{1}{N(K)} \tag{4.4}$$

where $N(K)$ is the recovery period, years.

Once Eq. (4.4) is used with Eq. (4.3), we have the *straight-line* method, where salvage value is assumed as zero.

Assume a \$100,000 asset, which for economic reasons we choose to depreciate over a 5-year life.

Year	Cost	Straight-Line Percentage, $P(j)$	Book Value at Year Beginning	Yearly Depreciation, D_j
0	\$100,000		\$100,000	
1		20	100,000	\$20,000
2		20	80,000	20,000
3		20	60,000	20,000
4		20	40,000	20,000
5		20	20,000	20,000

In view of its worldwide popularity and for general understanding, a salvage value is often associated with straight-line depreciation.

$$D_j = \frac{1}{N(K)}(P - F_s) \tag{4.5}$$

where F_s denotes the future salvage value of investment, dollars.

Reconsider the investment of \$100,000 with a \$10,000 salvage at the end of 5 years.

Year	Cost Less Salvage	Straight-Line Depreciation (%)	Book Value at Year Beginning	Yearly Depreciation, D_j
0	\$90,000		\$100,000	
1		20	100,000	\$18,000
2		20	82,000	18,000
3		20	64,000	18,000
4		20	46,000	18,000
5		20	28,000	18,000

Another method, sometimes used for depreciation accounting, is the *sum-of-the-years' digits*. It acts to provide a declining periodic depreciation charge over an estimated life. This is achieved by applying a smaller fraction recursively each year to the cost less its salvage value. In the recursive relationship the numerator of the changing fraction is the number of remaining years of life, while the denominator is the sum of the digits representing the years of life. With an asset having an estimated life of 5 years, the denominator of the fraction is 15 (= 1 + 2 + 3 + 4 + 5). For the first year the numerator is 5, for the second 4, and so forth.

$$D_{sd} = \frac{2}{N}\left(\frac{N + 1 - K}{N + 1}\right)(P - F_s) \tag{4.6}$$

where D_{sd} = sum-of-the-years-digits' depreciation charge, dollars
$\quad K$ = current year
$\quad N$ = life defined for depreciation, years

Reconsider the investment of $100,000 with a $10,000 salvage at the end of 5 years.

Year	Cost Less Salvage	Rate	Book Value at Year Beginning	Yearly Depreciation, D_{sd}
0	$90,000		$100,000	
1		5/15	100,000	$30,000
2		4/15	70,000	24,000
3		3/15	46,000	18,000
4		2/15	28,000	12,000
5		1/15	16,000	6,000

Still another method of depreciation is based on the premise that an asset wears out exclusively as demands are placed on it. Called the *units of production* method, the computation is given as

$$D_{up} = \frac{1}{N(i)}(P - F_s)N_i \tag{4.7}$$

where D_{up} = unit of production depreciation charge, dollars
$\quad N(i)$ = units for ith year

This method has the advantage that expense varies directly with operation activity. Retirement in these cases tends to be a function of use. An estimate of total lifetime production is necessary. The $100,000 cost and $10,000 salvage value example is estimated to have 200 units of output over the 5-year period.

Year	Cost Less Salvage	Units of Production, $N(i)$	Book Value at Year Beginning	Yearly Depreciation, D_{up}
0	$90,000		$100,000	
1		15	100,000	$ 6,750
2		45	93,250	20,250
3		50	73,000	22,500
4		55	50,500	24,750
5		35	25,750	15,750
		200		

The advantages of accelerated methods of depreciation are compatible with the logic that the earning power of an asset is created during its early service rather than later, where upkeep costs tend to increase progressively with age. Accelerated methods offer a measure of protection against unanticipated contingency such as excessive maintenance, and they return the investment more quickly and simultaneously, decreasing the book value at the same rate. A high book value would tend to deter the disposing of unsuitable equipment even when the need for replacement is pressing. Rapid reduction of book values, provided the owner overlooks the tax benefits from capital loss, leaves the owner more free to dispose of inefficient and unsatisfactory equipment.

Depreciation of costs is collected under the control of general ledger accounts, such as accumulated depreciation or allowance for depreciation. Periodic fixed charges resulting from these accounts are analyzed and charged departmentally under the proper cost classification through the application of worksheet analysis. Distribution of depreciation of machinery and equipment is thus made to different departments based on factors such as cost of factory equipment, rates of depreciation applicable to each unit of equipment, and departmental location of each unit. In the case of plants and buildings, various property ledgers would show location of cost and accumulated depreciation. The proration of depreciation on buildings to departments may be based on the cost of the building, the total area of the building, and the area occupied by each department of the building.

A *reserve for depreciation* account contains the accumulated estimated net decrease in the value of the particular asset account to which it pertains. In most industries the amount shown in the depreciation account does not appear as cash unless a special fund is set aside specifically for this purpose. To create a fund of this nature suggests that a fund is actually invested outside the company to earn interest. However, interest rates found on the outside are less than the earning rate enjoyed by the company. It is wiser to employ the money for some operations. The amount equal to the depreciation will appear as other assets such as working capital, raw materials, or finished products in storage. When it becomes necessary to buy new equipment or replacements, management must convert physical assets into cash (unless sufficient cash is on hand) or use existing profit to pay for the new equipment. The appearance of a depreciation reserve on the balance sheet, as with other types of assets, represents capital retained in the business, ostensibly for the ultimate replacement of the capital asset being depreciated.

It has been suggested that a number of factors in any depreciation model are subject to estimation: salvage value and, particularly, life. If for some reason the estimates prove faulty, then it is possible to retire an investment before its capital has been recovered. In the circumstance where net income received is less than the amount invested, an unrecovered balance remains. This unrecovered balance is referred to as *sunk cost*. The term "sunk cost" may be defined as the difference between the amount invested in an asset and the net worth recovered by services and income resulting from the employment of the asset. As an illustration of the above statements, consider a case where a capital investment of $5000 is to be recovered in 5 years with a remaining $1000 salvage or $4000 depreciation. Based on straight-line depreciation the amount invested and to be recovered per year will be $800. As a result of excessive use, the machine was sold after 3 years, for $1400, and had actually consumed $3600 in 3 years or $1200 per year on the average. The sunk cost is equal to the difference in the actual depreciation and the depreciation charge, in this case $3600 − $2400 = $1200. Stated yet another way, sunk cost is determined to be the estimated depreciation value (or book value) minus the realized salvage of the asset. Sunk costs cannot be affected by decisions of the future and must be faced with reality.

The act of exhausting a natural resource and converting it to a saleable product is called depletion. The natural resources which are subject to depletion are oil, natural gases, metal and mineral mines, orchards, fisheries, and forests. Not all natural resources are subject to depletion, for example, soil fertility and urban land. In accounting for depletion, it is the allocation of the value of the quantity of natural resources extracted from a deposit that is considered. Like depreciation, it is a noncash expense that is an allowed tax deduction.

4.9 OVERHEAD

By definition *overhead* is that portion of the cost which cannot be clearly associated with particular operations, products, projects, or systems and must be prorated among all the cost units on some arbitrary basis. Broad details regarding the posting of direct-labor cost, time, material, and other indirect costs have been given earlier. What will be discussed here are those overhead aspects which pertain to estimating. The key to this puzzle is the way in which indirect expenses are allocated, unitized, and charged to individual estimates; the direct costs, such as direct labor and direct materials, present little if any allocation problem. These costs do not exist unless the product is made.

The underestimating or overestimating of overhead rates is serious in view of the proportion of the total estimated cost. As an illustration, consider two different operations where the labor rates are $21.25 per hour. Machine A, a numerical controlled milling machine, is initially worth $150,000, while machine B, a standard general-purpose milling machine, is worth approximately $15,000. Using an average burden rate of 200%, it would be indicated that machines A and B would each cost, on a machine-hour basis, $63.75 per hour. However, this is false machine-hour costing, as the investment in machine A is 10 times that in machine B. It is evident that the proper cost base and sensible allocation of overheads to handle discrepancies of this sort are necessary. Years ago machine investment per worker was lower, and it was not uncommon that overhead rates were uniformly distributed over the direct-labor base. In recent decades, the ratio of fixed cost to variable cost has risen, and the simple expediency of overhead distribution via the single rate is misleading.

A primary distribution of overhead consists of assigning the various overhead costs to several departments or defined divisions within the unit, or factory, for example. Sometimes *cost centers* combine or separate departments to form homogeneous groups and are a logical point for the accumulation of costs. In making this distribution there is no distinction between a producing department (the milling machine department) and a service department (first aid). This distribution is followed by a redistribution in a secondary manner. Overhead is allocated to a designated base. A base for distribution of manufacturing overhead may be floor area, kilowatt hours, direct-labor dollars or hours, machine hours, or number of employees. The redistribution of costs originally assigned to service cost centers (first aid, for example) to the production cost centers is termed *secondary* distribution. This bookkeeping transfer technique of overhead costs to production departments is for subsequent recovery within operation or product cost. A secondary distribution, in the case of first aid, might be to prorate the total medical center costs to the production department on the basis of the number of employees within that department. If the milling machine department had two times as many employees as the lathe department, one could reason that the costs that it receives should be borne on a 2:1 ratio. Building depreciation, building insurance, building maintenance, and building taxes are often distributed on a floor area basis. Electrical power poses a confusing choice. It may be distributed on the basis of machine weight, machine-hours, horsepower hours, or even direct labor hours. Overhead costs become complicated whenever they have a joint or commonness with different levels of variability. Joint costs, or costs incurred jointly, are depreciation, insurance, property taxes, maintenance, and repairs. They are dependent on one another. But joint costs are handled differently for accounting analysis, than for direct labor and direct material of Chapters 2 and 3. *Accounting joint* costs are handled entirely by the overhead process.

The four steps of overhead analysis are graphically given by Fig. 4.4. The horizontal axis is "period," where E is the *now-time* of the estimate. Past periods are -1 and -2, while future periods are 1, 2, and 3. Sketch (a) plots overhead charges versus period. Obviously, actual charges can only be collected up to the current time, but charges can be estimated or gathered for future periods. This gathering is sometimes referred to as "pooling." Note that the behavior of the charges can be linear, flat, or nonlinear. In sketch (b) the vertical axis is identified with the general term "basis," which is a popular accounting term meaning simply "denominator." The basis can be one of several things, such as direct labor cost or time. The basis is gathered for equivalent periods, as shown in sketch (b). In sketch (c) we have the general definition of overhead, or

$$\text{overhead rate} = \frac{\text{overhead charges}}{\text{basis}} \tag{4.8}$$

Notice that *actual* charges, basis, and rates do not coincide with the *estimated* value. This is usually what happens, and an effort is made to have coincidence. It is the total area of sketch (a) divided by (b) that gives a constant rate value shown in (c). But the overhead rate is *applied* by estimating. While an accountant will do sketches (a), (b), and (c), it is usually an estimator who handles the application of sketch (d).

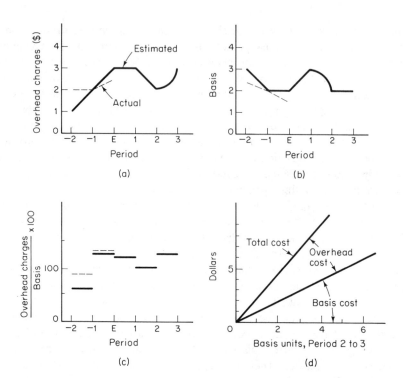

Figure 4.4 Overhead sequence: (a) collecting and plotting overhead charges; (b) collecting and plotting the basis; (c) calculating overhead rate; (d) applying overhead rate.

4.9.1 General Classification of Overhead Methods

The exact nature of the overhead rate differs from one company to the next; it is not uncommon to find various overhead methods used within one firm. A classification is given as

1. The basis used to determine and apply overhead, such as direct-labor dollars, direct-labor hours, machine hours, or material costs
2. Whether the rate includes fixed costs, as in absorption, or not, as in direct costing
3. The scope of the rate to the plant, to a cost center, or to a specific machine
4. Whether the rate applies to all designs (such as product lines) or to one line of the design, or to a unit of product

An actual burden rate has the merit of distributing among the jobs the incurred factory overhead. It is subject to certain defects, as it is unavailable until the close of the accounting period. Historical rates delay cost calculations until the end of the month and often later and fluctuate because of seasonal and cyclical influences acting on the actual overhead costs and on the actual volume of activity for which overhead cost is spread. In view of the dependency on predetermined overhead rates, our discussion will disregard historical rates.

In most situations overhead rates are determined from data developed from operating budgets. We will use Tables 4.7, 4.8, and 4.9 to determine several kinds of rates.

The method of finding overhead as a ratio of the direct-labor dollars is one of the oldest and most popular, or

$$R_{dl} = \frac{C_o}{C_{dl}} \tag{4.9}$$

where R_{dl} = overhead rate on basis of direct-labor cost

C_o = overhead charges, dollars

C_{dl} = direct labor, dollars

The numerator and denominator may be the factory or department or cost center. While it would appear that Eq. (4.9) is dimensionless, it is more useful to remember R_{dl} as dollars of overhead charge per dollar of direct labor cost. Now examine Tables 4.7, 4.8, and 4.9 for the following information:

	Overhead Charges Fringes		Direct-Labor Costs	
Production center				
Light machining	$4.92 × 58,000 =	$285,360	$16.40 × 58,000 =	$ 951,200
Heavy machining	5.93 × 8,000 =	47,440	19.75 × 8,000 =	158,000
Assembly	4.70 × 20,000 =	94,000	15.65 × 20,000 =	313,000
Finishing	5.12 × 16,000 =	81,920	17.05 × 16,000 =	272,800
			102,000 hr	$1,695,000
General factory				
Space		$ 256,000		
Power		239,625		
Indirect labor		229,000		
Equipment, etc.		639,600		
		$1,881,945		

$$R_{dl} = \frac{1,881,945}{1,695,000} = \$1.11 \text{ overhead charge per dollar of direct labor}$$

Note that engineering and general management overhead costs were not spread against direct labor cost, although it could have been handled that way. We will later spread engineering and general management against cost of goods sold.

It is sometimes assumed that many factory overhead charges are proportional to labor time. This situation occurs if labor is paid on an hourly basis and the rate per hour is substantially the same for all workers. The rate of overhead per direct-labor hours is calculated as

$$R_{\text{dlh}} = \frac{C_o}{H_{\text{dl}}}$$ (4.10)

where R_{dlh} = overhead rate on basis of direct-labor hours

H_{dl} = budgeted direct labor, hours

The scope may include the factory, department, or cost center. The dimensions for Eq. (4.10) would be dollars overhead charge per hour of direct labor. Now examine Tables 4.7, 4.8, and 4.9 and notice that C_o = \$1,881,945, which was previously found, and H_{dl} = 102,000 hours. Then

$$R_{\text{dlh}} = \frac{1,881,945}{102,000} = \$18.45 \text{ per hour of direct labor}$$

Engineering and general management were not spread against direct labor time. The rate per direct labor hour represents the ideal in methods of overhead proration, as overhead accumulates on a time basis, while the rate per direct labor hour distributes on a time basis.

Another method uses prime cost as the denominator, or

$$R_p = \frac{C_o}{C_p}$$ (4.11)

where R_p = overhead rate on the basis of prime cost

C_p = prime cost, dollars

Prime cost is defined as direct materials plus direct labor. Still another case of absorption costing involves dividing the expected volume of product output into the total budgeted overhead to get cost per unit. This method will work for a few industries which have identical product units, such as cement, petroleum, and foodstuffs.

When the machinery used in production is not reasonably equal in value, the machine-hour rate method is useful. This method has the formula

$$R_{\text{mh}} = \frac{C_o}{H_m}$$ (4.12)

where R_{mh} = overhead rate on the basis of machine hours

H_m = machine hours

Equation (4.12) can be computed on a specific machine or machine grouping, as the following example demonstrates. The steps in computing the rate are similar. Budgets shown by Tables 4.7, 4.8, and 4.9 are necessary. But now we consider the physical factors associated with the production centers, such as number of machines, floor space, machine horsepower hours, depreciation, and tooling expenses. These data are shown by Table 4.7, which deals with the production center budget. From Table 4.8 we use the manpower cost requirements to operate those machines, such as number of direct-labor employees, wage, fringe rate, budgeted direct-labor hours, and the total direct-labor cost. From Table 4.9 we use factory overhead, engineering and development, and general management charges. The machine hour and gross hourly cost spread sheet is shown by Table 4.11. Observe in Table 4.11 the distribution of space costs ($256,000) to each of the four production centers. The floor space cost to each center is on the basis of its area to the total area. For instance, the allocation fraction $256,000/8300 = \$30.84/ft^2$ would result in $86,361 (= 2800 \times 30.84)$ for light machining. The $256,000 is total charges for space, while 8300 ft^2 is total area. The allocation factor is described for the several columns, and may be floor space, horsepower hours, direct-labor hours, and depreciation and tooling. The depreciation and tooling ratio is computed differently. The equipment depreciation ($ = \$170,000$), tooling ($ = \$355,000$), and services ($ = \$114,600$) are removed from that portion of factory overhead. We presume that these services are incurred on the basis of the sum of depreciation and tooling. Light machining services are $55,117 (\doteq 0.22 \times 252,500)$. This ratio is the same as $(52,500 + 200,000)/(170,000 + 355,000) \times 114,600 \doteq \$55,117$.

The results of the machine-hour overhead rate are $17.84, $65.30, $11.84, and $20.16. For example, $17.84 (= 1,034,540/58,000)$ is the machine-hour cost on the basis of light machining budgeted hours. The average gross hourly cost for direct labor is added to each machine center. Comparison of this column on Table 4.11 shows that heavy machining costs about three times as much as finishing. Machine-hour rates afford an accurate method of allocating overhead expenses, and from the engineering point of view, are suitable for estimating manufacturing from specifications and route sheets. The machine-hour rate method is best used whenever operations are performed by machinery which is significant in terms of the final cost of the design.

Cost can be identified as either variable or fixed with respect to changes in output. Materials and direct labor are variable costs, and as a practical expedient it is sometimes desirable to distinguish overhead costs as variable and fixed also. To achieve this distinction each cost center has identified variable and fixed overhead. The following cost items are a sample of how overhead might be classified into variable or fixed:

Variable Overhead Cost	Fixed Overhead Cost
Indirect materials	Indirect labor
Labor-related costs	Labor-related costs
Power and light	Depreciation
Inspection	Property taxes

Labor-related costs are included as both variable and as fixed costs. It is conceivable, if they are related to direct labor, that they are variable overhead, and conversely, if they are related to indirect labor, a fixed cost, they become fixed overhead. Overhead can be established that is variable, or

$$R_v = \frac{C_{ov}}{C_{dl}} \tag{4.13}$$

Table 4.11. CALCULATION OF MACHINE-HOUR RATE COMBINED WITH GROSS HOURLY WAGE

Machine Center	Space	Power	Indirect Labor	Depreciation	Nonperishable Tools, Expenses	Services	Engineering and Development	Management	Total
Light Machining	$ 86,361	$ 82,738	$130,216	$ 52,500	$200,000	$ 55,117	$140,451	$287,157	$1,034,540
Heavy Machining	92,530	139,703	17,961	95,000	80,000	38,200	19,373	39,608	522,375
Assembly	27,759	4,482	44,902	—	10,000	2,183	48,431	99,020	236,777
Finish	49,349	12,700	35,722	22,500	65,000	19,100	38,745	79,216	322,533
	$256,000	$239,625	$229,000	$170,000	$355,000	$114,600	$247,000	$505,000	$2,116,225
Allocation Basis	Floor Space	Horsepower Hour	Budgeted Direct-Labor Hours	Depreciation and Tooling			Budgeted Direct-Labor Hours	Budgeted Direct-Labor Hours	
Fraction	$\frac{256,000}{8,300}$	$\frac{239,625}{1,283,000}$	$\frac{229,000}{102,000}$			$\frac{114,600}{525,000}$	$\frac{247,000}{102,000}$	$\frac{505,000}{102,000}$	

Machine Center	Budgeted Assigned Direct-Labor Hours	Machine Hour Cost	Gross Hourly Wage Rate	Wage and Machine Hour Cost
Light Machining	58,000	$17.84	$21.32	$39.16
Heavy Machining	8,000	65.30	25.68	90.98
Assembly	20,000	11.84	20.35	32.19
Finish	16,000	20.16	22.17	42.33

where R_v = variable overhead rate on basis of direct-labor cost

$\quad\quad C_{ov}$ = variable overhead charges, dollars

Examining Table 4.9, we observe that the factory overhead items have been separated into fixed and variable choices.

$$R_v = \frac{843225 + 508720}{1,695,000} = \$0.798 \text{ per direct labor dollar}$$

The fixed overhead costs are not forgotten, and become a consideration of the pricing method, which is covered in Chapter 8. In the accounting procedure of *direct costing,* the overhead charges are separated into fixed and variable choices. Note that direct *costing* is not the same as direct *cost.* The distinction to *absorption costing* is this separation; in absorption, lumped charges are divided by a basis. In many circumstances we can see that the fixed quantity, when divided by a basis that is more or less variable, causes future difficulties to arise, as overhead may be substantially different than the resulting actual overhead. A variable cost quantity divided by a variable cost basis is more uniform and responsive. A difference between actual and projected overhead is called *over-* or *under*absorption and is a consequence of poor budgeting or operation.

Overhead charges can be separated into those which are factory, management, engineering and development, and selling. Factory overhead charges are spread using Eqs. (4.10) to (4.13). The total of direct materials and labor and factory overhead charges necessary for the operation of the producing units is sometimes referred to as *cost of goods manufactured.* Management, engineering, and selling expenses are distinct functions in the business enterprise, and we segregate those costs and apply them on the basis of cost of goods manufactured. These are general expenses for the conduct of many products, and their overhead model is

$$R_{sga} = \frac{C_{sga}}{C_{gm}} \tag{4.14}$$

where R_{sga} – overhead rate on basis of cost of goods manufactured

$\quad\quad C_{sga}$ = overhead charges for selling, general, and administrative, dollars

$\quad\quad C_{gm}$ = cost of goods manufactured, dollars

The phrase "selling, general, and administrative," is often abbreviated SG&A, where we understand that engineering, development, and management expenses are also implied.

4.10 JOB ORDER AND PROCESS COST PROCEDURES

Cost accounting procedures are established to provide historical cost information, and are known as *job order* or *process* cost. The procedures allocate material, labor, and burden charges to control accounts. If many different types of products are made and there are various customers, a job order accounting procedure is found.

In job or lot production every "run" of product is assigned a production order number. This number is a convenient way to collect the material requisitions and labor job tickets. A typical job cost sheet describes the costing points to which the run refers. A job order may cover the production of one unit or a number of identical units. Examples might be a large seagoing ship or several similar electric generators when the items are complex or costly. The total quantity may be divided in smaller production lots and the job order for the total contract may be supported by a separate job order for each lot. In job order, the production cycle and the cost cycle are equal in the time allowed for gathering the costs.

Process cost procedures are used whenever there is large volume or a repetition of a highly similar process. The completed item is a consequence of a series of processes, each of which produces some change in the material. These procedures are found in industries that operate 24 hours per day, such as oil, steel, and chemicals. The production cycle continues without interruptions, but the cost cycle is terminated for each accounting period, such as a month, to determine the results of operations. Costs are accumulated on process cost sheets which show input and output material and labor.

Upon completion of the job order and the process accounting period, the overheads are applied using actual information if it is available. Thus average cost per unit information is obtained from both procedures, although they are substantially different approaches. Both procedures fundamentally divide the total manufacturing cost by the number of product units produced, and compute the unit costs of the individual processes and total them. In both cases, these historical unit values can be forecast into the future to provide a *rough* glimpse of estimated cost.

SUMMARY

Cost accounting is important to the performance of diverse estimating functions. As colleagues in the gathering, analysis, and reporting of business data, the accountant provides overhead rates, some historical costs, and budgeting data. The estimator reciprocates with manpower and material estimates for the several designs. In many situations, the estimate will serve as a mini profit and loss statement for products or projects. Thus there is mutual dependence between these two professions. The estimator is less interested in balance sheets, profit and loss statements, and the intimate details of the structure of accounts. Overhead rates are vital for the estimating functions, however, as the estimator will apply these rates. By definition overhead is that portion of the cost which cannot be clearly associated with particular operations, products, projects, or systems designs and must be distributed among the cost units in some arbitrary way. The overhead rate is simply

$$\text{overhead rate} = \frac{\text{predicted indirect costs associated with a design}}{\text{predicted direct costs associated with a design}}$$

Accounting costs, if they are purely historical and derived from job order or process cost procedures, are usually inadequate as estimates of future costs. The design may have changed or costs may have increased or decreased, but one of the essentials for intelligent cost estimating is the continuous flow of reliable information from all activities of the organization. Accounting is an important contributor of past data. The next chapter deals with the future speculation of labor, materials, and accounting data.

QUESTIONS

4.1. Give an explanation of the following terms:

Asset	Account balance	Charges
Liability	Depreciable value	Income
Net worth	Book value	Expenses
Accounting equation	Service life	Overhead
Balance sheet	Trial balance	Basis
Net assets	Closed account	Machine-hour overhead
Capital stock	Open account	Absorption overhead
Surplus	Declining balance	Direct costing
Debit	Accrual	Job order costs
Credit	T-account	Process costs

4.2. For a business with which you are familiar, list 10 kinds of assets and 5 kinds of liabilities.

4.3. Why do expense accounts normally have debit balances, and income accounts normally have credit balances?

4.4. What is the purpose of a trial balance? Into what main groups are trial balances accounts divided?

4.5. Distinguish between the cash and accrual bases of accounting. Discuss the conditions under which each is acceptable.

4.6. What are the functions of special and general journals?

4.7. What is the purpose of the budget? How would you define a cost center for an engineering budget? How do you prevent the budget from being meaningless?

4.8. Why is equitable distribution of cost essential throughout the organization to cost finding, analysis, and prediction?

4.9. Distinguish between a cost account and a cost code. How does the nature of the organization determine whether a cost code or cost account system of classification is used?

4.10. Define overhead. What is the essential and philosophical purpose of overhead?

4.11. What is the difference between direct costing and absorption? How does that affect overhead calculation?

4.12. Prescribe and contrast several methods for the distribution of indirect cost.

4.13. How do job order and process cost procedures differ?

PROBLEMS

4.1. Evaluate the effects of transactions by constructing a daily balance sheet showing an asset side and an equities side. *January 1:* John Smith starts a sheet metal business producing metal products for the home. The business is called John Smith Sheet Metal. Mr. Smith deposits $10,000 of his own money in a bank account which he has opened in the name of the business. *January 2:* The business borrows $5000 from a bank, giving a note, therefore increasing the assets and cash and the business incurs a liability to the bank. *January 3:* The business buys inventory in the amount of $10,000, paying cash. *January 4:* The firm sells material for $300 that cost $200.

4.2. Given the following ledger T accounts from Weichman Mfg. Co., set up a balance sheet for the month of March.

		Cash					
March	1	Capital	$1000	March	5	Rent	$200
	10	Consulting fee	250		20	Salaries	350
	25	J. A. Wilson on acct.	500				

		Customers (Accts. receivable)					
March	10	J. A. Wilson	$1200	March 25		Cash on acct.	$500

		Supplies on Hand				
March	3	Accts. payable	$360	March 31	Supplies used in March	$110

		Equipment		
March	4	Notes payable	$3200	

		Accts. Payable			
			March 3	Supplies	$360

		Notes Payable			
			March 4	Equipment	$3200

		Weichman Mfg. Co. Capital					
March	5	Cash	$200	March	1	Cash investment	$1000
	20	Salaries	350		10	Consulting	250
	31	Supplies used	110		10	J. A. Wilson	1200

4.3. Using the following closed ledger, construct a profit and loss statement:

		Equipment		
June	1	Balance	$3200	

Accts. Payable

June	2	Cash Myers Co.	$360	June	1	Balance	$360
					6	Supplies	600
					28	Misc. exp.	40

Notes Payable

				June	1	Balance	$3200

Capital

				June	1	Balance	$1790
					30	From P & L	1570

Income

June	30	To P & L	$2500	June	4	Accts. pro.	$2200
						A. B. Jones	
					15	Cash I. N. Smith	300

Lease Expenses

June	1	Cash	$200	June	30	To P & L	$200

Misc. Office Expenses

June	10	Telephone, cash	$60	June	30	To P & L	$100
	28	Elec.	40				

Salaries

June	20	Cash	$350	June	30	To P & L	$350

Supplies Expense

June	30	Supplies used	$280	June	30	To P & L	$280

4.4. Evaluate the effects of each transaction by constructing a balance sheet showing an assets side and a liabilities + net worth side.

1. Samuel Specthrie established the SS Company, paying in $250,000 cash for the entire capital stock.
2. Paid $50,000 cash for a building site.
3. Erected a building costing $200,000, paying $50,000 cash and issuing a $150,000 first mortgage for the balance.
4. Borrowed $60,000 cash from First National Bank.
5. Bought furniture, costing $15,000, on an open account from Wood Furniture Co.
6. Purchased $50,000 of tools from Universal Tool on credit.
7. Bought $30,000 worth of computer equipment from Byte Co. for cash.
8. Return $15,000 of faulty tools to Universal Tool.
9. Paid $25,000 in reduction of the bank loan.
10. Bought $40,000 of U.S. Treasury bonds for cash.

4.5. Evaluate the effects of each transaction by constructing a balance sheet showing an assets side and a liabilities + net worth side.

1. The Eastwood Machine Co. is organized with a capital stock of $250,000, which is paid for in cash.
2. Bought from Culpepper on credit $100,000 of merchandise.
3. Borrowed $80,000 cash from City Bank.
4. Paid Culpepper $30,000 on account.
5. Return $10,000 of defective merchandise to Culpepper.
6. Loaned $50,000 cash to Robert Gondring.
7. Paid $20,000 cash for a building site.
8. Erected a building at a cost of $120,000 cash.
9. Borrowed $70,000 from Friendly Insurance, giving a mortgage for that.

4.6. Analyze the following transactions using the approach given by Table 4.2.

1. Founded the AJAX supply business, paying $300,000 cash for capital stock.
2. Bought merchandise from supplier Caterpillar on credit for the amount of $150,000.
3. Paid rent for the month, $4000.
4. Sold four units to M. Meyers for $35,000 cash.
5. Paid $50,000 to Caterpillar on account.
6. Retired $60,000 of capital stock.
7. Borrowed $80,000 cash from First National Bank.
8. Sold merchandise on account to K. Wilson for $60,000.
9. Returned $20,000 of merchandise to Caterpillar.
10. Paid salaries and wages, $3000.

4.7. Short Corporation started the year with the following balances:

Account	Balance as of January 1
Cash	$100,000
Inventory	100,000
New plant and equipment	400,000
Accounts payable	50,000
Owner equity	550,000

Transactions during the year were limited to the following: Pay $100,000 for labor; purchase $150,000 worth of materials; note equipment depreciation of $50,000, adding to inventory 300,000 units costing $1 to the manufacturer; sell 300,000 units for $2 each, cash; purchase new equipment costing $200,000. Accounts payable at the end of year were the same as at the beginning of the year. Neglect income taxes. Make an end-of-year balance sheet. Make an income statement for the year just ended.

4.8. Construct a balance sheet for Dynamics Corp. based on the following information:

Retained earnings	$610,000
Cash	150,000
Outstanding debt	450,000
Raw materials	100,000
Finished goods	50,000

Current liabilities	40,000
Stock ownership	400,000
Fixed assets	1,100,000
In-process materials	100,000

4.9. Prepare a profit and loss statement using the following account balances of E. Biller-beck for the nine months ended September 30.

Sales	$700,000	Rent	$ 80,000
Sales returns	40,000	Salaries	120,000
Inventory, January 1	120,000	Interest earned	2,000
Purchases	270,000	Sales discounts	10,000
Purchase returns	20,000	Interest expense	5,000
Inventory, September 30	160,000		

4.10. The following data are the assets, liabilities, incomes, and expenses of Warren Andrews, contractor.

(a) Prepare an income and expense statement for the 6-month period ending June 30.

(b) Prepare a balance sheet at June 30.

(*Hint:* Since the profits amount is needed for completing the balance sheet, it is necessary to prepare the income and expense statement first.)

Cash in bank	$ 85,000	Office fixtures owned	$ 50,000
Income from fees	150,000	Bank loan	100,000
Interest income from	5,000	Accounts payable	70,000
owned securities		Interest expense on bank	2,500
Rental income on owned	30,000	loan	
properties		Receivable from clients	90,000
Staff salary expense	120,000	Automobiles owned	40,000
Traveling expense	7,500	Capital stock	415,000
Telephone expense	2,500	Surplus, January 1	85,000
Drafting supplies expense	7,500	Securities owned	200,000
Real estate owned	250,000		

4.11. Following are data for assets and liabilities at December 31, and incomes and expenses for the year of Wilmer Hergenrader, industrial consultant. Using this information, prepare **(a)** an income statement and **(b)** a balance sheet.

Cash in bank	$ 80,000	Office furniture and fixtures	$ 30,000
Fees earned	420,000	Rental income on building	26,000
Interest received from bonds	2,500	lease	
Land	60,000	Bonds owned	120,000
Receivable from clients	50,000	Traveling expenses	35,000
Staff salaries	270,000	Taxes paid	15,000
Building	180,000	Office expenses	10,000
Bank loan payable	70,000	Telephone expense	5,000
Capital stock	275,000	Accounts payable	25,000
Surplus, January 1	65,000	Automobiles owned	20,000
Interest expense on bank	4,000	Association dues	2,500
loan		expenses	
		Donation to charity	2,000

4.12. An asset has a cost of $43,000, salvage value of $3000, and an asset life of 10 years. Compute the depreciation expense for the first 3 years under **(a)** accelerated cost recovery, **(b)** straight line, and **(c)** sum-of-the-years digits.

4.13. Company *A* purchased a machine that costs $250,000. Economic life is estimated as 5 years with a salvage value of $15,000. This company chooses the accelerated cost recovery method for depreciation. Company *B*, in competition with company *A*, purchased the same machine at identical cost. The management of company *B* uses straight-line depreciation. Determine the yearly depreciation charges and the end-of-year book value. Compare the two methods for this competitive situation and comment on the importance of the depreciation method for cost estimating.

4.14. A manufacturer recently acquired a numerical control long-bed lathe. Due to the high initial cost and setup charges, he is in doubt as to the appropriate depreciation method to apply. He considers three methods: or straight line, sum-of-the-years digits, and units of production. For the following data, plot the book value against time and justify your selection as to the manufacturer's best choice. Initial cost, $140,000; installation and programming, $6000; and estimated useful life, 10 years, with 20% salvage value. Production outputs for the 10 years are 600, 800, 1000, 1000, 1200, 1200, 1200, 1100, 1000, and 900 consecutively.

4.15. A construction company will buy a tire-mounted excavating machine for a delivered price of $250,000. Life is 6 years, 12,000 hours, and salvage is expected to be nil. At the end of the life, the machine will be retired to secondary and emergency service. Determine the depreciation charge and book value for **(a)** accelerated cost recovery, **(b)** straight-line, and **(c)** sum-of-the-years-digit methods.

4.16. A standard-sized sedan purchased for $17,516 will cost its owner $54,212 by the time it has been driven 10 years and 100,000 miles. Besides depreciation to zero, this sum includes $10,396 for repairs and maintenance; $8384 for gas and oil; $7236 for garaging, parking, and tolls; $5400 for insurance; and $5280 for state and federal taxes.
(a) Find the depreciation cost per mile.
(b) What are the yearly and per mile costs?
(c) What are the percentages for the elements?

4.17. Car value and upkeep costs were found to follow this schedule:

Year	Drop in Value (%)	Drop in Value	Upkeep Costs
1	28	$ 4904	$ 412
2	21	3600	540
3	15	2700	1076
4	11	2000	1372
5	9	1504	1288
6	6	1036	1388
7	4	756	1828
8	3	484	968
9	2	340	1216
10	1	192	308
		$17,516	

(a) How many years does it take for a car to depreciate two-thirds and three-fourths of its value?

(b) If the car is driven 13,500 miles per year, what are the operating yearly costs in dollars per mile? Plot these operating costs. When is the advantageous time to trade a car assuming that the chief criterion is per mile economy?

(c) *Discuss:* If the immediate cost of repairing an old car is less than first-year depreciation on a new one, is the best policy to buy a car and drive it until it is ready to be junked?

4.18. Develop direct-costing overhead and absorption overhead rates on the basis of direct labor dollars for the following production levels:

Production load	80%	100%	125%
Labor costs	$100,000	$125,000	$156,250
Number of units	20,000	25,000	31,250
Variable overhead cost	$ 60,000	$ 75,000	$ 93,750
Fixed overhead costs	$120,000	$120,000	$120,000

4.19. An assembly area has floor space allocation as follows:

(a)	Drop area	300
(b)	Conveyor 1	100
(c)	Conveyor 2	150
(d)	Bench area	800
		1350 square feet

Total overhead costs are $8000 for this area. Determine the allocation ratio and overhead costs for each assembly production center.

4.20. A company is composed of five cost centers. Each month a budget is prepared anticipating the primary distribution of certain costs. Let C_w = costs incurred within the cost center such as depreciation and supplies and indirect labor (for producing centers only) and C_m = miscellaneous costs.

Cost Center	C_w	C_m	Area (ft^2)	Direct-Labor Dollars	Direct-Labor Hours
Fabrication	$30,000	$1,000	25,000	$20,160	1,600
Assembly	8,000	500	6,000	7,296	640
Finishing	2,000	4,000	1,900	3,744	320
Engineering	4,000	9,000	1,600	—	—
Administration	2,000	1,000	2,100	—	—

Make a secondary distribution for engineering and administration to the producing departments, designated C_0, on the basis of space, dollars, and hours and determine cost center and plant-wide overhead ratios. Discuss the merits of these allocation schemes.

4.21. (a) Assume the following simple overhead model: $C_b = C_w + C_0 + C_m$, where C_b = overhead costs; C_w = costs incurred within department such as depreciation, indirect labor, and supplies; C_0 = costs incurred outside the department but allocated to it, such as engineering design, building depreciation, and administration; and C_m = miscellaneous overhead account.

| Department | Monthly Costs | | | Hours | Direct-Labor Dollars |
	C_w	C_o	C_m		
Fabrication	$30,000	$7,000	$1,000	1,600	$20,160
Assembly	8,000	5,000	500	640	7,296
Finishing	2,000	4,000	500	320	3,744

Determine departmental overhead rates on the basis of hours and direct-labor dollars. Find the overall plant rate on the basis of dollars.

(b) Now a product cost model can be defined as $C_p = C_{dm} + C_e + C_b$, where C_{dm} = direct material cost and C_e = direct labor cost. Let fabrication, assembly, and finish departmental C_e's be $6, $2.25, and $0.75, respectively, for a unit of product—also 0.48, 0.20, and 0.064 standard hour per unit. If C_{dm} = $1 per unit, what is the product unit cost based on departmental overhead rates? If we let C_e = $9 per unit, what is the product cost based on an overall plant rate? Discuss the reasons for the differences in product cost.

4.22. Assume that a job is routed through Machining and Finishing. Machining is heavily mechanized with costly numerical control and other automatic equipment, while Finishing has only a few simple tools. Obviously, burden costs are high in Machining and low in Finishing. Job 1 takes 1 labor hour in Machining and 10 hours in Finishing. Job 2 takes 9 labor hours in Machining and only 2 in Finishing. If a single blanket rate based on labor hours is applied to both jobs, the burden allocation would be the same in both cases (11 hours for each job). The following illustrates the previous discussion:

| | Blanket Rate | | Department Rate | |
	Machining	Finishing	Machining	Finishing
Budgeted annual burden	$100,000	$ 8,000	$100,000	$ 8,000
Direct labor hours	10,000	10,000	10,000	10,000
Blanket rate per DLH	$5.40			
Department rates per DLH			$10.00	$0.80

Determine the overhead costs for jobs 1 and 2 using blanket and department rates. Discuss the necessity for selecting the correct base.

4.23. Management is attempting to maintain an overhead rate of 175% for an assembled product. The "problem" area is the machining process. Here the overhead rate is 225%

based on $23,000 direct labor. Total direct dollars excluding machining is $89,000. Overhead charges excluding machining are $150,000. What overhead rate will the company achieve based on this information? Use direct labor dollars as a base.

4.24. Given the following data:

Machine Center	Area	Hours	Horsepower Hours	Depreciation	Tooling	Workers	Direct-Labor Budget
Fabrication	25,000	1600	2200	$27,000	$1000	10	$20,160
Assembly	6,000	640	325	7,200	500	4	7,296
Finishing	1,900	320	650	1,800	4000	2	3,744

Item	Amount
Indirect overhead	$16,000
Power	4,200
Indirect labor	4,000
Engineering	13,000
Administration	3,000

(a) Find a plant-wide rate on the basis of direct labor dollars.
(b) Find a machine center rate on the basis of hours.

4.25. The following problem illustrates variable machine hour costing. A spread sheet for five production departments is given as follows:

Production Center	Direct Labor	Power	Packaging	Variable Indirect Material	Variable Indirect Overhead	Total
Vertical boring	$ 63,000	$ 6,458	$ 8,253	$ 2,000	$ 4,000	$ 83,711
Light machining	275,500	12,227	36,090	5,000	20,000	348,817
Heavy machining	44,000	20,699	5,764	8,000	3,000	81,463
Bench work	113,900	644	14,920		8,000	137,464
Finishing	66,400	1,877	8,698	3,000	4,000	83,975
	$562,800	$41,905	$73,725	$18,000	$39,000	$735,430

In addition to these variable costs there are other variable related labor costs of $20,000 which are unallocated and direct product materials of $462,500. These product materials are uniform.

(a) What is the total out-of-pocket cost or variable cost?
(b) Fixed costs are $736,000. What is the full cost of overhead?

CASE STUDY:
MACHINE SHOP

Mr. Dennis Schultz is owner of a modern precision job shop. In recent years he has made more estimates, but the "capture" percentage of estimates won to estimates made has fallen. Even worse, he has noted that he is able to keep his higher-priced equipment loaded but the less expensive equipment is not operating at full capacity. Dennis has said: "I know my direct labor costs are competitive," but he is suspicious of his overhead computation, which is a general plant rate with a basis of direct-labor hours. Dennis wants to compute a machine-hour rate for his factory. A budget is prepared and shows the following:

Machine Center	Machine Center Budgeted Hours	Horsepower Hours	Tooling Expenses	Direct-Labor Operators	Gross Hourly Wage	Budgeted Direct-Labor Hours
Lathe	13,328	160,000	$15,000	8	$17.50	15,680
Threading	6,664	66,000	5,000	4	16.00	7,840
Milling	6,664	53,000	12,000	4	21.75	7,840
Drilling	19,992	100,000	8,000	12	16.00	23,520
Bench	26,656	—	—	16	15.75	31,360
Grinding						
Horizontal	3,332	50,000	28,000	2	24.50	3,920
Rotary	1,666	13,000	16,000	1	21.50	1,960
Heat treat	6,664	—	30,000	4	17.50	7,840

	Undepreciated Amount/Machine Center	Remaining Depreciable Years	Department Expenses	Utilities and Power	Repairs
Lathe	$ 25,000	5	28,000	$18,000	45,000
Threading	60,000	10	36,000	8,000	21,000
Milling	80,000	8	19,000	6,500	21,000
Drilling	60,000	10	29,000	15,000	15,000
Bench	2,000	5	28,000	1,000	5,000
Grinding					
Horizontal	25,000	10	15,000	6,035	5,000
Rotary	120,000	10	15,000	1,950	15,000
Heat treat	15,000	5	10,000	6,000	8,000

The factory is separate from the engineering and management offices, and Dennis anticipates that these charges will spread at 25% of the machine cost per hour. Raw Stores, Shipping, and Inspection are factory overhead charges. Their budget gives the following:

Indirect Department	Wages	Supplies	Supervision
Raw stores	$120,000	$80,000	$22,000
Shipping	85,000	70,000	26,000
Inspection	210,000	35,000	38,000

The factory layout is shown in Fig. C4.1, and the 200 × 150 ft (60 × 45 m) is equally departmentalized. The undepreciated factory value is $1.6 million and 20 years of depreciable life remain. Ordinary straight-line methods of depreciation have been used.

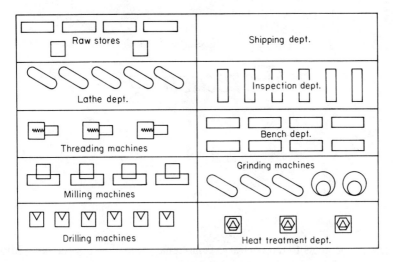

Figure C4.1.   Plant layout of precision job shop.

(a) Help Dennis by recommending his combined wage and machine-hour rate for his machine shop.

(b) Reconsider (a) by applying the accelerated recovery depreciation schedule.

5

Forecasting

Despite all statements to the contrary, "emotional estimating," or the other idiom, "guesstimating," has not disappeared from the cost-estimating scene. Nor has its substitute, estimation by formula and mathematical models, been universally nominated as a replacement. Somewhere between these extremes is a preferred course of action. In this chapter we consider the ways by which cost estimating can be enhanced by graphical and analytical techniques.

Business forecasting comprises the prediction of market demands, prices of material, cost of conversion, cost and availability of labor, and the like. Every major engineering decision is influenced by business forecasts. The usual approach to business forecasting involves extrapolation of past data into the future using linear or nonlinear curves and mathematical relationships. Future demands are expected to follow some pattern of growth and decay. Most business forecasts are made for the short-run period of up to 2 years. Medium-term forecasts cover 2 to 5 years, while long-term forecasts are for more than 5 years.

In this chapter we consider statistical methods, moving averages, and indexing. Our intention is to be basic, and to point out the special connection to cost estimating. Forecasting does not mean estimating. Forecasting is dependence on statistical or mathematical methods, and is only a small part of the professional field of estimating.

5.1 GRAPHIC ANALYSIS OF DATA

The field of descriptive statistics is concerned with methods for collecting, organizing, analyzing, summarizing, and presenting data as well as drawing valid conclusions and making reasonable decisions on the basis of analysis of the data. In a more restricted sense, the term "statistics" is used to denote the data themselves or numbers derived from the data, as, for example, averages.

The data that are gathered for descriptive statistics and graphical presentation may be either discrete or continuous and are usually the result of a series of observations taken over time or another controllable or noncontrollable variable. Raw data, however, communicate little information. One way to communicate information develops a frequency distribution which compacts the data into manageable proportions.

A frequency distribution begins with the collection of observations into a tabular arrangement by intervals. For instance, a market study has been made of the price for a roll of plastic film, and the number of observations are stated for the price interval.

Price Interval ($/roll)	Number of Observations	Relative Frequency	Cumulative Frequency
12.35–12.75	1	0.003	0.003
12.75–13.15	6	0.019	0.022
13.15–13.55	33	0.102	0.124
13.55–13.95	51	0.157	0.281
13.95–14.35	121	0.373	0.654
14.35–14.75	50	0.154	0.808
14.75–15.15	44	0.136	0.944
15.15–15.65	13	0.040	0.984
15.65–16.05	3	0.016	1.000
	324	1.000	

The price of 12.35 to 12.75 is called an *interval* and the end numbers are called *limits*. The size is 0.40 ($= 12.75 - 12.35$). The first *midpoint* is 12.55 [$= (12.35 + 12.75)/2$]. *Relative frequency* is the number of observations for each interval divided by all observations. Graphical representations of relative frequency distributions are called *histograms*. Figure 5.1, which plots percent observations against price ($/roll), is a histogram. If the relative frequencies are consecutively summed, a *cumulative frequency* results. That is shown by the dashed line and right-hand scale of Fig. 5.1. If these data are considered representative of the parent population, the term *cumulative probability of occurrence* is used. If the midpoints of the histogram cells are joined by a line, and smoothed, the frequency curves will appear as in Fig. 5.2. Figure 5.2 shows several types of frequency curves obtainable from analysis of data. A common type of title for the y-axis would be percentage of observations or count. All these graphical plots can be constructed in a manner similar to Fig. 5.1. Curve construction calls for a trained eye. For instance, if a wealth of data exists, the bimodal or multimodal plot may be evident. But in the absence of an abundance of data, graphical conclusions of this sort are seldom found. For this and other reasons mathematical analyses are resorted to. After the plot has been concluded, it is common to calculate a measure of central tendency, such as

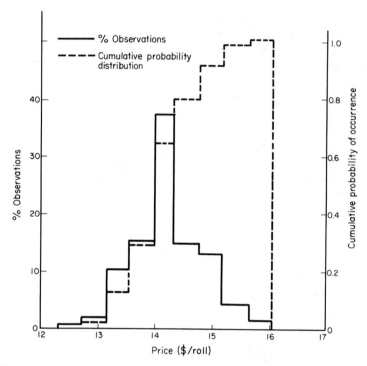

Figure 5.1 Relative frequency curve and cumulative probability of occurrence curve for data.

mean, median, or mode, and a measure of dispersion, such as the standard deviation or range.

An average is typical or representative of a set of data, and is sometimes called the arithmetic *mean,* and is found as

$$\bar{x} = \frac{x_1 + x_2 + \cdots + x_n}{n} = \frac{\sum\limits_{i=1}^{n} x_i}{n} = \frac{\Sigma x}{n} \qquad (5.1)$$

The *median* of data arranged in order of magnitude is the middle value for an odd number of data, or the mean of the two middle values if the set number is even. The *mode* of data is that value which occurs with greatest frequency. The mode may not exist or may not be unique. The set $-1, 0, 2, 4, 6, 6, 7, 8$ has the mean 4, median 5, and mode 6. The set $-1, 0, 2, 4$ has no mode, while the set $-1, 0, 0, 4, 6, 6, 7, 8$ is bimodal with the values 0 and 6.

The degree to which numerical data tend to spread about a mean value is called the dispersion of the data. Various measures of dispersion are available, the most common being the range and standard deviation. The *range* of a set of data is the difference between the largest and smallest numbers in a set. The *standard deviation* of a set of n numbers, $x_1, \ldots, x_n$, is denoted by s and is defined by

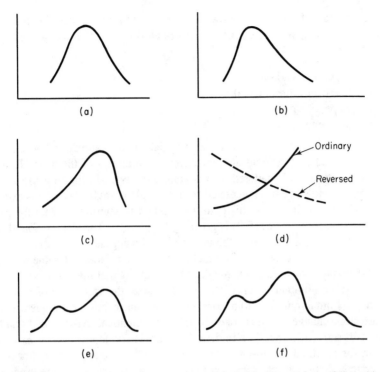

Figure 5.2   Several types of frequency curves obtainable from analysis of data: (a) symmetrical; (b) skewed to the right; (c) skewed to the left; (d) J-shaped; (e) bimodal; (f) multimodal.

$$s = \sqrt{\frac{\Sigma(x_i - \bar{x})^2}{n - 1}} \qquad (5.2)$$

The standard deviation is determined from the mean of the sample. The *variance* of a set of data is defined as the square of the standard deviation or s^2. The set (-1, 0, 2, 4) has the range of 5, $s = 2.22$, and $s^2 = 4.92$.

Plotting of data is an important step in graphical analysis. Despite the ease with which data can be mathematically and statistically analyzed, plotting of two variable data, y versus x for example, is useful for the estimator to gain a "feeling" from the actual data. For mathematical relationships, void of a visual or real-life experience, can lead to misjudgment in estimating. Knowledge, skill, or practice derived from direct observation of or participation in the statistical analysis helps to develop judgment so necessary for estimating.

A graph is a pictorial presentation of the relationship between variables. Most graphs are two-variable, where we presume that x is the independent or controlled variable and y is the dependent variable. Once raw data are gathered, the next steps select the axes and divisions, locate the points, and draw the straight line. A rule of thumb to follow in plotting by eye is to have one-half of the points above the line, and one-half of the points below the line, excluding those that lie on the line. With the line drawn, we find the graphical straight-line equation using

$$y = a + bx \qquad (5.3)$$

where y = dependent variable
a = intercept value at $x = 0$
b = slope, rise/run
x = independent or control variable

Both arithmetic and logarithmic axes are popular in cost estimating and are given by Fig. 5.3. Trial plots should attempt different groupings of the axes. That plot which "straightens out" scattered data is considered best. In Fig. 5.4(a), the axes are arithmetic, and slope b is calculated from the right triangle. The line is extended to the y-axis at $x = 0$, and at this point the value a is determined from the graph. The logarithmic copy of Eq. (5.3) is given by Fig. 5.4(b). The slope is found using the points (x, y) and (x_1, y_1) after the line is plotted using the rule of thumb above.

Figure 5.5 is an example of a practical linear plot. Notice that the points are left on the graph, which indicates the typical variability that may exist with time or cost data. At the nominal 10-in. (250-mm) pipe size, the variability of man-hours is four times from a minimum to maximum, not an unusual event. Frequently, there is a sharp slope change which is not evident by mathematical analysis, and graphical plotting will show this knee-jerk in data. The simple formula $y = a + bx$ is often sufficient for practical day-to-day work, but when the line appears nonlinear or is logarithmic straight, curves other than those using arithmetic scales are used. After the plot and the graphical equation are concluded, attention turns to mathematical analysis; for graphical plots and equations will vary between two estimators, but their mathematical equations should be identical. The graphical plots do identify the type of straight line and the method of least squares is the usual way to analyze data for their equation.

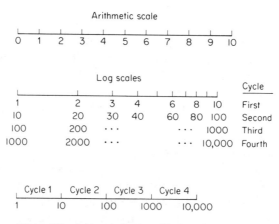

Figure 5.3 Arithmetic and logarithmic scales compared.

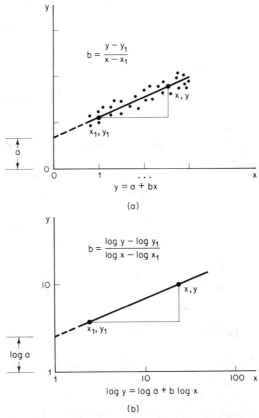

Figure 5.4 Plotting straight lines on (a) arithmetic and (b) logarithmic scales.

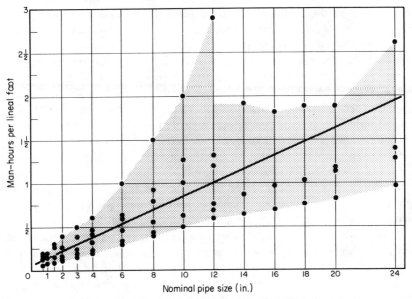

Figure 5.5 Man-hours to handle and install standard pipe.

5.2 LEAST SQUARES AND REGRESSION

The descriptive statistical methods described so far have been concerned with a single variable and its frequency fluctuation. However, many of the problems in the estimating field involve several variables. The next several pages explain simple methods for dealing with data associated with two or three variables. These methods are known as regression models and are useful tools. In regression, on the basis of sample data, the estimator wishes to know the value of a dependent variable, say y, corresponding to a given value of a variable, say x. This can be determined from a least-squares curve which fits the sample data. The resulting curve is called a regression curve of y on x as y is determined from a corresponding value of x. If the variable x is time, the data show the values of y at various times and are known as a time series. Regression lines or a curve y on x or the response function on time is frequently called a trend line and is used for the purposes of prediction and forecasting. Thus regression refers to the average relationship between variables.

5.2.1 Least Squares

The notion of fitting a curve to a set of sufficient points is essentially the problem of finding the parameters of the curve. The best known method is the method of least squares. Since the desired curve or equation is to be used for estimating or predicting purposes, it is useful to require that the curve or equation be so modeled as to make the errors of estimation small. An error of estimation means the difference between an observed value and the corresponding fitted curve value. It will not do to require the sum of these differences or errors to be as small as possible. It is a requirement that the sum of the absolute values of the errors be as small as possible. However, sums of absolute values are not convenient mathematically. The cause of the difficulty is avoided by requiring that the sum of the square of the errors be minimized. If this procedure is followed, the values of parameters give what is known as the *best curve* in the sense of least-squares difference.

This principle of least squares states that if y is a linear function of an independent variable x, the most probable position of line $y = a + bx$ will exist whenever the sum of squares of deviations of all points (x_i, y_i) from the line is a minimum. These deviations are measured in the direction of the y-axis. The underlying assumption is that x is either free of error (a controlled assignment) or subject to negligible error. The value of y is the observed or measured quantity, subject to errors which have to be "eliminated" by this method of least squares. The value y is a random variable value from the y population values corresponding to a given x. For each value x_i we are interested in corresponding $\overline{y}_i$; suppose that our observations consist of pairs of values as x_i, y_i, which are assumed to give a linear plot as in Fig. 5.6. The symbol $\overline{y}_i$ reads "y-bar" and is the average value resulting from the x_i controlled variable. For instance, if the value of $x_i = 5$ and the experiment were repeated 10 times, $\overline{y}_i$ would be the mean value of 10 observations. If a very large number of

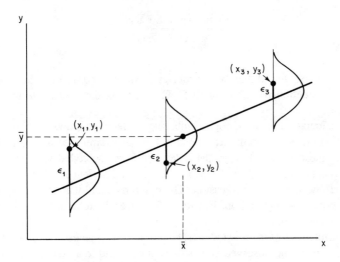

Figure 5.6   Regression line of $y = a + bx$.

experiments were made, a histogram and eventually a normal curve, or bell-shaped curve, could be constructed, as is evident in Fig. 5.6. The bell-shaped curve is positioned with respect to the y-axis value and is considered a random variable. The area under each normal curve is 1. Our problem is to uncover a and b for a best fit. For a general point i on the line, $y_i - (a + bx_i) = 0$, but if an error ϵ_i exists, then $y_i - (a + bx_i) = \epsilon_i$. For n observations we have n equations of

$$y_i - (a + bx_i) = \epsilon_i \tag{5.4}$$

where ϵ_i is the difference between actual observation and regression value of Eq. (5.4). Summing, we can write the sum of squares of these residuals as

$$\sum_{i=1}^{n} \epsilon^2 = \sum_{i=1}^{n} [y_i - (a + bx_i)]^2 \tag{5.5}$$

For a minimum, we insist on

$$\frac{\partial \sum \epsilon^2}{\partial a} = 0, \qquad \frac{\partial \sum \epsilon^2}{\partial b} = 0 \tag{5.6}$$

or

$$n\sum xy - \sum x \sum y = n\sum (x - \bar{x})(y - \bar{y}) \tag{5.7}$$
$$= n(\sum xy - \bar{x}\sum y + \bar{x}\sum y - \bar{y}\sum x)$$

and solving these two normal equations for a and b we have

$$a = \frac{\sum x^2 \sum y - \sum x \sum xy}{n\sum x^2 - (\sum x)^2} \tag{5.8}$$

and

$$b = \frac{n\Sigma xy - \Sigma x \Sigma y}{n\Sigma x^2 - (\Sigma x)^2}$$

These values would then be appropriately substituted into $y = a + bx$. This least-squares equation passes through $(\bar{x}, \bar{y})$, which is the coordinate mean of all observations.

The calculation of these coefficients may be handled manually, with an electronic calculator, or by computer. Table 5.1 is an example of a tabular form in determining these values. If $Y =$ the index and $X =$ the coded year, the equation of the least-squares line is $Y = 84.875 + 2.389 X$. The four left-hand columns of Table 5.1 are necessary for regression. The columns x and y are the data, while x^2 and xy are required computation. Equation (5.8) uses the total of these columns for finding constants a and b.

The limitations of the method must be pointed out. The method of least squares is applicable when the observed values of y_i correspond to assigned (or error-free) values of x_i; the error in y_i (expressed as a variance of y) is assumed to be independent of the level of x. If inferences are to be made about regression, it is also necessary that the values of y_i corresponding to a given x_i be distributed normally, as shown on Fig. 5.6 with the mean of the distribution satisfying the regression equation. It is required also that the variance of the values of y_i for any given value of x be independent of the magnitude of x. While the evidence of this statement can be statistically shown, experience shows that only a comparatively small number of the distributions met within cost estimating can be described by normal distributions. Cost data are limited at the zero end. Distributions influenced by business, engineering, and human factors are generally skew. Despite these drawbacks, the method is widely used. Imperfection, apparently, does not reduce popularity.

5.2.2 Confidence Limits for Regression Values and Prediction Limits for Individual Values

If variations around the universe regression are random, the method of least squares permits the computation of sampling errors and provides for the determination of the reliability of the estimate of the dependent variable from the fitted line. Confidence limits for regression values can be constructed through the extension of simple statistics. The confidence limits for individual regression values and for the straight line are quadratic in form around the sample line of regression. The confidence band for the slope is fan-shaped with the apex at the mean while the confidence limits for the intercept are parallel lines.

The variance of an estimate permits the forming of confidence limits of the estimate. The approach, similar to the variance of a sample, in this case reckons the deviations from a line instead of a mean. The variance of y, estimated by the regres-

Table 5.1. CALCULATION OF REGRESSION COEFFICIENTS

Year, x	Index, y	x^2	xy	$\hat{y}$	$\epsilon = y - \hat{y}$	ϵ^2
0	87	0	0	84.875	2.125	4.516
1	89	1	89	87.264	1.736	3.014
2	90	4	180	89.653	0.347	0.120
3	92	9	276	92.042	−0.042	0.002
4	93	16	372	94.431	−1.431	2.047
5	99	25	495	96.820	2.180	4.752
6	97	36	582	99.209	−2.209	4.879
7	100	49	700	101.598	−1.598	2.554
8	101	64	808	103.987	−2.987	8.922
9	106	81	954	106.376	−0.376	0.141
10	106	100	1,060	108.765	−2.765	7.645
11	109	121	1,199	111.154	−2.154	4.640
12	115	144	1,380	113.543	1.457	2.123
13	118	169	1,534	115.932	2.068	4.277
14	122	196	1,708	118.321	3.679	13.535
105	1524	1015	11,337			63.167

For $Y = a + bx$, the constants

$$a = \frac{\Sigma y \Sigma x^2 - \Sigma x \Sigma xy}{n \Sigma x^2 - (\Sigma x)^2} = \frac{(1524)(1015) - (105)(11,337)}{15(1015) - (105)^2} = 84.875$$

$$b = \frac{n \Sigma xy - \Sigma x \Sigma y}{n \Sigma x^2 - (\Sigma x)^2} = \frac{15(11,337) - (105)(1524)}{15(1015) - (105)^2} = 2.389$$

$\hat{Y} = 84.875 + 2.389X$ or if X is year, then index $= 84.875 + 2.389X$. The forecast mean value for year $x_i = 15$ is $Y = 84.875 + 2.389(15) = 120.71$.

$$S_y = \left(\frac{\Sigma \epsilon^2}{n - 2}\right)^{1/2} = \left(\frac{63.167}{13}\right)^{1/2} = 2.204$$

$$S_{y_i} = S_y \left[\frac{1}{n} + \frac{(x_i - \bar{x})^2}{\Sigma (x - \bar{x})^2}\right]^{1/2} = 2.204 \left[\frac{1}{15} + \frac{(15 - 7)^2}{280}\right]^{1/2} = 1.198$$

For degrees of freedom $= 13$ and a 5% level of significance, $t = 2.160$. The confidence interval is $120.71 \pm 2.160(1.198) = (118.122, 123.298)$. For a single estimated value of y_i for $x_i = 15$,

$$S_{y_i} = S_y \left[1 + \frac{1}{n} + \frac{(x_i - \bar{x})^2}{\Sigma (x - \bar{x})^2}\right]^{1/2} = 2.204 \left(1 + \frac{1}{15} + \frac{64}{280}\right)^{1/2} = 2.508$$

The prediction interval is $120.71 \pm 2.160(2.508) = (115.293, 126.127)$. The confidence interval for the slope and intercept are

$$S_b = \frac{S_y}{[\Sigma (x - \bar{x})^2]^{1/2}} = \frac{2.204}{(280)^{1/2}} = 0.132$$

slope interval $= 2.389 \pm 2.160(0.132) = (2.103, 2.674)$

$$S_a = S_y \left[\frac{1}{n} + \frac{x^2}{\Sigma (x - \bar{x})^2}\right]^{1/2} = 2.204 \left(\frac{1}{15} + \frac{49}{280}\right)^{1/2} = 1.083$$

intercept interval $= 84.875 \pm 2.160(1.083) = (82.536, 87.214)$

sion line, is the sum of squares of deviations divided by the number of degrees of freedom available for calculating the regression line, or

$$s_y^2 = \frac{\Sigma \epsilon_i^2}{\nu} \tag{5.9}$$

where s_y^2 is the variance around the regression line and ϵ_i is as defined previously by Eq. 5.5. Only two bits of information are required to determine the regression line: means $(\bar{x}, \bar{y})$ and either slope b or intercept a. With n as the number of paired observations, ν is defined as

$$\nu = n - 2 \tag{5.10}$$

where ν represents the degrees of freedom. Also,

$$s_y^2 = \frac{\Sigma \epsilon_i^2}{n - 2} \tag{5.11}$$

Defining

$$s_{\bar{y}}^2 = \frac{s_y^2}{n} \tag{5.12}$$

where $s_{\bar{y}}^2$ is the variance of the mean value of y or $\bar{y}$.

It is now possible to write the confidence limits for $\bar{y}$. A table of Student's t-distribution and of the values of t corresponding to various values of the probability α (level of significance) and a given number of degrees of freedom ν is found in Appendix II. With this t-value we state that the true value of $\bar{y}$ lies within the interval

$$\bar{y} \pm t s_{\bar{y}} \tag{5.13}$$

The probability of being wrong is equal to the level of significance of the value of t. As the regression line must pass through the mean, an error in the value of $\bar{y}$ leads to a constant error in y for all points on the line. The line is then moved up or down without change in slope.

If limits for an individual value are desired, a different approach must be asserted. The statement that usually describes the *limits* for individual values goes like this: If we use the sample line of regression to estimate a particular value for y, we add to the error of the sample line of the regression some measure of the possible deviation of the individual value from the regression value. For individual values a new set of parabolic loci may be viewed as prediction limits. Figure 5.7 shows the prediction loci for individual values as well as the confidence loci for average values. It will be noted from the figure that the prediction limits for y get wider as x deviates from its mean, both positively and negatively. This means that predictions of the dependent variable are subject to the least error when the independent variable is near its mean and are subject to the greatest error when the independent variable is distant from its mean.

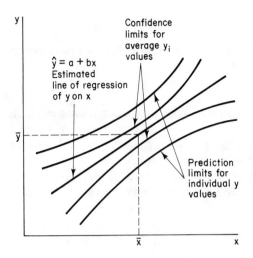

Figure 5.7 Confidence bands for average values and prediction limits for individual values.

If we require an estimate of the confidence limits corresponding to any x_i, we calculate the limits for $\hat{y}_i$ (strictly speaking, an estimate). The variance of the estimate of this mean value is

$$s^2_{y_i} = s^2_y \left[\frac{1}{n} + \frac{(x_i - \bar{x})^2}{\Sigma(x - \bar{x})^2} \right] \tag{5.14}$$

where $s^2_{y_i}$ denotes the variance of each mean value of y. A new $s^2_{y_i}$ is computed for each x-value. The confidence interval for the mean estimated value of y_i corresponding to specific x_i is

$$y_i \pm ts_{y_i} \tag{5.15}$$

The interior confidence limits of Fig. 5.7 correspond to Eq. (5.15).

For a predetermined level of significance we are able to predict the limits within which a future mean estimated value of y_i will lie with an appropriate chance of error.

We can find the prediction interval of a single estimated value of $\hat{y}_i$ using the variance of a single value, which has as its variance

$$s^2_{y_i} = s^2_y \left[1 + \frac{1}{n} + \frac{(x_i - \bar{x})^2}{\Sigma(x - \bar{x})^2} \right] \tag{5.16}$$

where $s^2_{y_i}$ is the variance of individual value of y. This variance is larger than $s^2_{y_i}$ because the variance of the single value is equal to the variance of the mean plus the variance of $\hat{y}$ estimated by the line or

$$s_{y_i}^2 = s_{y_f}^2 + s_y^2 \tag{5.17}$$

Each x requires a separate value of $s_{y_i}^2$. The prediction interval for a single value is greater too, or

$$y_i \pm ts_{y_i} \tag{5.18}$$

In Fig. 5.7 the external lines are computed using Eq. (5.18). The terms *confidence* and *prediction* interval have different meanings. A confidence interval deals with an expected average Y value. A prediction interval deals with a single Y value. The prediction interval is greater in magnitude.

The variance of the intercept a is a particular case of the variance of any mean estimated $\hat{y}_i$. If we substitute $x_i = 0$ in Eq. (5.14), the variance of intercept a is

$$s_a^2 = s_y^2 \left[\frac{1}{n} + \frac{\bar{x}^2}{\Sigma (x - \bar{x})^2} \right] \tag{5.19}$$

Its confidence band is given by

$$a \pm ts_a \tag{5.20}$$

and note Fig. 5.8(a) which corresponds to Eq. (5.19).

The variance of slope b is given as

$$s_b^2 = \frac{s_y^2}{\Sigma (x - \bar{x})^2} \tag{5.21}$$

Its confidence band is given by

$$b \pm ts_b \tag{5.22}$$

and note Fig. 5.8(b) which corresponds to Eq. (5.21).

The confidence band for the slope is represented by a double-fan-shaped area with the apex at the mean.

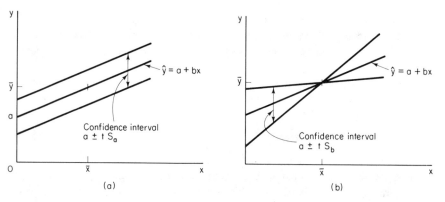

Figure 5.8   (a) Confidence interval for intercept a; (b) confidence interval for slope b.

For all confidence intervals in this section, the number of degrees of freedom is $v = n - 2$.

Table 5.1 demonstrates the manual calculation of regression values, namely, the parameters a and b; the $\hat{y}$ column is calculated using the regression equation $\hat{y} = 84.875 + 2.389x$. For example if $x = 1$, $\hat{y} = 87.264$. This calculation is repeated for each observation of x. The $\epsilon = y - \hat{y}$ column is the error difference between the observed and regression value. The right column is the square of the error. The sum 63.167 is used to calculate s_y. Confidence and prediction intervals are found for $x = 15$ and given in Table 5.1.

5.2.3 Curvilinear Regression and Transformation

The world of linearity, largely an imaginary one, is a tidy and manageable world about which generalizations can be asserted with confidence. Many prefabricated tools are known that can be used with these assumptions. The function $y = a + bx$ is a characterization which is frequently employed for known nonlinear situations. It seems that electronic computers and a greater awareness are forcing a reevaluation of linearities. A listing would show for cost estimating purposes the following nonlinear relationships:

$$y = ae^{bx} \quad \text{semilog*} \tag{5.23}$$

$$y = ab^x \quad \text{exponential} \tag{5.24}$$

$$y = ax^b \quad \text{power} \tag{5.25}$$

$$y = a + \frac{b}{x} \quad \text{reciprocal } x \tag{5.26}$$

$$y = \frac{1}{(a + bx)} \quad \text{reciprocal } y \tag{5.27}$$

$$y = \frac{x}{(a + bx)} \quad \text{hyperbolic} \tag{5.28}$$

$$y = a + b_1 x + b_2 x^2 + \cdots \text{polynomial} \tag{5.29}$$

The exponential and power fit Eqs. (5.24) and (5.25) are used frequently. The regression formulas of Sec. 2.1 can be made to work with these curvilinear models. First, it is noted that these equations appear like $y = a + bx$ if transformed. The exponential function $y = ab^x$ transforms to

$$\log y = \log a + x \log b$$

*The three exponential curves $y = ae^{bx}$, $y = 10^{a+bx}$, and $y = a(10)^{bx}$ are equivalent. If any two points are chosen and the constants for each curve determined so it passes through these points, the curves are equal.

We let $y = \log y$, $a = \log a$, $b = \log b$, and $x = x$. This plots as a straight line when plotted on arithmetic–logarithmic scales. Similar to Eq. (5.8), the values of the parameters of Eq. (5.24) can be solved using

$$\log a = \frac{\Sigma x^2 \Sigma \log Y - \Sigma x \Sigma x \log y}{n \Sigma x^2 - (\Sigma x)^2}$$

(5.30)

$$\log b = \frac{n \Sigma x \log y - \Sigma x \Sigma \log y}{n \Sigma x^2 - (\Sigma x)^2}$$

The power function $y = ax^b$ is transformed from a curved line on arithmetic scales to a straight line on log-log scales if we let $y = \log y$, $a = \log a$, and $x = \log x$. Intercept and slope equations can be found making these substitutions into Eq. (5.8).

$$\log a = \frac{\Sigma (\log x)^2 \Sigma \log y - \Sigma \log x \Sigma (\log x \log y)}{n \Sigma (\log x)^2 - (\Sigma \log x)^2}$$

(5.31)

$$b = \frac{n \Sigma (\log x \log y) - \Sigma \log x \Sigma \log y}{n \Sigma (\log x)^2 - (\Sigma \log x)^2}$$

The power equation is often used to model *learning*. If we repeat the production of an article, it takes less time to manufacture subsequent products, which is known as learning.

Assume that we have five sets of experiences, or the unit number x and the man-hours, y, to make that unit. Data are (10, 510), (30, 210), (100, 190), (150, 125), and (300, 71). Thus the 10th and 300th units require 510 and 71 hours, respectively. Table 5.2 shows the calculation. The first two columns are the original units, while the four right columns are the transformed calculations. The transformed and original unit equations also give identical results. Let $x = 500$th unit; then

$$\log y = 3.1921 - 0.515 \log 500 = 1.8021$$
$$\text{antilog } y = 63.4 \text{ hours}$$

Also

$$y = 1556(500)^{-0.515} = 63.4 \text{ hours in original units}$$

which shows the agreement.

Each of these functions can be statistically evaluated for the fitted data, such as

Coefficients of the equations

Listing of calculated estimates

Standard error of y, $\Sigma \epsilon_i^2 = (y_i - \hat{y})^2$

Squared correlation coefficient

95% confidence limits values for y

Computer programs do this calculation where the work is large.

Normally, the *best fit* line is judged by the smallest value of the standard error, while other computed values provide an intuitive feel for how good the correlation

Table 5.2.   LEAST-SQUARES ANALYSIS OF ACTUAL COST DATA TO FIND INITIAL VALUE
AND LEARNING SLOPE

Given: $y = ax^b$

or

$$\log y = \log a + b \log x$$

which is of the form

$$y = a + bx$$

Let $y = \log y$, $a = \log a$ intercept, $b = b$ slope, $x = \log x$, and $n =$ sample size.

Unit, x	Man-Hours, y	$x = \log x$	$y = \log y$	$(\log x)^2$	$\log x \log y$
10	510	1.0000	2.7076	1.0000	2.7076
30	210	1.4771	2.3222	2.1818	3.4301
100	190	2.0000	2.2788	4.0000	4.5576
150	125	2.1761	2.0969	4.7354	4.5631
300	71	2.4771	1.8513	6.1360	4.5859
		9.1303	11.2568	18.0532	19.8443

$$\log a = \frac{\Sigma (\log x)^2 \Sigma \log y - \Sigma \log x \Sigma (\log x \log y)}{n \Sigma (\log x)^2 - (\Sigma \log x)^2}$$

$$\log a = \frac{(18.0532)(11.2568) - (9.1303)(19.8443)}{5(18.0532) - (9.1303)^2} = 3.1921$$

$$b = \frac{n \Sigma (\log x \log y) - \Sigma \log x \Sigma \log y}{n \Sigma (\log x)^2 - (\Sigma \log x)^2}$$

$$= \frac{5(19.8443) - (9.1303)(11.2568)}{5(18.0532) - (9.1303)^2} = -0.515$$

Then

$\log y = 3.1921 - 0.515 \log x$ (in logarithm units)

antilog $a = 1556$ (initial value at $x = 1$)

$y = 1556x^{-0.515}$ in original units

What is the estimate for $x = 350$ units?

In logarithm units:

$\log y = 3.1921 - 0.515 \log 350 = 1.8819$

antilog $y = 76.19$ hours

In original units:

$$y = 1556(350)^{-0.515} = 76.19 \text{ hours}$$

obtained really is. Polynomial regression, that is, where for any x the mean of the distribution of y's is given by $a + b_1x + b_2x^2 + b_3x^3 + \cdots + b_px^p$, is used to obtain approximations whenever the functional form of the regression curve is a mystery. Estimators plot data a variety of ways hoping to "straighten out" an arithmetic curve via semilog or log-log plots, for example. If sets of paired data straighten out on semilog paper, the analyst would conclude that the form is exponential or $y =$

ae^{bx} and he would be tempted to apply least-squares methods that utilized this form to the data.

Suppose that coded data were obtained as follows, where y, or dollars, was assumed to be related to small gas-engine horsepower as $y = a + bx^2$:

x	Observed Value, y_i	Error-Free Value, $\hat{y}$	Deviation, $y_i - \hat{y}$
0	1	a	$1 - a$
1	1.4	$a + b$	$1.4 - (a + b)$
2	1.8	$a + 4b$	$1.8 - (a + 4b)$
3	2.2	$a + 9b$	$2.2 - (a + 9b)$

The sum of the squares of the deviations is

$$\Sigma \, \epsilon^2 = (1 - a)^2 + (1.4 - a - b)^2 + (1.8 - a - 4b)^2 + (2.2 - a - 9b)^2$$

For a minimum we are required to satisfy

$$\frac{\partial \Sigma \, \epsilon^2}{\partial a} = 0 \quad \text{and} \quad \frac{\partial \Sigma \, \epsilon^2}{\partial b} = 0 \tag{5.32}$$

or $(1 - a) + (1.4 - a - b) + (1.8 - a - 4b) + (2.2 - a - 9b) = 0$ and $(1.4 - a - b) + 4(1.8 - a - 4b) + 9(2.2 - a - 9b) = 0$. This reduces to the normal equations

$$4a + 14b = 6.4$$
$$14a + 98b = 28.4$$

Hence $a = 1.175$ and $b = 0.122$. When substituted back into the general form, the fitted equation becomes $y = 1.175 + 0.122x^2$. A better fit may be obtained from an equation of a different form or $y = a + bx + cx^2$.

The previous little problem was straightforward, but the application of the method of least squares to nonlinear relations usually requires a good deal of computational effort, computers notwithstanding. In most cases we are able to transform or rectify a nonlinear relation to a straight-line relation. This manipulation simplifies handling of the data and permits a graphical presentation which may be revealing for certain facts. With a rectified straight line, extrapolation is simpler, and the computation of certain other supportive statistics, such as the standard deviation or confidence limits, is simpler.

Now these previous functions indicated a regression of y on x which was linear in some fashion. Sometimes a clear relationship is not evident, and a general polynomial is selected. A predicting equation of the polynomial form [see Eq. (5.29)] requires a set of data consisting of n points (x_i, y_i) and we estimate the coefficients $a, b_1, b_2, \ldots, b_p$ of the pth-degree polynomial by minimizing

$$\sum_{i=1}^{n} [y_i - (a + b_1x + b_2x^2 + \cdots + b_px^p)]^2 \tag{5.33}$$

according to

$$\frac{\partial \Sigma \epsilon^2}{\partial a}, \frac{\partial \Sigma \epsilon^2}{\partial b_1}, \frac{\partial \Sigma \epsilon^2}{\partial b_2}, \cdots, \frac{\partial \Sigma \epsilon^2}{\partial b_p} = 0 \qquad (5.34)$$

which is the least-squares criterion by minimizing the sum of squares of the vertical distances from the points to the curve. This results in $p + 1$ normal equations of the shape

$$\Sigma y = na + b_1 \Sigma x + \cdots + b_p \Sigma x^p$$
$$\Sigma xy = a \Sigma x + b_1 \Sigma x^2 + \cdots + b_p \Sigma x^{p+1}$$

$$\cdot \qquad (5.35)$$
$$\cdot$$
$$\cdot$$

$$\Sigma x^p y = a \Sigma x^p + b_1 \Sigma x^{p+1} + \cdots + b_p \Sigma x^{2p}$$

where summation notation has been eliminated. This is now $p + 1$ linear equations in $p + 1$ unknowns $a, b_1, \ldots, b_p$.

As an example, consider the following: An aircraft manufacturer has accumulated data on the chem-milling operation of steel panels, and paired sets of data are cost per square foot, dollars per square foot, and depth of cut, inches—(0.01, 7.0), (0.02, 8.4), (0.03, 9.2), (0.04, 10.1), (0.05, 10.3), (0.20, 26.2)—and resultant tabulations, very similar to previous least-squares calculations of Table 5.1, reveal $\Sigma x = 0.35$, $\Sigma x^2 = 0.0455$, $\Sigma x^3 = 0.008225$, $\Sigma x^4 = 0.00016979$, $\Sigma y = 71.2$, $\Sigma xy = 6.673$, and $\Sigma x^2 y = 11.0225$. With these values we are ready to solve the following system of three linear equations,

$$6a + 0.35b_1 + 0.0455b_2 = 71.2$$
$$0.35a + 0.0455b_1 + 0.008225b_2 = 6.673$$
$$0.0455a + 0.008225b_1 + 0.0016979b_2 = 11.0225$$

for which $a = -31.73$, $b_1 = 1660$, and $b_2 = -7025$ and the predicting equation becomes

$$y = -31.73 + 1660x - 7025x^2$$

In practice it may be difficult to determine the degree of the polynomial to fit data, but it is always possible to find a polynomial of degree at most $n - 1$ that will pass through each of n points, although what we want is the lowest degree that describes our problem.

5.2.4 Correlation

It has been seen how the method of regression shows the relationship to one independent variable which can be considered linearly related. There is a closely related measure, called correlation, which tells how well the variables are satisfied by a linear relationship. If the values of the variables satisfy an equation exactly, then the variables are perfectly correlated. When two variables are involved the statistician refers to simple correlation and simple regression. When more than two variables are involved it is referred to as multiple regression and multiple correlation. In this section only simple correlation is considered.

Figure 5.9 indicates the location of points on an arithmetic coordinate system. If all the points in a scatter diagram appear to lie near a line as in Fig. 5.9(b) or (d), the correlation is presumed to be linear and a linear equation is appropriate for regression or estimation. If there is no relationship indicated between the variables as in Fig. 5.9(c), there is no correlation; i.e, the data are uncorrelated. In the case of Fig. 5.9(b), the correlation coefficient is negative linear, while for Fig. 5.9(d) a positive linear correlation coefficient is found.

With a fitted curve from data it is possible to distinguish between the deviations of the y-observations from the regression line and the total variation of the y-observations about their mean. A calculated difference between the two variations gives the amount of variation accounted for by regression, and the higher this value, the better the fit or correlation. For $y = a + bx$ no correlation exists if $b = 0$ as in Fig. 5.9(c) and the line plots as a horizontal line. Thus x and y are independent.

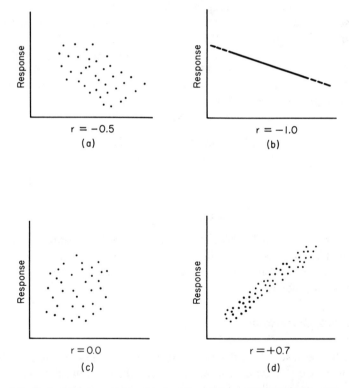

Figure 5.9 Scatter diagrams showing levels of correlation coefficients: (a) negative linear correlation; (b) negative linear correlation; (c) no correlation; (d) positive linear correlation.

There is no correlation of x on y if x is independent of y. These two statements are mathematically

$$\frac{n\Sigma xy - \Sigma x\Sigma y}{n\Sigma x^2 - (\Sigma x)^2} = 0 \tag{5.36}$$

and

$$\frac{n\Sigma xy - \Sigma x\Sigma y}{n\Sigma y^2 - (\Sigma y)^2} = 0 \tag{5.37}$$

For no correlation the product of Eqs. (5.36) and (5.37), or the product of the slopes, is zero. Conversely, for perfect correlation all the points lie exactly on each of the two regression lines and their lines coincide, or

$$\frac{n\Sigma xy - \Sigma x\Sigma y}{n\Sigma x^2 - (\Sigma x)^2} \times \frac{n\Sigma xy - \Sigma x\Sigma y}{n\Sigma y^2 - (\Sigma y)^2} = 1 \tag{5.38}$$

We call the square root of this product the correlation coefficient and denote it by r:

$$r = \frac{n\Sigma xy - \Sigma x\Sigma y}{\{[n\Sigma x^2 - (\Sigma x)^2][n\Sigma y^2 - (\Sigma y)^2]\}^{1/2}} \tag{5.39}$$

which is a computation equation form. Correlation is concerned only with the association between variables, and r must lie in the range $0 \le |r| \le 1$. Using the data from Table 5.1, the correlation coefficient may be found as an example. Recollecting that $n = 15$, $\Sigma xy = 11{,}337$, $\Sigma x = 105$, $\Sigma y = 1524$, $\Sigma x^2 = 1015$, and $\Sigma y^2 = 156{,}500$, then

$$r = \frac{(15)(11{,}337) - (105)(1524)}{\{[(15)(1015) - (105)^2][15(156{,}500) - (1524)^2]\}^{1/2}}$$
$$= +0.98$$

which is a high score for correlation. The magnitude of the correlation coefficient r determines the strength of the relationship, while the sign of r tells one whether the dependent variable tends to increase or decrease with the independent variable. The estimator may realize that r is a useful measure of the strength of the relationship between two variables—only if, however, the variables are linearly related. The value of r will be equal to $+1$ or -1 if and only if the points of the scatter lie perfectly on the straight line, which is unlikely in cost estimating.

The interpretation of the correlation coefficient as a measure of the strength of the linear relationship between two variables is a purely mathematical interpretation and is without any cause or effect implications.

5.2.5 Multiple Linear Regression

It may happen that the method of least squares for estimating one variable by a related variable yields inadequate success. Although the relationship may be linear, frequently there is no single variable sufficiently related to the variable being estimated to yield good results. The extension is natural to two or more independent variables. As linear functions are simple to work with and estimating experience shows that many sets of variables are approximately linear related, or assumed so for a short period of time, it is reasonable to estimate the desired variable by means of a linear function of the remaining variables. Problems of multiple regression involve more than two variables but are still treated in a manner analogous to that for two variables. For example, there may be a cost relationship between differential profit (DP), investment (I), and market saturation (MS) which can be described by the equation $DP = a + b_1 I + b_2 MS$, which is called a linear equation in the variables DP, I, and MS. The constants are noted by a, b_1, and b_2. This kind of analysis can explain variations in one dependent variable by adding together the effects of two or more independent variables. It is not limited to problems involving a time trend. Time is a catchall, and it takes into account gradual changes that may be due to different factors both known and suspected. For three or more variables, a regression plane is a generalization of the regression line for two variables, as previously considered. We are concerned with the linear regression function of the form

$$y = a + b_1 x_1 + b_2 x_2 + \ldots + b_k x_k \qquad (5.40)$$

where $x_0 = 1$, a is a constant, and b_1, b_2, . . . , b_k are partial regression coefficients. This is a plane in $k + 1$ dimension. We do not say that the result so obtained is the best functional relationship. We simply state that, given this assumed function and criterion, we have chosen the best estimate of the parameters.

Regression analysis requires the following assumptions:

1. The x_j-values are controlled and/or observed without error. Perfection remains a difficult requirement within cost-estimating practices, but it is nominally met.
2. The regression of y on x_j is linear.
3. The deviations $y - [j|x_j]$ are mutually independent.
4. These deviations have the same variance whatever the value of x_j.
5. These deviations are normally distributed.
6. The data are taken from a population about which inferences are to be drawn.
7. There are no extraneous variables which make the relationship of little intrinsic value.

The plane in the $k + 1$ dimension passes through the mean of all observed values, similar to the two-variable case, and

$$\bar{y} = a + b_1 \bar{x}_1 + b_2 \bar{x}_2 + \ldots + b_k \bar{x}_k \qquad (5.41)$$

Reworking Eqs. (5.40) and (5.41), we have

$$a = \bar{y} - b_1 \bar{x}_1 - b_2 \bar{x}_2 - \ldots - b_k \bar{x}_k \qquad (5.42)$$
$$y - \bar{y} = b_1(x_1 - \bar{x}_1) + b_2(x_2 - \bar{x}_2) + \ldots + b_k(x_k - \bar{x}_k) \qquad (5.43)$$

As before, the coefficients are determined using the method of least squares. To illustrate we consider the case of two independent variables, and we have

$$y = a + b_1 x_1 + b_2 x_2 \tag{5.44}$$

with n sets (y, x_1, x_2) of points at this point. In each set the error is given as

$$\epsilon = y - (a + b_1 x_1 + b_2 x_2) \tag{5.45}$$

and the sum of squares of errors in the n sets is

$$\Sigma \epsilon^2 = \Sigma [y - (a + b_1 x_1 + b_2 x_2)]^2 \tag{5.46}$$

We minimize $\Sigma \epsilon^2$ as before, which requires that the partial derivatives of $\Sigma \epsilon^2$ with respect to a, b_1, and b_2 be zero:

$$\frac{\partial(\Sigma \epsilon^2)}{\partial a} = \Sigma [y - (a + b_1 x_1 + b_2 x_2)] = 0$$

$$\frac{\partial(\Sigma \epsilon^2)}{\partial b_1} = \Sigma x_1 [y - (a + b_1 x_1 + b_2 x_1)] = 0 \tag{5.47}$$

$$\frac{\partial(\Sigma \epsilon^2)}{\partial b_2} = \Sigma x_2 [y - (a + b_1 x_1 + b_2 x_2)] = 0$$

Subscripts for summation were dropped for convenience. If we keep x_2 constant, the graph of y versus x_1 is a straight line with slope b_1. If we keep x_1 constant, the graph y versus x_2 is linear with slope b_2. Due to the fact that y varies partially because of variation in x_1 and partially because of variation in x_2, we call b_1 and b_2 the partial regression coefficients of y on x_1 keeping x_2 constant and of y on x_2 keeping x_1 constant. The normal equations corresponding to the least-squares plane for the y-, x_1-, and x_2-coordinate systems are

$$\Sigma y = na + b_1 \Sigma x_1 + b_2 \Sigma x_2$$

$$\Sigma x_1 y = a \Sigma x_1 + b_1 \Sigma x_1^2 + b_2 \Sigma x_1 x_2 \tag{5.48}$$

$$\Sigma x_2 y = a \Sigma x_2 + b_1 \Sigma x_1 x_2 + b_2 \Sigma x_2^2$$

The solution of this system of three simultaneous equations gives the values of a, b_1, and b_2 for Eq. (5.44) and is referred to as y on x_1 and x_2. This is a regression plane, but more complicated regression surfaces can be imagined with four-, five-, ... dimensional space. The problem given earlier as a polynomial has been solved again by multiple linear regression. Table 5.3 shows the procedure to distinguish the gross product in manufacturing, $\$10^9$, the index of output per man-hour, and worker productivity. These were assumed to be the influencing variables.

5.2.6 Computer Statements

The arithmetic in the simple linear or nonlinear regression equations is digestible, but when an equation is to consider many variables the situation seems impossible. The electronic computers, capable of making short work out of massive computations, make it possible to find linear and nonlinear regression equations of 150 variables or more with all the accompanying statistical measures of reliability and to select the best equation meeting the statistical attributes. This has without a

Table 5.3. MULTIPLE LINEAR REGRESSION

Gross Product in Manufacturing, y ($\$10^9$)	Index of Output per Man-Hour, x_1	Productivity, x_2	Computations Required in Solution for y on x_1 and x_2
92.6	81.5	1.48	$\Sigma\, y = 1756.30$
102.0	83.7	1.64	
105.0	86.1	1.74	$\Sigma\, x_1 = 1520.1000$
111.9	87.6	1.84	$\Sigma\, x_1^2 = 156{,}872.75$
103.8	91.2	1.89	$\Sigma\, x_2 = 32.37$
116.7	96.3	1.96	$\Sigma\, x_2^2 = 72.01092$
116.4	95.0	2.07	
117.8	100.0	2.20	$\Sigma\, x_1 y = 180{,}565.04$
109.7	103.9	2.28	$\Sigma\, x_2 y = 3860.8860$
121.8	107.2	2.34	$\Sigma\, x_1 x_2 = 3357.3750$
122.0	108.8	2.44	
122.0	113.1	2.49	
134.1	118.4	2.57	
138.5	121.6	2.67	
142.0	125.7	2.76	

The normal equations are

$$17{,}563.30 = 15a + 1520.10b_1 + 32.37b_2$$
$$180{,}565.04 = 1520.10 + 156{,}872.75b_1 + 3357.3750b_2$$
$$3860.886 = 32.37a + 3357.3750b_1 + 72.0109b_2$$

for which

$$a = 29.1181$$
$$b_1 = 0.7052$$
$$b_2 = 7.658$$

and the multiple linear equation becomes

$$y = 29.1181 + 0.7052x_1 + 7.6458x_2$$

doubt created many benefits to cost estimating, but unfortunately also many pitfalls. Perhaps the greatest danger is encountered at the outset when the source and type of data are being selected. Despite the excellence of computation, final results are entirely dependent on the reliability of data used, the interpretation of the computations, and judgment as to reasonableness of the conclusion. Thus an idea of causation must precede statistics.

5.3 MOVING AVERAGES AND SMOOTHING

The estimator may be concerned with periodic observations of labor, material cost, overhead, product demand, and other prices. The characteristics of these observations are described as constant, variable, trend cycle, seasonal, or regular. A *trend cycle* or *seasonal* term suggests a *time series* to a set of observations taken at specific times. Examples of time series are the monthly demand for motorcycles, and the total of monthly costs of expenses in a manufacturing department.

The simplest of the time-series cases is the algebraic model using the mean. For the trivial case of constant mean, or nearly so over the time interval for which the forecast is required, the dependent variable is nonsensitive. Samples of pictorial graphs where time is the abscissa and a response is the ordinate are given by Fig. 5.10. The simple case, constant with no trend, has already been discussed. The linear model with a trend is found more widely than the quadratic and exponential models.

Movements are generally considered to be cyclical only if they recur after constant time intervals. An important example of cyclical movements are the so-called business cycles representing intervals of boom, recession, depression, and business recovery. Seasonal movements are well known and refer to identical or nearly identical patterns which a time series appears to follow during corresponding months of successive years. These events may be illustrated by peak summer production preceding the Christmas demand. Certain of these effects are sometimes superimposed on other effects, for example, Fig. 5.10(f) where a linear and a cyclic pattern are superimposed.

Consider the following data:

PLASTIC SHEET COST DATA

Years Ago	Price ($/100 lb)
6	$60.20
5	60.50
4	68.70
3	60.24
2	60.55
1	62.32
Now	75.71

The analyst may assume that the computation of moving average at any single point in time should ideally place no more weight on current observations than those achieved some time previously. This is the major logic for the moving average. A reasonable estimate, given by the average price per plastic sheet, is $64 and the forecast for any future observation could be that same value. The actual average of N most recent observation computed at time t is given by

$$M_a = \frac{x_t - x_{t-1} + \cdots + x_{t-N-1}}{N} \tag{5.49}$$

where M_a = moving-average value

  x = observation

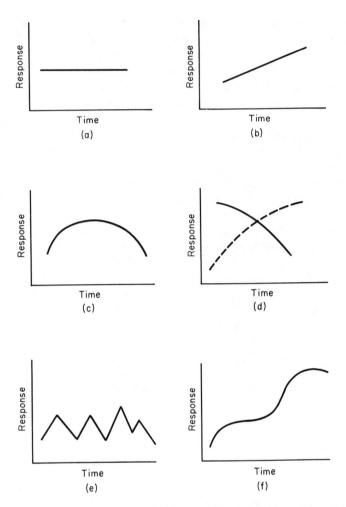

Figure 5.10 Typical time-series models: (a) constant (no trend); (b) linear; (c) quadratic; (d) exponential; (e) cyclic or seasonal; (f) linear and cyclic.

$$t = \text{time-series period number}$$
$$N = \text{number of observations}$$

with the restriction that the number of terms in the numerator be equal to N and x_t be the latest term added. Another arrangement, of course, is to use the most recent three, four, or five observations and divide the sum by 3, 4, or 5. For example, the model can be arranged to another form

$$M_a = M_{t-1} - \frac{x_t - x_{t-N}}{N} \tag{5.50}$$

for t, $N = 1, 2, 3, \ldots$, and $t > N$. If a 3-year moving average were required, the data would be arranged as follows:

Date, t	Data, x_t	3-Year Moving Total	3-Year Moving Average
1	60.20	$\cdots$	$\cdots$
2	60.50	$\cdots$	$\cdots$
3	68.70	189.40	63.13
4	60.24	189.41	63.14
5	60.55	189.43	63.14
6	62.32	187.30	62.43
7	75.71	192.46	64.15
8	$\cdots$	$\cdots$	$\cdots$
$\cdots$			

It is seen that the matter of computing a moving average is simple and sufficiently straightforward for computer processing or for manual computation.

One of the difficulties with moving averages is that the rate of response is sometimes difficult to change. The rate of response is controlled by the choice of N of the observations to be averaged. If N is arbitrarily chosen large, the estimate is stable. If N is selected small, fluctuations due to random error or some other cause can be expected. The estimator is able to take advantage of these properties, for if the process is considered constant, he or she may wish to choose a large value of N to have accurate estimates of the mean. However, if the process is fluctuating, small values of N provide faster indications of response.

For most estimating problems some type of moving average is desired that reflects historical and current trends. A smoothing function may be defined as

$$S_t(x) = \alpha x_t + (1 - \alpha)S_{t-1}(x) \tag{5.51}$$

where $S_t(x)$ = smoothed value

α = smoothing constant, $0 \le \alpha \le 1$.

The α is like but not exactly equal to the fraction $1/N$ in the moving-average method. Whenever this operation is performed on a sequence of observations, it is called exponential smoothing. The new smoothed value is a linear combination of all past observations. Statistically speaking, the expectation of this function is equal to the expectation of the data, which is its average.

When the smoothing constant α is small, the function $S(x)$ behaves as if the function is providing the average of past data. When the smoothing constant is large, $S(x)$ responds rapidly to changes in trend. While no precise statements can be made regarding this smoothing, the following generally describes the effect of smoothing constant on time-series data:

	Variation in α Values		
Drift in Actual Data	Small $\alpha \approx 0$	Little $\alpha \approx 0.5$	Large $\alpha \approx 1$
None	None	None	None
Moderate	Very small	Small	Moderate
Large	Small	Moderate	Large

As an example of the exponential smoothing for $\alpha = 0.2$, the following is presented:

EXPONENTIAL SMOOTHING

Date, t	Data, x_t	Smoothed Data, $S_t(x) = 0.2x_t + 0.8S_{t-1}(x)$
...	...	...
10	...	67.38
11	63.2	66.54
12	68.3	66.89
13	65.7	66.66
14	78.4	69.00
...	...	...

For exponential smoothing there are initial conditions that must be established, as a previous value of the smoothing function S_{t-1} is required. If data exist at the time one begins to use exponential smoothing, the best initial value is the average of the most recent end observations $S_{t-1} = M_{t-1}$. If there are no past data to average, smoothing starts with the first observation, and a prediction of the average is required. The prediction may be what the process intended to do. These predictions can also be based on similarity with other processes that have been observed for some time. If there is a great deal of confidence in the prediction of initial conditions, a small value of the smoothing constant, $\alpha \to 0$, would be satisfactory. On the other hand, if there is very little confidence in the initial prediction, it is appropriate to have α as a larger value, $\alpha \to 1$, so that the initial conditions are quickly discounted. This argument is the counter to the argument about flexibility of response to a change of the process. If the estimator believes that the real process is like the prediction, there is little reason to have a change. On the other hand, the contrary viewpoint would have a quick response between the prediction and the real process.

Cycles may be interpreted either of two ways: as deviations from established long-term trend or as significant fluctuation due to some time-series effect. In the case where the cycles are interpreted as deviations from a trend, the peaks and troughs are normally referred to as errors from the estimate and are caused by a collection of unknown factors. However, dependence on long-term data, such as industry-wide sales for a particular product, can also be faulty.

Table 5.4 and Fig. 5.11 picture the monthly rise and fall of the cycles about an increasing linear demand. The high point for annual sales occurs during March (purchased for the summer months ahead) and to a lesser magnitude during the month of December. The least-squares line for these data is total monthly sales = 105,070 + 1392X, where X is the base month 0 at October 2 years ago.

Months following this time reference would be 1, 2, 3, . . . , while months previous would be −1, −2, −3, ... The historical data conclude with July of the present year, and the time index for the next month of August would be 22. The demand would be August sales = 105,070 + 1392(22) = 135,694 motorcycles. Noticing the deviation of the cycles from the trend line, little faith can be given to this estimate for August. In view of the monthly variation, adjustments are called for. The following discusses one method whereby arithmetic adjustments can be made to account for the seasonal or monthly pattern. The quarterly sales are converted to percentage of the yearly sales.

PERCENTAGE OF TOTAL YEARLY SALES BY QUARTERS

	Quarter				
	First	Second	Third	Fourth	Total
3 Years ago	19.4	35.6	28.5	16.5	100
2 Years ago	19.4	34.0	27.6	19.0	100
Last year	19.0	33.6	27.4	20.2	100
Total	57.8	103	83.3	55.7	300
Average, %	19.3	34.3	27.8	18.6	100
Range, %	−0.3, +0.1	−0.9, +1.3	−0.4, +0.7	−2.1, +1.6	

Table 5.4. THOUSAND MOTORCYCLE SALES IN THE UNITED STATES

	3 Years Ago	2 Years Ago	Last Year	This Year
January	46	45	60	54
February	62	78	91	89
March	78	111	121	132
April	99	125	145	154
May	124	154	172	180
June	118	132	161	155
July	102	122	142	135
August	96	119	139	
September	75	93	111	
October	51	82	96	
November	39	51	62	
December	68	96	133	
	950	1208	1433	1584 (projected)

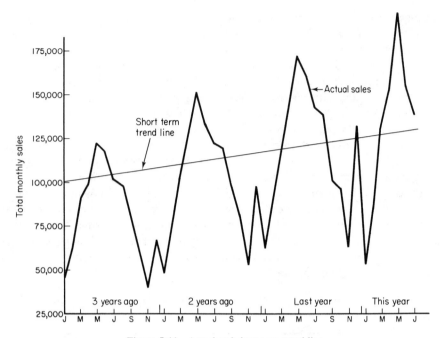

Figure 5.11 Actual and short-term trend line.

The first quarter averages 19.3% of the year's sales with a range of -0.3 and $+0.1\%$. If the range is assumed to represent random fluctuation, the analyst may wonder if this randomness can account for the difference between the first quarter and the fourth. If the analyst compares the first quarter against the second quarter, there is greater justification to suppose a seasonal pattern of sales. The logic of a March quarter sales peak for a product that is essentially a summer vehicle could overcome timidity in view of a lack of data. However, if the range of the data were, say, to illustrate a point, 10% either way for the four quarters, the analyst would be in a weaker position to put much credence in seasonal factors. Nonetheless, the differences are assumed to be relevant, and the next step is to translate the percentages into factors. For example, the first quarter averaged 19.3% of the year, while an average quarter would be 25% of the year. The percentages are translated to a base of 1.0 by multiplying by the number of periods in a year. (If the comparison is on the basis of 3 months, multiply by 4; if on months of the year, by 12, and so forth.) The first quarter with an average of 19.3% of the year would have a seasonal factor of $4 \times 0.193 = 0.772$:

	Quarter			
	First	Second	Third	Fourth
Seasonal factor	0.772	1.372	1.112	0.744

The quarterly sales figures would be converted to the average quarter by dividing by 0.772, 1.372, 1.112, and 0.744, respectively. The next step is the incorporation of exponential smoothing, which uses formula (5.51):

$$\alpha(\text{adjusted sales}) + (1 - \alpha)(\text{previous smoothed value}) \qquad (5.52)$$

If the adjusted sales were 249,000 units for the second quarter and the previous smoothed value was actually 216,000 units, the forecast (with an α of 0.6) for the second quarter is $0.6 \times 249,000 + 0.4 \times 216,000 = 236,000$ units. Although the selection of α has been discussed, it is worthwhile for any real-world problem to forecast sales for a sample of items using different α-values and to compare the results. The value which results in the lowest absolute forecast error is superior.

After the parameters have been chosen (α-value and seasonal factors), the forecast can be made. The actual sales are backcast several periods in the past to provide a basis for smoothing. They are seasonally adjusted by dividing by the seasonal factor, and the smoothing technique is applied to give the next forecast value. The forecast is then readjusted to put the seasonal factor back in by multiplying by the factor. The process is continued for each period as sales are reported. Table 5.5 uses $\alpha = 0.6$. The figure of 216,000 units for the first quarter for "3 Years Ago" was provided by the use of the least-squares equation for the previous 3 months. In starting up the system, the initial figure can be based on the average of the previous 3 or 6 months or another value acceptable to the estimator.

A typical calculation for the adjusted sales of the second quarter for "This Year" is given as

$$\text{actual sales for second quarter} = 489,000 \text{ units}$$
$$\text{adjusted sales} = \text{actual sales} \div \text{seasonal factor for}$$
$$\text{the current period}$$
$$\text{adjusted sales} = 489,000 \div 1.372 \doteq 356,000 \text{ units}$$
$$S_t(x) = 0.6(356,000) + 0.4(363,000) \doteq 359,000$$
$$\text{forecast sales for second quarter} = \text{smoothed value} \times \text{seasonal factor}$$
$$= 359,000 \times 1.372 \doteq 493,000 \text{ units}$$

The comparison to the actual sales is fortunate at this point since the deviation approximates 400 for this period. Actually, up to this point, the calculations did not provide forecasts, as there were real-life data for a comparison. The adjusted seasonal forecast can now attend to a legitimate forecast for the forthcoming third period of "This Year":

$$\text{smoothed value} = \alpha(\text{second period smoothed value})$$
$$+ (1 - \alpha)(\text{first period smoothed value})$$
$$= 0.6(359,000) + 0.4(363,000) \doteq 360,000 \text{ units}$$
$$\text{forecast sales} = 360,000 \times 1.112 = 401,000 \text{ units}$$

In any real problem it is advisable to keep a running count of the magnitude and sign of the error to alert the estimating management to deficiencies in the planning.

Table 5.5. FORECAST USING EXPONENTIAL SMOOTHING AND SEASONAL ADJUSTMENT (100 UNITS OF MOTORCYCLES)

	3 Years Ago				2 Years Ago				1 Year Ago				This Year			
	First	Second	Third	Fourth	First	Second	Third	Fourth	First	Second	Third	Fourth	First	Second	Third	Fourth
Seasonal factors	0.772	1.372	1.112	0.744	0.772	1.372	1.112	0.744	0.772	1.372	1.112	0.744	0.772	1.372	1.112	0.744
Actual sales	186	341	273	158	234	411	334	229	272	478	392	291	275	489		
Adjusted sales	241	249	246	212	303	300	300	308	352	348	353	391	356	356		
Smoothed value[a]	216	236	242	224	271	289	295	303	332	342	349	374	363	359	360	
Forecast sales	167	324	270	167	209	397	330	226	256	469	389	278	280	493	401	
Error	−19	−17	−3	+9	−25	−17	−4	−3	−16	−9	−3	−13	+5	4		

[a] $\alpha = 0.6$.

178

5.4 COST INDEXES

A *cost index* provides a comparison of cost or price changes from period to period for a fixed quantity of goods or services. It permits the estimator a means to forecast the cost of a similar design from the past to the present or future period without going through detail costing. Provided that the estimator uses discretion in choosing the proper index, a reasonable approximation of cost should result. Extrapolation through time-series analysis of cost indexes is possible for future periods. Index numbers have been used for these purposes for a long time. An Italian, G. R. Carli, devised the index numbers about 1750. He used index numbers to investigate the effects of the discovery of America on the purchasing power of money in Europe.

Index numbers are useful in other respects. With time for estimating usually scarce, the cost estimator is forced to make immediate use of previous designs and costs which are based on outdated conditions. Because costs vary with time due to changes in demand, economic conditions, and prices, indexes convert costs applicable at a past date to equivalent costs now or in the future. A cost index is merely a dimensionless number for a given year showing the cost at that time relative to a certain base year. If a design cost at a previous period is known, present cost can be determined by multiplying the original cost by the ratio of the present index value to the index value applicable when the original cost was obtained. This may be stated formally as

$$C_c = C_r \left(\frac{I_c}{I_r} \right) \tag{5.53}$$

where C_c = present or future or past cost, dollars

C_r = original reference cost, dollars

I_c = index number at present or future or past time

I_r = index number at time reference cost was obtained

In selecting an index to upgrade an estimate, the estimator should consider the design, region, elements of the index, and the individual elements indicated in the original estimate. If major items are ignored in the index as compared to the estimate, adjustments in the composition of the index are necessary. An index seldom considers all factors such as technology progress or local and special conditions.

Consider the following example. Construction of a 70,000-square-foot warehouse is planned for a future period. Several years ago a similar warehouse was constructed for a unit estimate of $162.50 when the index was 118. The index for the construction period is forecast as 143, and construction costs per square foot will be

$$C_c = 162.50 \left(\frac{143}{118} \right) = \$196.93$$

While many indexes are published and have become accepted, their construction, alteration, and application are worthy subjects because the cost estimator needs to recognize that it may be better for the firm to develop its own index. Arithmetic development of indexes falls into several types: (1) adding costs together and dividing by their number, (2) adding the cost reciprocals together and dividing by their number, (3) multiplying the costs together and extracting the root indicated by their number, (4) ranking the costs and selecting the median value, (5) selecting the mode cost, and (6) adding together actual costs of each year and taking the ratio of these sums. The weighted arithmetic method is the most popular. But in most cost-estimating situations, the best method develops the index using a tabular approach. While formulas are straightforward, determination of engineering indexes bears little resemblance to formulas because of the variety, number, and complications involved.

A cost index is a dimensionless number representing the change in cost of material or labor or both over a period of time. Prices, which are the input of an index, must relate to specific material or labor. An index for lumber is based on the price of a specific quantity and type of lumber, such as board foot of 2 × 8 in. (50 × 200 mm) utility-grade pine. Quantity and quality must remain constant over the periods so that price movements represent a true price change rather than a change in quality or quantity. This is difficult for indexes that are charted over many periods.

A cost index expresses a change in price level between two points in time. A cost index for lumber in year 1990 is meaningless alone. An index for material A has no relationship to the index for material B. Similarly, the cost index for material A in two geographical areas may not be directly comparable.

To compute a price index for a single material, a series of prices must be gathered covering a period of time for a specific quantity and quality of the material. Index numbers are usually computed on a periodic basis. The prices gathered for the material may be average for the period (month, quarter, half-year, or year) or they may be a single observed value, as found from invoice records for one purchase.

Assume that the following prices have been collected for a standardized unit of a laser glass material: Let the origin of the data be labeled period 1.

				Period		
				Bench Mark		
	1	2	3	4	5	6
Price	$43.75	$44.25	$45.00	$ 46.10	$ 47.15	$ 49.25
Index	94.9	96.0	97.6	100.0	102.3	106.8

Index numbers are computed by relating each period to one of the prices selected as the denominator. If period 4 is the *bench-mark* period, period 3 price divided by period 4 price = 45.00/46.10 = 0.976. When period 4 price is expressed as 100.0, period 3 price is 97.6. The index can be expressed on the basis of 1 or 100 without any loss of generality. The *bench-mark period* is defined as that period which serves as the denominator in the index calculation.

Movements of indexes from one period to another are expressed as percent changes rather than changes in index points:

Current index	106.8
Less previous index	102.3
Index point change	$+4.5$
Divided by previous index	102.3
Equals	$+0.044 = +4.4\%$

The average periodic change resulting from these indexes can be found using

$$r = \left[\left(\frac{I_e}{I_b} \right)^{1/n} - 1 \right] \times 100 \tag{5.54}$$

where r = average percentage rate per period
   I_e = index value at end of period, number
   I_b = index value at beginning of period, number
   n = number of periods

For an index beginning with 94.9 and ending with 106.8 over a 5-year period, the average rate is 2.4%. If the average index rate is expected to persist, Eq. (5.54) is reformed to give

$$I_e = I_b \left(1 + \frac{r}{100} \right)^n \tag{5.55}$$

This will give an approximate future value. Suppose that we want an index for period 8, or

$$I_8 = 94.9(1 + 0.0239)^7 = 112.0$$

If cost $C_3 = \$3700$ is known, use of Eq. (5.53) will give for $n = 8$,

$$C_8 = 3700 \left(\frac{112.0}{97.6} \right) = \$4246$$

A composite index is often required, say for adjustment of "quote-or-price-in-effect" types of purchase contracts. Equally important is the updating of estimates of complicated assemblies, buildings, and plants.

Assume that a product called "10-cm-disk aperture laser amplifier" is selected for a composite index. The 10-cm-disk amplifier was produced only during period 1 and cost tracking of selected items has continued. To worry about all amplifier components is too involved, so major items are picked for individual tracking and prices have been gathered for 4 years. Observe Table 5.6 as an example of a tabular construction of an index. The "material" column identifies those items that are significant cost contributors to the laser. Usually, a representative set is selected if the product is complex. However, for a simple product all the materials may be chosen. The "quantity" column is proportional to the requirements of the product. The "quality specification" column identifies the technical nature of the material. Once these three columns are determined, cost finding begins. Year 1[a] is the first determination of the cost facts, and once we divide the total by itself, the index 100.0 is determined. Cost facts are collected for each subsequent period and each total is divided by the bench-mark total to obtain the index. Thus the indexes for

Table 5.6. Calculation of Index for Material, Quantity, and Quality Specifications

Material	Quantity	Quality Specification	Period			
			1[a]	2	3	4
1. Laser glass	3–10 cm disk	Silicate	$26,117	$24,027[b]	$22,345	$21,228
2. Stainless steel turnings	18 kg	AISI 304	1,913	2,008	2,129[c]	2,278
3. Aluminum extrusion	4 kg	3004	418	426	439	456
4. Fittings	3 kg	MIL STD 713	637	643	656	657
5. Harness cable	4 braid, 4 m	MIL STD 503	2,103	2,124	2,134	2,305[d]
6. Annular glass tube	12 m	Tempered $\frac{3}{16}$-in. wall PPG-27	4,317	4,187	4,103	4,185
		Total	$35,505	$33,415	$31,806	$31,109
		Index (%)	100.0	94.1	89.6	87.6

[a]Bench mark year

[b]Change in laser glass subsequently observed in year 2. Note Table 5.7

[c]Change in quantity of stainless steel observed in year 3. Note Table 5.8

[d]Change in specification of material observed in year 4. Note Table 5.9

182

Table 5.6 are 100.0, 94.1, 89.6, and 87.6. A general decline in prices is suggested by these indexes. Apparently, there is improvement in technology reducing prices.

One may argue that materials, quantities, and qualities are not consistent. Indeed, if technology is active, a decline in the cost and index is possible. Indexes should reflect basic price movements alone. *Index-creep* results from changes in quality, quantity, and the mix of materials or labor. Assume now that three changes occur and these are denoted by superscripts b, c, and d on Table 5.6. Effects of material mix, quantity, and quality changes need to be handled; this requires recomputing the index to keep it current. The effects of these three changes are made in the year they are noted.

In period 2 of Table 5.7 there is a quality change in glass, improving from silicate to fluorophosphate. Instead of $24,027 for silicate glass, a value of $37,621 is quoted for a comparable quantity. To substitute $37,621 in place of the old silicate value would cause distortion unless the bench mark year was appropriately repriced for the new glass. If a new glass price is unavailable for period 1, the bench mark $37,621 can be adjusted by the overall index as uncovered, such as $37,621/0.941 = $39,980. But it is more correct to adjust the new glass by the history between periods 1 to 2 for silicate glass, or $26,117/24,027 \times 37,621 = $40,893$, and this value is entered in Table 5.7 for period 1 and a new bench mark total is computed and new indexes are computed. This going-backward is termed *backcasting*.

In period 3 of Table 5.6 there is a change in the weight of stainless steel. Instead of 18 kg, a new design has increased to 23 kg. The backcasting adjustment from 18 kg to 23 kg is calculated for the bench mark year and for intervening years. At period 3 of Table 5.8, the new price entry would be $23/18 \times 2129 = 2720. This value is deflated to periods 1 and 2 using the index values for the material, and those entries are shown in Table 5.8. Totals and new indexes are shown again.

In period 4 of material 5 (Table 5.6) a substitution is made as harness cables are changed to flexible printed circuit wires. Using a vendor's quotation, the value is substituted into period 4 of material 5. New quantity and quality specifications are stated, and bench mark and intervening values are backcast. The last schedule of index changes is shown in Table 5.9. All indexes were subsequently reviewed

Table 5.7. RECALCULATING INDEXES FOR QUALITY CHANGE IN PERIOD 2

Material	Quantity	Quality Specification	Period 1	Period 2
1. Laser glass	3–10 cm	Fluorophosphate	$40,893	$37,621
2. No change			1,913	2,008
3. No change			418	426
4. No change			637	643
5. No change			2,103	2,124
6. No change			4,317	4,187
		Total	$50,281	$47,009
		Index (%)	100.0	93.5

Table 5.8. RECALCULATING INDEXES FOR QUANTITY CHANGE IN PERIOD THREE

Material	Quantity	Quality Specification	Period 1	Period 2	Period 3
1. No change			$40,893	$37,621	$39,423
2. Stainless steel	23 kg	AISI 304	2,444	2,566	2,720
3. No change			418	426	439
4. No change			637	643	656
5. No change			2,103	2,124	2,134
6. No change			4,317	4,187	4,103
		Total	$50,812	$47,567	$49,475
		Index (%)	100.0	93.6	97.4

and revised again. These changes for indexes of designs which are technologically active are necessary to keep the index values accurate.

The effects of changes in mix, quantity, and quality on the index scheme are called "technology creep." Unless they are evaluated at time of occurrence, indexes are unsuitable for high-technology products. Product indexes can be maintained by noting the changes when they occur, inputing changes for previous data, and backcasting the previous year's indexes. Every so often it may be necessary to reset the bench mark year whenever delicate effects are influencing the index and are not being removed.

The several kinds of indexes are

1. Material
2. Labor
3. Material and labor
4. Regional effects for material, labor, or composite mixes
5. Design
6. Quality

Virtually any combination of materials, labor, services, products and projects can be evaluated for an index, as the intent is to show relative price changes. An interesting contrast is a quality index. Instead of noting price changes, the purpose is to remove price effects and show quality changes between the periods.

Several characteristics distinguish indexes. In the construction of the index, there is a choice in the selection of the information. Wholesale prices or retail prices, wages or volume of production, proportion of labor to materials, and the number of separate statistics used are typical alternative choices. Indexes apply to a place and time, that is, period covered or region considered, base year, and the interval between successive indexes, yearly or monthly. Additionally, indexes are varied as to the compiler and sources used for data. A variety of objectives create diversity for the many indexes.

A variety of cost indexes is available to the estimator. Virtually every industrialized nation regularly collects, analyzes, and divulges indexes. A government index listing is given by *The Statistical Abstract of the United States,* a yearly

Table 5.9. RECALCULATING INDEXES FOR MATERIAL-MIX CHANGE

Material	Quantity	Quality Specification	Period				
			1	2	3	4	5
1. No change			$40,893	$37,621	$39,423	$42,617	$48,507
2. No change			2,444	2,566	2,720	2,910	3,085
3. No change			418	426	439	456	479
4. No change			637	643	656	657	689
5. Flexible printed circuit cable	4m	MIL STD 711	3,743	3,733	3,762	3,861	3,900
6. No change			4,317	4,187	4,103	4,185	4,311
		Total	$52,452	$49,176	$51,103	$54,686	$60,971
		Index (%)	100.0	93.8	97.4	104.3	116.2

185

publication that includes materials, labor, and construction. A yearly publication of the U.S. Department of Labor is the *Indexes of Output Per Man-Hour for Selected Industries*. This volume contains updated indexes such as output per man-hour, output per employee, and unit labor requirements for the industries included in the U.S. government's productivity measurement program. Each index represents only the change in output per man-hour for the designated industry or combination of industries. The indexes of output per man-hour are computed by dividing an output index by an index of aggregate man-hours. For an industry the index measures changes in the relationship among output, employment, and man-hours.

The Bureau of Labor Statistics publishes monthly *Producer Prices and Price Indexes* and covers some 3000 product groupings. In building construction alone, there are many public and private indexes covering from 1 to 20 types of buildings in 1 to 200 different locations. Some of these indexes are available at a charge from their compiler, while others are published regularly. There are special indexes covering railroad stations, airport hangers, hospitals, refineries, equipment, and so on.

SUMMARY

As is now evident, forecasting is analysis using imperfect information. Estimating, when coupled with the forecasting process, takes the analysis of imperfect information and adds to it the ingredients of judgment and knowledge about engineering designs to provide the setting for decisions. In forecasting processes it should be remembered that data provide the information, although imperfect and incomplete, that pretend to be the situation in the future. Thus the forecasting methods of statistics and analysis are used to uncover the relationships that exist for products, production costs, prices, sales, and technology. The application of time series, single and multiple linear regression, correlation, and graphical analysis are the principal statistical techniques used in forecasting for the future. Moving averages involve a consideration of time and fluctuations that occur during these periods. Cost indexes are useful adjustments that permit estimating over lengthy periods of time.

QUESTIONS

5.1. Give an explanation of the following terms:

Relative frequency	Best curve	Moving average
Histogram	Confidence limits	Time series
Mean	Prediction limits	Smoothing constant
Standard deviation	t-table	Cycles
Regression	Rectification	Trend line
Least-squares criterion	Power function	Indexes
Intercept	Correlation	Backcasting
Slope	Multiple-linear regression	Creep

5.2. "Statistics never lie, yet liars use statistics" is a common statement. Discuss.

5.3. Why are graphical plots preferred initially over mathematical analysis of data?

5.4. Is cost estimating more concerned with empirical evidence or theoretical data? Illustrate both.

5.5. Cite instances when a cumulative curve would be necessary.

5.6. Discuss what regression analysis is. What are its underlying assumptions?

5.7. What is minimized in a least-squares approach?

5.8. What is meant by correlation analysis? What does $r = 0$ or 1 imply?

5.9. Distinguish between correlation and causation. Could you have causation without correlation?

5.10. What is the purpose of a moving average? How does smoothing relate to a moving average?

5.11. If the estimator was confident of his past data, would the smoothing constant be large or small?

5.12. What are the differences between cycles and trend cycles?

5.13. Define a cost index.

5.14. Why would an estimator use a cost index? What qualifications are necessary before a building index is chosen?

PROBLEMS

5.1. A labor survey was conducted for the area firms, and the following classification is given:

Wage	Number	Wage	Number
8–10	5	17–19	36
11–13	11	20–22	52
14–16	28	23–25	15

Construct the frequency distribution table, relative frequency curve, and cumulative frequency curve. (Note that wage interval end numbers are open.)

5.2. Time studies were examined for a specific handling element, and their observations are given as follows:

Time	Observations	Time	Observations
0.04	2	0.16–0.20	14
0.04–0.08	12	0.20–0.24	13
0.08–0.12	14	0.24–0.28	12
0.12–0.16	15	0.28–	6

Construct the frequency distribution table, relative frequency curve, and cumulative frequency curve.

5.3. Raw data of unemployment are gathered for two separate years in community A and shown below.

RAW DATA OF UNEMPLOYMENT FOR COMMUNITY A

Age Range	March First Year	March Second Year
14–15	20	26
16–17	87	93
18–19	636	709
20–21	206	191
22–23	202	50
24–25	81	229
26–27	15	37
28–29	13	29
30–31	19	73
32–33	25	83
34–35	38	47
36–37	53	42
38–39	36	85
40–44	89	30
45–49	101	97
50–54	86	107
55–59	111	67
60–64	117	173
65–69	144	180
70+	101	102
	2180	2450

(a) Construct the frequency distribution table, relative frequency curve, and cumulative frequency curve for both years. Describe their appearance.

(b) Repeat (a) using intervals 14–19, 20–24, 25–34, 35–44, 45–54, 55–64, and 65 +. Describe the appearance of the curve. Comment about non-uniform-sized classes and deliberate or unintentional statistical distortion.

5.4. Find the mean, median, mode, range, standard deviation, and variance of the following sets of data:

(a) 3, 5, 2, 6, 5, 9, 5, 1, 7, 6

(b) 41.6, 38.7, 40.3, 39.5, 38.9

(c) 2, −1, 0, 4, 6, 6, 8, 3, 2

(d) 16, 23, 82, 41, 16, 0, −3

(e) $\frac{1}{8}, \frac{1}{16}, \frac{1}{4}, -\frac{1}{2}, 0.125, 0$

(f) 11, 13, 13, 16, 16, 16, 20, 21, 23

5.5. Market surveys have determined the U.S. value of the ship-building industry over a ten-year period.

Year	1	2	3	4	5	6	7	8	9	10
10^6 value	1467	1216	1360	1400	1518	1678	1818	2160	2200	2460

Graph the data on arithmetic coordinates using the "one-half" rule. Find the graphical equation $y = a + bx$ of the line. Forecast the value in year 11 using the curve and equation.

5.6. The index for the union wage rate for carpenters has followed this pattern:

Year	1	2	3	4	5	6	7	8	9	10
Index	100.0	104.4	107.8	112.3	117.2	122.5	132.8	145.6	159.3	171.6

(a) Plot the straight line of the data on arithmetic coordinates using the "one-half" rule. Find the graphical equation $y = a + bx$ of the line. Forecast the value in year 11 using the curve and equation.

(b) Visually determine the year for which there is a change in slope and construct two new straight lines for the data, finding their graphical equations. Also forecast the value in year 11.

5.7. The life of a cutting tool is determined by testing under standard conditions and observing flank wear. Taylor's tool-life equation is $VT^n = K$, where V is the velocity in ft/min (m/s), T the time in minutes, n the slope, and K the intercept. The test log is AISI 4140 steel, depth of cut, 0.050 in. (1.27 mm) feed, 0.010 in./revolution (0.25 mm/rev), and tool wear limit, 0.005 in. of flank wear (0.13 mm). Once the flank wear length is reached, the time is recorded against a controlled cutting surface in feet per minute (m/s). The data are as follows:

Cutting Speed, (surface feet/min)	Tool Life, T (min)
400	7, 9, 8
450	6, 8.5
500	5.5, 7.5, 6
550	4, 7, 6
600	5
650	3
700	2.5, 3, 3 4
750	3

(a) Plot the data as $\log V = \log K - n \log T$ and find the graphical equation.

(b) Forecast the value for 300 fpm (1.52 m/s) and 800 fpm (4.06 m/s).

(c) Repeat parts (a) and (b) in metric units.

5.8. Determine the least-squares regression line for Problem 5.5. Find the dependent value for year 11.

5.9. Determine the least-squares regression line for Problem 5.6. Forecast the value for year 11.

5.10. (a) Find t_α if $\alpha = 0.10$ and $v = 10$ degrees of freedom.

(b) Find t_α if $\alpha = 0.05$ and $n = 20$.

(c) Compare t_α and Z (from Appendix I) for $\alpha = 0.05$ and $n = 120$.

(d) If $t_\alpha = 2.8$, find α for $v = 16$.

5.11. (a) Find the mean and individual dependent value for Table 5.1 for year 16.

(b) Determine the variance of the mean value y and the individual y for $x = 16$ from Table 5.1.

(c) Determine the confidence and prediction limit for parts (a) and (b).

5.12. A price index for labor is given for 7 years:

Year	1	2	3	4	5	6	7
Index	100.0	106.0	111.1	117.2	121.3	125.2	128.0

(a) Graph the data using the one-half rule.

(b) Compute trend values and find a least-squares line fitting the data and construct its graph.

(c) Predict the price index for year 8 and compare with the true value 132.6. What is the range for the individual year 8 using a 95% prediction interval?

5.13. From the following data, determine the values of parameters a and b using the method of least squares. Assume that the data can be plotted as $y = a + bx$.

Year	Retail Price Index, y
0	95.1
1	97.7
2	98.4
3	100.0
4	101.1
5	102.2
6	103.5
7	104.9
8	106.6
9	109.7

Find the 90% prediction interval for the year 10 value. Estimate the 95% confidence interval for the slope.

5.14. A time study is conducted on a spot-welding operation. Three elements are summarized:

Time Study	Number Spots	Spot Time	Load L + W + H	Load Time	Unload L + W + H	Unload Time
1	8	0.28	29	0.08	37	0.10
2	3	0.13	46	0.10	46	0.17
3	9	0.34	101	0.27	106	0.28
4	14	0.87	60	0.21	60	0.32
5	36	2.06	53	0.19	53	0.51

(a) Find regression equation for number of spots (x) versus decimal minute spot time (y). Determine the 95% confidence limits for 15 spots.

(b) Determine regression equation for load $L + W + H$ (x) versus time (y). Find the 95% confidence limits for $x = 50$.

(c) Determine the regression equation for unload $L + W + H$ (x) versus time (y). Find the 95% confidence limits for $x = 100$.

5.15. Solve Problem 5.7 using regression methods. Find the equation in transformed and original units. What is the value at $V = 600$ fpm (3 m/s)?

5.16. Product cost learning has been found to follow the function $T_u = KN^s$, where $T_u =$ unit time for Nth unit, $K =$ man-hours estimate for unit 1, and $s =$ the slope of the improvement rate. Transform this into a log relationship and determine the log regression line. Also determine the equation in original units. Estimate the man-hours at $N = 50$ in both log and original units.

(a)	N	Man-hours, T	(b)	N	Man-hours, T
	5	155		7	210
	8	143		13	160
	13	137		21	142
	17	97		26	128
	25	75		31	121

5.17. Direct labor for a 12-kW four-cylinder diesel generator set has been plotted on arithmetic graph paper and shown as Fig. P5.17.

(a) Replot these data on semilog paper where $y =$ logarithm man-hour.

(b) Find the regression equation.

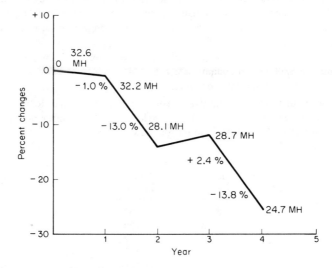

Figure P5.17   Evidence of direct labor learning for a 12-kW four-cylinder diesel generator set.

(c) What is the expected value for year 5 from your log plot and equation?
Use the theoretical equation $T = Kx^s$, where T is the man-hours, x the year, K the intercept, and s the slope.

5.18. A firm that manufactures totally enclosed capacitor motors, fan-cooled, 1725-rpm, $\frac{5}{8}$-in. (15.9-mm) keyway shaft, has known costs on $\frac{1}{4}, \frac{1}{3}, \frac{3}{4}$, and 1 hp (0.20, 0.25, 0.55, and 0.75 kW) of $67.50, $75.00, $88.50, and $105.00. Determine the cost equation using
(a) the semilog equation, and
(b) the power equation.
(c) Which equation using the test of $\Sigma(y - \hat{y})^2$ is best?

5.19. Find the correlation for Problem 5.5.

5.20. A study of past records of installed insulation cost (including labor, material, and equipment to install) for central steam-electric plants revealed the following data:

Equipment Cost (x10⁵)	Insulation Cost (x10⁴)	Equipment Cost (x10⁵)	Insulation Cost (x10⁴)
$ 5.5	$ 3.5	$14.1	$ 9.2
10.7	5.5	14.8	9.3
34	28	15.1	14.1
2	1.4	15.3	13.8
6	6.4	21.3	15.0
1.5	2.1	34.0	15.8
8.1	7.2	24.1	9.8
10.1	6.4	26.0	15.8

(a) Plot a chart of this information on arithmetic coordinates. On log-log coordinates. Which do you think is more suitable for cost-estimating purposes? Major equipment costs have been estimated as $300,000 for a new project. What is the estimate for the installed insulation cost?
(b) Find the arithmetic regression equation and correlation r. What is the insulation cost value for $300,000 of equipment?
(c) Find the logarithmic equation and the value for $300,000.

5.21. A company that has been converting manual production methods to automatic means wants to evaluate its efforts. Is there correlation for this number of employees and shipment value? What assessment do you make?

Shipments ($\times\ 10^6$)	Number of Employees
$573	1573
606	1550
648	1530
720	1550
765	1540
798	1550
848	1560

5.22. Analyze the following data using multiple linear regression:

Weight	Cost/1000 Units for Length:		
	1.50	1.75	2.00
60.5	5070	4770	4540
52.6	4540	4215	3930
42.3	3660	3660	3120
33.3	2390	2390	2100

5.23. In a study of scrap and production rate, the following information was collected:

Production, x (units/period)	1000	2000	3000	3500	4000	4500	5000
Scrap, y (% of production)	5.2	6.5	6.8	8.1	10.2	10.3	13.0

(a) Determine an exponential model and a second-degree polynomial.
(b) Which model gives the smallest error sum of squares?

5.24. Material costs were collected from historical purchase orders, and the information was categorized by period and quantity. The quantity represents the volume of units purchased, but the data are listed as dollars per unit. (See Table 3.2 for a practical example.)

Period	Quantity		
	1	2	3
−3	10.00	8.00	7.00
−2	10.70	8.60	7.50
−1	11.10	8.95	7.85
0	11.25	9.00	7.90

(a) Use multiple linear regression to find the unit cost equation equation y where $x_1 =$ period and $x_2 =$ quantity.
(b) Find the unit cost for period 1 and quantity 2.

5.25. Requirements for identical materials are consolidated and purchase requests are issued for a quantity each period. The following table is a summary of the purchased cost history of a single material. y is identified as cost per unit. There is no information for values not shown.

Period	Quantity		
	1	2	3
−3	10.00	—	—
−2	—	—	7.50
−1	—	8.95	—
0	—	—	7.90

(a) Use multiple linear regression and find the equation where x_1 = period, x_2 = quantity, and y = material cost per unit.

(b) Find unit cost for period 1 and a quantity of 2.

5.26. A company uses extensive amounts of plastic film for one of its automatic processes. This purchased film constitutes the major cost for machine-hour cost.

Budget Period	Unit Price	Budget Period	Unit Price
1	$60.20	11	$63.20
2	60.50	12	68.30
3	68.70	13	65.70
4	60.20	14	78.40
5	60.50	15	81.20
6	62.30	16	82.10
7	75.70	17	82.10
8	73.10	18	84.60
9	80.10	19	83.10
10	77.40	20	82.10

(a) Plot a four-period moving average and actual unit price.

(b) Using an exponential smoothing function, determine the smoothed data for α = 0.25.

5.27. (a) Plot the following data:

Period	Value	Period	Value
1	7.5	11	4
2	8	12	2.5
3	9.5	13	1.8
4	9.7	14	0.8
5	10	15	0.2
6	9.9	16	0.1
7	9.8	17	0.3
8	9	18	0.9
9	7.6	19	2
10	6	20	4

(b) Using a smoothing function with α = 0.1, determine smoothed data and over-plot the raw information. What familiar function does the information resemble?

5.28. The cost of a purchased component used in the assembly of a product was analyzed on a time series. Make a table for a 3-year moving total and average price. Plot the average price versus time and describe the movement.

Years Ago	10	9	8	7	6	5	4	3	2	1	Now
Cost (cents/each)	23.2	24.1	26.3	25.7	26.8	27.2	28.0	27.8	28.0	28.5	28.3

5.29. Hot-rolled $\frac{7}{32}$ -in. (5.6-mm) coils of low-carbon steel have the following cost history:

Year	Quarter	Cost	Year	Quarter	Cost	Year	Quarter	Cost
1	1	$ 7,761	3	3	$13,059	6	1	$15,854
	2	7,844		4	12,786		2	16,127
	3	7,844	4	1	12,786		3	15,953
	4	7,844		2	12,952		4	15,953
2	1	9,577		3	14,195	7	1	15,622
	2	9,668		4	14,195		2	17,031
	3	9,668	5	1	14,195		3	17,247
	4	9,668		2	14,195		4	17,247
3	1	9,668		3	14,958	8	1	18,043
	2	13,391		4	14,958		2	18,673

Plot these time-series data point to point, and eyeball a straight line through the data. Identify the cycles. Provide a smoothing equation.

5.30. A warehouse construction job is anticipated in 2 years. A similar layup steel-walled warehouse was constructed for a unit price of $105 per square foot of wall when the index was 107. The index now is 143, but in 2 years it is expected to be 147. What will be the unit estimate for the construction? What is the bid cost of a warehouse with 700,000 square feet of wall?

5.31. A production man-hour index based on 1967 = 100 is given as 1949, 41.9; 1959, 48.0; 1969, 107.6; and 1979, 205.8. Convert the index to a 1979 basis = 100.

5.32. A construction index for Los Angeles is

Year	Index
5	1200
15	3108

and a structure built in year 10 cost $1,000,000. How much will the same structure cost in year 20?

5.33. Indexes for buildings in Denver and New York are as follows:

Year	Denver	New York
1	400	500
5	600	750

(a) If the building cost $400,000 in year 1, what is its cost in year 6?
(b) If the building costs $400,000 in year 2, find its cost in year 6.

5.34 A company receives an order for a large quantity of drill steel to be used in mining. The delivery point is equally spaced between its plants in the United States and France.

Material and transportation costs are assumed to be equivalent for both countries. The efficiency index is 1.3 French man-hours = 1.0 U.S. man-hours for the same job. Indirect cost percentages are 120% France = 75% United States. The direct unit cost (labor only) is $99.65 France = $153.53 United States. Which of the two plants should this company build and ship from?

5.35. Determine the fabrication base cost for a pressure vessel. A pressure vessel is a cylindrical shell capped by two elliptical heads. The base cost estimates the vessel fabricated in carbon steel to resist internal pressure of 50 psi with average nozzles, manways, supports, and design size. Design: diameter, 8 ft; height, 15 ft; shell material, stainless 316 solid; and operating pressure, 100 psi. Estimating data: Construction 3 years hence with a 5% material increase per year, carbon steel material costs = $24,000, factor for non-carbon steel material = 3.67, factor for nonstandard pressure = 1.05. What is the expected cost?

5.36. A cast-steel foundry uses indexes to price its raw materials. They are purchased over a period of time and stored in open inventory, but they are priced out on a current index basis to remain competitive. Find the indexes for periods 2 and 3 with the reference period as 1. Speculate on the next period index.

	1-Ton Finished Casting, Proportion (%)	Period		
Item		1	2	3
1. Pittsburgh scrap steel, No. 1 heavy	80	$37.00	$37.50	$38.00
2. Metal alloy No. 1	15	48.00	48.50	50.00
3. Metal alloy No. 2	5	57.00	56.25	55.00

5.37. Basic union wage rates and indexes for major construction trades are given.

		Month		
Trade	Weight	1	2	3
Carpenter	31.4	100.0	104.4	107.8
		20.40	21.30	22.00
Electrician	13.6	100.0	102.2	104.3
		23.00	23.50	24.00
Laborer	10.1	100.0	106.1	110.9
		14.70	15.60	16.30
Plumber	15.3	100.0	107.6	110.3
		22.30	24.00	24.60
Painter	11.5	100.0	105.7	108.5
		17.60	18.60	19.10
Others	18.1	100.0	105.0	107.9
		19.80	20.80	21.30
Weighted average index		100.0	105.0	107.9

(a) What is the next period index for carpenters? For the total trade?

(b) A new job is to be estimated, but it will have no painting component. Construct a revised index free of the painting trade and determine next period index.

(c) *Discuss*: While the rates relate to the amount paid the tradesman for 1 hour, the indexes do not encompass the efficiency with which that hour is utilized in successive years.

5.38. A construction firm uses indexes to price wall-footing forms. Material quantities and labor man-hour data and/or material unit costs have been gathered for three periods.

		Rate for Period:		
Item	Quantity	1	2	3
1. Materials:				
Sides: 2 × 12 in.	200 BF[a]	0.06	0.057	0.053
Stakes and braces	75 BF[a]	0.055	0.053	0.052
2. Labor:				
Carpenter	3.5 hr	24.60	27.52	31.02
Laborer	1.75 hr	21.85	23.66	26.12
3. Stripping forms,				
laborer	1.5 hr	21.85	23.66	26.12

[a]1000 BF.

(a) Find the indexes and determine the value for year 5.

(b) A cost is $17,500 at period 2. Calculate the cost for period 5.

5.39. Estimate the cost to a utility company in supplying power to a new housing development. A similar housing development with the same type of home, lot sizes, and street layout in period 1 cost the utility $504,000. The following table gives the basic material required for the period 1 development and price changes in the past 4 years.

Material	Quantity Required	Quality Specification	Period			
			1	2	3	4
1. Pad-mounted three-phase switch	1	Standard	6,000	6,500	7,000	7,500
2. Conduit	1000 ft	$4\frac{1}{2}$ in. metallic	60,000	69,000	78,000	87,000
3. 12.47-kV primary cable (one-phase)	10,000 ft	No. 0/AWG	85,000	89,000	98,000	100,000
4. 120/240 Vac secondary cable	20,000 ft	350 KCMIL	180,000	190,000	200,000	220,000
5. 120/240 Vac service cable	20,000 ft	No. 4/0 MWG	160,000	170,000	180,000	200,000
6. 25-kVA pad-mounted transformers	10	Standard	13,000	13,900	14,000	15,000
			504,000	538,400	577,000	629,500

(a) Calculate the indexes. Find the average increase per year. What is the index for period 5?

(b) Now assume that the following design changes were enacted by the utility company for their underground residential distribution during year 2 and then in year 3.

1. From period 2 onward the utility eliminates the conduit, item 2, under driveways and sidewalks, requiring conduit only under streets. This will reduce the amount by 50%.

2. From period 3 onward the company will use a new trenching method which will reduce costs for cables by 25%. This deals with material items 3, 4, and 5.

Adjust the data and backcast the index using period 1 as the bench mark for each year, including the material, installation, and quality changes above, and then estimate the period 5 cost for the new housing development.

CASE STUDY:
MARKET-BASKET INDEX

Construct a "market-basket" index of these items. The base year is 1. The prices of these items were collected under similar circumstances over a 5-year period.

Item	Price, Yearly					
	1	2	3	4	5	Total
1. Milk, homogenized, $\frac{1}{2}$ gal	\$ 1.13	\$ 1.23	\$ 1.62	\$ 1.63	\$ 1.71	\$ 7.32
2. Ice cream, regular vanilla, $\frac{1}{2}$ gal	1.67	1.92	1.87	1.96	2.16	9.58
3. Eggs, grade A large, 1 dozen	0.95	1.16	1.17	1.21	1.43	5.92
4. Margarine, 1 lb, regular Blue Bonnet, Parkay	0.85	0.99	1.11	1.36	1.47	5.78
5. White bread, 1-lb loaf, sliced	0.75	0.83	1.02	1.10	1.14	4.84
6. Instant coffee, 10-oz jar	2.83	3.13	3.47	4.61	5.83	19.87
7. Flour, 5 lb, all-purpose Pillsbury	1.67	1.69	1.73	2.01	2.27	9.37
8. Ground beef, less than 25% fat, 3-lb package	7.15	8.13	8.47	9.16	10.11	43.02
9. Potatoes, U.S., one 5-lb bag	1.15	1.18	1.39	1.43	1.89	7.04
	\$18.15	\$20.26	\$21.85	\$24.47	\$28.01	\$112.74

(a) Determine yearly indexes.

(b) What is the average percentage rise over the 5-year period?

(c) What are the major and minor items contributing to this increase?

(d) Construct a time-series plot of the index.

(e) Determine a least-squares-equation fit for this time series.

(f) If these items constitute 3% of the grocery bill for a hypothetical time period and family, what are the gross dollars lost to inflation?

(g) Using inquiry methods at your local grocery store, determine current prices for these items and compare to year 1.

6

Preliminary and Detail Methods

Estimating methods are remarkably similar even though designs may differ. We see that in this chapter, which introduces various methods useful for all kinds of design. A preliminary method is used in the formative stages of design. Attention turns to detail methods as designs and information become complete. We shall discuss general estimating methods and point out their advantages and shortcomings. These methods range from experience and judgment as the dominant requirement to ones with mathematics.

6.1 DESIGN AND EVALUATION

A design is without specific form and shape in the early stages of its evolution. For instance, design engineers may have progressed through problem definition, concepts, engineering models, and evaluation with only the final design step remaining. The preliminary estimate is requested at some point in the initial evaluation. With a lack of facts and specific information the cost estimator is asked to provide this first estimate. Using various methods, rules of thumb, and simple calculations, a quick and relatively inexpensive estimate is provided. Obviously the accuracy of the estimate depends on the amount and quality of information and the time available to prepare the estimate. The preliminary estimate may cause the firm to take some sort of action. An estimate, such as an operation cost, product price, project bid, or system effectiveness, can have serious financial overtones. More frequent, however, is the case where the preliminary estimate is used to screen designs and aid in the formulation of a budget. They are used by engineering and management to commit or stall additional design effort, or for appropriation requests for capital equipment, or for culling out uneconomic designs at an early point. Although decisions based on the preliminary estimate may not lead to legal obligations or authorization for capital spending, mistakes can be costly by eliminating potentially profitable designs.

We define a preliminary estimate as one which is made in the formative stages of design. Overlooked in this definition is the accuracy, type of design evaluated, nature of the organization, dollar amount, and the purpose for the estimate. A precondition of accuracy for preliminary estimates cannot be imposed, as special designs or objectives create a unique set of requirements. An estimate involving, say, pennies is no less of a challenge than an estimate involving millions of dollars, for many of the same methods are used at both ends of the dollar scale. Other terms used in practice include conceptual, battery limit, schematic, order of magnitude, and mean preliminary estimate.

Their purpose is to screen and eliminate unsound proposals without extensive engineering cost. If these estimates lead to a continuation rather than a dismissal decision, additional methods are required. Now we confine our attention to methods that are more thorough in preparation and accurate in results as well as costly in design and estimating. At this point in time the designer would have extended his own preparations, and the estimator can construct an estimate on enlarged quantities of verified information. In some cases the detail estimate may be a reestimate, as only limited updating needs to be done.

The man-hours devoted to estimating the operation, product, project, or system design naturally varies with circumstances, and we have no rules that can guide management. The case for increased accuracy from a detail estimate is often made. Some practitioners claim that detail estimates are within $\pm$ 5% about a future actual value. Whether the particular value is $\pm$ 5% or $\pm$ 50% is not significant now; however, we want to assert that methods that generally are more accurate have a commensurable increase in cost of preparation. Thus, data are purified, design has increased detail, and in actual estimating situations management stipulates that the estimate be within an interval about the future actual or standard value.

Detail estimating methods are more quantitative. Arbitrary and excessive judgmental factors are suppressed, although they are never eliminated, and emphasis shifts to comprehensiveness. Whether the model is a recapitulation columnar sheet, a set of computational rules, or a functional model, the intent is the same: We want to find the value of the detail estimate through formal and rigid rules.

6.2 OPINION

Personal opinion is inescapable in estimating. It is easy to be critical of opinion, but in the absence of data and shortage of time, there may be no other way but to use opinion in the evaluation of designs. The estimator is selected for the job because of his or her observational experience, common sense, and knowledge about the designs. In judging the economic want of a design, the mettle of the estimator is tested. Estimators respected as "truth-tellers" are sustained in this activity; others are not. Time, cost, or quantities about minor or major line items are estimated using this inner experience. That the estimator be objective in attempting to measure all future factors that affect the out-of-pocket cost is understood. Opinion estimating is also done collectively.

6.3 CONFERENCE

The conference method is a nonquantitative method of estimation. It provides a single value or estimate made through experience. The procedure, although it has many forms, involves representatives from various departments conferring with estimating in a round-table fashion and jointly estimating cost as a lump sum. Sometimes labor and material are isolated and estimated with overhead, and profit added later through various formula methods by the estimator.

The conference method may also be used within the cost-estimating department. Estimators having specialized knowledge confer on a design and determine a cost figure without counsel from other departments.

The way in which the method is managed depends on the available information. Various gimmicks can be used to sharpen judgment. A *hidden-card* technique has each of the committee experts reveal a personal value. This could provide a consensus. If agreement is not initially reached, discussion and persuasion are permitted as influencing factors. Sometimes this is called estimate-talk-estimate, or E-T-E. The hidden-card idea prevents a brain-storming session, which generally tends to provide optimistic estimates. In a conference on estimating, the estimator will serve as a moderator and provide questions such as "What is the labor and material cost for this part?"

A ranking scheme along the "good–better–best" lines of Sears, Roebuck & Co. can be applied in a cost sense. The estimators rank two or more designs and then give their cost value. Provided that the set is not large, the ranking method seems to work. Major drawbacks to the conference method are the lack of analysis and a trail of verifiable facts leading from the estimate to the governing situation. Although little faith and accuracy can be assigned to the method, the lack of procedural rigor seldom deters usage.

6.4 COMPARISON

The comparison method is similar to the previous method except that it attaches a formal logic. If we are confronted with an unsolvable or excessively difficult design and estimating problem, we designate it problem a and construct a simpler design problem for which an estimate can be found. The simpler problem is called problem b. This simpler problem might arise from a clever manipulation of the original design or a relaxation of the technical constraints on the original problem. Thus we attempt to gain information by branching to b as various facts may already exist about b. Indeed, the estimate may be in final form, or portions may exist and there need only be a minor restructuring of data to allow comparison. The alternative design problem b must be selected to bound the original problem a in the following way:

$$C_a(D_a) \leq C_b(D_b) \tag{6.1}$$

where $C_{a,b}$ = value of the estimate for designs a and b

   $D_{a,b}$ = design a or design b

Also, D_b must approach D_a as nearly as possible. We adopt the value of our estimate as something under C_b. The sense of the inequality in Eq. (6.1) is for a conservative stance. It may be management policy to estimate cost slightly higher at first and once the detail estimate is completed with D_a thoroughly explored we comfortably find that $C_a(D_a)$ is less than the original comparison estimate.

An additional lower bound is possible. Assume a similar circumstance for a known or nearly known design c, and a logic can be expanded to have

$$C_c(D_c) \leq C_a(D_a) \leq C_b(D_b) \tag{6.2}$$

We assume that designs b and c satisfy the technical requirements (but not the economic estimate) as nearly as possible.

Consider an example of comparison estimating. It is desired to decrease the rolling speed of a ball bearing relative to the rotational speed of the shaft. Among other factors the maximum operating speed of a ball bearing depends on its size and the rolling speed of the balls within the raceways. A preliminary design solution is to add an intermediate ring with raceways on its inner and outer peripheries for light radial loads. This would cut the relative rolling speed to approximately half that of the balls in an unmodified bearing. Figure 6.1(a) indicates a possible arrangement of design A. The adaptation of an additional outer roll of balls achieves many of the similar features required of design A and is known as design B [Fig. 6.1(b)]. Velocities are reduced and other technical advantages are achieved. The design requirements for B satisfy most of A. The cost of B can be determined as the outer roll of balls is in many ways similar to single-roll ball bearing technology. The technology for conventional double-row ball bearings [Fig. 6.1(c)] has known costs and is our design C. With costs determined for designs B and C, comparison becomes possible.

Precautions which consider up-to-date costs, processing variations, similar production quantities, and spoilage rates are factors which call for insight in picking a specific value for design A between the B and C range. The comparison method is sometimes called *similarity* or *analogy*.

6.5 UNIT

The unit method is the most popular of the preliminary estimating methods. Many other titles exist that describe the same thing—average, order of magnitude, lump sum, module estimating—and involve various refinements. Extensions of this method

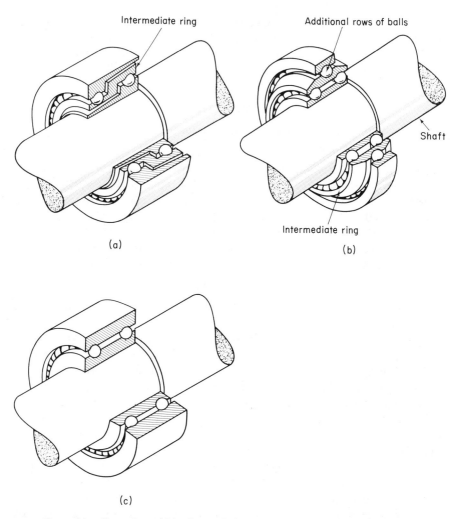

Figure 6.1. Comparison of (a) unknown design to (b) higher-cost design and (c) lower-cost design.

lead to the factor estimating method, discussed later. Examples of unit estimates are found in all activities. For instance:

Cost of house construction per square foot of livable space
Cost of metal casting per pound
Cost of electrical transmission per mile
National-norm cost of university education per student year
Chemical plant cost per barrel of oil capacity
Factory cost per machine shop man-hour

While typically vague in these contexts, the strongest assumption necessary is that the design to be estimated is like the composition of the parameter used to determine the estimate. Notice that the estimate is "per" something. Thus if the unit value of a casting is $1.22 per pound ($2.72 per kilogram), a 5-lb (2.3-kg) casting will cost $6.10 each.

Unit estimates are easily figured. Consider the manufacturing operation of metal turning. Using job tickets, the total time for several jobs and many parts for a lathe are known. Divide this total time by the number of inches (centimeters) turned. Thus we have a unit estimate, or hours/in. (cm) of length. Even though this is simplistic when expressed in this context, unit estimating methods are widely used.

A unit estimate is defined as the mean, where the divisor is the principal cost driver, or

$$C_a = \frac{\Sigma C_i}{\Sigma n_i} \tag{6.3}$$

where C_a = average cost per unit of design

C_i = value of design i, dollars

n_i = design i unit (lb, in., kg, mm, count, etc.)

Consider the design of cast iron sphere where there are three observations:

Design Weight lb (kg)		Cost
2	(0.9)	$ 2
3	(1.4)	3
4	(1.8)	6
9	(4.10)	$11

The cost per pound (kilogram) is $1.22 (− 11/9)($2.71 kg). A new casting design would be estimated by finding sphere weight, and multiplying this value by $1.22/lb. While the estimating value is obviously improved with more observations, it suffers from other more fundamental faults. Note Fig. 6.2(a), where the data are plotted and a regression equation would give $C = -2.33 + 2.00/lb$. Effectively, the unit value is nothing more than the general slope b where $a = 0$, or $y = 0 + bx$. For in the estimating of $1.22/lb to a design, the cost is zero for no weight, as 1.22 is a linear multiplier. An improvement is made when the data are fitted to $y = a + bx$. When using $C_a = 1.22$, the unit method either over- or underestimates the design when compared to $y = a + b_1x$. The only location where there is no *policy error* of the choice of the estimating model occurs at $\bar{x}$ and $\bar{y}$ of the data, or weight = 3 lb and $C_a = 3.67, which for $y = a + b_1x$ and C_a are equal. Notice that the regression equation has a negative intercept, which as a practical matter suggests negative fixed costs, an unlikely situation. When $a < 0$, the estimator is signaled for faulty data or the equation model is suspect.

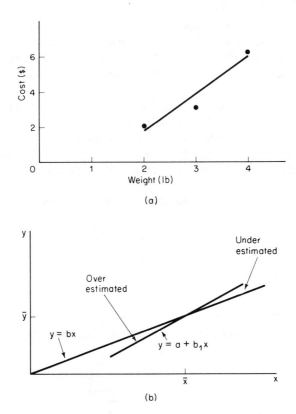

Figure 6.2. (a) Plot of three observations; (b) unit model compared to $y = a + b_1 x$ results in an over and under estimate error except at $\bar{x}$, $\bar{y}$ of the data.

The unit method fails to use the principle of *economy of scale*. For example, a 2-lb sphere costs \$2.44, while a 4-lb sphere costs \$4.88. At least a linear regression improves on the value as \$1.67 and \$5.67, which is not simple doubling.

6.6 COST- AND TIME-ESTIMATING RELATIONSHIPS

Cost-estimating relationships (CERs) and time-estimating relationships (TERs) are mathematical models or graphs that estimate cost or time. CERs and TERs are popular jargon within the U.S. Department of Defense and other national political organizations.

The word *parameter* is often used in the CER context. A parameter usually refers to empirical coefficients in an equation [e.g., $C_a = -2.33 + 2.00(\text{lb})$]. But after the development of a CER, and in the application phase, we substitute the particular parameter values for the design and calculate a cost, such as the parameter of a casting weighing 5 lb (11.1 kg) and costing \$7.67. Simply, CERs and TERs are statistical regression models that mathematically describe the cost of an item or activity as a function of one or more independent variables. Previous discussion of these principles was covered in Chapter 5, but forecasting tends to deal with time serial and minor analytical problems. However, CERs and TERs are formulated to give estimates for end items. Rules of thumb, such as the unit method, are not recognized as CERs.

These approaches are not new, but for product, project, and system estimates, the ideas use output design variables (i.e., physical or performance parameters such as weight, speed, power thrust, etc.) to predict cost since the design parameters are available early. Estimates are preliminary and their analysis adopts historical information. These equations are statistical relationships between cost or time and physical or performance characteristics of the past designs. Sometimes, these characteristics or parameters are termed *cost drivers*. As in all functional estimating models, there must be a logical relationship of the variable to cost, a statistical significance of the variables' contribution, and independence of the variables to the explanation of cost. This is sometimes referred to as "causality." CERs can be developed using a variety of steps, but we suggest this approach: obtain actual costs, interview experts having knowledge of cost and design, find cost/time drivers, plot data roughly and understand anomalies, final plot and regression analysis, review, publish, and distribute the CERs to cost estimators. These steps constitute the basis for much of cost-estimating analysis, of course.

6.6.1 Learning

It is frequently recognized that repetition with the same operation results in less time or effort expended on that operation. This improvement can be sufficiently predictive through ordinary estimating techniques. The observed characteristic of the improved performance is called *learning*. The first applications of learning were in airframe manufacture, which found that the number of man-hours spent in building a plane declined at a constant rate over a wide range of production.

Other names abound for learning model, including manufacturing progress function and the experience or dynamic curve. They suggest that cost can be lowered with increasing quantity of production or experience. Knowing how much product cost can be lowered and at what point learning is applied in estimating procedures are reasons for studying learning prior to product estimating methods. The learning model rests on the following observations:

1. The amount of time or cost required to complete a unit of product is less each time the task is undertaken.
2. Unit time will decrease at a decreasing rate.
3. Reduction in unit time follows a specific estimating model such as $y = ax^b$, an equation studied in Chapter 5.

To state the underlying hypothesis, the direct labor man-hours necessary to complete a unit of product will decrease by a constant percentage each time the production quantity is doubled. While the hypothesis stresses only time, practice has extended the concept to other types of measures. A frequent stated rate of improvement is 20% between doubled quantities. This establishes an 80% learning and means that the man-hours to build the second unit will be the product of 0.80 times that required for the first. The fourth unit (doubling 2) will require 0.80 times the man-hours for the second; the eighth unit (doubling 4) will require 0.80 times the fourth; and so forth. The rate of improvement (20% in this case) is constant with regard to doubled production quantities, but the absolute reduction between amounts is less.

The notion of constant reduction of time or effort between doubled quantities can be defined by a unit formula:

$$T_u = KN^s \tag{6.4}$$

where T_u = effort per unit of production, such as man-hours or dollars required
to produce the *Nth unit*
N = unit number
K = constant, or estimate, for unit 1 in dimensions compatible to T
s = slope or a function of the improvement rate

The slope is negative because the effort decreases with increasing production. Equation (6.4) plots as a curved line on arithmetic coordinates but as a straight line on logarithmic coordinates. Taking logarithms of both sides, we get

$$\log T_u = \log K + s \log N \tag{6.5}$$

which in terms of $y = \log T_u$, $x = \log N$, and $a = \log K$ has the form $y = a + bx$, the equation of a straight line. Figures 6.3 and 6.4 show the arithmetic and logarithmic plot.

To understand the graphic presentation of the learning curve on logarithmic graph paper, first compare the characteristics of arithmetic and logarithmic graph paper. On arithmetic graph paper equal numerical differences are represented by equal distances. For example, the linear distance between 1 and 3 will be the same as from 8 to 10. On logarithmic graph paper the linear distance between any two quantities is dependent on the ratio of those two quantities. Two pairs of quantities having the same ratio will be equally spaced along the same axis. For example, the distance from 2 to 4 will be the same as from 30 to 60 or from 1000 to 2000.

The learning curve is usually plotted on double logarithmic paper, meaning that both the abscissa and the ordinate will be a logarithmic scale. For an exponential function $T_u = KN^s$ the plot will result in a straight line on log-log paper. Because of this, the function can be plotted from either two points or one point and the slope (e.g., unit number 1 and the percentage improvement). Also, by using log-log paper the values for a large quantity of units can be presented on one graph, and these can be read relatively easily from the graph. Arithmetic graph paper, on the other hand, requires many values to sketch in the function.

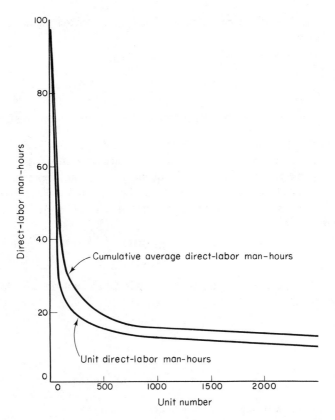

Figure 6.3.   80% learning curve with unit 1 at 100 direct-labor man-hours, arithmetic coordinates.

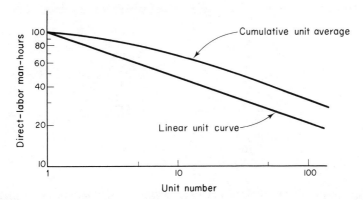

Figure 6.4.   80% learning curve with unit 1 at 100 direct-labor man-hours, logarithmic coordinates, and unit line assumed linear.

Equation (6.4) implies a constant reduction for doubled production. For any fixed value of s,

$$T_1 = K1^s, \qquad T_2 = K2^s$$

and

$$\frac{T_2}{T_1} = \frac{K(2^s)}{K(1^s)} = 2^s$$

Also, $T_2 = K(2^s)$, $T_4 = K(4^s)$, and $T_4/T_2 = 2^s$, and similarly, $T_8/T_4 = 2^s$. Every time quantity is doubled, the time per unit is a constant 2^s of what it was. As s is negative, the time per unit decreases with quantity. It is common practice to express learning in terms of the gain for double production. A 80% learning requires only 80% of the time per unit every time production is doubled. Note Fig. 6.5 for this relationship. Define

$$\phi = \frac{T_{2N}}{T_N} = \frac{K(2N)^s}{K(N)^s} = 2^s \tag{6.6}$$

where ϕ is the decimal ratio of time per unit required for doubled production. Taking logarithms, we have

$$\log \phi = s \log 2 \tag{6.7}$$

or

$$s = \frac{\log \phi}{\log 2}$$

A table of decimal learning ratios to ϕ is given as follows:

ϕ	Exponent, s
1.0 (no learning)	0
0.95	-0.074
0.90	-0.152
0.85	-0.234
0.80	-0.322
0.75	-0.415
0.70	-0.515
0.65	-0.621
0.60	-0.737
0.55	-0.861
0.50	-1.000

Application of Eq. (6.4) can be illustrated by an 80% learning curve with unit 1 at 1800 direct-labor man-hours. Solving for T_8, the number of direct-labor man-hours required to build the eighth unit gives

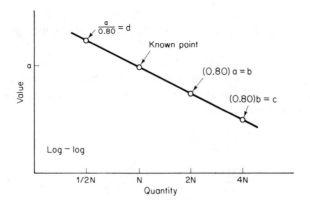

Figure 6.5. Constructing learning line on basis of known data for 80% curve. Note: 50 to 100 is the same distance as 500 to 1000 or 5 to 10 on log-log paper.

$$T_8 = 1800(8)^{\log 0.8/\log 2}$$

$$= 1800(8)^{-0.322} = \frac{1800}{1.9535} = 922 \, \text{hours}$$

For unit 1 requiring 1500 hours and a projected learning of 75%, the time for unit 90 is

$$T_{90} = 1500(90)^{-0.415} = \frac{1500}{6.471} = 232 \, \text{hours}$$

It may be desired to find out if learning has materialized, and if it has, to determine the function for which other unit estimates can be found. Where only two points are specified it may be desirable to find the learning curve that extends through them. Let the two points be specified as (N_i, T_i) and (N_j, T_j). At each point

$$T_i = KN_i^s \text{ and } \qquad T_j = KN_j^s$$

Dividing the second into the first gives

$$\frac{T_i}{T_j} = \left(\frac{N_i}{N_j}\right)^s \tag{6.8}$$

and taking the log of both sides we have

$$\log \frac{T_i}{T_j} = s \log \frac{N_i}{N_j} \tag{6.9}$$

$$s = \frac{\log T_i - \log T_j}{\log N_i - \log N_j}$$

K may be found by substituting s into $T_i = KN_i^s$ and solving for K:

$$\log T_i = \log K - s \log N_i \tag{6.10}$$

This has a linear form like $y = a + bx$, one of the linear models described in Chapter 5. It is seen that on log-log paper the intercept is K while the slope of the line is equal to $-s$.

An example will now illustrate this concept. A company audited two production units, the twentieth and fortieth, and found that about 700 hours and 635 hours were used, respectively. Now at the seventy-ninth unit, they want to estimate the time for the eightieth unit:

$$s = \frac{\log 700 - \log 635}{\log 20 - \log 40}$$

$$= \frac{2.8451 - 2.8028}{1.3010 - 1.6021} = \frac{0.0423}{-0.3011} = -0.1406$$

and

$$\log \phi = s \log 2$$
$$= (-0.1406)(0.3010) = 9.9577 - 10$$

Taking the antilog of both sides gives $\phi = 0.907$. The percentage learning ratio is 90.7%. Using the data for the twentieth unit, we obtain

$$700 = K(20)^{-0.1406}$$
$$\log 700 = \log K - 0.1406 \log 20$$
$$\log K = 2.8451 + 0.1406(1.3010) = 3.0279$$

Taking the antilog, $K = 1066$ hours. The learning curve function is

$$T_u = 1066N^{-0.1406}$$

The unit time for any unit can now be calculated directly. For the eightieth unit

$$T_{80} = 1066(80)^{-0.1406} = 576 \text{ hours}$$

Usually, learning is calculated using regression models since historical data of many points are required. For instance, see page 163 and Problem 5.16.

The unit formulation can be extended to other types of functional models. It may be necessary to determine a cumulative average number of direct-labor man-hours. This can be found by the cumulative total and is

$$T_c = T_1 + T_2 + \cdots + T_N = \sum_{u=1}^{N} T_u \qquad (6.11)$$

where T_c is the cumulative total effort from unit 1 to N.

$$T_a = \frac{\sum_{u=1}^{N} T_u}{N} = \frac{T_c}{N} \qquad (6.12)$$

where T_a denotes the average total effort from unit 1 to N. A good approximation of the cumulative average number of direct-labor man-hours for 20 or more units is given by

$$T_a \doteq \frac{1}{(1 + s)} KN^s \qquad (6.13)$$

The cumulative average curve is above the linear unit curve (see Fig. 6.6).

Unit 1 is estimated to require 10,000 hours and production is assumed to have an 80% learning curve. What will be the unit direct-labor man-hours, the cumulative direct-labor man-hours, and the cumulative average direct-labor man-hours for unit 4?

$$T_1 = 10,000$$
$$T_2 = 10,000(2)^{-0.322} = 8000$$
$$T_3 = 10,000(3)^{-0.322} = 7021$$
$$T_4 = 10,000(4)^{-0.322} = 6400$$

The cumulative direct-labor man-hours are

$$\sum_{u=1}^{N=4} T_u = 31,421$$

while the average using Eq. (6.12) is

$$T_a = \frac{1}{4}(31,421) = 7855$$

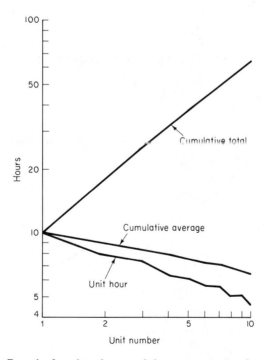

Figure 6.6.   Example of raw data where cumulative average appears to be a straight line.

Also

$$T_a \doteq \frac{6400}{1 - 0.322} = 9440$$

Equation (6.13) is not accurate in this quantity range since it is on the upper left-hand hump of the curve. This can be seen by examining Fig. (6.4).

What has been shown so far is only one-half of the learning. The previous development assumed that the *unit learning line* is linear.

Two other curves, T_c and T_a, were derived from this basic one. Sometimes these formulas are called the Boeing concept. Another frequently encountered learning curve model is the cumulative average, which is the original model first described by T. P. Wright in 1936. The theory states that as the total quantity of units doubles, the average cost per unit decreases by a constant percentage. In this case the *average learning line* is linear and the unit line curves under the average until 20 to 30 units, at which point they become parallel. Figure 6.7 is a graph of the two sets of curves. If the two learning theories start at the same K intercept and have the same learning rate, different values will result.

It is necessary to state which basic theory is chosen for any application. Various proponents adopt one practice or the other. Either will work, but values may not be directly comparable.

Define

$$T_a' = \frac{KN^{s+1}}{N} = KN^s \tag{6.14}$$

where $T_a' = $ average effort per unit given T_a' is a straight line.

$$T_c' = KN^{s+1} \tag{6.15}$$

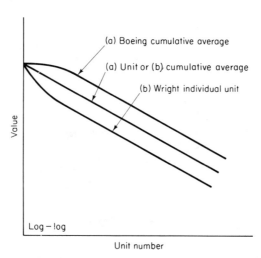

Figure 6.7. Comparison of two theories: (a) unit line is assumed linear or (b) cumulative average line is assumed linear.

where $T_c' =$ cumulative total effort from unit 1 to N.

$$T_u' = KN^{s+1} - K(N-1)^{s+1} \qquad (6.16)$$

where $T_u' =$ unit effort given that T_a' is the linear line.

Unit 1 is estimated to require 10,000 hours and production is assumed to have an 85% learning curve. What will be the cumulative average hours, unit hours, and cumulative hours at 45 units?

$$T_a' = 10,000(45)^{-0.234} = 4103 \text{ average hours}$$
$$T_u' = 10,000(45)^{-0.234+1} - 10,000(44)^{-0.234+1}$$
$$= 186,654 - 181,503 = 3151 \text{ hours}$$
$$T_c' = 10,000(45)^{-0.234+1} = 184,654 \text{ hours}$$

Because of their frequent use, the formulas are converted into tables provided in Appendix III. Columns 1–4 are developed using Eqs. (6.4), (6.11), and (6.12), having the unit line as the straight-line line.

The following is typical for 93%, where $s = \log 0.93/\log 2 = -0.105$.

STRAIGHT-LINE UNIT

(1) N	(2) T_u	(3) T_c	(4) T_a
1	$K = 1.0000$	1.0000	1.0000
2	0.9300	1.9300	0.9650
3	0.8913	2.8213	0.9404
4	0.8649	3.6862	0.9216
5	0.8449	4.5312	0.9062
10	0.7858	8.5604	0.8560
15	0.7531	12.3856	0.8257
Equation	KN^s	$\sum_1^N T_u$	T_c/N

Appendix III also provides values for the learning curve where the cumulative average is the straight line on logarithm scales. Tabulation for the 93% slope is as follows:

STRAIGHT-LINE AVERAGE

(1) N	(2) T_a	(5) T_c'	(6) T_u'
1	$K = 1.0000$	1.0000	1.0000
2	0.9300	1.8600	0.8600
3	0.8913	2.6740	0.8140
4	0.8649	3.4596	0.7856
5	0.8449	4.2246	0.7650
10	0.7858	7.8579	0.7073
15	0.7531	11.2969	0.6767
Equation	KN^s	KN^{s+1}	$KN^{s+1} - K(N-1)^{s+1}$

The learning curve has been successfully applied to engineering change-order calculation, follow-on estimating, break-even analysis, and spare-parts production. These practical applications are discussed in Chapter 8. Learning deals with the *economy of quantity* principle, which differs from size or scale.

6.6.2 Power Law and Sizing Model

The power law and sizing model is frequently used for estimating equipment. This model is concerned with designs varying in size but similar in type. The unknown costs of a 200-gallon kettle can be estimated from data for a 100-gallon kettle provided both are of similar design. No one would expect that the 200-gallon kettle would be twice as costly as the smaller one. The law of economy of scale assures that. The power law and sizing model is given as

$$C = C_r \left(\frac{Q_c}{Q_r} \right)^m \tag{6.17}$$

where C = cost value sought for design size Q_c

C_r = known cost for a reference size Q_r

Q_c = design size expressed in engineering units

Q_r = reference design size expressed in engineering units

m = correlating exponent, $0 < m \le 1$

If we let $m = 1$, we have a strictly linear relationship and deny the law of economy of scale. For chemical processing equipment m is frequently near 0.6, and for this reason the model is sometimes called the *sixth-tenth* model. The units on Q are required to be consistent as it enters only as a ratio.

Let us assume that 6 years ago an 80-kW diesel electric set, naturally aspirated, cost \$160,000. The plant engineering staff is considering a 120-kW unit of the same general design to power a small isolated plant. If the value of $m = 0.6$, we have

$$C = 160,000 \left(\frac{120}{80} \right)^{0.6} = \$204,000$$

The model can be altered to consider changes in price due to inflation or deflation and effects independent of size, or

$$C = C_r \left(\frac{Q_c}{Q_r} \right)^m \frac{I_c}{I_r} + C_1 \tag{6.18}$$

where C_1 is the constant unassociated cost. The price index for this class of equipment 6 years ago was 187 and now is 194. Assume that we want to add a precompressor, which when isolated and estimated separately costs \$18,000 or

$$C = 160,000 \left(\frac{120}{80} \right)^{0.6} \left(\frac{194}{187} \right) + 18,000 \doteq 230,000$$

The determination of m is important to the success of this model, and methods of curvilinear regression and rectification given in Chapter 5 are cogent. If the statistical analysis assumes constant dollars, then the index ratio I_c /I_r is used for increases or decreases for inflation or deflation effects.

The model usually does not cover those situations where the estimated design Q_c is greater or less than Q_r by a factor of 10. Some typical exponents for equipment cost versus capacity are given below.

Equipment	Size Range	Exponent, m
Blower, centrifugal (with motor)	1–3 hp	0.16
Blower, centrifugal (with motor)	$7\frac{1}{2}$–350 hp	0.96
Compressor, centrifugal (motor drive, air service)	20–70 hp drive	1.22
Compressor, reciprocating (motor drive, air service)	5–300 hp drive	0.90
Dryer, drum (including auxiliaries, atmospheric)	20–60 ft^2	0.36

The value of m is important in several ways. If $m > 1$, we deny the economy of scale law,* as is shown with the centrifugal compressor. If $m = 0$, we can double the size without affecting cost, an unlikely event.

An equation expressing unit cost C/Q_c can be found, or

$$C\frac{Q_r}{Q_c} = C_r\frac{Q_r}{Q_c}\left(\frac{Q_c}{Q_r}\right)^m = C_r\left(\frac{Q_c}{Q_r}\right)^{-1}\left(\frac{Q_c}{Q_r}\right)^m$$

(6.19)

$$\frac{C}{Q_c} = \frac{C_r}{Q_r}\left(\frac{Q_c}{Q_r}\right)^{m-1}$$

As total cost varies as the mth power of capacity in Eq. (6.17), C/Q_c will vary as the $(m - 1)$st power of the capacity ratio.

6.6.3 Other CERs

Other relationships exist, such as

$$C = KQ^m$$

(6.20)

where K = constant for a plant, equipment, part
Q = capacity expressed as a design dimension

There are difficulties in using Eq. (6.20) because it is necessary to know the capital cost of an identical plant. The scale factor m is not constant for all sizes of the

*In fact, when $m > 1$, we have "diseconomy" of scale.

design. Generally, scale-up or scale-down by more than a factor of 5 should be avoided.

The problems of Eq. (6.20) can be overcome by differentiating between the direct capital costs, which are subject to the economy of scale rule, and the indirect or fixed element, which is not. Another relationship can be expressed as

$$C = C_v \left(\frac{Q_c}{Q_r}\right)^m + C_f \tag{6.21}$$

where C_v = variable element of capital cost, dollars

C_f = fixed element of capital cost, dollars

A multivariable CER is also possible. For instance,

$$C = KQ^m N^s \tag{6.22}$$

where the symbols are as previously. In these cases the coefficients are determined by regression methods. Equation (6.22) is a relationship dealing with the cost estimating principles of quantity and scale.

CERs can be plotted together with all points, allowing the estimator a feeling for the data and the line. Removing the points destroys the sense of variation. Are the data a scattergram or are the data lying neatly on a line? Figure 6.8 is an example of the plot of pressure vessels, where the x-axis is "gallons per minute" multiplied by "feet head."

6.7 PROBABILITY APPROACHES

As usually prepared, the estimate represents an "average" concept. It does not reveal anything about the probability of the expected values, however, and uses information which is called certain, or *deterministic*.

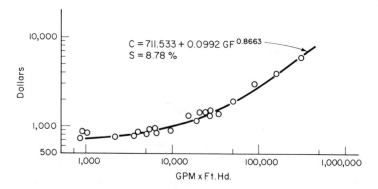

Figure 6.8. Example of a CER plot and equation using physical variables.

Much has been written on the topic of statistical decision theory, also called Bayesian analysis. Despite the subject's importance, delving into details is too encompassing for a text of this sort.

6.7.1 Expected Value

For this simpler discussion we assume that the estimator can give a probability point estimate to each element of uncertainty as represented by the economics of the design. This assignment has nonnegative numerical weights associated with possible events, such that if an event is certain its associated probability equals 1. If two events A and B are mutually exclusive, the probability of the event "either A or B" equals the sum of the probability for each of the events. These probabilities are really a numerical judgment of future events, and the techniques for deriving probabilities are the following: (1) analysis of historical data to give a relative frequency interpretation, (2) convenient approximations like the normal and (3) introspection, or what is called opinion *probability*. Opinion probabilities call for judgmental expertise and a pinch of luck. Better success is assured when past data are analyzed; on the other hand, data may be unavailable, and it should be remembered that data are past, while these probabilities should be indicators of the future. Sometimes both past data and a reshuffling of probabilities are jointly undertaken. This type of discrimination is not new to professional cost-estimating practice, as that is what estimating is all about.

For the most part estimators have preferred to deal with the simplest case of *certainty*. When we say that "material cost is $1," we imply, but leave unstated, that the probability is 1, a certain event. Any other material cost has the probability of zero. Despite this practice, it seldom exists. The category involving *risk* is appropriate whenever it is possible to estimate the likelihood of occurrence for each condition of the design. These probabilities describe the true likelihood that the predicted event will occur. Formally, the method incorporates the effect of risk on potential outcomes by a weighted average. Each outcome of an alternative is multiplied by the probability that the outcome will occur. This sum of products for each alternative is entered in an expected value column, or mathematically for the discrete case,

$$C(i) = \sum_{j}^{n} p_j x_{ij} \tag{6.23}$$

where C = expected value of the estimate for alternative i

p_j = probability that x takes on value x_j

x_{ij} = design event

The p_j's represent the independent probabilities that their associative x_{ij}'s will occur with $\sum_{j=1}^{n} p_j = 1$. The expected value method exposes the degree of risk when reporting information in the estimating process.

Consider the following example: An electronics manufacturing firm is evaluating a portable TV having special design features. Market research has indicated a substantial market available for a small lightweight set if priced at $850 retail. This implies that the set will have to be sold for approximately $650 to wholesalers. Before the decision can be made to enter the market, several questions need to be answered. Three important ones are: What will be the first year's sales volume in units? How much will the sets cost to produce? What will be the profit? To answer these questions, marketing furnishes an estimate of the first year's sales in units. Subsequently, the cost estimators provide a total cost per unit. Marketing presented the following forecast:

Annual Sales Volume	Probability of Event Occurring
15,000	0.2
20,000	0.2
25,000	0.6[a]

[a]Most frequent case.

After inspecting the sales forecast, cost estimating provided the following estimates:

Cost per Unit ($)	Probability of Event Occurring
450	0.7[a]
500	0.2
550	0.1

[a]Most frequent case.

The illustration can now be divided into (1) risk not apparent and (2) risk apparent. Assume that marketing and estimating use the most probable figure from their studies and do not report any uncertainty. The profit is calculated as

$$\text{profit} = (650 - \text{cost})\text{volume}$$

where cost = \$450
   volume = 25,000 units
   profit = $(650 - 450)25,000 = \$5,000,000$

On the other hand, assume that the organization encourages a policy of reporting risk in estimates. The probability numbers are used without the effects of editing. Since there are three possibilities for cost and three for volume, we calculate nine profit possibilities:

The reader may argue that simple mathematics need not be complicated. Both cost estimating and marketing could have computed an expected value as 470 ($=$ 450 $\times$-0.7 + 500 $\times$ 0.2 + 550 $\times$ 0.1) and 22,000 ($=$ 15,000 $\times$ 0.2 + 20,000 $\times$ 0.2 + 25,000 $\times$ 0.6). The expected profit becomes 22,000 (650 $-$ 470) $=$ \$3.96 million. In the case of risk not apparent the total profit was overstated. The calculations for this example require that the cost per unit be independent of volume and that cost be inversely related to volume, which is generally not the case.

(650 − Cost)Volume	Joint Probability of Occurrence	Expected Value Profit
(650 − 450)15,000 = 3,000,000	0.14	420,000
(650 − 450)20,000 = 4,000,000	0.14	560,000
(650 − 450)25,000 = 5,000,000	0.42	2,100,000
(650 − 500)15,000 = 2,250,000	0.04	90,000
(650 − 500)20,000 = 3,000,000	0.04	120,000
(650 − 500)25,000 = 3,750,000	0.12	450,000
(650 − 550)15,000 = 1,500,000	0.02	30,000
(650 − 550)20,000 = 2,000,000	0.02	40,000
(650 − 550)25,000 = 2,500,000	0.06	150,000
	Total = 1.00	Profit = 3,960,000

One of the difficulties in applying expected value is the inability of estimators to guess opinion probabilities. Seldom are there sufficient experiences that allow for a gradual development of this ability.

6.7.2 Simulation

Simulation is defined as the manipulation and observation of a synthetic model representative of a real design which for technical or economic reasons is not susceptible to direct experimentation. This synthetic model ideally represents the essential characteristics of the real design with the frills excluded. The computer is mandatory in analysis of this sort. "What if?" types of questions can be examined.

Simulation models are classified into several groupings:

1. Real versus abstract. A real design would be a prototype aircraft or a pilot plant, for example, versus mathematical or logical statements.
2. Deterministic versus probabilistic. All business and engineering is probabilistic; however, these situations are conveniently described by constant-value models. In probabilistic situations it is possible to introduce random events such that the various parameters of operation are affected, while in deterministic situations we assume that the value used for the parameter is an ideal approximation for that particular design. Sometimes probabilistic simulation models are termed *Monte Carlo*, which is a simulation tool and convenient with digital computers.
3. Machine versus man–machine. The "machine" is a pure computer simulation in which all eventualities are programmed into the computer. The man–machine simulation allows program interruption by the human being and permits intervention at strategic points. This division of labor allows the computer to do what it can do well and encourages the ability of people to interpret qualitatively rather than quantitatively.

Although simulation uses mathematics, it is not mathematics per se. In simulation, you *run* problems, not *solve* them as you do in mathematics. The intent is the collection of pertinent data from the experiment as one runs and watches the outcome of many simulation trials. Figure 6.9 is a description of the methods that

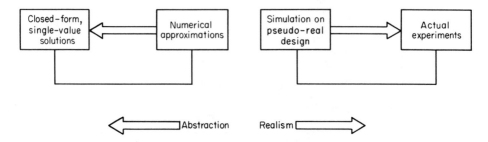

Figure 6.9. Simulation-direct solution approach to cost-engineering problems.

are useful to engineering-economic analysis. On the one hand, the actual experiment of a cost-engineering design provides realism. On the other, the orthodox mathematical solution to business and engineering problems remains an abstraction. This "running" and "watching" by simulation is described further by Fig. 6.10.

In simulation a model is formulated that looks like the procedures described in later estimating chapters. These procedures use addition of cost elements such as labor, materials, and multiplication for overhead application. This is the pattern for simulation.

Presume that a cost can be expressed as $A = x + y$, where x and y are probability distributions. The distribution of $f(x)$ is found by field data methods and is given as

Cost of x $\times\ 10^6$	Relative Frequency	Monte Carlo Numbers
$1.1	0.05	0.00–0.05
1.2	0.10	0.06–0.15
1.3	0.15	0.16–0.30
1.4	0.20	0.31–0.50
1.5	0.20	0.51–0.70
1.6	0.15	0.71–0.85
1.7	0.10	0.86–0.95
1.8	0.05	0.96–1.00

The Monte Carlo numbers are found similarly to the construction of the cumulative frequency intervals for empirical distributions in Sec. 5.1. Thus 1.1×10^6 million has an interval of 0.00 to 0.05. In simulation we assume that random numbers are the probability of the cost item. If a random number of 0.18 is drawn, we say that this corresponds to 1.3×10^6 million after entry in the Monte Carlo numbers,

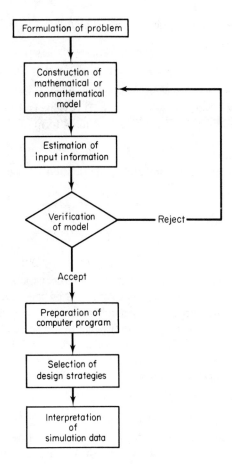

Figure 6.10.   Typical flowchart for simulation studies.

because it falls within that range. Tables of random numbers can be found in other texts. We provide a sample grouping when required for any problem.

The collection of field data and determining Monte Carlo numbers is one approach. A second method uses theoretical distributions fitted with empirical coefficients. We assume, for example, that a negative exponential function represents a cost. A *probability density function* for the continuous random variable X is defined as

$$f(x) \geq 0$$

$$\int_{-\infty}^{+\infty} f(x) \, dx = 1 \tag{6.24}$$

$$P(a \leq x \leq b) = \int_{a}^{b} f(x) \, dx$$

As an immediate consequence, the *cumulative distribution F(x)* of the random variable is given by

$$F(x) = P(X \le x) = \int_{-\infty}^{x} f(x) \, dx \qquad (6.25)$$

In simulation we let various random numbers, 0 to 1, substitute for $F(x)$ and solve for the upper value of integration, x. This value is the simulated value. Assume that $f(y)$ is given by a density with a functional form of

$$f(y) = \tfrac{1}{8} e^{-y/8}, \qquad y \ge 0$$

To find the cumulative probability distribution we use

$$F(y) = \int_{0}^{Cy} f(y) dy = \int_{0}^{Cy} \tfrac{1}{8} e^{-y/8} \, dy$$

$$= 1 - e^{-C\hat{y}/8}$$

$$C_y = -8 \ln [1 - F(y)]$$

Our example requires that the random variable x be added to the random variable y. This requirement is established by the model under study. If a random number is found from a random number table or a computer file and has the properties of being between 0 and 1, it is set equal to the cumulative probability distribution. A random number 0.73 is drawn for design x, and the corresponding value of the random variable is $1,600,000. In a similar way we supply a random number 0.18 to the functional model for y:

$$C_y = -8 \ln (1 - 0.18)$$
$$C_y = 1.587 \quad \text{or} \quad \$1,587,000$$

Our solution is cost $A = 1,600,000 + 1,587,000 = \$3,187,000$ and is accepted as a sample value of our cost A. This procedure is repeated many times, and finally a distribution of cost A can be found. This distribution can be tested for its cost estimate average, range, standard deviation, and other statistical properties. In using simulation techniques to estimate design cost, it is usually required that the input relationships be independent.

A cost trial A is the consequence of a random event for x and y. After many trials, distribution A can be developed, which would appear as shown in Fig. 6.11, and could be compared to another alternative design B, which would be simulated separately.

Suppose that two designs are to be judged and that cost is the criterion. Figure 6.11 illustrates four cases where the cost estimates are shown as probability distributions. For case (a) all probable costs of A are lower than B and there is no difficulty in choosing A. The situation for (b) has a possibility that the actual cost of A will be higher than B. Given that this is a small chance, the estimator would select A. As the amount of overlap increases, the expected cost estimate C_a may not be given a clear choice. For (c) the average cost estimates are equal, although their distributions are not. Certainly, the cost distribution of B is greater and there is an

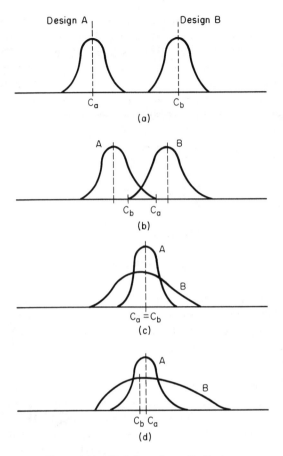

Figure 6.11. Variations of cost distributions.

associated risk of having a lower cost than A. On the other hand, A is less variable; the estimator's assessment of cost return and risk will serve as the guide here. In (d) the expected cost estimate of B is lower but less certain than A. If only the expected value estimate is used in this case, the estimate would likely choose the more desirable alternative B.

6.7.3 Range

Estimators knowing the weaknesses of information and techniques recognize that there are probable errors. The indication that cost is a random variable opens up the topic of range estimating. A *random variable* in statistical parlance is a numerical-valued function of the outcomes of a sample of data. Another approach to single-valued estimating involves making a single estimate and bracketing this estimate for each cost element. This forms the basis for range estimating.

The following procedure is based on a method developed for PERT (program evaluation and review technique). It involves making a most likely cost estimate, an optimistic estimate (lowest cost), and a pessimistic estimate (highest cost). These estimates are assumed to correspond to the beta distribution shown by Fig. 6.12. This particular figure is skewed left. Symmetric and skewed-right distributions are also possible. The total area under the curve is 1. The mathematics of the beta probability density are complicated, but their expected values lead to simplified equations.

With the three estimates made, a mean and variance for the cost element can be calculated as

$$E(C_i) = \frac{L + 4M + H}{6} \tag{6.26}$$

and

$$\text{var}\,(C_i) = \left(\frac{H - L}{6}\right)^2 \tag{6.27}$$

where $E(C_i)$ = expected cost for element i, dollars
$\quad\quad\ L$ = lowest cost, or best case, dollars
$\quad\quad M$ = modal value of cost distribution, dollars
$\quad\quad\ H$ = highest cost, or worst case, dollars
$\text{var}\,(C_i)$ = variance of element i

If a dozen or more elements are estimated this way and are assumed to be independent of each other and are added together, the distribution of the total cost is approximately normal. This follows from the *central limit theorem:* The mean of the sum is the sum of the means, and the variance of the sum is the sum of the variances. The distribution of the sum of costs will be normal despite the individual shape of cost elements. This is shown by Fig. 6.13.

$$E(C_T) = E(C_1) + E(C_2) + \cdots + E(C_n) \tag{6.28}$$

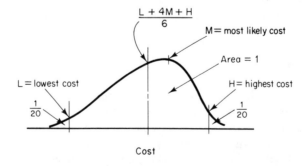

Figure 6.12. Location of estimates for PERT-based beta distribution.

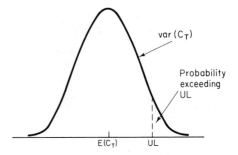

Figure 6.13. Normal curve assumed to be a result of sum of many individual beta probabilities.

and

$$\text{var}\,(C_T) = \text{var}\,(C_1) + \text{var}\,(C_2) + \cdots + \text{var}\,(C_n) \tag{6.29}$$

where $E(C_T)$ = expected total cost, dollars
$\quad\text{var}(C_T)$ = variance of total cost, dollars

Table 6.1 shows an application of this approach. The expected cost is \$10,600 and the variance representing probable error is 22,300. Now various statements regarding the interval for the future value can be made, such as some cost will not be exceeded and probability boundaries can be established.

With the normal curve developed, it is possible to examine this distribution and ask the question: What is the probability that a certain cost will be exceeded, or $P[\text{cost} > E(C_T)]$? This is found using

$$Z = \frac{\text{UL} - E(C_T)}{[\text{var}\,(C_T)]^{1/2}} \tag{6.30}$$

Table 6.1. CALCULATION OF EXPECTED COST AND VARIANCE FOR THE RANGE-ESTIMATING METHOD

	Lowest Cost, L	Most Likely Cost, M	Highest Cost, H	Expected Cost, $E(C_i)$	Variance, var (C_i)
1. Flashlamp	\$ 370	\$ 390	\$ 430	\$ 393.33	100.00
2. Data grid	910	940	1,030	950.00	400.00
3. Computer	200	210	270	218.33	136.11
4. Optical isolator	170	180	190	180.00	11.11
5. Power supply	260	290	350	295.00	225.00
6. Switch	171	172	176	172.50	0.69
7. Capacitor	875	925	975	925.00	277.78
...	...	...	...	...	...
n. Frame	2,000	2,100	2,600	2,166.67	10,000.00
			$E(C_T) =$	\$10,601.66	var $(C_T) =$ 22,301.39

where Z = value of the standard normal distribution, Appendix I

  UL = upper limit cost arbitrarily selected, dollars

The location of UL is shown by Fig. 6.13 in relation to $E(C_T)$.

The square root of var (C_T) is the standard deviation. The value of Z is entered in Appendix I and an upper-tail probability can be determined. Consider Table 6.1 and find the probability that the cost will exceed \$10,850, which is

$$Z = \frac{10,850 - 10,602}{(22,301)^{1/2}} = 1.66$$

and $P(\text{cost} > 10,850) \doteq 0.05$.

According to PERT practices, the optimistic and pessimistic costs would be wrong only 1 time in 20 if the activity were to be performed repeatedly under the same conditions. Usually, the job is estimated only once, so these requirements are never met. We suggest that these costs be viewed as *best, most likely,* or *worst cost.* Furthermore, it is unlikely that a distribution of major actual cost elements can ever be constructed. Costs, if they are internal to a firm, are seldom independent of each other, although for a project estimate of various contractors' costs, independence is more valid. The expected value method discussed earlier required selection of opinion probabilities, which we believe is unsound. However, the range method requires three values of cost, and if rational methods are employed, the range method is acceptable as a preliminary technique. This method is discussed in Chapter 9, where it is useful for contingency analysis.

6.8 STANDARD TIME DATA

We have discussed several methods whereby work measurement data are collected. Time data in their raw form are not usable by the cost estimator. Frequently these data include bad methods, unwarranted conditions, or non-average operators. Sometimes it is lacking due to the limitations of a narrow range of observed work. The estimator uses regression analysis to extend these raw data into a more digestible form. For it is not the original time measurements that the estimator ultimately desires; rather it is a set of engineering performance data, or standard time data, or more briefly standard data, that he or she uses for estimating. *Standard time data* may be viewed as a catalog of standard tasks that are used for performing a given class of work. Parenthetically, it should be indicated that standard time data are arranged in a systematic order and are used over and over again. The advantages over direct observation methods such as time study, predetermined motion time data, work sampling, and man-hour reports are lower cost and greater consistency. Description is provided in advance of the need for the data, and more estimators can use standard time data. Standard time data may be divided into preliminary or detail. The estimator is more likely to be concerned with a preliminary standard data early in estimating; later, detail data become more important. Standard time data are ordinarily determined from any of the various methods of observing work.

In manufacturing, time-study and predetermined motion data are the major sources. In construction and hospitals, work-sampling and man-hour reports are the principal sources of information. In certain government work, such as that of the post office or armed forces, work-sampling and man-hour methods are used. Whatever the source of work data, the development of standard data is similar.

Standard time data are now defined as the time values in a concise final form from which a standard time can be obtained reflecting the cost of a given operation performed under usual conditions. The key word in this definition is *usual*. It is unwise to devise standard time data without first knowing conditions, specifications, methods, and procedures. If these precautions are heeded, the time values are based on the local conditions in which the standard is to apply.

Although the number of basic studies used for standard time data is a statistical question, it is realized that accuracy is a function of the number of observations. Assuming that the basic data were correctly and uniformly determined, one of the decisions that faces the analyst is to determine whether a particular element is *constant* or a *variable*. A constant is accepted by convenience and assumed to have less than an arbitrary percentage P_1 slope between the limits of work scope. It is admitted that very little work is ever constant, but in order to get things done we overlook some variability. If the time slope, say a positive 2%, from the minimum to the maximum is found, the analyst arbitrarily chooses to classify this element as a constant if the P_1 limit value amounted to 5%. In this case a constant value would be found. If the increase of slope between the limits of the defined element is greater than 5%, the element is classified as a variable. The dependent variable time can be related to an independent variable by a graph, a table, or regression formula. A particular element may be one of many elements that define a set of standard time data for some operation. Moreover, if the element is P_2 or less of the standard time of the total expected mean operation time, it could be classified as a constant irrespective of its elemental variability.

A TER element is judged "constant or variable" on the outcome of two rules. The technician will measure conditions that include extremes, minimum to maximum, of the design. The two rules are as follows:

1. An element is conditionally variable if

$$\frac{\hat{y}_{max} - \hat{y}_{min}}{\hat{y}_{min}} \times 100 \geq P_1\% \tag{6.31}$$

where $\hat{y}_{max}$ = maximum dependent value related to time
      driver x_{max}
  $\hat{y}_{min}$ = minimum dependent value related to time driver
      x_{min}
  P_1 = percentage, arbitrarily fixed

The $\hat{y}$ values are preferred over actual raw y data because the least-squares time value minimizes observational errors. If test $1 < P_1$, the element is constant, otherwise

2. An element is variable if

$$\frac{\hat{y}_{ave}}{\hat{y}_t} \times 100 \geq P_2\% \tag{6.32}$$

where $\hat{y}_{ave}$ = average dependent value for x_{ave}

$\hat{y}_t$ = total dependent value for $\bar{x}$'s of operation elements

P_2 = percentage, arbitrarily fixed

Rule 1 is concerned with inner element variability, while rule 2 evaluates the effect of the element average to the total average for the operation. An element could be variable on the basis of rule 1, but it might have so little effect on the average outcome that it would be more practical to consider it constant and overlook small variability. Both of these rules are subject to discretion by selection of P_1 and P_2.

After the TER standard time data elements are judged constant or variable, the analyst organizes the information into tables.

Standard time data tables are developed in the following way. Constant elements are combined and an average time value is calculated. One or several elements will be found constant for the operation. An abbreviated description of the elements is written, together with the best value, and is prepared as printed or typed material. Obviously, constant values are easy to use, but they are insensitive in estimating cost. A trade-off between ease of estimating and sensitivity is necessary. Each variable element is converted to a table. What is adequate and accurate for one variable element could be too detailed for the next. The simplest method of tabulating the variable element is to divide the time driver into classes (i.e., small, medium, large, etc.) and select a time value for each class. This can be improved by subdividing the y's into several or many unequal cells, or equal percentage jumps, and finding the x-value corresponding to each specific y. One efficient way of doing this is given by

$$x_i = \frac{\hat{y}_i - a}{b}(1 + P_3) \tag{6.33}$$

where x_i = independent variable value recursively determined

$\hat{y}_i$ = minimum starting dependent value

P_3 = percentage for step, arbitrarily fixed

Assume a TER $y = 0.0642 + 0.0133x$, where $\hat{y} = 0.131$ for $x_{min} = 5$. For $P_3 = 20\%$ and $y = 0.131 \times 1.2 = 0.157$, for which $x = 7.0$; $0.157 \times 1.2 = 0.189$, for which $x = 9.4$; and $0.189 \times 1.2 = 0.227$, for which $x = 12.2$. Summarizing, we have

x	5.0	7.0	9.4	12.2
y	0.131	0.157	0.189	0.227

The y increases in absolute time from 0.026 ($= 0.157 - 0.131$) to 0.038 ($= 0.227 - 0.189$), while the neighboring steps jump at 20% increments.

For ease and consistency in using standard time data tables, "look-up" rules of thumb are followed:

1. If the value of the independent variable, or time driver, of the design is less than shown in a standard time data table, the look-up will choose the minimum value as listed. This minimum is equal to or greater than the positive fixed intercept *a* of the TER.
2. If the time driver falls between listed table values, the estimator will choose the next higher value. This rule discourages tabular interpolation, a time-consuming step often ineffective in improving accuracy.
3. If the time driver exceeds the tabular listed value, the maximum of the values is used. This presumes a natural process barrier that may have been uncovered during measurement.

These rules, while admittedly inflexible, encourage later verification of an estimate by someone other than the original estimator.

Construction of a standard time table is by trial and error. Ease of understanding, speed in labor estimating, compression of tables into the fewest number, and accuracy are desirable features. After the tables are tentatively constructed, the tables are compared back to the original time measurements using the three rules of table look-up. Three measures to evaluate accuracy are

$$E_g = \frac{\Sigma H_s - \Sigma H_a}{\Sigma H_a} \times 100 \tag{6.34}$$

where E_g = gross overall percentage error
H_s = time for design from tables using "look-up" rules of thumb
H_a = time from original measurements

$$E_{ad} = \Sigma \left(\frac{H_s - H_a}{H_a} \times 100 \right) / N \tag{6.35}$$

where E_{ad} = average deviation percentage error
N = number of measurement studies

and

$$E_{at} = \Sigma \frac{(H_s - H_a)}{N} \tag{6.36}$$

where E_{at} is the average time error per estimate. Accuracy in these formulas relates the original measurement to the table look-up value. If these three measures of error are found unacceptable, the process is repeated with different P_1, P_2, and P_3 until satisfactory tables are constructed. Now consider the construction of standard time data for a manufacturing operation.

Spot welding is a form of resistance welding in which two sheets of metal are held between copper electrodes. A welding cycle is started with electrodes contacting the metal under pressure before current is applied, then a squeeze time under pressure with current, and finally a pressure dwell without current. Five time studies have been tabulated below. Among the many choices of an independent variable, *girth*, or length plus width plus height ($= L + W + H$), and the number of spots are selected for handling and welding. Five elements are identified. The number of spots is specified as x_1. In spot welding, a second and third part, if necessary, are assembled and welded to the first or major part. Girth for handling the major is shown below as x_2. Spot-welding time includes position part for spot weld, spot weld, and occasional cleaning of the electrodes. The load-major-part time includes moving part from skid to the electrodes. The secondary part and third part time includes moving the part from skid and positioning on major part with clamps and fixtures, and the variables are identified as x_3 and x_4. The unload time starts after the last spot and includes removing fixtures and clamps and moving the welded part onto the skid. Time is normal, i.e., observed time study elemental time which has been rated. The time in units of minutes are associated with their causal variables.

Time Study	Number Spots, x_1	$L + W + H$ Major Part, x_2	$L + W + H$ Secondary Part, x_3	$L + W + H$ Third Part, x_4	$L + W + H$ Final Part, x_5
1	8	29	16	—	37
2	3	46	8	—	46
3	9	101	17	5	106
4	14	60	28	33	60
5	36	53	23	44	53

Time Study	(1) Spot-Weld Min	(2) Load Major Part Min	(3) Load Additional Parts Min Second	(4) Load Additional Parts Min Third	(5) Unload Min	Total Time Study Min
1	0.28	0.08	0.12	—	0.10	0.58
2	0.13	0.10	0.14	—	0.17	0.54
3	0.34	0.27	0.21	0.10	0.28	1.20
4	0.87	0.21	0.59	0.61	0.32	2.60
5	2.06	0.19	0.29	0.57	0.51	3.62

Thus 0.28 minutes identified under spot-weld minutes corresponds to Time Study 1 where the number of spot is 8. The 0.28 was measured by a time study.

Assume that management selects $P_1 = 50\%$, $P_2 = 15\%$, and $P_3 = 20\%$. As the independent variable "number of spots" is an integer, it is necessary to show natural numbers for spot welds. Table 6.2(A) shows the steps to select constant or variable elements. The regression equation and independent variable are shown for each element. The values x_{min} and x_{max} are determined from the data, and corresponding $\hat{y}_{min}$ and $\hat{y}_{max}$ values are found using the equations. Data points x_{ave} and

Table 6.2.(A) REGRESSION EQUATIONS AND CONSTANT AND VARIABLE ELEMENTS
FOR SPOT-WELD MEASUREMENTS

Element	Independent Variable	Regression Equation
1. Spot-weld	Number of spots, x_1	$-0.1156 + 0.0608x_1$
2. Load major part	Major part girth, x_2	$0.0139 + 0.0027x_2$
3. Load second part	Second part girth, x_3	$-0.1282 + 0.0216x_3$
4. Load third part	Third part girth, x_4	$0.0642 + 0.0133x_4$
5. Unload	Final part girth, x_5	$0.1907 + 0.0014x_5$

Element	x_{min}	x_{ave}	x_{max}	$\hat{y}_{min}$	$\hat{y}_{ave}$	$\hat{y}_{max}$
1	3	19.5	36	0.067	1.070	2.073
2	29	65	101	0.092	0.189	0.287
3	8	18	28	0.045	0.261	0.477
4	5	24.5	44	0.131	0.390	0.649
5	37	71.5	106	0.243	0.291	0.339
				$\hat{y}_t =$	2.201	

Element	Test 1: $\dfrac{\hat{y}_{max} - \hat{y}_{min}}{\hat{y}_{min}} \times 100$ (%)	Test 1 Type Element	Test 2: $\dfrac{\hat{y}_{ave}}{\hat{y}_t} \times 100$ (%)	Test 2 Type Element
1	2995	Variable	49	Variable
2	212	Variable	9	Constant
3	960	Variable	12	Constant
4	396	Variable	18	Variable
5	40	Constant	—	—

Table 6.2.(B) TRIAL VALUES

Number of Spot Welds	Normal Time	Number of Spot Welds	Normal Time	Number of Spot Welds	Normal Time
3	0.067	9	0.432	21	1.162
4	0.128	10	0.493	24	1.344
5	0.188	12	0.614	28	1.588
6	0.249	14	0.736	33	1.892
7	0.310	16	0.858	36	1.959
8	0.371	18	0.979		

Load Third Part, $L + W + H$	Normal Time	Load Third Part, $L + W + H$	Normal Time
5.0	0.131	24.2	0.385
7.0	0.157	30.0	0.462
9.4	0.189	36.9	0.554
12.2	0.227	45.2	0.662
15.4	0.268	55.2	0.796
19.4	0.321		

y_{ave} are calculated. Test 1 shows that only element 5 is constant. Test 2 confirms that elements 1 and 3 are variable.

With elements 2, 3, and 5 as constant, their total regression mean time is 0.741 normal minute. Now we use Eq. (6.33). Element 1 is variable, and while requiring increasing steps of 20%, the number of spot welds is also required to be integer. Element 4 is variable and increases by 20% from minimum $\hat{y}$ value. Trial values are as follows:

Table 6.2.(C) COMPARISON OF TRIAL VALUES TO TIME STUDY TIME.

Time Study	Constant	+	No. Spots	+	Third Part	=	H_s	Time Study Total Time, H_a
1	0.741	+	0.371	+	0	=	1.112	0.58
2	0.741	+	0.067	+	0	=	0.808	0.54
3	0.741	+	0.432	+	0.131	=	1.304	1.20
4	0.741	+	0.736	+	0.554	=	2.031	2.60
5	0.741	+	2.257	+	0.664	=	3.662	3.62
							8.917	8.54

These trial values are compared to measured values using the table-look-up rules of thumb and are shown in Table 6.2(C).
Errors can be assessed, or

$$E_g = \frac{8.917 - 8.54}{8.54} \times 100 = 4.4\%$$

$$E_{ad} = \frac{91.7 + 49.6 + 8.7 - 21.8 + 1}{5} = 25.9\%$$

$$E_{at} = \frac{0.532 + 0.268 + 0.104 - 0.569 + 0.042}{5} = 0.075 \, min$$

Usually, standard time data are tested against new measurements in addition to original information. It appears that while gross errors are small, average deviations are larger, and the average magnitude of estimating exceeding measurement is 0.075 min. Improvements can be expected with more studies and other trial values of P_1, P_2, and P_3. For this example we assume that the data meet evaluation criteria. At this point, the normal time data are converted to standard minutes ready for widespread use. If the allowances are 14%, the allowance multiplier F_a is 1.163 [= 100/(100 − 14)]. Finally, the standard time data are distributed to labor estimators. Table 6.3 is a small example of *detail* standard time data. The estimator would visualize the elements knowing the design and operation and select time values for the labor estimate. Application of standard time data is demonstrated in Chapter 7.

But standard time data such as Table 6.3 can be further compressed and this summary is called *preliminary*. The average value of the constant elements plus the

Table 6.3.   Example of Detail Standard Time Data

Setup hours						1.2 hr

Operation elements in standard minutes

1. Load major part, load secondary part and clamp if necessary,
   and unload spot-welded part   0.86
2. Load third part, if required, and clamp

$L + W + H$			$L + W + H$		
in.	mm	min	in.	mm	min
5.0	130	0.16	24.2	615	0.46
6.9	175	0.19	30.0	760	0.55
9.2	235	0.22	36.9	940	0.66
12.0	305	0.27	45.2	1150	0.79
15.4	390	0.32	55.2	1400	0.95
19.4	495	0.38			

3. Position parts, spot-weld, and occasional electrode cleaning

Spots	min	Spots	min	Spots	min
3	0.08	9	0.51	21	1.38
4	0.15	10	0.59	24	1.60
5	0.22	12	0.73	28	1.89
6	0.30	14	0.88	33	2.25
7	0.37	16	1.02	36	2.33
8	0.44	18	1.17		

intercepts for variable elements are added. It may be necessary to prorate a share of an irregular element such as element 4, loading of the third part. A sample of preliminary standard time data is given by Table 7.4. A single line is devoted to spot-weld estimating on that table. Preliminary TERs can be collected for many operations on a few sheets. Detail standard time data are collected in a loose-leaf book and used by estimators for operations. Problem 6.28 asks the student to apply the standard time data for a labor estimate using Table 6.3.

6.9 FACTOR

The factor method is a basic and important method for project estimates. Other terms such as *ratio* and *percentage* methods are about the same thing. Essentially, the *factor method* determines the estimate by summing the product of several quantities, or

$$C = (C_e + \sum_i f_i C_e)(f_I + 1) \tag{6.37}$$

where C = value (cost, price of design)

C_e = cost of selected major equipment

f_i = factor for the estimating of buildings, instrumentation, etc.

f_I = factor for the estimating of indirect expenses such as engineering, contractor's profit, and contingency

$i = 1, \ldots, n$ factor index

The factors f are uncovered by historical, measured, or policy methods. Data from internal reports, industry at large, or from the government may be the principal source.

A natural simplification leads to the preliminary unit estimating model $C = fC_e$, where one factor is used to find the composite cost. This factor-estimating formula has variants such as $C = \Sigma_i f_i D$, where D is the particular design parameter, e.g., material machining time, combat force, and capital investment, and f_i is the factor in units compatible to the design.

The unit-cost estimating method was limited to a single factor for calculating overall costs. The factor method achieves improved accuracy by adopting separate factors for different cost items. For example, the approximate cost of an office building can be estimated by multiplying the area by an appropriate unit estimate such as the dollars-per-square-foot factor. As an improvement, individual cost-per-unit-area figures can be used for heating, lighting, painting, and the like, and their value C can be summed for the separate factors and designs.

Plant cost can be estimated by the factor method. The hydrobromination process is one step in the sequence of making an intermediate product for a liquid soap formulation. The hydrobromination flow chart, given by Fig. 6.14, is a microprocess plant.

The flowchart and the specification sheet are input data to the project estimator. With the flowchart, the basic item (or items) of the process is identified. This basic item should be a major item for a building such as the structural shell, or tons of concrete for a highway, or process equipment in a chemical plant. After the cost of the basic item has been determined, the next step is to find the cost relationship of other components as a percentage, ratio, total cost, or factor of the basic item. For the building structural shell, the factors would be brick, concrete, masonry, architectural and reinforced concrete, carpentry, finish trim, electrical work, plumbing, and so forth. For the chemical process project, equipment erection, piping and direct materials, insulation, instrumentation, and engineering can be correlated to process cost. These correlations can be statistically found using the methods of Chapter 5. In some instances the variations in the cost of components being analyzed are independent of the variation in the cost of the basic item. These independent components (e.g., roads, railroad siding, and site development for a new plant) must be estimated separately by other methods.

There are practical considerations in applying the factor method. For the chemical plant problem, variation between estimates are due to

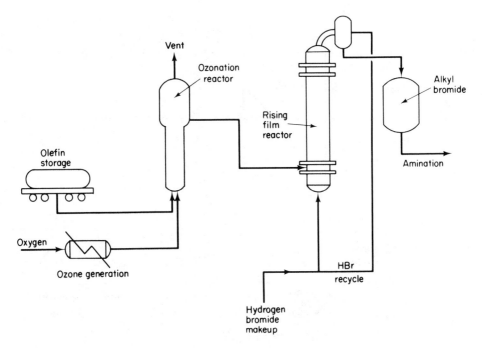

Figure 6.14.   Flowchart for hydrobromination process.

- Size of the basic equipment selected
- Materials of construction
- Operating pressures, temperatures
- Technology such as fluids processing, fluids–solids processing, or solids processing
- Location of plant site
- Timing of construction

Practically speaking, if the physical size of the basic item becomes larger and therefore more costly, the factor relating, say, the engineering design cost is marginally smaller. If the basic item is constructed with more expensive materials such as stainless steel or glass-lined materials, the factors become nonproportional to the item being estimated. This factor behavior is described by Fig. 6.15. The basic item cost is the entry. Intersection with the line leads to a factor. If the entry value is doubled, we assume that the factor is not doubled, thus assuring economy of scale. This is also apparent as the line is nonlinear in Fig. 6.16. Frequently, a popular industry-wide or government bench-mark year is used and all data is reflected to this constant base year. The uses of indexes are important in this method.

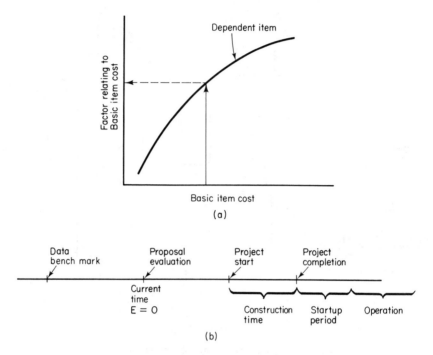

Figure 6.15.   (a) Economy of scale for factor method; (b) time line for project evaluation.

The first step is to evaluate the basic item costs. In the flowchart, the rising film and ozonation reactors are chosen. As this process is high-pressure and high-temperature, we would expect the piping, supports, instrumentation, foundation, and so on, to reflect correlated costs. If the material were carbon instead of stainless, the factor would reflect the distinction. The two reactors are evaluated for current-time costs, which corresponds to the time of the estimate or $E = 0$. The evaluation could be internal, or vendors can be asked for bids, and the average or a reasonable value gives

Major Process Item	Cost
1. Rising film reactor	$2,200,000
2. Ozonation reactor	700,000
	$C_e = \$2,900,000$

In doing this estimating, a company would maintain indexes such that the C_e value could be backcast to the data bench mark year. The f_i factors are read off the curve. At this point, the indexed value is multiplied by $f_i C_e$. Next the bench-mark cost is indexed forward to that point in time when the cost is expected out-of-pocket,

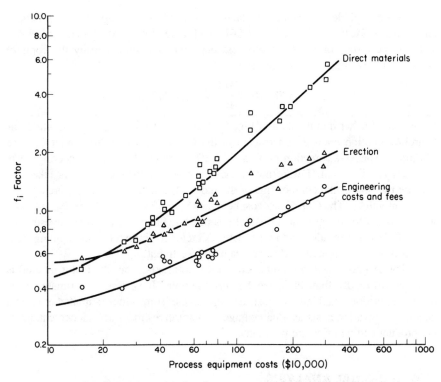

Figure 6.16. Typical factor chart based on process equipment costs for bench mark year.

project start, completion, or progress-payment periods as stipulated by the contract. The data for chemical plants are often stated in terms of the Gulf Coast. Construction at other locations requires regional indexing to adjust for differences in labor and material cost.

Using Eq. (5.53), we revise it to show that

$$C_r = C_c \left(\frac{I_r}{I_c} \right) \tag{6.38}$$

where C_r = bench-mark cost, dollars
    C_c = current cost, \$2,900,000
    I_r = 100 for bench-mark year
    I_c = current index as 114.1 for equipment
    C_r = \$2,900,000(100/114.1) = \$2,541,630

With this adjusted major component cost, from a curve plotted for the base year, Fig. 6.16 yields engineering costs and fees, 1.1; erection, 1.7; and direct materials, 4.1.

Observe Table 6.4, where the factors are used as a multiplier for the bench-mark cost, or $4,320,770 = 1.7 \times 2,541,630$ for erection. Next, this cost is inflated to the project start point or the progress-payment time stipulated by the contract clauses. This would, for instance, be

$$4,320,770 \times \frac{189}{100} = \$8,166,250$$

Let us state further that the data of Fig. 6.16 are Gulf Coast information, while our hydrobromination plant is constructed in the Midwest, where direct materials are 8% more expensive, erection costs are 13.2% more costly, and engineering costs and fees are identical. Furthermore, these regional adjustment factors take into account the mix of the components of the index. These regional factors are applied to current values. The Gulf Coast cost becomes $8,166,250 \times 1.132 = \$9,244,200$, which adjusts for geographical distinctions of cost. Finally, the capital investment, $34,630,210, is provided as the estimate. A factor for indirect costs, contingency, and profit can be applied to this raw capital investment.

The example dealt with plant equipment estimating, but the factor method is used more broadly than indicated by this example. It is used to estimate labor, materials, utilities, and indirect costs as a multiple of some other estimated or known quantity. Operating costs as a percentage of plant investment or as a percentage of the product selling price are popular.

6.10 MARGINAL ANALYSIS

Cost estimating provides estimates about designs to make future decisions. There is the premise that the action recommended by the estimate will add to the benefits of the enterprise to make it worth the trouble. Typical situations in which estimating weighs the proposition "will it add to the benefits" include the following: A firm is considering a new plant producing an intermediate soap chemical or a special product has been designed and will be marketed shortly. Not all situations assure that the originator will be better off. Consider this case. An electric utility serving several separated geographical regions employs transmission repair crews for high-voltage line failures. The manager has permission to add another maintenance operator to a crew. In district A the average of the cost of repair per operator is estimated as $780, while in district B the unit estimate is $470. Our manager chooses to assign the operator to district B. But it is possible that the difference in the estimates occurred because the size of the repair crew in B was better adapted. If so, the new line mechanic may add little to cost reduction, while in A he may lead to a greater decrease in cost. The reasoning that would lead to the right choice is based on marginal cost and is a method of analysis important to cost estimating. Too often decisions are made on the basis of average cost or average return rather than marginal cost or marginal return.

Table 6.4. Factor Estimate for a Chemical Plant Process

Estimated Item	Current Time Cost	Current Index	Bench mark Cost	f_i	Bench mark Cost	Project Start Index	Gulf Coast Project Start Cost	Midwest Regional Index	Project Start Plant Site Cost
1. Equipment:									
Major process items	$2,900,000	114.1	$2,541,630	1.	$ 2,541,630	118.0	$ 2,999,120	—	$ 2,999,120
Erection				1.7	4,320,770	189.0	8,166,250	1.132	9,244,200
Direct materials				4.1	10,420,680	127.0	13,234,260	1.08	14,293,000
2. Engineering costs and fees				1.1	2,790,000	145.0	4,053,890	1.0	4,053,890
3. Building site development									
Site development									1,250,000
Process building									2,100,000
Railroad spur									40,000
Utilities									650,000
									$34,630,210

Marginal costs are the added costs incurred as a result of adopting a change in operations or making an engineering-change order for a product. The change in operations usually implies increasing or decreasing production. Marginal cost is used interchangeably with *differential cost* or *incremental cost*. In a broad sense all estimates are marginal estimates inasmuch as they are concerned with creating changes from a current course of action. Only after a detail estimate is made can the estimator exploit the advantages of marginal analysis.

We explain the arithmetic of marginal analysis with a simple illustration.

Quantity	Estimated Total Cost	Analyzed Marginal Cost	Analyzed Average Cost
0	0	0	—
1	$1000	$1000	$1000
2	1900	900	950
3	2700	800	900

The hypothetical cost is zero before any production. Marginal cost, by convention, is also zero and average cost is undefined at this point. At two units, marginal cost is the amount which is added by the production from one to two units, or $1900 - 1000 = \$900$. Average cost (arithmetic mean) is as usually determined. The principles of marginal cost are better explained by calculus, which is the more precise way to cope with these matters. The brute-force way to explain marginal analysis is through an extensive table, where total cost is enumerated for successive units, i.e., 61, 62, 63, . . . in the region of interest. However, the approach recommended is to have a scattering of cost-estimated points and then proceed to fit linear and nonlinear regression lines. To illustrate we fit a first-, second-, and third-order polynomial regression line through the estimating data for the product. Total cost data are given in Table 6.5. We analyze the marginal properties of these data from fitted regression models.*

A simple model relating variable and fixed costs to production rate n is given as

$$C_T = nC_v + C_f \qquad (6.39)$$

where C_T = total cost dollars per period

n = number of production units per period

C_v = lumped variable cost per unit

C_f = lumped fixed cost per period

If at various values for n, C_v is the same, we have the linear cost model; if C_v is permitted to vary, we are concerned with nonlinear models. For the constant C_v,

---

*Higher-ordered polynomials sometimes create problems. Usually, it is acceptable practice to fit a polynomial regression equation of low order. The number of data points for the equation may be three to eight times the order of the equation.

Table 6.5. TOTAL COST ESTIMATE FOR PRODUCT

Six-Month Production	Total Cost
5,000	$ 6,875
10,000	10,460
15,000	13,260
20,000	16,400
25,000	21,125
30,000	29,250

nC_v is a straight line increasing at a constant rate per unit, and C_v is the slope of the variable cost line. The linear model statistically fitted for the product data is $C_T = 0.84n + 1527$, where $C_v = 0.84$. The fixed cost is $1527 and is the vertical-axis intercept.

The average cost model is given as

$$C_a = \frac{nC_v + C_f}{n} = \frac{C_T}{n} \tag{6.40}$$

where C_a is the average cost, dollars per unit. If C_v is constant, we have the linear case again. Equation (6.40) is still valid if C_v is nonconstant and we have the nonlinear case, which is the usual fare.

For linear cost situations marginal cost equals C_v and is a constant. For the general case we define *marginal cost* as

$$C_m = \frac{dC_T}{dn} \tag{6.41}$$

where C_m = marginal cost, dollars per unit

dC_T/dn = derivative of total cost function with respect to quantity n

By similar reasoning, if the output n is increased by an amount Δn from an established level n and if the matching increase in cost is ΔC_T, then the increase in cost per unit increase in output is $\Delta C_T/\Delta n$. Marginal cost is the limiting value of this ratio as Δn gets smaller (i.e., marginal cost as the derivative of the total cost function). It measures the rate of increase of total cost and is an approximation of the cost of a small additional unit of output from the given level. Sometimes marginal cost is called the slope or tangent of the total cost curve at the point of interest.

For the data of Table 6.5 fitted to a second-order polynomial or $C_T = 6594.+ 0.08n - 0.0000217n^2$, marginal cost dC_T/dn becomes

$$C_m = 0.08 - 0.0000434n$$

The marginal cost is a linear line inclining downward with a slope 0.0000434. A third-order polynomial fit of the same data is

$$C_T = 840 + 1.527n - 7.418 \times 10^{-5}n^2 + 1.827 \times 10^{-9}n^3$$

and the marginal cost function becomes

$$C_m = 1.527 - 14.836 \times 10^{-5}n + 5.481 \times 10^{-9}n^2$$

from which a marginal curve is plotted directly. The marginal cost curve is a parabola and is shown on Fig. 6.17.

Plotting the average cost and marginal cost curve, we notice that the marginal cost line intersects the lowest point of the average cost curve. At this particular value of n, average cost is minimum and equal to marginal cost. This is shown by Fig. 6.17.

The decision for the maintenance operator was made on the average cost estimate. It should have been made on the marginal yield which it promises. If district A has a greater marginal cost reduction by the addition of the maintenance operator, it is the preferred location. The choice between the two districts would be based on the greatest negative C_m.

The parallel to marginal cost is *marginal return*. It associates with many of the same concepts. In an operation design, marginal return would be marginal

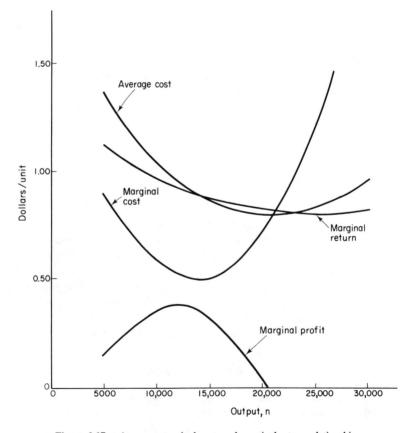

Figure 6.17.   Average, marginal cost, and marginal return relationships.

savings; in a product design we use the popular term marginal revenue; in a project design the word marginal rate of return connotes some of the same concepts; finally, in system design the term marginal effectiveness is frequently employed. It is assumed that a specific economic measure can be chosen that will reflect important differences among different values of the design variables. In a market situation total return may be the total money revenue of the producers supplying the demand and the total money outlay of the consumers providing the demand. For our purpose we assume that a total return function is estimated with knowedge about input price and demand and that it increases or decreases with increasing output according to whether the demand is elastic or inelastic. Elastic demand implies a demand which increases in greater proportion than the corresponding decrease in price, and vice versa.

For continuation of our product problem the total return or revenue is given in Table 6.6. A zero-sale estimate is a trivial requirement, but it aids the construction in a least-squares sense. The total return column contains no reference to the price. It can be computed by dividing total return per unit of output. We tacitly require for any further analysis that production equal sales volume. In a similar fashion we can fit polynomial regression curves to these data and analyze these determined models on the basis of marginal principles.

For a product design we construct a model of the form

$$R_T = nR_v + R_f \tag{6.42}$$

where R_T = total return dollars per period
$\quad n$ = number of units per period
$\quad R_v$ = lumped variable return per unit
$\quad R_f$ = lumped fixed return per period

This is a linear or nonlinear model as either R_v is a constant multiplier or a nonlinear term. If we are considering the sale of a product, no receipts are obtained until the sale of at least one product or $nR_v > 0$. For a no-sale condition $R_f = 0$, too. If the total return curve is linear, the marginal return is a constant and equals R_v. For a product sold commercially this is the sales price.

Table 6.6.   ESTIMATED TOTAL REVENUE FOR PRODUCT

Estimated Sales Quantity	Total Revenue
0	0
5,000	$ 6,000
10,000	11,125
15,000	15,200
20,000	19,300
25,000	23,500
30,000	27,000

For an average return the model becomes

$$R_a = \frac{nR_v + R_f}{n} = \frac{R_T}{n} \tag{6.43}$$

where R_a is the average return dollars per unit.

Marginal return is defined in a way similar to marginal cost, or

$$R_m = \frac{dR_T}{dn} \tag{6.44}$$

where R_m = marginal return, dollars per unit

dR_T/dn = derivative of total return function with respect to quantity n

For the data of Table 6.6 fitted to a second-order polynomial,* or $R_T = 90 + 1.138n - 8.13 \times 10^{-6}n^2$, the marginal return becomes

$$R_m = 1.138 - 16.26 \times 10^{-6}n$$

and thus marginal return is a linear line inclining downward with a slope -16.26×10^{-6}. For a third-order polynomial fit,

$$R_T = -48 - 1.23n - 1.64 \times 10^{-5}n^2 + 1.833 \times 10^{-10}n^3$$

the marginal return function would be $R_m = 1.23 - 3.28 \times 10^{-5}n + 5.499 \times 10^{-10}n^2$ from which a marginal return parabolic curve is plotted in Fig. 6.17. In the usual circumstance the second-order marginal model is considered more accurate than a first-order model.

Marginal estimating depends on calculus. The marginal models are for the most part derived functions from fitted data. Occasionally natural physical functions are employed. For either case the functions C_T or R_T are assumed continuous and differentiable. A good deal of information can be uncovered from these basic models. Returning to the maintenance operator problem, the decision should be made on the marginal yield which it promises. Indeed, the addition of maintenance operators can proceed until the net yield is zero. The greatest negative marginal cost indicates the design with greatest cost reduction for least input resources (a negative cost change is a gain). Given adequate resources, both crews should be expanded until the yields are zero. If resources are not present, the next strategy to adopt is to achieve the same marginal cost for both districts, and this may be done by reassigning operators from one district to another district.

---

*This second-order polynomial does not pass through the origin. It might be assumed that at $n = 0$ there should be no revenue, which is correct; however, the data of Table 6.6 are least-squares approximations, and a displaced origin is not uncommon with estimated data. Furthermore,

$$R_T = \begin{cases} 0 & \text{if } n \leq 0 \\ R_v n + R_f \text{ if } n > 0 \end{cases}$$

With curves and mathematical models, like those described for the product it is possible to optimize sales revenue and cost. The question should be asked, What shall we optimize? Maximizing sales revenue may not guarantee maximum profit, nor does minimizing cost balance other factors for maximum profit. In some cases these actions may in fact reduce profits. One of the traditional ways to study this interaction is by *break-even* analysis. A *break-even point* is defined as the point of production or operation at which there is neither a loss nor profit nor savings. Several points of neutrality are possible, and the location of these points is a straightforward exercise after the curves and models have been formulated from the data.

Using models (6.39) and (6.42) we assume that the linear approximation of a *point of indifference* occurs whenever $C_T = R_T$. Ignoring profits tax and solving for n, we have

$$n = \frac{C_f - R_f}{R_v - C_v} \tag{6.45}$$

Model (6.45) is for the class of problems where R_f is not zero; for a product that is commercially sold no income is received until products are sold and R_f as a fixed residual income does not exist, so $R_f = 0$. In the case of fitted models to estimated data R_f may exist to satisfy the best fit in a least-squares sense; moreover, when using linear models $C_T = 0.84n + 1527$ and $R_T = .887n + 1284$ the break-even point is

$$n = \frac{1527 - 1284}{0.887 - 0.84} = 5170 \, \text{units}$$

This is pictured in Fig. 6.18. The denominator of the foregoing is unit profit without fixed cost or return. But as fixed cost must be absorbed in the production and sales volume, the net unit profit when divided into fixed dollars yields the break-even point in terms of dollars and units sold.

Several comments about linear break-even analysis are worth noting. These relationships are valid only for the short-term period. *Short term* for one activity may be only weeks, while another firm may view *short term* over an extended period of months and even years. To establish arbitrary rules about what is short or long term is dangerous unless specific cases are analyzed. As was demonstrated by the example, the mathematics and graphics involving linear (or nonlinear) costs and incomes provide information for break-even production.

In the linear example a narrow wedge of profits begins at 5170 units and continues indefinitely. The defect of pure linear models is obvious: Reduced revenue or unit price as an additional quantity is produced can occur from a variety of economic happenings. Increased unit costs of production beyond that which is normal are typical as production increases indefinitely. Although linear methods can be used for production above or below normal capacity and for cost-cutting tactics, the simplest way is to examine the plots of the original data. This can be done by straightforward plotting of Tables 6.5 and 6.6. This is shown by Fig. 6.19 where

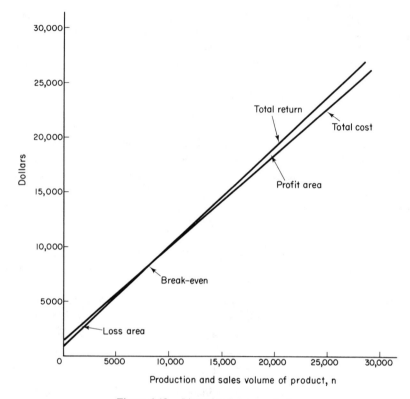

Figure 6.18.   Linear break-even analysis.

two break-even points, a lower and upper, are indicated. C_v is an increasing function, while R_v is a decreasing function. With this dual intersection of the return and cost lines, additional analysis of the meaning of optimum profit is called for.

The intersection of the slopes of the total cost and total return functions is given as

$$\frac{dR_T}{dn} = \frac{dC_T}{dn} \tag{6.46}$$

The finding of this intersection is the point at which marginal profit equals zero or $dZ/dn = dR_T/dn - dC_T/dn = 0$. If n increases beyond this point, the cost of each unit exceeds the revenue from each unit and total profits begin to decline as they do beyond the upper break-even point of Fig. 6.19. The profits do not become zero until the *profit-limit point,* which is the beginning of a loss area. When the marginal profit is zero we have the *critical production rate* and *maximum profit.* This critical production does not necessarily occur at the rate corresponding to the minimum average unit cost, nor does it necessarily occur at the point of maximum profit per unit.

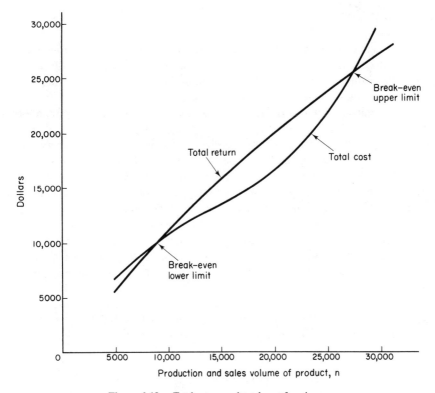

Figure 6.19.   Total return and total cost functions.

A plot of $dR_T/dn - dC_T/dn$ is given in Fig. 6.17. The point at which $dR_T/dn = dC_T/dn$ is also zero for marginal profit or dZ/dn. The critical production rate may be determined directly from differentiation of the profit function Z. This critical production rate is zero at $n = 20,800$ units, which is the point of maximum gross profit. But it is not the rate corresponding to minimum average unit cost or the maximum profit per unit. The maximum profit per unit may be estimated from the level dome of the marginal profit curve, or approximately 12,200 units. Using Fig. 6.17 minimum marginal cost is estimated as 14,500 units, and maximum marginal return is at the minimum sales projection of 5000 units.

Although several points of operation can be obtained from minimizing total or unit cost, maximizing total or unit return, or maximizing gross or unit profit, one should not conclude that all is lost if these exact objectives are never precisely realized. There is a redeeming feature for the estimator if the actual and the ideal n do not coincide. Fortunately, most optimums are relatively flat near the optimum. For these domes operation on either side is insensitive. Naturally, a converse example can be found that demonstrates a sharp peak as optimum. In this case operation at this point becomes important.

SUMMARY

Estimates are constructed on available information. If there is no information, there can be no estimate. Conversely, an estimate is unnecessary if actual costs are available. The estimator operates within these limits. In this in-between region we separate estimating methods into preliminary and detail.

Preliminary methods are less numeric than detail methods. Accuracy of the estimate is improved by attention to detail, but balancing this is the speed and cost of preparation which favor preliminary methods. The methods are preliminary because they correspond to a design which is not well formulated. Frequently a preliminary estimate leads to the management decision of further consideration for the design. Before detail methods of estimating are attempted, information that has been deliberately collected, structured, and verified to suit the method of estimating must be available. Most estimates are made using detail methods.

In the next four chapters the methods of detail estimating are examined further. The concern becomes one of using various cost-estimating relationships, ranging from simple cost factors to functional models, to estimate operations, products, projects, and systems.

Here we return to the question, How do you select the right method for a particular application? Regrettably, no textbook can supply an infallible set of rules— you will have to rely on experience and continuing analysis.

QUESTIONS

6.1. Give an explanation of the following terms:

Preliminary estimating	Straight-line average
Detail estimating	Power law
Conference method	Economy of scale
Hidden card	Standard time data
Unit method	Opinion probability
Cost driver	Simulation
CERs and TERs	Monte Carlo
Parameter	Density function
Learning	Economy of quantity
Cumulative average	Marginal cost

6.2. Discuss the timing of preliminary estimates. Is the timing a precise point in a well-ordered organization?

6.3. Use the conference method to estimate
  (a) The price for a clean-air car using a turbine drive.
  (b) The ticket price for a 5000-mile one-way air trip.
  (c) The cost of a year's college education in 1990.
  (d) The time to dig a trench 2 × 4 × 10 feet in soft clay.
  (e) The improvement in the efficiency of handing mail of a central post office near you after converting to automated methods.

6.4. What advantages can you cite for the conference method? Disadvantages?

6.5. Assume that design A can be redesigned into designs B and C with known costs. What safeguards can you suggest to assure that A is properly estimated?

6.6. Discuss some substitute unit measures for "cost per square foot of residential construction." What are your local values?

6.7. What are the ways in which probabilities are determined? What is the distribution of the rolls of one six-sided die considering only the face-up event? Consider two dice, and determine the distribution of numbers from 2 to 12.

6.8. Point up the human frailties in determining opinion probabilities. Would you think that one would under or overestimate these point probabilities?

6.9. Describe the kinds of applications that are suitable for the factor method. What kinds are suitable for standard time data?

6.10. What is meant by the law of economy of scale? Apply it to the factor method. Does the unit method follow this law?

6.11. Outline the method to be followed in marginal analysis. What distinguishes linear from nonlinear margins?

6.12. Define mathematically the point of indifference, the upper and lower break-even points, the maximum profit point, and the profit-limiting point.

PROBLEMS

6.1. Use the conference method to estimate some product or sample statistic which is familiar to the entire team but whose exact value is unknown, for instance, cost of interstate highway construction per mile or number of automobiles in your town. Then check its value.

6.2. A manufacturer of factory-built houses has collected raw data for flooring and has converted them to a common square-foot basis:

Material	Size	Material Cost	Labor Cost
Laminated oak blocks	$\frac{1}{2} \times 9 \times 9$ in.	$2.30	$0.85
Parquet	$\frac{5}{16} \times 12 \times 12$ in.	2.10	1.65
Strip flooring, oak	$\frac{25}{32} \times 2\frac{1}{4}$ in.	2.60	1.25
Resilient tile			
A grade	$9 \times 9 \times \frac{1}{8}$ in.	0.60	0.70
B grade		0.85	0.70
C grade		0.90	0.70
Vinyl asbestos	$9 \times 9 \times \frac{1}{16}$ in.	1.05	0.70
Softwood, C grade	S4S, 1×6 in.	1.65	0.80
Linoleum	$\frac{1}{8}$ in., plain	1.50	0.75
Slate, irregular flags	Irregular flags	6.00	4.00
Terrazzo	$\frac{1}{4}$ in. thick	4.75	3.95

Using only your opinion, where would you cost cork tile? Where would you cost carpet? These houses are delivered to the site by company trucks. What are the non-feasible alternatives? Conduct an analysis after your opinion to help sharpen your value.

6.3. An inventor has fashioned a new mailbox design with an interesting feature. When the mailman closes the hinged cover, a spring-loaded flag pops up at the back of the box telling the owner that he has received mail. A survey of popular catalogs has revealed the following data:

Size	Weight	Material	Cost	Features
14 × 7 × 4	4 lb, 4 oz	Steel	$ 23.60	Holds magazine, wall mount
13 × 7 × 3	3 lb, 6 oz	Steel	15.60	Holds magazine, wall mount
14 × 6 × 4	4 lb, 15 oz	Aluminum	35.96	Holds magazine, wall mount
14 × 7 × 4	4 lb, 12 oz	Steel, aluminum	27.60	Holds magazine, wall mount
6 × 2 × 10	4 lb, 8 oz	Forged iron	32.40	Letter-sized
6 × 2 × 10	2 lb, 11 oz	Steel	17.60	Letter-sized
5 × 2 × 11	2 lb, 11 oz	Steel	10.20	Liberty bell emblem
10 × 3	1 lb, 8 oz	Brass	23.60	Mail slot
10 × 3	1 lb	Steel	7.08	Mail slot
10 × 3	1 lb, 5 oz	Aluminum	23.60	Mail slot
18 × 7 × 6	8 lb, 8 oz	Steel	26.76	Red signal flag, mount post
19 × 7 × 6	10 lb	Steel	39.16	Black wrinkle finish
18 × 6 × 9	10 lb	Steel	37.16	Name holder
18 × 7 × 6	8 lb, 1 oz	Steel	9.48	Size no. 1
18 × 7 × 6	8 lb, 1 oz	Steel	19.60	Rural mailbox
18 × 7 × 6	4 lb	Aluminum	15.40	Rural mailbox
17 × 9 × 10 unit		Steel	200.00	Apartment type

(a) In using a comparison method, where would you place the inventor's design?

(b) Construct a rough unit estimate from the data to help in the evaluation.

(c) Discuss various reasons that might lead to a different analysis.

6.4. The cost of a residential home with 2000-square-foot livable space and a basement and garage is $146,000. The house dimensions are such that 1200 square feet are on the first floor. The volume including house, garage, and basement is 30,200 cubic feet. Determine unit estimates.

6.5. For the following problems, assume that the unit line is linear.

(a) Find the first unit value when the 100th unit is 60 hours with 81% learning.

(b) Find the value for unit 6 when the value for unit 3 is 1000 hours at 74% learning.

(c) If the unit value at number 1 is $2000, find the unit dollars for units 20 and 40 with learning rates of 93% and 100%.

(d) Units 1 through 100 have accumulated 10,000 hours. Calculate the unit time for number 50 with a learning ratio of 71%.

(e) If the cumulative average time at unit 100 is 100, find the unit, cumulative, and average time at unit 101 for a learning rate of 92%.

6.6. For the following problems, assume that the average line is linear.

    (a) Find the cumulative average value for the 20th unit when the 10th unit has an average of 100 hours for 68% learning.

    (b) The cumulative average cost for the 100th unit is $10,000. Find the average cost for the 50th and 200th unit for a learning rate of 87%.

    (c) If 400 cumulative average hours are required for the 3rd unit and 350 hours for the 6th unit, find the slope, T_a', T_u', and T_c' for the 10th unit. What can you say about these calculations?

    (d) If 800 average man-hours are required for the 10th unit and 750 hours for the 20th unit, find the percentage learning ratio, T_a', T_c', and T_u' for the 5th and 40th units.

    (e) If the unit time at unit 100 is 100, find the unit, cumulative, and average times at unit 101 for a learning rate of 92%. Compare to Problem 6.5(e).

6.7. Unit man-hours are reduced by 20% every time production is tripled. Find the slope.

6.8. Find the slope for the following conditions:

    (a) A company assumes that the unit line is linear. Two points uncovered by a shop study show a pair ($N_1 = 15$, $T_1 = 80$), ($N_2 = 25$, $T_2 = 70$) of unit values. Find the slope, T_a and T_c for N_1 and N_2.

    (b) A cumulative average linear line study has revealed that at 10 units, $T_a' = 1550$ hours, while at 25 units, $T_a' = 1010$ hours. Find s, T_u' and T_c' for 50 and 100 units.

6.9. **(a)** The cost-estimating department has determined an estimate of 10,000 hours at unit 100. They believe an improvement of 10% can be expected from unit 1 onward. Find the unit time to build units 1 and 2. Assume that the unit line is linear.

    (b) Unit 1 = 10,000 hours and unit 8 = 5120 hours. What unit and cumulative times can be expected at 16 and 32 units?

6.10. **(a)** For management proposal A, cost at unit 1 is $8000, and the learning rate is 80%. For management proposal B, unit 1 cost is $6000 and the learning rate is 90%. Which is the best proposal at unit 15? At unit 13? Assume that proposal B was adopted. Cost estimating discovers that at unit 15 the actual cost was really $3975, while for unit 1 it was as initially estimated. What was learning performance? Assume that the unit line is linear.

    (b) An audit of learning curve performance revealed that at the 18th product unit the direct product cost was $181,000, while at the 24th product unit it was $169,000. What is the estimated direct product cost for the 27th product unit?

6.11. Use Appendix III and plot T_u, T_a, and T_c for 1, 5, 10, 20, and 100 units for 80% learning on arithmetic and logarithmic graph paper. Find graphical values for unit 500.

6.12. Use Appendix III and plot T_a', T_c', and T_u' for 1, 5, 10, 20, and 100 units for 80% learning on arithmetic and logarithmic graph paper. Find graphical values for unit 500.

6.13. Calculate new tables like Appendix III for units 1 to 4

    (a) for 83% learning.

    (b) for 63%.

6.14. Calculate new tables such as those of Appendix III for units 1 to 4

    (a) for 73% learning.

    (b) for 77%.

6.15. **(a)** An 80-kW diesel electric set, naturally aspirated, cost $160,000 8 years ago. A similar design, but 140 kW, is planned for an isolated installation. The exponent m

$= 0.6$ and index $I = 187$. Now the index is 207. A precompressor is estimated separately at \$19,000.

(a) Using the power law and sizing model, find the estimated equipment cost.

(b) Repeat (a) for $m = 0.7$.

6.16. A cost estimate is desired for a 34-cm disk laser amplifier. A previous reference design of 22 cm has been made for a cost of \$16,459. Inflation indexes for this design are unavailable, but the annual Consumer Price Index of 7.5% will be used for a 3-year escalation. A calculation of $m = 0.7$ was found.

(a) Find the cost of the new design.

(b) Repeat the above for $m = 0.8$.

6.17. A product is known to follow the power law, which can be used to estimate the cost of new design. Four sizes of the turbine have been analyzed as to cost:

kW	Cost ($\times 10^6$)
3500	\$1.8
5000	2.5
7000	3.2
8000	3.5

A similar design, except that it is larger at 8750 kW, is to be estimated. Determine the slope m and estimate the cost of the new unit. (*Hint:* Use $\log C = \log C_r + m \log Q/Q_r$ and let $Q_r = 3500$. Plot the relationship on logarithmic graph paper.)

6.18. A firm that manufactures totally enclosed capacitor motors, fan-cooled, 1725-rpm, $\frac{5}{8}$-in.-O.D. keyway shaft has known costs on $\frac{1}{4}$, $\frac{1}{3}$, $\frac{3}{4}$, and 1 hp as \$90, \$100, \$118, and \$140. A 3450-rpm, 1-hp motor costs \$134. Determine m for the 1725-rpm motor series, and estimate the cost for a $1\frac{1}{2}$-hp motor. Should the 3450-rpm motor be included in the sample to estimate the 1725-rpm motor?

6.19. **(a)** A company sells two different designs of one item. A study discloses that 65% of its customers buy the cheapest design for \$75. The remaining 35% pay \$110 for the expensive model. What is the expected purchase price?

(b) A salesman makes 15 calls without a sale and 5 calls with an average sale of \$200. What is his expected sales per call?

(c) A machine tool builder takes old lathes as trade-ins for new models and sells the returned lathes through a second-party outlet. Analysis shows that the markup is \$2500 on 70% of the lathes and \$4000 on the rest. What is the expected markup?

(d) An insurance company charges \$20 for an additional \$50 increment of insurance (from \$100 to \$50 deductible). What is their assessment of the risk for the increment of insurance?

6.20. A student is interested in selling his car instead of trading it in. His estimating model, he reasons, is the sale price of a new car − (depreciation + major maintenance cost). Other costs for driving are the same regardless of whether he drives a new car or not. The original sticker price is \$13,137 and a major maintenance cost is \$2000. His opinion probability for a major maintenance cost is given as follows:

Life	Cumulative Probability of Major Maintenance	Cumulative Decline in Depreciation
2	0.2	0.49
3	0.4	0.64
4	0.7	0.75
5	1.0	0.83
6	0.1	0.89
7	0.2	0.93
8	0.4	0.96
9	0.7	0.98
10	1.0	0.99

When should he sell his car? Initially assume that the next car, whenever he buys it, will be equal to his first car's price. Next assume that the new car's price increases by 3% compounded per year.

6.21. A company is considering redesign of one of its basic products. The engineering cost and the manufacture of new tooling will cost $25,000. Three alternatives are to be evaluated, and the estimators determined the profit and opinion probability of success. Production costs for designs A and B are the same:

No Change		Design A		Design B	
Profit	Probability	Profit	Probability	Profit	Probability
$200,000	0.4	$400,000	0.3	$300,000	0.2
250,000	0.3	450,000	0.5	450,000	0.3
300,000	0.3	500,000	0.2	600,000	0.5

Determine the expected value of the profit—new tooling for each of the three alternatives. Which one is preferred?

6.22. Work the problem in Sec. 6.7.2 using these random numbers:

Random Number x	Random Number y
0.07	0.59
0.33	0.30
0.16	0.10
0.75	0.96
0.58	0.88
0.23	0.98
0.89	0.14
0.08	0.43
0.10	0.76
0.96	0.70

Determine the mean cost A. Plot the distribution of cost A and determine its standard deviation.

6.23. Work the problem in Sec. 6.7.2 using these random numbers:

Random Number x	Random Number y
0.24	0.64
0.82	0.98
0.83	0.25
0.18	0.94
0.66	0.03
0.76	0.23
0.07	0.96
0.62	0.80
0.61	0.64
0.96	0.99

Determine mean cost A and its standard deviation.

6.24. (a) A is distributed exponentially with a mean of 3 and B is distributed from a continuous distribution as $f(x) = \frac{2}{9}x$, where $0 \le x \le 3$. Find the cost of the distribution where $C = A + B$. (*Hint:* Integrate the two functions and assume random rectangular variates for substitution.)

(b) A simulation model is defined as $c = x + y$, where x is given by

$$f(x) = \begin{cases} \dfrac{1}{b-a}, & 2 \le x \le 8 \\ 0, & \text{elsewhere} \end{cases}$$

and the continuous variable y is given by the frequency:

Cost of y	Occurrence
\$1	0.15
2	0.25
3	0.40
4	0.15
5	0.05

Determine cost c after five simulation trials.

(c) Distribution A has the form $f(x) = \frac{1}{4}e^{-x/4}$, where $0 \le x$, and distribution B has the following estimated data:

B_i	f	B_i	f
1	4	5	18
2	15	6	8
3	22	7	2
4	30	8	0

If $C = A/B$, find the mean of C after five trials. Use the first five random numbers of Problem 6.23.

6.25. (a) Use the technique of range cost estimating to find the expected total mean cost and variance.

Cost Element	Optimistic Cost	Most Likely Cost	Pessimistic Cost
1. Direct labor	$79	$95	$95
2. Direct material	60	66	67
3. Indirect expenses	93	93	96
4. Fixed expenses	69	76	82

(b) What is the probability that cost will exceed $325?

6.26. A five-element cost program has been summarized as follows:

Cost Item	Optimistic Cost	Most Likely Cost	Pessimistic Cost
1	$ 4	$ 4.5	$ 6
2	10	12	16
3	1	1	1.5
4	4	8	12
5	2	2.5	4

(a) Determine the elemental mean costs, the total cost, and the elemental and total variances.

(b) Find the probability that cost will exceed $26.

6.27. Construct standard data like Table 6.3 for the spot welding regression equations. Use the three rules of thumb for applying standard time data tables and find the errors. Let allowances be 15% and develop one page of data.

(a) $P_1 = 50\%$, $P_2 = 15\%$, and $P_3 = 10\%$

(b) $P_1 = 50\%$, $P_2 = 10\%$, and $P_3 = 25\%$

(c) $P_1 = 50\%$, $P_2 = 20\%$, and $P_3 = 25\%$

6.28. (a) A spot-weld design has a primary, secondary, and third part, where the third part girth = 20 in. A total of 34 spot welds are necessary. The gross hourly direct labor wage is $25. Find the estimated cost per unit, cost per 100 units, and pieces per hour. Follow the three rules of thumb in applying Table 6.3. What purposes do these rules serve?

(b) Repeat (a) for another design where third-part girth = 10 in., and the number of spots = 19.

(c) Repeat (a) for another design where third-part girth = 24, and the number of spots = 37. Let lot quantity = 75 and find lot cost.

6.29. An element, "move casting, and aside part to tote pan," has been time studied and information recorded. Three possible independent variables are weight, girth, and fixture locating points.

(a) Determine three linear regression equations. Indicate criteria to allow selection of the best time driver for the preparation of standard time data. Which of the three equations is the "best line"? For your best line, provide a table of 25% increasing steps in time.

(b) Repeat (a) for metric dimensions of weight and girth.

Time Study	Time (minutes)	Weight lb kg	Girth $L + W + H$ [in. (mm)]	Fixture Locating Points
1	3.4	15 (6.8)	7 (178)	3 (3 buttons)
2	1.4	5 (2.3)	6 (152)	4 (nest)
3	2.8	12 (5.4)	7 (178)	3 (2 edges, 1 pin)
4	2.2	10 (4.5)	3 (76)	4 (nest)
5	4.8	20 (9.1)	11 (280)	1 (pin only)
6	4.2	17 (7.7)	9 (230)	2 (2 edges)

6.30. Develop standard data for an operation of "sawing and slitting" $\frac{1}{4}$-in.-O.D. maple dowels in a furniture factory. Several time studies are available from which normal times are removed for a recap sheet. It is assumed that methods engineering has standardized workplace layout. Time is in decimal minutes. Elements 1 and 4 are variable. Use steps of 25% for variable time.

Element	1	2	3	4	5
1. Pickup dowel	0.023	0.023	0.035	0.041	0.051
Reach distance	8 in.	8 in.	13 in.	16 in.	17 in.
2. Position for slotting	0.031	0.035	0.029	0.030	0.032
3. Move 14 in. and piece aside in tote box	0.024	0.021	0.031	0.030	0.030
4. Saw slot to length	0.093	0.126	0.103	0.210	0.193
Length	$\frac{1}{4}$ in.	$\frac{1}{4}$ in.	$\frac{1}{4}$ in.	1 in.	$\frac{7}{8}$ in.

Allowances are 15%. Develop the standard data in a tabular format.

6.31. Develop standard time data using the following information. Maximum and minimum part sizes are 32 and 288 in.^{2} Elements have been summarized into four linear equations and are

Element	Normal-Minute Equation
1	89.2 + 0.069 (square inch)
2	11.0 + 0.590 (square inch)
3	0.312 (square inch)
4	49.4 + 0.764 (square inch)

Use these rules:

1. A constant element is defined as one with less than a 20% increase in time from minimum to maximum size of the independent variable.

2. A variable element is defined as one with more than a 20% increase in time from minimum to maximum size and a time greater than 15% of the total time for average size work; otherwise, the element is constant.

3. Tabular time values for variable time increase 25% for each step, starting with minimum size and concluding with maximum size.

4. Tabulated values are expressed in standard hours. Allowances for personal, fatigue, and delay are 10%.

6.32. Provide one page of final standard time data for construction of reinforced concrete culverts. Measurements were made of five jobs. Time values are man-hours. Identification of independent variables are below task description.

	(1) 2 × 2 × 48	(2) 3 × 3 × 48	(3) 3 × 3 × 46	(4) 4 × 4 × 48	(5) 4 × 5 × 26
1. Excavation	8	16	19	28	18
ft³ removed	195	410	650	814	572
2. Forms	17	73	50	78	40
1000 board ft	300	1440	1160	1610	900
3. Place steel	23	91	95	85	62
lb	335	1369	1490	1617	1072
4. Place concrete	30	34	44	47	30
yd³	13	21	29	33	19
5. Cleanup	6	7	7	8	10
Top area ft²	96	144	184	192	130

Let $P_1 = 25\%$, $P_2 = 20\%$, and $P_3 = 20\%$.

6.33. A residential builder constructed a 2000-ft², two-story home on sandy loam soil for $124,000. This cost was exclusive of lot, taxes, and utility hookup costs. What is the unit estimate for his next home? An additional breakout of his costs revealed the following percentages for this same job:

Item	Percent	Item	Percent
Rough lumber	13.0	Earthwork	2.6
Rough carpentry	9.2	Flooring	6.4
Plumbing	13.6	Hardware	2.1
Finish lumber	1.2	Heating	3.0
Finish carpentry	2.8	Insulation	1.5
Cabinets	6.4	Lighting	0.5
Concrete	5.8	Painting	7.1
Wallboard	6.0	Roofing	2.2
Electrical wiring	5.5	All other	11.1

A 3200-ft², two-level home is to be built. Estimate his total and item costs. What elements would you adjust if this were a single-story home? Up or down?

6.34. The hydrobromination bid received for another rising film and ozonation reactor is $1,750,000 and the current index is 121.5. Use the method discussed in Sec. 6.9.

(a) What is the bench-mark cost?

(b) What are the factors for engineering, erection, and direct materials?

(c) An overall index of 123 is assumed for costs during construction. The regional factor is 7% more than the Gulf Coast for all factors. Items independent of the estimating process are found to cost $2,000,000. What is the total factor estimate for the chemical plant?

6.35. A food factory is planned near a large area of truck farms. These farms sell to stores, but a surplus is generally available. A small general-purpose production plant is planned, and the following equipment is engineered and priced out by bidding:

Process	Cost	Process	Cost
Roller grader	$10,000	Extractor	$ 36,000
Peeling and coring	18,000	Two cookers	7,000
Pulping	30,000	Can seaming	54,000
Instrumentation	57,000	Packaging	22,000
Conveying	37,000	Six motors	35,000
Filler press	14,000	Heat exchanger	44,000
Tanks	10,000		$374,000

Factors to obtain installed cost, including cost of site development, buildings, electrical installation, carpentry, painting, contractor's fee, foundation, structures, piping, engineering overhead, and supervision, are listed for various equipment as

Process centrifuges	2.0	Can machines	0.8
Compressors	2.0	Cutting machines	7.0
Heat exchangers	4.8	Conveying equipment	2.0
Motors	8.5	Ejectors	2.5
Graders	1.6	Blenders	2.0
Tanks	2.1	Instruments	4.1
Fillers	0.8	Packaging equipment	1.5

Estimate a plant cost based on this information. What other way would there be to improve on the quality of this estimate?

6.36. (a) An opportunity sale of an additional 200 units is received above an existing production level. The buyer is prepared to pay $350 for these 200 units. Cost for the current 500 units is $950. Total cost for producing 700 units is $1277. What is the marginal total cost? The unit marginal cost? What is the profit or loss? What is the minimum opportunity sale price to break even?

(b) The total cost of producing a given output varies according to the following estimated data:

Output	Total Cost	Output	Total Cost
0	$ 0	5	$192
1	100	6	205
2	150	7	230
3	175	8	280
4	187	9	380

Plot the estimated total cost curve, average cost curve, and marginal cost curve.

(c) A cast iron sphere has the following design weight (x) and cost (y): (2, 2), (3, 3), (4, 5), and (5, 8). Plot the cost curve, average cost curve, and marginal cost curve. Do these data comply with the economy of scale law?

6.37. Given the marginal return function $= 500 + 0.10n$, marginal cost $= \$1000$, point of maximum profit $= \$5000$, and fixed cost $= \$10,000$, find the demand function for price, quantity per period, and total cost function for the same period.

6.38. A motorcycle manufacturer is considering producing a new model of motorcycle designed for a specific market. Management has determined the total fixed cost for the plant and design to be $\$10^5$. The cost of producing the cycle after the initial investment has been made is estimated as a function $V(n)$ of the total number n of cycles produced.

(a) If $V(n) = 200n - 3 \times 10^{-3}n^2 + 10^{-7}n^3$, determine the marginal cost.

(b) What is the minimum marginal cost? How many cycles does this correspond to, and what is the average cost per cycle at this level of production?

(c) If the total return from sales $S(n)$ is given by $S(n) = 250n$, find the marginal return, the total profit, and the marginal profit.

(d) How many cycles should be produced to maximize profit?

6.39. Market studies of three locations, X, Y, and Z, show a demand of 20,000, 7000, and 6000 units of the same product per day in each location for 6 days per week. At the time of this estimate, two alternatives are being planned to meet this demand. In plan A, one plant with a daily capacity of 40,000 units could be located equidistant between the locations and produce with a fixed cost of $\$2000$ per day and a variable cost of $\$0.15$ per unit. Alternatively, plan B has mini-operations in each location with capacity of 24,000, 8000, and 8000 units, respectively. Fixed costs would be $\$1500$, $\$700$, and $\$700$ per day, respectively. Because of reduction in transportation costs and differences in labor costs, variable costs per unit are $\$0.10$, $\$0.11$, and $\$0.12$ per unit.

(a) Which alternative is more desirable?

(b) If sales were to increase to production capacity, does the best choice change?

(c) What variable cost per unit may plan B increase to for a break-even to A, at demand capacity? At full capacity?

CASE STUDY:
MARGINAL LABOR AND TOOL COST

The Don Boyle Co. makes zinc die castings. It has one 300-ton machine with a trim press located at the end of the quench conveyor. The machine is a hot chamber type and is capable of running automatically.

Andy James, Inc., manufactures leather goods. The purchasing agent for Andersons, Inc., calls Andy James (and several other manufacturers) for a quote on a 3-in.-wide belt. The belt is to be made with an adjustable buckle. The James engineers design a zinc die cast chrome-plated buckle, and call Don Boyle (and several other die casters) to quote on the buckle. Andersons, Inc., has estimated a volume of 75,000 belts annually for the next 3 years, at which time it is thought the item will be phased out.

Don Boyle must quote Andy James a unit price and a tooling price. He has a 300-ton machine capable of casting up to 16 buckles at one shot. His trim press is also capable of handling a shot this size. How does he quote this part to stay competitive? A 16-cavity die would minimize the unit price, but the tooling cost would be enormous. A single-cavity die maximizes the unit price but minimizes the tooling price. Which alternative should Don choose?

A single-cavity casting die, Don estimates, would cost about $4500. A trim die would cost an additional $900. Direct labor and overhead to cast one shot, no matter how many parts it has, is 6 cents. In other words, to cast the required 225,000 buckles in the next 3 years, the lowest cost for tooling is $5400. However, the unit cost (excluding tooling) is 6 cents per part, or $13,500 for the total of 225,000 units (no allowance is made for scrap).

Now, the marginal costs and marginal revenues must be examined. Marginal revenue is defined as the increment of total revenue (plus or minus) that results when the number of cavities is increased by one unit (or fraction thereof). Marginal cost likewise is defined as the increment of tooling cost that results from a similar increase in cavities. (Total revenue does not refer to the amount of money to be paid by Andy to Don. That would be a pricing problem, whereas this discussion concerns the problem of an efficient design.) Total revenue here is the total dollars saved by using a two-cavity die compared with a one-cavity die, or three cavities against two, and so forth. This total revenue may be called unit savings.

To cast the buckle for Andersons, Inc., the minimum starting point is single-cavity tooling. Total revenue at this point is zero. Don has not yet experienced a saving as a result of his tooling choice.

A two-cavity design, Don estimates, would cost an additional $600 for the die-casting die and $200 for the trimming die. The marginal cost is $800, and this does not include unit cost. Unit costs are considered only in respect to changes that create a savings or loss. A two-cavity die will produce two parts per shot, reducing the unit cost to 3 cents per part, or $6750 for the 3-year requirement. This is a reduction from $13,500 to $6750, or a unit saving of $6750.

For each additional cavity added to the tooling, Don estimates that the tool cost will increase by an additional $800. With 16 buckles per shot, the maximum capacity of the machine has been reached. Anything over 16 buckles per shot would require a larger die-casting machine.

Where does Don maximize the profits from a tooling standpoint? How many cavities does this decision call for? What is the full cost for this decision? How does raw material affect your decision?

7

Operation Estimating

This chapter stresses operation estimating. The heart of operation estimating is, in a substantive measure, a talent for breaking a task into essential elements. A design formulated sufficiently for this analysis is available, and the operation estimator uses functional cost equations and standard time data that model the details of the design.

In manufacturing the design is a part print and a processing plan; in chemical industries a flowchart and layout with engineering calculations are at hand; in engineering construction a set of drawings and specifications is a part of the given information. These designs are used for purposes such as estimating, planning, scheduling, methods improvement, and production or construction. They communicate the description and sequence of operations and are the hub on which individually and collectively many decisions, both great and small, are made.

Outmoded practices of operation estimating take the total cost of operating the plant for a period of time and divide by a total production quantity. Other practices determine a labor and material cost for an operation from a test run or prototype. Historical records of like operations are used. These methods are unsuitable for predictive cost estimates.

The operation estimator begins by subdividing the design task into large portions of labor and material. Progressively finer detail is determined until a description of labor and materials is very broad. At this point dollar extensions of labor and material are made to reflect the cost of the design.

There are many thousand kinds of labor and material operations. Regrettably, our choice of explanation extends only to few. Trade books, handbooks, internal sources of data, and so on, must be consulted for data for any real-life estimating. Some sources are listed in the references.

7.1 OPERATION COST

Before an operation estimate is started, some authority must initiate this activity. A request for quote, work order, production planner, foreman's request, work-simplification savings, employee suggestion, or architect or marketing request are reasons to prepare the operation estimate. These reasons are written on a *request for estimate* form, or RFE, which is the commissioning order to begin work. The RFE will describe or include the design, period of activity, specification, quality, and give other assumptions.

Economic evaluation follows many forms. In all these approaches, microanalysis is necessary. A facility for subdividing an operation design into elements—both physical and economic—is a characteristic. As detail estimates are relatively costly to prepare, the risk of achieving success must be offset by the cost of preparation. If risk were not minimal, the estimates for the operations would not be started. This risk is measured by a *capture percentage,* which we define as (estimates won)/(estimates made) × 100. For job shops the capture percentage may be low, and quotations are prepared using preliminary procedures. If the capture percentage is high, or the cost of estimating cost is not proportionately high to the benefits from success, detail estimating is mandatory.

While the labor and material may differ from design to design, techniques for evaluation are based on the same principles and practices. Operations are necessary to produce a change in value, and as a way of working the basic combination of a man and tool is the primary ingredient. Through man and tool activities the economic value of material is altered. The measure of the change in economic value is cost.

Cost in this instance implies a consumption of labor, materials, and tools to increase the value of some object. The use of expensive fixed assets involving capital cost in operations, while a consumption activity of wealth, is deferred until Chapter 9 where methods are introduced. In some cases automatic equipment produces units of output and may not require labor. These operations, however, consume materials and utilities and constitute the operation cost estimate. But operation designs may require tools, fixtures, or test equipment. Without these indirect materials, the operation is not possible. These tools are also estimated while direct labor and material are being considered. Our term that describes these "tools" is nonrecurring initial fixed costs.

Operation evaluations are limited as to the time horizon. The immediate future period rather than an extended time period is intended. The nature of labor is for a period of time such as "units of labor time per piece" or "units of labor per month or year."

The estimate may be undertaken to establish the operation cost for components, subassemblies, and intermediates of a product; to initiate the means of cost reduction; to provide a standard for production and control; and to compare different design ideas. It may be used to verify operation quotations submitted by vendors and to help determine the most economical method, process, or material for manufacturing a product. Whenever an operation is material- or labor-intensive, rather than capital-intensive, the methods of this chapter are primary. Figure 7.1 is a description of the items estimated in the context of manufacturing and construction work. In these situations the measure of economic want is *operation cost.*

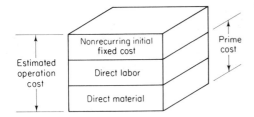

Figure 7.1. Descriptive layer chart of items included in an operation estimate.

7.2 MANUFACTURING WORK

Manufacturing of durable goods, such as toys to turbines, can be broadly classified as mass or moderate or job lot production. In *mass production,* sales volume is established and production rates are independent of single orders. In *moderate production* parts are produced in large quantities, and perhaps, irregularly over the year. Output is more dependent on single sales orders. *Job-lot* industries are more flexible and their production is closely connected to individual sales orders. Lot quantities may range from 1 to 500 for example. For cost estimating these distinctions are superficial because a similar logic is necessary for mass, moderate, or lot quantity operations despite the sales volume.

In manufacturing, operations are conducted at a machine, process, or bench. These are *workstations* involving direct labor. A *machine* is capable of metalworking; examples would be a turret lathe, milling machine, drill press, or punch press. A *process* tends to be chemical or fusion in character, such as spray painting, silver plating, welding, or casting. *Bench work* is pictured by an assembler doing joining, fastening, and assembly at a table. Figure 7.2 is a sketch of metalworking operations of turning, milling, drilling, and shearing metal with a punch and die.

Before detail estimating can begin, it is necessary to have engineering drawings, marketing quantity, specifications of the workpiece material, machines, processes and benches, and standard time data. Preparation of the operations sheet occurs simultaneously with direct-labor estimating. Once the operations are listed, the estimator refers to standard time data, which coincides with the machine, process, or bench identified by the operations sheet for doing the work. Each operation is detailed into elements that correspond to the standard time data. These elements may be on a form standardized by the company or marginal jottings or scratch-pad calculations may be followed. Computer spreadsheets are used also.

For the operation and workstation, and after visualizing the elements of an operation, the estimator will select times from the standard time data for setup and cycle. *Setup* includes work to prepare the machine, process, or bench to produce parts or run pieces. Starting with the workstation in a neutral condition, setup

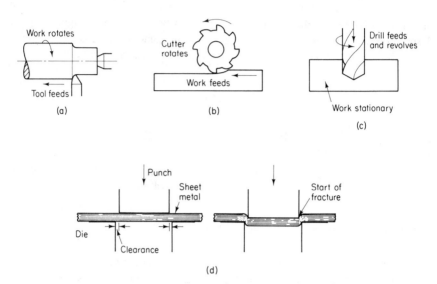

Figure 7.2. Various metal working operations: (a) turning; (b) milling; (c) drilling; (d) punching.

includes operator punch in or out, paperwork, obtain tools, position unworked materials nearby, adjust, and inspection; and after the parts are cycled, it includes teardown, return tooling, and cleanup of the workstation to a neutral condition ready for the next job. The setup does not include time to make parts as that is included in the cycle time. Estimating setup time is done for job shops and moderate quantity production. In mass production setup costs are of less unit importance, although its absolute value remains unchanged for large quantities. Setup is handled as an overhead charge for mass production. *Cycle time* or *run time* is the work to complete one unit after the setup is complete.

7.2.1 Metal Cutting

Involved in a metal cutting operation cycle is load work (LW), advance tool (AT), machining, retract tool (RT), and unload work (UW). These elements are shown in Fig. 7.3(a) and are labeled "One Work Cycle." After a number of parts are machined, tool maintenance is required, which includes removing the tool and replacing or regrinding the tool point and reinserting the tool ready for metal cutting. This is shown by Fig. 7.3(b). The mathematical model most frequently used in the study of machining estimating describes the cost of a single-point-tool rough-turning operation.

Setup standard time data for metal cutting operations are listed in hours as this is customary in the United States. For instance, Table 7.1A shows greatly

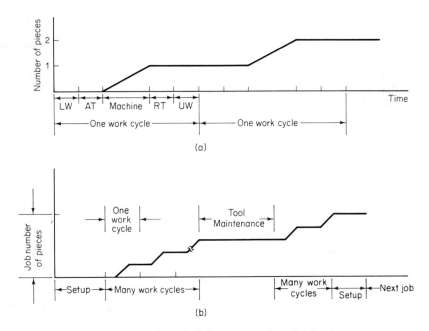

Figure 7.3. Operation items including setup, cycle, and tool maintenance.

abbreviated and typical values for turret lathes, mills, and drill presses. The time driver is the number of different tools and holding fixtures. Setup values, which include allowances, are posted once for each occurrence on the operations sheet. Setup element values are additive; that is, a type of holding device and a tool are added, and these would be read from the standard time data and posted on the operations sheet.

Operation unit cost is a function of handling, machining, tool changing, and the tool cost.

Handling time is the minutes to load and unload the workpiece from the machine. It can also include the time to advance and retract the tool from the cut and the occasional dimensional inspection of the part. It is unrelated to cutting speed and is a constant for a specified design and machine. Table 7.1E is an example of cycle standard time data shown in decimal minutes, which includes the personal, fatigue, and delay allowances. Decimal minutes are adopted for cycle work rather than seconds or hours because it is more widely understood. We define

$$\text{handling cost} = C_o t_h \qquad (7.1)$$

where C_o = direct-labor wage, dollars per minute

t_h = time in minutes for handling

Figure 7.4(a) is an example of this element plotted against cutting speed. C_o does not include overhead.

Table 7.1. Various Standard Time Data* For Turret Lathe; Milling Machine And Drill Press, Speeds And Feeds, Tool Life (Includes Allowances)

A. Setup expressed in hours

- 1. Punch in and out, study drawing   0.2
- 2. Turret lathe
  - First tool   1.3
  - Each additional tool   0.3
  - Collet fixture   0.2
  - Chuck fixture   0.1
- 3. Milling Machine
  - Vise   1.1
  - Angle plate   1.4
  - Shoulder-cut milling cutter   1.5
  - Slot-cut milling cutter   1.6
  - Tight tolerance   0.5
- 4. Drill press
  - Jig or fixture   0.1
  - Vise   0.05
  - Number of numerically controlled turrets
    - First turret   0.25
    - Additional turrets   0.07/each

B. Machining speeds and feeds

| | Turning and Facing (fpm, ipr) | | | |
| | High-Speed Steel | | Tungsten Carbide | |
Material	Rough	Finish	Rough	Finish
Stainless steel	150,0.015	160,0.007	350,0.015	350,0.007
Medium carbon steel	190,0.015	125,0.007	325,0.020	400,0.007
Cast iron, gray	145,0.015	185,0.007	500,0.020	675,0.010

| | HSS | | HSS | |
| | Slab Milling | | Slot   1 in. | |
Material	Rough	Finish	Rough	Finish
Stainless steel	140,0.006	210,0.005	85,0.002	95,0.0015
Medium carbon steel	170,0.008	225,0.006	85,0.0025	95,0.002
Gray cast iron	200,0.012	250,0.010	85,0.004	95,0.003

Drill Diameter[a]	Stainless Steel	Medium-Carbon Steel	Cast Iron, Gray
$\frac{1}{4}$	0.55	0.20	0.20
$\frac{5}{16}$	0.61	0.23	0.23
$\frac{3}{8}$	0.65	0.25	0.25

[a]Times are minutes per inch for power-feed drilling; threading times are minutes per inch.

Table 7.1.   (cont.)

Threads/in.[a]	Steel	Stainless Steel
32	0.18	0.33
20	0.15	0.30
16	0.19	0.33
10	0.32	0.48

C. Taylor tool-life parameters

Material	High-Speed Steel		Tungsten carbide	
	K	n	K	n
Stainless steel	170	0.08	400	0.16
Medium carbon steel	190	0.11	150	0.20
Cast iron, gray	75	0.14	130	0.25

D. Tool changing or indexing and costs

Time to index a turning type of carbide tool	2 min
Time to set a high-speed tool	4 min
Large milling tool replacement	10 min
Remove drill, regrind and replace	3 min
Cost per tool cutting corner for turning, carbide	$3
Cost for high-speed steel tool point	$5
Cost per milling cutter, 6-in. carbide	$250
Drill	$3

E. Handling and other constant cycle-time elements expressed in minutes

All machines	
Start and stop machine	0.08
Change speed of spindle	0.04
Engage spindle or feed	0.05
Air-clean part and fixture	0.06
Inspect dimension with micrometer	0.30
Brush chips	0.14
Turret lathe	
Advance turret and feed stock	0.18
Turret advance and return	0.04
Turret return, index, and advance	0.07
Cross slide advance and engage feed	0.08
Index square turret	0.04
Cross slide advance, engage feed, and return	0.14
Place and remove oil guard	0.08
Milling machine	
Pick up part, move, and place; remove and lay aside	
5 lb	0.13
10 lb	0.16
15 lb	0.19
Open and close vise	0.14
Seat with mallet	0.11

Table 7.1. (cont.)

Wipe off parallels	0.26
Pry part out	0.06
Clamp, unclamp vise, $\frac{1}{4}$ turn	0.05
Quick clamp collet	0.06
Clamp and unclamp hex nut	0.21 each
Numerically control turret drill press	
Pick up part, move, and place; pick up and lay aside	
To chuck:	
2.5 lb	0.10
5.0 lb	0.13
10.0 lb	0.16
Clamp and unclamp	
Vise, $\frac{1}{4}$ turn	0.05
Air cylinder	0.05
C-clamp	0.26
Thumb screw	0.06
Machine operation	
Change tool	0.06
Start control tape	0.02
Raise tool, position to new x-y location,	
advance tool to work	0.06/hole
Index turret	0.03/tool

*See *American Machinist Manufacturing Cost Estimating Guide,* 1983 edition, Phillip F. Ostwald, McGraw-Hill Book Co., for more information.

Machining time is the minutes that the tool is actually in the feed mode or cutting and removing chips. We define

$$t_m = \frac{L}{fN} = \frac{L\pi D}{12Vf} \tag{7.2}$$

$$\text{machining cost} = C_o t_m \tag{7.3}$$

where t_m = machining time, min
     L = length of cut for metal cutting, in.
     D = diameter, in.
     V = cutting speed, ft/min
     f = feed rate, in./rev

$$N = \text{rotary cutting speed} = \frac{12V}{\pi D}, \text{ rpm} \tag{7.4}$$

Each material will have special turning and milling cutting speeds and feeds as determined by testing or experience. Values will be different for roughing or

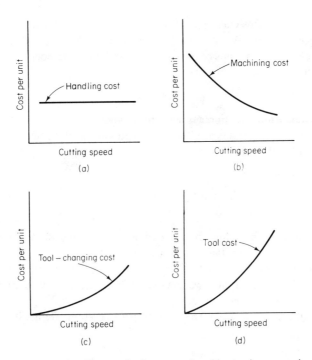

Figure 7.4.   Graphic costs for four parts of machine turning economics.

finish. A roughing pass will remove more material but does not satisfy dimensional and surface finish requirements. The material removal rate is min/in. for drilling and tapping. Table 7.1B is an example of standard time data for machining. As cutting velocity increases, the unit cost decreases, and this is shown by Fig. 7.4(b).

The turning length, which is being machined in a lathe, is at least equal to the final drawing dimension and is usually more because of additional stock for roughing or finishing. In a lathe facing element, the diameter will vary from the center of the barstock circle to the outside diameter (or the stock O.D.), and the facing length is at least equal to one-half of the diameter.

The diameter, D, may be either the workpiece or the tool. When a lathe turning operation is visualized, the diameter is the largest unmachined barstock dimension. In turning the periphery, it is the maximum diameter resulting from the raw stock or previous element. For milling and drilling, the diameter is the cutting tool diameter. A drill $\frac{1}{2}$ in. (12 mm) in diameter or a rotary milling cutter 1 in. (25 mm) in diameter are examples. The cutting speed velocity, V, has the dimensions of surface feet per minute (metres per second). Its value depends on many factors, and standard time data will consider these effects. Table 7.1B shows a small sampling which will be used for the examples and problems.

Cutting tools become dull as they continue to machine. Once dull they are replaced by new tools, or they are removed, reground, and reinserted in the tool holder. Empirical studies can relate tool life to cutting velocity for a specified tool and workpiece material. Two popular tool materials are high speed steel (HSS) and tungsten carbide. Most studies of tool life are based on the famous Taylor's tool-life cutting-speed equation.

$$VT^n = K \tag{7.5}$$

where T = average tool life, minutes per cutting edge
n, K = empirical constants resulting from regression analysis and
field studies, $0 < n \le 1, K > 0$

The average tool life, T, can be found as

$$T = \left(\frac{K}{V}\right)^{1/n} \tag{7.6}$$

Problem 5.7 deals with finding the regression values n and K for a tool-wear-out study. Table 7.1 C provides Taylor tool-life data.

If a tool life equation is $VT^{0.16} = 400$, we can find either V or T given the other variable. If $V = 200$ fpm, we can expect 76 minutes of machining before the tool must be indexed to a new corner.

The third cost is the tool changing cost per operation. Define it as

$$\text{tool changing cost} = C_o t_c \frac{t_m}{T} \tag{7.7}$$

where t_c is the tool-changing time, minutes. The tool-changing time, t_c, is the time to remove a worn-out tool, replace or index the tool, reset it for dimension and tolerance, and adjust for cutting. The time depends on whether the tool being changed is a disposable insert or a regrindable tool for which the whole tool must be removed and a new one reset. In lathe turning and milling there is the option of an indexable or regrindable tool. The drill is only reground. In Fig. 7.4(c), we see the relationship of tool-changing cost to cutting speed.

Define the following as

$$\text{tool cost per operation} = C_t \frac{t_m}{T} \tag{7.8}$$

where C_t denotes the tool cost, dollars. Tool cost, C_t, depends on the tool being a disposable tungsten carbide insert or a regrindable tool for turning. For insert tooling, tool cost is a function of the insert price, and the number of cutting edges per insert. For regrindable tooling, the tool cost is a function of original price, total number of cutting edges in the life of the tool, and the cost to grind per edge. As the cutting speed increases, the cost for the tool increases, as shown in Fig. 7.4(d). Table 7.1D provides tool costs and changing times.

The total cost per operation is composed of these four items. Machining cost is observed to decrease with increasing cutting speed while tool and tool changing costs increase. Handling costs are independent of cutting speed. Thus we can say that unit cost C_u is given as

$$C_u = \sum \left[C_o t_h + \frac{t_m}{T}(C_t + C_o t_c) + C_o t_m \right] \qquad (7.9)$$

Upon substitution of t_m and T by Eqs. (7.2) and (7.6), and after taking the derivative of this equation with respect to velocity and equating the derivative to zero, the minimum cost may be found as

$$V_{min} = \frac{K}{\left[\left(\frac{1}{n} - 1 \right) \left(\frac{C_o t_c + C_t}{C_o} \right) \right]^n} \qquad (7.10)$$

which gives the velocity for the unit cost of a rough-turning operation. In this development, we give no recognition to revenues that are produced by the machine. Had we found the marginal cost and marginal revenue, similar to Sec. 6.10, their intersection provides a higher value of velocity than that demonstrated by Eq. (7.10). This intersection is the profit maximum point. Consequently, Eq. (7.10) identifies the minimum velocity.

Occasionally, to avoid bottleneck situations there is a need to accelerate production at cutting speed greater than that recommended for minimum cost. In these expedited operations, we assume the tool cost to be negligible, or $C_t = 0$. If the costs in the basic model are not considered, the model gives the time to produce a workpiece, and we develop

$$T_u = t_h + t_m + t_c \frac{t_m}{T} \qquad (7.11)$$

where T_u is minutes per unit. The production rate (units per minute) is the reciprocal of T_u. The equation that gives the cutting speed that corresponds to maximum production rate is

$$V_{max} = \frac{K}{\left[\left(\frac{1}{n} - 1 \right) t_c \right]^n} \qquad (7.12)$$

The tool life that corresponds to maximum production rate is given by

$$T_{max} = \left[\left(\frac{1}{n} - 1 \right) t_c \right] \qquad (7.13)$$

Now consider an operation optimization problem of machining 430 F stainless steel, 1.750-in. (44.45-mm)-O.D. barstock. The cutting length is 16.50 in. plus a $\frac{1}{32}$ in. for approach giving 16.53 in. (419.8 mm). The turning operation will use a tungsten carbide, insertable and indexable eight-corner tool (about the size of a dime) which costs $3 per corner. Time to reset the tool is 2 minutes. Handling of the part is 0.16 minute and the operator wage is $15.20 per hour. The Taylor tool-life equation is $VT^{0.16} = 400$ (in U.S. customary units) for the tool and workpiece material. Feed of the rough-turning element is 0.015 ipr (0.38 mm/rev) for a depth of cut of 0.15 in. (3.8 mm) per side. These data are included in parts B, C, and E of Table 7.1. If the four items of the cost equation are plotted with several velocity values as the x-variable, we have Fig. 7.5, which shows the optimum at 200 fpm (0.2 m/s).

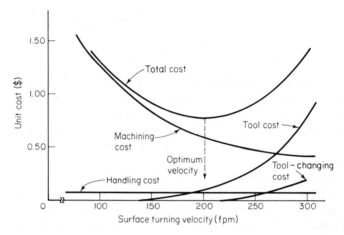

Figure 7.5.   Study of the various effects of cutting speed upon handling, machining, tool, and tool changing cost to give optimum.

Similarly, using Eq. (7.10), we have for the information

$$V_{min} = \frac{400}{\left[\left(\frac{1}{0.16} - 1\right)\left(\frac{0.25 \times 2 + 3}{0.25}\right)\right]^{0.16}} = 201 \text{ fpm}$$

and $T_u = 2.74$ at V_{min}, $V_{max} = 275$, and $T_{max} = 10.5$ min.

Typical metal-cutting problem.   A pinion is given by Fig. 7.6, and a long-term quantity of 1000 is planned with a lot requirement of 200 units. Raw material is 1.750-in. (44.45-mm)-O.D. 430 F stainless steel. Raw stock is purchased in 12-ft (3.7-m) lengths. Observe in Fig. 7.6 that the finished dimension is 18.750 in. (476.25 mm), and with a 0.015-in. (0.38-mm) facing length plus a 0.125-in. (3.18-mm) cutoff results in a minimum length of a 18.89 in. (479.81 mm).

The procedure for identifying the route of the pinion is known as an *operation sheet*. Table 7.2 identifies workstation, sequence number, description, setup time, and cycle time in hours per 100 units, together with other technical and cost-estimating information. The manufacturing cost estimator will determine the routing or sequencing of the workstations to produce the part. Following this the estimator will indicate the elements for each operation. The elements often correspond to standard

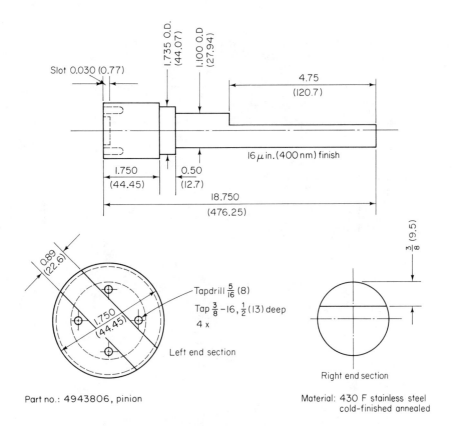

Figure 7.6. Typical part studied for cost estimating.

time data elements. At this point, the estimator studies the material requirements. Raw material amounts depend on scrap, waste, and shrinkage losses, which in turn are related to manufacturing operations.

Each 12-ft bar will produce 7.6 pieces, and allowing for gripping, we expect 7 units per bar. Shape yield from Eq. (3.4) gives about 91% when considering waste losses for facing, cutoff width, and end gripping of the last pinion. This material costs $1.24/lb ($2.76/kg). Each 200-quantity lot will require 29 bars, and each bar foot weighs 8.178 lb (3.71 kg). The unit cost of material is $17.38 (= 8.178 × 12 ÷ 7) which is posted in Table 7.2.

The estimator studies the drawing, machine specifications, and posts the machining elements, descriptions, workstation, and operations. After the machining elements are concluded for stock removal, dimensions, feeds, and speeds, handling is added, using standard time data for the machine. Other constant elements to cover start and stop, inspection, and machine adjustment are added. Concluding the operation estimate is the evaluation of setup. This is summarized for operation 10 in Table 7.3.

Table 7.2. Operation Sheet For Typical Part, Giving Estimate

Part no. 4943806
Part name: Pinion

Ordering quantity: 1000
Lot requirement: 200

Material: 430F Stainless steel 1.750 ± 0.003 in. cold finished 6S-12 ft bars = 1000 pieces
Unit material cost: $17.38

Workstation	Operation no.	Description of operations (list tools and gauges)	Setup hour	Cycle hour/100 units	Unit estimate	Labor rate	Labor + over-head rate	Labor + overhead
Turret lathe	10	Position Face 0.015 Turn rough 1.45 Turn rough 1.15 Turn finished 1.110 Turn 1.735 Cut off to length 19.750 (Carbide tools)	3.2	10.067	0.117	18.35	1.70	3.65
Vertical mill	20	End mill 0.89 slot with 3/4 H.S.S. end mill (Collet fixture)	1.8	7.850	0.088	19.65	1.85	3.20
Horizontal mill	30	Slab mill 4.75 x 3/8 (Nesting vise, H.S.S. tool)	1.3	1.500	0.022	19.65	1.80	0.78
N.C. turret drill press	40	Drill 5/8 holes - 4 x Tap 3/8 - 16 (Collet fixture)	0.66	5.245	0.056	17.40	2.15	2.10
							Unit material, labor, and overhead cost	$27.11

Table 7.3.   DETERMINING CYCLE AND SETUP ESTIMATES FOR OPERATION 10, TABLE 7.2.

A. Calculation of machining elements

Element	Dim. (in.)	Depth of Cut, (in.)	Length of cut L_d, (in.)	Safety Stock (in.)	Length (in.)	Diameter (in.)	Velocity (fpm)	Feed (ipr)	Time t_m
Facing		0.015	0.875	1/32	0.906	1.750	350	0.015	0.08 min
Rough turn	1.45	0.15	16.5	1/32	16.53	1.750	350	0.015	1.44
Rough turn	1.15	0.15	16.5	1/32	16.53	1.45	350	0.015	1.20
Fine finish	1.10	0.025	16.5	1/32	16.53	1.15	350	0.007	2.03
Turn	1.735	0.0075	0.5	1/32	.53	1.750	350	0.007	0.10
Cutoff		0.125	0.875	1/32	0.906	1.750	350	0.015	0.08

t_m = sub total machining time = 4.93 min

B. Selection of handling and other machine standard time data

Start and stop machine	0.09 min
Advance turret and position raw stock	0.18
Place and remove oil guard	0.08
Speed change, assume 4 times, 4 × 0.04	0.16
Advance, index, and return turret, 6 times, 6 × 0.08	0.48
Inspect part with micrometer, irregular element, $0.30 \times \frac{1}{5}$	0.06
Air-clean part	0.06

t_h = subtotal handling and other machine data = 1.11 min

total cycle = 6.04 min

C. Setup development

Punch in and out, study drawing	0.2 hour
First tool	1.3
Five additional tools	1.5
Collet fixture	0.2

Total setup = 3.2 hour

D. Entry values for operations sheet

Setup = 3.2 hours
hr/100 = 10.067

Each turret lathe machining element will use a single tool on a square or hexagon turret, for example, and handling of the turrets to advance, engage, and retract the turrets from the workpiece depends solely on machining elements. Similarly, setup will depend on the number of tools, tolerance, and so on, which are dependent on machining elements.

Consider the elements of operation 10, which uses a turret lathe machine. A turret lathe is a turning metal-cutting machine and the principal characteristic is that the tools can be positioned in readiness on the turrets for consecutive elements. There are usually two turrets, a six-position hexagonal type mounted on the ways, and a four-position square type mounted on a carriage. Ten different cutting tools can be preset.

Figure 7.7 is a description of the consecutive machining elements. In Fig. 7.7(a), a facing cut is made. Note Table 7.3, where the design factors are given to

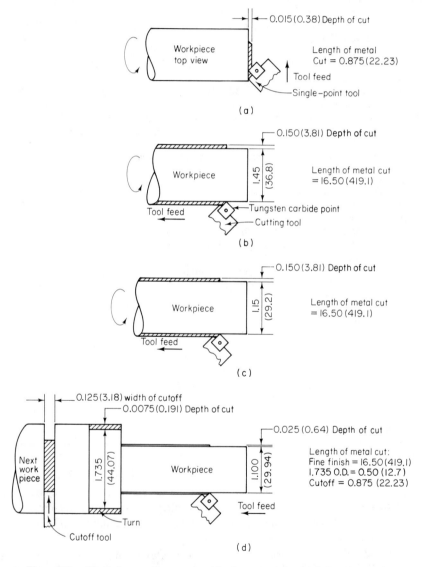

Figure 7.7. Machining cuts for operation 10 using turret lathe: (a) facing element; (b) first pass, rough-turning element; (c) second pass, rough-turning element; (d) final turret lathe elements.

calculate t_m using tungsten carbide. Values of t_m are calculated using Table 7.1 values and Eq. (7.2). As these computations are frequent, special slide rules are available; computers or electronic calculators are programmed to do this work quickly. Observe that values of t_m are posted to Table 7.3(A). Note that the diameter is successively reduced as a result of two rough and one finish turning passes. These differing values of diameter would theoretically require different values of N, according to Eq. (7.4), or

$$N = \frac{12 \times 350}{\pi \times 1.75} = 764 \text{ rpm versus} \quad N = \frac{12 \times 350}{\pi \times 1.45} = 922 \text{ rpm}$$

Each of these rpms calls for a speed adjustment, which requires additional time. If the time saving is small, an average rpm will be used and no speed adjustment made. But for long cuts the savings in machining time is worth the time to change the rpm. That is the plan we use in our examples. Observe that these rpms exceed those required from previous minimum-cost velocity calculations.

Knowing the number of different cuts, we assume that each cut will use a separate tool and require an "advance, engage, and retract" turret handling time for either the hex or square turret. Handling and other manual elements are now selected from standard time data of Table 7.1 and posted in Table 7.3(B).

Setup is estimated after the cycle time is determined. Observe that setup values are shown as Table 7.3(C). The entry for the cycle is listed in the hours per 100 units column to a three-place decimal using rules of *exaggerated precision* discussed in Chapter 2. For example, $(6.04/60) \times 100 = 10.067$ hours per 100 units. The setup of 3.2 hours and 10.067 hours per 100 units are transferred to Table 7.2, operation 10.

In operation 20, a $\frac{3}{4}$-in. (19-mm) end mill will machine the 0.89-in. (22.6-mm)-wide by 0.030-in. (0.77-mm)-deep slot. A collet fixture will be used to grip the part. The width of the slot is slightly wider than the end-mill diameter. An end-mill cutter is similar to a drill except that the bottom is flat and has four cutting flutes on the bottom and side, and a milling machine capable of holding the end mill vertically is used. Two passes are necessary for the width and a rough cut will remove 0.025 in. (0.64 mm) while the finishing cut will remove 0.005 in. (0.13 mm) with a high-speed steel tool. Figure 7.8 describes the machining.

In operation 30, a 4-in. (100 mm) plain milling cutter, high-speed steel, with a 6-in. (150-mm) face and eight teeth will slab-mill the 4.75-in. (120.7-mm) dimension given on the pinion. This milling flat is relative to the slot cut in operation 20, and a special nesting vise will be designed and constructed to ensure dimensional compliance. Because of the greater rigidity of this tool, along with the horizontal-arbor milling machine, only one pass is necessary to reach finish dimension. Figure 7.9 shows an end view of the basic features of the machining operation.

In operation 40, four holes are first drilled, and then followed by tapping. A collet fixture that has bushing guides for the four holes is required. The design of the fixture will satisfy the hole locational requirements. Figure 7.10 describes the drilling and tapping element.

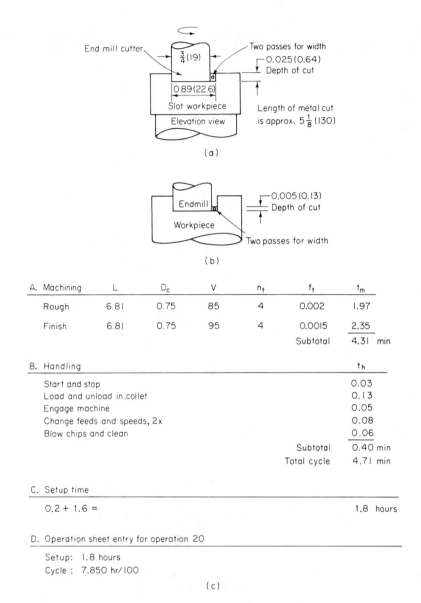

(a)

(b)

A. Machining	L	D_c	V	n_t	f_t	t_m
Rough	6.81	0.75	85	4	0.002	1.97
Finish	6.81	0.75	95	4	0.0015	2.35
					Subtotal	4.31 min

B. Handling	t_h
Start and stop	0.03
Load and unload in.collet	0.13
Engage machine	0.05
Change feeds and speeds, 2x	0.08
Blow chips and clean	0.06
Subtotal	0.40 min
Total cycle	4.71 min

C. Setup time

0.2 + 1.6 =   1.8 hours

D. Operation sheet entry for operation 20

Setup: 1.8 hours
Cycle : 7.850 hr/100

(c)

Figure 7.8. Operation 20: (a) rough end-mill slotting element; (b) finish end-mill slotting element; (c) calculation of estimate.

The end milling, slab milling, and drilling-tapping elements have different length of cut requirements. Note Fig. 7.11 as an illustration. The length of cut L is the distance for which the cutting tool is moving at feed f velocity. This is much less than the "rapid traverse" velocity, which may be as high as 200 to 500 in./min. The general relationship is

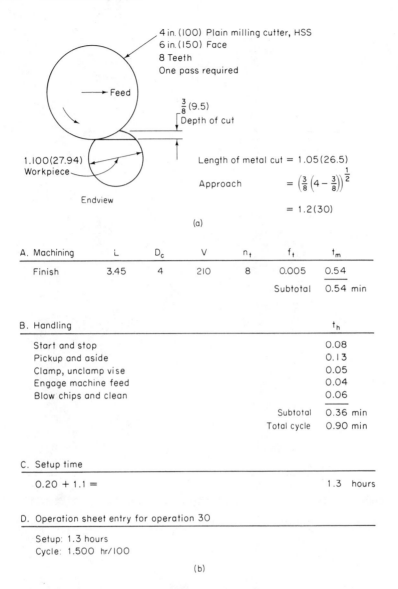

Figure 7.9.   Operation 30: (a) slab milling operation, end view section; (b) calculation of estimate.

$$L = L_s + L_a + L_d + L_{ot} \tag{7.14}$$

where L = length of cut at velocity f, in.

L_s = safety length, in.

L_a = approach length due to cutter geometry, in.

L_d = design length of workpiece, in.

L_{ot} = overtravel length, in.

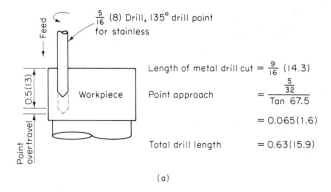

Length of metal drill cut $= \frac{9}{16}$ (14.3)

Point approach $= \dfrac{\frac{5}{32}}{\text{Tan } 67.5}$

$= 0.065$(1.6)

Total drill length $= 0.63$(15.9)

(a)

A. Machine	L	D_c	f_{dt}	Lf_{dt}	No. holes	t_m
Drilling	0.63	$\frac{5}{16}$	0.61	0.38	4	1.54 min
Tapping	0.5	$\frac{3}{8} - 16$	0.33	0.17	4	0.66
					Subtotal	2.20 min

B. Handling	t_h
Load part	0.13
Start machine	0.08
Start tape	0.02
Change tools, 2x	0.12
Raise tool, position to new location, advance x 8	0.48
Index turret, 2x	0.06
Blow off chips	0.06
Subtotal handling	0.95 min
Total cycle	3.15 min

C. Setup time

0.2 + 0.14 + 0.25 + 0.07 =   0.66 hours

D. Operation sheet entry for operation 40

Setup: 0.66 hours
Cycle: 5.245 hr/100

(b)

Figure 7.10. Operation 40: (a) drilling element, end view section; (b) calculation of estimate.

L is the value required for finding t_m in machining calculation. Safety length, L_s, is necessary for any possible stock variations; if the stock is oversize and the cutter is at rapid-traverse velocity, damage could result upon the cutter striking the workpiece. Values are $0 < L_s \leq \frac{1}{2}$ in. Approach length depends on cutter-workpiece geometry. Note Fig. 7.11, which shows the three cases of operation 20, 30, and 40.

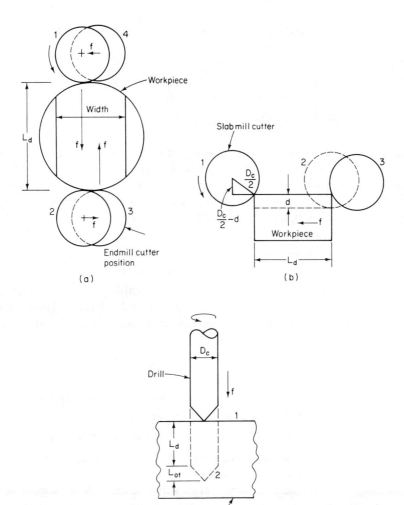

Figure 7.11. Approach and over-travel length for (a) end milling (top view); (b) slab milling (elevation view); and (c) drilling (elevation view).

For operation 20, a $\frac{3}{4}$-in. (19.1-mm) end mill is vertically milling the 0.89-in. (22.6-mm) slot. Observe that the cutter will start in position 1 and mill to 2, 3, and 4, and finally back to position 1, ready to begin end-milling the next workpiece. L_a is approximately two diameters plus the distance from 2 to 3 and 4 to 1 or $2(0.89 - 0.75) = 0.28$ in. Let $L_s = \frac{1}{64}$ in. (0.4 mm) $= L_{ot}$, and $L_d = 1.75$ (44.5 mm). Then cutting length, noting Fig. 7.11(a), $L = \frac{1}{64} + 4(0.75) + 0.28 + 2(1.75) + \frac{1}{64} = 6.81$ in. (173 mm). In this calculation the design length is about 50% of total length. Operation 30 can be simplified and shown as sketch (b). The chip removal of the cutter is on the periphery of the 4-in. (100-mm) O.D. It has an approach given by

$$L_a = \sqrt{\left(\frac{D_c}{2}\right)^2 - \left(\frac{D_c}{2} - d\right)^2} = \sqrt{d(D_c - d)} \tag{7.15}$$

where D_c = cutter diameter, in.
d = depth of cut, in.

For this operation we assume that $L_a = L_{ot}$. If the operation were only roughing, we could let $L_{ot} = 0$, since the full depth would have been removed at position 2. But the operation design calls for only one pass, so the cutter will feed from position 1 to 3. At position 3, it will reverse and return to position 1, however at rapid-traverse velocity. For operation 30, we let

$L_s = 1/16$ in. (0.4 in.)
$L_d = 1.05$ in. (26.7 mm)
$L = 1/16 + 2(0.375(4 - 0.375))^{\frac{1}{2}} + 1.05 = 3.45$ in. (87.5 mm)

Operation 40 requires four $\frac{5}{16}$-in. (8-mm) holes. Drilling will have an overtravel distance required for the length of the 135° conical drill point. Stainless steel uses a different conical point than other materials, as the usual included point angle is 118°.

$$L_{ot} = \frac{D_c}{2 \tan 67.5} = 0.2D_c \tag{7.16}$$

where D_c is the drill diameter, in. For drilling we use $L_s = \frac{1}{16}$ in. (1.6 mm) and $L_a = 0$. For operation 40 the length for machine feed is

$$L = \tfrac{1}{16} + 0 + 1/2 + 0.2\,(5/16) = 0.63 \text{ in. (15.9 mm)}$$

Tapping usually does not require additional distances and only L_d is necessary.

With the cutting lengths determined, we turn next to finding cycle and setup times using standard time data. As before, the steps proceed with the various machining elements, handling, setup, and converting estimated values to setup and cycle hours per 100 units. For a multitooth milling cutter, Eq. (7.2) is converted to

$$t_m = \frac{L\pi D_c}{12Vn_t f_t} \tag{7.17}$$

where n_t = number of teeth on cutter
f_t = feed per revolution-tooth

For the rough-milling element of operation 20, $L = 6.81$ in., $D_c = 3/4$ in., $V = 85$ fpm, $n_t = 4$, and $f_t = 0.002$ in/rev.-tooth, then $t_m = 1.97$ min. For the finish milling element, the same cutter and setup is used, except that $V = 95$ fpm, $f_t = 0.0015$ iprt, and $t_m = 2.35$ min. These are marked in Fig. 7.8, where other standard time data entries are made. Finally, for operation 20, the setup and cycle time values are posted on the operations form.

Operation 30 is horizontal milling, and varies somewhat from operation 20. The metal cutting values are $L = 3.45$ in., $D_c = 4$ in., $V = 140$ fpm, $n_t = 8$, $f = 0.006$ iprt, and $t_m = 0.54$, which is entered on Fig. 7.10. Other values for handling and setup are selected from Table 7.1, and finally setup and cycle time are posted to the operation sheet for operation 40.

The drilling and tapping element of operation 40 uses a different formula for machining, as these kinds of metal cutting are expressed as rates, or

$$t_m = L f_{dt} \tag{7.18}$$

where f_{dt} is the drilling or tapping feed rates, min/in. The metal cutting rates are classified by standard time data, and typical values are given by Table 7.1B. Entry information is drill diameter and workpiece material. Other handling time is collected for Fig. 7.10 and final cycle information is posted on Table 7.2.

7.2.2 Sheet Metal

Manufacturing work is concerned with thousands of different operations in addition to metal cutting. Sheet metal work is an interesting example and shows the diversity. Setup and cycle estimates are required and standard time data are applied to operations sheets as before. For variation we want a preliminary estimate using preliminary information. These standard time data are developed by summarizing detail information, as was discussed for resistance spot welding in Sec. 6.8. Preliminary estimates must be prepared more quickly than detail estimates, and they are not as accurate. Dimensions for preliminary standard time data for setup and cycle are listed as hours. Data provided to the estimator are single- or two-variable linear equations and were discussed as time-estimating relationships in Chapter 6. Sometimes the preliminary data are "flat." This is like the *flat rates* used by auto repair shops, which are constant hours for repair. Flat rates or average operation hours are posted from the preliminary time data tables without any calculation and are the simplest. They are insensitive to design variation and are used for operations which have constant output. The drilling data of Table 7.4 is an example of preparing data differently for preliminary estimates. Previously for Table 7.1B and Fig. 7.10(a) feed rate and length of cut were multiplied to give time. When dealing with sheet metal material the length of metal cut is often less than the overtravel required by the drill point, and, furthermore, sheet metal materials are easily machined. Drilling and many other machining operations performed on sheet metal materials use average observed values and deliberately ignore complicated formula or tabular approaches.

Consider the isometric sketch of Fig. 7.12. This chassis, part number 674, is a spot weld of two individual parts, 672 and 673. The operations sheets for a preliminary estimate will supply minimum information. Unlike detail operation estimates, which are determined for each operation, the total of the setup and cycle time is calculated for preliminary operations as element analysis is not required for the individual operation. Once the totals are available, they are multiplied by an average plant direct-labor wage rate.

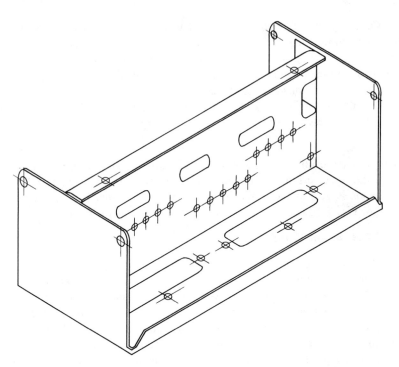

Figure 7.12.   Sheet metal assembly part number 674 composed of parts 672 and 673.

Notice in Table 7.4 that the data are dimensioned in hours, although dollars are possible. With time as the dependent value, the data are insensitive to changes in labor rates. Little supplemental information is provided, as the estimator is expected to know the physical characteristics of the machine, process, or bench work. The *setup* covers the initial and terminating work for a lot of anywhere from one to many units. The *cycle* is the operation time to complete one unit. The information may have been originally measured by time study, predetermined motion time data systems, or job tickets and includes the personal, fatigue, and delay allowances.

The estimator will write setup and cycle totals from the component P/N 672 and 673 on the assembly preliminary operation sheet. Following the selection and writing of the operations, time values are transferred from Table 7.4 to Table 7.5. For example, the flat rates of 0.1 hour setup and 0.004 hour cycle are entered in operation 10. Observe operation 20, spot weld. The cycle constant is 0.011, 10 spots, and $L + W + H$ girth dimensions are 13, and cycle = 0.047 (= 0.011 + 0.00 × 10 + 0.002 × 13), which is posted for operation 20. The student may want to compare this estimate by referring to Table 6.3.

Two tools for drilling are necessary and setup is 0.3 hr (= 0.2 + 0.05 × 2) and cycle is 0.049 hr (= 0.015 + 0.003 × 2 + 0.001 × 28) for 28 holes. The drill and countersink are equivalent time consuming elements for preliminary estimating of sheet metal materials. The constant time 0.015 hr of the drill press esti-

Table 7.4.   Preliminary-Type Standard Time Data For Sheet Metal Operations

Operation	Setup (hours)	Cycle (hours per unit)
Shear	0.1	0.001
Punch press	0.4	0.0015
Numerical control punch press	0.2 + 0.03 (tool)	0.008 + 0.0005 (hit)
Press brake	0.3	0.001 + 0.002 (lay no.)
Drill press	0.2 + 0.05 (tool)	0.015 + 0.003 (tool) + 0.001 (hole)
Spotweld	1.2	0.011 + 0.001 (spot) + 0.002 (third part $L + W + H$)
Degrease	0.1	0.001
Deburr	0.1	0.005
Tumble	0.1	0.005
Chromate finish	0.1	0.003
Silk screen	0.3	0.004
Deoxidize	0.1	0.004

Table 7.5.   Preliminary Operations Sheet And Estimate

Part no. ____674____   Material _Unit_   0.41 + 1.12 = $1.53

Name _Electrical chassis_

Lot quantity ____37____

	Part no.	Setup	Cycle
	672	2.3	0.132
	673	2.35	0.087
	Total	4.65	0.219

Operation no.	Operation	Setup	Cycle
10	Deoxidize	0.1	0.004
20	Spot-weld 10 spots two parts, $L + W + H = 13$	1.2	0.047
30	Drill 18 1/8-in. hole through countersink 0.138 in., 10 holes	0.3	0.049
40	Deburr holes	0.1	0.005
50	Degrease	0.1	0.001
60	Chromate	0.1	0.003
70	Silk screen	0.3	0.004

	Setup	Cycle
Part no. 674	2.2	0.113
Total assembly	6.85	0.332
Assembly lot hours		19.134
Average plant labor cost		$19.353
Assembly material cost, unit		$1.53
Lot labor cost		$370.24
Unit material and direct-labor cost		$11.53

mating data covers loading and unloading of the part, start machine, clean part and drill press table, and so on, and is an average time for these elements when the operation deals with sheet metal parts. "Constants" are always included with preliminary estimates. The spot-weld and drilling operations are examples of a two-variable linear estimating model which require a minimum of calculation. Note the flat rate of 0.001 hour per unit for "shear" in Table 7.4. If a shear operation of a sheet results in a strip having 100 pieces, the estimator will divide 0.001 by 100 and post 0.00001 hour for operation time, but this practice requires judgment because shear time is already relatively small.

7.2.3 Nonrecurring Initial Fixed Costs

In manufacturing it is necessary to design tools and test equipment to adapt machinery to a specific operation or product design. At the moment of the operation sheet preparation, the estimator will evaluate these designs for their cost. Officially, we term these devices as *nonrecurring initial fixed costs*. They are one-time-only costs despite the number of lots or continuous production quantity requirements. This is unlike setup costs, which occur for each batch, or setup for mass production requirements. The part or product could not be manufactured without these tools, and thus they are front-end or *initial costs*. These designed devices are classified as *fixed costs* rather than variable and are a depreciable asset subject to taxation laws. Additionally, the devices are classed as *permanent* as contrasted to *perishable,* such as lathe turning tools, milling cutters, and drill bits. Perishable tooling incurs an indirect operational expense and is included as an overhead charge. Examples of nonrecurring initial fixed costs are jigs, fixtures, molds, dies, electronic testing and quality control gauges, and special handling devices. These items require engineering design.

At every stage in manufacturing, tool engineers are confronted with dollar signs. The tool designer should know enough of cost estimating to determine whether temporary tooling would suffice even though funds are provided for more expensive permanent tooling. He or she should be able to comprehend design plans so as to initiate or defend decisions when amortizing the tooling on a single run as opposed to amortizing distributed against probable future reruns.

Many types of jigs, fixtures, tools, gauges, and dies have fundamental details in common. This fact permits simplification in methods of estimating. The factor method is usually employed; the factors are larger than used for labor estimating for mass production. That is too time consuming. In some cases the tool estimator may resort to the comparison method, which is the quickest but not the most accurate way.

In terms of test equipment and inspection devices, it too is weighed on equal footing with ordinary tooling. The estimator should be aware of what exists and is available for production and that which is special, requiring design or purchase. Special processing tools may be required for general-purpose or special-purpose equipment. In operation and postoperation inspection, tooling before assembly could include gauges, holding devices, cutting tools, universal jigs, specially designed and constructed fixtures, and other purchased tooling. Inspection requirements for the estimate include such necessary tools for the receiving department, in-process inspection, postfabrication inspection requirements, and postassembly requirements. Environmental needs where engineering specifications call for peculiar ambient, weather, or shock tests cannot be overlooked.

These initial costs will be estimated either before their design, or following design but prior to manufacture. If estimating precedes design, an experienced estimator will use comparison estimates for the cost value. If a design is at hand, he or she will use standard time data. This information can be developed for a variety of designs. A typical and reduced sample of estimating data for manufacturing sheet metal tooling is given as Table 7.6. The data are listed in hours and are specifically for the manufacturing of dies using oil-hardenable steel components precision machined and assembled by a journeyman tool and die maker.

Figure 7.13 is an example of a part that is estimated using Table 7.6. The tool will blank the external shape and pierce the holes. A second tool is necessary to

Table 7.6.   STANDARD TIME DATA FOR THE MANUFACTURE OF TOOLING
FOR SHEET METAL OPERATIONS (Time in Hours)

1. Pierce hole tooling

Diameter (in.)	First Hole	Each Additional Hole
0.0156–0.1245	21	3.5
0.125–0.500	16	2.5
0.501–1.000	21	9.0
1.001–1.500	31	10.0

2. Blank external contour tooling

Periphery (in.)	Straight Contour	Curved Contour
Up to 3	24	30
3–4	27	40
4–5	29	50
5–8	40	80

3. Form tooling

Length of Bend (in.)	Width of Bend (in.)	90° Bends
Up to 1	Up to 1	30
Over 1 to 2	Up to 1	32.5
Up to 1	Over 1 to 2	32.5
Over 1 to 2	Over 1 to 2	35
Over 2 to 3	Over 2 to 3	40

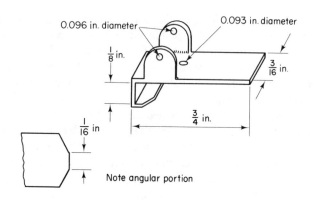

Tool Element	Calculation	Time
1. Pierce holes		
2 – 0.096 in.	21 + 3.5	24.5 hours
1 – 0.093 in.	21	21
2. Blank		
Straight contour ≈ 2 in.		24
Curved contour ≈ 0.1 in.		30
	Total	99.5 hours
	Machine-hour rate	$75
	Tool cost	$7462.50

Figure 7.13. Manufactured part, 303 stainless steel, $0.031 \times 9/16 \times 1.0$ in. developed size. Example of nonrecurring initial fixed cost estimate.

bend the tabs, but that is left as a chapter problem. Another possible design can perform piercing, blanking, and forming in one tool having several stations, which is then called a progressive die. The data should be sufficiently flexible to estimate many types of die designs. The estimated hours are multiplied by the machine-hour rate, which was discussed in Chapter 4.

The cost of these designs is significant. The cost is handled by amortization, direct sale to customer, or general overhead application. *Amortization* is an estimating calculation, meaning the division of the cost by the quantity of the operational lot or market total. Selecting this quantity presents a trade-off problem. If this quantity is too small, amortization will be overstated, causing greater cost and increased price, perhaps resulting in fewer sales of the product. If the quantity is too large, other errors may result or the tooling could be made obsolete due to unfortunate design changes required by the part and sunk costs are created. The cost of the tooling may not be completely amortized, due to actual production falling short of expectations. Problems involved in evaluating trade-off policies are left for the student. But the simplest expedient is to add the prorated cost of the tooling to operation cost. A model for amortization is given as

$$C_{ot} = \frac{C_{nif}}{N} \qquad (7.19)$$

where C_{ot} = operation cost for tooling, dollars per unit
$\quad C_{nif}$ = nonrecurring initial fixed-cost dollars
$\qquad N$ = quantity used for amortization which may be lot, model, or year

In some business situations a manufacturer may sell the tools directly to the customer. Vendors will design and build the tool, and separately quote the cost of the tooling independent of the unit part price to a customer. A *separate tooling charge* sidesteps the trade-off problem involved with amortization, as the customer receives the tooling upon delivery of the product. In other situations the estimator will add tooling costs to overhead, which spreads the cost to all products. This is not a recommended practice.

The operation estimator is able to evaluate several alternative designs. A part can be manufactured with or without tooling. Tooling will allow less direct-labor time in the operation but will increase initial costs. This break even can be evaluated using

$$C_{nif} = \frac{Na(1 + t) - SU}{I + T + D + M} \qquad (7.20)$$

where N = number of units manufactured per year
$\quad a$ = savings in labor cost per unit compared to another operation
$\quad t$ = percentage of overhead applied on labor saved
$\ SU$ = yearly cost of setup, dollars
$\quad I$ = annual allowance for interest on investment, decimal
$\quad T$ = annual allowance for taxes, decimal
$\quad D$ = annual allowance for depreciation, decimal
$\quad M$ = annual allowance for maintenance, decimal

Consider the chassis shown by Fig. 7.12. Each lot produces 37 units, while annual requirements are 370 units. P/N 672 setup requires 2.3 hours and 0.132 hour for run time. From operations analysis of other routing plans, tools can be substituted for improved methods and a savings of 0.7 hour setup and 0.05 hour cycle will occur if a special tool estimated to cost $750 is made. Other data are $a = 0.05 \times \$19.35 = \$0.97$ savings per unit, $t = 30\%$, 10 setups of tool will save SU = 0.7 hour $\times \$19.35 \times 10 = \$135.45$, $I = 25\%$ allowance for interest, $T = 5\%$ taxes, $D = 25\%$ for depreciation, and $M = 20\%$ annual allowance for maintenance. The permissible first cost for a tool is

$$C = \frac{370 \times 0.97\,(1.30) - 135.45}{0.25 + 0.05 + 0.25 + 0.20} = \$441$$

As the estimated cost of the proposed tooling ($750) is more than the potential savings it promises, we choose to have a higher direct-labor cost rather than initial fixed costs.

7.2.4 Calculating Operation Cost

Operation cost can be found once the operations sheet is determined and standard time data applied. Observe Table 7.2. After setup and cycle are determined, we find the *unit estimate* using

$$T_u = \frac{SU}{N} + H_s \qquad (7.21)$$

where T_u = unit estimate, hours
SU = setup hour for operation
N = lot quantity
H_s = standard hours per unit

For example, operation 10 of Table 7.2 indicates setup = 3.2 hours, hours per 100 units = 10.067, and N = 200 lot requirement. Then $T_u = 0.117$ (= 3.2/200 + 0.101). The next step is to post the labor rate and labor plus overhead rate on the operation sheet. With this done, it is possible to find unit cost as given by

$$C_{dl} = \left(\frac{SU}{N} + H_s\right)R \qquad (7.22)$$

where C_{dl} = cost of direct labor operation per unit
R = labor rate, dollars per hour

Then we multiply by the overhead rate and labor rate to eventually determine operation cost of labor and overhead, or

$$C_{dlo} = \left(\frac{SU}{N} + H_s\right)R(1 + R_{oh}) \qquad (7.23)$$

where C_{dlo} = direct labor and overhead cost
R_{oh} = overhead rate on the basis of per unit operation direct labor

In operation 10 of Table 7.2, this is really one calculation using one equation, 3.65 = (3.2/200 + 0.101)(18.35)(1.70). When we add R_{oh} to 1, we are, in effect, combining the labor and overhead rate. The 1.70 labor plus overhead rate is 70% overhead and 100% labor. The total unit cost for the operation sheet is given as

$$C_u = \Sigma C_{dlo} + C_{dm} + \Sigma C_{ot} \qquad (7.24)$$

where C_u = unit cost of manufacturing operations.

Finding the preliminary operation cost is simpler than a detail estimate, although not as accurate. Notice Table 7.5, where we sum the total setup and cycle time, and use

$$NT_u = \Sigma SU + N\Sigma H_s \qquad (7.25)$$

which is the lot time for the operations. After multiplying by average direct labor cost, we find direct-labor cost for the lot. From that point it is a simple matter to find unit cost, material additions, or factory cost.

Unit costs are used in many important ways, such as pricing or make-versus-buy. Pricing is considered in Chapter 8. In *make-versus-buy* the estimator is required to determine if it is cheaper to self-manufacture the part or "make," versus purchase from an external source, or "buy." The objective is selection of the cheapest source of supply. If the part can be purchased cheaper, the firm will subcontract the design. Factors beside cost which influence the subcontract decision are vendor capability, schedule to complete and deliver, and future activity. If these factors are more or less equal, it is to the firm's economic advantage to choose the decision on the results of a make-versus-buy analysis. The estimator uses the price as promised by the vendor on a quotation and calculates the make value.

Table 7.7 is a summary of the cost items that are included in the make side of the comparison. Their inclusion depends on the level of plant capacity; that is, the heading "fixed capacity" refers to whether or not the plant is operating at less than full or greater than 100% of fixed capacity. A plant below capacity will have fewer employees than normal. Idle equipment is increased and sales are less than in previous periods.

Direct labor, direct material, and variable overhead are always included despite the level of capacity. An optional choice implies that management policy will dictate if the item is included. Omitting an item implies that the "make" side is less, giving the advantage to the estimator's company. The marginal cost component is a special calculation that results from the decision to make or buy, which can be positive or negative. Consider an example where the plant is at less than 100% capacity. If the decision "to buy" will result in employee terminations, the unit cost approximation for marginal cost is positive to reflect increased workmen's unemployment insurance. As the choice is relative between a price-versus-make value, it causes little difference in the outcome if the marginal cost is subtracted from price, except that it is better estimating discipline to leave price unaltered. A plant with greater than 100% capacity will have overtime, rushed work, and be hiring employees. If the plant capacity is greater than 100% and the decision "make" will require overtime, new equipment,

Table 7.7. SUMMARY OF THE COST ITEMS TO CONSIDER IN THE "MAKE" SIDE OF THE MAKE-VERSUS-BUY COST ESTIMATING ANALYSIS

	Plant Load	
Cost item	Less than 100%	Greater than 100%
Direct labor	Include	Include
Direct material	Include	Include
Variable overhead	Include	Include
Fixed overhead	Omit	Include
Marginal cost	Include	Include
Sunk cost	Omit	Omit
Profit	Omit	Optional

plant space, or additional shifts, the marginal cost addition to the make side is positive. Problems are provided for make-versus-buy.

7.3 CONSTRUCTION WORK

We have identified manufacturing and construction work as the two major applications of operation estimating. These business sectors are about equal in monetary size; however, there are about 250,000 manufacturing estimating units versus 600,000 construction estimating units in the United States. The construction entities are smaller, however. Construction estimates range from $1000 to $1 billion. Many of the same estimating fundamentals are used at these extremes. We have suggested that the intellectual estimating requirements of a $0.25 product to a $250 million project are not really different, as the author has dealt with these extremes. The designs that construction estimators consider are naturally different from manufacturing—not any more or less complicated, however. The design is fundamentally different between manufacturing and construction, but many estimating practices are similar. Construction estimators are employed by either an owner or contractor. Estimating distinctions between these two kinds of employers are superficial.

Construction estimating considers the preparation of estimates of probable costs, budgets, financing, and bidding. The person most likely to do this work is a cost estimator having costwise knowledge of construction. His or her job is to know where the money is going, what operations are costing more than estimated, where possible savings can be made, and what the total probable cost of the operation will be. Accordingly, the cost estimator plans the construction job considering the features such as transportation and hauling equipment (trucks, carryalls, tractors) and loading and hoisting machines. The estimator must determine what on-site plant units (including size and capacity) the job will require, such as concrete mixing, sand and aggregate crushing, classifying, and conveyor units; what administrative and shop buildings will be necessary; and where construction roads, raw and fresh water systems, air, and power lines will be necessary.

7.3.1 Manufacturing–Construction Distinctions

The construction estimator prepares an estimate which is eventually used for a bid. A bid is the cost and profit that the contractor requires for various labor, services, materials, overhead, and so on, from the owner or major contractor. If the bid wins, the contractor will buy materials, hire workers, and go about meeting the obligations of the designs, specifications, and schedule. There is similarity to the manufacturing job shop, which really is a construction plant where the plant is fixed and the output is mobile. In contrast, the construction plant is mobile and the output is fixed.

In construction crew work is usual but in manufacturing it is uncommon. In manufacturing the estimator *dejoints* the crew labor and shared material. In construction, we do not dejoint crew work, and operation estimates are left as joint. We define *crew work* to be at least two operators working on the same operation. One of the workers could be a supervising or working foreman. In manufacturing the foreman is termed indirect labor, but in construction the foreman could be classified as direct even though he or she may be a permanent employee and not hired from the union hall like the remainder of the crew.

Except for the larger construction or owner companies, estimating information is usually from external sources. There are many annually published manuals which are listed in the references. There is seldom any time study or other consistent recording scheme of direct work observation, even though nonrepetitive long-cycle-time study is appropriate for construction. Information is historical, and sometimes there is an effort to rationalize the data to an allowed man-hour base, as discussed in Chapter 2. These construction hours are known by various terms, but in this text the construction operation estimating data are called *standard man hour* data. Similar to manufacturing the data can be preliminary or detail. Preliminary data tend to be listed as *man days,* while detail is *man hours.* In previous years the day was selected as the unit of time and labor estimates were based on the amount of work done per day. Nowadays the hour is used, which eliminates days of varying working length. The hour is the primary unit. If the hour has been measured by any of the several methods, or adjusted for inefficiency and published, we refer to the hour as *standard.* Its usual reference is 100% productivity. Adjustments for productivity are discussed in Chapter 11.

The estimating data are arranged by the construction cost code as discussed in Chapter 2. These codes maintain consistency from recording of actual data to observation to estimating. This segregation will allow tracking of costs against the estimate. The cost code is an assigned number to operational or task work and labor, as it is a reflection of job execution and the way costs will be collected. The cost codes are a detailing of the work; and documenting is made difficult without it.

7.3.2 Operation Description

An estimator should possess knowledge of construction work. The work of estimating can be divided into finding (1) material quantities and costs, (2) labor hours and costs, (3) amounts and kinds of equipment and costs, and (4) determining overhead items. The *operation description* is a step-by-step plan that describes the tasks for a job.

In manufacturing, the operation was estimated for setup and cycle. These are unfamiliar terms in construction operations. For manufacturing the quantity is usually greater than 1, but in construction the output is ordinarily 1. Thus setup and cycle have less meaning, and are merged as a single value. The plan will include the material takeoff. The preparation of a list of materials is known as the *takeoff.* He or she tabulates on quantity sheets the materials as to kind, number, size, and shape. The quantity takeoff sheet is ruled in a way to encourage systematic and legible work. It may be later priced according to the nature of the work and current or projected material prices and wage rates. This takeoff approach is much like a bill of material or a family shopping list. If the job is large, a summary is collected as the top sheet of the many takeoff sheets. In some non-U.S. locations, a licensed quantity surveyor compiles the materials list, which is called a *quantity survey.* Contractors will use this shopping list when doing their estimating. However, the application of a quantity survey is uncommon in the United States, as each bidding contractor prepares his or her own. There are various "tricks of the trade" that have shortcuts or other advantages claimed for them in this work, but are too numerous or minor to discuss here.

7.3.3 Man-Hour and Unit Quantity Estimating

Construction estimating adopts some of the methods described in Chapters 2, 3, and 6. The principal methods are quotation, power law and sizing, curves, equipment, standard man-hour data, and unit quantity. The power law, curves, and equipment methods are expanded in Chapter 9 because these principles deal more with capital estimating.

A contractor may have a subcontractor who promises to perform work to meet design and specification. A contractor will also submit a quotation to an owner. Frequently, the cost of this work is stated in a *quotation,* a contract to perform work and services and install material quantities for a stated dollar value. A quotation is not an estimating method, but the result of estimating. But historical quotations, design and work are the historical information upon which estimating data are developed. Quotations have been discussed in Chapter 3 with respect to materials and are covered again in Chapters 9 and 12.

Standard man-hour data are the simplest of the detail labor estimating methods. The techniques used to measure time are man-hour reporting, time study, and work sampling. Standard man-hour data are developed using the ideas in Sec. 2.2.2. The data would lead to an estimate in the following way.

The example illustrates a construction operation design of simple hand labor in a country without mechanical equipment. The estimator is to estimate the cost of labor required to excavate earth by hand under different conditions. For the first operation the soil is a sandy loam which requires light loosening with a pick prior to shoveling. The maximum depth of the trench will be 4 feet. Climatic conditions are good with the temperature averaging about 70°F. The laborer should easily loosen 5 cubic yards of earth per hour using a long-handle round-pointed shovel; it should require about 150 loads to move a cubic yard of earth. If a laborer can handle 2.5 shovel loads per minute, he will remove 1 cubic yard per hour. These rates of production were for 2 man-hours to loosen and 1 man-hour to remove a cubic yard of earth of the trench or a total of 3 man-hours per cubic yard. For the second operation, the soil is a tough clay which is difficult to dig and lumps badly. The maximum depth of the trench would be 5 feet. The temperature is estimated to be about 100°F without shade. Under these conditions a laborer may not loosen more than 0.25 cubic yard per hour. Because of the physical condition of the loosened earth, it is estimated to require about 180 shovel loads to move a cubic yard of earth. It is estimated that a laborer can handle 2 shovel loads per minute or 120 shovel loads per hour, which is equivalent to 0.67 cubic yard per man-hour or 1.5 man-hours per cubic yard. Given these rates of production, it is necessary to have 4 man-hours to loosen and 1.5 man-hours to remove a cubic yard, or a total of 5.5 man-hours per cubic yard. Perceiving as he did varying rates of production for hand operations, the estimator computed the total number of man-hours per cubic yard. For a given labor cost per hour, including certain fringes and other factors, the cost estimator is able to compute per yard the cost of excavation using functional cost models and standard man-hour data.

An example of standard man-hour data for electrical distribution construction is shown by Table 7.8.

Once the estimator is aware of the job requirements he or she will select the appropriate man-hour data that match the operation. Consider the following problem. An isolated home is to be connected to the main electrical system. Two poles will be set in soil and four are in rocky terrain. A total of two soil anchors are sufficient. Framing will be single-phase armless tangent when deenergized on ground. One transformer and a lightning arrester are required. A crew of three and a line

Table 7.8.   EXAMPLE OF STANDARD MAN-HOUR DATA FOR ELECTRICAL DISTRIBUTION CONSTRUCTION AT JOB SITE (Travel to Job Site Not Included)

	Man-Hours		
Equipment: Line truck *Crew:* 3	Dirt	Sand	Rock
1. Setting wood pole, 30–50 ft high			
Truck dig and set	1.5	5.5	11.6
Hand dig and set	10.2	16.0	15.3
Back hoe dig and set	3.0	3.0	3.4
Back hoe dig and truck set	2.1	3.4	8.0
2. Setting anchor			
Truck set	1.6	5.5	—
Hand set	7.1	10.2	—
Back hoe set	2.9	3.4	2.9
3. Framing			
a. Single-phase armless tangent			
Deenergized line on ground		1.6	
Energized line in air		2.0	
Dead-ending line and hot tap		2.0	
b. Three-phase wood cross-arm tangent			
Deenergized line on ground		3.0	
Energized line		5.2	
4. Miscellaneous work			
Transformer mount		4.4	
Install single aerial conductor per single span		1.7	
Street light		1.3	
Lightning arrester		1.8	

truck are planned, and total crew and truck cost is $95 per hour. What is the cost of the labor at the site?

Operation Element	Man-Hours	
	Unit	Total
Set pole in soil	1.5	3.0
Set pole in rock	11.6	23.2
Anchor	1.6	3.2
Framing	1.6	6.4
Transformer	1.8	1.8
Run wire	1.7	6.8
		44.4
Job-site cost		$4218/job

The extension of standard man-hour data to the unit quantity method is natural. For the estimator in making a takeoff will associate requirements to design. The basic model is given by

$$C_o = \sum_{i=1}^{m} \sum_{j=1}^{n} n_i(R_i + H_{ij}R_{ij}) \tag{7.26}$$

where C_o = operation cost for construction cost code
n_i = quantity for design material i, in dimensional units or count compatible to design
R_i = unit cost rate for material i
R_{ij} = unit cost rate for requirement i, j
H_{ij} = unit man-hours for requirement i, j
i = material 1, 2, . . . , m from takeoff associated with operation
j = requirement to satisfy installation of material i for design, 1, 2, . . . , n

Overhead and profit are not included in the operation estimate at this point. These matters are delayed until Chapter 10.

Consider the example of a foundation wall shown by Fig. 7.14. Corners, offsets, or openings are not a part of this wall. Total masonry for material and labor is required for this operation. The design is one of many possible ones. A spread sheet of the cost is given by Table 7.9. Three different materials are included. The symbol n_i is the quantity required for the several components for the design. It includes excavation, forms, reinforcing steel, concrete, and backfill. Observe that 59.3 yd^3 of excavation is necessary for a $4 \times 4 \times 100$ ft trench. R_i is the unit cost of material and R_{ij} are rates for labor and equipment. Obviously, excavation does not need material and $R_1 = 0$, but it does require labor and equipment. Forms, on the other hand, have a material and labor component, but equipment is unnecessary, so $n_2H_{23}R_{23} = 0$. H_{ij} is the standard man-hour per unit of n_i quantity. For example,

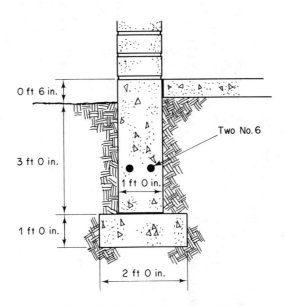

Figure 7.14. Typical foundation wall.

$H_{12} = 1.6 (= 0.027 \times 59.3)$. R_{12} is the unit labor cost, which may be for single or crew work. A n_i quantity does not always require materials or equipment. Concrete has been identified as requiring contractor labor in Table 7.8, but the delivery truck is provided by the concrete supplier in the cost of concrete. The subtotal labor amount of $60.84 is required for excavation. This matches equipment requirements as $H_{12} = H_{13}$. Depreciation or rental cost for the equipment is identified as R_{13}. The row total is the cost of the work, material, and equipment. Row and column totals are extended and 100 ft of a wall will require a grand total of $3785.77. A cost per lineal or cubic foot is found and used for subsequent design estimating. If engineering or business changes are subsequently necessary, the estimator will choose between adjusting the table or accepting it as "close enough."

SUMMARY

Cost is the major objective for operation estimating, and material and labor are the principal elements. If the labor is designated and engineering performance data are available, time estimates are found which are subsequently multiplied by the wage or the productive hour cost. Tools can be estimated and appraised for their economic justification. In the next chapter we consider product estimating. Manufacturing operation estimates are a prerequisite and provide information to cost and price products. Construction operation estimates are required for Chapter 9, which deals with project estimating. These construction estimates are basis of the bid.

Table 7.9. Unit Quantity Table For Foundation Wall, 100 Foot Long

Work and Material Takeoff	Quantity, n_i	$j=1$ Materials Unit Cost, R_i	Subtotal Amount, n_iR_{i1}	$j=2$ Labor Unit Man-Hours, H_{i2}	Total Man Hours, n_iH_{i2}	Unit Cost, R_{i2}	Subtotal Amount, $n_iH_{i2}R_{i2}$	$j=3$ Equipment Unit Hours, H_{i3}	Total Hours, n_iH_{i3}	Unit Cost, R_{i3}	Subtotal Amount, $n_iH_{i3}R_{i3}$	Row Total
Excavation, 4 × 4 × 100 ft	59.3 yd³	0	0	0.027	1.6	$38.00	$ 60.84	0.027	1.6	$112.50	$180.12	$ 240.96
Forms, 2 at 4-6 × 100 ft	900 ft²	0.45	405.00	0.035	31.5	36.50	1149.75					1554.75
Reinforcing steel, 2 No. 6, 100 ft + 10%	330 lb	0.90	297.00	0.004	1.3	35.00	46.20					343.20
Concrete, 2 × 1 × 100, 1 × 3-6 × 100	20.4 yd³	72.9	1487.16	0.065	1.3	30.00	39.00	0.020	0.8	115.00	92.00	1526.16
Backfill, compact	41 yd³			0.02	0.8	35.00	28.70					120.70
Column total			$2189.16				$1324.49				$272.12	$3785.77
Cost per lineal foot			21.89				13.24				2.72	37.86
Cost per cubic foot of concrete			107.31				64.9				13.34	185.58

300

QUESTIONS

7.1. Give an explanation of the following terms:

RFE	Speeds and feeds	Milling
Operation cost	Machining cost	Length of cut
Moderate production	Rough pass	Approach
Process	Tool life	Flat rates
Operation	Tool changing	Make-versus-buy
Setup	Amortization	Construction work
Cycle	Operation sheet	Standard man-hour

7.2. What role does the RFE have in the management of cost estimating?

7.3. Separate the types of production according to volume. How else can you classify production?

7.4. Why is setup, a fixed direct-labor cost, divided by the quantity of the lot?

7.5. Describe the origin of flat rates. Why are some labor hour estimates flat?

7.6. Name examples of nonrecurring initial fixed costs. How are these costs handled? Does the act of separating a tooling charge from the unit cost of the product for a buyer eliminate the amortization problem?

7.7. If a tool has been designed, constructed, and paid for, would it be included as an item on the "make" side of a make-versus-buy analysis?

7.8. Define marginal costs for a make-versus-buy analysis.

7.9. Compare manufacturing and construction plants.

7.10. List the pros and cons of trade-off policies dealing with the selection of quantity in the amortization of nonrecurring initial fixed costs.

PROBLEMS

7.1. (a) An operator earns $15 per hour and handling and other metal-cutting elements total 1.35 minute. What is the cost for the element?

(b) The length of a machining element is 20 in. and the part diameter is 4 in. O.D. Velocity and feed for this material 275 fpm and 0.020 ipr. What is the time to machine?

(c) The Taylor tool-life equation is $VT^{0.1} = 172$. What is the expected average tool life for $V = 275$ fpm?

(d) Tool-changing time is 4 minutes, tool-life equation is $VT^{0.1} = 172$, $V = 275$ fpm, $C_o = \$0.25/min$, $L = 20$ in., $D = 4$ in., and $f = 0.020$ ipr. Determine the tool-changing cost.

(e) Using the information in part (d) and $C_t = \$5$, find the tool cost per operation. Would you recommend these machining conditions?

7.2. (a) Operator and variable expenses are $60 per hour and handling is 1.65 minutes. Find the handling cost for this element.

(b) The length and diameter of a gray iron casting are $8\frac{1}{2}$ in. by 8.6 in. Velocity is 300 fpm and feed is 0.020 ipr. Find the machining time.

(c) The Taylor tool life equation is $VT^{0.15} = 500$. Find the expected tool life for 300 fpm.

(d) The time to remove an insert and index to another new corner is 2 minutes, the tool-life equation is $VT^{0.15} = 500$, $V = 300$ fpm, $C_o = \$1/\text{min}$, $L = 8.6$ in., $D = 8$ in., and $f = 0.020$ ipr. What is the cost to change tools?

(e) Using the information in part (d), and that an eight-corner insert is \$24, find the tool cost per operation.

7.3. **(a)** Stainless steel material is to be rough- and finish-turned. Diameter and length is 4 in. × 30 in. Recommended rough and finish cutting velocity and feed for tungsten carbide tool material are $(350, 0.015)$ and $(350, 0.007)$. Determine rough and finish cutting time.

(b) Medium carbon steel is to be rough- and finish-turned using high-speed-steel tool material. The part diameter and cutting length are 4 in. and 20 in. Using Table 7.1, determine the total time to machine.

(c) Gray cast iron is to be rough- and finish-turned with tungsten carbide tooling. Part diameter and cutting length are $8\frac{1}{2}$ in. and 8.6 in. What is the part rpm for the rough and finish? Using Table 7.1, find the turning time.

7.4. **(a)** The top of a square 250-mm block is to have a 65-mm slot machined on it. The end mill is 25 mm and only one pass is traced over the slot. Calculate the length of cut if a safety stock is 5 mm.

(b) A slab milling cutter is 6 in. in diameter. The design length is 15 in., and two machining passes of $\frac{3}{8}$ in. and 0.015 in. depth of cut are necessary. Safety stock is $\frac{1}{4}$ in. If the cutter is required to move its vertical center line to the edge of work for roughing and completely leave the work for finishing, determine the length of cut for roughing and finishing.

(c) Find the length of cutting for a 25-mm drill in soft steel where the design length is 13 mm.

7.5. **(a)** The top of a 250-mm circle anvil is to have a 60-mm slot through the cross-hair center of the circle. Find the length of cut for a 25-mm end mill if the safety stock is 5 mm.

(b) Find the length of cut for a 2-in. slab milling cutter removing $\frac{1}{4}$ in. of thickness for a workpiece length of 10 in. The milling cutter is to mill completely off of the stock. Safety stock is $\frac{1}{16}$ in.

(c) Calculate the overtravel required for a $\frac{1}{2}$-in. drill in stainless steel; in cast iron.

7.6. **(a)** A stainless steel surface 1 in. × 10 in. is to be end-milled with a 1-in. four-flute end mill for a depth of 0.015 in. The end mill will pass entirely over the material and have a safety stock of $\frac{1}{8}$ in. Velocity is 85 fpm and chip load per tooth is 0.002. What is the length of cut? How much time is necessary for machining? What is the cutter rpm and feed rate in in. per min?

(b) A 1-in. slot is to be end-milled in gray cast iron for a depth of $\frac{1}{4}$ in. A rough and finish pass is required for the high-speed-steel four-fluted cutter. The cutter must pass entirely over the surface and a safety stock of $\frac{1}{8}$ in. is necessary. What is the machining length of cut for rough or finish? Determine rough and finish machining time. Use Table 7.1 for machining data, where data are cutting velocity and tooth load. Find cutter rpm and cutting rate in in. per min.

7.7. **(a)** A surface 8 in. wide by 20 in. long is rough-milled with a depth of cut of $\frac{1}{4}$ in. by a 16-tooth cemented carbide face mill 6 in. in diameter. The material is gray cast iron. What is cutting length? Estimate the cutting time if $V = 120$ fpm and $f_t = 0.0012$ in./tooth-rev. Find the cutter rpm.

(b) A high speed steel vertical milling cutter with 12 teeth is 100 mm in diameter and 125 mm long. It is used to mill a soft-steel surface 75 mm wide by 225 mm long with a depth of cut of 20 mm. A cutting speed of 0.5 m/s and a feed of 0.25 mmpt are selected. What are the cutting time and cutter rpm?

7.8. **(a)** A stainless steel part is to be drilled $\frac{5}{16}$ in. for a depth of 1 in. It is followed by a $\frac{3}{16}$-16 tap for a depth of $\frac{7}{8}$ in. Find the drilling length and the drilling and tapping time. Use Table 7.1. Repeat for steel.

(b) Steel is tapped-drilled $\frac{3}{8}$ in. for a depth of 1 in. It is followed with a tapping element of $\frac{5}{16}$-10 hole for $\frac{7}{8}$ in. Find the drilling length and the drilling and tapping time. Repeat for stainless steel.

7.9. **(a)** Find the cutting time for a hard copper shaft 2 × 20 in. long. A surface velocity of 250 fpm is suggested with a feed of 0.009 in. per revolution.

(b) An end facing cut is required of a 10-in.-diameter workpiece. The revolutions per minute of the lathe are controlled to maintain 400 surface feet per minute from the center out to the surface. Feed is 0.009. Find the time for the cut.

(c) If the tool is K-3H carbide, the material is AISI 4140 steel, depth of cut is 0.050 in. and the feed is 0.010 in. per revolution, what is the surface feet per minute for a 4-in. bar and a 6-minute life if the tool-life equation $VT^{0.3723} = 1022$? Also rpm.

(d) Consider the Taylor tool-life model, $VT^n = K$ for the following tool materials and work materials:

Tool	Work	n	K
High-speed steel	Cast iron	0.14	75
High-speed steel	Steel	0.125	47
Cemented carbide	Steel	0.20	150
Cemented carbide	Cast iron	0.25	130

For a tool life of 10 minutes for each of these combinations, what is the cutting velocity?

7.10. Note the tool-life curve of Fig. P7.10 for SAE 3140, feed of 0.013, depth of cut of 0.50, and a HSS tool material.

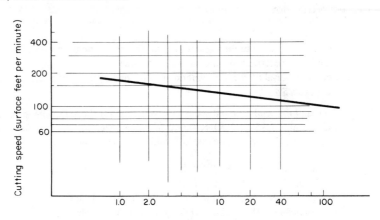

Figure P7.10   Tool life (min)

(a) Using the curve, find the parameters for $VT^n = K$.
(b) What is tool life for 100 feet per minute?
(c) What are the revolutions per minute for 2-in. bar stock and $V = 100$ fpm?
(d) Repeat for 150 fpm.

7.11. A rough-turning operation is to be performed on medium-carbon steel. Tool material is high-speed steel. The part diameter is 4-in. O.D. and the cutting length will be 20 in. The tool point will cost $5. Time to reset the tool is 4 minutes. Part handling will be 2 minutes and the operator wage is $20 per hour. The Taylor tool-life equation $VT^{0.1} = 172$. Feed of the turning operation is 0.020 ipr for a depth of cut = 0.25 in.
(a) Plot the four items of cost to find total cost curve and select optimum velocity.
(b) Determine the minimum velocity analytically.

7.12. Let the cost of $C_t = 0$ for Problem 7.11 and plot the elements of time to find optimum time. Compute V_{max} and T_{max} and T_u.

7.13. Construct individual cost curves similar to Fig. 7.5 for the following machining work. A gray iron casting having a diameter of $8\frac{1}{2}$ in. is rough-turned to 8.020/8.025 in. for a length of 8.6 in. A renewable square carbide insert is used. The insert has eight corners suitable for turning work and costs $24. Operator and variable expenses less tooling costs are $60 per hour. The feed for this turning operation is 0.020 ipr. Taylor's tool-life equation for part and tool material is $VT^{0.15} = 500$. The time for the operator to remove the insert and install another new corner and qualify the tool ready to cut is 2 minutes. Part handling time is 1.65 minutes for a casting mounted in a fixture.
(a) If the y-axis is unit cost and x-axis is fpm, plot the curves and locate optimum velocity.
(b) Determine optimum velocity analytically.

7.14. Assume that the cost of $C_t = 0$ for Problem 7.13 and graphically find optimum time, V_{max}, and T_{max}.

7.15. Find the material cost and setup and cycle time for the operations of a stainless steel pinion similar in all respects to Fig. 7.6 except for the following changes: Work each part separately. Complete the operations process sheet and find the unit cost as demonstrated by Table 7.2.
(a) Let the 18.750-in. dimension be 8.750 in., the 1.100-in. dimension be 1.125 in., and no holes.
(b) Let the 4.75-in. flat dimension be 8.00 in., and the raw material be 2 in. O.D. instead of $1\frac{3}{4}$ in. O.D.
(c) Let the 4-in. plain milling cutter be 3 in. in width, and operation 10 will use high-speed tool material instead of tungsten carbide.
(d) Let the material be medium-carbon steel instead of stainless steel. Medium-carbon steel costs $0.72/lb.

7.16. Find the unit material cost and setup and cycle time for P/N 672. The material is 5052-H34 aluminum, $7.75 \times 3.50 \times 0.042$ in. blank size, and the cost factor is $0.015/in.^{2} Use Table 7.4 for estimating the following operations. Refer to Fig. 7.12.

1. Shear strips from 48×120 in. sheet stock, 7.75 in. wide
2. Shear blanks from strip
3. Numerically controlled pierce and notch, 10 tools and 60 hits
4. Countersink 18 0.120-in. O.D. and 4 0.125-in. holes
5. Degrease

6. Deburr
7. Press brake lips, two lays
8. Press brake lips, two lays
9. Ream two 0.125-in. and four 0.132-in. holes
10. Degrease
11. Deburr

7.17. Find unit material cost and setup and cycle time for P/N 673. Material is 5052-H34 aluminum, $12.50 \times 4.35 \times 0.062$ in. blank size, and the cost factor is $0.0205/in.^2 Use Table 7.4 and refer to Fig. 7.2 for the operations, given as:

1. Shear strips from 48×120 in. sheet raw material
2. Shear blanks from strips
3. NC pierce and notch, 10 tools and 75 hits
4. Counterbore two 0.128-in. holes
5. Degrease
6. Deburr
7. Press brake, one lip
8. Press brake, one lip
9. Press brake, one lip
10. Press brake, one lip

7.18. Find time and nonrecurring initial fixed costs to construct a form die required for Fig. 7.13, a 303 stainless steel part using Table 7.6. The machine-hour rate is $75 per hour. This tool is used after piercing and blanking, and will form the two ears and end lip.

7.19. Find the unit and total operational cost for the design in Fig. P7.19. The sheet metal part is processed according to the following plan:

Shear strips from 48×96 in. sheet using shear.
Shear blanks from strips using shear.
Punch four holes using punch press.
Form two lips using form die on punch press.

(a) Determine the unit material cost if the raw materials cost $0.020. Estimated quantities are 12,000.
(b) Find the tooling cost using Table 7.6 and $75 per hour. The tool design cost is $360. Labor costs $19.20 per hour.

7.20. Find the unit and total operational cost for the design problem in Problem 7.19. A preliminary processing route sheet is

Shear strips 1.450-in. wide from 48×96 in. sheet.
Punch and form complete with one progressive die.

A die design costs $2000. Tooling construction labor and overhead costs $75 per hour and operational labor costs $19.20 per hour. Quantities are 12,000 units. Use Table 7.6 and sheet metal standard time data (Table 7.4).

7.21. Estimate the operation cost per unit for design Fig. 3.10. 1018 CRS stock is purchased in a 48×96 in. sheet size. The total quantity required is 20,000 units. In stamping fabrication the distance between blanks is restricted to 0.75 of thickness while margins between the edge of the strip and blank is $0.9 \times$ thickness for each side. The density of steel is 0.28 lb/in.^{3} The cost of this material is $0.60/lb. Use Table 7.4 for the following preliminary operation sheet:

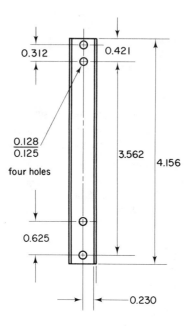

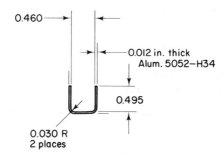

Figure P7.19

1. Shear strips 1.363 × 96 in. long using shear.
2. Punch 0.500-in. hole using punch press.
3. Blank 1.25 × 2 in. part with blank die using punch press.
4. Deburr.

The die design cost is $1200. Use Table 7.6 to estimate tool manufacture for the blank die at $75 per hour. Average shop direct labor cost is $20 per hour.

7.22. Construct a preliminary processing plan to produce 40,000 of the soft-brass springs shown in Fig. P7.22, 0.005 in. thick, for which material costs 0.028 per square inch. Determine the tooling cost, standard labor cost (dollars of labor cost = $20 per hour), and toolroom labor cost (= $75 per hour). Material cost for the nonrecurring initial tooling cost is $250. A hardening operation performed by an outside vendor costs $0.016 per spring.

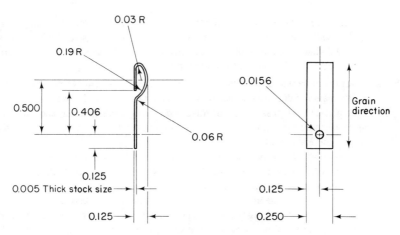

Figure P7.22

7.23. Let the estimated unit savings in direct labor be $0.30, burden on labor saved = 50%, cost of each setup = $100, interest rate = 20%, allowance for taxes and insurance = 10%, allowance for maintenance = 25%, and yearly allowance for depreciation and obsolescence = 50%.

(a) The cost of a fixture is $4000. With one run per year, how many pieces must be made per year to have the fixture pay for itself?

(b) Let depreciation be 100%, as the fixture must pay for itself within a year. How large must that run be?

(c) Using the data above, how much money can we afford for a fixture for a single run of 15,000 units at an estimated savings of $0.30 per piece?

(d) How many years will a $4000 fixture require to pay for itself for an annual quantity of 20,000 units?

7.24. PN 8871 is to be analyzed for a make-versus-buy decision. The labor estimate is

Operation	Unit Cost
1	$0.0006
2	0.0130
3	0.0130
4	0.0007
5	0.0068

Direct material and material overhead = $0.0084 per unit. Variable overhead is 75% of direct labor, while fixed cost is $0.05 per unit. This company believes that the part deserves a profit of $0.025.

(a) If the company's plant capacity is underutilized, is the decision "make or buy" for a vendor's price = $0.075?

(b) For 100% plant utilization, what is the decision for a $0.118 price?

(c) If the plant chooses to make the article while at undercapacity, it will incur a 15% increase in direct wages due to marginal costs of inefficient production. What is the decision for a $0.125 price?

(d) Evaluate the choices above for a nonrecurring initial fixed price of tooling which is designed, manufactured, and paid for. These initial costs for 2500 units were $25.00. What are the nonquantitative considerations of this sunk cost? Also do the analysis as if the $25 has not been spent.

7.25. (a) A farm is to be wired from the main-line distribution system. The electrical distribution planning department indicates that 10 poles set in soil, four anchors, seven three-phase wood cross-arms, one transformer, a lightning arrester, and a farm light are to be included in the bid. If crew and equipment costs $90 per hour, what is the job cost? Use Table 7.8.

(b) Let the crew size be two instead of three and unit man-hours be increased 60% because of unbalanced crew work. If crew labor and the line truck are $40 and $25 per hour, what is estimated cost for part (a)?

(c) A storm has ravaged an area, and unit man-hours for a task are acceptable if increased by 65%. A light commercial building needs four poles in rock, three phase cross-arms, four anchors, a transformer, and two parking-lot lights. Costs for the crew and back line are $75 per hour. Find the job cost.

7.26. (a) A cement contractor is asked to bid on a small concrete retaining wall along a sidewalk. The wall, on the average 2 ft high, will rest upon a 2 × 1 ft foundation. The length will be 75 ft. What is the expected cost? Adjust Table 7.9 to accommodate to the new wall height.

(b) An electrical contractor is required to install a conduit according to the sketch in Fig. P7.26. His hours-per-foot standards, which do not conform exactly to the requirement, are on page 309.

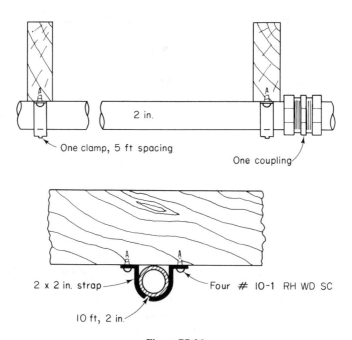

One clamp, 5 ft spacing

2 in.

One coupling

2 x 2 in. strap

10 ft, 2 in.

Four # 10-1 RH WD SC

Figure P7.26

Size	Exposed	Slab Deck Wood Frame	Trench	Furred Ceiling	Notched Joists	Weight lb/100 ft
$\frac{3}{4}$	0.046	0.033	0.023	0.030	0.039	50
$1\frac{3}{4}$	0.080	0.062	0.040	0.054	0.063	100

Labor costs $26.25 per electrical journeyman-hour, and material is $0.84 and $1.20 per pound for the $\frac{3}{4}$ and $1\frac{3}{4}$-in. sizes. He is required to install 7000 ft. What is his operational labor and material cost?

7.27. A large office with 10-ft ceilings by 250-ft sides is to be initially painted. Redecoration will be required every 4 years. Initially all holes will be filled and sanded, and one prime coat and one finish coat will be applied by spray gun. Initial protection will be nominal. The redecoration process calls for the walls to be washed and one finish coat to be applied with brush and rollers. A crew of three will be employed (one foreman and two journeymen). A three-section scaffold is 21 ft long × 5 ft wide × 5 ft high. Perform an operation estimate to forecast labor expenses for both the initial and redecorating processes and compare labor cost per square foot. Job elements are:

1. Scaffolding time: 0.90 man-hour per scaffold, erection; 0.60 man-hour per scaffold, dismantle.
2. Sealing and sanding time: 195 ft^2/hr, 0.50 man-hour per 100 ft^2.
3. Spray paint concrete surfaces: 465 ft^2/hr, 0.22 man-hour per 100 ft^2.
4. Paint concrete surface by roller: 155 ft^2/hr, 0.54 man-hour per 100 ft^2.
5. Washing walls time: 0.87 man-hour per 100 ft^2, 147 ft^2/hr.

Assume that the scaffold will be moved 10 times per wall and that it will take 10 minutes to move for a new unpainted wall and 12 minutes for redecorating. The foreman has a job labor rate of $24.00 per hour, and each journeyman has a job rate of $22.35 per hour.

7.28. **(a)** A new job is similar to Table 7.9 except for the excavation rate, which is increased to 0.05 and cost of $105. Concrete is a different specification costing $82.50 per unit. The backfill crew cost is $38. Find the cost per cubic foot of concrete.

(b) The foundation wall footing will be poured without forms, against earth walls. Excavation is narrowed to a 2-foot trench to accommodate the footing. Recalculate Table 7.9 to compensate the newer design.

7.29. A straight concrete gutter of 1000 linear feet is necessary for the edging of a parking lot. Equipment selected for the job is a Case 580 loader with a 36-in. bucket and output of 28.84 ft^3/hour at an hourly cost of $39.50. The field crew consists of a foreman (50% at $13.75 per hour), operator (100% at $26.00 per hour), laborer (100% at $21 per hour), and checker (50% at $12.75 per hour). The curb and gutter requires 55 yd^3 concrete at $115/yd^3; 1000 feet of forms at $0.25/ft, 33 expansion joints at $2 each, and miscellaneous curbing material for $75. The curb and gutter crew will require 12 hours for 1000 lineal feet. Prepare the unit quantity table to show the unit cost per cubic yard and per lineal foot for 1000 ft.

7.30. A 10,000-ft^2 parking lot is to be estimated from a unit quantity table. The fine-grading crew and equipment will need 8 hours at $280 per hour for the total area. The building of forms uses a forming crew and their equipment and needs 12 hours at $252 per hour. To complete pouring and finishing, a crew will require 16 hours at $296 per hour.

Reinforcing material of 10 × 10 mesh and No. 4 bars (12 in. each way) are at $0.09/ft^2 and 0.40/ft^2. Requirements and cost of concrete are 200 yd^3 at $61/yd^3. Form material, $\frac{1}{2}$-in. premolded expansion joints, and concrete curing material costs are $500, $112, and $172. Precast concrete bumpers, 39, are $8 each. 840 ft of 4-in.-wide painted lines are estimated to cost $0.10/ft. Find the cost per unit square foot from the unit quantity table.

7.31. A 2000 × 25 ft road is to be constructed. Cut and fill is necessary and 5000 ft^3 of roadbed and soil will be hauled an average 200 ft. The road will have a 4-in. aggregate base and 2 in. of asphalt. Excavation will require: a bulldozer that can remove 145 ft^3/hour, and two are necessary for $115 per hour. A water truck and a packer-roller will be used at $13.50 per hour and $69 per hour for 5 hours. Hour labor cost for this excavation is foreman ($27.50 per hour), three operators ($79.20 per hour), truck driver ($21.60 per hour), and grade checker ($26.40 per hour). Grading and asphalt laying will require: Fine grading and crew for 12 hours at $434 per hour, base equipment and crew for 10 hours at $390 per hour, paving equipment and crew 6 hours at $424 per hour, prime equipment and crew for 5 hours at $223 per hour, and seal equipment and crew for 8 hours at $166 per hour. Material requirements for 50,000 ft^2 of road are

> Asphalt, 619 tons at $25 per ton
> Seal oil, 3.5 tons at $170 per ton
> Sand, 27.8 tons at $8 per ton
> Aggregate base, 1233 tons at $8 per ton
> Prime, 5.6 tons at $170 per ton

Prepare a unit quantity table, and determine total cost, cost per 100 feet, and cost per square foot.

7.32. A printed circuit blank is 300 × 450 × 1.6 mm in size. The surfaces are copper laminated to a pressed plastic core. The blank is eventually sheared into six 100 × 125 mm pieces. The remainder of the blank is necessary for margins and is material lost as waste. Production of the printed circuit pieces may require a setup for the operation, a setup for each blank, and a cycle time for each piece on the board or blank. Setup for the operation is one-time recurring for the lot. A blank setup is one-time recurring for the blank, while cycle time may be for the blank or piece.

Operation	Wage Rate ($/hour)	Operation Setup (hours)	Blank Setup (hours)	Cycle Time (hours per 100)
Clean blank	$15.25	0.5	0.2	1.677/b.
Photo resist	16.75	0.2	0	0.835/p.
Develop	16.75	1.0	0.1	3.345/b.
Etch	16.75	0.4	0.05	0.167/b.
Clean	15.25	0.1	0.1	0.085/p.
Pierce holes	14.50	0.1	0	0.250/p.
Shear	17.50	0.1	0	0.100/p.

A lot of 250 blanks is started at the clean blank operation and after shearing, only 95% will be satisfactory.

(a) Find the joint labor cost for the lot.

(b) Find the joint and unit labor cost for each operation.
(c) Determine the net unit labor cost for the piece.
(d) Develop an estimating formula for answering questions (a), (b), and (c).

CASE STUDY:
P/N 8871

Endicott Components is bidding on P/N 8871 and a design is shown in Fig. C7.1. The contractor is interested in 2500 units to be shipped in one order. The operation routing appears

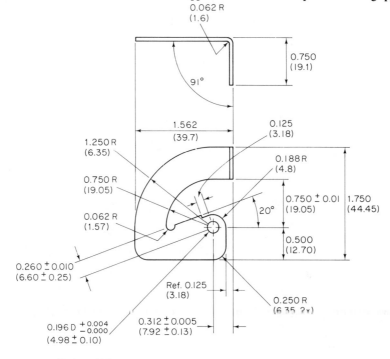

Part no: 8871
Title: Hinge bracket
Material: 0.048 (18 ga.) C.R.S., 4 X 8 ft sheet

No.	Operations	Machine
1	Shear in strips 2.750 (69.89) wide X 48.0 (1220) long; makes 21 pcs.	Shear
2	Blank and pierce complete	Punch press
3	Form 89° on 0.062 in. (1.57 mm) radius	Punch press
4	Tumble	Tumbler
5	Degrease	Degreaser

Figure C7.1

on the drawing. Material costs $0.28 per in^3. Average direct labor cost is $17.75 per hour. A pierce and blank die design will cost $1500. The machine hour rate for the tooling is $65. First, estimate tooling cost and determine the unit amortization. What is the operation cost, including material, labor, and tooling? Finally, describe what cost elements you would consider for a make-versus-buy analysis in this part if (a) the firm's business was below or above capacity, and (b) if the tool was already available.

8

Product Estimating

With design details at hand the product estimator begins the task of estimating. While providing information for the pricing step is the object of the estimate, other documents are vital for management strategy. To permit the preparation of a product estimate, sales, marketing, and operation estimates must be concluded. Enroute to price setting, various procedures work on the task so as not to overlook the objectives of stockholders and consumers as well as management and estimating. The preliminary estimate provided early screening. Now a detail product estimate is necessary to help the pricing step and determine cash flow, rate of return, and profit and loss statements for a second look. The appraisal is made on new or continuing products and product lines.

8.1 PRICE

The product effort is ongoing, all-inclusive, and basic to company survival. The care and stimulus for the product and its success rests on research, engineering, manufacturing, marketing, legal, and management. A product strategy calls for a wide assortment of decisions. This is a large undertaking for any firm. The hazard is high as of some several hundred fresh ideas only one will congeal into a successful new product. In view of these complications we now direct our efforts toward cost-estimating aspects related to the product.

Even this portion of confined study is vast. In addition to price and cost of the product, there are problems concerning cash flow, rate of return, and meeting obligations to investors, owners, and shareholders.

Who is responsible for setting price? Practice varies, for are we talking about an old or new product? What precisely is the cash flow problem? As products provide income, the realization of revenue from the sale of newly introduced or established products must be offsetting of costs of these same products. Is the new or old product small in proportion to total income? If it is significant, individual products and product lines constitute an important factor to the cash flow problem. Some new products require a large outlay of cash for new plants and processing equipment in addition to engineering and construction costs. Investment analysis, called *profitability,* is one way to conduct an investigation. The capital obligations for this expansion may come from profit, current depreciation, loans, or new issues of stock. Expansion may be necessary to produce the product.

The conclusion of a product estimate is price. Along the way to this result are a number of analyses, not the least of which is cost. There is a school of thought that asserts that "price is not related to cost." An argument begins by assuming that houses A and B are identical as to neighborhood, appearance, and the like. Price A is $100,000 while price B is $90,000. Now owner A argues that his cost for house A is $100,000. The buyer, however, considers this as irrelevant and so would choose B. But what about owner B? If his cost is under $90,000, he has made a profit, but if his cost is $90,000 or more, his prosperity is weakened. What the buyer is willing to pay is influenced by the lowest competitive price and is determined at the point of sale, not in the factory. If price is less than cost, the company must take steps to reduce cost or abandon the product. Of course, cost is not the only factor that sets a price, but it is a vital one. For long-term survival it is imperative to recover the full consumption of resources; a price strategy must accommodate this policy.

Older products for which an existing market is well defined present a different situation. Here competition plays a bigger role. Custom products for one customer require different treatment than do products for which a large market exists.

A cost estimate for a product undergoing redesign requires a different treatment than a new product. The components of the redesigned product are compared to the old design and classified as changed, added, or identical parts. The costs of the unchanged parts are found from records and may or may not be altered to reflect future conditions. Operation estimates are prepared for the altered and new parts. In each of these several product conditions, methods of product costing and pricing vary.

8.2 INFORMATION REQUIRED FOR PRODUCT ESTIMATING

Upon receiving a *request for estimate* the estimator analyzes the information, which includes:

1. Due date for completion of estimate
2. Quantity, rate of production, and schedule
3. Engineering bill of materials, specifications, and designs
4. Special test, inspection, and quality control requirements
5. Packaging and shipping instructions
6. Marketing information

Figure 8.1 describes the estimating elements with price as the ultimate objective. The bottom layer, operation costs, consisting of direct material, direct labor and nonrecurring initial fixed cost, provides the grist for an operation estimate and was covered in Chapter 7. Addition of the upper blocks is achieved by the several methods of this chapter.

In some cases engineering costs for a product are not covered by overhead and must be estimated separately. These companion estimates would include research and development and engineering. For instance, high-technology firms calculate engineering, development, and design as a separate line item cost.

The determination of administrative, marketing, distribution, and selling rates are found like overhead rates. However, the denominator for this calculation is the *cost of goods manufactured*. Costs for administration and sales are structured and totaled, and finally the appropriate ratios are determined. Refinements such as separating divisional and corporate expenses or marketing from sales can be undertaken. These refinements are usually worth the trouble because these costs can be more accurately absorbed to a product for its eventual recovery.

Contingencies are another category in Fig. 8.1. Uncertain costs may be estimated here. Although this is not a desirable category, there are circumstances where

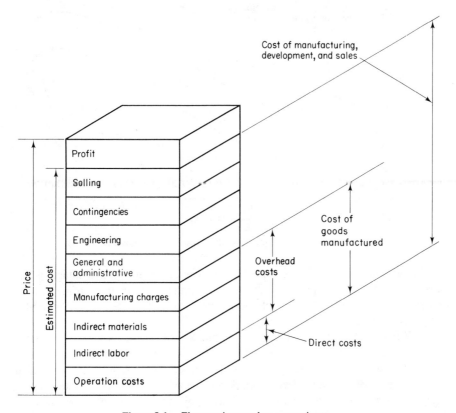

Figure 8.1.   Elements in a product cost estimate.

it may be used. For instance, government imposed safety requirements may be required for product reliability. The firm, uncertain of this future behavior and unprepared to introduce this feature until the government has provided the specifications, uses this category for a visible cost. The contingency feature as an estimating practice has the advantage of providing special provisions for future legitimate costs. The use of the contingency, say, to cover careless detailed estimating practices, is not encouraged. Products having extraordinary research, development, and design problems are candidates for contingency.

The elements of Fig. 8.1 vary in importance depending upon the business sector. Some industries may be labor intensive and thus direct labor may be important; or material, such as standard purchased parts, raw materials, and direct utilities may dominate. In capital-intensive industries, the recovery of capital money is important. The relative importance of these major elements may be seen by examining Fig. 8.2. The example in this figure is an expensive product. The estimating

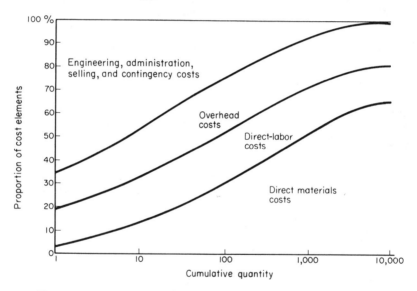

Figure 8.2.   Proportion of major segments of costs as production volume varies.

emphasis given to the basic elements usually depends upon their percentage of total cost. The estimating department accommodates their information profile requirements, functional estimating models, and spread sheets as dictated by their individual product situation.

When is product estimating done? Figure 8.3 shows the location of this effort relative to design, production, and delivery. This is a simple time scale defining the point at which information is processed. The now time, or $E = 0$, is the moment when the estimate is made. Periods are denoted as positive or negative integers, and may be days, weeks, months, or years. It is pointed out that some products will

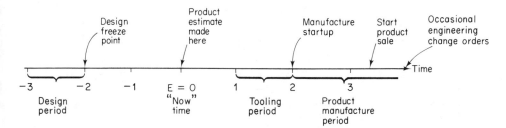

Figure 8.3.   Time scale line showing chronology of product estimate events.

require only a few weeks from moment of estimate to delivery, but the majority are for several months' or many years' duration. Estimating methods must accommodate to these diverse requirements. The time scale of Fig. 8.3 shows the important events to be considered in product estimating.

8.2.1 Estimating Research and Engineering Costs

When products are comparable to existing products, or when there is a reasonable assurance about the state of art in terms of engineering, ordinary techniques useful in judging the costs of engineering may be adopted. For these conventional situations, engineering can be estimated on the basis of similar and past historical records. This includes an appraisal of past performance on similar work and from it the determination of the probable efforts required for the proposed task.

Engineering provides services measured in terms of the design of the product, specifications, bill of materials, and maybe physical models. In addition, preliminary engineering may be done for a job for which orders are not received. The engineering task may embrace evaluation and production liaison, field and construction service, and maintenance engineering during the life of the product. For these specific functions, hours and a cost factor containing provisions for hourly rates for wages and salaries of the group, charges for supervision, housing, light, and heat are estimated. Engineering costs to develop proposals that do not materialize in orders are additionally collected into the conglomerate hourly rate and used as the multiplier for the estimated number of hours. The total of this cost is amortized to the product by

$$C_e = \frac{\text{total engineering expenses}}{\text{projected product quantity}} \tag{8.1}$$

where C_e represents the engineering cost per unit. Model (8.1) is for exceptional charging that is not included in overhead practices. This model can be expanded into a spread sheet such as Table 8.1. The design engineering estimate is categorized by type of labor and rate per hour and is finally extended to total design engineering labor. The estimate can be associated with a custom design or for one lot of products.

There are cases where an engineering effort is large in proportion to a contract, or in special cases an engineering firm will be hired to do the engineering and, say, manage a large-scale construction job. Estimating these costs may become a com-

Table 8.1.   ESTIMATING FOR DESIGN ENGINEERING

Design engineering estimate for _Speed Reducer_ products

Description _Design for Left hand speed reducer_

Customer _Not Known_ _____ Inquiry or quote no. _____ Date _____
Based on quantity of _480 units_ _____ During period of _____

Type of labor	Hours	Rate per hour	Extended labor
Scientist, research			
Engineer, senior design	40	$33.00	$1,320
Engineer, design	800	$30.00	$24,000
Technician, electrical			
Designer / engr. aide	160	$18.75	$3,000
Tech. writer			
Illustrator			
Draftsman	80	$17.00	$1,360
Provisioning specialist			
Model shop			
Total design engineering labor	1080		$29,680

petitive bid among engineering firms. If major equipment is installed, say, in the range of $500,000 to $50 million, engineering costs for complex pilot and chemical plants range from 20 to $7\frac{1}{2}$%. In repetitive types of construction, engineering costs vary from $3\frac{1}{2}$ to 13% of total installed cost.

These engineering costs may be negotiated on a lump-sum turn-key basis where the cost of engineering is included in the erection package for a entire plant; sometimes, the engineering contracts are negotiated on some cost-plus basis. Variations would include:

1. Cost plus a negotiated fee or profit for the engineering contractor.
2. Cost plus a fixed fee contract with a guaranteed maximum.
3. A contract for engineering design manpower to be supervised by the client's engineering staff.

These contractual variations are discussed in Chapter 12. No matter what the contract type, design engineering contains these elements of total cost:

$$C_t = \Sigma S + \Sigma E + \Sigma OH + \Sigma F \tag{8.2}$$

where C_t = sum of engineering expenses
     S = salaries
     E = variable expenses such as travel, living away from home, communication
    OH = overhead, rent, depreciation, heat, light, clerical supplies, workman's compensation, and so forth
     F = fees paid to other specialists and engineers

In view of the proportion of salaries to the total cost, it is usual to find factors that multiply expected salaries to arrive at the estimate. These factors vary from 1.8 to 3.0 depending on complexity, novelty, or secrecy of the work. In chemical and architectural work, the ratio of design drafting is of the order of two or three times other types of engineering. In electronics this is reversed. Standards for engineering work have related size of drawing and design productivity. In tooling of dies, for instance, the size of the drawing can be associated to so many hours of design time. Other similar rules of thumb have been established. In any one industry there seems to be a tendency toward standardization in drawing size as well as the kind and quantity of information recorded on the print. To determine the cost of engineering, it must be estimated in order to be prorated to product charges like any other cost. Its impact may amount to very little, or it can be a major factor, particularly when a product, new or revised, calls for a new process or plant.

8.3 FINANCIAL DOCUMENTS REQUIRED FOR PRODUCT DECISION

The appraisal of products, old, newly introduced, or ones at the detail stage, is handled by analysis. What money is necessary for the venture and what will come out of it? Management, stockholders, and money lenders are interested in this question. Operating capital, loans, and notes for new equipment or plant enlargement may be needed before there is any revenue from the products. Thus it is mandatory to prepare several documents on products. Management takes action on the product on the basis of what these documents say. These documents are listed as:

1. Product estimate
2. Cash flow statement
3. Rate of return analysis
4. Profit and loss statement

Product estimate.   The product estimate indicates a full cost and selling price that the product will have to command for a profitable future. Almost all of this chapter is concerned with this first document.

Cash flow statement.   The cash flow document considers the value of transactions in and out of a firm. It may be likened to a reservoir receiving a stream of water. At certain times more water is received than at other times. Concurrently the demands placed on the reservoir fluctuate with a controlled quantity leaving. Money to a company behaves very much like this illustration and is frequently called a *stream*.

If the cost of the product venture is small in proportion to the inflow or accumulated surplus, the cash flow document may be unnecessary. If, on the other hand, the venture is a big one, the company must evaluate its cash position to meet obligations. If the product requires a tooling up period, long pilot runs, expensive equipment, and extensive engineering and preoperation break-in, the construction of a cash flow document is vital. A small company may require operating capital before product revenue is received. They would find a cash flow document necessary.

A cost estimate involving price and quantity schedules, production rates, and marketing and sales rates, and capitalization costs for new equipment and plant enlargement is necessary in order to construct a cash flow statement. A sample is provided by Table 8.2. For this chemical plant operation the percent of capacity increases up to 100%, at which point it is assumed that capacity would continue to grow due to learning effects. Obviously to have net profits after taxes, a market quantity and price are known. Depreciation is a tax-sheltered fund while a tax credit (a product of the depreciation times the firm's tax rate) helps to provide the inflow of funds. Depreciation in the table is simple straight line over 10 years or 70,000 ($= 700,000/10$). Preoperating expenses and investment costs are first year cash out. Working capital is made up of several items such as accounts receivable, raw material inventory, work in process, and finished goods inventory. Increases in inventory require immediate cash outlays that delay cash flow from generating sales revenue. Ordinarily a higher requirement for cash on hand occurs during periods when operations are increasing. Determination of what constitutes working capital is usually meant to be incremental capital (i.e., differential capital between present and prior year). The arithmetic for net and cumulative cash flow is evident in Table 8.2. A *payback time* calculation can be performed which measures the number of years required to regenerate, via profits, depreciation, and tax credits, the total investment of the fixed assets and preoperating expenses that we required to launch the product. The payback time of 5 years illustrates that it will take this number of years to recoup the capital investment and pretax operation expenses. For a cash flow statement we define

$$F_c = (G - D_c - C)(1 - t) + D_c \qquad (8.3)$$

where F_c = total source of funds, dollars, year
$\quad\ \ G$ = estimated annual gross product income, dollars
$\quad\ D_c$ = annual depreciation charge, dollars
$\quad\ \ C$ = annual costs not estimated elsewhere, dollars
$\quad\ \ t$ = tax rate, decimal

The payback time and cash flow is based on a *nondiscounted basis* (i.e., the face value of the cash flows for each year). Methods taught in Chapter 9 show how these values are discounted.

Table 8.2. Cash Flow Statement

	Year 1	Year 2	Year 3	Year 4	Year 5	Year 6
Percent of capacity	25	50	75	100	110	116
Production, 10,000 lb/yr	12	25	37	50	55	58
Net profit after taxes	$51,000	$148,500	$188,500	$248,500	$269,500	$282,500
Depreciation	70,000	70,000	70,000	70,000	70,000	70,000
Total inflow of funds[a]	$121,000	$218,500	$258,500	$318,500	$339,500	$352,500
Startup expenses after taxes	75,000					
Fixed assets (from project estimate)	700,000					
Working capital per year (from operation estimates)	125,000	100,000	90,000	80,000	80,000	80,000
Total outflow of funds	$900,000	$100,000	$90,000	$80,000	$80,000	$80,000
Net cash flow, annual	−779,000	118,500	168,500	238,500	259,500	272,500
Cumulative cash flow	−$779,000	−$660,500	−$492,000	−$253,500	+$6,000	$278,500

[a]Equation (8.3) can be equivalently $F_c = (G - C)(1 - t) + tD_c$.

Rate of return analysis.   A broad view of rate of return analysis is one that considers the net effective profitability of a product over its life span. Sometimes this analysis is called *profitability*. This must evaluate the return for a price-volume situation over a period of time that will be maintained. A principle requires that a product, including equipment and plant enlargement, capital costs and working capital, must, during the product's life, return to the firm a suitable fixed interest on the unpaid balance of outstanding cash flows. A company can value a product in terms of a constant annual rate of interest that will be produced on the unreturned balance of investment during a product's life. Thus profitability is an analysis technique that measures the desirability of risking money for new products, and the basic factors are capital, expense, revenue, and time. The end result of a rate of return analysis predicts the discounted net changes in the company's cash position. This topic is covered in the next chapter.

Profit and loss statement.   The final document important to making decisions on whether to go ahead with commercialization of a product is the profit and loss statement. Chapter 4 introduced this statement along with several formats. Now we direct our attention to its role in the evaluation of a product. It is an important product that merits P & L attention. Uneventful products that do not impinge significantly on the profit and loss statement can be evaluated by other criteria.

The P & L takes into account sales volume, manufacturing costs, and research and design costs. For the analysis of a proposed product one must have an estimate of production level and an annual accrual of sales income. Direct manufacturing cost is a tabulation of the various cost components that are estimated. A P & L statement shows management the commitments that marketing, sales, and manufacturing operations must make in order to reach the predicted gross sales. P & L statements are made for several years ahead for significant products. Any method that estimates product cost, must also be a *mini P & L*.

8.4 LEARNING APPLICATIONS

The theory of learning was introduced in Sec. 6.6. Now our attention turns to the applications for product estimating. Applications are found in procurement, production, and the financial aspects of a manufacturing enterprise. In purchasing, a function can be used to negotiate purchase price or it may be used for the *make-versus-buy* decision. In estimating, decisions related to cost are based in part on the concept. Contract negotiation is sometimes reopened after a first satisfactory model has been produced. With the experience of time and cost for the prototype unit known, the contract for later units is based on learning reductions.

There are explanations for this behavior and verification has been uncovered by independent researchers and companies. Principally, the reduction is due to direct-labor learning and the management process. The direct-labor learning process assumes that as a worker continues to produce, it is natural that he or she should require less time per unit with increasing production.

The management processes are those engineering programs which improve production, encourage quality, reduce design complexity, create technology progress, and foster product improvement. These programs inspire time and cost reduction beyond that which direct-labor learning would provide.

This author suggests that the operator is responsible for approximately 15% of the total reduction, while management and their programs contribute the remaining 85%. In the manufacturing industries the 85% has been broken down into 50% due to the product engineering endeavors, while manufacturing and industrial engineering activities are credited with the remaining 35%.

Ships, aircraft, computers, machine tools, and apartment and refinery construction have in common high cost, low volume, and discrete item production and can be treated by learning. Although the same principle applies to TV production, for instance, the effects may take years to uncover because of the large production volume. The learning curve is usually not applied to high-volume or low-cost products.

8.4.1 Follow-on Procurement

Costs for *follow-on production* are noticeably lower than original costs. The learning curve may be defined if the number of direct-labor hours required to complete the first unit is established and if the subsequent rate of improvement is specified. Alternatively, the learning curve may be defined if direct-labor man-hours for a downstream unit and the learning curve rate are estimated. Other possibilities for defining the curve can be selected. The number of direct-labor hours required to complete the first production unit depends on these circumstances:

1. The previous experience of the company with the product. If it had little or no experience, the first unit time would be greater than for a product with considerable experience.
2. The amount of engineering, training, and general preparations that the organization expends in preparation for the product. In some cases the first several units are custom-made and tooling is not designed and constructed until more sales can be assured. This "hard-way" production would inflate the first unit time.
3. The characteristics of the first unit. Large complex products would be expected to consume more direct-cost resources than something less complex.

Figure 8.4 describes the follow-on estimating for procurement. In this development we assume that the cumulative average is the linear line.

The follow-on estimating problem can be stated as follows: Given that historical values are available for unit number and the associated direct labor man-hours, find the value for the cumulative quantity of a follow-on estimate. This is

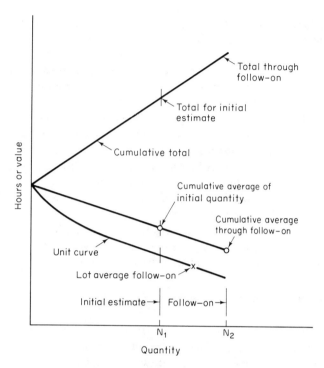

Figure 8.4.   Follow-on learning for procurement.

shown by Fig. 8.5 for a 10-kW product and a graphical solution is possible. However if at unit 18 the hours are 73.5 and learning is 95%, the first step finds K using Eq. (6.14),

$$K = \frac{73.5}{18^{-0.074}} = 91.0$$

Finding the average time at unit 500, $T'_a = 91.0(500)^{-0.074} = 57.5$ cumulative average through follow-on. This should compare to a graphical value. The lot time for the follow-on shipment is found using Eq. (6.16), except that the subtraction is between shipments N_1 and N_2.

$$
\begin{aligned}
T'_c &= KN_1^{s+1} - KN_2^{s+1} \\
&= 91(50^{-0.074+1} - 18^{-0.074+1}) \\
&= 27,413 \text{ hours}
\end{aligned}
$$

The follow-on estimate may indicate a value that is too high for competitive reasons. Management may change the 500th value to 53.0 from 57.5 hours, for instance. It is necessary to find the slope and assess whether the challenge is reasonable. Using Eq. (6.9),

$$s = \frac{\log T_i - \log T_j}{\log N_i - \log N_j}$$

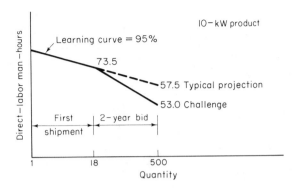

Figure 8.5.   Follow-on learning.

we have

$$s = \frac{\log 73.5 - \log 53.0}{\log 18 - \log 500} = -0.0984.$$

Applying Eq. (6.6), $2^s = 0.934$. Thus we have changed the slope parameter from 95% to 93.4% and its attainability would have to be assessed by management.

8.4.2 Engineering Change Orders

Engineering change orders (ECOs) can be evaluated by learning. ECOs may occur after the product is estimated, priced, and perhaps a contract exists between a buyer and seller. Delivery may have started. Engineering change orders are the result of design improvements. It becomes necessary to estimate an equitable adjustment to product cost and price, if the contract terms allow. Now consider Fig. 8.6(a) and (b), which show curves for the *nonretrofit* and *retrofit* cases. ECO learning line could be above or below the follow-on line. In the nonretrofit portion of the curve in (a), no adjustment is required for products supplied prior to ECO action. In (b), retrofit work is required for units prior to the ECO point. Additional time or value is also required after the ECO action and an ECO learning line with different slope is shown. At the unit point of the ECO, the estimated ECO and actual learning lines do not intersect. The difference between the two lines at the ECO point is the unit time or cost to effect the ECO. It is simpler to estimate unit effects at the ECO point rather than cumulative average values. Thus the unit line is assumed linear.

Assume for Fig. 8.6(b) that the actual and projected learning line is $T_u = 1066N^{-0.1520}$ hours, similar to page 212. The cumulative average learning line is $T_a \doteq 1257N^{-0.1520}$ hours using Eq. (6.13) and ϕ is 90%. An ECO is planned for the 101th unit. Retrofit is scheduled for units 1 to 100 and units 101 to 500 are manufactured consistent with the ECO design. Using a similar experience, the slopes of the ECO configured designs are estimated at 95% prior to the ECO point and 93% afterward. Now we determine the amount of the contract change.

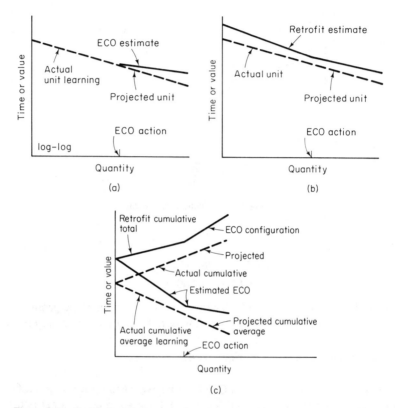

Figure 8.6. Engineering change order learning curves: (a) nonretrofit; (b) retrofit. (c) Finding total cost for ECOs.

At $N = 100$ the retrofit line and the ECO design line meet, but not at the original time. At $N = 100$, $T_u = 529$ hours and $T_a \doteq 620$. The time necessary for the ECO at only $N = 100$ is 75 hours. For units 1 to 100 and a slope of 95%, $s = \log 0.95/\log 2 = -0.074$ using Eq. (6.7). The retrofit intercept K for unit 1 is 105.5 hours. Notice that the learning line is assumed linear because it is easier to estimate the unit difference at $N = 100$ than the cumulative average value. Cumulative retrofit hours $= 8080 (= 105.5 \times 75.5864)$ using Appendix III.

The slope for ECO configuration product is $s = \log 0.93/\log 2 = -0.1047$ and the unit time at 100, $T_u = 529 + 75 = 604$. Its intercept $K = 978.2$ hours and $T_u = 978.2N^{-0.1047}$, which is effective for units 101 to 500. Note that when using equations, we deal with a unit as if it is continuous, as calculation will be from $100 +$. In the use of tables, we use the discrete quantity.

With these equations found, we now find the total time for the ECO product. Notice Fig. 8.6(c), which shows cumulative average and total cumulative lines while still recognizing that the unit line is assumed linear. The convex portion of the cumulative average line is shown straight even though we know it is curved, as shown in Fig. 6.7. The dashed lines of Fig. 8.6(c) represent the actual and projected time without an engineering change. The solid lines represent cumulative average and cumulative total learning prior and subsequent to ECO action. Note the change in slope for the retrofit and the ECO configured product, and at the ECO point there is an incremental cost for the change. It is plausible that the ECO configuration product line could be less than the original projected line. But an ECO causing retrofit would not be less than the original actual, of course.

Now we calculate the time for the ECO retrofit. The retrofit cumulative total is NT_a for the 100 units, or $T_c = 978.8N^{0.8953}$, and the cumulative hours are 194,884 for these future units. The original projected time is $1257(500^{0.848} - 100^{0.848})$ and becomes 181,968 hours. The total difference of 12,917 ($= 194,885 - 181,968$) is the hours of retrofit. The total hours for the ECO for the two pieces become 20,994 ($= 8,077 + 12,917$). This amount would be multiplied by the machine-hour rate, for example, and becomes an addition to the contract.

8.4.3 Break-Even

Break-even analysis was first discussed on Sec. 6.10. Usually, these methods solve for the quantity where cost and price are equal. These earlier methods did not consider learning. Now our study expands on those linear methods with single- and multiple-effect product learning break-even models. We define

$$P = KN_{be}^s \qquad (8.4)$$

where P = price of product, dollars

N_{be} = break-even unit

Equation (8.4) assumes that the unit line is linear. The right side of the equation may be cost and a profit exists when $N > N_{be}$. Note Fig. 8.7(a), which shows this idea. Let the price of a product be \$4762, its cost $12,500N^{-0.2172}$, and $N_{be} = 86$. Profit develops if $N > 86$. The problem is more involved by having a value for P less contribution, margin, or other deductions.

Often product learning is a composite of several separate learning models, as shown in Fig. 8.7(b). Each of these models could be identified with different major assemblies, or the single model may be itemized into labor, material, and overhead. The former is a hardware classification, while the latter is functional. Which approach is chosen will depend on the historical information. We assume knowledge of two learning curves for labor and material:

$$T_{ul} = 25 \times 106N^{-0.1405} = 2650N^{-0.1405}$$
$$T_{um} = 9850N^{-0.2435}$$

where T_{ul} = direct labor dollars per unit

T_{um} = direct material dollars per unit

The "25" shown in the T_{ul} model is labor cost per hour as the $106 = K$ hours.

A composite model is determined by finding T_{ul} and T_{um} at two points, say 1

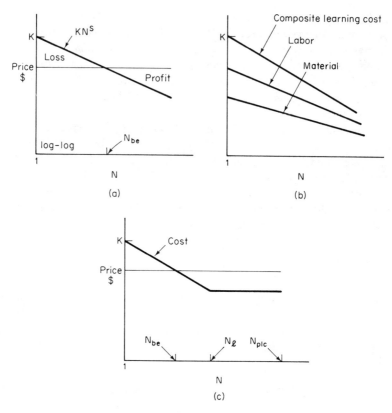

Figure 8.7. (a) Learning break-even; (b) composite learning constructed from individual learning models; (c) learning model with bottom-out effects.

and 100, and adding their values. This is an approximation and more points would allow a new regression curve to be fitted to the data.

Equation	$N = 1$	$N = 100$
$2650N^{-0.1405}$	2650	1388
$9850N^{-0.2435}$	9850	3209
	12,500	4597

$$s = \frac{\log 12,500 - \log 4597}{\log 1 - \log 100} = -0.2172$$

and $2^s = 2^{-0.2172}$ and $\phi \doteq 86\%$.

The composite learning model becomes $12,500N^{-0.2172}$, from which we find break-even, as indicated by Fig. 8.7(a).

Product learning may not continuously decline and may bottom or level out. This happens if management finds it uneconomic to continue cost-reduction programs indefinitely. Cost levels out and the product is manufactured until the product life cycle, which is an estimate of the number of units that will be ultimately sold. This is shown by Fig. 8.7(c).

Interest then turns to uncovering cash flows or profit and loss over the duration of the product life. Loss cash flow for $1 \leq N \leq N_{be}$ is given by

$$\text{loss cash flow} = \frac{KN_{be}^{s+1}}{1+s} - N_{be}P \qquad (8.5)$$

Gain cash flow for $N_{be} < N \leq N_1$, where N_1 is the limit of learning unit number and is given as

$$\text{gain cash flow} = (N_1 - N_{be})P - \frac{K}{1+s}(N_1^{s+1} - N_{be}^{s+1}) \qquad (8.6)$$

Level-cost cash flow for $N_1 < N \leq N_{plc}$, where N_{plc} is the product life cycle unit number, and is given as

$$\text{level-cost cash flow} = (N_{plc} - N_1)(P - KN_1^s) \qquad (8.7)$$

Recall the previous example having $N_{be} = 86$ and price $= \$4762$. Marketing suggests that $N_1 = 125$ and $N_{plc} = 325$. The cash flows are found as follows:

$$\text{loss cash flow} = \frac{12{,}500(86)^{0.7828}}{0.7828} - 86(4762) = \$112{,}365$$

$$\text{gain cash flow} = (125 - 86)4762 - \frac{12{,}500}{0.7828}(125^{0.7828} - 86^{0.7828})$$

$$= 185718 - 177495 = \$8223$$

$$\text{level cash flow} = (325 - 125)(4762 - 4380) = \$76{,}426$$

The total cash flow over the product life $= -\$112{,}365 + \$8224 + \$76{,}426$
$= -\$27{,}716$.

8.4.4 Cost Application

In predicting costs it is useful for estimators to know the recurring costs of production and the learning slopes for the several aspects of production (e.g., manufacturing direct labor, raw material, manufacturing engineering, tooling, quality control, and other indirect charges). In our next application we consider learning for direct labor and factory overhead. Materials are now assumed to be insensitive to the learning curve.

$$C = \frac{KN^s}{s+1}(R) + \frac{KN^s}{s+1}(R)(R_{oh}) + C_{rm} \qquad (8.8)$$

$$= \frac{KN^s}{s+1}(R_{dl})(1 + R_{oh}) + C_{rm}$$

where C = product cost per unit
    R = direct-labor hourly wage, plant average, dollars per hour
   R_{oh} = overhead rate including engineering, tooling quality
        control, and other indirect charges expressed as a
        decimal of the direct-labor hourly rate
  C_{rm} = direct material cost

Our example considers a situation in which 200 units are to be produced. R is \$25 per hour, raw material cost is \$250, and the overhead rate is 50%. The first unit is estimated to require 350 direct-labor man-hours, and a 90% learning curve slope where the unit line is linear. The average cost per unit is

$$C = \frac{350 \times 200^{-0.152}}{0.8482}(25)(1 + .050) + 250 = \$7167$$

For a lot of 200, the total cost is 200(7167) = \$1,433,400. We will return later to learning and show an important extension for estimating product cost.

8.5 METHODS

The product estimate determines the *full cost* of the product using operation estimates, wage rates, overhead, and other companion estimates. A preliminary estimate may have preceded, but that effort served for screening or feasibility. The product estimate is a *pro forma* (a Latin word meaning "for the sake of form"), which is the company's official cost estimating form, which summarizes total direct labor, material, and overheads of various kinds. It is the single most important document of the product estimating effort. It is often approved by the owner, president, or senior executive officer. The pro forma should be contained on one sheet, and thus may be summary of other information. It must provide the total of the manufacturing, development, and sales items, which is the *full cost*.

Four methods of product estimating are studied:

1. Operation
2. Machine center
3. Variable cost
4. Learning

Worldwide firms that produce a product number in the millions. In the United States there are over 250,000 firms. Variations in these methods can be expected; but generally, these methods represent typical industrial practices. All are widely practiced, and each has advantages that makes it superior to others at certain times. They depend on disclosure of detail operational estimates, engineering data, and marketing information. The marketing information, although it may be vague and tentative for new products, must be available.

The bill of material is a fundamental design document, and the following data useful for estimating are obtainable from it:

1. Part number
2. Description or title of part of subassembly
3. Quantity required per unit of product
4. Material specifications
5. Other products in which components may be used
6. Cross reference to similar part numbers

The various methods for preparing and issuing bill of material lists may be partially or wholly done on the corner of the drawing or may be separately listed on other documents. Whenever there is a separate bill of material, the list may be typewritten or appear on a computer printout. It contains information such as the number of the drawing, the name of the part or assembly, the material to be used for the part, and the quantity per unit of the final product.

The control and assignment of numbers for various engineering data such as drawings, bill of material lists, and engineering instructions is a function of design engineering. Cost estimating accommodates to the design numbering system, which is hopefully comprehensive enough to serve engineering, manufacturing, and sales and yet unique enough to indicate readily specific conditions. The bill of material provides an abundance of information leading to other existing documents, products, and cost estimates. New product designs incorporate some parts, subassemblies, or major subassembly units of other manufactured products, and the product estimator uses the bill to find previously prepared estimates. These older estimates are updated using indexes or new wage rates and the like. It may not be necessary to estimate the parts of a product from scratch, as similar parts can reduce the estimating requirements.

For new parts the estimator prepares new estimates. Thus the bill is a complete listing of parts, including standard commercial materials, parts, subcontract, and raw material. Using a bill, the product estimator can be assured that all materials, both purchased and fabricated, will not be inadvertently overlooked.

8.5.1 Operation

This is the oldest of the product estimating methods. Manufacturing operation sheets are prepared for each part, subassembly, and assembly. These operation sheets provide the manufacturing procedure and give the operation setup and cycle standards, labor wage, and operational overhead rate. The total unit cost for a part (and hence a part number) is given as

$$C_u = \Sigma C_{\mathrm{dlo}} + C_{\mathrm{dm}} + C_{\mathrm{ot}} \tag{8.9}$$

where the symbols are as defined on pages 291 and 292. Practice dictates that setup and cycle standards for operations be determined from any of the methods of time measurement discussed in Chapter 2. If the lot quantity N is large, C_{dlo} will not include setup-time considerations, as SU/N becomes negligible on a unit basis, and under these circumstances cycle time H_s is the only one considered. Setup for large volume is costed on an overhead distribution basis.

It is custom for the cycle H_s to be standard time, including allowances for personal, fatigue, and delay. Composition of this *standard* was discussed in Chapter 2. On the other hand, performance against these standards invariably requires adjustment to actual time. The adjustment is either up or down and divides the operational cost by efficiency, or adjustments in the operation overhead rate by a predetermined performance variance.

Notice Table 8.3. The bottom line is found using

$$C_p = \Sigma C_u(1 + R_{ga} + R_s) + C_e + C_c \qquad (8.10)$$

where C_p = unit product cost of manufacturing, development, and sales
where C_u = unit costs of direct labor, direct material
$\quad R_{ga}$ = overhead rate of general and administrative costs, decimal
$\quad R_s$ = overhead rate of sales, decimal
$\quad C_e$ = prorated engineering costs, dollars per unit
$\quad C_c$ = contingency cost, dollars per unit

The summation sign includes all of the components that are a part of the product bill of material.

On Table 8.3 the material cost is summed down starting with $18.36 for subassembly P/N 7150 and includes $0.26 for shipping documents as material for operation 20. This gives a total of $156.60. Concurrently, P/N 7150 requires $109.38 for direct labor and overhead. The column total is $256.99. The cost of goods manufactured is $413.59 (= 156.60 + 256.99). General and administrative, and selling overhead, are a fraction of this base. A companion engineering estimate for line 3 is also necessary. Table 8.3 is the final full cost incorporating labor, material, and overhead.

The operation method is accurate and useful for job shops or companies with proprietary products where there is a reasonable assurance of doing the work. Because of the way the costs are built up, the method relates to a *costed* bill of materials.

8.5.2 Machine Center

This method is simpler than the operation method. While operation sheets can be input information, it is possible to prepare the pro forma without them. However, direct labor time must be estimated for each machine center. This implies the application of standard time data or historical values. The hours per lot are thus found for each machine center, which in turn is multiplied by a machine-hour rate. This rate was determined by methods of Sec. 4.3. Note especially Table 4.11, which provides the calculation of the machine-hour rate combined with gross hourly rate. It is important to recognize that some machine rates can be several times more costly: for example, heavy machining as compared to simple bench assembly.

Table 8.3. OPERATION METHOD OF PRODUCT ESTIMATING

Final Sheet metal radio

Part no. 492 7151
Quantity 250
Estimator PFD
Date 3/12
Estimate expires on 6/9

Part name Chassis Assembly
General notes Has / four subassemblies

Work center	Operation no.	Description of operation (list tools and gauges)	Subassembly Part no.	Setup hours	Hr/100 units	Unit estimate	Labor rate	Labor + over- head rate	Material cost	Labor + overhead cost
			7150						$13.36	$109.36
			7149						27.46	42.15
			7148						102.18	87.33
			7147						7.47	17.24
									Cost of material	Cost of labor + overhead
Stockroom	–	Supply subassemblies								
181-3	10	Finish Box-pack		0.2	1.955	0.020	16.65	1.45	0.87	0.48
2700	20	Pack shipping documents		0.1	1.056	0.016	16.45	1.40	0.26	0.39
									$156.60	$256.99

1. Total cost of goods manufactured   372.23
2. General and administrative costs @ 90% of 1   33.83
3. Engineering cost   —
4. Contingencies
5. Selling costs @ 40% of 1   165.44
   Total unit cost of manufacturing, development, and sales $985.09

333

Table 8.4 is an example of the machine center method. Additional companion estimates are required for materials, custom engineering labor, and the like. This machine center method has the advantage of lower cost for cost estimating, and it is easy to understand.

Table 8.4.   MACHINE CENTER METHOD OF PRODUCT ESTIMATING

Estimate for _Multilaser_ product

Description _Speed decreaser_   Quantity _480 unit_

Customer _Eastwood Electronics_ Quote no. _718_

Machine center	Hour/lot	Machine center rate/hour	Machine center cost
Light machining	172.24	$ 39.16	$ 6744.89
Heavy machining	68.0	90.98	6186.64
Assembly	45.0	32.19	1448.55
Finishing	25.0	42.33	1058.25
			$ 15,438.33

Item	Description		Unit	Lot
1	Machine centers		$ 32.16	$ 15,438.33
2	Raw, standard, subcontract materials		28.80	13,825.73
3	Overhead on materials at 15%		4.32	2073.86
4	Custom engineering labor		61.83	29,680.00
5	Overhead on engineering at 40%		24.73	11,872.00
6	Research and development		—	—
7	Contingencies		—	—
8		Subtotal	$ 151.81	$ 72,889.92
9	Selling costs at 25% of 8		37.96	18,222.48
10	Total cost		$ 189.82	$ 91,112.40
11	Profit at 13% markup on total cost		24.68	11,844.61
12	Selling price		$ 214.49	$ 102,957.01

8.5.3 Variable Cost

The third method depends on separation of costs into fixed and variable. The variable cost method determines all variable costs associated with the product. The method receives its title because of this emphasis. Direct labor and direct material are obviously included in the variable cost portion. But the variable costs included in the overheads of manufacturing, engineering, administration, and sales must also be determined by analysis of the charges. We define *variable cost* as those costs that vary with the quantity of production or sales of the product. With the variable charges of overhead separated from the fixed charges, the next step is to classify the fixed cost into product related and standby. The finding of the variable overhead was described by formula (4.12).

Product fixed costs are related to the making of the product. Product line *A* would have different fixed costs from product line *B*, for instance. These are fixed in the sense that small variation in output causes no change in the budget of a future period. These costs are related to the decision of producing the product and include engineering costs for design and manufacture. If the product is made, they exist, and vice versa. *Standby fixed costs* are incurred regardless of producing the product. The standby description suggests a "bare bones" type of cost. It is independent of current managerial policy or whether any particular products are produced. Interest costs on loans, property taxes, depreciation on plant and equipment, plant protection costs, rental, and certain salary expenses are typical.

Table 8.5 is a sample of a variable cost pro forma. This method is popular for large-volume consumer products. Variations of estimates can be rendered for changes in volume. Note the estimate originally given for the product on page 243. For Table 8.5 it is seen that the total unit cost decreases and then eventually begins to increase due to penalty factors at high levels of production. The estimator judged that plant limitations would impede lower costs and these penalty costs outweighed advantages

Table 8.5.   VARIABLE-COST METHOD OF PRODUCT ESTIMATING

Manufacturing Estimate Summary

Cost estimate no. _182_   Description of product _Special Wrench_ Date _6/21_
Estimator _D80_   Plant _Boulder_   Estimate expires _8/21_

Quantity		5,000	10,000	15,000	20,000	25,000	30,000
Variable manufacturing costs:							
Direct labor		$0.251	$0.229	$0.201	$0.200	$0.200	$0.200
Direct material		0.600	0.500	0.440	0.384	0.380	0.380
Variable overhead rate on labor		(0.20)	(0.12)	(0.10)	(0.10)	(0.13)	(0.25)
Variable overhead rate on material		(0.10)	(0.02)	(0.01)	(0.01)	(0.01)	(0.03)
Variable manufacturing expenses		0.053	0.027	0.020	0.020	0.026	0.050
Variable material related expenses		0.060	0.010	0.008	0.007	0.010	0.011
	Total	$0.964	$0.766	$0.669	$0.611	$0.616	$0.641
Variable marketing costs:							
Trade discounts							
Allowances							
Variable selling expenses							
	Total	0.109	0.001	0.002	0.004	0.006	0.110
Variable administrative costs		0.100	0.077	0.011	0.013	0.021	0.022
Total variable costs		$1.173	$0.844	$0.682	$0.628	$0.643	$0.773
Standby (fixed) costs:							
Manufacturing							
Selling and marketing							
Administrative							
	Total	$0.120	$0.120	$0.120	$0.120	$0.120	$0.120
Product (fixed):							
Manufacturing							
Selling and marketing							
Administrative							
	Total	0.082	0.082	0.082	0.082	0.082	0.082
Total variable and fixed costs		$1.375	$1.046	$0.884	$0.820	$0.845	$0.975

of greater volume. Both labor and material decline for reasons of learning efficiency and material price breaks. In both cases learning reaches a *floor* and then levels off. The variable overhead rates decline until midway in the production quantity range and then begin to increase. A similar pattern is seen for variable administrative and marketing costs. To reach these conclusions it is required to have concrete historical comparisons or several variable overhead rate calculations for various production quantities.

8.5.4 Learning

A sample of the learning pro forma is given by Table 8.6. The cost elements are *operation estimates* consisting of direct labor, direct material, and nonrecurring initial fixed costs. The estimate is made for the first unit, which subdivides the cost into fixed and variable portions. By definition for this method direct labor and direct material are considered variable only. In Chapter 7, the nonrecurring initial costs were considered fixed. Now we acknowledge that tooling and test equipment may have a variable component such as perishable tooling which varies with the quantity.

Table 8.6. LEARNING METHOD OF PRODUCT ESTIMATING

Cost element	First unit Cost estimate		Estimated learning slope	150-unit cumulative factor	Total
	Fixed	Variable			
Direct labor					
Machining	—	$85,000	85%	46.44	$3,947,400
Sheet metal	—	170,000	90	70.04	11,906,800
Assembly	—	650,000	75	18.75	12,187,500
Quality	—	45,000	80	29.88	1,344,600
Direct material					
Raw	—	68,000	90	70.04	4,762,720
Standard	—	15,000	95	103.53	1,552,950
Sub contract	—	240,000	95	103.53	24,847,200
Nonrecurring					
tooling	175,000	500	95	103.53	226,765
Test	20,500	100	98	129.62	33,462
				Subtotal	$60,809,397

1. Plant overhead at 75%	45,607,048
2. Total cost of goods manufactured	106,416,445
3. General and administrative at 20%	21,283,289
4. Engineering	8,500,000
5. Selling at 5%	5,320,822
6. Contingencies	.0
Cost of manufacturing, development, and sales	$141,520,556

Its proportion to nonrecurring initial fixed-cost sum is small for Table 8.6. The learning slopes are estimated using historical evidence. The 150th cumulative average factor is found from Appendix III or using Eq. (6.15). Each cost element total is found using the following formula:

$$\text{cost element total} = C_f + C_v \times T_c' \qquad (8.11)$$

where C_f = cost element considered fixed, dollars
$\quad\ C_v$ = cost element considered variable, dollars
$\quad\ T_c'$ = cumulative factor where cumulative average line is assumed linear

A plant overhead is applied to the total of the operation estimates. The sum of direct costs and plant overhead gives the cost of goods manufactured. General and administrative, and selling overheads are applied on the basis of the cost of goods manufactured. Engineering costs require a separate estimate. The total of the five major costs leads to the *full cost,* or the cost of manufacturing, development, and sales. The learning method is required for major contractors selling to the agencies of the U.S. government. The method is also used for expensive low-quantity industrial products such as computers, turbines, boilers, and airplanes.

8.6 PRICING METHODS

The major purpose of an estimate is to provide information for price setting. In small companies the estimator is also charged with price setting. But in large or diversified or technological-oriented companies, price setting is handled by sales or marketing, which is separate from cost estimating. The division of estimating and price-setting functions is useful in other respects. The product estimators have a desire not to understate or overlook any costs. In price setting there is the urge to have price as low as possible to encourage sales, meet competition, and so on. If cost-estimating and marketing functions are merged, the cost estimate tends to become a "guesstimate" rather than a technically determined fact.

"Tension" between estimating and sales can be useful. A constructive understanding between estimating and sales will lead to better cost estimates and prices if the functions remain separate.

There is seldom a price solution that is without complexities. The problems that appear first are those of competition and the consumer. Setting a price causes reactions by competition as well as a knotty evaluation of the kind of response to be expected from the consumer. Additionally, the law impinges on some price decisions. Prosecution is not unknown for prices established through industry-wide collusion. In times of fierce competition salesmen exert pressure to reduce prices. A number of practices exist and are closely related to price setting and add to the complexities. For instance, promotional pricing, premiums, coupons, trade-ins, extras, fire-sale gimmicks, volume discounts, repeat discounts, geographic price differentials, lease–buy arrangements, and reciprocal agreements are deals that squarely affect the price choice.

The pricing situations presented to the price setter are diverse. They may range from a price for a one-of-a-kind product to one where there are identical units offered to many buyers. The firm may have only a single product or it may have a multiple-product line. The product may be brand new to the firm, or on rare occasions may be a product of research or invention. The product may have been manufactured for decades in the same form, or minor modifications may be introduced every so often.

There may be market distinctions. There is the *open market* in which products are sold to an unknown buyer. Competition among products is based on price and nonprice factors. A second market distinction is the *bid or order market,* in which manufacturers produce an item for a specific buyer. The type of contract, specification, and engineering design, in addition to price, are factors. In some cases price is the single means of competition; in others price may be relatively unimportant. In all these situations one pricing method is superior and others are not. To make a rational price decision, we attempt to foresee the effects on the objectives of the company and on the several groups of people affected by the price. In view of these complications, we justify several concepts to determine a price. At this point we define *price* as the value of the economic want of a product design given, received, or asked in exchange. Of course, the value is monetary and expressed in the currency of the country (i.e., dollars, deutsche marks, yen). We have deferred a rigorous definition of profit up to this point, allowing its general understanding. For the purpose of cost estimating, *profit* is the future monetary excess between price and the estimated cost by the producer of the product design. The actual or historical profit that is realized is of more importance to accounting than engineering. Estimated and historical profit may not be equal.

Concepts of pricing are as follows:

1. The first concept has prices proportional to cost. If the concept produces the same percentage profit for all elements of cost, it is full cost plus a *markup*. Another variation would have different markup percentages on the several cost elements.

2. Prices can be established that are proportional to conversion cost. This concept ignores the effects of the several kinds of material cost in its calculation. A conversion cost concept emphasizes *value added,* or direct labor plus overhead.

3. Prices can be proportional to variable cost (i.e., that result in the same percentage contribution over variable costs). This concept can lead to different proportions for different designs. Fixed costs and profit are the parts of the *contribution.* The concept may use direct labor and direct material (and variable overhead in some situations) as its base. It emphasizes marginal cost of producing additional units.

4. Prices can be systematically related to the stage of market and competitive development of the product. Price and cost-estimating relationships are necessary features of the concept.

5. Prices can be established that depend on the elasticity of demand, a topic discussed in Sec. 6.10.

Costs are stressed in the first four concepts. In the fifth concept, the theoretical desire to provide elasticity of information in time and quality for pricing meets with frequent failure. This concept seldom leads to practical methods.

Four methods of product pricing are studied:

1. Opinion, conference, and comparison
2. Markup on cost
3. Contribution
4. Price estimating relationships

8.6.1 Opinion, Conference, and Comparison

These nonanalytic methods involve the people who know the product's market and its price and understand the technical factors. They meet as a consequence of competitors' actions, or someone may notice that the price of an item may be out of line. Perhaps costs have gone up or down and adjustments are felt necessary. Discussion regarding the volume effect that each of the alternative prices would have and the product's profit as a result of alternative prices would be undertaken. Data on competitors' prices will usually be available, as well as comparisons of strengths and shortcomings of competing products. Cost estimates, past sales figures, and the history of price changes will be at hand.

To assess the number of units that might be sold and their price we try to imagine the customer response to each alternative. Furthermore, the response of distributors and salespersons, changes in the sales of other products, and probable response of competitors, and the effect on the share of the market are evaluated. The predictions will be shaky, and we must recall their shortcomings. While we discern the future actions of our customers and competitors we can be certain that their reactions in the future will differ from those in the past. Analytic methods to determine a price are overlooked. Despite their absence, opinion, conference, and comparison remain essential to price setting.

8.6.2 Markup on Cost

This method, variously called the *cost plus* or *markup,* sets prices proportional to cost. It is probably the most popular method. The method identifies the types of the costs from the pro forma, and adds an additional percentage of those costs as a markup. If the total cost of manufacturing, development, and selling is used, it is a *full-cost* base. The formula for a full-cost markup is

$$P = C_t + R_m(C_t) \tag{8.12}$$

where P = unit price, dollars
C_t = total cost of manufacturing, development, and sales, dollars
R_m = markup rate on cost, decimal

Examine Table 8.4, where $C_t = 230.021$ and $R_m = 13\%$. Then $P = \$259.92$.

Simple as this appears, there are literally dozens of variations. For instance, the C_t term can be broken down to material, labor, burden, and engineering with each term having its own markup. This is found in government contracting where limitations on the markup of the cost components are sometimes required. Some companies use the same add-on percentage year after year. Others use markups which reflect the preceding year's actual percentages. For the most part these percentages vary with business conditions, and this feature along with its ease of understanding are its best features. As business falls the add-on is reduced and vice-versa. When large companies use these procedures, it is usually as a starting place for a price decision. In some companies the sales managers in the territory eventually decide what price they will actually quote and the markup percentage serves as background.

Conversion-cost pricing emphasizes *value added* or direct labor plus overhead in the base for a markup calculation. In some cases material will be provided *cost-free* to the manufacturer, as it may not be competitive to add markup on materials. We can define a price using the following:

$$P = \Sigma C_{dlo}(1 + R_{oh})(1 + R_m) + C_{dm} \tag{8.13}$$

where C_{dlo} = direct-labor cost on operations, dollars
    R_{oh} = general overhead rate, decimal overhead dollars to
         direct labor dollars
    R_m = markup rate, decimal
    C_{dm} = direct material cost, dollars

In some cases C_{dm} may equal zero. Using a plan like Eq. (8.13) shifts the emphasis to products with high material costs and economizes on company labor and overhead.

If the cost base is direct labor and direct material, the price objective is the incremental cost of additional units, or

$$P = (\Sigma C_{dlo} + C_{dm})(1 + R_m) + C_{oh} \tag{8.14}$$

where C_{oh} denotes the costs of overhead, dollars. In some cases C_{oh} can equal zero. Equation (8.14) would require a larger markup on a smaller base than in the case of the full-cost base.

It is basic that if a new venture or a major improvement is desirable, the net return from it must exceed the cost of capital required. This philosophy provides a pricing method that depends on invested cost. This requires that the cost of operation and the consumption of fixed assets and an acceptable rate of return be estimated. The acceptable rate of *return on investment* varies with numerous economic factors, but overall cumulative values have emerged. They range from a low of 10% to over 50%. A simplified markup pricing model based on investment cost is

$$P = \left(\frac{iL}{N_Y} + C_f + C_v N\right)/N \tag{8.15}$$

where i = desired return on investment, decimal
    I = investment, dollars

N_y = number of years for payback of investment
C_f = product fixed costs, dollars
C_v = product variable cost unit, dollars
N = number of units sold

In this model the return on investment substitutes for the markup rate.
Another cost-based approach to pricing includes methods to achieve a *markup on sales* value. It may be formalized as

$$P = \frac{C_t}{1 - R_s} \qquad (8.16)$$

where C_t = total cost of manufacturing, development, and sales, dollars
R_s = markup on sale value, decimal

Refer to Table 8.4 again. If C_t = \$189.82, R_s = 13%, then P = \$218.19. This compares to \$214.49 for a markup of 13% of total cost. Terms found in sales have *discount* synonymous with margin, *list* with selling price, and *net* with cost.

8.6.3 Contribution

As we have said, some costs vary with changes in production quantity, while others do not. Pricing is then related to this variable cost as a percentage of the full variable cost. We continue the study of the product estimate originally developed for marginal cost and marginal revenue (Sec. 6.10), and subsequently estimated as one of the major methods (page 335). In this development we find the principal items of variable cost, including labor, material, marketing, and administrative costs. Upon this C_v value, we find the contribution based on sales price, or

$$P = \frac{C_v}{1 - R_c} \qquad (8.17)$$

where P = list price for manufacturer, dollars
C_v = full variable cost, dollars
R_c = contribution rate, decimal

For instance, examine the variable cost estimate (Table 8.5) for 5000 quantity, and note that total variable cost is \$1.173 per unit. If a contribution percentage of $2\frac{1}{4}\%$ is assumed, then P = 1.200 (= 1.173/0.975). This is shown as line 3 of Table 8.7. Each list price of Table 8.7 is similarly computed. Line 4 is total revenue and is found as *NP.* But this manufactured product is sold retail using a commercial discount of 40%, and a typical calculation for line 6 of Table 8.7 is \$2.00 [= 1.20/(1 − 0.4)]. Line 7, standby and product overhead per unit, is estimated as \$0.202 and is shown repeated from Table 8.5. Line 8, total cost per unit, is the sum of the variable and fixed costs. *Contribution* is the amount left over from revenue after paying the variable costs and is used first to pay the fixed expenses. Any overage is a contribution to profit. Noting Table 8.7, we see that every level of possible sales quantity

Table 8.7. Contribution Method For Establishing Price on Basis of Variable-Cost Estimate

	Quantity, N					
	5000	10,000	15,000	20,000	25,000	30,000
1. Estimated variable cost/unit, C_v	1.173	0.844	0.682	0.628	0.643	0.773
2. Contribution percentage, R_c	2.25	24.4	32.1	34.9	31.6	14.1
3. Manufacturer's list price, P	1.200	1.116	1.005	0.965	0.940	0.900
4. Total revenue, NP	6000	11,125	15,200	19,300	23,500	27,000
5. Discount, 40%	0.800	0.744	0.670	0.645	0.630	0.600
6. Retail price, $\dfrac{P}{1-0.40}$	2.00	1.86	1.68	1.61	1.57	1.50
7. Standby and product overhead/unit, C_f	0.202	0.202	0.202	0.202	0.202	0.202
8. Total cost/unit, $C_v + C_f$	1.375	1.046	0.884	0.820	0.845	0.975
9. Total cost, $N(C_v + C_f)$	6875	10,460	13,260	16,400	21,125	29,250
10. Contribution/unit, $P - C_v$	0.027	0.272	0.323	0.337	0.297	0.127
11. Total contribution, $N(P - C_v)$	135	2720	4845	6,740	7,425	3,810

does contribute, but reaches a maximum at the quantity $25,000. Note Fig. 6-17 for other viewpoints on optimization on the production of this product.

Obviously, the percentages for the several kinds of pricing rates (i.e., markup, contribution, etc.) are not comparable. The percentages have meaning only in relationship to a pricing method.

8.6.4 Price-Estimating Relationships

Price-estimating relationships (PERs) are mathematical models or graphs that estimate price. Similar in construction to cost-estimating relationships (Sec. 6.6), a *price driver* is the independent variable. Time is usually chosen, although quantity and other variables are possible. A variety of functional forms are available and the reader can refer to Chapter 6 for details.

Now consider PERs in the application of a price ceiling and a price floor. The marketplace determines the price at which products will sell and sets a *price ceiling*. The cost, profit, and price determined by the firm establishes a *price floor*. In this context we define an *opportunity margin* offered by the market. Opportunity margin is the difference between the ceiling and the floor. If the policy is to accept the marketplace as determining the price at which products will sell, then when the two meet, the firm may choose to stop manufacturing of the product or reduce price or cost. Price for a product will remain static in constant dollars if production and demand remain in equilibrium. Excess demand tends to increase prices, while excess supply suppresses prices. If profit and opportunity margin are high, more competitors are apt to enter the market.

We define

$$\text{opportunity margin} = P_o e^{-k_m t} - P_f e^{-k_f t} \qquad (8.18)$$

where P_o = price of the initial unit at inception of production, dollars

k_m = decay experience for the product, decimal

t = time, typically years

P_f = price floor initially, dollars

k_f = decay experience of the price floor, decimal

A typical graph for a product selling price would be as shown in Fig. 8.8. The floor price is the point at which the most efficient producer will make a reasonable profit. With a fairly stable floor price the margin over this floor price decays rapidly as more competitors attempt to capture the market.

A new product has been developed. Novelty will sustain early sales but long-range estimates have concluded that competing designs with a constant retail price of $9 will provide a floor. The initial price of the firm is $21 and a decay of 0.25 is expected on the basis of experience. The number of years for the intersection is

$$9 = 21 e^{-0.25t}$$
$$t = 3.4 \text{ years}$$

Figure 8.8.   Opportunity margin, projection for the model $M_0 e^{-k_m t} - F_0 e^{-k_f t}$.

8.7 SPARE PARTS

Spare parts are defined as product for separate production and procurement that are required for maintenance or repair. This would exclude end items which have redundancy designed into the product to avoid failure. Spare parts could range from piece parts to minor assemblies to end items. Production scrap and waste are not included in spare parts. Cataloged and off-the-shelf replacement spare parts occurring in a purchase action are trivial and will be overlooked.

We will not consider methods to calculate failure rates or the number of spare parts required, except to point out that historical averages, mean-time-between-failure types of statistics for similar equipment or opinion are employed. An estimate of the number of replacement spare parts is required before a cost estimate can be made.

Usually, spares are quoted after a product has been sold, although the product may not have been delivered. Actual cost may be available to allow a basis for making the new estimate. When using actual costs, material and labor costs must be updated. If changes in setup quantity are noticeably different, adjustments in this, too, may be necessary. For companies who deal in selling spares, either on a single or lot basis, many of the same techniques as described in this chapter are used.

Figure 8.9 graphically describes policies for spare-part and regular production. Policy (a) is constant production followed immediately by spare-parts production but at a lower rate. In (b), spare parts are concurrent to regular production. For policy (c) the production of spare parts is prior to regular production. In some situations spare-parts production may continue during regular production. Policy (c)

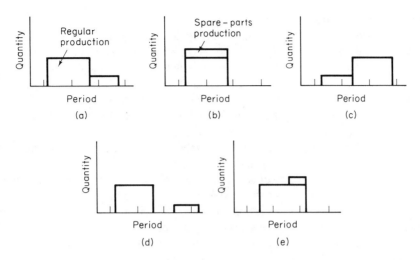

Figure 8.9.   Production plans for spare parts.

is found in the auto industry, where spares are in the hands of car dealers prior to introduction of a new model. Policy (d) shows a period of time before spare-parts production is started. In (e) we see spare-parts production starting after initial production and concluding with the regular production.

According to our definition, spare parts require separate production. Sketch (b), while it has provision for spare parts beyond a basic production number, would not qualify for special cost-estimating treatment because the spare parts are piggyback to the production requirement. The spare parts in this case would be identified as spare parts certainly, but cost-estimating procedures and formulas do not recognize them as a distinctive group if they are joined to the basic group. Special estimating treatment is given to spare parts scheduled apart from basic production. In sketch (a) the spare parts are produced after regular production, which may not be the same as spare-parts production. In (d) there is a significant period of time between regular and spare-parts production. Sketch (c) shows a change between regular and spare-parts production and indicates a lower throughput rate for spare parts. Another nuance could be imagined which would be a combination of sketches (b) and (c), or a delayed start for a slower scheduled rate for spare parts.

Spare parts are estimated using the methods of Sec. 8.5. Regular production is considered first, and modifications are examined later. Adjustments by setup quantity, indexing, rates of labor, material, or overhead are possible depending on the pro forma method. Inasmuch as the nonrecurring costs are amortized by regular production, these costs may not appear in spare parts. Contrariwise, an increase in quantity broadens the base for amortization of fixed costs, permitting more economical production methods. But better practice will acknowledge that spare parts are dependent on full variable cost. A learning theory approach for assembly or major items is possible. The learning theory approach concentrates on the variable cost per unit and any effects of nonrecurring cost are progressively diminished. Figure 8.10 gives the thinking for a learning theory approach. Sketch (a) is similar to a follow-on estimate. Sketch (b) demonstrates the situation where there is a significant time period between regular and spare-parts production. In sketch (c), spare-parts production is at a lower scheduled rate. These practices are demonstrated by chapter problems. Spare-parts pricing and profits are often attractive. But buyers who purchase spare parts are aware of these potential lucrative prices and they may negotiate smaller profit markups.

Repair estimating is unlike the spares problem. Until the product is examined, the work needed to restore the product to an acceptable condition cannot be fully identified. A number of practices are found with repairs. The product may be stripped at the site and estimated by a person experienced in identifying the work necessary. Or a time, material, and profit contract between the original supplier or repair company and the owner may be specified. The product may be shipped back to the factory and a repair inspection undertaken there. The time is estimated and a unit cost per hour is applied.

8.8 DESIGN-TO-COST

For the most part, product estimators "build up" an estimate starting with operation estimates and concluding with either product cost or price. Sometimes a reverse procedure is required. Beginning with a competitor's market price for a given product, the estimator works backward to find total cost and the cost for various design elements. This practice is called *design-to-cost*. Design-to-cost is the early estimating of the product prior to preliminary design. These design-to-cost targets are for engineering, management, procurement, or production.

In the conventional approach estimators build up an estimate starting with direct material, direct labor, overhead, and concluding with full cost. In design-to-cost, a reverse procedure is required. Beginning with the potential price, the esti-

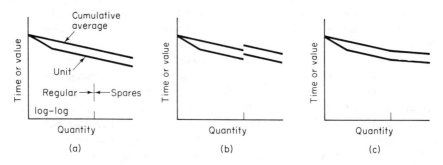

Figure 8.10. Learning curve approches for spare parts.

mator works backward to find the cost for various design elements. The potential price may be a competitor's market price for a product.

What is meant by "early cost" estimating? If the intent is as an incentive for better procurement, fabrication, or assembly, estimating prior to these actions is early. If we wish to encourage design people to be cost conscious, early may be prior to their design. Design-to-cost provides a target of direct labor and direct material costs for significant hardware. A reward system to encourage design and other engineers to meet target can be associated with its attainment.

Major and minor cost elements are uncovered by estimating or by the use of factors. The level of detail may even extend to components and hardware. In the design-to-cost procedure, and when detail exists, learning curve theory, tooling philosophies, quantities, rates of manufacture, and escalation or de-escalation of costs can be introduced in the process.

The apportioning of cost is in accord with a logical design structure for the product. Designers may consult with the estimator in developing the logical structure. Each design is given a *target;* thus the designer knows that he or she controls the design and hopefully is able to design to match the goal. The purpose is to ensure that the product will meet a designated price to allow product competition.

Note Fig. 8.11. Estimating ascertains that a product is sold for $555 per unit. The estimator reduces the price by the profit markup (about 10%) leaving a cost of manufacturing, development and sales of $500. In turn, general and administrative, selling, engineering, and cost of goods manufactured are determined. The same factors that were used to build up a cost are used in a reciprocal way. With an overhead of $195 the process changes. At this point the division of remaining value is divided into direct materials and direct labor along the principal design lines.

This breakdown is identified and, in conference with the designer, the components and costs are estimated. The designer now has a cost goal. Figure 8.12 shows what these goals are for one section of a design.

Naturally, it is important that the total goal be distributed fairly and that no subassembly or component be favored at the expense of another. As the design effort progresses, the usual pattern of preliminary and detail product cost estimates is undertaken. A cost and price would ultimately be found using methods given in this chapter. Obviously, it would be desirable that the final price harmonize with design-to-cost goals.

SUMMARY

In this chapter we considered product-estimating procedures. Important as other motives may be in price setting, the cost of a product must be fully recovered with profit to assure that the firm will ultimately survive. Financial documents are important in the appraisal of the worth of a product to a firm. Learning curve theory, useful for large-scale production goods, impinges on the product estimate in impor-

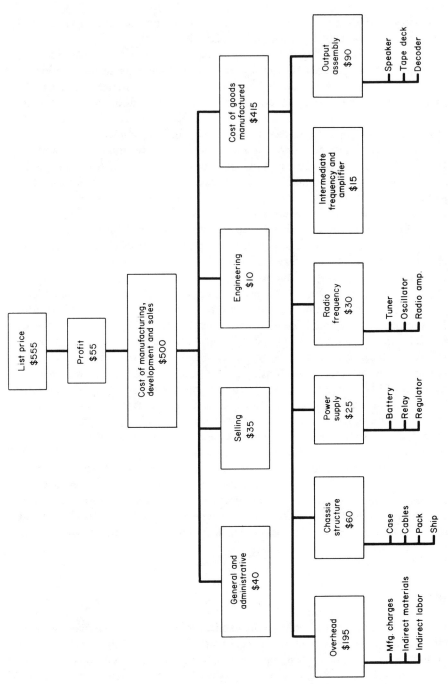

Figure 8.11. Distribution of price to design-to-cost goals for major assemblies of a product.

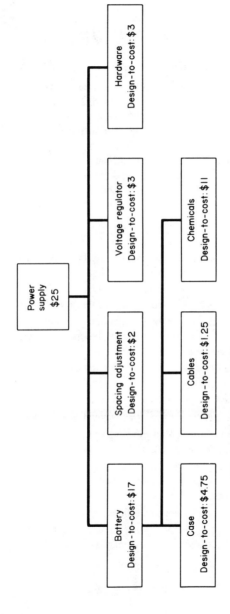

Figure 8.12. Estimating typical subassembly and component design-to-cost goals.

tant ways. Methods of product costing and strategies of pricing lead to the information required for various financial documents and help to improve the product's success.

QUESTIONS

8.1. Give an explanation of the following terms:

Price	Machine hour method
RFQ	Standby fixed costs
Cost of goods manufactured	Markup
Amortization	Investment price
Cash flow	Margin
Follow-on estimate	Contribution
Engineering change orders	Opportunity margin
Bill of material	Payback
Operation method	Design to cost

8.2. What are the ways a product estimate will be used? List others not included in the chapter.

8.3. What kinds of information are required for a product estimate? Which is internally determined by the product estimator?

8.4. Relate the flow of information between the various financial documents. At what point would these documents be required? When would they be unnecessary?

8.5. Describe the purpose of learning for a cost estimate. In addition to production quantity, what other things show learning correlation? Where in the cost estimating process is the learning theory applied?

8.6. How may the shape of the learning theory be defined? What factors contribute to this shape?

8.7. Segregate the methods of product costing. Outline these differences.

8.8. Indicate the complexities of pricing. Rank several objectives of a pricing policy.

8.9. When is the full cost method of pricing appropriate? What are its failings? Devise a new model that uses the full cost and investment method of pricing.

8.10. Is contribution pricing a marginal method of analysis? How important is it to have a contribution? What are the problems involved in determining fixed costs and associating them with various product lines?

8.11. Describe the distinction in spare-part estimating.

8.12. What is design-to-cost? How does this procedure aid the control of costs during the design process? What features of this management procedure bear watching?

PROBLEMS

8.1. An investor is considering an invention, and costs and revenue have been estimated. Calculate the net cash flow representing this investment. Disregard taxes and discounting.

Year	Cost	Revenue
0	$50,000	0
1	5,000	$ 2,500
2	5,000	10,000
3	2,500	25,000
4	0	25,000
5	0	20,000

8.2. The cash flow for a product entering production is given as follows:

Year	Cost	Revenue	Amount for Depreciation
0	$60,000	0	0
1	5,000	$ 2,500	$9000
2	5,000	10,000	9000
3	2,500	25,000	9000
4	2,500	25,000	9000
5	2,500	20,000	9000

Fixed assets are $45,000, and initial operating expenses are $15,000. If the company is in the 25% tax bracket, determine the net cash flow. When is the payback point based on a nondiscounted cash flow?

8.3. Construct a cash flow document. Investment and preoperating charges are $100 and $25 × 10^5 for the first year; production is 10 million pounds and is expected to increase by 2 million pounds per year for the next 5 years. Net profit after taxes amounts to $20 × 10^5 for the first year, depreciation is straight line for 10 years, and working capital is $8 × 10^5 dollars per year for year 1. Costs are assumed constant over the period. What is the payback period?

8.4. If the 2-year bid of Fig. 8.5 is estimated to decline to 52 hours, what is the slope? How many hours does this result in?

8.5. A company that produces engine generator sets is planning follow-on bidding with the learning model. At the 980th unit a 5-kW product required 68 man-hours of direct labor with a slope of 95% learning. The company adopts the cumulative average learning line as linear.
   (a) Plot the cumulative average line between units 1 and 980 on log-log paper.
   (b) Follow-on will involve 2460 units. Extend the constructed line to include this second shipment. What is the value of unit 3440 graphically? Repeat analytically.
   (c) Now management believes that the 5-kW product must reduce to 56.3 hours at the 3440th unit. Find the new slope and the lot time for the second shipment. What is the average time per unit for the follow-on lot?

8.6. A company uses the learning concept to cost products. A summary of one product is given on page 352. The average hour is assumed linear and its best-fit equation is $T'_a = KN^s = 365N^{-0.256}$, which is the regression equation for columns 6 and 7.

Lot	Lot Quantity	Recorded Total Hours	Average Hours Each	Cumulative Hours	Cumulative Quantity	Cumulative Average Hours
1	5	1300	260	1300	5	260
2	22	2600	118	3900	27	144
...	...	...	...	...	...	...
8	55	3520	64	24020	267	90
9	45	2760	61	26780	312	86

(a) How many hours will be required for lot 10 if 42 units are to be built?

(b) What is the average unit estimate for the lot?

(c) If the full cost per hour is $35.00, what is the total lot cost?

8.7. For the engineering change proposal A, the cost at unit 14 is $8000 and the learning rate is 80%. For EC proposal B, the unit 14 cost is $6000 and the learning rate is 90%. Which proposal is best at unit 15 or 20? Assume the unit line as straight.

8.8. The actual and follow-on learning equation is $T_u = 1000N^{-0.322}$, where the unit-hour line is assumed linear. An engineering change order is planned for $N = 4$ and the slope parameter $\phi = 75\%$ is estimated. Find the total hour effect for units 4 and 5. Retrofit is not required. Repeat for $\phi = 85\%$. (*Hint:* Units 1, 2, and 3 are unchanged.)

8.9. The actual and follow-on learning equation is $T_u = 1000N^{-0.322}$, where the unit-hour line is considered linear. At $N = 4$ an engineering change is planned with a slope of 85%. At $N = 4$ an additional 50 hours will be necessary. The slope for the retrofit portion is 90%. Find the total time for the ECO for units 1 through 5.

8.10. The equation $T_u = 35,000N^{-0.322}$ is actual and projected hours for a design, and the unit line is considered linear. An ECO is planned at the 50th unit. Retrofit is scheduled for units 1 to 50 and units 50 to 100 supplied according to ECO configuration. From a similar experience 90% and 85% are estimated as learning prior and subsequent to the ECO action. 150 hours are estimated at the ECO point. Find the number of hours resulting from the ECO for the ECO and projected units 50 to 100. Use Appendix III.

8.11. A new product will sell for $6250 each. Unless a learning curve approach is adopted, the product will be scrapped because the cost summary indicates that the full cost exceeds the potential price initially. Management wishes to determine the break-even point N between price and full cost. The following facts are gathered:

Selected Cost	Value at 500 Units	Cost per Hour	Percent Learning
Direct labor	105 man-hours	$17.76	95
Purchased Materials:			
Engine	$ 850		95
Semifinished	250		90
Raw	700		80
Other	650		100
Other	$2450		

Overhead is at 100% of direct-labor cost. Find the break-even point N_{be} to recover full costs. Use an approximation for a composite learning curve with units 1 and 500. What is the unit profit available at 1000 units? Use the unit line as the linear line.

8.12. A product, PN 8871, has these operational times summarized:

Operation	Setup	Hours per 100 Units	Direct-Labor Wage
1. Shear	0.1	0.0048	16.50
2. Punch press	0.4	0.150	19.00
3. Punch press	0.4	0.150	19.00
4. Tumbler	—	0.010	16.05
5. Degreaser	0.1	0.100	19.45

The quantity is 2500 to be shipped in one order. We assume no learning for this product. Find the full cost for manufacturing, development, and sales using the following pro forma:

(a) Use the operation method. Operational overhead rates for 1, 2, 3, 4, and 5 are 45%, 76%, 76%, 60%, and 75%. These overhead rates are exclusive of labor cost. Material unit cost including material overhead = $0.0966. General and administrative overhead is 25% on the basis of direct labor, material, and overheads for operation and material. Sales is 15% on the same basis as G & A.

(b) Use the machine hour method. Fringe labor costs are a part of the manufacturing overhead, which is 75%. General and administrative cost is 20% of the manufacturing labor and overhead. Unit material cost is $0.084 per unit and overhead on materials = 15%. Selling costs are computed as 25% of plant labor, material, and overheads.

(c) Use the variable cost method. Variable direct labor and material unit costs are $0.0864 and $0.084. Their variable overheads are 30% and 15%. Variable marketing and administrative overhead rates are 10% and 25% of the total variable direct cost of labor and material. Standby and product fixed cost are $0.015 and $0.030 per unit.

8.13. A single-component product is to be estimated for cost and price for a lot of 175 units. The operation estimates for this product are as follows:

Operation	Setup Hour	Cycle Hours per Unit
1. Shear	0.1	0.001
2. Pierce	0.5	0.038
3. Countersink	0.3	0.043
4. Brake	0.6	0.010
5. Weld corners	0.2	0.035
6. Grind weld	0.1	0.020
7. Deburr	0.4	0.006

Average shop labor is $17.25 per hour. Factory overhead is 75% of direct labor, material cost and overhead unit is $0.075, and G & A is 25% of the cost of goods manufactured. There is no selling or contingency cost. The percentage markup upon full cost is 20%.

(a) Find the unit and lot cost, and price.

(b) Which operation is most costly? If a 50% reduction can be achieved in this operation, what addition to profit would you expect at the same selling price? (Assume that profit is increased only by direct-labor costs reduction.)

8.14. A universal projection screen mount is to be estimated. This product provides a means of suspending a screen from the ceiling and eliminates the tripod support. The device permits rotation of 360° and tilting of a maximum of 30°. Various vendors supply parts to the company. Figure P8.14 shows an installation sketch. An indented bill of material is used to summarize cost facts.

No. Req'd				Part Name	Material Cost per Unit	Labor Estimate (hours/ units)	Gross Hourly Wage (dollars per hour)
1				Complete assembly		0.01	$20.05
	1			Gear pivot assembly		0.03	20.05
		1		Pivot, geared	$2.25	0.005	18.75
		1		Bolt	0.25	0.004	16.00
		2		Nut	0.10	0.002	15.00
	1			Adjustment shaft	0.75	0.01	20.05
	1			Worm	1.15	0.01	18.75
		1		Shaft	0.60	0.01	16.00
	1			Connector	0.50	0.02	17.75
		2		Thumbscrews	0.20	0.01	15.00
		2		Rod	0.40	0.03	16.00
	1			Housing		0.02	20.05
	1			Cover plate	0.60	0.005	16.00
	2			Side plate	0.30	0.015	16.00
	1			End plate	1.40	0.010	16.00
	1			Top plate	1.75	0.010	16.00
	1			Bottom plate	1.65	0.020	16.00

(a) Find the direct costs for labor and material.
(b) Define the cost of manufacturing as labor and material. Let the costs of general, administrative, and sales be at 200% of the cost of manufacturing. Find the full cost.
(c) If markup is 25% of full cost, find the profit and price.
(d) Repeat part (c) if the margin is 25% of the sales price.

8.15. Electronic components must be protected during manufacture. Spurious electric charges can destroy microelectronic chips, for example. To avoid these problems, a tote-box liner is designed that uses a static-free plastic material. An assembly sketch is given by Fig. P8.15. A vendor has provided a quotation for items 3 and 4 as follows:

Quantity	Item 3	Item 4
500	$4.10	$5.22
1000	3.51	4.47
2500	3.28	4.17
Material	0.28	0.33

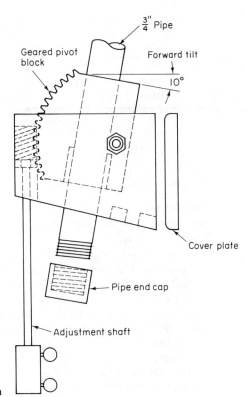

Figure P8.14. Universal projection screen mount.

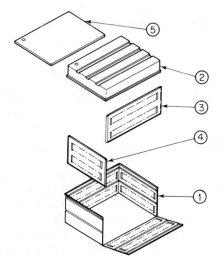

Figure P8.15. Tote-box liner.

Items 1, 2, and 5, assembly, and packaging are estimated by the company. Additional cost factors are as follows:

Item	Unit Material Cost	Tooling Cost	Direct Labor Setup (Hours)	Direct Labor Hours/Unit	Gross Hourly Cost
1	$1.22	$3500	6.5	0.025	$18.75
2	0.92	1750	4.0	0.013	18.75
5	0.67	1200	3.0	0.012	19.00
Assembly			0.5	0.005	17.00
Packaging	0.20		0.5	0.005	17.50

General administrative and sales costs are at 100% of operational costs. Develop a pro forma system to estimate full cost, and then use it for quantities of 500, 1000, and 2500.

8.16. (a) A company's experience in building gear transmissions indicates that the first unit will consume 100 hours of fabrication and assembly time. A learning rate of 75% is anticipated. A contract is being estimated in which 40 units will be supplied. Labor cost of $24 per hour covers labor time and indirect manufacturing expense and material expenses should be $25 per unit. If a 20% add-on for profit is historically applied, what should the bid price be? How much must the time estimates be off to consume the profit? Assume that the unit line is linear.

(b) A prototype unit has been constructed with 45,000 hours of work recorded on job tickets. The direct labor hourly average rate is $24, and the overhead rate on the basis of labor is 100%. Raw material costs charged to the job were $20,000. The company, after a period of time for design changes, will build units 2, . . . , 10 for sale. Customizing for specific customers is negligible. They anticipate a learning rate of 90% for direct labor and 95% for material. What are the total estimated costs for this product, the average, and the 10th-unit cost? The unit line is linear.

8.17. A company uses the learning curve approach to estimate its product. The cumulative average line is assumed linear.

Cost Item	Prototype Cost Estimate Fixed	Prototype Cost Estimate Variable	Estimated Learning (%)
Direct labor	—	45,000 hr	90
Direct material	—	$20,000	95
Manufacturing support	25,000	$5,000	95

Labor costs $18 per hour, fixed and miscellaneous overhead is 100%, distribution and administrative overhead is 20%, and selling costs are at 2% of direct labor and manufacturing support. The company uses the full-cost method with profit at 10%. Find the price for the 10th unit. Find total price for 10 units.

8.18. (a) If the margin on sales is 20% and cost is $160, find the selling price.

(b) If the margin on sales is 30%, find the markup percentage.

8.19. The cost estimator has found the following costs per unit:

Direct labor	$0.10
Direct material	0.20
Overhead	0.06
	$0.36

(a) Find the price if the markup of full cost is 50%.

(b) If the markup of direct labor and material is 100%, determine the price for an objective of incremental cost of additional units.

(c) Disregard the cost of materials for a markup of 200% upon conversion cost. Find the price.

(d) Find price for a margin of sales as 50%.

8.20. An estimate is as follows: direct labor, $4.50 per unit; direct material, $8.00 per unit; overhead, $12.50 per unit. Find the price for a margin on sales as 25%.

8.21. A firm desires a return on investment of 30% before taxes. A project estimate indicates that the required investment is $100,000, fixed costs = $20,000, and variable costs are $2000 per unit. The firm desires that its investment is to be paid back within 5 years. Sales are anticipated as 500 units per year. Find the price per unit.

8.22. A product is priced at three levels:

Unit price	$4	$5	$6
Projected quantity	40,000	30,000	15,000

The full variable cost is $3. For each unit price find the following:

(a) Contribution and contribution percentage.

(b) Total revenue and contribution.

(c) Which price level is preferred?

8.23. A revolutionary product has been developed. It is believed that novelty will sustain early sales, but long-range estimates have concluded that competing designs with a constant retail price of $30 will provide a floor. An initial price of $70, and a decay of 0.25 is expected. How many years will elapse until the new product intersects the competing price of $30 per unit?

8.24. A price dictated by formula (8.18) has the following information given: initial price = $10, decay = 0.25, floor price = $6, and decay = 0.15.

(a) Using these estimates, at what year will there be an intersection of the selling price with competitive floor price?

(b) At a floor price of $3.50, what is the opportunity margin? At what year will this level be reached?

(c) Discuss what your pricing policy should be after the intersection of prices.

8.25. A multinational company designs and manufactures products, both complete and semi-finished, for sale to international divisions scattered throughout the world. While specific cost estimating practices depend upon which two trading companies are dealing, consider the following: A non-U.S. firm wants to buy a product for use as a standard purchased material for its own finished product. The American international division buys the product from the manufacturing division using a variable pricing formula, or variable cost plus 35% for the firm's contribution (price = variable cost ÷ (1 − .35)). The international division adds 20% for its own overhead based upon the manufacturing division's price. This transaction is F.O.B. (*free on board* at the U.S. plant, and requires the consignee to pay all transportation costs from factory to destination). Export and import duty at the border is 0 and 20% of the *ad valorem* (invoice price at the port of shipment). Freight cost from the U.S. plant is $0.18 per unit. If the manufacturing variable cost = $1 per unit, what is the price that the importer ultimately pays? Recall that during production of this product, the importer will add labor, material, overhead, and contribution to the standard purchased material. Discuss what happens to the trade of this exported product if the rate and efficiency of production are approximately equal between these trading partners.

8.26. A multinational company is considering a "twin-plant" project where two plants are adjacent in the sense of low-cost transportation (separated by a national border, or the material is nonbulky and transportation costs both ways are negligible on a per unit basis). On the U.S. side, labor rates and productivity conform to typical standards, while in the foreign country labor rates vary from 1/10 to 3/4 as much. The U.S. plant will process the material, transport the semifinished material to the twin plant, whereupon the foreign plant adds labor value to the product, and returns the product to the U.S. plant. The U.S. manufacturing unit cost for the semiprocessed material is $1. At the border, *custom fees* amount to 5% and return custom fees are 5%, and an ad valorem of 20% of value added is assessed. In the foreign plant the labor work value is $.25 for an equivalent $1.25 per unit of U.S. work. Once back in the United States, a 35% contribution is added to give final price. Find the product price for a twin-plant and a single-plant operation. Discuss the implications of a policy that sends goods for intermediate processing to other countries. What must the labor cost of the non-U.S. labor be to make the decision indifferent between the twin plants?

8.27. Regular production is defined by $T'_a = 38,204N^{-0.152}$ dollars for 50 units.
   (a) If units 50 to 100 are expected as spare parts, find their cost.
   (b) A period of 1 year will elapse at the conclusion of the 50th unit before spare-part production is started. An increase of 10% over the 50th unit is estimated for the 51st unit. If there is no change in slope from regular production, find the cost for units 50 to 100.
   (c) Spare-parts production is expected to change to 95% at the 50th unit. Find the cost for units 50 to 100.

8.28. Determine the factors that the estimator used in Fig. 8.11 to uncover design-to-cost for the product. Future competition will probably drive price down as technology improves and more firms enter the market. What component costs do you expect for a $375 product price? Profit is computed on the basis of full cost.

CASE STUDY:
UNIJUNCTION TRANSISTOR METRONOME

Ray Enterprises has released a new design and hopes to market it through a well-established chain of catalog houses. President Art Ray says that the key to the quality of the product lies in its new electronic circuitry, given by Fig. C8.1. The bill of material is given by the parts

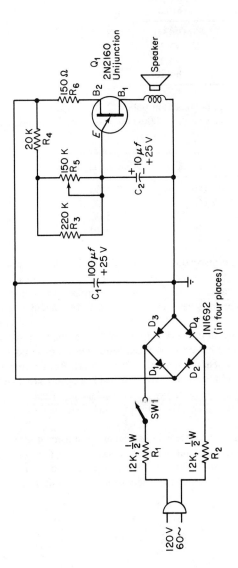

Parts List

Qty	Unit price	Extended	Remarks
2	0.12	0.24	Any
3	0.13	0.39	Any
1	1.02	1.02	Mallory U42
4	0.49	1.96	Newark
—	0.66	0.66	Cutler Hammer 7580K4
—	0.81	0.81	Cornell–Dubilier Electrolytic BR100–25
—	0.60	0.60	Cornell–Dubilier Electrolytic BR10 –25
—	1.49	1.49	Allied
—	1.85	1.85	Quam 30A05

12–KΩ, $\frac{1}{2}$ W resistors
20–KΩ, 150Ω, 220 KΩ, $\frac{1}{4}$ W resistors
150–KΩ, log taper potenticmeters
Signal diode
SPST switch
Capacitor, 25 V, 100 µf
Capacitor, 25V, 10µf
Unijunction transistor, 2N2160
Speaker, 3.2Ω, 2 W

Figure C8.1. Unijunction transistor metronome.

list, and other materials cost $1.25 per unit which covers the case, plug, and vector boards. Marketing, accounting, finance, and sales have been asked for information and the following preliminary suggested P-V is received:

Annual Volume	Potential Market Price
200,000	$95.90
210,000	93.30
235,000	90.40
260,000	89.20

New investment: $20,000 in tooling; depreciation policy, 2 years. Current tax rate: 40%. Standards for production are determined for the 2000th unit from operation estimates as follows:

	Hours per 100	Rate per Hour
Finishing	18.00	$14.60
Machine shop	7.00	15.00
Assembly	6.25	15.00
Inspection	2.80	16.20

The learning curve for finishing and inspection is estimated at 90%, while all else is 75%. Learning stops at the 2000th unit. The manufacturing burden is broken into variable and fixed with a rate of 75% and 25%. Administrative and marketing burden costs amount to 50% fixed only. Engineering development costs have amounted to $24,000. Manufacturing startup expenses will be about $15,000.

The distributor's charge for a product of this sort is usually 40% less than list price. A full-cost practice of adding 25% to all costs has been practiced before but is now used as a guide. A 20% return on appropriate investment is a minimum desired level. Ray Enterprises has used quality assurance techniques, and for products like this one has empirically determined that about 1 failure in 50 is expected. Its warranty policy is adamant: "Replace with new model if the old unit fails during the first year." The company reimburses the distributors for a new unit.

Construct a cost estimate and determine a price based on the full-cost method. Provide a cash flow statement over the next 2 years and a profit and loss statement for this product. Should this product be made and sold? In view of the preliminary marketing data on price and volume and estimating data on cost, what recommendations on price and cost can you make to President Art Ray?

9

Project Estimating

Project design is concerned with investment and is dissimilar to other designs because of the need for money appropriation. If the money is immediate expense rather than a capital cost, we are concerned with an operation design; otherwise we have a project design. A project design is for a one-of-a-kind end item. Appropriations are lumped-sum or first-cost type. The principal concern about investment evaluation is due to its long-range impact on the financial health of the firm.

Examples of project designs are numerous: plant, turbine, high-voltage transmission line, and major equipment. It is noted that these things are physical. When one considers a task-dominated design to improve paperwork flow through an office, it is recognized as a one-time design certainly, but in the absence of capital expenditures we call this an operation design. A product design is time-dependent on production of units and is of different character.

To clarify the discussion for the remainder of this chapter, it is assumed that the technical feasibility of equipment, plants, and other physical services has been determined but that the project cost estimate is not yet revealed.

Project estimators are frequently the first to recognize the need for new equipment, processes, plants, or their replacement. As the preliminary engineering plan is originated, and as a matter of good practice, the estimator contributes information to the budget defining the costs that may be required. Should the preliminary estimate call for additional planning, a detail estimate is made. If the estimate looks encouraging, the question to spend money becomes an executive-coordinated decision, particularly if the capital money is large when compared to readily available resources. Thus there is a special responsibility that rests within the project-estimating function.

Of the decisions which executive management makes, few affect the financial stability and the future earnings of the firm more than those pertaining to capital investment. These decisions commit the firm to manufacture or distribute certain products, to construct plants at certain locations, and to utilize certain materials, processes, methods, machines, or groups of machines. They establish the structure within which the organization will operate for years to come. These decisions involve thousands if not millions of dollars to any one firm. The design decision has a substantial impact on cost. Although engineering is able to influence the efficiency of the transformation of the design into the actual product or service, the approximate level of cost is nominally fixed after the plans and functional engineering concepts have been finalized. This holds true because these concepts and designs determine the limits and cost of the processes, materials, and labor that are used. Each of the various original design concepts results in a different final cost. It is important that the design concept be initially chosen in the light of the cost of the processes and the methods that it dictates and the capital investment requirements that result from these processes.

Although project designs calling for evaluation differ, the economic techniques are common despite seemingly large differences in the engineering design. Nor are there distinctions in methods for estimates ranging from several thousand dollars to several billion dollars. An equal intellectual challenge awaits the owner's or contractor's estimator. Ideas in this chapter are germane to either an owner or contractor and all sizes of projects.

9.1 PROJECT BID

The project estimator prepares an estimate which is eventually required for a bid. This preparation responds to a *request for estimate* (RFE) from management if the estimator is employed by the owner. Similarly, the *request for proposal* (RFP) is the response by the contractor's estimator to an owner, major contractor, or other business opportunity. In either case, the effort leads to a bid. Very simply, a *bid* is the cost and profit that a project requires for labor, materials, and overhead. Sometimes a bid is known as a quotation, proposal, investment, price, or even cost, as terms are used loosely in practice.

Cost elements of a project vary widely. Their selection differs between a plant, electrical transmission line, or turbine even though the design is for a single end item. One approach recognizes that these costs can be divided into fixed capital and working capital. *Fixed capital* investment is the amount of money required from concept to the finished end item. Jargon for a complete estimate of this type is known as a "grass roots" or "greenfield" estimate. But once the plant is ready to operate, working capital is required.

Net *working capital* is the difference between current assets and current liabilities. Sometimes we calculate working capital as the allowance in a capital estimate for necessary operating inventory (raw, in-process, and finished materials), cash, and net receivables. Working capital requires immediate cash outlays that are not realized until the sales revenue is generated. Thus *timing* is involved. The following should be tabulated and totaled to obtain total working capital: changes in current payables and accounts receivable, change in inventory of raw materials and supplies, changes in cash-on-hand balances, and changes in current liabilities and nondepreciable items. Increases in working cash are required to support the operations resulting from the investment. A higher requirement exists during periods of expansion, and a lower requirement exists during contracting periods. Working capital is important because of the time delay in its recovery. At the termination date of the project, a credit for working capital is estimated to offset, although not equally, the initial requirements for working capital at the start of the project. But classifying project cost into fixed and working capital diminishes the complexity of a project estimate. Instead, we symbolically define project cost as given by the layers of Fig. 9.1. Not all the layers may be required. It depends on the design.

Operation and product estimates may be available as information in the preparation of a project estimate. In operation estimating the emphasis is upon man-hours and man-days, which were defined as standard, and are estimated for tasks. These were explained for a unit quantity method. The reader may refer to Sec. 7.3.3 for additional information. Chapter 8 dealt with methods of estimating product designs. A project design could be a turbine which has thousands of turbine blades. These blades could be estimated using principles of product estimating. The project estimator in gathering cost facts may estimate the man-days for an operation or the price for product; or these may be provided as a consequence of a RFP.

Direct labor is work associated with the materials required for an engineering project design. Alternatively, we can define labor as the initial or ongoing labor required for plant operation. This second definition is for working-capital or operating requirements of a plant once it had been constructed. The work of pouring concrete footings for a turbine base is direct, while indirect labor would be the

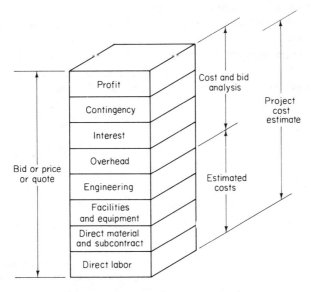

Figure 9.1 Components of project cost estimate.

guards or clerks on duty. Turbine operation and turbine maintenance would require direct and indirect labor.

Initially the direct labor is expressed in time units, man-hours, man-months, or years. An individual or crew wage multiplies the units of time, leading to direct cost. Previous chapters have dealt with this computation. If these costs are identified as "allowed," or "standard," an adjustment by productivity becomes necessary. The productivity factor adjusts allowed time to actual time. The productivity factor varies with time of season, location, worker experience, and so on. See Problem 9.1 for an example.

Direct materials are subdivided into raw, standard commercial items, and subcontract items. They appear in the end item. The amounts must be increased for losses stemming from waste, scrap, and shrinkage. Indirect materials are supplies, lubricants, and small tools, for example, necessary for the construction of direct materials. Standard commercial materials are hardware or items generally selected from designers' catalogs or materials having common specification and design. These materials are broadly available. Subcontract materials are custom designed, and a RFQ instructs an offeror to submit a bid to the project estimator.

Depending on the particular plant process, raw materials can constitute a major portion of operating costs. A list is developed from the process flowsheet. Information obtained for each raw material would include units of purchase, unit cost, sources of supply, quantity required per unit time and unit of output of product, and quality (concentration, acceptable in purity level, etc.) of raw material. Naturally, the quantity is increased for waste and yield. Fuels involved in the process or catalysts and other processing material are raw materials. The initial fill of fuels and catalysts is a part of the capital cost, while refill materials at the conclusion of the first year is ongoing direct material. Process by-products, including wastes and pollutants, must be considered for the operating cost estimate of direct materials. Every input and output stream must be considered in the operating cost estimate. These costs may be credits (for salable or usable by-products) or debits (for wastes or unsalable by-products).

Consider a simple flowsheet for processing raw milk. A dairy is designed to convert raw milk into 2% milk and 40% cream. The percentages refer to fat content.

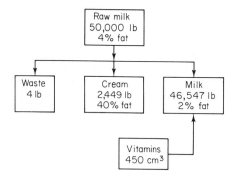

Figure 9.2. Simple flowchart for converting raw milk to 2% vitamin fortified milk.

A flowchart is shown by Fig. 9.2. Input materials are raw milk and vitamins. A charge of $0.50 per pound is required for this milk plant to dispose of its cream to a butter plant. Vitamins are added to the 2% milk. There is 98% yield, or 2% shrinkage, for three items. A 4-pound waste is a sludge removed to a landfill dump. This raw milk problem is not a joint cost problem, as discussed in Chapter 3, because there is only one marketable product. Cream is a result of the process, but this plant has no equipment to process or market its cream. As it is not feasible to drain the cream, $0.50 per pound is a charge for tanker truck removal to a butter plant. A tanker truck supplies 50,000 pounds of raw milk daily to the dairy.

Material	Cost per Unit	Quantity	Cost
Raw milk	$32/100 lb	50,000 lb	$16,000
Vitamins	$20/450 cm^3	450 cm^3	20
Processed cream	$0.50/lb	2449 lb	1,225
			$17,245

The output cost of 46,547 pounds is $0.37 per pound, or about $3.19 per gallon if 1 gallon = 8.61 pounds. This considers the cost on the output amount.

In addition to operating materials, an expanded flowsheet could provide a listing of the equipment. This raw milk processing is handled by equipment that must be estimated. If this equipment is standard, a quotation can be obtained, or it may be conceivable that the process is novel and that special equipment must be designed and manufactured.

Facilities and equipment cost is a term that can be broadly defined. For a uranium-ore-processing plant, the pieces of capital equipment, such as conveyors, tanks, and rod mills, are examples. A high-voltage transmission line may require a field office or facilities. Equipment for the construction of the transmission line may be used for other lines. In this case, equipment is an overhead charge. Indirect materials and labor are other charges that are conveniently handled by overhead.

Engineering costs are the costs incurred for design, drawings, specifications, or reports. Included are the salaries and overhead for engineering administration, drafting, reproductions, and cost engineering. This was discussed in Sec. 8.2.1, and differences for project design are minor. These overhead and engineering costs are also called "development."

Contingency costs are for those situations having no prior experience or data. Projects requiring extraordinary research, development, and design are the best candidates for contingency. Unfortunately, contingency is sometimes a cover-up for poor estimating practices.

Because projects are a large financial undertaking, interest charges are usually charged against the contractor or owner during construction progress. These interest charges can be substantial and are a part of doing business. The layers of Fig. 9.1 from direct labor to interest are the elements of a project cost estimate. Profit is calculated on these items. The sum of cost and profit constitutes a bid. The remainder of this chapter uses these terms and definitions.

9.2 WORK PACKAGE

Steps for project estimating are given by Fig. 9.3. A precise sequence is not intended. The likely way is a simultaneous maneuver, but a project estimator develops this style only after experience.

The proposal plan gives the technical statement, preliminary designs, and preliminary estimate. An encouraging plan will lead to additional effort. This results in the RFE/P, which initiates the work. Bills of material and designs are the principal technical information for cost-estimating products. A project, however, may have significant nonhardware costs. The project design, by itself, is insufficient for estimating. Other necessary information is consolidated with the project designs. The collected project information is called a *work package*. Forms included within a work package are the definition, designs, work breakdown structure, schedule, and estimates. If the project is large, the amount of information in a work package is extensive. Even small projects require a thick notebook.

The *definition* gives a workable scheme to achieve the end item. The design engineer is concerned with a design that will satisfy the specifications at least cost. The results of this effort become the definition that translates performance objectives

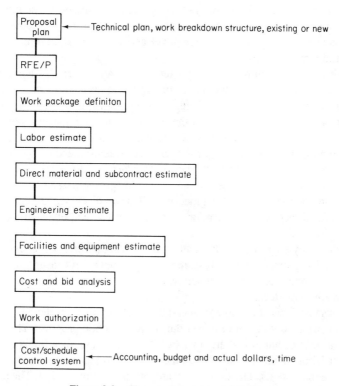

Figure 9.3.   Flow chart for integrated project.

into a project design. A project engineer will take an overall project definition and assign items of the work breakdown structure to cognizant engineers of the proposal team. A "definition" is a *planning form* which identifies what is to be done, when, and by whom it is to be done. There is a numbering system which relates the definition to other forms and shows a baseline initiation date. For the remainder of this chapter we assume that the definition phase has been completed, but that the cost estimate remains.

Data collection for the definition can follow one of two approaches. It is possible to gather data for a specific estimate as the estimate is unfolding. This may be accomplished by contacting vendors for quotations for each part of the estimate, and the data are recollected for each job. A second way is to identify, collect, analyze, and divulge data that are more-or-less permanent, and while adjusted for technology and price changes, once they have been initially collected they are standard. Indexes change but the base standard information remains consistent. Standard information is then used over and over again.

The definition subdivides the end item into large-scale tasks and eventually operations for physical items. For example, a reinforced concrete wall may be a one task, or it may be divided into erect outside forms, tie reinforcing steel, erect inside forms and bulkheads, pour concrete, remove forms, and clean. The latter items are called *operations* and were estimated by methods described in Sec. 7.3.3.

The work breakdown structure (WBS) is a graphical display. It results from reduction of an end item into logical components. These components can be arranged into a treelike figure to allow visibility and analysis of a single component or they can be grouped into larger tasks or the end item itself. The WBS is used for estimating, planning, and performance measurement and control. In some cases they link accounting charges to the design via WBS. Further, it can be arranged to show manpower. The WBS is widely accepted by contractors and U.S. Department of Defense.

Subdivision of a large complex end item into smaller, less complex, and more manageable tasks is not new. This has been basic to production for a century or more. The work breakdown structure is composed of hardware, software, services, and other work tasks. "Levels" are used to specify the WBS. Level 1 is the entire project. Level 2 elements are the major elements, such as "Land." A contract WBS is the complete WBS for a contract developed and used by the contractors. It may contain three or more levels as found necessary. Five levels are usually considered adequate. Figure 9.4 is a example of a six-level WBS. Each lower level adds another digit, and 1321 is a fourth-level minor cost item of major hardware. The numbering of the WBS corresponds to the definition and the estimates. The definition is the source of the original WBS number system. Finally, the WBS can be closely identified with *cost codes* initially described in Chapter 3. However, cost codes are hardware oriented while WBS deals with nonhardware costs as well.

After the project summary WBS is formulated and numbered, individual contract WBSs are used for procurement actions for vendors. The vendor may extend the WBS to lower levels as the basis of an RFP. When attached to the project

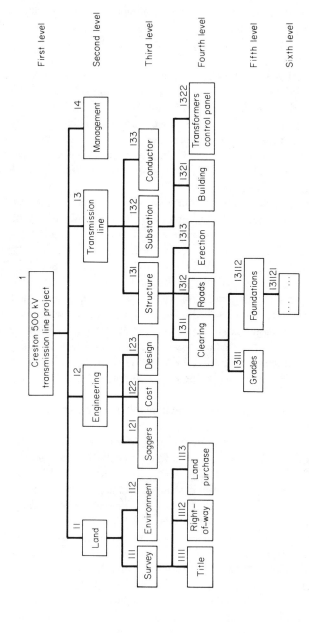

Figure 9.4. Work breakdown structure (WBS) of a project to the sixth level.

summary WBS, the project WBS is formed. The project summary WBS and its derivatives are used throughout contract definitions, construction, design, and operation for technical and management activities. Reporting of progress, performance, and financial data are often times based on the project WBS. In some instances it is possible to have specifications and drawings conform to the numbered WBS.

Schedules are an important part of the work package. While the definition is the planning document and says what must be done, scheduling determines the calendar dates for the start and conclusion of the WBS activity. Details of scheduling like CPM (critical path method), PERT (program review and evaluation technique), or other network methods are considerable and we refer the reader to the many excellent texts available for that. Instead, refer to Fig. 9.5 which symbolically shows

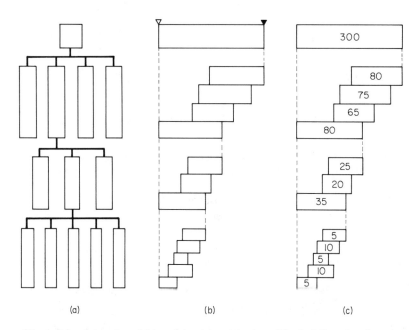

(a)   (b)   (c)

Figure 9.5.   Integration of (a) work breakdown structure, (b) scheduling of work, and (c) estimating tasks.

the integration of the WBS, schedule, and costs. The fourth level of the WBS is estimated at $5, $10, $5, $10, and $5 for each task. The third-level summary is $35. Two other third-level tasks are estimated at $20 and $25 for a second-level summary of $80. The first-level summary is $300. In sketch (b), open and darkened triangles indicate the start and conclusion of the major task. Each task can be similarly scheduled. The length of the bar is an indication of its time requirement, not its cost.

If we add period designation to the horizontal axis, we can match the costs for levels of the WBS as shown by Fig. 9.6. In sketch (a), the $150 bid is broken

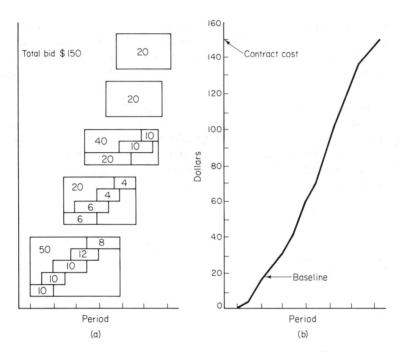

Figure 9.6. Definition leading from (a) estimated tasks to (b) scheduled cash flow called the baseline.

down for the WBS. In turn, sketch (b) shows the *baseline* defined as the time-scheduled out-of-pocket cash flow for the estimate. If the estimator works for the owner, this will represent the owner's cash flow. Similarly, it may represent the estimated cash flow for a sub or major contractor. The contract cost of $150 is noted. The baseline is similar to an ogive curve. It is useful for estimate assurance and cost control.

Commitments for a project vary with the type of material. Notice Fig. 9.7 where the axes are period and dollars per period. *E* indicates the moment of the estimate, *M* is the elapsed time for construction, fabrication, assembly, or test, while *D* is the moment of delivery or startup of operation. Open and darkened triangles are the starting and ending *milestones*. It is worth noting that the division of material into four types depends on the project. Seldom will any two projects have the same mix of materials.

In sketch (a), facilities and equipment are committed earliest after the point of the estimate. In this example, facilities and equipment make up 20% of the value committed. The long-lead-time components and subcontract materials, as in (b), are committed next, and they account for 30%. In (c) and (d) the standard commercial materials and raw material and stock items are committed successively. Using addition of areas, the actual area is summed for all four types in sketch (e). An approximate triangle is shown with the peak at midpoint. The data for these commitments are determined from the Work Package.

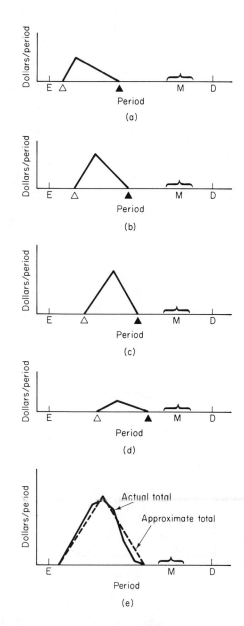

Figure 9.7. Purchase commitment for a project: (a) facilities and equipment, 20%; (b) long-lead-time materials, 30%; (c) standard commercial materials, 40%; (d) raw materials and stock items, 10%. (e) Sum of the actual areas.

Commitment dates are not the same as delivery or payment dates. The commitment date allows a time lag for a subcontractor for delivery and payment. Scheduling of expenditure differs from scheduling commitment. A reverse order is sometimes necessary when time-staging expenditures to commitments. Notice Fig. 9.8, where expenditures of those items previously committed are now examined. The factors that impact scheduling of expenditure for a major program are initial funding,

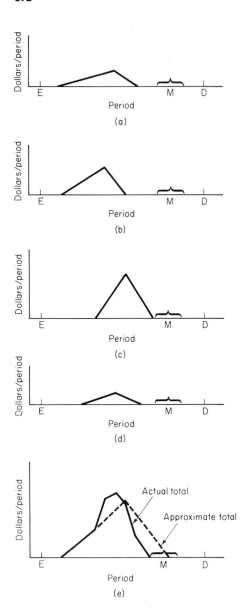

Figure 9.8. Expenditure scheduling for a project: (a) facilities and equipment, 20%; (b) long-lead-time materials, 30%; (c) standard commercial materials; 40%; (c) raw materials and stock items, 10%. (e) Sum of the actual areas.

progress payments, type of contract, and billing practices (such as 2% discount if paid within 30 days). Obviously, expenditures are discrete and lump sum, yet a continuous line and area is assumed. For major projects this smoothing assumption is acceptable but for smaller projects discrete payments cannot be ignored.

The order for expenditure scheduling implies several ideas. For purchase commitments, the center of gravity of the area of the cash flow triangles is before the midpoint of the time span. For expenditure scheduling, the center of gravity is after the midpoint of the period axis. Also, raw material will be required to allow construction or production an earlier start. Standard commercial materials and long-lead-time components will be required. They should be stocked and the accounts paid as work-in-progress. Payments on long-lead-time items often start early due to required progress payments. Payments for minor raw materials may be on a letter contract or a voucher system. Thus scheduling of expenditure relates to the commitment, yet it has different time staging and a cash flow triangular shape.

An isosceles triangle is used to approximate the actual total area where the midpoint of the isosceles triangle is halfway between the initial and final expenditure milestone. The approximation allows simpler and earlier estimating of the points or periods of expenditure. If commitments and expenditures can be estimated and scheduled, management is able to measure performance against project goals. These ideas are extended in Chapter 11 dealing with cost/schedule control. But the isosceles triangle can be divided into periods and the percentage determined for each period. Selection of the isosceles shape and midpoint is arbitrary. The period length is longer than the actual project length and ending points are chosen based upon policies of self-funding by the contractor and subcontractor.

Consider Fig. 9.9 which shows the approximating isosceles triangles for commitment and expenditure. The y-axis is designated dollars per period. The numbered x-axis is labeled "period" with the origin E set equal to zero. The numbered period axis implies fiscal half-years, but other calendar periods are also suitable. Some organizations define a scheduling month as four weeks (or 160 hours) and an estimating year as 13 months to avoid the problem of short and long months. A half-year or quarter period does not proportionately have these scheduling-period differences.

Observe Fig. 9.9, where the commitment triangle is five periods long and is divided into fiscal half-year percentages using geometry. Similarly, the expenditure

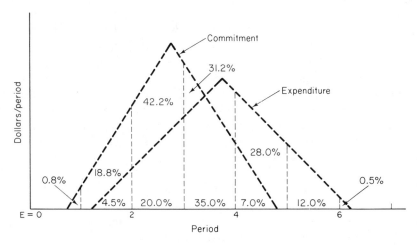

Figure 9.9. Matching commitment and expenditure to period.

triangle is six periods long and its amount can be synchronized to the fiscal half-year percentages. These half-year percentages shown on the figure are repeated in the following table:

Fiscal Half-Year	Percent Commit-ment	Percent Expen-diture	Contractor Dollar Commitment	Owner Dollar Expenditure
0	0.8	—	$ 94,000	—
1	18.8	4.5	2,209,000	$ 528,750
2	42.2	20.0	4,958,500	2,350,000
3	31.2	35.0	3,666,000	4,112,500
4	7.0	28.0	822,500	3,290,000
5	—	12.0	—	1,410,000
6	—	0.5	—	58,750
			$11,750,000	$11,750,000

Total project funds can be distributed using these percentages. If the project is estimated as $11,750,000, the committed and expenditure dollars for each half-year are given by the product of the percentage and the total project funds. With these ideas and continuity of periods, it is straightforward to find monthly commitment and expenditure percentage and dollar amount.

Approximating curves to the actual commitment and expenditure curves other than the isosceles triangle can be used. Rectangular, trapezoidal, and bell shapes are possible.

If the committed or expenditure dollars as found in the previous table are progressively accumulated for the periods and a smooth line drawn through the points, an ogive curve results. This is shown in Fig. 9.10. A third line, available funds, is included. Available funds represent the money received periodically from the owner and used by the major contractor to pay subcontractors or themselves. The funds available line is herky-jerky as shown in this figure because discrete payments are received. These three lines are important in financing a project. At the midpoint commitments lead available funding dollars, and if the graph had divisions this lead time could be measured. Expenditures lead available funds by so many periods, although less than committed. Current liabilities represent the difference between the expenditure and available funds line. One can define current liabilities for material as total dollars that must be assumed if the contract were terminated. Unliquidated commitments comprise the unpaid balance between commitments and expenditures. These three lines are used in cost/schedule control. Now we turn to cost scheduling of direct labor.

The discussion so far in cost scheduling has been with materials, but many of these ideas are effective with direct labor. There are several ways to spread direct labor cost. The distinction is whether or not the work package has been concluded.

The labor estimate is used for spreading direct labor cost. Recall that the labor estimate provides entry opportunity for labor craft, period and year, total hours,

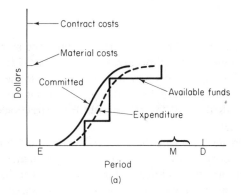

Period

(a)

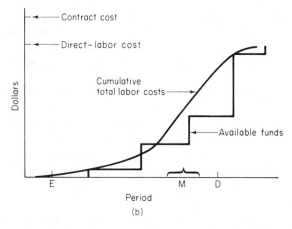

Period

(b)

Figure 9.10. Collection of many cost estimates to form (a) smooth committed, expenditure curve and available funds and (b) labor costs and funds available.

average hourly rate, and total dollars. The labor hours are also totaled for the period. For any modest or major project, these data from the labor estimate are already spread. This kind of spreading is acceptable and can be done either in hours or dollars. Hours are more useful for work planning, while dollars are necessary for financial planning and control. Hours are not subject to escalation because of inflation effects although dollars are. The labor estimate integrates the elements of the estimate, learning theory if it exists, schedule, and proper lead times to accomplish the tasks in their order. After summing the labor estimates for various periods, Fig. 9.10(b) an ogive curve can be drawn. During the construction, assembly, and test phase, the curve is steeper, indicating more manpower.

Estimates are another major part of the work package. They are done concurrently with the work package development and are the most important documents relating to the project bid.

9.3 ESTIMATING

A project estimate is composed of labor, direct material and subcontract, facilities and equipment, and engineering. Procedures vary because of application or dollar amount. The larger-valued projects may have addendums to these forms. Distinctions exist between construction, either building, road, plant, and so on. An owner or contractor has needs that call for variety. But for instructional purposes, these four forms are sufficient.

The labor estimate deals with the bidder's labor or work force. This assumes that labor will be direct hire for the duration of the project rather than a subcontract arrangement. Direct-hire labor is hired and paid on a per hour basis to the worker. Consequently, the form may involve effective gross hour wages, payroll overhead, and productivity. In those situations where union labor is used, the term "off the bench" implies that the hiring is though a union-controlled hiring office, and that the labor is waiting for a "call." Where union labor is not used, the firm will conduct its own hiring. Whether the labor is union or nonunion, the company pays the workers directly. Subcontract labor works for a subcontractor and his costs are estimated and quoted on a fixed-unit price or lump sum, often including material costs.

An abbreviated labor estimate is shown by Table 9.1. The labor estimate is cross-referenced to the WBS and the definition. Various information can be posted such as start date, duration, conclusion and labor types, hours, and their wages. Some forms will include a check-off that indicates how hours were estimated (i.e., opinion, comparison, standards, cost estimating relationship, etc.). The project estimator determines if the work is recurring or nonrecurring. Recurring work for project estimating is cyclic; that is, it is done and estimated with repetition in mind, such as the erection of transmission towers.

The estimated time may be adjusted for productivity. The same job may require more time in Alaska than Texas because of weather conditions. While a standard for a job is consistent, effects of location, crew skill, native or green, and so on, are factors that the estimator weighs in his or her opinion. Productivity for the bidder's and subcontractor's work force can vary, and some experience suggests that

Table 9.1. LABOR ESTIMATE

Project High-voltage transmission line

WBS	Description	Total hours	Periods 3	4	5	6	Gross wage	Cost
1311	Clearing	4,000	4,000				$30	$120,000
1312	Roads	8,000		4,000	4,000		35	280,000
1313	Tower erection	55,743	8,862	22,297	16,723	7,861	40	2,229,720
1321	Substation building	24.285		5,000	15,000	4285	35	850,000
								$3,479,720

subcontractors have a more favorable productivity. Chemical plant construction estimates consider the U.S. Gulf Coast as a standard location. The preferred approach is to estimate separately the allowed man-hours (or man-days) and their productivity, rather than posting a lump sum which is the product of the two quantities. These features are a part of the usual labor estimate, but are not demonstrated by Table 9.1.

The direct material and subcontract estimate requires similar title-block information as the labor estimate. It is cross-identified to the WBS and labor estimate. There is a difference between direct material and subcontract. Direct materials end up in the project design and are usually installed by the bidder's work force. These include bulk materials or structural steel, piping, concrete, wiring, and so on. We have consistently referred to these materials as raw or standard commercial materials. These direct materials do *not* include the contractor's work force in their cost.

On the other hand, the WBS and the definition may indicate that a subcontractor will be hired. Subcontract materials are specially designed or standard commercial materials. Especially important is the notion that subcontract materials use subcontractor labor, and this dual nature makes it different from direct materials which uses the contractor's work force. A subcontract may include both the material and subcontractor's labor. A basic quantity of the item is posted. Additions for scrap, waste, shrinkage, and spares can be included for direct material. The subcontract materials may be item-estimated or handled as a lump sum.

The source of the direct material estimate may be opinion, comparison, takeoff for shape and rate, statistical relationship, and so on. The information for a subcontract may be similar, but additionally a quotation may be available. Selection of the subcontractor may be based on low bidder, technical competence, or best delivery schedule. Table 9.2 is an abbreviated example of the direct material and subcontract estimate.

Table 9.2.   DIRECT MATERIAL AND SUBCONTRACT ESTIMATE

Project *High-voltage transmission line*

WBS	Description	Direct material or subcontract	Periods 2	3	4	5	Cost
1312	Road	Direct material	15,000				$15,000
1313	Tower	Direct material	1,000,000	940,625			1,940,625
1321	Substation building	Direct material			90,000	90,000	180,000
1322	Substation transformers, control	Subcontract		200,000	150,000	50,000	400,000
133	Conductor	Subcontract		195,000	195,000	195,000	785,000
							$3,215,625

Facilities and equipment are also direct materials but of a different character. This category is delivered and erected equipment, such as large storage tanks or field-fabricated vessels involving both material and labor as a single lump sum. These items are specified in detail and are custom manufactured for the project. These items may be produced and estimated like a product. They are made in shops by vendors who specialize in this equipment. Sensitive to demand, these job-shop manufacturers adjust prices to accommodate demand. Price fluctuations can be expected in these costs, especially for external suppliers.

It is also necessary to estimate any raw or bulk materials which may be necessary with the facilities and equipment. For example, an electric transmission tower will require concrete foundations. Will the foundations be estimated with the transmission towers? Usually not, and a cost connection must be made between the WBS, definition, and the estimate. The concrete foundations are estimated as direct material using the contractor's work force.

Because facilities and equipment are custom designed, a quote becomes necessary; but often a predesign estimate is made. Thus the source for these data can be external to the estimating team or may be based on internal information.

Facilities and equipment estimates can include land and building and processing equipment. Equipment supporting a subcontractor in his work is included in the subcontractor's quotation. Rental charges for construction support equipment can be included in the labor estimate but usually are included in project overhead. Table 9.3 is an abbreviated example of a facilities and equipment estimate.

Table 9.3.   FACILITIES AND EQUIPMENT ESTIMATE

Project High-voltage transmission line

WBS	Description	Type	Period 1	2	3	4	5	6	Cost
111	Land, Survey	Facility	75,000	11,575					$86,575
112	Environment	Facility		6,425					6,425
1321	Substation building	Facility						50,000	50,000
1322	Substation transformer	Equipment				400,000	400,000		800,000
									$943,000

Engineering estimates have been previously discussed in Chapter 8. These costs are significant for a project design and their separate consideration points to this importance. Table 9.4 is an example of an engineering estimate for project designs. Productivity can vary and should be forecast. Overtime, job size, and specific working conditions can affect productivity.

These estimating procedures have similar advantages. The uniformity encourages consistency for estimate assurance. The source of information, auditing, a

Table 9.4.   Engineering Estimate

Project High-voltage transmission line

WBS	Description	Hours	Hourly rate	Applied overhead	Period 1	2	3	Total cost
12	Engineering	750	$44.61	25%	35,000	5,000	1,875	$41,875
121	Saggers	150						
122	Cost	80						
123	Design	520						

standardized communication format, cross-reference, and the central WBS management document make these estimating methods of value throughout the project.

9.4 COST AND BID ANALYSIS

The four kinds of estimates provide the factual basis for cost and bidding analysis. If the estimates are poorly done, no amount of superficial analysis will improve the estimates. But we separate the task of estimating from its later analysis. It is important that the bid be in line competitively as well as compatible to the firm's ability.

More information becomes available to the estimator during the estimating and analysis period. Tips may be found in the local newspapers, budget disclosure, or the owner or major contractor may even indicate boundaries for the bid. Rebidding may occur in large projects, and first bids are known. By law, past winning bids are open knowledge for public works. Business magazines and trade newspapers publish information regularly. Even rumors are sought. It is in this environment that cost and bidding analysis is conducted.

Competitive bidding is usual for projects. In the simplest case, the offeror will announce a deadline date for the bid and sealed envelopes containing the bid and other information are opened and the winner announced. In technical projects the bidder will provide a design along with the bid. Evaluation may take a long time before the winner is selected. When formal advertising and competitive bidding are impractical, a bargaining process begins between the parties, each having its viewpoint and objective. This is termed *negotiation*. Cost and bidding analysis may be done differently for each of these situations. The estimating procedures should be identical, however. Eventually, the bid is "laid on the table," so to speak, and its acceptance or denial depends on many factors.

The bid is the sum of the estimates, overhead, contingency, interest, and profit. As a *pro forma* document, it is the center of much interest. If the project estimate is a public document subject to audit by an owner, major contractor, or the government, and this depends on the contract, analysis may be done by a contracting officer, negotiator, or estimator on an "arm's-lengths" basis (i.e., each side having a competitive and self-serving interest). The audit may be from several vantage points—engineering, accounting, purchasing, and estimating. Thus the cost and bidding analysis must satisfy many objectives.

9.4.1 Overhead

Overhead costs were discussed in Sec. 4.9, which pertained to operation and product overhead. Many of those principles apply to projects. Overhead for projects is of two types, office and job. These charges are exclusive of direct labor, direct and subcontract materials, and facilities and equipment. Items appearing in overhead must not be included in these estimates. However, for practical reasons, some minor costs that could be treated as direct are classified and handled as overhead.

Office overhead includes general business expenses, such as home office rent, office insurance, heat, light, supplies, furniture, telephone, legal expenses, donations, travel, advertising, bidding expenses, and salaries of the executives and office employees. These charges are incurred for the benefit of the owner's or contractor's overall business. In office overhead, the final cost objective is multiple (i.e., several projects). They cannot be isolated as specific estimating amounts. While variety is possible in the calculation, one approach would use

$$R_o = \frac{C_o}{C_p} \times 100 \qquad (9.1)$$

where R_o = office overhead rate on basis of direct costs, percentage

C_o = overhead charges summed for office activity of contractor, dollars

C_p = cost of direct labor and direct and subcontract materials, dollars

A company has had an annual value of direct cost of construction as $60,000,000 and a general office overhead of $2,400,000. $R_o = 4\%$, which is applied against those estimated future costs, provided that it is felt that the future will be similar to these past historical costs. While the rate would be guided by historical patterns, it is necessary that these computations be for future periods, specifically budgeted for the duration of the project. It is necessary that both the base and the overhead charges be forecast and computed for identical periods.

Job overhead pertains to the project. If a firm has only one field project in mind, a consolidation of office and job overhead is a convenience. On the other hand, improved accuracy and other advantages become apparent if separate job overheads are found for one or all projects. Job expenses are those costs incurred which do not become an integral part of the construction. They are directly chargeable to the contract and must be separated in the accounting journals from overhead expenses, which are general. Typical items of job overhead are listed below. Each project will require a special analysis to determine its own items.

Permits and fees	Insurance
Performance bonds	Electricity at job location

Job office expense	Water at job location
Office salaries	Barricades
Cost clerk	Badges
Timekeeper	Survey
Supplies	
Telephone	Parking areas
Working foremen	First aid
Depreciation	Storage and protection

These overhead charges do not include mandatory contributions for direct labor such as FICA, workman's compensation insurance, or unemployment insurance, or any of the union contract contributions. Employee related costs are included in the gross hourly cost of direct labor, for example Table 2.12.

$$R_j = \frac{C_j}{C_p} \times 100 \qquad (9.2)$$

where R_j = job overhead rate on basis of direct cost, percentage

C_j = overhead charges summed for project, dollars

C_p = cost of direct labor and subcontract

materials for project, dollars

As a rule of thumb, if the base is increasing, the overhead rate should be decreasing. Conversely, if the base is decreasing, the overhead rate generally will be increasing. These short-term fluctuations depend on cost control and estimate assurance. Comparison of rates between projects may make no sense, remembering that the rate is a ratio of two cost sums. A low rate may indicate a project involving manual labor. As a result the direct labor base is high. The overhead account is less because it includes little or no charges for depreciation or rental of equipment.

The overhead is applied to the project using

$$C_{op} = C_p'(R_o + R_j) \qquad (9.3)$$

where C_{op} = overhead charged to future project, dollars

C_p' = cost of future direct labor and direct and subcontract

materials estimated for forthcoming project

This value is posted to the estimate summary.

9.4.2 Contingency

Contingency is another cost element. Sometimes this element is called "management reserve" and uncertainties in developmental projects are included by this self-insurance. Especially in the early stages of a project where technology detail and its cost are absent, contingency estimating is preferred to careless estimating or unjustified padding of cost elements. Contingency cost estimating is practiced for projects albeit by various techniques.

As the project design matures and as more information becomes available, the contingency estimate becomes less in absolute value and percentage of the total proposal value. In large-scale project cost planning, contingency amounts are more important during early estimating. Eventually a detail estimate is determined using a work breakdown structure. Thus contingency dollars follow the rule: more information and less contingency. In high-risk high-dollar projects, contingency is usually present and can appear as a line item in the bid. As the project spends money for materials, direct labor, subcontracts, and so on, the dollars of budgeted contingency are available for the payment of unexpected problems that arise.

Two methods of assessing contingency are considered. The first recognizes the importance of experience and opinion, while the second treats it analytically.

In discussing an *informal* method of assessing contingency, we assume that dollar amounts for the major WBS levels are already estimated. Using opinion the cost engineer estimates an additional dollar amount for major elements. For instance, laser glass is risky development and prudent evaluation would determine an incremental cost for possible overrun. This increment is contingency.

Contingency analysis can also be associated with the estimating of the major elements, as is shown by a second method. It is an extension of range estimating discussed in Sec. 6.7.3. Note Fig. 9.11 for the steps.

Contingency cost estimating begins with estimating a lowest value (L), most likely value (M), and the highest cost value (H) of the cost elements of the WBS. The most likely value is the modal or most common value that would be repeated in an unlikely repetition of this cost element. Similarly, the lowest and highest cost values are not to be exceeded either downward or upward with a probability of 1/20. Seldom, if ever, are these instructions exactly executed, but three values are necessary to allow the use of the beta probability distribution. The form of this general distribution has properties that make for simple calculation, which is important for early estimates of the project. It is unnecessary to specify the probability distribution of the individual cost elements, which is fortunate, since their behavior is nonnormal and unknown. After many elements are added, according to central limit theory and practice, the resulting distribution is normal and can be manipulated using conventional probability rules.

The three values for each major cost element are estimated at today's costs even though it is future expenditure that is desired. If information is available, it is often at current value; further, in conference and round-table estimating, current values are easier to estimate intuitively than future values.

Now assume that the expected cost of Table 6.1 $E(C_t) = \$10,600$, and its variance var $(C_t) = 22,300$ dollars^2 are to be analyzed for contingency. Recall Eq. 6.30:

$$Z = \frac{UL - E(C_T)}{[\text{var}(C_T)]^{1/2}} \tag{9.4}$$

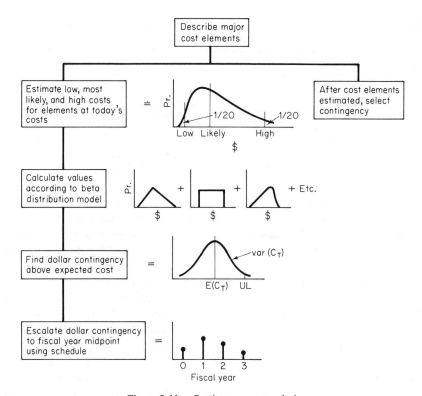

Figure 9.11.   Contingency cost analysis.

where Z = standard normal variable

   UL = upper limit cost, arbitrarily selected, dollars

$E(C_T)$ = expected cost of range estimating model, dollars

var(C_T) = expected variance of range estimating model, dollars^2

The square root of the variance is called the standard deviation. $E(C_T)$ and var(C_T) were calculated using Eq. 6.23 and 6.29.

Values of UL are selected by the project estimator and cover the potential range of over- or underrun cost of the project. The range of these values depends on the risk of the project. With several values picked, Table 9.5 is completed using Eq. 9.4 and Appendix I, standard normal distribution tables. The Appendix provides probabilities as measured from the reference $Z = 0.00$. Overrun and underrun are defined with respect to this reference. At this symmetrical location, 50% of the probability is above and below $Z = 0.00$. For example, if $Z = 1.00$, the table reads 0.3413, which is the area or probability from $Z = 0.00$ to 1.00. If we want $P(Z \geq 1.00)$, an upper tail area is given by $0.5 - 0.3416 \geq 0.16$. If we are interested in the probability that cost exceeds \$10,300, we would have

$$Z = \frac{10,300 - 10,600}{(22,300)^{1/2}} = -2.00$$

Table 9.5. CALCULATION OF PROBABILITY GIVEN THAT A COST UPPER LIMIT EXCEEDS A MEAN VALUE

UL	Z	P(cost ≥ UL)	UL	Z	P(cost ≥ UL)
$10,300	−2.00	0.98	$10,750	.99	0.16
10,400	−1.35	0.91	10,800	1.32	0.09
10,500	−0.68	0.75	10,850	1.66	0.05
10,600	0	0.50	10,900	2.00	0.02
10,650	0.32	0.37	10,950	2.33	0.01
10,700	0.66	0.25	11,000	2.67	0.004

As we are interested in $P(\text{cost} \geq 10{,}300)$, the Appendix would be used as 0.5 + 0.4772 ≐ 0.98, which is observed as the first entry in Table 9.5.

Observe Fig. 9.12, which gives the probability of exceeding the expected project cost. Note that the expected value, $10,600, gives a 50% probability. The probability that cost will assume values less than $10,600 is greater than 50% naturally. From this analysis the estimator gains an opinion for the risk with this curve. Several contingent maximum costs are considered, keeping in mind the uncertainty, design, technology, and construction conditions. Eventually, one upper limit cost is selected as the *contingent maximum cost*. This selection is made with management approval. For example, suppose that management selects $10,700 as this value, which will be exceeded with a 25% probability. The next step is to schedule the increment of contingency of $100 ($= 10{,}700 - 10{,}600$) over the project periods. The contingent maximum is at current cost. If inflation or deflation is suspected, this value is adjusted via indexes relating to the project. Indexes such as those provided by Table 5.6, which assumes declining costs due to active technology, are now used. Additionally, expenditure scheduling given in percent terms is known. This information is shown as Table 9.6. The scheduled contingent amount for period 2 is 23.5 ($= 100 \times 0.25 \times 0.941$).

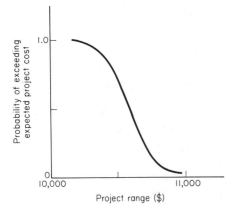

Figure 9.12. Risk graph of contingency.

Table 9.6.   SCHEDULING CONTINGENCY AMOUNT OF $100 FOR PERCENT EXPENDITURE
AND INDEXES

	Period				Total
	1	2	3	4	
Expenditure (%)	15	25	40	20	100%
Period cash flow ($)	15	25	40	20	$100
Index	1.000	0.941	0.891	0.876	
Contingent cash flow ($)	15	23.5	35.6	17.5	91.6

The total of $91.60 is posted to the project summary as a line item for contingency. Similarly, the $10,600 is entered as the project estimate amount. Note that contingency is shown for the total project rather than single cost elements. Even though it is element variability that gives project contingency, it is as likely that other cost elements may be overlooked and this contingent amount becomes available for unspecified requirements. Opinion and technical experience are inescapable in estimating contingency amounts. On the other hand, algebraic refinements such as those presented do not substitute for effective methods in project estimating. Unfortunately, in practice, contingency is a device that replaces qualified cost estimating methods.

Depending on the contract type, if unjustified contingency is added to the cost, the bid becomes noncompetitive. In some cases, should a surplus of contingent dollars be available at the conclusion of the project, they are returned to the owner—according to provisions of the contract.

9.4.3 Interest

Projects may involve periodic payments between the owner and contractor, or between the contractor and subcontractors. These payments are known as partial or *progress payments* and reimburse for work. Often the owner will hold back an amount and not immediately pay for work concluded. This amount is called *retainage*. The contract may require that retainage be placed in an escrow account with a bank, thus assuring the contractor of its availability. An escrow account removes any unfair advantage and the motivation is contractual. Eventually, the owner will pay all monies, but with a sufficient delay to assure that the project design is concluded according to the terms and specifications of the contract. Projects may exceed cash-on-hand and bank loans are necessary to meet the ongoing cash flow requirements. Before interest is calculated for the estimate pro forma, it is necessary to establish a prepayment plan. The difference between payment for work concluded and available funds is the amount required for bank loans and is the *principal* upon which short term construction interest is charged. Both an owner and contractor are required to establish this cash flow stream.

Figure 9.13 shows project cash flows where the x-axis is the contract time scaled as a percent. The y-axis is baseline dollars per period. The triangle approx-

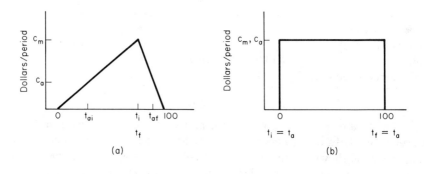

(a)

(b)

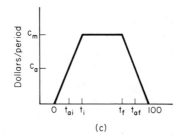

(c)

Figure 9.13.   Cash flow models: (a) triangular; (b) rectangular; (c) trapezoid.

imation has been previously discussed. A rectangular cash flow approximation may result from a pipe-laying project, for example. A trapezoid is the more common approximation. These sketches assume continuous cash flow. Let

t_i = initial time when baseline dollar per period is maximum as a percentage of contract time

t_f = final time when baseline dollars per period is maximum as a percentage of contract time

C_a = average baseline dollars per period and equal to the total value of contract divided by frequency of progress payments

C_m = maximum baseline dollars per period

Geometrically, for the trapezoid, Fig. 9.13(c),

$$\frac{C_m}{C_a} = \frac{200}{100 + t_f - t_i} \qquad (9.5)$$

Values of C_m/C_a can be calculated as follows:

t_i	t_f			
	50	60	70	80
20	1.54	1.43	1.33	1.25
40	1.82	1.67	1.54	1.43
60	—	2.00	1.82	1.67

where $0 \leq t_i < t_f \leq 100$.

An early step in the analysis is to assume the geometrical approximation, t_i, t_f, and C_m/C_a. These assumptions may be based on prior experience.

The periods of contract time during which the baseline dollars per period is equal to the average value can be shown by similar triangle geometry to be

$$t_{ai} = \frac{t_i}{C_m/C_a}\frac{N}{100} \qquad (9.6)$$

and the final instance for an average cash flow rate is found when

$$t_{af} = \left(100 - \frac{100 - t_f}{C_m/C_a}\right)\frac{N}{100} \qquad (9.7)$$

where N = number of project payments

t_{ai} = period when average is initially reached

t_{af} = period when average is finally reached

A construction estimate is $150,000 and has a contract time of 10 months and payment is monthly. If the cash flow assumption is trapezoidal and t_i = 40% and t_f = 70%, we have

$$\frac{C_m}{C_a} = \frac{200}{100 + 70 - 40} = 1.54$$

as the ratio of maximum to average cash requirements.

C_a = 150,000/10 = $15,000 per period average cash flow

C_m = 15,000 × 1.54 = $23,100 per period from t_i to t_f

t_i = 0.40 × 10 = 4th month, when maximum cash flow rate starts

t_f = 0.70 × 10 = 7th month, when maximum cash flow rate concludes

$t_{ai} = \dfrac{40}{1.54} \times \dfrac{10}{100}$ = 2.6th month, when initial average cash flow rate is reached

$t_a = \left(100 - \dfrac{100 - 70}{1.54}\right)\dfrac{10}{100}$ = 8th month, when final average cash flow rate

is reached

As the project progresses, the cumulative cash flow appears as an ogive or S curve. These cumulative curves are the integral of the curves given in Fig. 9.13. But it is also possible to have the cumulative baseline value as a percentage of the total contract amount, y-axis, to the percentage of the total contract time, x-axis. This is shown by Fig. 9.14. Both the triangular and trapezoid of Fig. 9.13 give the S-shaped curve. The rectangular model, sketch (b) of Fig. 9.13, will give a straight line. For a trapezoid cash flow model we have after integrating

$$\text{CBV} = \frac{C_m}{2C_a} \frac{t^2}{t_i}, \qquad\qquad 0 \le t \le t_i \qquad (9.8)$$

$$\text{CBV} = \frac{C_m}{C_a}\left(t - \frac{t_i}{2}\right), \qquad\qquad t_i \le t \le t_f \qquad (9.9)$$

$$\text{CBV} = \frac{C_m}{2C_a}\left[2t_f - t_i + (t - t_f)\left(1 + \frac{100 - t}{100 - t_f}\right)\right], t_f \le t \le 100 \qquad (9.10)$$

where CBV denotes the cumulative baseline value, percentage. Application of these formulas requires t to be a percentage number. With these equations and $t_i = 40\%$ and $t_f = 70\%$, we have the following:

t (%)	CBV (%)	t (%)	CBV (%)
0	0	60	61.52
10	1.92	70 (t_f)	76.90
20	7.69	80	89.72
30	17.30	90	97.53
40 (t_i)	30.77	100	100.00
50	46.15		

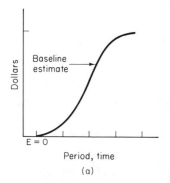
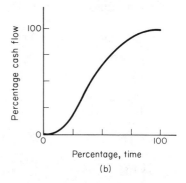

Figure 9.14. Cumulative baseline curve plotted as (a) period versus dollars and (b) percentage time versus percentage cash flow.

The cash flow requirements for this project need additional information. For example, there may be a delay from work concluded to money paid. Now assume that for the $150,000 project there is a 1-month delay, and profit is 10% of the project bid by the major contractor. A different profit would result if the 10% were a markup rate on cost. Refer to Table 9.7. In column 1, each period is a progress payment and begins with zero. It ends with the total number of periods of contract time plus those periods before all monies, including retainage, will be received. Column 4 is the product of column 3 and the project contract value. Profit, column 5, is found by multiplying column 4 by 10%, the markup profit rate. Expenditure is the difference between columns 4 and 5. Available funds depends on contract terms. For our example, there is a 1-month delay for the owner to certify that the work is done, and is paid on the basis of 85%. For example, at $t = 2$, column 7 is found by multiplying the cumulative baseline one period earlier by 85%, or 2448 ($= 2880 \times 0.85$). Retainage, column 8, is found by subtracting available funds from the cumulative baseline value for each period. For period 2, column 8 is $9087 ($= 11,535 - 2448$). The last column describes contractor's net cash flow. It is found as the difference between columns 7 and 6 or 5 and 8. For period 2, (7934) denotes a negative value and a loan equal to this amount is required. It is only the last period, $t = 12$, when the apparent profit of $15,000 is available to the contractor. Note that column 9 is a cumulative deficit or surplus. Values in this column are a guide to the amount to which the contractor must finance the project with a bank loan. Interest must be paid for this interim financing.

The net cash flow column when plotted against the month provides the S curve. Note Fig. 9.14. The y-axes can be identified in dollars per month in actual or percentage terms.

While labor scheduling can be done directly using the work package, it is also possible to schedule with geometrical models. Both the trapezoid and S-curve would deal with manpower in this case. We slightly change the example, and we add information as follows. Assume that the general contractor's markup for overhead and profit is 20% of cost, and he subcontracts all work. Subcontractor's markup for overhead and profit is 25% of cost. Labor accounts for 60% of cost and is paid $20 per hour. Now let the contract total be $1,500,000 and $t_i = 40\%$ and $t_f = 70\%$.

The cost to the general contractor is $1,500,000/1.2 = $1,250,000$. Cost to the subcontractors is $1,250,000/1.25 = $1,000,000$. Total cost of labor is $1,000,000 \times 0.60 = $600,000$. Manpower requirements $= 600,000/20 = 30,000$ man-hours. Man-months $= 30,000/173.3 = 173.1$, where $173.3 (= 52 \times 40/12)$ is the available hours per month. The average number of direct-labor workers is $30,000 \div (10/12 \times 2080) = 17.3$. If the maximum on the job manpower is 154% of the average manpower, the maximum number of direct-labor employees is $27 (\doteq 1.54 \times 17.3)$. A manpower curve is shown by Fig. 9.15(a).

Another variation to labor scheduling can be approximated by Fig. 9.15(b). Assumptions leading to this sketch are that the maximum-on-the-project manpower is 154% of the average. The maximum first occurs after 30.8% has been expended and when 40% of the project time has elapsed. The period of maximum force

Table 9.7. Determining Project Cash Flow, Retainage, and Expenditure

(1) Month	(2) Contract Periods (%)	(3) CBV (%)	(4) CBV	(5) Profit	(6) Expenditure	(7) Available Funds	(8) Retainage	(9) Net Cash Flow
0	0	0	0	0	0	0	0	0
1	10	1.92	$ 2,880	$ 288	$ 2,592	0	$ 2,880	$ (2,592)
2	20	7.69	11,535	1,154	10,382	0	9,087	(7,934)
3	30	17.30	25,950	2,595	23,355	2,448	16,145	(13,550)
4	40	30.77	46,155	4,616	41,540	9,805	24,097	(19,482)
5	50	46.14	69,210	6,921	62,289	22,058	29,978	(23,057)
6	60	61.52	92,280	9,228	83,052	39,232	33,451	(24,223)
7	70	76.90	115,350	11,535	103,815	58,820	36,912	(25,377)
8	80	89.72	134,580	13,458	121,122	78,438	36,532	(23,074)
9	90	97.53	146,295	14,630	131,666	98,048	31,902	(17,273)
10	100	100.0	150,000	15,000	135,000	114,393	25,649	(10,649)
11	110	100.0	150,000	15,000	135,000	124,351	22,500	(7,500)
12	120	100.0	150,000	15,000	135,000	127,500	0	15,000

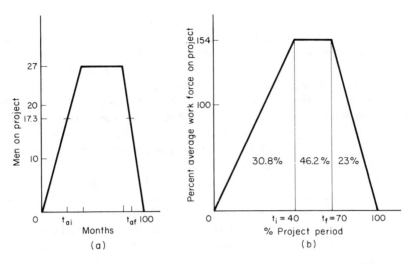

Figure 9.15. Project trapezoidal models for (a) manpower requirements and (b) percentage requirements with respect to timing.

accounts for 46.2% of total manpower. The cumulative manpower curve for time would appear as an S-curve, as typically shown by Fig. 9.10.

As projects involve large dollar undertakings, the owner or contractor may have insufficient cash on hand to meet all financial requirements. Borrowing may be necessary. Once the project is concluded, the contractor is paid, but the owner has incurred a long-term debt. For project analysis there are two components to owner's interest. The first is during the period of the construction phase and the second is following the conclusion of construction. The owner deals with both, but the contractor is concerned with project-construction cash flow requirements only.

The owner will use a cash flow analysis such as Table 9.7. In particular, the owner will pay attention to column 7. Initially, there will be some cash-on-hand available for progress payments. If we assume that the owner has 25% available money to finance the project, then from period 5 on, a loan for the remainder is required. This is construction financing and terminates at project end. It is usually more expensive, interest-wise, than ordinary long-term debt for which collateral and other securities are pledged. The short-term loan is converted into long-term debt.

In a similar way, the contractor needs money to meet obligations. Table 9.7 was prepared from an owner's viewpoint, as the owner held back contractor's profit in retainage. Realistically, the contractor may need short-term financing measured by the difference between columns 6 and 7 up to period 10, or column 9. The money out-of-pocket is the same as indicated by column 9. Repayment by the contractor to the lender would be concluded following final payment by the owner. The amount of paid interest by a contractor to a lender also depends on initial working capital.

Consider Table 9.8, which demonstrates the calculation of interest for short-term financing by a contractor. In this evaluation we assume total financing by the contractor, and that column 9 of Table 9.8 reflects the net cash flow requirement to be financed monthly. Line 1 is the total loan requirement at the start of the period, say a month in our case. Line 1 is the balance of the loan at the start of the period. Line 2 is the money needed for construction during the upcoming month. It is found from Table 9.7, column 9, and is the difference between the current and previous month. Deficit quantities are considered positive for the purpose of a loan requirement. The total loan is the sum of lines 1 and 2 and is the quantity on which interest is charged. For this example we use a 1% monthly interest rate. Line 4 is the product of the total loan and the interest rate. The outstanding loan is the sum of lines 3 and 4, which becomes line 1 in the next period.

Observe in Table 9.8 that the outstanding loan is paid off in month 12. The total of the monthly interest, $1831, would be posted to interest on the pro forma. In this situation it reduces the apparent profit of $15,000 to $13,169.

The owner would use a similar procedure and interest is based on column 7 of Table 9.7. This quantity is converted to long-term debt at the conclusion of the project construction.

9.4.4 Pricing and Bid

Pricing for project designs differs from product in several ways. Many products are sold on the open market to an unknown buyer. In the bid market, however, a manufacturer or contractor produces or constructs an end item for a specific buyer.

Projects are procured by contract. Methods of pricing depend on the type of contract selected by the owner or buyer and pricing is in accordance with the contract. For products, price adjustments are routine based on market or technology or cost movements. This choice is made every so often for the same or similar products. A bid requires a unique analysis where opportunity for repetition is unlikely. Some product estimators develop many prices, while project estimators submit bids infrequently.

The winning or losing of a bid award may give no hint about how well the project was estimated and priced. A competitor may "low ball" a bid to keep a project work force busy. Contrariwise, the winning of a bid may be against uninterested competition who submit high bids. In the product market a 3% increase may reduce the number of sold units by 5%, for example. A similar increase in the bid may lose the contract. Contracts can be broadly divided into two groups. In the first, risk is borne by the contractor and the contract is called "firm price." The contractor may determine a contingency or not which is added to the estimate. Second, an owner or buyer may assume all economic risk, and the contract is called "cost plus." In this type costs are reimbursed by the owner. A profit percentage or a fee is usually agreed to between the parties, which increases the total amount. In view of these contract complexities we defer their discussion to Chapter 12. This author recommends that estimates be prepared similarly for either type of contract. Preparation of the price and bid analysis will depend on the contract type, however.

The procurement objective of an owner or buyer is to buy the end item from

Table 9.8. SHORT-TERM FINANCING OF LOAN BY CONTRACTOR

	Month											
	1	2	3	4	5	6	7	8	9	10	11	12
1. Loan, start of month	0	2,618	8,040	13,792	19,921	23,731	25,146	26,563	24,503	18,889	12,388	9,331
2. Monthly net cash flow	2,592	5,342	5,615	5,932	3,575	1,166	1,154	−2,303	−5,401	−6,624	−3,149	−9,331
3. Total loan	2,592	7,960	13,655	19,724	23,496	24,897	26,300	24,260	18,702	12,265	9,239	0
4. Interest amount	26	80	137	197	235	249	263	243	187	123	92	Σ = $1,831
5. Outstanding loan	2,618	8,040	13,792	19,921	23,731	25,146	26,563	24,503	18,889	12,388	9,331	0

Net profit = $13,169

393

a responsible source for a reasonable bid. We define *bid* to be the value of the economic want of a project design given, received, or asked in exchange. The value is monetary and expressed in the currency of the country. The bid is also called other things, such as price or quote. It does not include costs of operation and maintenance for the end item. Procurements are usually competitive and may result from formal advertising or from a request for proposal to an individual firm. In bidding competition, the quote, which may be lowest, may not be selected. Quality, specification adherence, delivery, and performace may be more important than price. Contrariwise, the lowest price from a responsible bidder may be selected.

Many view project pricing as an interpretive art. They say "price can be anything you want to make it." Others would change this art to a routine calculation where price is found by formula. In engineering and estimating, while opinion is unavoidable, several pricing strategies are important but none guarantee success. Pricing success, when achieved, is a consequence of technical and estimating factors of moderate importance. Seldom is it a result of brilliant strategy. But to evaluate potential bid prices, analysis, and the use of formulas are required. As the spread between cost and price is an indication of value, there is a temptation to base cost on price alone. In this book we stress that pricing proceeds once cost is estimated. The estimated cost is the *most* significant and recognizable component of price.

The most common approach is to use cost plus a *markup*. A formula would be

$$P = C_t + R_m(C_t) + C_m \tag{9.11}$$

where P = project bid, dollars
$\quad C_t$ = total cost of direct labor, direct and subcontract
$\qquad$ materials, facilities and equipment, etc. dollars
$\quad R_m$ = markup rate on cost, decimal
$\quad C_m$ = miscellaneous costs which may be inappropriate for
$\qquad$ markup (i.e., contingency), dollars

Another variation would use various markup factors on the several cost elements.

A less frequent approach is to base the markup on the price. For instance, see Table 9.7, where the calculation of profit was found by multiplying a rate with the contract value, that is, $0.10 \times$ cumulative baseline value.

Table 9.9 is the bid summary for the 500-kV voltage transmission line project. Information from the estimates, Tables 9.1 to 9.4 are removed and posted. The estimating analysis for overhead, contingency, interest, and profit is conducted after this posting. Eventually, a bid value of \$9,098,653 for 5 miles of a high-voltage transmission line is found.

9.5 ENGINEERING ECONOMY

The purpose of converting money into plants and equipment is to return an amount of money that exceeds the investment. This statement assumes that capital is productive and earns a profit for the owner of this capital. In efficiency terms this is

Table 9.9.   PROJECT BID SUMMARY

Project   High-voltage transmission line
Customer   Bonneville Power Administration

Direct labor	$ 3,479,720
Direct material	2,035,625
Subcontract items	1,180,000
Facilities	143,000
Equipment	800,000
Engineering	41,875
Overhead	
1. Office, applied to direct cost $R_o = 4\%$, direct costs = $6,695,345	267,813
2. Job, applied to direct costs $R_j = 5\%$, direct costs = $6,695,345	334,767
Subtotal	$8,282,800
Contingency, $\frac{1}{2}\%$ of subtotal	41,414
Interest with retainage	103,500
Total	$8,427,749
Profit 8% (on cost less contingency)	670,904
Bid	$9,098,653

related to a ratio of output to input. Unlike physical processes, the economic efficiency of capital, assuming long-term success and a capitalistic society, must exceed 1. The productivity of capital comes from the fact that money purchases more efficient processes for making goods and supplying services than consumers could employ themselves. These products are then offered to the public at attractive prices which pay a profit to the manufacturer.

In earlier chapters stress was placed on cost and price as the measure of importance. For purposes of capital investment, the owner uses a term called *return*. Like cost and price, return can be expressed in several ways. Among these are total dollars, percent of sales, ratio of annual sales to investment, or return on investment. The last one is favored by most project estimators. The methods for calculation of return on investment are (1) average annual rate of return, (2) payback period, and (3) engineering-economic rate of return. Naturally, the selection of a method must be consistent with management's goals of profitability. The goal of any project estimate is to predict the net change in the company's overall cash position. The estimator makes studies of alternatives, looking for the change in cost and revenue that must be considered. These studies provide factual quantitative data to measure the interaction of future events.

In this text we favor the compound-interest-based investment computation that considers the *time value of money*. Many other fine texts expand upon engineering economy. However, as a background let us look at methods which are used because of simplicity.

9.5.1 Average Annual Rate of Return Method

In some economic studies return on investment is expressed on an annual percentage basis. The yearly profit divided by the total initial investment represents a fractional return or its related percent return. This method recognizes that a good investment not only pays for itself but also provides a satisfactory return on the funds committed by the firm. There are several variations, of which the following is one:

$$\% \text{ return} = \frac{\text{earnings per year}}{\text{bid value}} \times 100 \qquad (9.12)$$

The earnings are after tax, and deductions for depreciation usually represent some average future expectation. For instance, consider the following example: The bid for new equipment is $175,000, salvage will provide $15,000, and an average earnings of $22,000 after taxes is expected.

$$\% \text{ return} = \frac{\$22,000}{160,000} = 13.75\%$$

Now assume that a private investment opportunity of $25,000 has been brought to your attention. This is broken down to $20,000 for the investment and $5000 for initial working capital (cash, accounts payable, and so forth). Annual operating and other expenses are estimated at $10,000 and income at $15,000 per year. This investment is analyzed as follows:

Income	$15,000
Expenses	10,000
Net income	$ 5,000

$$\% \text{ return} = \frac{\$5000}{\$25,000} = 20\%$$

Another variation is expressed as

$$\% \text{ return} = \frac{\text{average earnings} - (\text{total investment} \div \text{economic life})}{\text{average investment}} \times 100 \qquad (9.13)$$

The earnings in the formula are the average annual earnings after taxes plus appropriate depreciation charges. It is seen that the original investment is recovered over the economic life of the proposal by subtracting the factor of total investment ÷ economic life from average earnings. This difference denotes the average annual economic profit on the investment. The average investment is defined as the total investment times 0.5. The method acknowledges that the life of an investment for tax purposes and its true economic life are not the same. The first is based on the normal physical life or as legally defined by the Internal Revenue Service, while the second represents the profitable life of the investment, which is frequently a different period of time. If management desires, it may incorporate a risk element by further shortening economic life. For example, an average after-tax earning of

$22,000 is expected from an investment of $175,000 with an economic life of 10 years. Straight-line depreciation is assumed for 12 years and salvage is $15,000.

$$\% \ \text{return} = \frac{22,000 + (160,000/12) - (175,000/10)}{160,000 \times \frac{1}{2}} = 22.29\%$$

9.5.2 Payback Period Method

The payback method is easy and widely adopted. Essentially, the method determines how many years it takes to return the invested capital return. The formula as normally given is

$$\text{years payback} = \frac{\text{net investment}}{\text{annual after-tax earnings}} \qquad (9.14)$$

The payback method recognizes liquidity as the basis for the measure of economic worth of capital expenditures.

The method separates proposals of doubtful validity from those which call for additional economic analysis. Obviously, the method signals the immediate cash return aspect of the investment which may be desirable for corporations where a high-profit investment opportunity and limited cash resources exist. In some situations the payback is used for those investment situations where it is felt that the risk does not warrant earnings beyond the payback period. Let us use an example to illustrate this. The installed cost for new equipment is $175,000 and old equipment will be sold for $15,000. Better productivity of the new equipment will return $40,000. For a composite 55% corporate tax rate earnings amount to $22,000.

$$\text{years payback} = \frac{175,000 - 15,000}{22,000} = 7.3$$

Consider now two investment opportunities:

	Equipment A	Equipment B
Total investment	$ 60,000	$60,000
Revenue:		
Year 1	20,000	30,000
Year 2	20,000	30,000
Year 3	20,000	30,000
Year 4	20,000	—
Year 5	20,000	—
Total annual after-tax earnings	$100,000	$90,000
Payback period	3.0 years	2.0 years

In this case equipment B is preferred over A because of the smaller payback period. If sufficient resources were available, a management fiat could allow any investment that was under an arbitrary level such as 5.

The average annual rate of return is acknowledged to have faults. It assumes equal distribution of earnings throughout the economic life of the asset. Even if this were true, there is a significant difference between the value of the dollars earned in the first year and those earned in later years. This method ignores the time value of money. A project yielding savings in early years of its life is more beneficial, as these funds become available for additional investment or for alternative use and often are subject to less risk than savings projected many years ahead. This method overlooks the differences in salvage values and their relation to the time element. Nor is interest on borrowed money in any way reflected.

The payback method suffers similarly. It is noted that the life pattern of earnings is ignored in payback formulas. In the example equipment B had a shorter payback period than equipment A, yet A will return $10,000 more. New equipment may not be profitable during the early part of the payback period; on the other hand, it may be quite profitable in the future. This method does not provide for a system of ranking with other investment possibilities, nor does it take into account depreciation or obsolescence, nor does it consider the earnings beyond the payback period. For example, it does not recognize that one investment with an earning of $10,000 the first year and $2000 the second year is more desirable than another which earns $6000 in each of the 2 years. The situation for which payback is suited, and then only provisionally, is as a rough measure of evaluation.

The engineering-economic method of determining return overcomes these shortcomings. This method is applicable to every possible type of a prospective investment and can yield answers that permit valid comparisons between competing projects.

There are many methods of capital investment analysis, and, unfortunately, only a few will be studied in detail. It is the analysis that leads to a strategy which in turn leads to the decision. The time value of money is the application of compound interest formulas to the additional cash flow produced by the investment. This concept enables management to place a value on the money which will become available for productive use in the future as well as for the money which is available today. Fundamentally, the time value of money begins with simple interest, or

$$I = Pni \qquad (9.15)$$

where I = interest earned, dollars
$\quad P$ = principal sum, dollars
$\quad n$ = number of compounding periods
$\quad i$ = interest rate, decimal

This formula can be restated as the amount including principal and simple interest which must be repaid eventually, or

$$F = P + I = P(1 + ni) \qquad (9.16)$$

where F is the principal and interest sum collected at some future time. In the payment of simple interest, the interest is paid at the end of each time period or the sum total amount of money is paid after a given length of time. Under the latter condition there is no incentive to pay the interest until the end of the contract time.

If interest were paid at the end of each time unit, the lender could put his money to use for earning additional profits. Compound interest considers this point and requires that interest be paid regularly at the end of each interest period. If the payment is not made, the amount due is added to the principal and interest is charged on this converted principal during the following time unit. An initial loan of $10,000 at an annual interest rate of 5% would require payment of $500 as interest at the end of the first year. If this payment were deferred, the interest for the second year would be ($10,000 + $500)(0.05) = $525, and the total compound amount due after 2 years would be $10,000 + $500 + $525 = $11,025. When interest is permitted to compound, as in the following computation, the interest earned during each interest period is permitted to accumulate with the principal sum at the beginning of the next interest period. This compounding is shown in Table 9.10. The resulting factor, $(1 + i)^n$, is referred to as the single-payment compound-amount factor. The total amount of principal plus compound interest due after n periods is

$$F = P(1 + i)^n \tag{9.17}$$

where F is the future amount, dollars. The single-payment compound-amount factor may be used to solve for a future sum of money F, the interest rate i, the number of interest periods n or a present sum of money P when given the other quantities.

It has been stated that the engineering economic methods were preferred because they depend on time-value-of-money concepts. One should not conclude that all methods employing interest computations are useful for all occasions. Some have limited applicability. We present here four distinct variations; when these methods are given correct information and properly understood their answers are equally valid. They are:

1. Net present worth
2. Net future worth
3. Equivalent annual cost
4. Rate of return

Table 9.10.   DERIVATION OF BASIC COMPOUND INTEREST FORMULA

Year	Principal at Start of Period	Interest Earned During Period	Compound Amount F at the End of Period
1	P	Pi	$P + Pi = P(1 + i)$
2	$P(1 + i)$	$P(1 + i)i$	$P(1 + i) + P(1 + i)i = P(1 + i)^2$
3	$P(1 + i)^2$	$P(1 + i)^2 i$	$P(1 + i)^2 + P(1 + i)^2 i = P(1 + i)^3$
n	$P(1 + i)^{n-1}$	$P(1 + i)^{n-1}i$	$P(1 + i)^{n-1} + P(1 + i)^{n-1}i$ $= P(1 + i)^n$

Each of these methods measures a different factor of the investment; they can give quite different evaluations. Nonetheless, they will all give the same recommendation for consistent decision making.

Each method is demonstrated with the same standard problem. Cents are dropped from calculations for ease of understanding.

Year	Cost	Revenue
0	$1025	$ 0
1	0	450
2	0	425
3	0	400

The annual compounding and end-of-year convention are used to simplify understanding. It is assumed that the nonuniform revenue is instantaneously received at the end of year.

9.5.3 Net Present Worth Method

This method is also known as net present value or venture worth. The present worth of future revenue is compared with initial capital investment. It assumes a continuing stream of opportunities for investment at a pre-assigned interest rate. The procedure is to compare the magnitude of present worth of all revenues with the investment at the datum time 0. One way of defining the method is as the added amount that will be required at the start of a proposed project using a preassigned interest rate to produce receipts equal to, and at the same time as, the prospective investment. For a given interest rate of 10%, the net present worth of the previously given problem is computed by discounting all revenues to year 0 at this rate and subtracting the proposed investment, or

Period	$\dfrac{1}{(1 + i)^n}$ Present Worth Factor at 10%		
Year 1 to zero	$450 × 0.9091	=	$ 409
Year 2 to zero	425 × 0.8264	=	351
Year 3 to zero	400 × 0.7513	=	301
		Total	$1061
	Less proposed investment		1025
	Net present worth		$36

The $36 is the amount that must be added to the $1025 to set up the amount that would have to be invested at 10% to achieve receipts equal to and at the same time as those predicted for the recommended investment, or

$$(\$1025 + \$36) \quad \times \quad 1.1 = (\$1061) \times 1.1 \quad = \quad \$1167$$

Less payment $\quad \underline{\quad 450 \quad}$

$\$\ 717$

$717 \times 1.1 \qquad\qquad\qquad\qquad\qquad\qquad = \quad \$\ 789$

Less payment $\quad \underline{\quad 425 \quad}$

$\$\ 364$

$\$364 \times 1.1 \qquad\qquad\qquad\qquad\qquad\qquad = \quad \$\ 400$

Less payment $\quad \underline{\quad 400 \quad}$

0

9.5.4 Net Future Worth Method

The standard application of compound interest using $F = P(1 + i)^n$ is highlighted in this example. It uses the notion that assets and revenues can be invested at the preassigned interest rate where there is a continuous exposure of investment opportunities. A comparison of investment of the original sum plus reinvestment of revenues at the preassigned interest is made against the standard alternative of investing only the original asset value. The calculation results in that added amount that is obtained at the end of the project economic life if the project's anticipated revenues were invested instead of the proposed investment. A common comparison uses the same stipulated interest rate.

For the sample problem and 10%, the net future worth is computed by compounding future revenues to the terminal year and then subtracting from this the amount that would have resulted from the other alternative of investing the original asset at the same preassigned interest rate to the terminal year:

Period	$(1 + i)^n$ Compound Amount Factor at 10%		
Year 1 to 3	$\$450 \times 1.10^2$	=	$\$\ 545$
Year 2 to 3	425×1.10	=	468
Year 3	400×1.00	=	$\underline{400}$
			$\$1413$
Less disbursement compounded to terminal year at 10%			
Year 0 to 3	$\$1025 \times (1.10)^3$	=	1364
	Net future worth		$\$\ \ 49$

The calculations point out that if the project is funded and if the revenues materialize as estimated, then a surplus of $49 will be expected over the simple alternative of investing only the asset of $1025. The same period of time and equal interest rates are parts of this comparison.

9.5.5 Net Equivalent Annual Worth Method

Management often wants a comparison of annual costs instead of, say, present worth of the costs. Here we refer to net costs, that is, the net difference between any cost or revenues or credits. This method considers a supply of opportunities for investment of both assets and receipts at the predetermined interest rate plus a supply of capital at the same interest rate. Now the sample problem does not have uniform annual receipts, and they first must be converted to total present worth and then to annual equivalents. The total present worth at time zero is $1061 (from page 400). The annual equivalent is found by dividing by the sum of the present worth factors, or

$$\text{annual equivalent} = \frac{1061}{(0.9091 + 0.8264 + 0.7513)} = \frac{1061}{2.4868} = \$427$$

$$\text{net annual equivalent worth} = 427 - \frac{1025}{2.4868} = \$14$$

This $14 is the amount by which the anticipated revenues from the proposed investment, rated at 10% interest, exceed the annual equivalent of the proposed investment:

Anticipated equal annual receipts		$ 427
Less equal annual equivalent worth at 10%		14
Equal annual receipts to be generated by investing		$ 413
1025 × 1.10	=	$1128
Less payment		413
		715
715 × 1.10	=	$ 787
Less payment		413
		374
374 × 1.10	=	$ 413
Less payment		413
		0

Starting with the investment which earns interest and subsequently subtracting payments leads to a balance of zero dollars at the end.

9.5.6 Rate of Return

This procedure evaluates the rate of interest for discounted values of the net revenues from a project to have these present worths of the discounted values exactly equal to the present value of the investment. The method thus solves for an interest rate to bring about this equality. Other titles, such as *ROI (return on investment), true rate of return, profitability index,* and *internal rate of return,* also exist. The adjective *true* distinguishes it from other less valid methods that have been labeled rate of return, for instance, Eqs. 9.13 and 9.14. For this method there is no assumption of an alternative investment and no predetermined interest rate. We define this interest rate at which a sum of money, equal to that invested in the proposed project, would have to be invested in an annuity fund in order for that fund to be able to make payments equal to, and at the same time as, the receipts from the proposed investment.

The solution for the interest rate is by repeated trials or by graphical or linear interpolation. For the sample problem

Year, n	Revenue	$\dfrac{1}{(1+i)^n}$ PW Factor at 15%		Discounted Value
1	$450	×	0.8696	=	$391
2	425	×	0.7561	=	321
3	400	×	0.6575	=	263
					$975

Year, n	Revenue	$\dfrac{1}{(1+i)^n}$ PW Factor at 5%		Discounted Value
1	$450	×	0.9524	=	$ 429
2	425	×	0.9070	=	385
3	400	×	0.8638	=	346
					$1160

The two trial values bound the initial asset value of $1025. Either graphical or interpolating methods can be used to locate the rate of return, or from which

$$\frac{0.05 - i}{1160 - 1025} = \frac{0.05 - 0.15}{1160 - 975}$$

it follows that $i = 12.3\%$. This rate of return is the interest rate at which the original sum of $1025 could be invested to provide returns equal to, and at the same time as, the receipts of the prospective investment:

$$1025 \times 1.123 = \$1151$$
$$\text{Less payment} \qquad \underline{450}$$
$$\$ 700$$
$$700 \times 1.123 = \$ 787$$
$$\text{Less payment} \qquad \underline{425}$$
$$\$ 362$$
$$362 \times 1.123 = \$ 400$$
$$\text{Less payment} \qquad \underline{400}$$
$$0$$

This shows that the earning rate is true and is the actual return of the invested money. It has the important advantage of being directly comparable to the cost of capital.

9.5.7 Comparison of Methods

A summary of the four different methods provides:

1. Net present worth at 10% $36
2. Net future worth at 10% $49
3. Net annual equivalent worth at 10% $14
4. Rate of return   12.3%

We can demonstrate that the first three are commensurable answers. For instance, the net present worth of $36 can be compounded to the terminal year using Eq. 9.17 or

$$F = 36(1.10)^3 = \$49 \tag{9.17}$$

The preassigned interest rate, 10%, gives the net future worth or $49. The net annual equivalent worth of $14 can be uncovered by dividing the net present worth value of $36 by a sum of present worth values, of 10% or

$$\frac{36}{2.4867} = \$14$$

On the other hand, the rate of return cannot be calculated from the foregoing answers. It is found directly from the data. Equivalency among the first three can be found for any arbitrary interest rate, and if these are equivalent to the rate of return, then it is equivalent at only one preassigned interest rate. The first three methods are only differences based on the choice of an interest rate. This arbitrary selection of an interest rate makes the three methods little more than decision tools for comparing projects. The rate of return is the only one that can provide a consistent measure of the extent of the economic productivity of prospective investments. The answer can be compared directly with the cost of capital. However, no one single method or criterion of profitability analysis is preferred for all situations.

9.6 EXAMPLE

A 500-kV transmission line is to be estimated. An owner provides an RFQ to the project estimator stating that a double-circuit electrical transmission line will be about 5 miles in length from a power station buss wall to the Creston Substation. "Double circuit" implies two parallel transmission conductors and hardware which are constructed side by side. The aluminum conductor is 3 × 1.6 in. O.D. per circuit. Performance is 0.28 voltage drop per mile at 525 kV. Fig. 9.16 describes the route and tower. Figure 9.4 has already provided the WBS. The second, third, and fourth levels of the WBS need to be determined for a pro forma bid. These higher-level estimates are preliminary, and if lower levels are evaluated, we are dealing with a detail or takeoff bid.

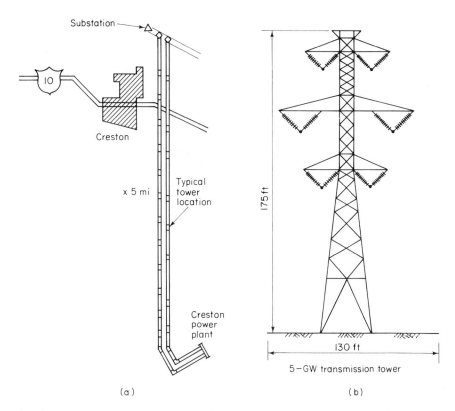

(a)   (b)

Figure 9.16. Preliminary design of Creston 5-GW transmission line: (a) sketch of double-circuit transmission; (b) transmission line tower.

The RFQ will give the design, schedule, location, and specifications. It will indicate that the estimate is preliminary and discuss the purpose, which may be for study, budget, or bid. As the transmission line is a single end item and will require significant money, a project estimate is clearly needed.

The project estimator first establishes the definition and WBS. Organizational policy may require that other company units assist him or her in this work. Complicated projects require a team. There is no single approach, as many management styles can be successful.

We show several methods for making estimates. These methods have been introduced previously. Table 9.11 is a summary of the data, methods, and references. Figure 9.17 is a summary of curves useful for the transmission line. Although the problem is a simplification of real data, it demonstrates the ideas necessary for project estimating.

Observe Table 9.11. Note that entry is WBS and type of estimate. This summary is instructional only. Estimating data, curves, and equations can fill many notebooks. Similar information may also be obtained from nationally published data

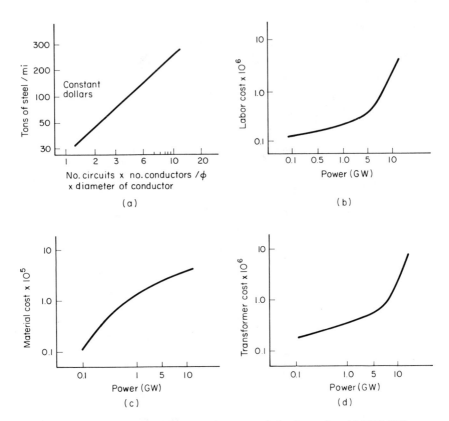

Figure 9.17. Typical curves for high-voltage transmission line project: (a) WBS 1313; (b) WBS 1321; (c) WBS 1321; (d) WBS 1322.

manuals. The application of the data depends on design parameters. Note WBS 111, land survey, which uses a unit estimate. As the average cost is $17,315 per mile, and the distance from the power plant to substation is 5 miles, $86,575 is entered in the facilities estimate, Table 9.3. Road clearing, WBS 1311, is a comparison and opinion estimate, and a value of $120,000 (= 4000 × 30) is posted on the labor estimate, Table 9.1. Road clearing does not require materials beyond that of overhead supplies and the road equipment is covered by the job overhead. This labor is the contractor's work force. Construction equipment necessary for clearing is covered by job overhead. Construction equipment is different from equipment installed in the substation.

  WBS 1312, Roads, has two entries on Table 9.11. The first deals with direct labor, while the second provides for the material base, asphalt, and so on, for the road. Note that these two results, $280,000 and 15,000, are entered in two different estimates, Tables 9.1 and 9.2.

  WBS 1313, Erection of Tower Structure, shows a labor estimate using the average learning theory. Parameters are listed by Table 9.11. For 26 towers, the

Table 9.11. SUMMARY OF ESTIMATING DATA FOR HIGH-VOLTAGE TRANSMISSION PROJECT

WBS	Type of Estimate	Method of Estimating	Data, Curve, Equation	Reference
111	Facilities	Unit	$C_a = \$17,315/\text{mi}$	Eq. 6.3
112	Facilities	Unit	$C_a = \$1285/\text{mi}$	Eq. 6.3
12	Engineering	Linear regression	$a = 25,000$; $b = 1700/\text{mi}$; rate $= \$44.67$; overhead $= 25\%$	Eq. 5.3
1311	Labor	Comparison, opinion	4000 hours; \$30/hr	Secs. 6.2, 6.3
1312	Labor	Comparison, opinion	8000 hours; \$35/hr	Secs. 6.2, 6.3
1312	Direct material	Opinion	\$15,000	Sec. 6.2
1313	Labor	Learning	$K = 3,518$; $\phi = 90\%$; average line linear, $N = 26$	Sec. 6.6.1
1313	Direct material	Curve	See Fig. 9.17(a); $I_c = 1.15$; cost/lb = \$0.75	Eq. 5.53 Eq. 6.3
1321	Labor	Curve	See Fig. 9.17(b)	
1321	Direct material	Curve	See Fig. 9.17(c)	
1321	Facilities	Historical quote, comparison	\$50,000	
1322	Subcontract	Power law and sizing model	$Q_r = 1.2$ GW; $C_r = \$200,000$; $m = 0.9$; $I_r = 1$; $I_c = 1.18$	Eq. 6.18
1322	Equipment	Curve	See Fig. 9.17(d)	
133	Subcontract	Cost estimating relationship	$22,800 x_1^{2.38898} x_2^{1.15675}$; $x_1 =$ diameter of conductor, $x_2 =$ number of conductors per phase	Eq. 6.22

entry of 55,743 hours (also $2,229,720 = 55,743 \times 40$) is posted on the Labor Estimate (Table 9.1).

Direct material, WBS 1313, is found using Fig. 9.17(a). The cost driver for this curve is "no. circuits $\times$ no. conductors/circuit $\times$ diameter" or $9.6 (= 2 \times 3 \times 1.6)$, and the curve value of 225 tons of steel per mile is read. When multiplied by the unit cost of material and welded fabrication for tower manufacture, we have $1,940,625 (= 225 \times 5 \times 2000 \times 0.75 \times 1.15$) for the direct material estimate (Table 9.2). Since Fig. 9.17(a) is for constant dollars of a bench-mark year, the value is multiplied by an index 1.5 to inflate the material cost to the period of out-of-pocket cash flow.

WBS 1321, Substation Building, involves a labor, direct material, and facilities estimate. Figure 9.17(b) and (c) provides $850,000 and $180,000 and are entered for Tables 9.1 and 9.2 for a value of 5 GW. A minor facilities value of $50,000 is judged on the evidence of a past quote and comparison for Table 9.3.

Together with other information, the four estimates, Tables 9.1 to 9.4, are concluded. With various overhead rates, contingency, construction interest, and a profit markup, a bid value of $9,098,653 is found for Table 9.9.

This value of $9,098,653 is the investment charge for a utility. The life of this transmission line is 50 years, which is approximately perpetuity because of the nature of the time-value-of-money tables. It is possible that this investment will be subjected to an engineering economy analysis to determine its profitability.

SUMMARY

The project estimator has the job of forecasting capital investment and operating expenses. This aids the management process in choosing and evaluating one-of-a-kind end items. There are several kinds of estimates for projects. Once these estimates are concluded, a bid and pricing analysis is conducted. Eventually, alternative designs and their estimates are analyzed using engineering-economy methods. Accurate estimates are crucial to any type of time-value-of-money computation.

QUESTIONS

9.1. Give an explanation of the following terms:

RFP	Pro forma document
Fixed capital	Job overhead
Working capital	Contingency
Standard commercial items	Optimistic cost
Facilities cost	Retainage
Work package	Baseline
WBS levels	Markup
Commitment	Time value of money

Subcontract estimate   Payback
Cost spreading   Equivalent annual cost
Bid summary   Venture worth

9.2. What is the purpose of a project estimate? Why are project estimates important?

9.3. What kinds of information are necessary to undertake a project estimate?

9.4. Illustrate fixed capital, working capital, and direct and indirect costs.

9.5. Distinguish between direct material and subcontract in a project bid.

9.6. Give the purpose of a work package. What is the definition part?

9.7. How do commitment and expenditure differ? What causes this difference?

9.8. Describe and construct a new labor estimating form.

9.9. Why is the bid document important for project designs?

9.10. Why is overhead separated into office and job?

9.11. Is there a difference between the interest calculated for project funding and the interest included in time-value-of-money concepts?

9.12. Describe two pseudo-return methods and indicate why they are faulty. What advantages do they serve?

9.13. What is meant by "equivalent or equality" with methods of net present worth, net future worth, and net annual equivalent worth?

9.14. What criteria do you suggest for making project decisions? Will a shortage of capital influence your decision? Do you believe that a successful company is cash poor and bank mortgage rich?

9.15. Suppose that at a certain date an organization had a listing of engineered projects each showing the amount of capital required and the rate of return and that these can be plotted as shown in Fig. Q9.15. Given a limited amount of equity capital, it asks the bank to cover these capital ventures, and you show them your curve. Now the bank, knowing your financial credit, offers its own curve with increasing interest because of

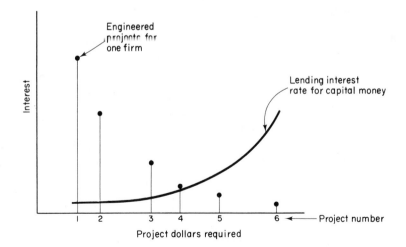

Figure Q9.15.

their risk as more capital is loaned. What is the favorable aspect about this approach to the firm? Unfavorable? What does this method say about the marginal interest to be earned? At what point should one stop borrowing?

PROBLEMS

9.1. A task requires 17,000 allowed hours. Location of the work is above the Arctic Circle and the productivity factor is estimated as 45%. If the gross hourly cost is $45.00, what is the estimated cost? If the work is in Texas, hourly cost is $25, and a productivity factor of 85% is used, what is the cost of direct labor?

9.2. Five similar bridges are to be constructed under the direction of one field office. Facility costs for the field office are $250,000. Overhead on the basis of direct labor and material cost is 45%. Additional data for each bridge are as follows:

Task	Hourly Rate		Estimated Time (months)	Estimated Material	Professional Estimate
	Wage	Equipment			
Masonry and concrete	$25	$40	15	$30,000	
Forms, scaffolding	20	30	6	20,000	
Asphalt	20	80	3	15,000	
Grading	15	40	2		
Surveying	30	10	3		
Engineering					$50,000

Each month is a $173\frac{1}{3}$-hour period. Develop a simple project cost estimate using items of Fig. 9.1. Find the project cost and the cost for one bridge.

9.3. The flowchart for the manufacture of printed polyethylene food bags is given by Fig. P9.3. Costs for this process are

Polyethylene, $3/kg
Color chips, $5/kg

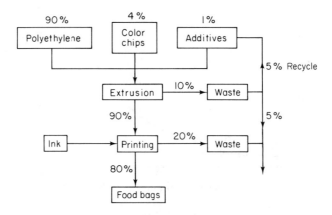

Figure P9.3

Additives, $4/kg
Ink, $9/liter
Waste removal, $1.50/kg

Find the cost of 1 million good bags if 1 kg = 500 bags, and 1 liter of ink will print 10,000 bags. (*Hint:* Work from good bags upward to requirements. Assume that ink has a 20% loss.)

9.4. A flowchart for a hydrocracker is proposed. A simplified version is illustrated by Fig. P9.4. There are a large number of physical materials, such as gas-oil input, catalyst, hydrogen, fuels, and so on.

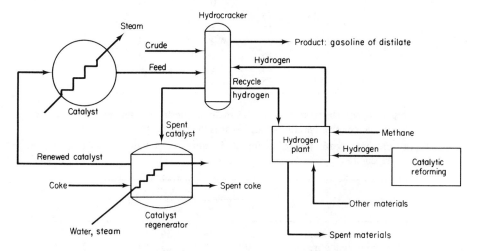

Figure P9.4.   Schematic model for hydrocracker.

(a) Develop a listing of the materials.
(b) Tabulate a qualitative material balance.
(c) What input and output material costs do you identify?

9.5. From an experience of yours, provide a work breakdown structure showing and describing the principles used in its construction. Decompose a project to the fifth level, where one block in each level is further reduced to a lower level. Indicate the numbering and title for each block.

9.6. A satellite repeater link has the following definition:

WBS	Definition Title	WBS	Definition Title
1	Satellite repeater	15	Equipment
11	Management	16	Training
12	Engineering	151	Preamplifier
13	Documentation	152	Mixer
14	Integration	153	IF, amplifier, filter
		1511	Other hardware

Construct a graphical WBS. How many levels are used?

9.7. A project is defined as follows:

WBS	Cost	Starting Milestone	Ending Milestone
1		0	11
11	165	6	11
12	225	0	8
13	140	7	10
14	160	6	9
121	55	3	8
122	95	0	6
123	75	3	7
1221	15	3	6
1222	25	2	5
1223	15	2	3
1224	25	1	4
1225	15	0	3

Prepare a graphical work breakdown structure. Construct a graphical schedule of work. Plot the cumulative baseline costs. What is the total cost?

9.8. (a) Prepare a cash flow plan for $6.5 million, matching dollars commitment to expenditure.

	Period					
	0	1	2	3	4	5
Percent commitment	10	18	36	28	8	0
Percent expenditure	0	8	25	39	21	7

(b) A project costs $200,000 and the isosceles triangles of Fig. 9.9 are an approximation for the cash flow plan. If the periods now represent quarters, prepare a cash flow plan matching dollars commitment to dollars expenditure. When is the approximate midpoint of the commitment and expenditure triangles? What is the difference in money at this time?

9.9. A project definition for conversion of a plant, and the design, manufacture, and assembly of a kerosene heater product line, is given.

WBS	Definition Title	Start Period	Ending Period	Cost Estimate ($\times 10^3$)
1	Kerosene project	0	10	
11	Design	0	2	$1,000
12	Model assembly	2	8	750
13	Plant conversion	1	3	8,000
14	Reliability	4	10	1,600
121	Body assembly	2	6	400

continued

WBS	Definition Title	Start Period	Ending Period	Cost Estimate ($\times 10^3$)
122	Tank assembly	2	6	200
123	Burner assembly	2	5	150
1211	Lower body	2	5	300
1212	Upper body	3	5	100
1221	Upper tank	2	4	150
1222	Lower tank	3	6	50
1231	Glass cylinder	2	3	100
1232	Net	3	4	50

(a) Prepare a graphical work breakdown structure.
(b) Construct a schedule of work similar to a bar chart.
(c) Plot the cumulative baseline costs. Determine project cost.

9.10. A contractor has the following historical costs, expressed in dollars $\times 10^6$, for the last 4 years:

Year	C_p	C_o	C_j
1	$240	$12	$7
2	320	14	5.6
3	280	13	8
4	300	15	7.6

(a) Calculate office and job overhead rates and determine the rates for year 5.
(b) If in year 5 a project is estimated to have a direct labor and material cost of $150 million, calculate the overhead amount.

9.11. Historical costs for one project have provided the following data:

> Equipment, $600,000
> Direct and subcontract materials, $10,000,000
> Direct labor
> > 100 employees at $25 per hour for 525 hours each
> > 500 employees at $20 per hour for 875 hours each
> > 200 employees at $15 per hour for 1050 hours each

General expenses include office rent, $250,000; insurance, $160,000; furniture and supplies, $150,000; telephone and computers, $50,000; and salaries, $500,000. Project expenses include permits, $25,000; superintendence, $100,000; storage and protection, $75,000, and other project expenses, $400,000. Find the office and job overhead rate. (*Hint:* Consider equipment as an overhead cost.)

9.12. Find direct cost and job overhead rate and amounts from the following information: Direct materials, $200,000. Labor hours for project = 2000 hours and labor wage without fringes and mandatory contributions = $20 per hour. Fringes and mandatory contributions = 40%. Office overhead rate = 50% on basis of full direct labor and materials. Permits and fees = $2500, bonds = $5000, job office expenses are salaries,

$18,000; supplies, $1500; and telephone, $1200. Insurance $= $15,000, utilities $=$ $8000, and surveys $=$ $28,000. What is the full cost of the job?

9.13. A developmental project has an expected cost of 25×10^6 and a variance of 9×10^{12} dollars^2.

   (a) Plot a risk graph of contingency.

   (b) Find the upper limit cost for 25% overrun. For 25% underrun.

9.14. **(a)** A preliminary estimate is considered uncertain. Management directs a contingency plan as insurance to the conceptual estimate. Mean cost and standard deviation are $100,000 and $50,000. Construct a risk graph of contingency for the current time.

   (b) Project life is 4 years and money flow is scheduled as 25, 50, 15, and 10%. Escalation indexes for these years as related to bench mark year are 1.000, 1.015, 1.050, and 1.100. Find the total contingency cash flow amount necessary to add to the project estimate where the contingent maximum cost is selected at 25% risk.

9.15. An owner requests the contractor create a *bias contingency* in his estimate, that is, artificially calculating a high estimate to avoid asking for additional funding from a bank and thus giving the impression of a project in control. Assume an expected cost of $100,000 and a standard bias contingency of 10%. Project cash flow and indexes are identical to Problem 9.14. Construct a risk graph and find the deviation of $50,000. Assume a contingency for a current period as well as inflated periods. Use a 25% overrun risk level. Discuss the pros and cons of this manipulation.

9.16. A construction estimate is $200,000 and has a contract period of 5 months. The cash flow is trapezoidal and $t_i =$ 40% and $t_f =$ 80%.

   (a) Draw the cash flow trapezoid similar to Fig 9.13c. Find average and maximum cash flow and when they occur.

   (b) Earned profit is 10% and there is a 1-month delay for payment by the owner. Retainage is 20%. Construct a table similar to Table 9.7.

9.17. A construction bid is $8 million and has a contract period of 5 months. Cash flow is trapezoidal and $t_i =$ 20% and $t_f =$ 60%.

   (a) Draw the cash flow trapezoid. Find average and maximum cash flow and when they occur.

   (b) Profit earned by the contractor is 20%. Retainage is 10% and there is a 1-month delay in payment by the owner. Find the project cash flow table.

9.18. A contract of $150 million is estimated. A trapezoid model of cash flow is assumed with $t_i =$ 30% and $t_f =$ 80%. Project life is 15 months. Other assumptions are as follows: profit $=$ 10%, owner retainage $=$ 5%, and money as paid from owner to contractor is 1 month late.

   (a) Find the net surplus or deficit for each period from the contractor's viewpoint.

   (b) Plot the cumulative baseline dollars against the months.

   (c) Plot the cumulative baseline percent against the cumulative contract percent. When does the cumulative baseline percentage equal the elapsed contract percentage?

9.19. Schedule and geometrically model the labor for Problem 9.16. The general contractor's markup for overhead and profit is 20% of cost and he subcontracts all work. Subcontractor's markup for overhead and profit is 25% of cost. Labor accounts for 60% of cost and is paid $20 per hour.

9.20. A construction contract has an overall value of $8 million and a contract period of 5 months. Cash flow is trapezoidal, where t_i = 20% and t_f = 60%. The general contractor's markup for overhead and profit is 10% of cost and he subcontracts all work. The average subcontractor's markup for overhead and profit is 20% of cost. Labor accounts for 50% of cost and is paid $30 per hour. Plot manpower requirements for the project and as a percent of average work force. For how long does the maximum work force last as a percentage?

9.21. A project that costs $150 million total is scheduled to be constructed in 15 periods. The major contractor markup on labor for overhead and profit is 20% of cost. All work is considered subcontracted. The subcontractor's markup for overhead and profit is 25% of labor cost. Labor accounts for $50 million and is paid at $40 per hour (includes wage and fringe costs). Maximum on-the-job manpower first occurs after 30% of the total manpower requirement has been paid. The period of maximum labor occurs for 50% of the project duration. Consider only the $50 million.
   (a) Plot the percent of average work force on project versus percent elapse time of project.
   (b) Plot men on project versus project time, periods.
   (c) Provide an ogive curve for labor cost versus periods.

9.22. Let the interest rate be $1\frac{1}{2}$% per month for Table 9.8. Determine the interest and net profit.

9.23. Calculate the interest and net profit amount where interest is 1% per period: (a) For problem 9.16; (b) For problem 9.18.

9.24. Calculate the interest amount, where interest is 2% per month for the net cash flow given in millions of dollars.

Month	1	2	3	4	5	6
Net cash flow	(1.92)	(2.10)	(1.83)	(1.05)	(0.64)	1.60

(Hint: The net cash flow is cumulative. A bank loan of $2,100,000 − $1,920,000 = $180,000 is the amount necessary for month 2.)

9.25. You, as a contractor, find that monthly estimates for payment increase uniformly for the first quarter, decrease uniformly for the last quarter, and are level for the middle half of the job. The job will require a $2,400,000 contract lasting 12 months. The first monthly estimate will be paid 2 months after the start of the job less 10% retainage, and monthly thereafter. It is necessary to pay all expenses promptly. Profit is figured at 15% of direct and indirect costs. Prepare a monthly cash flow schedule of the project. Determine timing and amount of debt. When does the percentage of work in place equal the percentage of elapsed contract time?

9.26. Consider a project where materials are divided into four categories: (a) facilities and equipment, (b) long-lead-time materials, (c) standard commercial materials, and (d) raw materials and stock items. The estimator is required to set levels of commitment. Ultimately, subcontractors and vendors supply the materials to the contractor and demand their money. The commitment and expenditure cash value per period can be geometrically modeled against period number. $E = 0$ is the point of the estimate and 16 is the point at which manufacture will be started. Assume that cash flows are instanta-

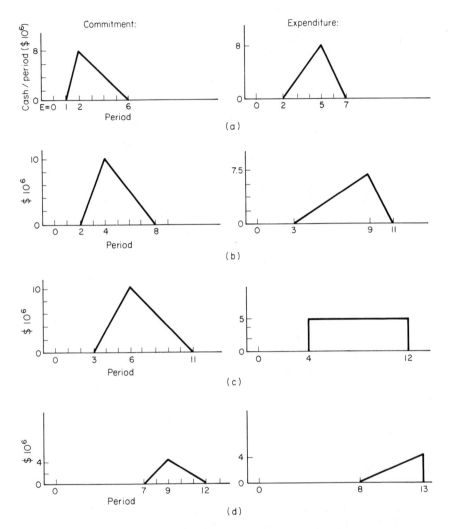

Figure P9.26. Commitment and expenditures for (a) facilities and equipment; (b) long-lead-time materials; (c) standard commercial materials; (d) raw materials and stock items.

neous because the project is large and there are many suppliers, so a continuous cash flow model is considered reasonable. The four categories, graphical value per period and period numbers, are given as Fig. P9.26.

(a) Plot the total commitment dollar ogive beginning at period 1 and concluding at period 12. Describe the method.

(b) On the same curve, plot the total expenditure ogive beginning period 2 and ending period 13. Show the method.

(c) Graphically or analytically determine the effective retainage for the major contractor for periods 2, 7, and 13.

In the curves above, title the commitment and expenditure axes as budgeted cost material committed and budgeted cost material expended. To the contractor all material costs are money-out-of-pocket.

(d) Using the same curves, redefine the range from 1 to 100% for both the *x*- and *y*-axes.

9.27. (a) A new capital item will cost $225,000, salvage is $25,000, and an average earning of $20,000 after taxes is expected. Find the average annual rate of return. If earnings are doubled, what is the rate?

(b) Consider part (a). The investment has an economic life of 10 years. Straight-line depreciation for 8 years is used. Find the percent return.

9.28. (a) Investment for new equipment is $100,000 and salvage will be $10,000 eight years hence. An earning from this equipment will be $15,000 on the average after taxes. What is the non-time-value of money return? What is the payback?

(b) Two investment opportunities are proposed.

	Process *A*	Process *B*
Total investment	$60,000	$60,000
Revenue (after tax)		
Year 1	20,000	30,000
Year 2	20,000	30,000
Year 3	20,000	30,000
Year 4	20,000	
Year 5	20,000	

For an interest of 10%, which has the least period of time before capital recovery is complete?

9.29. Two bids are compared for performing the same design.

	Bid *A*	Bid *B*
Total bid	$100,000	$150,000
Revenue (after tax)		
Year 1	25,000	25,000
Year 2	30,000	40,000
Year 3	35,000	55,000
Year 4	30,000	40,000

(a) Determine the payback.

(b) For an interest of 5%, which bid has the least period of time before the bid value is returned?

9.30. (a) What is the principal amount of interest at the end of 2 years on $450 for a simple interest rate of 10% per year?

(b) If $1600 earns $48 in 9 months, what is the nominal annual rate of interest?

(c) An investment of $50,000 is proposed at an interest rate of 8%. What is the future amount in 10 years?

(d) What is the present worth of $1000 6 years hence if money is compounded 10% annually?

(e) What is the compound amount of $3000 for 15 years with interest at 7.25%?

(f) Find the annual equivalent value of $1050 for the next 3 years with an interest rate of 10%.

(g) How many years will it take for an investment to triple itself if interest is 5%?

(h) An interest amount of $500 is earned from an investment of $7500. What is the interest for 1 year? For 2 years?

9.31. (a) Find the principal if interest at the end of $2\frac{1}{2}$ years is $450 for a simple interest rate of 15% per year.

(b) A loan of $5000 earns $750 interest in $1\frac{1}{2}$ years. Find the nominal annual rate of interest.

(c) In 1626 the Indians bartered Manhattan Island for $24 worth of trade goods. Had they been able to deposit $24 into a savings account paying 6% interest per year, how much would they have in 1990? At 7% interest?

(d) What payment is now acceptable in place of future payments of $1000 at the end of 5, 10, and 15 years if interest is 5%?

(e) What is the compound amount of $500 for 25 years with interest at 15%?

(f) Calculate the annual equivalent value of $1000 for the next 4 years with interest rate at 5%.

(g) How many years will it take for an investment to double itself if interest is 10%?

(h) An investment of $10,000 earns an interest amount of $750. Find the rate if the amount is earned over 1, 2, or 3 years.

9.32. (a) Reconsider the cash flow of cost and revenues provided on page 400. Provide the net present worth, net future worth, and net annual equivalent worth if interest is 11%.

(b) Repeat part (a) for an interest of 9%.

9.33. (a) Reconsider the cash flow of bid A in Problem 9.29. Find the net present worth, net future worth, and net annual equivalent worth if interest is 4%. Find the rate of return. Present a summary of the four methods.

(b) Reconsider the cash flow of bid B in Problem 9.29. Repeat part (a) and present a summary of the four methods. Which bid is preferred, A or B?

9.34. Reconsider the cash flows of equipment A and B given on page 397. Present a summary of the four methods. Assume an interest of 20%. Is A or B preferred?

9.35. A project estimate has the following cost and revenue cash flows. The cash flows are end-of-period.

Year	Cost	Revenue
0	$800	$ 0
1		450
2		425
3		400

(a) If interest is 10%, find the net present worth, net future worth, and net annual equivalent worth.

(b) Find the rate of return.

(c) Present a summary of the four methods.

9.36. A prospective venture is described by the following receipts and disbursements:

Year End	Receipts	Costs
0	$ 0	$800
1	200	0
2	1,000	200
3	600	100

For $i = 15\%$, describe the desirability on the basis of present worth.

9.37. (a) Evaluate the cash flow diagram, Fig. P9.37. Arrows pointing down represent end-of-the-year costs and upward arrows are revenues. Determine a present sum, an equivalent annual payment, and a future sum. Use $i = 25\%$.

(b) Repeat part (a) with $i = 10\%$.

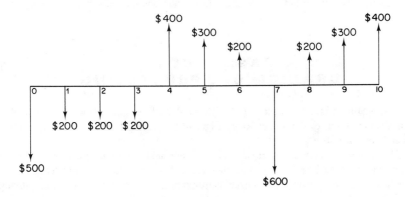

Figure P9.37

9.38. (a) Evaluate the cash flow diagram, Fig. P9.38. Downward-pointing arrows are costs

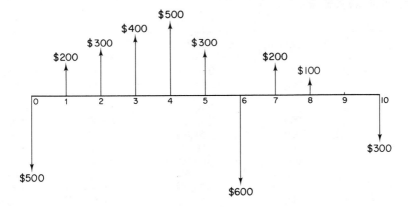

Figure P9.38

and upward arrows are revenues. Find present value, annual value, and a future value. Use $i = 15\%$.

(b) Repeat part (a) with $i = 10\%$.

9.39. Using Tables 9.1 to 9.4, construct the cumulative baseline cost ogive curve plotted against period. In what period will roughly 50% of the estimated costs be spent?

9.40. Assume that a transmission line is to be estimated. Apply the data using Table 9.11 and the following assumptions: Length of transmission, 8 miles; 525 kV, single circuit, 1.5 GW capacity, 3×1.3 in. O.D. conductor per phase, 30 towers, and other data the same. Determine the labor, direct material and subcontract, facilities and equipment, and engineering estimates. Conclude by finding the bid value similar to Table 9.9.

9.41. Estimate the following data for 735-kV double-circuit transmission line. The transmission line length is 25 miles. The conductors are 4×1.38 in. O.D. per phase. Capacity is 5 GW, and there are 90 transmission towers. Other data of Table 9.11 remain the same. Find the four project estimates and the bid similar to Table 9.9.

CASE STUDY:
URANIUM ORE PROCESSING

Chamberlin Mining Ltd. has discovered a rich ore deposit in Saskatchewan, Canada. Prospector Chamberlin hires consultant Ralph Light to provide him with preliminary estimate facts and flowsheet data.

Light reports that three process methods are used: acid-leach countercurrent decantation solvent type, acid-leach resin, and an alkaline leach. Operating costs are affected greatly by the grade of ore, mill capacity, and reagent consumption for a particular operation. Although sulfuric acid costs are decreasing, labor costs are not, and the general trend is upward. Construction costs are increasing with new plants requiring pollution controls.

Because Chamberlin is unwilling to disclose his proprietary facts such as profits above costs, transportation, depreciation rates, overhead rates, and assets, Light is forced to submit only preliminary data for his client:

Type of Plant	Plant Capacity (tons of ore feed per day)	Capital Cost Installed ($ per ton)	Direct Operation Cost ($ per ton)	Uranium Purity
Acid-leach,	500	$110,000	$57.00	0.90
CCD	1000	75,000	45.50	0.93
	2000	55,000	38.00	0.95
Acid-leach,	500	90,000	53.50	0.88
resin	1000	60,000	46.00	0.90
	2000	42,500	38.00	0.94
Alkaline-	500	120,000	61.00	0.93
leach	1000	80,000	49.50	0.95
	2000	60,000	41.50	0.96

Now the prospector determines that a plant runs 300 days per year and he figures a model that incorporates the full cost of capital and operation will be good for a starter. Based on these preliminary estimating data, what will be the direct operating dollars per recovered pound of U_3O_8 if the ore grade of feed is 0.20% U_3O_8? What conclusion as to capacity and flow sheet do you recommend on this basis?

From a separate exploration report Chamberlin knows that the ore body is limited to $10-12 \times 10^6$ tons before primary grades are exhausted. New processing equipment will then be required. What is the capital investment cost for the nine plants? Ignoring depreciation, which type of plant minimizes total capital and operating costs over the life of the ore? Which flowsheet should be analyzed by detail estimating methods?

10

System Estimating

In this chapter we outline methods for applying system estimating to system designs. Unfortunately, a procedure cannot be set out beforehand in some recipe fashion. If that were possible, and after we have learned these procedures and by strict adherence to them, we would be guaranteed absolute confidence of result. The preparation of each estimate is unique and, to a large extent, the methods are adapted to the design. Each system estimate is a result of the skill, experience, and resourcefulness of the estimator. Nevertheless, there is a methodology and a set of principles that aid the construction of system estimates.

We shall show that the measure of system estimating is effectiveness. Previously we considered cost, price, and bid as the appropriate measure for operation, product, and project types of designs. To make a cost-effectiveness evaluation, it is necessary to contrive and then construct an information flow structure. Given the information flow structure and the corresponding model it becomes possible to use various analytical aids to arrive at system effectiveness. Finally, several small-scale system estimates are provided.

Concepts inherent in system estimating have been applied successfully to a broad listing of problems, such as water resources, health systems, social welfare programs, hospital planning, space systems, community relations interaction, industrial growth, and weapons development and production. The techniques have been applied at levels ranging from preliminary to detail.

What is meant by the word *system*? Three classifications are normally suggested, executive, operational, and physical. For the first we have in mind procedures and organizational forms that connect organized effort. In operational systems the central thought is about responsibilities, authority, and aspects of functional relationships as they deal with minor or major problems. Our concern is for the engineering and the social system, which we collectively term *physical*. Because this is a book about cost estimating our system shall deal with a configuration of operations, products, and projects; thus scrutiny of these divisions is possible by the means of the previous three chapters.

10.1 EFFECTIVENESS

In system estimating the word *effectiveness* is the focus of a great deal of attention. Effectiveness is something like efficiency. In the traditional sense efficiency is non-dimensional and as a quantity it approaches one. In engineering the object is to have as high efficiency as possible. But effectiveness means more than efficiency. For one thing it may have dimension.

Efficiency reports usually express performance in terms of a percentage of a predetermined norm or standard. If the daily standard for a production operation is 100 units and actual production is 97 units, efficiency for that day's operation is 97%. If the standard is properly determined, the efficiency indicates this operation close to expectation, but there is room for improvement. Even though the efficiency may be close to 100%, it does not necessarily prove that the operation is effective. *Efficiency* describes the ability to do things right, while *effectiveness* is the ability to do the right thing efficiently.

The finding of system effectiveness measures is not easy. Although many effectiveness measures are possible, only a few ever serve a practical purpose. For any meaningful evaluation, analysis cannot be conducted on lofty levels because of the lack of detail inherent in the general terms, and consequently more specific measures are desirable. To choose between two energy systems by listing the things we value, such as satisfaction, dependability, and lack of pollution, is not very helpful. This does not indicate that we should not form such a list early in the analysis. Effectiveness measures such as cost, heat loss, waste-heat recovery cost, and equal-marginal fuel cost are more specific in meaning. With narrow measures of effectiveness, there is a greater chance of finding information to allow analysis.

While we could associate system effectiveness with a narrow meaning, this would restrict the actual character of the concept. There is no one best measure of effectiveness. With the present state of knowledge which obscures our perfection, we settle for something less. For cost estimating, that something less implies a dimension in monetary units such as dollars. This is our basic dimension of effectiveness.

There are ways to overcome the philosophical problem of effectiveness. The first is to make the effectiveness more specific. A major design can be reduced to elemental designs. For each of the elemental designs we assume that a special effectiveness measure can be constructed. This permits individual attention. A firm or governmental agency cannot have one system estimator examine all the designs simultaneously and pick each course of action in light of all the decisions. The magnitude of the task requires that the design be broken into its elements. The consequence of this action is to make broader policy choices by high-level officials, while others are delegated to lower levels. The piecemeal analysis makes it possible for more attention to detail. However, dangers are inherent in piecemeal analysis, as lower-level effectiveness may be unrelated to the higher-level designs. If the chosen effectivenesses provide only approximate results for smaller sub-optimal designs, a hierarchy of crude effectiveness measures would be considered simultaneously, and potential inconsistencies are abundant.

10.1.1 Cultivation of Alternatives

A system estimator is expected to consider a broad range of alternatives in his or her study. The estimator is encouraged to visualize most alternatives that are in the realm of practicality, denying acts such as perpetual energy, for instance. Although ideal opportunities are appealing, it is really not worth the effort. The estimator rules out other less rewarding possibilities due to the shortage of time, effort, and money. The remainder are reasonably exhaustive. For some situations it may be necessary to initially describe a list of possible alternatives that is at first quite large. Preliminary estimating methods will abridge the list to something more valuable. The converse is also true. As the analysis continues, opportunities may present themselves which were not known at the start.

Selection of appropriate alternatives for further study is guided by several rules. First, the scope of the system to be compared in conjunction with the selection of the effectiveness will tend to deny alternatives of doubtful value. When called on to narrow the selection of alternatives the estimator may want to logically state restrictions that had only been verbalized. This will prevent certain alternatives from creeping into the evaluation process. Naturally, a good rule is familiarity with overall system objectives.

10.1.2 Intangibles

An estimator may be unable to commit some aspect of a design into ordinary monetary units. Function, beauty, safety, quality of life, and ease are difficult to evaluate. These factors are *intangible* or irreducible. Although special and nonfundamental units for a scale of measurement or ranking might be forced on the intangibles, the estimator usually believes that it is not worth the effort and that it is truly imponderable in terms of ordinary units.

If intangibles are not treated in monetary units, there are other ways to consider them. If the stakes are not high, it may be convenient to ignore them. While intangible may be advantageous to some, there may be a contrasting disadvantage to others. A mere listing of the intangibles, both pro and con, may be a sufficient examination. Despite the ability to render, although superficially, various intangibles to a deterministic scale, the preponderance of practice chooses to accept most intangibles as closed to numerical estimating. Thus, it leaves the estimator in the position of considering what is tractable in dollars and that which is not.

10.1.3 Long-Term Uncertainty

The cost estimates in Chapters 7, 8, and 9 can be called average or expected outcomes. When viewed as a *random variable* they may be off their mark. For this present discussion there are two types of uncertainty. In the first case the uncertainty may be about the state of the world in the future and is called long-term uncertainty. It includes factors like technology uncertainty or strategic uncertainty by competitors. Statistical uncertainty is different and it results from purely chance elements. This exists even if the uncertainties of the first type are zero. They are usually less troublesome to handle in system studies. Attention to detail, meticulous care, and other techniques deal with statistical fluctuations. Discussion about random statistical variation is found in Chapter 5.

Probabilistic techniques and sensitivity analysis are tools for long-term uncertainties. Analysis to recognize these long-term uncertainties can be involved or simple. If the design warrants attention for this reason, the analyst may choose to provide a low, modal and high value for critical input variables. This range estimating would determine how sensitive the results are to variations in certain information. The number of combinatorial variations rises at remarkable rate for a statistical evaluation of this kind. Policies that are dominant irrespective of minor or major variations in input data are desirable solutions. However, it is an unusual system design that is so simple.

10.1.4 Time Horizon

Most decision making is a part of the prior history of decisions. Previous choices have affected the now time, and current decisions will influence future actions. Viewed this way all system estimates can be classified as having no time limit. Sometimes dynamic models have an unbounded horizon while others have a terminating date. Project-estimating models are mostly terminating. Time-value-of-money policy actions are examples. Obsolescence and depreciation are two factors that influence systems significantly. As a rule the particular system design is posed in a dynamic context, and the estimator considers time explicitly.

With time-phased costs from the cost streams of different alternatives, the irregular amounts may be discounted using an appropriate interest rate. Methods dealing with this idea were introduced in the last chapter, and they fit system-estimating problems.

10.1.5 Policies

Discussion has been leading up to the manner in which system studies are undertaken. The two approaches are either fixed effectiveness or fixed cost. For a *fixed-effectiveness* system, various alternatives for achieving a prescribed capability or level of effectiveness are studied to determine how such effectiveness can be attained with the least amount of resources. In other words, there is a given objective and the question is to find that alternative or feasible combination of alternatives to achieve the objective. The second type of system analysis deals with a *fixed budget* or specified cost. Given a fixed resource, the estimator looks for the most efficient manner to achieve the level of effectiveness.

In either of these approaches, there are two ways of conceiving the effectiveness measure. The analyst can consider either relative or absolute effectiveness. For relative effectiveness, the measure is viewed more as an index, and only differences are considered important. For comparisons between competing systems, it is simpler to use relative differences to make the decision. The second method is that of the absolute effectiveness or the total cost measure. In addition to the selection among alternatives, it indicates the magnitude and is an additional bit of wisdom for the decision maker.

10.2 DEFINITIONS

A *system design* is a configuration of operations, products, and projects in any combination. There are characteristics that separate system design from other engineering practices. There seems to be an urgency to design configurations based on performance, general requirements, equipment specifications, and their compatibility. Interwoven in system design are the management requirements directing an integrated effort. Every design is a new combination of preexisting knowledge which satisfies an economic want. It is the system estimator who provides the measure of the economic want. Symbolically, the measure is *cost effectiveness,* where *cost* is in dollar terms while *effectiveness* is a design measure.

To a large degree a system estimate is determined by the information that can be obtained. In this respect the system estimate is like other types of estimates, as accuracy, precision, and its general goodness are no less dependent on the available information. There is one distinction, however. In system estimating the kind, quality, and amount of information are usually established after the start of the estimate. With an operation, product, and, to a lesser extent, project design, information is reused, and agencies outside of estimating are in the habit of supplying raw data, performance figures, and the like. This is not true for the system estimate. As this type of estimate is unique, the information is determined after the estimate is started. Usually, it is gathered by the system estimator.

A request for proposal (RFP) initiates the estimating procedure. Internally, the requestor may be systems engineering, or the U.S. government may initiate the activity. In either case, the procedure is similar and the estimator eventually responds with an estimating summary indicating system cost. If the estimator is employed externally to the government, the information is primary (i.e., gathered, analyzed, and estimated within the firm). Government system estimators usually depend on information provided by several or more contractors and use these secondary sources for preparation of their estimates. The system estimator is not so much concerned with comparisons between competing designs. For example, a transportation system for a growing metropolitan area may include concepts of bus, monorail or light rail, subway, subway-bus, and so on. Each of these concepts is to be estimated. Estimators find the economic want and leave optimization, comparison, and trade-off techniques to other members of the system engineering team.

The system estimate is composed of elements as shown by Fig. 10.1. Our intent is to define the terms to prevent semantic difficulties, as system estimating is different from a general business understanding. Our systems are large scaled and the estimating practice is from a governmental or not-for-profit viewpoint. The first difference is the absence of a specially defined profit element. Certainly, the components will include profit for the manufacturers, contractors, and so on, but a system estimate does not include an explicit profit entry. Naturally, the estimates are future values and thus accounting values are unacceptable because future costs will differ from historical values. Some costs may be *nonrecurring,* that is, occur only once for a system design. This type of cost is not the same as fixed cost, which implies a constant periodic cost such as annual debt, rent, or depreciation. Some costs are *recurring,* which is not similar to variable cost. Recurring costs "recur" relative to a performance specification of the system. The system estimate is measured in money terms, dollars. The four estimates are figured considering inflation, deflation, technology, and system performance effects. It is an inviolate principle to this author that these estimate cash-flows are out-of-pocket, or real.

While there is no specific order in considering the elements, a skilled team may begin with the engineering estimate. These costs occur early. They include research, development, design, production or construction, testing, service, and so on. Test models, research laboratory, and facility support may be included. Engineering costs are basically nonrecurring. Techniques discussed earlier in Chapters 8 and 9 are sufficient for calculating an engineering estimate.

A project cost is for a single end item given by a unique and special design. An aircraft carrier and subway construction are typical of the many possibilities. The measure of the economic want is called a bid. A project estimate is dominated by thinking on "first cost," which is only a part of the system cost. Chapter 9 provided methods for project estimating.

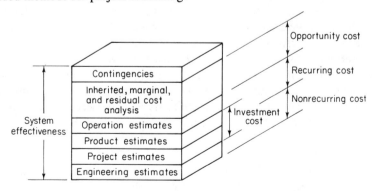

Figure 10.1.   Elements of system estimate.

Product estimates deal with several or many end items. Airplanes for an aircraft carrier or the people carriers for a subway are typical. Key to the logic of product estimating is the idea of replication of the design and the production of several or many units. The measure of the economic want of a product is price. Chapter 8 dealt with methods of product estimating.

The total of the project and product estimates is referred to as "investment" in system estimating jargon. Construction and products are simultaneously necessary for a system (i.e., people movers and the subway).

Operation costs include the costs associated with distribution, operational use, and the sustaining life-cycle logistical support of the system in the field. Maintenance of the investment, training, and utility costs are typical of many thousands of specific costs. Knowledge of whether the costs are borne by the seller or buyer (government in the case of the system estimate) is necessary. Fringe benefits, insurance, medical, retirement, and other overhead charges are a part of this cost pool. Both direct and indirect operational costs are included. Techniques provided by the discussions of operation estimating (Chapter 7) and overhead (Sec. 4.9) are necessary to understand this component. These costs, operation and maintenance (O & M), are figured on an annual basis, and the yearly distinctions required by the system are considered.

These four estimates are sufficiently understood and offer no new difficulties when reconsidered for incorporation into system estimates. However, a cost category unique to system estimating is inherited, marginal, and residual cost.

If a new system is able to adopt an existing subsystem, we have an inherited cost. We assume that the inheritance is already paid for, and thus is nonchargeable in the sense of future out-of-pocket monies. Existing missile silos for new missiles are an example. The missile silo does have economic value provided that a missile system will be used. The term *avoided cost* suggests a contradiction of definition, except in the sense that the silo is single purpose and will not be used unless the decision is made to design a contemporary weapon system compatible with the silo. Can a dollar value be assigned to an inheritance for which no commercial purpose is likely? The answer is yes if the silo prevents or displaces other monies to achieve the same function. The answer is no if substitution is unlikely, or if an equivalent amount of money will be spent anyway despite the incorporation of the missile system. However, the dilemma is partially resolved if the value of the inheritance is assessed to the system and placed in a fictitious account titled *opportunity*.

Opportunity cost is another concept peculiar to system estimating. The term is better understood if we recognize that a shortage of resources is ever present. Governments are no different from the governed—there are greater opportunities for spending than there are taxes or income. As a consequence of the scarcity of taxes and income the options for their use are limited. If we have $10, we could spend it proportionately on systems *A* and *B,* or invest it entirely on *C.* In either case one choice prevents the other.

There are two sides of an opportunity cost. We could spend the money on one system now and prevent its use for a choice now or later. The choice may be greater or smaller, and an opportunity cost is created. Perhaps urgency for some reason requires that we take immediate action even though it does not compare favorably with other actions.

Opportunity cost is a true cost that must be assessed to the system alternative selected and is germane to the selection. On the other hand, opportunity cost is not money-out-of-pocket. For example, inheritance cost of a missile silo is relevant to the system design choice and is a positive quantity that is reckoned in the special account of opportunity. Remember that the missile silos have been built and the money is spent. As another example, consider the relocation of a road for straightening purposes. The bypassed road has residual value and is assessed to the choice of the system that straightens the road in an opportunity account.

We point out that bookkeeping records will not keep track of these opportunity costs. These estimates of the opportunity are listed in a category separate from the other estimates and marginal costs which are real. The purpose of the opportunity category is to complete the total requirements for resources. Additionally, it avoids the "hidden" cost for a system. Conversely, if they were considered equal to the estimates, a possible distortion exists.

Opportunity cost should not be confused with sunk cost. *Sunk cost* is money spent which cannot be recovered by a current or future decision. If the missile silo is abandoned, its cost is sunk and unrecoverable. In fact, there may be a real residual cost for reclaiming the land.

Marginal costs are additional costs due to an alternative design. Section 6.10 already defined marginal cost in the context of production quantity, which is the usual variable. On the other hand, the marginal costs can be defined with respect to a system design change, policy selections, or effectiveness level. Note Fig. 10.2, which shows the system cost level for I. A change in design, policy, or effectiveness level indicates that marginal cost for II is the difference from the base level. It is also possible to have a negative marginal cost from a base level. Marginal costs are real costs and can be estimated by the chapters already discussed.

Residual costs are future values of an investment. A portable machine may have commercial value, or an automobile that has trade-in value, or materials that can be sold are examples of *salvage*. Residual value has different meaning, however. The initial value is determined by project and product estimates. Like salvage value,

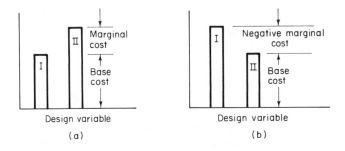

Figure 10.2.   Base cost and marginal cost for design levels I and II.

residual values may be negative, positive, or zero. It may be necessary to detoxify or reclaim a land area. Contrariwise a sale may be possible, thus providing revenue upon disposal of the asset. In some cases the value may be meaningless: for example, a highway that is bypassed by a newer road. It is also conceivable that a road may have residual value 20 years hence. The residual value is useful only if the function of the road persists. Thus residual value deals with governmental system estimates and may not have portability or a conventional market may be unavailable for its disposal. However, the dilemma for an evaluation is partially resolved if the residual value is assessed to the system and placed in a fictitious account titled opportunity.

10.3 ANALYTICAL AIDS

We shall now examine popular devices used to analyze system proposals. These are brief encounters, and the reader is encouraged to examine the references for greater detail on the mechanics of special methods. Often analytical aids for system estimating are necessary. These aids may be subroutines to the model, or they may be freestanding techniques useful for system estimating.

10.3.1 Discounting

Chapter 9 considered aspects of discounting as they related to project estimating. The methods presented there are sufficient for our current need. We now want to point out that which is relevant insofar as system estimating is concerned. The central conclusion that the time-value-of-money concepts can be selected for time-dynamic system models is valid. It allows a systematic method of comparing streams of costs and returns.

Generally the discounting or present worth model is used. If the annual rate is 5%, a dollar received 1 year from now is really worth $(1 + 0.05)^{-1}$ and in n years $(1 + 0.05)^{-n}$ dollars right now. Or if you presently had $\$(1 + 0.05)^{-n}$ and lent it at 5% interest compounded, you would have back $1 n years from today.

Regardless of the costing period chosen it is desirable to time-phase system cost throughout the total life period. Thus the annual cost model is not as appropriate as life cycle costs or the present worth of system design and development, acquisition, and operation costs. This raises the point, What is the life cycle? In public works 30 to 100 years can be used. In weapons system the horizon may terminate within a period of months to 20 years. In commercial enterprises, a system may logically extend between a fad period to an enduring life of 20 to 40 years. All kinds of priorities, political and social, affect the length of time. As the system life cycle becomes longer the actual length becomes less crucial, as the discounting factor drops rapidly if either i or n or both increase.

The total system life cycle is used for another reason. A trade-off analysis between design, investment for construction and acquisition, or operating cost becomes possible if the birth-retirement or death horizon concept is used. In this event it is possible to time-phase all costs and see if, say, additional costs in design might be warranted over excessively large investment and operating costs.

When considering present value, the higher the interest rate i, the smaller the discounted value. The interest rate pertinent for a system estimate is an important subject in its own right and is a lively topic among scholars and practitioners. An unrealistically low or high rate can give a distorted value to the proposed design. In addition, what are the rates for public and governmental units as compared to commercial enterprises? Inasmuch as the government is concerned with social good, there is an undeniable mixture of politics associated with economics. The general effect of an increase in the rate of discounting is not only to make it undesirable to engage in some investment but also to change the character of those system designs adopted, making them less capital-intensive and more labor-intensive.

10.3.2 System Boundaries

While discussion has been devoted to the effectiveness issue, little has been said in this chapter about boundaries or constraints that limit the effectiveness. Constraints, whether implied or unimplied, are always existent. These bounds may be in the form of a budget limit in terms of a fixed amount of cash, or a mathematical statement may be used. The finding of well-expressed constraints is not an easy task. Usually, the process starts by verbalizing a known constraint situation. Creating a notation and devising an algebra that translates the verbal statements may be the next step. Or the constraints may be well known, and empirical evidence may have substantiated its statistical behavior. The constraint may be theoretical, resting on mathematical hypothesis. However the constraint is derived, it is of major importance to system estimating.

Sometimes the constraints are obvious and thus easily overlooked. For instance, a constraint type of importance is nonnegativity (i.e., $x_i \geq 0$, $i = 1, 2, \ldots, n$), which says that the x variable cannot assume negative values. Negative production, meaning that the sunk cost of production could be recovered by a backward process such as disassembly of a product, is prevented by the statement that production $x_i \geq 0$.

10.3.3 Probability

The application of the probability art and science is commonplace in system estimating. In making system, product, project, or other design decisions, risk and uncertainty cloud future events. We deal with the future about which we cannot know, but certain things are inferred from what we know about the past. Time-series models, discussed in Chapter 5, are typical. It is information gained from past events used to predict future events. This involves the study of probability. To a small extent, probability has been discussed piecemeal throughout the previous chapters (see especially Chapters 5 and 6). But depth and rigor are necessary for system estimating.

As future events are random the insistence on single-valued determined data for input and output is misleading. It is frequently more meaningful to compare system alternatives in terms of a probability of being attained rather than by comparing mean values. As was shown in Fig. 6.11, cost estimates can be shown as probability distributions. The mean and variance are important in selecting between two system alternatives. The dilemma of total system cost of an alternative with a lower mean cost but a higher standard deviation—how much higher is naturally germane to the selection.

Given that neither system cost nor effectiveness can be calculated precisely, the determination of the amount of uncertainty is accorded a most-probable cost-effectiveness value. This requires finding the probability distribution of the major units of information. A cost estimate using this reckoning would be given as $250,000 ± $75,000 for a probability of 0.95 of being in this range.

One way to handle probability system cost is via Monte Carlo analysis. A simulation of the system elements is an effective way to model these problems. Many conditional combinations of random costs can be contrived to simulate the system.

10.3.4 Sensitivity

Analyses undertaken for system problems are rarely confined to single numerical values of the optimal solution. We want to know how much the input parameter values can vary without causing alterations in a computed optimal solution or the composition of some policy. An investigation of this sort is termed a sensitivity analysis. Shadow prices and dual variables are other terms used to describe sensitivity factors. In a sensitivity analysis study, fluctuations of the unit profit, or item cost, or time horizon, or product demand, or rainfall, or indirect secondary benefits are permitted. Sensitivity questions are sufficiently complicated to require electronic computation.

In the simplest case, say for straightforward computation of system data, each parameter is varied in turn to determine its effect on the model. Those parameters which are shown to have little or no effect may be treated as constant, or the analyst could be tolerant of variations in these data. Those parameters which when incremented show large variation in effectiveness and alter the optimal solution or reverse policy decisions are called sensitive and bear watching. These kinds of data should be examined in detail since they are important to system effectiveness.

10.4 METHODS

System estimating is relatively new. Even so, professional estimators have favorite practices. While widely divergent in detail, the thrusts of the practice are known as (1) benefit–cost, (2) life-cycle cost, and (3) system budgeting.

10.4.1 Benefit–Cost

Benefit–cost is a practical way of assessing the desirability of system alternatives where it is important to take a long-time and broad view. It is an effectiveness measure in its own right, as it implies the enumeration and evaluation of all or nearly all the selected costs and benefits. Benefit–cost has a long history, initially applied to the federal improvement of navigation back in 1902. It was used in France before that. For the most part benefit–cost is used by governmental agencies. B/C analysis is applied for water improvement and related land use and its application is controlled by federal statute. Costs have long been a factor in decisions made by highway engineers. From the many considerations of highway transportation, an economical road is achieved whenever the total cost is a minimum consistent with convenience, safety, transportation, and the ability to pay. The benefit–cost ratio method is a comparison of the difference in annual cost to highway users when there are vehicles using an existing road in one case and an improved road in another with the annual cost of making the improvement. The equation is

$$\text{benefit–cost ratio} = \frac{r_o - r_i}{(I_i - I_o) - (M_o - M_i)} \tag{10.1}$$

where $r_o - r_i$ = decrease in road user costs after improvements per year

$\quad I_i - I_o$ = increase in investment costs per year

$\quad M_o - M_i$ = decrease in maintenance costs per year

This would simplify to a ratio of decrease in user cost per year divided by net increase in investment costs per year. A similar approach is found for irrigation, recreational development, dams, and so forth. Benefit–cost ratios are calculated for the logical alternatives and are compared with the basic condition.

The current objective is to show how benefit–cost estimates are made, and methods of analysis that start after conclusion of the estimates. Criticism against the B/C method usually deal with the methods of analysis and overlook the schemes of estimating, their definition and logic.

The same input data, if applied consistently, will lead to similar decisions between alternatives. The benefits and costs can be analyzed by present worth and equivalent annual cost. The interest rate, sometimes called minimum attractive rate of return, is preestablished. These methods were discussed in Sec. 9.5 and many texts on engineering economy enlarge on that subject and provide tables to ease calculations. For simplicity, we adopt a present worth approach and confine discussion to that.

One of the confusing choices in benefit–cost analysis is that the benefit to some is a disbenefit to others, or a cost to a governmental agency serves as income to other firms. For purpose of this discussion, we rule that relevant consequences to the governmental units are classified as costs.

There are two methods of calculating the benefit–cost ratio. The first involves subtracting annual benefits from annual costs to establish a net annual benefit. Annual net benefits are discounted back to the date of the program's inception and summed to establish a present value of discounted net benefits. The benefit–cost ratio is then formed by relating this figure to the capital cost of the program. This approach is vaguely similar to a business calculation of the rate of profit that can be earned by capital. The second approach is to establish the gross benefits and costs for a typical year. The costs include annual operating costs and amortization of investment. No discounting is used.

Of the several ways to estimate a benefit–cost ratio, the one chosen here uses discounting. Principally, the B/C ratio has in the numerator the present worth of all benefits, while the denominator is the present worth of all costs. General notation is as follows:

B_n = future benefits in year n, dollars

C_n = future costs in year n, dollars

i = interest rate, decimal

n = year, $n = 0, 1, \ldots, N$

We adopt an end-of-the-year convention, meaning that benefits and costs, however they may occur, are assumed to be instantaneously received or paid at the end of the year. An investment or first cost occurs at time 0. The excess of the present worth of benefits over the present worth of costs is

$$\sum_{n=0}^{N} \frac{B_n}{(1+i)^n} - \sum_{n=0}^{N} \frac{C_n}{(1+i)^n} > 0 \tag{10.2}$$

Investment costs are already at time 0 and do not require discounting. If the difference in Eq. (10.2) is not positive, we presume that the contemplated action is unfavorable.

A present-worth approach to benefit cost ratios is determined by

$$P_b = \sum_{n=0}^{N} \frac{B_n}{(1+i)^n} \tag{10.3}$$

$$P_c = \sum_{n=0}^{N} \frac{C_n}{(1+i)^n} \tag{10.4}$$

and

$$B/C = \frac{P_b}{P_c} \tag{10.5}$$

Consider the stream of cash flows for project X and let $i = 8\%$.

		Year		
	0	1	2	3
Costs, C_n	6	3	4	5
Benefits, B_n	0	10	12	15

The analysis for project X would be

Year	$(1 + i)^n$	$\dfrac{B_n}{(1 + i)^n}$	$\dfrac{C_n}{(1 + i)^n}$
0	1	—	6.
1	1.080	9.529	2.778
2	1.166	10.292	3.431
3	1.260	11.905	3.968
		31.726	16.177

The value of the discounted cash flows of benefits and costs is \$31.726 and \$16.177. The excess of the present-worth benefits over costs is $15.549 \, (= 31.726 - 16.177)$ and the B/C ratio is $1.96 \, (= 31.726/16.177)$. In this example we assume that the benefits were amenities, such as might develop from increases in irrigation, recreation, and fish and wildlife revenues and assumes that they were nonexistent before.

In another situation, such as the straightening of a road, the benefits accrued to the user are reductions in road user costs and are a favorable consequence to road users. We then look upon the difference of the improved and the original road as a benefit to the road user.

Consider now projects X and Y, and determine their benefit–cost difference and ratio. Project X is in bad condition and reconditioning is planned. Project Y is new and involves higher investment but lower costs to the user. Operation and maintenance costs of the project also differ.

	Project X	Project Y
Investment	6.000	9.000
PW of maintenance	10.177	13.115
PW of user costs	31.726	25.267

Using present-worth calculations and using $P_b = P_{bx} - P_{by}$ as the difference in benefits,

$$P_b = 31.726 - 25.267 = 6.459$$

and the difference in costs as $P_c = P_{cy} - P_{cx}$

$$P_c = (9.000 + 13.115) - (6.000 + 10.177) = 5.938$$

The stipulation that $P_b - P_c > 0$ can also be expressed as the ratio 1.04. The conclusion is to adopt project Y, but barely, on the basis of the marginal B/C ratio.

As with other effectiveness measures, the B/C ratio has limitations which we cannot cover fully. It is a ratio—simply benefits divided by costs. At that point, however, complications set in. Which costs and whose benefits are to be included? How are they to be valued? At what interest rate are they to be discounted? What are the relevant constraints? There is bound to be arbitrariness in answering these questions.

In most cases the scope and nature of the system which is to be analyzed are clear. There is a wide class of costs and benefits which accrue to organizations other than the one sponsoring the system and an equally wide issue of how the parent agency should consider them. For instance, a hydroelectric dam can be costed and benefits determined, but what about the recreational amenities, water for farming, and improvements in scenery? The net rise in rents and land values is a result of the benefits of hydro power. These secondary benefits may be more important to one governmental agency than another, and calculations can impute these pecuniary spillovers in a more or less favorable way.

Some advocates suggest that a B/C analysis side-step the issue by requiring public agencies to operate on a commercial basis, leaving resource allocation to be resolved through an artifice of the pricing system. But welfare economics, the well-being of people, income redistribution, market imperfections, and the like make a reasonable demonstration of B/C in a commercial environment difficult. Thus a B/C philosophy has to have a comprehensive public viewpoint. When constrained by laws and appropriations, the B/C ratio is best used as a means of ranking various systems. Those which are higher are considered better from the B/C viewpoint.

As an example, consider the following. A project is planned largely to provide water for industrial, municipal, and domestic use in connection with anticipated development of coal and oil shale reserves. It would increase irrigation supplies for production of livestock feeds and also would benefit recreation, fish, and wildlife, and flood control.

Note Table 10.1, which is a summary of project and operation estimates and benefits. Project estimates which are determined using rules of Chapter 9 are posted for each of the separate projects. In turn, operation estimates which use the advice of Chapter 7 are averaged for the span of life, 100 years in this example. The project costs are nonrecurring. The operation estimate provides for the labor, materials, and overhead to operate and maintain the investment. Occasional replacement of minor capital requirements are, for convenience sake, included in the operation estimates.

The benefits are determined using price schedules of similar opportunities. For example, irrigation water has a market value and may be found using comparison methods. In circumstances where there may be no market advice, opinion estimates will lead to imputed values. It may be possible that some benefits reduce financial gain. For instance, the impounding of water into reservoir will reduce the grazing pasture for cattle and these efforts cause *disbenefits,* or benefits lost. It is a practice that benefits lost are charged against the benefits and not added to the denominator cost term.

With the benefits and cost posted to the pro forma summary (Table 10.1), it is possible to determine the net present worth of the cash flow and the B/C ratio. We use an interest rate of 6%.

$$P_b = \sum_{n=0}^{100} \frac{B_n}{(1 + i)^n} = \$5,845,300(16.618) = \$97,137,195$$

Table 10.1. SUMMARY OF BENEFIT–COST ESTIMATES

A. Costs	
Projects	
Dam 1	$11,850,000
Dam 2	6,400,000
Dam 3	5,100,000
Canals and diversion dams	23,870,000
Laterals and drains	5,350,000
Operating and equipment	330,000
Fish and wildlife equipment	610,000
Recreational facilities	1,246,000
Constructional total	$54,756,000
Operational costs	
Operation, maintenance, and replacement for 100 years, annual	$ 147,200
B. Benefits	
Average annual for 100 years	
Industrial, municipal, and domestic water use	$4,590,900
Irrigation	869,800
Recreation	245,800
Fish and wildlife	137,700
Flood control	11,000
Less benefits lost	9,900
Average yearly net benefits	$ 5,845,300

$$P_c = \sum_{n=0}^{100} \frac{C_n}{(1 + i)^n} = \$54,756,000 + 147,200(16.618) = \$57,202,170$$

The $P_b - P_c > 0$ and B/C $= 1.70$.

Once the tangible benefits and costs are recognized, classes of reimbursable and nonreimbursable cost allocations are made. We have seen the problem of cost allocation before. In a B/C situation though, it is the proper distribution of the costs of the features that serve several purposes that are the problem. This problem does not arise in the cost of a single purpose project, nor when national policy has determined in advance that the purpose to be served outweighs all costs. The costs of a multiple-purpose project are composed of the costs of individual project features such as irrigation canals, power houses, or navigational works, which serve only a single purpose. A dam, of course, serves these several single purposes and its cost must be allocated to both reimbursable and nonreimbursable services.

Broad principles of cost allocation are possible. Each purpose should share equitably in the savings resulting from multiple-purpose construction within the limits of maximum and minimum allocations. The maximum allocation to each purpose is its benefits or alternative single purpose cost whichever is less. The minimum allocation to each purpose is its specific or its separable cost. Joint costs are apportioned without regard to the ability of any particular purpose to pay.

In an oil shale water project as major as Table 10.1, it is necessary to recognize that many of the costs can be repaid by various public or private entities that will benefit. Land rents, payment for irrigation water, and recreational amenities by the general public are typical opportunities. Laws require repayment and practices have established the categories of reimbursable and nonreimbursable costs.

Reimbursable costs for Table 10.2 have a period of 50 years for repayment. Often, interest of a few percent may be added to these costs. Some expenses are considered nonreimbursable and are borne by the federal government, such as the expenses for project investigations. Note, however, that the total of both costs are used in determining the B/C ratio.

If there are several designs requiring a decision for one system, invariably the cost and benefits are different, and a marginal method must be used to find the best

Table 10.2. COST ALLOCATIONS AND REPAYMENT SUMMARY

	Project Costs	Annual Operation, Maintenance, and Replacement Costs
Reimbursable costs[a]		
Industrial, municipal, and domestic	$39,330,000	$ 61,200
Irrigation	10,160,000	40,100
Recreation	166,500	17,800
Fish and wildlife	375,000	
Subtotal	$50,031,500	$119,100
Nonreimbursable costs		
Recreation	$ 2,765,500	$ 27,500
Fish and wildlife	1,823,000	400
Flood control	136,000	200
Subtotal	$ 4,724,500	$ 28,100
Total	$54,756,000	$147,200
Repayment		
Industrial, municipal, and domestic use[b]		
Prepayment[c]	$ 474,000	
Water conservancy district	38,856,000	$ 61,200
	$39,330,000	$ 61,200
Irrigation		
Prepayment	$ 126,000	
Water conservancy district	6,720,000	$ 40,100
Apportioned to others	3,314,000	
	$10,160,000	$ 40,100
Recreation, fish and wildlife[b]		
Nonfederal interests	$ 541,500	$ 17,800
Total	$50,031,500	$119,100

[a]Reimbursed over 50 years.
[b]Repayment rate at 3.5% annually.
[c]Nonreimbursable expenses for project investigations.

system. Several guidelines are necessary. First, the same interest rate should be used to figure costs and benefits. The same period of life, N, is necessary for the system alternatives. We initially calculate the B/C ratio for each system, such as that which is given by Table 10.3. In this table there are four mutually exclusive choices. System choices that were less than 1 would be rejected.

Table 10.3. BENEFIT-COST RATIOS FOR FOUR MUTUALLY EXCLUSIVE SYSTEM CHOICES

System Design	Present Worth Benefits	Present Worth Costs	B/C
A	$120,000	$60,000	2.00
B	112,000	53,000	2.11
C	75,000	58,000	1.29
D	64,000	34,000	1.87

Inspection of these B/C ratios would suggest that alternative B is chosen because its ratio is the greatest. This is an improper selection. The proper choice depends on the principles of interest rate methods of engineering economy.

Table 10.4 shows the required calculations. The system choices are considered in order of increasing cost. System D is used as the initial base since it requires the minimum present worth cost. The first row of this table repeats row D from the previous table. Insofar as this first calculation is concerned, the decision is to accept D. Next, the marginal increase in cost and benefits is determined by using the next alternative above the least costly alternative. This would be C, and the C minus D values are indicated for the row. The marginal B/C ratio is 0.46, which is less than 1, and C is rejected. We proceed by considering the alternatives in order of increasing costs. Now choice B is compared to D and the B/C ratio exceeds 1 and design B is preferred to alternative D. System design B is the current best choice. Last, the marginal gain and loss of design A minus design B is computed. The ratio of marginal present worth benefits to marginal present worth costs is greater than 1, indicating that design A is preferable to B. The final choice is A, and it assures that the equivalent present worth benefits will be less than the equivalent present worth costs and the system return is maximized. Choice A is contrary to the initial selection B.

Table 10.4. MARGINAL BENEFIT-COST RATIOS

System Design	Marginal Present Worth Benefit	Marginal Present Worth Costs	Marginal B/C Rates	Decision
D	$64,000	$34,000	1.87	Accept D
C − D	11,000	24,000	0.46	Reject C
B − D	48,000	19,000	2.52	Accept B
A − B	8,000	7,000	1.14	Accept A

Thus B/C analysis deals with the first step of estimating the costs and benefits. If this is successfully achieved, the next step is to rank alternatives in order of increasing investment such as the present worth, and then check to see if the marginal investment is effective. This is tested by checking the differences between successive pairs of B/C alternatives against a status quo condition, or do nothing. A conclusion is reached whenever the last alternative is compared with the last acceptable alternative.

10.4.2 Life-Cycle Cost

Life-cycle cost (LCC) is the summation of all estimated cash flows from concept, design, construction and manufacture, operation, and disposal of the system at the end of useful life. The design is generally a system, but a product or project can also be evaluated. Intuitively, individuals have used LCC principles for economic evaluation of cars when they concern themselves not only with initial cost (sticker price) but with operating and maintenance expenses (gas mileage, worn parts, insurance, license) and residual value (resale price).

LCC attempts to estimate all relevant costs, both present and future, in the decision-making process for the selection among various choices. Figure 10.3 illustrates engineering, product, project, and operation costs as separate cash flows. These cash flows are determined using the estimating methods previously discussed. However, in LCC analysis, the estimates are scheduled as period cash flows starting with $E = 0, +1, +2$, where E = moment of the estimate, N_c = end of costing period, and N_l = end of life cycle. The periods are year designations. Note in Fig. 10.3 that design precedes project and product, which precedes the operating costs. It is not necessary that the curves be symmetrically shaped. Costs conclude at the end of cycle, of course.

Operating cash flows can easily be greater than the original R & D or the investment. Moreover, a system with higher engineering and investment costs but lower operation and maintenance costs may, depending on service life, be a least

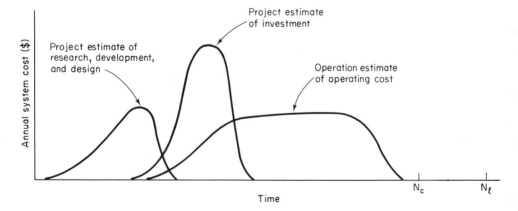

Figure 10.3. Cost time phasing for a system life cycle.

LCC system. It has been shown that for military hardware systems, approximately two-thirds of life-cycle costs are unalterably fixed during the design phase. LCC encourages trade-off analysis between one-time costs and recurring costs. This is described by Fig. 10.4, where either system *A, B,* or *C* is selected on the basis of minimum LCC and operating years. The analysis suggested by Fig. 10.4 is important in trade-off selection.

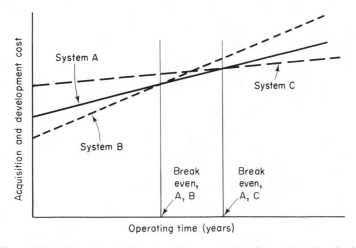

Figure 10.4. Life-cycle cost where operations over a period of years determine selection.

We shall consider a case study of LCC applied to an environmental chamber used to simulate high-altitude pressures for electronic equipment experimentation. See the case study in Chapter 1 for additional background. Figure 10.5 is a preliminary design of the product. The system is a retractable chamber which opens to allow the placement of various electronic equipment. Various vacuum pressures are possible. The design will have a life cycle of six periods because the experiment will conclude then. The length of life cycle is sensitive to wear-out, casualty or destruction, economic, or technology factors. For our case study, the life cycle is set by the contract period for the experiment of electronic equipment.

In preparation for the LCC system estimate the following data are required:

1. Engineering estimate
2. Product estimate
3. Operation estimate
4. Operating profile
5. Maintenance schedule

The operating profile has a repetition time and contains all the operating and non-operating modes of the equipment. It is sometimes possible to have operating profiles

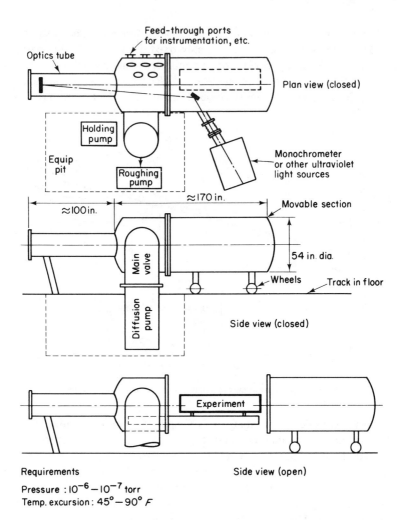

Figure 10.5. Vacuum chamber environmental conceptual test system.

internal to other operating profiles. For trade-off studies, candidates must be evaluated with the same operating profile. In our example, we must know what use we
are going to make of the vacuum chamber. The operating profile tells when or in
what way the equipment will be operating. For example, the diffusion pump will
run 60% of the time in the environmental chamber. It will not run in a shutdown
mode; instead, a roughing pump holds nominal vacuum.

Operating costs incurred during the life of the equipment are found using the
profile. Two unusual cost parameters are *mean time between failure* (MTBF) and
mean time to repair (MTTR). *Warranty costs* are customarily included in the product
estimate and depend on MTBF information. Time between overhaul, power con-

sumption rate, and preventive maintenance routines such as cycle and the preventive maintenance rates are required information.

For our case study, installation is estimated to cost $20,000 and is a one-time nonrecurring cost. The aerospace firm estimates its operating profile and determines that a continuous three-shift operation for about one-third of a year, or 2920 hours per year, is necessary. Using the schedule and a labor rate, 2920 hours per year $\times$ $28 per hour $\times$ 1 man per machine $=$ $81,760.

Labor for preventive maintenance (PM) actions is calculated using

$$\text{number of PM actions} = \frac{\text{scheduled operating hours}}{\text{PM cycle time}} \tag{10.6}$$

The number of preventive maintenance actions is

$$\frac{2920}{160} = 19 \text{ actions}$$

where each maintenance cycle is 160 hours. Since each maintenance action requires 4 hours, we have $19(4) = 76$ hours of PM time for a total yearly cost of $1976 ($= 76$ hours $\times$ $26 per hour).

The aerospace firm has studies that the system will fail every 500 hours. The 500 number is the mean time between failures. The cost of corrective maintenance is found using

$$C_{cm} = \frac{\text{SOH}}{\text{MTBF}}(\text{MTTR})C_m \tag{10.7}$$

where C_{cm} = cost for corrective maintenance per year

SOH = scheduled operating hours
MTBF = mean hours between failures
MTTR = mean hours to repair
$\quad C_m$ = cost of maintenance labor

We have

$$C_{cm} = \frac{2920}{500}(40)(26) = \$6074$$

Power consumption cost is found by multiplying input power in kilowatts by total hours of operation and the cost per kilowatt hour.

$$\text{power cost} = 2920 \text{ hours per year} \times 10 \text{ kW} \times \$0.20/\text{kW} = \$5840$$

Spare parts, discussed in Chapter 8, may also be estimated by a historical percentage factor of the original product cost. For $\frac{1}{2}\%$, we have

$$\text{spare parts cost} = 0.005 \times (125,000 + 210,000 + 65,000) = 2000 \text{ per year}$$

All of these costs are summarized on Table 10.5. Their sum of $656,200 is the undiscounted life-cycle cost. However, LCC analysis discounts all costs back to a time zero, sometimes considered to be the moment of the estimate or $E = 0$. A discount rate of 10% is applied to the data, where each estimate is assumed end-of-

Table 10.5. DESIGN, PRODUCT, OPERATION, AND MAINTENANCE CASH FLOW ESTIMATES SCHEDULE OVER LIFE CYCLE OF ENVIRONMENTAL VACUUM CHAMBER

Cost elements	$1000 Cash Flow for Period:					
	1	2	3	4	5	6
1. Design	25	11	5			
2. Product manufacture		125	210	65		
3. Operation						
Installation				20		
Manpower					81.8	81.8
Preventive maintenance					2.0	2.0
Corrective maintenance					6.0	6.0
Power					5.8	5.8
Spare parts					2	2
Discount factor, $\dfrac{1}{(1.1)^n}$	0.909	0.826	0.751	0.683	0.621	0.564

period. The discount factor is found from $1/(1 + i)^n$. Total discounted cash flow sums the product of the discount factor and cash flow for each year, or $470,237.

Life cycle may be determined from wear-out, casualty, economic, or technical obsolescence factors. When obsolescence is a factor, opinion is required, as the life of the equipment may suddenly be terminated by a change in company policy, buying habits, government legislation, competitive pressures, or new designs.

Another prediction that can be bewildering is salvage value. An experienced appraiser may give opinions of future land and factory values. If the life is not expected to be great, the estimator is in a position to trust this source of information. For the longer-lived equipment, information may be unavailable. Despite the fear of distant predictions, errors in evaluating salvage value are not normally serious. Error in the present or the near future should be given more concern or study because the effects of these conclusions are greater. Another prediction for equipment and plants is that of the efficiency of the utilization. This efficiency is important because it controls cost to some extent. Errors in the degree of efficiency of equipment are considered serious, and predictions of this nature should be studied closely.

In forecasting the life of an asset there are two major concerns: annual deterioration and obsolescence. Where physical life or annual deterioration establishes the life, statistical data from past records become the basis for future prediction. If *life* is regarded as economic, statistical methods find the probability that the economic life of a proposal will terminate during each year of its service life. In either of these two cases, deterioration or obsolescence, the life of a particular proposal terminates because it is worn out or because the product or service which it produces is no longer profitable.

In the first instance, the physical condition has deteriorated and it does not produce the desired quality, or the cost of maintenance exceeds the cost of replacement. In the absence of statistical data, reliance must be placed on the opinion of people having experience such as engineers, operators, and the people producing the equipment. In the case of obsolescence, competition may introduce substitute products, processes, or machines with better prices, qualities, or services.

Once the estimate is concluded, continuing analysis becomes possible. The estimate allows for visibility of "tall poles," a jargon implying significant cost elements. For the vacuum chamber, the tall poles are product manufacture and operating manpower.

10.4.3 Budgets

In the previous three chapters on estimating, it is seen that the summing of various cost elements is a popular method.* System estimating is no different. Aggregation of cost may be handled by a general summation model of the form

$$C = \Sigma E + \Sigma M + \Sigma L + \Sigma \text{OH} + \cdots \tag{10.8}$$

where E = sum of engineering cost
  M = sum of direct materials
  L = sum of direct labor
  OH = sum of overhead

Budgets are pro forma methods that provide the summing of costs, although not as formal appearing as intended by Eq. 10.8. Its importance is made clear by its popularity, for the budget is indispensable for planning and traceability.

We have previously mentioned fixed, variable, operating, and appropriation types of budgets in Chapter 4. Minor modifications for concepts of opportunity cost, inherited (sunk or residual) cost, and marginal cost make these standard procedures suitable for system budgets.

From the viewpoint of system estimating, cost continues to be broadly interpreted and can be considered to be the amount paid or given for anything whether it is labor or self-denial to secure a benefit. In the minds of many system estimators, cost is only one element of value forgone in order to secure a benefit. In short, cost is a negative benefit. In these terms, cost includes money, time, performance, consumption of scarce resources, and ordinary human skills.

It is relatively easy to determine a value scale which relates the relative worth of one resource to another if an interchange is indexed by the dollar. The money value of inputs is not difficult to establish, as the market place provides a mechanism for assessing these costs. For a commercial system the dollar value measure system applies, and competition aids in establishing the price. In other situations the market

---

*The use of Department of Defense Form 633 is popular for many major and minor subcontractors who deal with the U.S. Government. This form has many derivatives, and cost estimating and accounting standards, practices, and laws are associated with these forms. While form 633 is not basically a "budget," it is a summation cost model. Discussion of Form 633 is inappropriate for a textbook.

mechanism may be unavailable, for example, weapons system or river basin development. Electrical power, one component of a river basin development, may have market value, but recreation or flood risk do not have this advantage. Whenever a competitive market action and reaction is nonexistent the analyst can determine an opportunity cost function for those components which require a value. This is equivalent to imputing a price which might be comparable to a market price.

Inasmuch as resources are always scarce, the options for their application are limited. The selection of one system design precludes another. Thus an opportunity cost arises from the fact that the expenditure of money on one design pre-empts its use for another. Failure to take advantage of the other opportunity may result in foregoing a profit or benefit that otherwise might have been obtained. This is a true cost which can be assessed against the alternative selected. In this context it is called opportunity cost. This indirect cost measurement approach evaluates the resource, which may not have been clearly identified and measured for the selected alternative.

Inherited and marginal costs cannot be separately treated in matters of system budgeting. Inherited or residual cost is a value of earlier resources committed to the system, while marginal costs are the additional costs resulting from a change in objectives or level of the decision. In earlier chapters we suggested that a policy can be made based on marginal analysis irrespective of inherited values. For instance, an optimum operating point n existed when $dC_T/dn = 0$. It is not really this simple. Not all decisions can be made separate of inherited costs and values such as marginal cost theory seems to imply. Certainly the logic to ascertain a marginal decision is based in part on inherited values. To remove or ignore that base and to deny its importance for future decision making overlooks its value as a base representing existing capability. In determining how many additional resources are needed to acquire some specific capability or, conversely, how much additional effectiveness will result from some additional cost is a marginal cost budgeting problem.

How are these concepts incorporated into the budget? Opportunity cost can be a line item in the accounts of the budget, as it is certainly germane to the design selection. A clarification must be made as to what it precisely means on the budget form to avoid misleading interpretations.

Two budgeting extremes for inherited and marginal costs are total of inherited values plus marginal cost, or *full,* and marginal costs only. Because of their extreme position, both can be faulty or correct at various times. In the full method, the overstatement of fixed values may cause insensitivity. One means to overcome a disproportionate statement is to identify that which is fixed inheritance from that which is variable or proportional to the decision. In the latter case, an allocation of a part of the inherited system value tends to reduce the invariant part of the fixed budget.

If one uses an absolute budget, then full inherited values and their amortization are indispensable methods. If a relative general budget is to be employed, marginal cost values can be used. Of course, there is the type of budget that is in between these two. Caution in the preparation and understanding must be exercised.

SUMMARY

As system designs are configurations of operations, products, and projects in any manner, a standardized treatment is largely illusory. An estimating method is devised for the design, and the principal elements deal with operations, products, projects, and engineering. The methods have the rubric of benefit–cost, life-cycle cost, or budget. A measure, called symbolically effectiveness and having a dollar monetary unit, is the usual one for cost-estimating activities. The task of determining the kinds and sources of information is next. As always, data are vital, and careful methods of analysis can extend the usefulness of the information. If the system is long-range and complex, the effort for a system estimate is formidable.

QUESTIONS

10.1. Give an explanation of the following terms:

System	Opportunity cost
Effectiveness	Sunk cost
Efficiency	Residual value
Intangible	Discounting
RFP	Sensitivity
Recurring costs	Life-cycle costs
Nonrecurring costs	Benefit–cost ratio

10.2. Two approaches for system studies are fixed effectiveness and fixed cost. Describe how they work and contrast their differences. What are the advantages and disadvantages of specific effectivenesses?

10.3. How is salvage cost different from residual cost?

10.4. For a real life problem, write some system bounderies, and then find their equation.

10.5. State some disbenefits for water-navigation projects. What makes the benefit–cost ratio like an effectiveness measure?

10.6. When is a relative effectiveness superior to absolute effectiveness? If accuracy of data is a problem, how does this affect your discussion?

10.7. For an imaginary system design, list several intangibles. Indicate the pros and cons.

10.8. Why are budgets important in system estimating?

PROBLEMS

10.1. There is no uniform method for the analysis of system problems. If one were available and after we had learned the procedures and by strict adherence to the method, we would be assured of a good chance for a successful result. Thus system evaluation is dependent on the skill and resourcefulness of the estimator. Considering the system concepts of (1) effectiveness and system models, (2) cultivation of alternatives, (3) intangibles and tangibles, (4) time horizon, and (5) fixed, variable, inherited, and marginal cost streams, how do you propose to analyze a technical problem that you are or would be concerned with? State your own problem, give its ramifications, and provide the system procedure for its evaluation.

10.2. A system is conceived of in terms of three goals. Management considers each desirable and of equal importance. The available alternatives are mutually exclusive and are measured by a relative effectiveness consistent for the goals and alternatives. Higher effectiveness is considered more desirable.

	G_1	G_2	G_3
A_1	80	22	19
A_2	50	40	43
A_3	35	70	21
A_4	39	47	48
A_5	25	25	75

(a) Which is the preferred alternative for each goal?

(b) Assuming that goals G_2 and G_3 are equally desirable, what weighting would goal G_1 require to favor alternative A_1?

10.3. Your company is attempting to sell a system design to a client. The design will provide a profit of $50,000 once it is concluded. So far, your company has spent $20,000 promoting the sale. There is a sense of confidence that the sale will be assured by an added expense. What is the maximum amount of resources (over what your firm has already spent) you should spend to secure the sale? Discuss.

10.4. (a) In a period of rising prices, a contractor is maintaining an inventory at a constant level. A subsystem is purchased by a contractor for $20,000 and then resold as a part of a system for $30,000. It is replaced for $40,000. Comment on their unit cost estimating and pricing policies.

(b) Now assume a period of declining prices. A contractor buys a subsystem for $40,000 and then sells it as part of a system for $30,000. Immediately it is replaced for $20,000. Discuss these policies.

10.5. Suppose that a building owned by a business can be rented for $10,000 per year to another firm or used for the manufacture and construction of a system. After an initial cost for equipment, the new system will provide a net equivalent annual income of $20,000. However, the analyst did not charge for expenses for self-use of the building because "it was owned by the company." Discuss this action considering opportunity cost. Is there a more meaningful measure? What if there had been no interested renters, or the space is unsuitable for rent; would this affect your measure? What if there is only one renter who desires the space for 1 year but the system has a potential market for 2 years? Contrariwise, the renter will lease for 2 years while the market will last only 1 year. Will these situations require a time-dependent weighting factor? Discuss the point: "Once a decision is made, the advantage of the alternative is foregone and further consideration is useless."

10.6. There are two possible system designs. System 1 is refurbished, while system 2 is new. The second system is located away from the older system. Both systems are identical in meeting performance requirements. Following Fig. 10.1 we select symbols that represent the discounted sum of the cash flow and their comparison are as follows: Engineering ($E_1 < E_2$); product ($P_1 = P_2$); project ($W_1 < W_2$); operation and maintenance ($OM_1 > OM_2$); inherited ($I_1 > 0$, $I_2 = 0$), residual ($R_1 = 0$ if choice 1 or 2 selected, and R_2 is unavailable if choice one is selected, or $R_2 > 0$ if choice two is made); and contingency ($C_1 < C_2$). Construct a total symbolic effectiveness measure for choices 1 and 2. Find their marginal difference. Indicate non-recurring and recurring cost. Give their investment costs. What is the opportunity cost in the context of the circumstances of selecting options 1 or 2? Does opportunity cost differ before and after the decision of selecting the system?

10.7. (a) Cash flows for a project A are given as follows:

	Year				
	0	1	2	3	4
Costs, C_n	20	5	5	6	8
Benefits, B_n	0	25	20	15	10

For an interest rate of $i = 8\%$, find the present worth of costs and benefits. Also calculate the net present worth and benefit cost ratio.

(b) Cash flows for project A are given as

	Year				
	0	1	2	3	4
Costs, C_n	20	8	6	5	5
Benefits, B_n	0	10	15	20	25

Using an interest rate of $i = 8\%$, find the present worth of costs, benefits, their difference, and the benefit–cost ratio.

10.8. Two projects, B and C, have the following cash flows:

		Year			
		1	2	3	4
B	Maintenance	5	5	6	8
	User cost	25	20	15	10
C	Maintenance	4	4	4	4
	User cost	20	15	10	5

(a) Investment costs for B and C are 20 and 30, respectively. The interest used in the analysis is 9%. Find the present worth of cash flows. Determine the benefit cost difference and ratio between the two projects.

(b) Repeat part (a) for 10%.

(c) Repeat (a) for 15%.

10.9. A manager is considering a new project. Her possible choices and estimates of costs and benefits are shown in the table. Each project has a 5-year life. Interest is 9%.

Item	Project Value ($\times 10^5$)		
	A	B	C
Initial cost	$144	$50	$380
Annual net benefits, five years	40	16	100
Residual value	0	0	10

(a) For each project find the net present worth. Which project should be chosen? Find the benefit cost ratios.

(b) Find the marginal benefit–cost ratios. Which project should be chosen?

(c) Reconsider parts (a) and (b) with an interest of 15%.

10. A governmental agency that uses an interest of 5% is able to select one of three projects:

Item	Project Value		
	A	B	C
Initial cost ($\times 10^6$)	40	50	60
Annual benefits ($\times 10^6$)	15	20	25
Project life (years)	4	4	4

(a) Find the net present worth. Determine the B/C ratios. Rank the projects according to method of evaluation. Determine the marginal benefit–cost ratios. Rerank the methods. Which one do you prefer?

(b) Reconsider part (a) with 10%.

10.11. A welfare program that is to be discounted at a 5% factor costs $350,000 with a $20,000 annual operating cost. Benefits are anticipated to be $40,000 in the first year and to increase by $30,000 each year for 4 years. It will decline to no benefit in 2 years. What is the benefit–cost ratio with and without discounting?

10.12. A sociopolitical system has a first cost of $1 million and an annual maintenance cost of $25,000 each year over a 50-year life cycle. Benefits average out as $50,000 per year.

(a) At 5% interest, what is the system net present worth?

(b) What is the benefit–cost ratio?

10.13. An existing highway, ABC (Fig. P10.13), originally constructed in 1924, is 8.5 miles long. Average daily commercial traffic is 10,000 vehicles with 10% trucks. Now requiring reconstruction, the unit estimated cost of improvements to existing highway is $2 million per mile. The right-of-way will cost $550,000 per mile. A 7-mile supplemental location, ADC, can be constructed for $3 million per mile. The right-

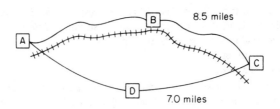

Figure P10.13

of-way costs $220,000 per mile. ADC requires two viaducts for $500,000 each. Long-term maintenance cost of either road is an average $10,000 per mile-year. This maintenance includes occasional resurfacing. Trucks cost $1 per mile, while cars are evaluated to cost $0.25 per mile. If ADC were constructed, it is estimated that 40% of the traffic between points AC will move to ADC and the remainder would use ABC. Describe the alternative plans.

(a) Based on a project estimate of capital cost only, which plan do you advise?

(b) What are the discounted and undiscounted traffic costs for 20 years for the two plans. Use $i = 5\%$.

(c) Let $i = 5\%$. Construct a B/C analysis for this total problem and advise a solution.

10.14. The B/C test has been applied to welfare and job training for underprivileged youth. In this case an undiscounted B/C ratio is given as

$$\text{benefit–cost} = \frac{B_p - B}{C_a - T_n}$$

where B_p is graduate earnings, B is original earnings of student, C_a is annual amortization payment, and T_n is taxes on net increased earning of student. The following items are estimated:

Direct program training cost	$ 725,000
Allocation of center overhead based	
on planned enrollment	950,000
Subtotal	1,675,000
Capital investment cost at 5%	83,750
Job corps cost at 25%	418,750
Total cost	2,177,500
Number of graduates	400
Total cost/graduate	5,443
Five-year amortization cost (C_a)	1,089
Average starting salary	4,222
Five-year average salary (B_p)	5,026
Five-year average taxes (T_n)	562
Original earning power of students (B)	1,040

(a) Find the undiscounted and discounted benefit–cost ratio.

(b) Let the interest rate be 5%. What happens to the B/C ratio as the interest rate increases? Decreases?

10.15. Construct a personal B/C ratio for your own education along the lines of the one in Problem 10.14.

10.16. Four mutually exclusive designs have their benefits and costs estimated.

	Present Worth	
Design	Benefits	Costs
A	$48.000	$38,000
B	35,000	24,000
C	37,000	31,000
D	45,000	34,000

Determine the individual B/C ratios and analyze the four choices on the basis of marginal yield to find the best one.

10.17. An aerospace firm has received a second bid for an environmental chamber. Design cost is estimated as $30,000 and $10,000, which occur in the first two periods. Installation will cost $30,000 at $n = 4$. Product manufacture is quoted as $90,000, $150,000, and $25,000 for $n = 2, 3$, and 4. The new bidder says that operation will require two operators. The preventive maintenance cycle time is 200 hours and each maintenance action requires 5 hours. MTBF = 650 hours and MTTR = 25 hours. Power requirements are 23 kW. Spare parts are $\frac{1}{4}$%. Find the LCC. Determine the discounted value of LCC where the opportunity interest rate = 10%.

10.18. A nonreparable electronic component is up for bid and an LCC approach is deemed mandatory. The purchasing agent advertises that an LCC model to select the winning bid will be based on the model

$$\text{cost per hour} = \frac{\text{unit price} + \text{unit stocking cost}}{\text{bid MTBF}}$$

The stocking cost of $110 per unit is the total cost for storage, installation, and dismantling. Each bidder supplies this information to the purchasing agent.

Bidder	Unit Price	Bid MTBF
1	$1000	800
2	1250	615
3	1175	917

Which bidder wins the contract?

10.19. The government tells potential contractors that a product will be evaluated according to a LCC model:

$$\text{LCC} = \text{unit operating cost}$$
$$= (\text{unit price} + \text{logistic cost}) \div \text{service life}$$

The selected contractor demonstrates service life in a post-award reliability acceptance test. If the reliability test does not meet the level stated by the contract, a penalty function deducts from the unit price as $(1 - \text{test value MTBF/quoted MTBF}) \times$ (unit price + logistic cost). The logistic cost is $200.

Company	Unit Price	Hours MTBF
A	$350	1000
B	400	1200
C	700	2100

Find the winning company. Now suppose that the contractor failed to meet the quoted MTBF by 10%. What is the penalty and the final price?

10.20. The government establishes an LCC model to evaluate tires. The model is given as LCC = quantity (unit price + shipping cost + maintenance cost per unit). Three tire manufacturers were invited to bid. Each was asked to provide a sample for simulated landing tests to determine the number of landings per tire. The government then determined the number of tires for each company's quote based on a tire-landing index which is given by number of required landings ÷ best performance:

$$\text{number of required landings} = 1,200,000$$

Shipping costs were evaluated from the manufacturer to a central inventory. Maintenance cost to change a tire is $47.50. Make a bid evaluation to determine LCC price. Which company do you select?

Company	Landings per Tire	Shipping Cost per Tire	Bid Price per Tire
A	110	$13.50	$1380
B	105	7.50	1280
C	95	13.00	1360

10.21. A purchasing agent announces that a system will be evaluated according to the following LCC model:

$$C_{cm} = \frac{SOH}{MTBF}(MTTR)C_m + \text{Unit Price}$$

The following bids were received. Which bid do you choose?

Company	Unit Price	SOH	MTBF	MTTR	C_m ($/hour)
A	$200	5000	1000	1.5	$25
B	280	4500	1500	1.4	25
C	260	4000	2000	1.3	25

CASE STUDY:
LIFE CYCLE OF PUMPING STATION

A new pump station is being designed by Mr. Jarrett, a municipal planning engineer. Jarrett secures the following information on the new pump:

Installation cost (1 year from design) – $22,000
Preventive maintenance cycle = 2190 hours
Operating hours per year = 2190 hours per year
Preventive maintenance action = 4 hours
MTBF = 10,950 hours
MTTR = 8 hours
Power demand = 60 kilowatts
Power cost = $0.07 per kilowatthour

Jarrett has estimated design cost as $40,000 for year 1. Maintenance labor will cost $26 per hour. In addition to the consumption charge of $0.07 per kilowatthour for power, there is a monthly demand charge of $390 for power. Find the LCC for the first 10 years of pump operation. What is the discounted LCC assuming an 8% interest rate?

11

Estimate Assurance

The cost estimator's interest in his or her estimate continues beyond the conclusion of the estimate. Its accuracy, reliability, and quality are important. If the estimate leads to a sale or winning bid, there is an opportunity to verify its general goodness. This chapter describes the analysis of estimates when compared to a so-called actual value. For there are lessons to be learned in improving the capture rate, understanding the importance of human behavior, and in various techniques.

It is an important dogma of this book that the cost estimate is more useful to the design than the actual or standard cost. Each of the four kinds of estimates, operation, product, project and system, requires modifying features to assure that reported costs concur with the estimate.

11.1 ANALYSIS OF ESTIMATES

Cost estimating is seldom done without an effort to check its success. A common method of verification is to find so-called actual costs and compare with the original estimates. That was done in a study of 157 cost estimates for tools in a manufacturing plant as shown by Fig. 11.1.

An error is measured as

$$E = \left(\frac{c_e}{c_a} - 1\right) \times 100 \tag{11.1}$$

where E = percentage error of estimate
c_e = estimate of cost, price, bid or effectiveness
c_a = actual cost, price, bid or effectiveness

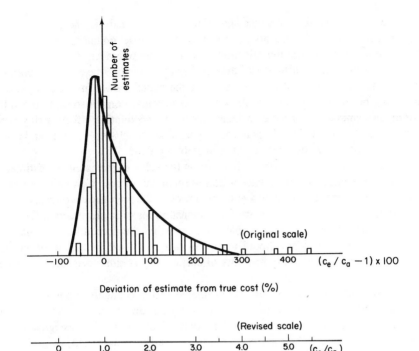

Figure 11.1.   Distribution of estimates for various tooling jobs.

Now if a firm determined this percentage error for a large number of estimates and plotted these findings on a histogram, we could, by assuming an infinite population of estimates, form a density distribution curve to these error estimates. In this actual study the deviations ranged from a low of 50% to a high of 450%, but the sum of the estimated amounts was less than 4% above the total actual cost. Obviously all the jobs that were estimated low did not yield as much as was expected. The others brought in more than was expected because they actually cost less than what was estimated. A natural question is: "What can be learned from an analysis of this sort to help improve the cost-estimating practice?" Should some amount be added to each estimate to reduce the losses from the low ones? If so, how much? Obviously to do so would raise the high estimates and diminish their chances in competition. The low estimates cannot be identified beforehand or there would not be any low estimates. While analysis of this sort is useful, it does not give information about jobs that did not meet competition. The actual costs of unsuccessful bids were never determined. Study of estimating policies must consider all estimates, not just the ones that have produced orders.

The goal of the estimating function is to produce estimates that are exact. While this is a commendable purpose, it is more realistic to say that the goal would have the estimate value fall within some acceptable range. This advances the notion of a tolerance. What this tolerance should be is open to analysis and consideration. Factors such as cost of preparation, time available, impact on the organization, and data requirements bear on the selection of an estimate tolerance. Inasmuch as estimates are prior to the fulfillment of the design, a passage of time exists between the estimate and the historical determination of the actual value. In some situations, data may never be gathered to allow even a nominal comparison. At the other extreme an abundance may be on hand; yet due to accounting effects a tidy comparison may be impractical. In practice a reconciliation between estimate and actual measure, while very desirable, is difficult to bring about.

There is yet another problem in assuring the value of the estimate. Estimators estimate, yet it is management that controls the elements of cost. Certainly estimators are a part of the general management team; however, the prerogatives of cost control, manning, budgets, and so forth are the responsibilities of nonestimators. One may argue that an estimator is responsible for forecasting the peccadilloes of management. Certainly estimators should try to be aware of these factors when costing designs; nonetheless, the responsibility of cost control is either delegated or shared with others.

In further discussion herein, the estimated cost c_e is understood to be the total price for a job. This includes the usual items of cost, direct and indirect, overhead, contingencies, and an expected profit. The contingency allows for unassignable extra costs that may occur. The total price is for the market, a quotation, or a bid. The actual cost c_a includes these same factors of cost and contingencies because they are inherent in the performance of each job.

For simplicity the deviations in cost estimates will be expressed by the ratio c_e/c_a. This does not change the shape of Fig. 11.1 to which a new scale may be applied to show the deviations in terms of c_e/c_a. Obviously, this ratio equals one where actual cost equals the estimated cost. This is the important break-even. Those points to the left on the horizontal axis are operationally undesirable because the firm will be operating at a loss. Depending on bidding policies and objectives, the distribution of estimates is to the right of the break-even point. Long-range survival depends on that.

But curves like Fig. 11.1 are seldom, if ever, found because actual costs may not match neatly with estimates. These nonsymmetrical data can be normalized for additional analysis but techniques are beyond the purposes of this text.

Our purpose in this chapter is not to deal with "cost control," as other books devote attention to that topic. But more important is the principle that *estimate assurance* is the critical factor. Cost control places emphasis on cost containment. But estimate assurance recognizes that the value of the estimate is the *best* value, and the objective becomes one of regulating costs to match the estimate.

Costs may be labeled estimate, actual, or standard. Actual costs are incorrectly assumed to be the more important. However, it is seldom that actual costs are accurately known, and furthermore they are not ordinarily indicative of future values. Actual costs are more expensive to determine than estimates and are not available until after the operation, product, project, or system is complete. Then they are too late except for analysis and reestimating. As is suggested throughout the chapter, actual costs are seldom known with precision.

Standard costs are hypothetical and in a sense are "should be" costs. This kind of cost is fashioned on accounting principles and is useful for income and expense recording, tax finding, and for other financial reports. Of course, these costs are never "true" except in the sense of a definition.

It is the point of this book that the estimate value, properly determined, is superior to either actual or standard values. It may be surprising to the reader that actual costs may never be determined, but it is interesting to speculate on the deviation with estimates that would be revealed if they were known. This difference is due to the error of the estimate. The three kinds of errors are mistakes, policy, and risk.

Mistakes result from imprecision, blunders such as $2 + 2 = 5$, and omissions. Typically, they pass unnoticed, but if they occur, "nature" may be kind due to compensating effects of offsetting mistakes. Prevention results from uncompromising arithmetic and strict attention to methods that inspire faultless computation. The use of a computer is a popular solution for overcoming mistakes. As a tireless machine, it removes the burden of routine calculation. But most estimates are not manipulated by a computer. Pad-and-pencil calculations for estimates are more common. Cross-checks by other estimators, or the stapling of a calculator's paper tape to the estimate, or row-and-column arithmetic simultaneously agreeing for the final value are simple ways to reduce mistakes. Preventing omissions in cost elements is encouraged by pro forma procedures, cross-talk within the estimating team, and checklists. Unfortunately, most management views errors as implying *only* mistakes.

Policy errors are errors of belief made through ignorance or inadvertence. Simplified illustrations include failure to recognize material price breaks for quantity purchase or overlooking a planned contractual increase in direct labor cost. Excessive or low values for overhead ratios, first cost, cost of operation, and other elements are typical. A cost-estimating relationship may have higher statistical correlation with a nonlinear relation instead of a linear model. Errors of policy are prevented by well-thought-out policies, practices and self-learning.

Risk errors are the least understood. Assume that in a competitive bidding situation, your value is "perfect" and yet a competitor submits a lower value. The lower value may be the result of their more productive business, and thus your failure to win is a consequence of your unproductive business. On the other hand, the competitor's bid may be a "low-ball," a bid simply to keep the work force busy. Thus your bid still lost. Contrariwise, your bid may win because your business is more productive or competitors are not really interested and submit high bids or they make mistakes and over bid. Maybe your bid is set intentionally low to keep your work force busy. Profit margins may be overlooked also. *Risk* error is the difference between the estimate and the winning value and is uncontrollable by the firm's estimator.

The winning bid may be known for public works, where the law dictates open disclosure. Some competitors' estimates may be proprietary and are unknown. On the other hand, some of these values can be determined by simply asking. Thus the deviation between the estimate and actual cost for estimates not realized may never be known.

Formula (11.1) to find the error by comparing to actual costs overlooks policy and risk errors. Finally, the comparison is not available until after the actual costs are reported.

An improved error measure uses a preliminary and a detail estimate and is given as

$$E = \left(\frac{c_p}{c_d} - 1 \right) \times 100 \tag{11.2}$$

where c_p = preliminary estimate of cost, price, bid, or effectiveness
    c_d = detail estimate of cost, price, bid, or effectiveness
Naturally, the preliminary and detail estimate are made for an identical design. The preliminary estimate is made quickly and independently of the detail estimate. A detail estimate uses a pro forma procedure and emphasis is on comprehensiveness. There are pitfalls to avoid. One problem is to prevent the preliminary estimate from becoming a self-fulfilling value where a detail estimate is guided to match a preliminary estimate. Two groups or individuals or alternative methods may make these estimates separately. The value of c_p should be restricted on a need-to-know basis so as not to influence the value of c_d.

Ultimately, estimates either win or lose in the sense that business is obtained. The purpose of a detail estimate is to determine an economic value of want that is desired by competing selfish interests. Contractors and job-shop manufacturers are frequently submitting cost estimates to potential customers. In the case of products, estimating is done to set cost and price. Estimates may win or lose in this case as well. Management may drop a proprietary product because it may not be economically successful, or a vendor may not be selected. Winning and losing business can be functionally related to cost estimating performance.

This analysis is called *capture rate* and is defined as

$$\text{capture rate} = \frac{c_w}{c_t} \times 100 \tag{11.3}$$

where c_w = cost estimates won, number
    c_t = total cost estimates, number
This capture rate may be determined monthly or yearly. Some firms may make hundreds of estimates per month, while for projects only a few are made yearly. The capture rate may differ between new and repeat business. Some firms adjust their costs or margins depending on the direction of the capture rate. If the capture rate falls, profit margins are reduced, and vice versa. This author knows of firms who operate successfully with 1% and unsuccessfully with a 90% rate. This measure alone does not give the entire picture of successful estimate assurance.

Actual costs deviate from estimates because of inefficiency or superior efficiency and many other reasons. While it is a goal to have actual costs approach the estimate, the usual term describing the reasons for this departure is *productivity.* Adjustments to the cost estimates are made using an overall productivity factor.* The productivity factor is found using

$$PF = \frac{\Sigma\ c_a}{\Sigma\ c_e} \tag{11.4}$$

where PF denotes the productivity factor, a dimensionless number. For instance, if $\Sigma\ c_a = \$5157.58$ and $\Sigma\ c_e = \$4715.07$, then $PF = 1.094$. If these data were considered representative of future work, the total estimated cost for a future design would be multiplied by 1.094 to anticipate the cost actually reported. The productivity factor may be found from a single sample or a time series of experiences. It is doubtful if a constant productivity factor is achievable. Ultimately, the estimator will use opinion and experience to state if a historical value can be used for the future.

Despite a variety of possible ways to make an estimate, resources for the preparation are always restricted as time, money, and the technical staff are limited. Eventually one reaches a point where the objectives must be satisfied with what time, money, and intelligence are available. The ideal policy would have the estimate coincide with the reconciled actual cost. Actual cost is, perhaps, never known. No procedure, mathematical technique, or policy employed in the engineering world is without its flaws and shortcomings or is able to guarantee perfect estimates. Although flaws in estimating may be obvious, these procedures and techniques are used for the simple reason that they are the best means at hand. Imperfection seldom deters usage.

11.2 BEHAVIORAL CONSIDERATIONS

The primary goal of estimate assurance is to develop and sustain business systems to inform management about the extent, type, and status of expenditures. The computer has given impetus to these systems enabling them to be more effective. While computerized business systems should lead to improvement of estimate assurance, it is recognized that this is only the routine part. While these enamored features are traditionally thought to be the essence of estimate assurance, it may be surprising to the reader that despite their development there remains a general lack of estimating success. Little heed is given to the problem that these systems operate in an organization. This is due to the difficulty of the task. Behavioral principles should be considered by the cost estimators since they encourage the better functioning of estimates.

The general "control" model consists of objectives and standards, measurement of actual results, comparisons of actual results to standards, and management

---

*Engineers usually think of productivity as analogous to efficiency, or output/input which is a number less than 1. It is the habit of this author to recommend the reverse ratio. But an output/input factor would divide the new estimate to indicate a "realized" estimate or as in language given by this book, "adjusted estimate."

action. Figure 11.2 describes a simple network. The "sensor" measures the output which is transmitted for comparison with a standard. If an unacceptable difference is noted, action is taken via an "actuator." Those control models that do not respond to external social or economic influences are known as *closed*. Systems that respond to poor labor efficiency, late material delivery. engineering changes, competition, price changes, and so on, are known as *open*. Open systems do not lend themselves to automatic regulation and are the more difficult and hence challenging. Less management time and finesse are necessary for a mechanistic or closed system. A detailed discussion of behavioral principles is beyond the scope of this text, but considerations are amplified throughout this chapter.

Let us relate these model components to cost estimating. Objectives and standards deal with performance, time, and cost. To be meaningful, unambiguous, and useful, objectives and standards must be quantitatively stated in measurable operational units. An objective could be the cost estimate, but there are many others. Measurement of results records actual cost and relates to the cost code, work breakdown structure, operation sheet, product task, and so on. This measurement may be supplemented by special reports and audits. Comparison of actual results to standards is done via reports. A simple example is the side-by-side comparison of estimate and actual costs for material, labor, and overhead, broken down in as fine detail as required. Much of this is done mechanically in conjunction with results management. Trending and charting of milestones are other techniques for this purpose. Management actions encourage performance to match the objective. If there is agreement, action is unnecessary. A match of this kind is unlikely. As estimates are "open" systems, change is commonplace and management is necessary to encourage conformance. This is the most crucial component in the cost-estimate assurance program.

There may be the policy issue of whether a cost estimate should be made tight or loose. Behaviorally, it can be argued that tight estimates will motivate attainment and lower cost, as Fig. 11.3 suggests. A counterargument is that loose cost estimates if easily attained will probably be exceeded with the generation of good feelings.

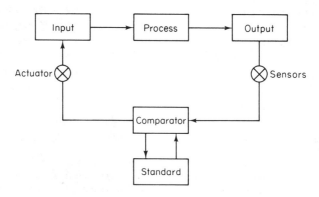

Figure 11.2.   Simple control model for cost assurance.

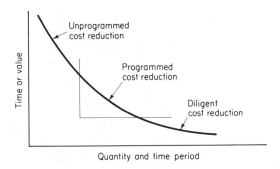

Figure 11.3. Reactions to match cost estimate.

Here the psychological motivation is needed for self-esteem. Research findings are biased toward tight estimates for productivity attainment. Unresolved is how tight the cost estimate should be, for if set too tight these act to demotivate and cause lower performance. This book, however, takes the viewpoint that the cost estimate should reflect the anticipated money-out-of-pocket that the element will require. Thus if a diligent cost reduction program is planned, lower cost is anticipated by the cost estimate.

In the cost-estimate assurance program, management must be aware of what is significant. A law, often attributed to Pareto, is the application to objective identification. It identifies that 20% of the parts, for instance, contribute 80% of the cost. Whether 20/80, 30/70, or another ratio is the correct *rule of thumb* is unimportant, but the rule relies on an analysis to determine the significant contributors.

11.3 OPERATION ESTIMATE ASSURANCE

An operation is the conversion of direct material by direct labor into various shapes. Indirect costs such as factory or construction overhead are necessary for the conversion. Operation estimates are for the immediate future period. Because of this brief time, comparison of actual to estimate values is sometimes possible.

A word "standard" is often used synonymously with "estimate" for operation work. Accountants are involved with standard costs. The engineer, when referring to *standards,* thinks in terms of a rigid specification, but analysts from other fields have dissimilar viewpoints. A *standard cost* as discussed here provides a dollar amount which is a "should be" amount and is not an immutable natural law. An attitude is necessary in viewing standard costs. Standard costs may be classified as perfection-level standards, and management encourages attainment of these standards as goals. Some businesses contend that perfection standards are preferable to attainable standards because they provide a stimulus to workers and management to achieve the best possible performance.

A standard unit cost of a labor operation, part, or product is a predetermined cost that may be computed even before operations are started. In constructing the standard unit cost of an item it is necessary to study the kind and grade of materials that should be used, how each labor operation ought to be performed, how much time each labor operation should take, how the indirect services should be best administered, and the entire specifications for the complete and total operation. The aim, of course, is to specify the most effective method of making the item and then through adherence to the specifications in the actual operations achieve the lowest practical unit cost. By now it should be realized that a system of this type may be expected to provide a calculated and anticipated cost of all products by cost elements; comparisons of the anticipated cost with actual results and the reasons for any differences; the effectiveness of all cost elements, including material, labor, and overhead; and measurement of departmental or individual performances against accepted standards. This is, of course, the method of estimating.

Despite the care used in establishing standard costs the actual costs as reported in any particular period or any particular job are very likely to deviate from the standard. These differences are known as *variances* and are expressed as dollar amounts or percentages. They are favorable variances when the actual costs are less than the standard costs and unfavorable when actual costs exceed standard costs. It should not be interpreted that excess of actual cost or of standard cost is adverse to the firm. Similarly, not all favorable variances represent actual benefits to the company. The terms *favorable* and *unfavorable* when applied to variances indicate the direction of the variance from standard cost.

Some businesses use variance analysis to understand inflation, deflation, schedule delays, engineering change orders, or rework. These variances may be the result of a buyer or seller action, or a governmental regulatory agency may be the cause. Many other causes are possible. A consistent approach allows for reconciliation and explanation of the total cost increase.

The elements used to estimate direct material cost are quantity, shape, and the raw material cost. Consequently, actual material cost may differ from the estimate because of a quantity variance or raw material cost variance or both. For instance

$$\text{Estimate: 200 units at } \$17.38 = \$3476.00$$
$$\text{Actual: 210 units at } \$17.05 = \$3580.50$$

It is apparent that an unfavorable variance of $104.50 resulted in part from an excess of 10 units and in part from a deficit unit cost $0.33. The analysis is described further by Fig. 11.4. There is a simple way to analyze the difference. The figure starts with actual material cost per unit times actual units. We change one of the factors (cost or quantity) to the estimate. The difference gives a variance due to the factor that was changed. The remaining difference is the variance for the other factor. In Fig. 11.4(a) the quantity factor is changed first, while for sketch (b) the material cost factor was changed first. These procedures result in a difference in the quantity or cost variance, depending on the order of calculation.

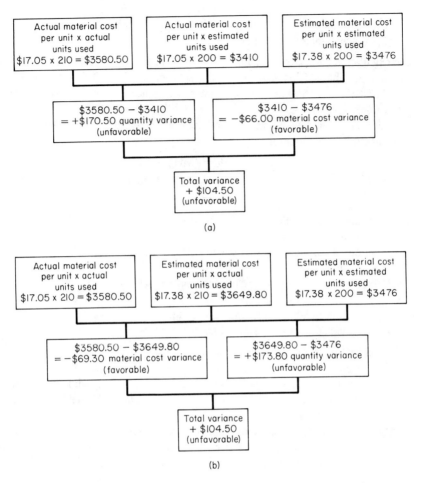

Figure 11.4. Finding variance on (a) quantity first and (b) material cost first.

This ambiguity can be significant in owner–contractor or contractor–subcontractor disputes. Terms of the contract may stipulate the manner in which variance analysis is undertaken. A typical resolution is as follows:

$$V_m = (N_a - N_e)C_e$$
$$V'_m = (C_a - C_e)N_a$$
$$\text{Net material variance} = V_m + V'_m$$

(11.5)

where V_m = dollar variance for material due to quantity change
  V'_m = dollar variance for material due to material cost
    per unit change
  N_a = actual quantity, number
  N_e = estimated quantity, number

C_e = estimated material cost per unit
C_a = actual material cost per unit

These calculations are shown by Fig. 11.5(a). Both favorable and unfavorable variances are possible. Using Eq. (11.5) the solution to Fig. 11.5 becomes V_m = $173.80 and V'_m = $-$$69.30. The net material variance is an unfavorable $104.50 (= 173.80 $-$ 69.30).

Labor costs can be analyzed for both man-hours and the labor dollar rate. Fig. 11.5(b) illustrates the notation.

$$V_1 = (MH_a - MH_s)R_e$$
$$V'_1 = (R_a - R_e)MH_a \qquad (11.6)$$
$$\text{net labor variance} = V_1 + V'_1$$

where V_1 = dollar variance for labor due to a difference from
     estimated hours
   V'_1 = dollar variance for labor due to a difference from
     estimated hourly rate
   MH_s = estimated total standard hours for operation
   MH_a = actual total hours for operation
   R_e = estimated labor hourly rate, dollar/unit
   R_a = actual labor hourly rate, dollar/unit

Consider the example where the estimated wage rate = $18.76, while hours are 283. The actual wage rate and hours were $17.32 and 325. The unfavorable variance due to changes in hours is $784 (= (325 $-$ 283) 18.67), while the favorable rate variance is $-$$439 [= (17.32 $-$ 18.67)325]. The unfavorable net labor variance is $345 (= 784 $-$ 439).

Man-hours are the product of a labor standard and the number of units. A three-dimensional variance analysis is possible for labor operation if we consider quantity, labor hourly rate, and the allowed or standard unit time. Define

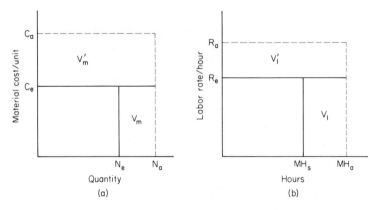

Figure 11.5   (a) Variance for material; (b) variance for labor.

$$V_{dl} = (N_a - N_e)H_s R_e$$
$$V'_{dl} = (H_a - H_e)N_a R_e \qquad (11.7)$$
$$V''_{dl} = (R_a - R_e)N_a H_a$$
$$\text{net direct labor variance} = V_{dl} + V'_{dl} + V''_{dl}$$

where V_{dl} = dollar variance for direct labor due to
        a difference from estimated quantity

$\quad V'_{dl}$ = dollar variance for direct labor due to
        a difference from estimated standard
        hour rate

$\quad V''_{dl}$ = dollar variance for direct labor due to
        a difference from estimated wage rate

$\quad H_s$ = estimated standard hours, hours per unit

$\quad H_a$ = actual hours, hours per unit

For a standard rate of 1.415 hours per unit and an estimated quantity of 200, the actual rate of 1.548 hours per unit and 210, and an estimated wage rate of $18.67 and actual of $17.32, the following facts are uncovered: V_{dl} = $264, V'_{dl} = $520, and V''_{dl} = −$439. The unfavorable labor variance is $345.

Indirect expenses are important for operations. Methods of their regulation and assurance are not as straightforward as direct material and direct labor, where variances are the focus of attention. Indirect costs, since they are in support of direct costs, are assumed to vary proportionately. A ratio of indirect to direct costs is one way to monitor these costs. Overhead can be analyzed for variances also.

Behavioral considerations are important for operation cost of labor and materials. Labor-cost reduction can be observed with the learning theory, as shown by Fig. 11.6. Reduction of direct labor hours is due to working harder, improved

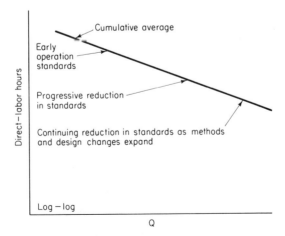

Figure 11.6. Typical effect of operation learning for standards. *Note:* Standards are lowered because of methods, design, or material changes only.

methods of design, or material changes. Contrariwise, slowdown, morale problems, unforeseen design changes, or destabilizing personnel reactions can alter the slope and *unlearning* may occur. For the most part, labor estimates are lowered because of improvements caused by technical productivity.

Direct materials are sometimes the major part of an operation. Figure 11.7 describes the percent increase for material. In this actual history, the cost of a material ran away for 1 year before engineering efforts were applied to regulate the material cost. The darkler line is the actual purchase cost of raw materials, while the dashed line is the compensating price. The difference is lost revenue. Figure 11.8 is a learning theory application for a subcontract material, diesel engines in this

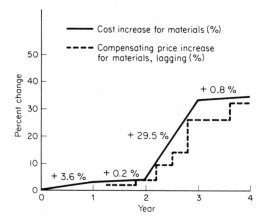

Figure 11.7.   Effects of material cost increases.

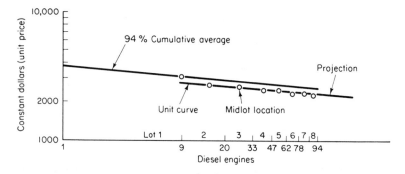

Figure 11.8.   Learning curve application for purchase of subcontract materials.

circumstance. These diesel engines were adapted for a special design, and thus are a subcontract material. It should be noted that the constant dollar cost of the engines declined because of the estimate assurance program.

11.4 PRODUCT ESTIMATE ASSURANCE

A product estimate deals with material, labor, and overhead cost elements for a design that is replicated. This notion, introduced in Chapter 1, suggests a similarity between subsequent designs. Model II is like model I, and we apply that principle to guide the logic of product estimating. This similarity is primary to the practice of product estimating. Product quantity may be anywhere from a few to millions and is another important factor. Seldom is a product design so novel that the firm has virtually no past experience. Estimate assurance programs for the product depend on similarity in design and quantity performance.

Introduced in Sec. 8.5 were four methods for estimating products. There are corresponding techniques for product assurance. Table 11.1 is an example continuing the variable cost method. This method was first discussed with marginal cost implications and Fig. 6.17 serves as a planning attempt to understand marginal cost analysis. Later in Sec. 8.5.3 distinctions of variable costs from product and standby fixed costs were examined and Table 8.5 is the pro forma. The pricing model (8.17) uses the notion of contribution. The student will want to review this background for understanding Table 11.1. At this development we assumed that 20,000 units of a special product model I have been produced, sold, and all cost facts have been historically determined. Observe in Table 11.1 that net sales are $19,300 and variable costs for labor, material, and various overhead are determined. A total variable cost $12,560 is found, which agrees (as it should) with the pro forma estimate (Table 8.5). Contribution at standard is 35%. At this point, it is noted that variances exist, both favorable and unfavorable, on the variable costs and purchase price. Profit contribution at actual reduces to $4065 and 21%. Period costs which are of a fixed nature occurring within the model I production period are identified with budgeted and variance values. Now total costs are estimated as $19,435, showing a loss of -0.7%. Apparently model I was not as successful as initially hoped.

It is at this point that a product estimate assurance program is necessary. Little can be done with the results of Table 11.1, as the money is already spent. Except that the results can lead to better operation methods, design, sales, and so on. Marketing and design engineering changes may lead to models II and III. Note Table 11.2, where an analysis of models I, II, and III is summarized. Clearly, model II is preferred as its percent of net sales is the highest.

Behavioral considerations, while not a root solution alone to product estimate assurance, leads to achieving desired results. Learning theory is appropriate for products having significant aggregate value and low volume. Figure 11.9 is an example of an actual history. This figure is evidence that the learning theory applies to this circumstance. Once this fact is established, learning can be used for estimating

Table 11.1.   VARIANCE ANALYSIS OF INCOME AND EXPENSES STATEMENT FOR MODEL I
OF SPECIAL PRODUCT

Net sales (20,000 units at $0.965)	$19,300
Variable costs	
Labor, 20,000 units at $0.20	$ 4,000
Material, 20,000 units at $0.384	7,680
Manufacturing expenses, 20,000 units at 0.02	400
Material overhead expenses, 20.000 units at 0.007	140
Administrative and marketing expenses,	
20,000 at 0.017	340
Total variable costs	$12,560
Profit contribution at standard	$ 6,740
Percent of net sales	35%
Variances on variable costs	
Labor	$ (450)
Material usage and scrap	(1025)
Manufacturing expenses	25
Material expenses	45
Administrative and marketing expenses	(20)
Purchase price	(1250)
Total variance	$ (2675)
Profit contribution at actual	$ 4,065
Percent of net sales	21%
Period costs	
Budgeted costs	4,060
Variances on period costs	(140)
Total period costs	$ 4,200
Total cost	$19,345
Net profit	$ (135)
Percent of net sales	0.7% loss

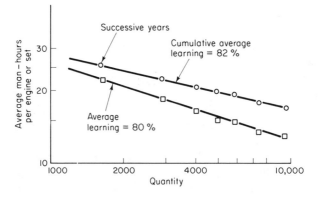

Figure 11.9.   Historical analysis of learning effects for engine-generator project.

Table 11.2.   ANALYSIS OF INCOME AND EXPENSES FOR MODELS I, II, AND III
OF SPECIAL PRODUCT

	Total	I	II	III
Sales	$97,300	$19,300	$36,000	$42,000
Variable costs				
Labor	$23,000	$ 4,000	$ 7,000	$12,000
Material	38,330	7,680	11,000	19,650
Manufacturing expenses	2,200	400	850	950
Material expenses	740	140	250	350
Administrative expenses	1,850	340	560	950
Total variable costs	$66,120	$12,560	$19,660	$33,900
Profit contribution	$31,180	$ 6,740	$16,340	$ 8,100
Percent of net sales	32%	35%	45%	19%
Variances on variable costs				
Labor	$ (830)	$ (450)	$ 120	$ (500)
Material usage and scrap	(1075)	(1025)	$ 750	$ (800)
Manufacturing expenses	(100)	$ 25	$ (75)	$ (50)
Material expenses	(90)	45	(85)	(50)
Administrative expenses	(45)	(20)	0	(25)
Purchase price	(2500)	(1250)	0	(1250)
Total variances	$(4640)	$(2675)	$ 710	$(2675)
Profit contribution at actual	$26,540	$ 4,065	$17,050	$ 5,425
Percent of net sales	27%	21%	47%	13%
Period costs				
Budgeted costs	$18,060			
Variances on period costs	(800)			
Total period costs	$18,860			
Total costs	$89,620			
Net profit	$ 7,680			
Percent on net sales	8%			

this or similar products produced by this company. Successful estimating with learning is a consequence of achieving results—learning should not be used as an estimating technique unless company history has demonstrated its success.

Design effort is necessary for learning-theory reduction. Figure 11.10 is an
example of the effect of an early or later estimate assurance engineering program.
The right vertical axis, engineering change notices (ECNS) and drawing change
notices (DCNS), may be related to a cost-reduction impact. This axis scale increases
downward. These engineering design programs are the investment in slope reduction.

Some products which have low value and high quantity may be inappropriate
for learning theory. Other techniques, such as design-to-cost, can be successfully
used. Note Figure 11.11, which shows a product work breakdown structure. Some
of the boxes have been completed and cost has been closed out, while for other
boxes costs are in-progress. The S-curves of Chapter 9 can be used to note the
trends. For long-term products, it may be possible to reduce the level of expenditure
and assure the value of the estimate.

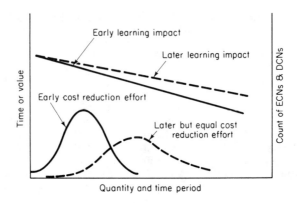

Figure 11.10.   Early and later engineering effort to assure product estimate.

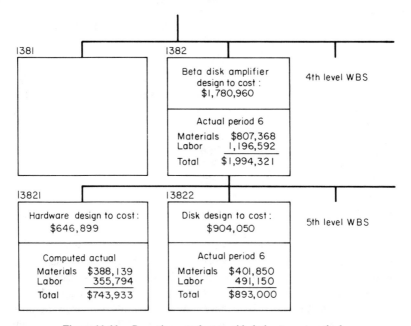

Figure 11.11.   Reporting actual costs with design to cost methods.

11.5 PROJECT ESTIMATE ASSURANCE

The capital investment for a single-end item is determined by a project estimate. The money required for a project is large compared to the available resources. Because of the importance of projects to the long-term financial health of the firm, considerable effort is devoted to assuring the success of estimate. Projects are scheduled over a long duration and opportunities exist to regulate the actual costs. Both the owner and contractor desire these objectives. However, an estimate-assurance program must be more than a mere objective. It must define details, provide a strategy, and indicate the steps. Owners sanction the project because of a profitable time-value-of-money concept, and money and time (or schedule) are the major factors of concern. The project estimator in preparing the work breakdown structure (WBS) package has already provided details, strategy, and steps. The WBS package is discussed in Chapter 9. That chapter developed the scope and definition, designs, work breakdown structure, schedule, and estimates. The WBS is used for estimating, planning, and performance measurement and to assure that actual costs achieve the estimate. Now we extend these principles for estimate assurance.

The elements of the project estimate are listed as direct labor, direct material and subcontract, facilities and equipment, engineering, overhead, interest, contingency, and profit. Contingency allows for unassignable extra costs that may occur and its eventual outcome is not known beforehand. Actual cost includes these contingencies because they are inherent in the performance of the cost element. The purpose of cost assurance is to guarantee the project profit. While estimate assurance deals with overall project cost, it is defined as the procedures where actual costs are controlled to the level of the elements. It makes little difference whether the budget is a scheduled commitment or a scheduled expenditure for the elements. Nor do values of dollar magnitude alter the approach.

The S-curves of Chapter 9 are developed first by plotting cumulative expenditure against the planned period. The subjects for the plot are the major elements of the project. The baseline values were determined using the trapezoidal or other models, or the WBS schedule. This ideal baseline expenditure is known as the "budgeted cost for work scheduled" or BCWS, and is available at the moment of the project start. This vertical axis may also be titled BCWS%, which is equivalent to cumulative baseline percentage. The contract period percentage is an alternate x-axis for cost/schedule performance reports. Once the project is under way the contractor's reporting methods will provide the "actual cost of work performed," ACWP, and by cross-checking actual work to the WBS will find the derivative "budgeted cost for work performed," or BCWP. Additionally, the cost/schedule status report will provide a forecast cost at completion, and budgeted cost at completion. These concepts are illustrated by Fig. 11.12. At the close of each period the estimator will graphically forecast the remainder of unfinished WBS elements for ACWP and BCWP. The extension depends on a graphical ability, and more important, that extra knowledge and opinion about delivery promises, potential strikes, bad weather, and so on. There is a problem, however, with work-in-process tasks having a long time period. If the reporting cutoff period slices into work-in-process for some task, the percentage of completion must be subjective. Estimating the percent of task complete must be done by the person responsible for the task. It is recognized that work packages vary. For example, fabrication work packages tend to be short and discrete. Engineering work packages are difficult to plan since the work is variable, making it difficult to judge for percentage completion. Contrariwise, work completion can be better judged over several reporting periods, as single-period judgment of percentage completion is a sticky wicket. A related problem deals with reporting cost and schedule variance on fixed-price subcontracts, since some subcontractors may not report internal progress on work. For those subcontractors who may not report progress, the estimator may do "vendor-talk" and learn informally of their progress and use that to keep the cost/schedule system informed.

Performance measurement is a comparison of budgeted versus actual accomplishment. Comparing the budgeted cost for work scheduled to the budgeted cost of work performed produces a dollar schedule variance. If the BCWP exceeds BCWS (i.e., is higher on the vertical axis), more work was accomplished than was planned and the favorable variance reflects the dollar (or percentage value) of the extra work. If BCWP is less than BCWS, less work was accomplished than was planned and an unfavorable schedule variance is indicated. The horizontal difference between BCWS and BCWP is the schedule variance expressed as periods or period percentage.

Contract cost performance is related to work done versus work planned. The BCWP when compared to BCWS indicates a schedule variance, but when compared to ACWP a cost variance is obtained. If the BCWP exceeds ACWP, a favorable variance is noted, and if ACWP is greater than BCWP, a negative cost variance, or an overrun, is currently observed. The cost and schedule variance are indicated on Fig. 11.12.

The dashed projection of BCWP to the contract cost level indicates the conjectured schedule completion. Project *slippage* is the number of calendar days or periods between the actual and planned project completion. The dashed projection of ACWP in Fig. 11.12 indicates the projected dollar overrun when compared to BCWP.

If the estimate assurance program reduces the magnitude of the actual expenditure, project attractiveness is enhanced. If the project decision was based on optimistic cost expectations, a cost assurance program should reveal this fact early enough for reassessment. Cost information must be available so that significant items of the project cost may be watched. The project budget is tabulated to have this record correspond to the WBS, definition, and estimates. It has happened that projects which had overly optimistic estimates, poor performance, and scheduled delays have been cancelled after reassessment.

Consider a construction bid of $8 million having a contract period of 5 months. Cash flow is trapezoidal, where $t_i = 20\%$ and $t_f = 60\%$. Profit earned by the contractor is 20%. The estimated cost total is $6,400,000. The owner has a retainage policy of 10% with a 1-month delay in the owner's payment. Table 11.3 provides the expenditure calculation as BCWS. Actual data have been provided for periods 1–4 as the work progresses. At period 4 there is a current unfavorable cost variance of $2,400,000 ($= 7,000,000 - 4,600,000$) and a project time delay of 1 month. The BCWP is extended to the contract cost. A horizontal difference between BCWS

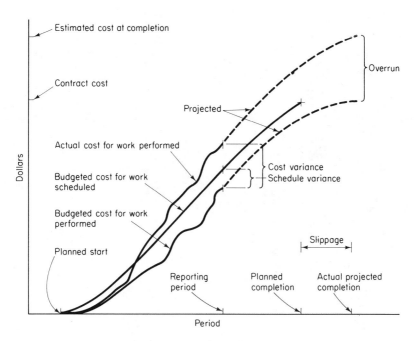

Figure 11.12.   Cost/schedule performance reporting.

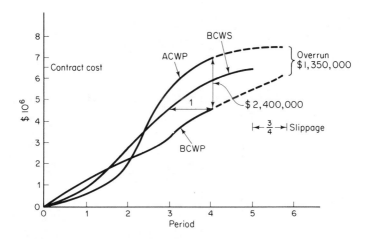

Figure 11.13.   Cost/schedule performance for contract of $6,400,000.

and BCWP gives a project slippage of $\frac{3}{4}$ month. The extended ACWP and BCWP indicates a project overrun of $1,350,000. The cost/schedule performance is shown as Fig. 11.13.

Table 11.3. Cost/Schedule Performance Report Where Costs Are $1000

Period	Period (%)	Cumulative				Schedule Variance		Forecast		
		BCWS (%)	BCWS	ACWP	BCWP	Months	Cost	BCWP	ACWP	Variance
1	20	14.3	$9150	$ 500	$1250					
2	40	42.9	2745	2000	2250					
3	60	71.5	4575	5500	3500					
4	80	92.9	5950	7000	4600	1	$2400			
5	100	100	6400			1.1	2250	$5600	$7500	−$1900
6	120	100	6400			3/4	1800	6400	7750	−$1350

11.6 SYSTEM ESTIMATE ASSURANCE

The system estimate is composed of operation, product, and project estimates. The collection of these estimates leads to a measure of the design called *effectiveness,* generally implying a benefit–cost ratio, life-cycle cost, or total cost for a large-scale design. System estimates are regularly made for weapon systems, water and navigation systems, and hospital and health care planning, to name a few. Preparation of a system depends on design circumstances and usually no two are alike. The time horizon from estimate start to life cycle is from several to 25 years or so. These ideas were first discussed in Chapter 10.

A spectrum of time relationships is possible for the three subestimates. They can vary from immediate or short-term operational requirements to the long-range planning of conceptual products and projects not even in the research and development stage. Many of the explanatory variables range from simple to complex. The crux of the difficulty in assuring the value of a system estimate cannot be routine or short term as is found with operation estimates. Effects of inflation or deflation, design changes, or definition alterations make a cost assurance program unlikely when one considers the complexity of system estimates.

Cost-estimating relationships are used to evaluate system design. Regardless of their complexity or simplicity, they can be derived only from historical data. The past may prove to be unreliable as a guide to the future. It is usual that some design characteristics are outside the range of the historical sample in dealing with advanced hardware systems. These dilemmas are not entirely resolved despite statistical procedures.

Not insignificant is the matter of legislative budget approval and eventual appropriation authority. Political pressures to shorten or lengthen schedules have an important role in whether the estimate is actually ever compared to the actual costs. A side-by-side comparison made between the estimate and actual costs for system estimates is seldom found.

Estimate assurance programs appropriate for operations, products, or projects are only partially successful when applied to a system design. As a consequence, emphasis shifts to increased mathematical analysis of the estimate. Techniques such as simulation, Monte Carlo, probability analysis, and sensitivity are used. These were discussed in Chapter 5 and Secs. 6.7, 9.4.2, and 10.3.3.

The preponderance of system estimates are used to make selections between alternative designs. The most popular technique is frequently identified as sensitivity. Once the *tall poles* are identified for a design, the values of the significant design factor are ranged over a wide magnitude to determine if a competing design becomes more cost effective. Note Fig. 11.14. Each alternative has a range for system cost at any value of a design factor. The region of preference for alternative 2 or 3 is clearly dominant for small or large values of the design factor. There is a region of overlap where one system's domination is a matter of probability. These circumstances are described by Fig. 6.11. Once this overlapping region is discovered, the system estimating team will enlarge its analysis to reduce the zone of uncertainty

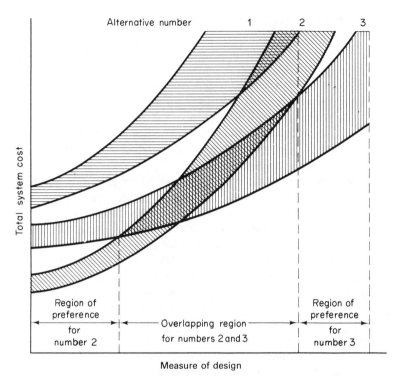

Figure 11.14. Sensitivity analysis with respect to system effectiveness.

by improved cost and design studies. Continuing analysis, it is reasoned, will make the alternative choice clearer. Thus estimates are assured by greater attention to detail prior to the spending of money.

SUMMARY

One purpose of an estimate is to secure business. Not all do, but those that are successful are matched against a comparison. The comparison could be an actual or preliminary value. Actual costs suffer from inaccuracy or lateness and do not always provide a valid future lesson. Nonetheless, a variety of techniques, including behavior considerations, variance, productivity, trend charting, and sensitivity, guide the actual cost values to become estimated values.

QUESTIONS

11.1. Give an explanation of the following terms:

Estimate error	True value
Contingency	Mistake error
Policy error	Standard

Risk error	Variance
Capture rate	Unlearning
Closed estimate assurance systems	ACWP
Pareto rule of thumb	BCWP

11.2. Why are estimates compared to actual cost or standard cost?

11.3. Describe the philosophical differences between an estimate assurance and a cost control program.

11.4. Management usually stresses the abolition of mistakes. Name practices to achieve this objective.

11.5. Describe management actions for a declining capture rate; for an improving capture rate. Why is a corrective policy based on a capture rate strategy alone defective?

11.6. Develop a list of behavioral principles that would be useful for cost estimating.

11.7. Give different formulas for variance calculations. Can ambiguity be completely overcome?

11.8. Why are system estimates difficult to cost-track? Cite some cost overruns from local or national circumstances. List the factors that cause these overruns.

11.9. Define a capture rate based on dollars won versus dollars estimated. What advantages does this have over Eq. (11.3)?

PROBLEMS

11.1. **(a)** A cement contractor bids a job of steps and risers for an apartment. His estimate is 125 hours at $15.25 per hour, material takeoff of 32 yd³ at $43.00/yd³, other materials are $145 for the job, and an overhead rate of 50% on the basis of direct labor. His pricing policy is 20% as a markup on sale value. Determine his bid for the job.

    (b) Reconciliation of all costs by the bookkeeper revealed the actual cost of $5250. Determine the error of the estimate. What was his final profit for the actual costs?

11.2. **(a)** A job-shop firm receives a confirmation order of 20,000 1018 CRS manufactured parts. Material cost per unit is $0.0293. Direct labor setup is 1 hour and cycle time is 0.009 hour per unit. The machine-hour rate, which includes labor and overhead, is $20. Pricing policy is a 25% markup on full cost. Determine the price for the part.

    (b) After the job is closed, an audit showed that material, labor and overhead, and tooling actually cost $6000, $3600, and $5500. Find the error of the estimate. What is the effective profit margin?

11.3. **(a)** A prototype unit has been constructed with 45,000 direct labor-hours and $20,000 of direct material. The direct labor rate is $18. The overhead rate is 100% of direct labor. The estimated learning rate is 90% and 95% for labor and material. The company has a policy of using a linear unit line. Pricing policy is 15% of total cost. Each unit is estimated and sold separately. Determine the 10th unit price.

    (b) Examination of the actual cost records showed a value of $1,250,000. Find the error of the estimate. Give the net profit and effective profit margin.

11.4. **(a)** The tooling vendor submitted 298 quotations for the winning jobs of Fig. 11.1. What is the capture rate?

(b) Of the winning jobs reported by this survey, 63 were for tools required by an engineering design change resulting from 109 quotes. The tooling vendor had supplied the original tools, which were not reported by this survey. What is the capture rate for new and repeat business?

(c) Discuss ways to improve his repeat business considering (1) profit margins which are 20% on repeat business and 2.5% on new business; versus (2) profit margins which are 2.5% on repeat business and 20% on new business.

11.5. A contractor reviewed last year's performance of bids left-on-the-table. What is the capture rate for 78 attempts? Because winning bids were openly announced, she was able to analyze her bidding strategy.

Bids Left-on-the-Table	Percentage above Winning Bid
2	0–2.0
1	2.1–4.0
3	4.1–6.0
7	6.1–8.0
10	8.1–10.0
10	10.1–12.0
5	12.1–14.0
2	14.1–16.0

(a) Discuss a strategy for no change in the future bidding environment.

(b) Assume that each quotation is about $1 million and includes $50,000 for profit. Discuss the strategy with this additional information. Are there adjustments that you can suggest?

11.6. An analysis of the estimating operation has been made for the previous fiscal year quarters:

Quarter	Estimates Made	Estimates Won	C_p	C_d	C_a	Business Value Lost ($\times 10^6$)	Profit on Detail Estimates ($\times 10^6$)
March	216	112	$195	$191	$193	$380	$17.4
June	237	118	201	198	202	426	17.2
September	293	138	219	224	233	544	16.8
December	338	149	221	227	244	625	10.2

Find quarterly and yearly estimating error on the basis of actual and preliminary estimates, capture rate, and productivity. What trends do you spot? Advise the management on cost-estimating policy for the next quarter. Evaluate the performance of estimating over the last year. Management has a goal of bidding 250×10^6 from detail estimates. What can be expected?

11.7. Repeat the variance calculation for Fig. 11.4 if actual material is $18.25 and quantity usage is 195.

11.8. Estimates for a material are 650 lb at $17.15/lb. The record shows an actual usage of 665 lb at $17.10/lb. Find the variance for material cost, quantity, and total.

11.9. A 1018 CRS material is estimated to cost $0.0293 per unit for 20,000 units. Actually, material costs $0.032 per unit and 20,500 units were necessary to allow for greater scrap and waste. Determine the material and quantity variance.

11.10. The estimates for labor are 72.6 hours at $13.76 per hour. The accountant's record indicated

> Kathy Holthaus, 20.2 hours at $13.50 per hour
> Radon Tolman, 14.3 hours at $13.75 per hour
> Louis Roth, 22.7 hours at $13.80 per hour
> Jim Morrison, 15.8 hours at $13.85 per hour

> Find the labor rate variance, hours variance, and total variance.

11.11. A labor estimate is 1.0 hour setup and 0.009 hour per unit for 20,000 units. The shop direct labor was expected to cost $15. In reality, total time for setup and cycle required 208.15 hours and shop labor was $14.50. Find the variance for the labor rate, hours, and total.

11.12. A time study demonstrated that assembly production of an electrical home outlet as 101.8 pieces per hour (see Fig. 3.2). Subsequent reports revealed an average of 1.062 hours per 100 units. An estimated job anticipated an order of 16,000 units, but actually 15,900 units were stocked. The labor rate was $14.75 instead of the expected $14.50. Determine the individual and net variances. Find the productivity factor. A future quantity of 20,000 units is anticipated.

(a) If operation improvement is not possible, what do you recommend as the future standard hour?

(b) If competitive reasons require a new labor time estimate, what percentage reduction is necessary for a methods engineering goal?

11.13. An aluminum part weighing 2.7 lb is drilled in 37 locations with a computer-directed drilling machine. The part is $\frac{7}{8}$ in. thick and hole diameters are $\frac{1}{2}$ in. and $1\frac{1}{2}$ in. Standard cost data expressed as setup dollars for the lot and cycle dollars for 100 units are given as follows:

$$\text{setup} = 1.90 + 0.78 \text{ (no. drill sizes)}$$
$$\text{cycle dollars/100 units} = 8.70 + 1.14 \text{ (no. lb)} + 1.10 \text{ (no. holes)}$$
$$+ 1.15 \text{ (no. sizes)} + 13.0 \text{ (ea. hole depth)}$$

The first term of the setup and cycle estimating linear relationship is the constant mandatory for estimating. The lot quantity is 250. Actual costs and quantity, as eventually determined, were $950 and 255. Find the variances and productivity factor.

11.14. A free-abrasive lapping machine is estimated to require 0.5 hour for setup and 1.721 minute per unit for the cycle. Estimated labor wage is $12.58. Actual man-hours and wage were 225 and $12.61. Let quantity = (a) 7500 units, and (b) 10,000 units.

(a) Find the dollar variances for hours and hourly rate.

(b) Calculate the net labor variance and productivity factor.

11.15. A dip-brazed assembly is estimated to require 0.15 hour for setup and 0.96 minute per unit. The estimated quantity is 625 units. But actual history was 9.85 hours for a lot of 620 units. Labor wage as estimated and as actually determined was $16.80 and $17.05. Determine the variances and productivity factor.

11.16. An 18-in.-long SAE 1020 steel bar weighs 83 lb. A lot estimate is required for 40 parts. Material cost is estimated as $0.73/lb. An invoice showed that 43 parts were consumed for $2960. Setup and cycle were estimated as 0.94 hour and 7.33 minutes. Records show that 6 hours were needed and the labor rate was $17.25 instead of the planned $16.90. Find the material, labor, and net variances for material and labor.

11.17. An actual-cost audit revealed that the labor had an unfavorable 20% variance, material was favorable by $0.001, and overhead was reported unchanged. If standard part cost was $0.35 for labor, $0.075 for material, and 200% on the basis of prime cost for overhead, determine the total standard cost and actual cost. What is the net variance?

11.18. An estimate resulted in $5.28 for labor, 150% for overhead on the basis of direct labor, and $17.38 for material. An actual fact-finding study revealed that labor had an unfavorable variance of 10%, material was favorable by $0.45, and overhead percentage was unchanged.
(a) Determine total estimated and actual cost. Find the net variance.
(b) Repeat if the overhead amount remains unchanged.

11.19. (a) Assume sales income for Table 11.1 as $20,300 and repeat calculations to find the net profit percent of net sales. All other values remain unchanged.
(b) Assume sales income for Table 11.2 as $20,300, $32,000, and $40,000 and repeat calculations to find the net profit of net sales. All other values remain unchanged. Which model suggests future emphasis?

11.20. (a) Sales income for Table 11.1 is $23,250 and repeat calculations to find the net profit percent of net sales. Other values remain unchanged.
(b) Sales income for Table 11.2 is $23,250, $36,000, and $38,000 and repeat calculations to find net profit percent of sales. Which model should be emphasized in the future?

11.21. A mining equipment manufacturer compiled the following data on three models of drill steel it produces:

Machine Center	Hourly Rate	Hours Required Per Unit for Model:			Cost per Unit for Model:		
		1700	1600	1500	1700	1600	1500
Cutoff	$14.20	0.01	0.01	0.01	$ 0.142	$ 0.142	$ 0.142
Upsetting	15.65	0.03	0.04	0.05	0.47	0.626	0.783
Machining	16.11	0.05	0.04	0.03	0.806	0.644	0.483
Heat treat	10.40	0.20	0.18	0.16	2.08	1.87	1.664
Bench	13.90	0.5	0.5	0.5	6.95	6.95	6.95
Finishing	15.02	0.1	0.1	0.1	1.50	1.50	1.50
				Unit labor cost =	$11.95	$11.74	$11.52
			Unit material cost ($0.20/lb) =		34.80	31.60	27.99
			Unit selling cost (5% price) =		3.75	3.20	2.50
				Total variable cost =	$50.50	$46.54	$42.01
				Selling price =	75.00	64.00	50.00
				Contribution/unit =	24.50	17.46	7.99
				Contribution percent =	33	27	16

Variances on variable costs are as follows:

Manufacturing labor and conversion, 3% unfavorable
Materials and scrap, 5% unfavorable
Selling and distribution, ½% unfavorable

(a) Make an income and expense statement if the manufacturer produces 200 1700-series, 100 1600-series, and 170 1500-series drill steel.

(b) If the total period costs (budgeted amount plus variance) were $5,500, what are the net profit and percent of net sales?

(c) What advice can you provide management for future production of these three products?

11.22. Determine the schedule and cost variance, graphically forecast BCWP and ACWP and find overrun and slippage assuming differing values for Table 11.3 as given by:

		Period			
(a)		1	2	3	4
	ACWP	250	1500	5000	6500
	BCWP	500	2000	3500	5000

		Period			
(b)		1	2	3	4
	ACWP	100	750	4000	5000
	BCWP	750	2250	3500	4250

11.23. Find the overrun and slippage for the following data and current and forecast variances.

	Period								
	1	2	3	4	5	6	7	8	9
BCWS	3	14	22	45	68	92	115	134	142
ACWP	4	10	19	60	83	113			
BCWP	1	4	15	28	52	82			

11.24. Refer to Table 9.7. Plot period number and period percent versus BCWS, BCWP, and ACWP, and BCWS% for the following additional data. Extend the data to completion and estimate cost at completion and project slippage. Determine schedule and cost variance, and budget, project, and difference until completion.

	Cumulative	
Month	ACWP	BCWP
1	$ 2,000	$ 3,000
2	5,000	12,000
3	13,000	18,000
4	28,000	27,000
5	41,000	32,000
6	54,000	52,000
7	92,000	78,000
8	122,000	108,000

Interpret the early periods. What action do you think might have been taken on the basis of the early periods?

11.25. Refer to Problem 9.26. Now assume that a project is under way and a material cost/
schedule procedure reports on budgeted cost material expended. Determine schedule
and cost variations for periods 4 and 5. Find project overrun and slippage. Use
graphical analysis.

			Period				
	1	2	3	4	5	6	7
BCWS	915	2745	4576	5946	6400	6400	6400
ACWP	250	1500	5000	6500			
BCWP	500	2500	3500	500			

CASE STUDY:
COST SCHEDULE PERFORMANCE REPORTING

When a contractor provides a proposal to an owner, he promises to perform work at a cost
within a time limit and to meet design requirements. For the contractor to fulfill a contract,
specific work is scheduled at various times of the project. Some contracts require periodic
preparation of cost–schedule performance reports which tell the owner what has been done
and when, and additionally what needs to be done and when. A graph such as Fig. C11.1 is
often a significant part of the report. This figure differs from other CSPR figures in that a
certain amount of ongoing project labor is considered fixed.

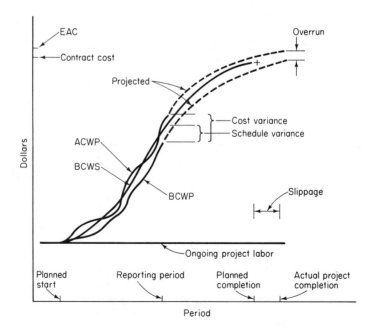

Figure C11.1.   Cost/schedule performance reporting with ongoing project labor.

Create the specifications for report system which builds on Fig. C11.1. Consider the following as necessary to your reporting procedure:

1. Alert management to conditions that might affect either cost or schedule.
2. Establish an orderly method of compiling supporting data.
3. Permit timely and corrective action to minimize negative effects or maximize positive breakthroughs on project cost and schedule.

12

Contract Considerations

If the cost estimate and the resulting price are selected by the customer, or the firm chooses to produce its product, the process of the business leads to contract considerations. Legal requirements become important and it is necessary that the estimator have an understanding about contracts.

A variety of contract types exists. The two major families are fixed price and cost reimbursable. Stipulations regarding changes, claims, disputes, and many other factors become possible with these contracts. An intermediate step to a completed contract may be negotiation. Auditing and ethics are other considerations for the cost estimator.

12.1 IMPORTANCE

By now the student has recognized that cost estimating is the para-business partner to design engineering. But the relationship also involves understanding contract law, ethics, and responsibilities to the employer, client, or customers, and professional obligations to society at large, and public law. While the estimator is not a lawyer, he or she needs a fundamental reasoning because preparation of the estimate is affected in many ways. Legal considerations are important.

The operation, product, project, and system estimates have differing legal requirements. But contractual distinctions are based on other factors. As the estimate is a measure of the economic want, a handshake, or amount of money in a legal contract may be the means of agreement between two parties. The notion of wants, initially described in Chapter 1, requires two people, companies, buyer and seller, vendor and contractor, and contractor and owner or government. Self-interest leads the parties to consent to an exchange which may be recognized by a handshake, money, or a formal contract. Negotiation may or may not be involved. In disputes, engineering changes, patents, warranty claims, and so on, litigation may follow, and the estimate may be a document of evidence.

We use the term "contract" to describe a variety of agreements or orders for the procurement of services or materials. A modification of this contract may be an alteration to the specification, delivery point, rate of delivery, contract period, price, quantity, or other provision of an existing contract, which is accomplished under one of the clauses, such as change order, notice of termination, supplemental agreement, or other options.

There is a variety of contract types. They refer to specific arrangements used for the employment of work, or the supply of materials, or compensation arrangements.

12.2 BASIC CONTRACT TYPES

There are two basic contracts to measure the value of the estimate: fixed price and cost reimbursable. These two arrangements lead to a variety of other types of contracts. Fixed-price arrangements have in common that one party, say a vendor or contractor, is to deliver a product or project or system, or perform an operation in accordance with the terms and conditions of the contract, and an agreement by a buyer, firm, agency, or government to pay a price equal to that specified by the contract. In contrast, cost-reimbursable contracts pay the vendor or contractor for money spent, subject to restriction and special negotiated understanding.

The element of risk, willingness of the parties, competition, advanced or ordinary technology, complexity of design, urgency, product cycle life, and many other factors influence which general type is selected. Highly complex development would permit a cost-reimbursable type of contract. Low technology, short time periods, well-developed production consumer products, large volume, and so on, argue for firm-fixed-price contracts. The cost-type contracts transfer the economic risk to the buyer or customer, while fixed-price contracts place the economic risk on the contractor, supplier, or vendor.

The fixed-price contract requires that the design (operation, product, etc.) be delivered as described on a predetermined schedule. Precluding changes allowed by the contract, the price is fixed for the life. However, the terms and conditions may allow for adjustment, and this is described shortly. While the firm-fixed-price contract provides the greatest risk, it also offers incentive and opportunity to realize the greatest profit. The vendor or contractor recovers fully savings due to cost reductions. Thus, if the actual costs are less than estimated costs, greater profit materializes.

Almost all public project contracts, as well as a large portion of private construction projects, are selected on the results of competitive bidding. Competitive-bid contracts for projects that are fixed price can have an interesting variation. A *unit-price* type of construction contract is based on the placement of certain well-defined items of work and costs per unit amount of each of these work items. For example, a price per linear foot of pile or cubic yard of excavation allows a reasonable variation to be made in the driven length of the individual piles or quantity of excavation. Thus a contractor will submit his bid on the basis of number and depth of the piles, which are verified by the cost engineer working in the field.

The fixed-price or lump-sum contract is popular from an owner or buyer's viewpoint, as the total project cost is known in advance. If the project cannot be accurately estimated, the fixed-price type may not be suitable.

The cost-type contract acts to place the risk on the buyer. This type is used whenever research, development, design, or urgency is necessary. The buyer will assure themselves that the contractor is reputable in quality, delivery, and design. Inherent in a cost-type contract is the *best effort* by the contractor in completing the work. Even so, the costs are passed on; it is often necessary that costs be as carefully estimated as for fixed price.

The cost-reimbursement family of contracts have provisions for payment of allowable, allocable, and reasonable costs incurred in the performance of the contract. Formulas, to be described shortly, permit adjustments for fees, incentives, and penalties.

Operations involve direct labor and direct material in the estimating process. They are the easiest to understand. Often the raw and standard commercial materials are listed in a catalog, price list, or schedule that is regularly maintained by a manufacturer or vendor. It may be published or made available for inspection by customers. The information may state prices of current interest or give prices to buyers. While these values may not be formal contracts, they are established in the usual course of business between buyers and sellers either free to bargain and agree, or not. Competition establishes the prices, and thus is a sufficient standard for a contract. These catalog prices, or the value of the estimate, say from $0.05 to $50 million, do not diminish the importance of the estimating, negotiating, or contractual procedure.

Labor costs may be contracted between the company and the union or between the company and an individual willing to work for the conditions as specified. Negotiations may be a factor. At the lower-wage level, federal laws may dictate the value of the wage. Labor laws were discussed in Chapter 2.

Some vendors may bid for work on the basis of a machine-hour cost. For example, the manufacturing company may specify the following schedule:

Heavy machining: $113.75 per hour
Light machining: $ 43.50 per hour

and then conduct the work. This is a form of fixed pricing. Note Table 4.11, where these rates were determined and formula (8.12), which adjusted the cost on the basis of 15% profit markup. In a sense, this is similar to the unit-price type of a construction. Obviously, the buyer needs to be satisfied that a fair and reasonable time was charged against the contract. Some contractor-vendors maintain an *open purchase* contract allowing this arrangement.

A *time and material contract* is used between a buyer and seller for work at a fixed and specified rate, say hourly, daily, and so on, that includes direct labor, indirect costs, and profit, and materials. The materials may be at cost or cost plus profit. This contract is suited for operations where the amount or duration of work is unpredictable or insignificant. Repair work is often handled on a time and material contract. The labor is considered a fixed part, but the material is cost-reimbursable since the nature of repair materials is unknown at the time of the contract.

12.3 FIXED-PRICE ARRANGEMENTS

The parties agree to the price before a firm-fixed-price (FFP) contract is awarded. The price is firm for the life of the contract unless it is revised according to the change clauses given in the contract. An example for a $1 million contract under varying consequences is given as

Contract price	$1,000,000	$1,000,000	$1,000,000
Actual cost	900,000	1,000,000	1,100,000
Realized profit	$ 100,000	$ 0	$ (100,000)

The contractor either gains or loses based on performance.

But in another fixed-price contract, a negotiated pricing formula can be agreed to that motivates and rewards the contractor for performance. In these *fixed-price incentive* (FPI) contracts, the process involves an estimated cost, target profit, target price, ceiling price, and profit sharing for costs incurred above or below the estimated cost. The example above with the $1 million contract price is a 0/100 sharing arrangement. This means that the buyer does not share and the contractor accepts 100% of the difference between price and cost. Figure 12.1 shows the basic fixed price with 0/100% sharing.

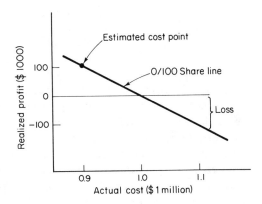

Figure 12.1. FFP arrangement with 0/100 sharing line.

The fixed-price incentive is written to have a target cost, and a target profit percentage along with a contract ceiling price and a price adjustment formula.

Estimated cost	$ 900,000
Target profit (11.1%)	100,000
Target price	$1,000,000
Price ceiling (125%)	$1,125,000
Cost sharing	80/20 above estimated cost
Cost sharing	90/10 below estimated cost

The owner will not pay above the ceiling price.

Assume that a contractor experienced an overrun of 15% of estimated cost, or $135,000 (= 0.15 × 900,000). The reimbursement would be as follows:

Estimated cost	$ 900,000
Plus 80% of $135,000	108,000
Total reimbursement cost	$1,008,000
Target profit	$ 100,000
Less 20% of profit	20,000
Total profit	$ 80,000
Cost plus profit	$1,088,000

Thus the owner covered 80% of the increased cost, but the contractor lost 20% of his profit. Instead of a 11.1% profit (= 100,000/900,000), profit declines to 7.9% (= 80,000/1,008,000).

Suppose that the contractor completed the job, but his costs were $820,000, or $80,000 less than estimated. Under the terms of cost sharing of 90/10 below estimated cost, the following is found:

Estimated cost	$900,000
Less 90% of $80,000	72,000
Total reimbursed cost	$828,000
Target profit	$100,000
Plus 10% of $80,000	8,000
Total profit	$108,000
Cost plus profit	$936,000

Instead of 11.1% profit, the profit increases to 13%. Note that profit is expressed as a percentage of the cost of the contract.

The FPI represents joint responsibility for ultimate cost. This arrangement shares in any dollar difference between the estimate and final cost. In an 80/20 example, the contractor is responsible for 20% of the difference either as an addition to or a deduction from target profit. The shares, while always a total of 100%, the proportions vary because of uncertainty, amount of target profit, and the spread between estimated cost and ceiling price. Expressions of the owner/contractor or government/contractor shares are 60/40, 75/25, 50/50, and so on.

The share line can be straight both above and below estimated cost. But an 80/20 above estimated costs can be matched with a 90/10 below estimated costs. Slope changes such as these depend on the design and negotiation.

Assume a 70/30 sharing proposition for the following cost facts:

Price ceiling	$11,500,000
Target price	$10,850,000
Estimated cost	$10,000,000
Final cost	$ 9,600,000
Difference	$ 400,000 underrun

The contractor receives $120,000 ($= 0.30 \times 400,000$) as an increase in profit. This is added to a target profit.

Target profit	$850,000
Contractor's share	120,000
	$970,000

The owner or government receives 70%, or $280,000 difference, as a reduction in price.

Final cost	$ 9,600,000
Final profit	970,000
Final price	$10,570,000
Target price	10,850,000
Price reduction	$ 280,000

Now assume a final cost of $10,500,000.

Estimated cost	$10,000,000
Final cost	10,500,000
Difference	$ 500,000 overrun

The contractor receives 30%, or $150,000, as a decrease in profit.

Target profit	$ 850,000
Less 30% of overrun	150,000
Final profit	$ 700,000

The owner receives 70%, or $350,000, as an increase in price.

Final cost	$10,500,000
Final profit	700,000
Final price	$11,200,000
Target price	10,850,000
Price increase	$ 350,000

If the final cost was $12,000,000, or $500,000 in excess of the ceiling, the ceiling of $11,500,000 is the final price.

A contract arrangement of fixed-price incentives with successive sharing ratios for early development, design, and production is possible.

Fixed price with redetermination (FPR) is another arrangement. The redetermination may be prospective or retroactive. In the prospective type, negotiation is undertaken for a fixed price in a future period, and then successive fixed prices are renegotiated periodically. Past costs, performance, and estimate assurance are data available for prospective contracts.

The retroactive type of FPR contracts provides for adjusting contract price after the work is completed. A ceiling price is initially determined and actual audited costs are the starting point for negotiation. The terms of the contract do not provide for mutual sharing. The retroactive type requires an opinion of the contractor's performance by the owner or government.

Quote or price-in-effect (QPE) types of contracts are also known as *escalation* contracts. They were introduced in Sec. 3.3. Long-term uncertainties which result from inflation or deflation effects are the reason for their use. The contractor will estimate his costs, and then establish a mutually agreed upon bench mark or index. Adjustment is mostly up, but downward adjustment is possible. The price adjustment clause must identify a base or bench-mark period, and one or more indexes to measure changes in price level in relation to the reference cost and reference period. If the contract provides for economic price adjustment, the contingency element of the cost estimate is ignored if it deals with inflation effects. Remember that contingency may be for considerations other than inflation.

12.4 COST REIMBURSEMENT ARRANGEMENTS

The *cost-plus-incentive fee* (CPIF) develops an incentive sharing formula. This is used in lieu of cost reimbursement with a 0/100 share. Cost reimbursement with incentive does use a ceiling price, and costs that comply with contract terms are reimbursed, and the total of reimbursed costs is the final cost of the contract. In fixed-price incentive plans the reasonableness and necessity of costs are established, and cost is finally found after negotiation. Under a cost-plus-incentive fee, the maximum and minimum fee are limited by negotiation. A cost level above and below estimated cost is negotiated for minimum and maximum levels; contract sharing ceases, and the contract reverts, in effect, to a cost plus fixed fee 100/0 sharing plan. In contrast, the ceiling price in a fixed-price contract establishes a point over target cost where the owner ceases to share and the contract becomes a fixed firm price with a 0/100 share model. The parties to a cost-plus-incentive fee contract believe the cost risk is too great for a realistic price ceiling. Cost-plus-incentive fee arrangements encourage incentive over a greater variation from estimated cost than would be expected with an FPI contract. The following is an example of a CPIF plan.

Estimated cost	$10,000,000
Target fee	750,000
Maximum fee	1,350,000
Minimum fee	300,000
Share formula	85/15

Assume a trial cost of $9,000,000.

Estimated cost	$10,000,000
Final cost	9,000,000
Difference	$ 1,000,000 underrun

The contractor receives 15%, or $150,000 (= 0.15 × 1,000,000), as an increase in fee.

Target fee	$750,000
Share	150,000
	$900,000

The owner receives 85%, or $850,000, between estimated and final cost as a reduction in price.

Final cost	$ 9,000,000
Final fee	900,000
Final cost plus fee	$ 9,900,000
Estimated cost plus fee	10,750,000
Reduction in price	$ 850,000 underrun

In this example the incentive is an effective overrun of $7,000,000, an underrun of 40% and an overrun of 30%. The contractor share of a $4,000,000 underrun is 15%, or $600,000. The share of a $3,000,000 overrun is 15%, or $450,000. These adjustments are added to or subtracted from a target fee of $750,000. The maximum and minimum fee ranges from $1,350,000 to $300,000. If the actual cost is greater than plus $3 million or minus $4 million from the estimated cost, the plan fixes the fee at either the maximum or minimum level.

Another cost reimbursement plan is the *cost-plus award fee*. It provides a base fee and an additional fee that may be entirely or partially upon performance. This plan does not include targets or automatic fee adjustment. The amount of the fee is subject to unilateral judgment by the government.

The *cost-plus-a-fixed fee* (CPFF) plan pays the contractor a fixed fee above reimbursable costs. The fee may change when the work breakdown structure changes. Conceptually, a CPFF is the opposite of a FFP arrangement. The FFP has a 0/100 sharing while CPFF has a 100/0 share.

Estimated cost	$15,000,000
Fixed fee	900,000
Estimated cost plus fixed fee	$15,900,000

The fee is unalterable with respect to actual costs. CPFF is used when the risk is great as when effort is inconsistent with performance.

12.5 CONTRACT CLAUSES

Organizations have procurement policies which are expressed as "standard" or "boiler plate" contract clauses. These printed statements are usually an attachment to the main body, and they should not be dismissed as unimportant to the estimator. Many clauses exist and only a few are discussed here.

The existence of real or potential competition before selection and award ends when the contract is signed. A competing offeror becomes a sole-source contractor or supplier. Contract clauses provide for circumstances that may alter some parts of the terms and conditions of an agreement. Contract changes are actions subsequent to the estimated cost and price and directly affect these documents.

Construction contracts give the owner the right to make changes in the design or work after the contract has been signed. Similarly, the U.S. government has the authority to initiate changes. A general commercial practice accepts what is known as the *change clause*. It is applicable to fixed-price and cost-reimbursable types of contracts. The customer may, without notice, make certain changes in the contract requirements if such changes are declared by the customer as not constituting a change in scope. If the change affects cost, delivery, schedule, performance, or other areas, the contractor must serve written notice to initiate a review, negotiation, and an equitable resolution of the claim. If the customer authorizes a change that may increase cost, it is assumed that there is adequate money to pay for the change. Construction contracts provide that the contractor is not to proceed unless there is written authorization.

When these change orders are issued, a supplement to the contract is prepared. The supplement can be made on the basis of a lump-sum or cost-reimbursable arrangement. A change order is a modification of the contract. The parties understand that modification has considered prior negotiations, terms, designs, and conditions.

A *disputes clause* of the contract provides procedures where resolution may be initially thwarted for a variety of reasons. The dispute clause provides that the customer will initially decide any dispute concerning a question of fact arising under the contract. Failure to agree to a price adjustment resulting from a change is considered to be a dispute concerning a question of fact. The contractor is expected to proceed with the contract as changed. Details differ between governmental and commercial activities. Construction contractors will first attempt to settle with the owner. There are levels of appeal from an adverse decision, including arbitration and courts, depending on whether the dispute involves questions of fact or law. In a similar way, the government will arbitrarily decide by written notice to the customer. After the decision is rendered by the customer, the contractor may appeal.

The addendum statement for cost-reimbursable contracts provides for control and regulation by the customer of costs that are accumulated. Costs caused by the contract are allowed and reimbursed. Criteria for determining *allowable costs* are defined in various documents that may be referenced by the contract. Or the terms of the contract may define the kinds of allowable costs. Reasonableness and prudence are governing practice in accepting allowable costs. For example, a subcontract material which was not competitively bid may not be allowable. Thus this material may be subect to negotiation to determine value.

The *inspection and correction* of defects, *warranty, full or conditional protection,* and so on, are clauses that obligate the contractor, vendor, or seller to correct defects, deficiencies, inability to meet specification, and so on, in various ways. These terms are so broad that we are unable to offer specifics, except that the cost estimate needs to include reasonable costs based on the wording of the clause. Mean time to failure and mean time to repair were concepts originally described in Chapter 10. Percent returns, conditional service contracts, customer assistance, field correction, recalls, and bulletins alerting the customer are features of a seller's costs that contractual terms that provide specificity. In a cost-reimbursable contract, costs are generally reimbursed.

Acceptance of the work by the owner or customer and payment may constitute waiver of his rights for damages if a claim is not made within a reasonable time. In construction work warranty work is normally covered by a performance bond. Exceptions are available to redress grievances by both a buyer and seller.

A subcontract is an agreement between a prime contractor and a subcontractor or a contractor and vendor. The subcontractor agrees to perform specialized work at a construction site or provide certain materials. A vendor, which is language more common to manufacturing, agrees to supply parts, subassemblies or assemblies, or subcontract material. A subcontract binds only the parties to the agreement. Many of the same clauses that are required of the prime contractor are applied similarly to a subcontractor, although the value of the contract will dictate its complexity. A $1 million subcontract has greater specificity than one with a $1000 value. Provisions of the general contract, including changes in work, minimum wage laws, warranty clauses, and other laws may extend to the subcontractor.

In fixed-price agreements, subcontracts are encouraged to be awarded as a result of competitive bidding. The *subcontract* clauses require the contractor to meet some stipulations in cost-reimbursable contracts. The contractor may be required to advise the owner or government of the anticipated subcontracts. Approval by the owner may be necessary, depending on the size of the award. Consent by an owner to use a specific subcontractor does not relieve the major contractor of failure to perform.

Contracts may be concluded in a variety of ways. The usual way is full and satisfactory performance by both parties. A contract discharge may result from a breach of contract. Failure of progress payments and unreasonable delays of the project are the most common by the owner. The contractor is entitled to *damages* caused by the owner's inability to discharge his responsibilities required by the contract. *Default or failure to perform* as required by the contract are the more common breaches committed by the contractor. Nonperformance, poor quality, failure to show progress, disregard of laws or instructions are actions that may allow the *termination* clause by an owner.

A convenience termination allows the customer the opportunity to decide that the material under procurement is no longer required and they are prepared to assume losses associated with termination. For convenience termination, the contractor ceases work, and issues cancellations on purchase orders and subcontracts. Eventually, the contractor provides a termination claim. The claim includes incurred costs of work performed, and special expenses associated with the termination effort. In cost-reimbursable types, the claimed costs are verified by an audit and the fee is negotiated. In a fixed-price contract, the legitimate costs and fees are determined both by submittal of evidence and negotiation.

There are many other contract clauses. Patent rights, value engineering, exclusable delays, retainage, progress payments, interpretation, excess material, shipping papers, insurance bonding, hiring of women and minorities, non-sex discrimination, and overtime requirements are typical.

12.6 NEGOTIATION, AWARD, AND AUDIT

Once the price and technical proposal have been conveyed to a buyer, negotiation may begin. Consider the situation where several bidders are responding to an RFQ. If the RFQ is for standard commercial materials and ordinary designs, the lowest bidder may be selected. Contrariwise, if the design is complicated and significant in terms of money, negotiation may be required. The negotiation could involve the buyer, contract administrators, design engineers, and cost estimators. The discussion may relate to technical areas, costs, schedules, and so on, for which the team approach may be useful. Prior to the negotiation, the representatives will be informed about price, schedule, contract type, and the design.

Negotiation is a term used broadly and has come to mean tactics and maneuvers by both parties in an effort to reach a decision on whether to contract together. Not all procurements are negotiated. But for technical and complex designs, the various bidders will make exceptions or claims regarding the RFQ and their technical response. It is an inviolate principle to this author that cost estimates are factual; however, profit and pricing are an opinion area. Pricing refers to the fair and reasonable values and is negotiable. "Horse trading" in negotiation is a simplistic picture when dealing with complicated designs and estimates; negotiation requires more complex maneuvers.

In small purchases, negotiation may consist of letters or telephone calls. In more significant procurements, the negotiation may be face to face and last many days. A plan or list of discussion points is necessary for effective negotiation. Issues regarding the design, RFQ, contract, terms, schedule, estimate, and performance are open to discussion. Each bidder may have exceptions or additional claims for the RFQ. For instance, two bidders on a high-voltage electrical transmission line may have a low cost but high voltage line losses, and vice versa.

The buyer in negotiation must be prepared to ask questions such as:

Are there issues that can be traded off if necessary?

How realistic is the delivery schedule?

If the delivery can be lengthened, is a lower price possible?

If a price reduction is desired, a vague statement that the "price is too high" represents a weak approach. A price reduction request must be plausible and businesslike. In certain situations the cost estimate is privileged information, yet in others, such as government work, it may be open to examination. The estimator should be prepared to defend his learning theory slope, wage rate, standards, and so on, on a factual basis. The buyer may perform a technical analysis upon the estimate.

A great variety of contract terms and contract types exist. Usually, standard contract terms are nonnegotiable, although an able negotiator takes nothing for granted. Terms of special clauses are another matter. These terms need to be carefully examined, as many of the contract terms and specifications may have financial and serious implications. *Specifications* mean additional practices, such as a particular type of quality control. It may place a burden on a factory or buyer who is unaware of the consequences.

Negotiation may deal with penalty clauses, retainage amounts, progress payments, and the like. Omissions, nebulous requirements, unclear accuracies, inconsistencies, and impossible or very expensive requirements are additional points of discussion.

A competitive negotiation will provide an opportunity for discussion by the offeror. It will conclude with the award of a contract to the one offeror whose price, design, and other factors are most beneficial to the buyer, owner, prime contractor, or government.

Once the contract is ongoing, terms of the contract may allow audits to verify allowable costs, possibility of fraud, compliance, documentation, and the like. Auditing is a common occurrence for government prime contractors. Audits may be by the customer, or they may be internal by the firm, or by a consultant hired by the organization. We are not referring to an accounting-firm auditor who examines the balance sheet and profit and loss statement and issues a public notice. The audit we are discussing deals with the estimating function, although it may be difficult to uncouple that from engineering, purchasing, accounting, or management. Internal audits imply the monitoring of cash flow, accounting, estimating, contracting, and the general business conduct of its operations. Internal audits of this type are commonplace in business. Prime contractors may also audit subcontractors.

Administrative audits deal with the several cost factors for a period of time. These factors include overhead cost rates, labor-hour rates, or efficiency factors which touch many contracts. These administrative action audits determine if present or future conditions negate the appropriateness of the cost factors.

Estimating audits are concerned with mistakes and omissions, procedures, and contingency assessment. Mistakes are $2 + $1 = $4 and are unavoidable, like a burp. Despite the popularity of mistakes, avoidance begins with attention to detail and checks by others and faultless arithmetic.

Procedures are a significant concern for audit. Consistency of estimate to the accounting system and to other estimates is important. The *audit path of verifiable facts* is conducive to reassessing consistency.

Separation of direct and indirect costs is watched closely. In general, direct costs are those which are identified as having been incurred for a particular product, work order, job, or contract. Indirect costs are composed of items of material, labor, and expenses which affect two or more products, work orders, jobs, or contracts, and the amount of cost charged to a specific one cannot be precisely determined. There is no universal rule that under every estimating and accounting system assures that items of cost be treated fairly as direct or as indirect cost. But it is essential that within estimating each item of cost be consistently treated. Some material costs may be confused as either direct or indirect, even though it is clearly incurred to the final project work order. Paint, for example, which appears on an end item, is an awkward thing to estimate, and may be called an indirect charge. Minor hardware is another optional choice. Estimators use $\frac{1}{2}$ to 5% of total direct material cost and claim that as the cost of minor hardware; or they may agree that it is charged as overhead. Because of these typical alternative choices, auditors check estimates for inconsistent treatment of direct and indirect costs.

Significant direct material cost estimates are audited carefully. Much of what is included as estimated direct material will have been purchased from outside sources. The auditor may examine the principal items within each material cost category and will check sources, quantities, unit prices, losses, and other specifics as shown on the direct material and subcontract estimate. Whenever engineering is completed and a bill of material is available, key part numbers are traced. For most engineering design efforts, estimates are prepared from less data than appear on a bill; and the WBS provides the skeleton for tracing, or the estimator may prepare a tentative bill of material from preliminary drawings. Estimating forms may serve as the preliminary bill. A less ideal means is the engineer's *project manual,* a bound record, where costs for the material and parts are estimated and tied to the design. For developmental work where costs are uncertain, planning quotations obtained from potential suppliers are verifiable.

Other options are open to auditing material costs. These distinctions range from routine supply problems to uncertain development efforts. Follow-on procurement provides realistic costs using earlier projects, and data can apply to projects even though they may be developmental. In follow-on procurement, reasonable projection of historical costs accounts for price reductions caused by removal of original design, tooling, rearrangement, excess spoilage, and other startup costs.

Economic factors, normal increases or decreases in price, and changes in production rates and quantities are considerations for follow-up estimating. Auditors are aware of these options.

A *priced bill-of-material* allows for scrutiny, especially in the amount of materials used. Once the design is fixed, auditors compare the quantity of material to that specified by the bill. This comparison is random, as an entire bill is seldom checked. Historical citations of scrap, waste, obsolescence, and spare-parts percentages are helpful in supporting estimates. A priced work breakdown structure can be audited. If a *contract work breakdown structure* is developed, estimates, subcontractor bids, purchase offers, vouchers, and bills of lading can be tracked from paper to physical hardware.

The third concern in auditing projects deals with contingency assessment. While we consent to the auditor's viewpoint that contingency can be negotiated and that he, the external auditor, is compassionate to these risks, we do not agree that contingency can be audited at the time of the estimate for developmental projects. Contingency for supply and production contracts may be questioned as to validity, certainly.

12.7 ETHICS

It is fitting that a book on cost estimating close with a discussion on ethics. It is no less important than the very first sections of the book, which dealt with the necessity of profit and wise stewardship. The task facing the estimator is one of providing a measure of the economic want. During the estimating period, it is not uncommon that various politics or pressures are applied on the estimating person. It is natural that an engineer will believe that the new design is "really cheaper," or the sales staff will promote a product that gives encouragement to marketing. While these motives are understandable, the estimator needs to maintain objectivity in fact-finding and his or her analysis. Subjectivity that may influence a policy of estimating out-of-pocket future costs seems to be unprofessional.

The estimate deals with elements of material, work, and money. As bargaining is the essence of competitive business, there are occasions in which the propriety of some trade practices is questionable. Revealing quotes to other contractors or vendors with the hope that a new bidder will submit an even lower bid is suggested to be improper. "Bid shopping" is the term applied to this practice. On the other hand, some contracts are required to be public knowledge, and on these occasions, integrity would require that the same value be disclosed equally to all candidate bidders.

Firms that are known to be unqualified to perform work or supply the product should not be invited to bid. Unless it is understood as a clause in the contract or is mandated by public law, the price and cost estimates of one competitor should not be made known to another competitor.

QUESTIONS

12.1. Give an explanation of the following terms:

Fixed-price arrangements	Cost plus incentive fee
Cost reimbursement	Cost plus award
Best effort	Subcontract
Open purchase contract	Change clause
Time and material contract	Allowable costs
Fixed-price incentive	Negotiation
Quote or price-in-effect	Audit

12.2. In the sharing arrangements for FPI, what are the pros and cons of a sharing plan such as 90/10 versus 50/50 to the contractor and owner for cost reductions below the estimated cost?

12.3. Contrast fixed-price versus cost-reimbursable types of contracts for **(a)** very high voltage transmission line over rugged terrain and **(b)** prototype manufacture of an ultra-high-vacuum-chamber environmental test unit.

12.4. When would an owner prefer an FPI contract? Why would a contractor desire an FPI arrangement?

12.5. List the advantages and disadvantages of CPIF from the owners' and contractors' viewpoint.

12.6. Prepare an outline of a negotiation strategy for the project estimate given in Sec. 9.6.

12.7. Assume that the project estimated in Sec. 9.6 was awarded. Itemize a list of documents that will be useful for an auditor on this project.

PROBLEMS

12.1. A construction contractor provides a unit price contract of the following:

Pile Diameter (in.)	Price per Foot Driver
12	$1250
18	2576
20	2685

The owner's cost engineer observed that 18 12-in. piles were driven to 60 ft, 14 18-in. piles were driven 52 ft, and 5 20-in. were driven 41 ft. What is the net realized contract value?

12.2. A vendor is considering a fixed-price contract where his machine-hour rates will be quoted. The vendor uses a markup-of-sales-value method of pricing. His markup rates are varied depending on his perception of negotiation stages.
(a) What are the fixed-price quotations?
(b) The customer indicates that a job is estimated and suggests the potential number of hours. What fixed-price contract is suggested?

Machine Center	Wage and Machine-Hour Cost	Markup (%)	Job Estimate (hours)
Light machining	$39.16	10	80
Heavy machining	90.98	20	40
Assembly	32.19	15	20
Finishing	42.33	5	15

12.3. **(a)** Reconsider the example given for fixed-price incentive in Sec. 12.3. What is the cost plus profit for an incentive of 75/25 above target cost where the overrun is $135,000?

   (b) Assume that the overrun is $150,000 and 75/25 sharing above target cost is negotiated. Find the cost plus for a fixed-price incentive contract. Use the example in Sec. 12.3.

12.4. **(a)** Reconsider the FPI example in Sec. 12.3, where the cost reduction is $80,000. For an 80/20 incentive contract, what is the cost plus profit?

   (b) Now let the cost reduction be $70,000 with a 75/25 incentive contract. Find the reimbursement by the owner.

12.5. A contractor estimates and negotiates the following fixed-price incentive contract:

   Estimated cost, $10,000,000
   Target profit, $850,000
   Target price, $10,850,000
   Price ceiling, $11,500,000

   There is 70/30 sharing of costs below estimates, and 0/100 sharing above the price ceiling. Sketch the contractor's FPI profit chart, where profit is the y-axis and cost dollars are the x-axis. Assume actual cost = $8,500,000.

12.6. Hot-rolled alloy-steel bar, $1\frac{1}{2}$ in. O.D. × 20 ft, AISI 4140 oil-hardening annealed grade, machine straightened, was quoted on a QPE contract.

Weight (lb)	Price ($/100 lb)
120 (= 1 item)	$115.00
2000	71.00
6000	66.50

   Steel is indexed according to a grade of scrap which has shown a 5%, 10%, and 8% increase per period. Find the price for the last period.

12.7. Repeat the example of CPIF in Sec. 12.4 for an 80/20 share. Plot a chart for a 75/25 sharing.

12.8. **(a)** An estimate has an estimated cost of $5 million, target fee of $600,000, maximum and minimum fee of $800,000 and $450,000. The share proportion is 80/20. Find the contractor's CPIF and the owner's cost for a final cost of 15% above estimate.

   (b) Repeat part (a) for 10% below estimated cost.

   (c) Plot a chart for 60/40 sharing.

12.9. The High Voltage Transmission Line Construction Company is under contract to build the transmission line estimated in Sec. 9.6. After agreeing to the price stipulated by Table 9.9, the owner invoked its right to two changes.

1. It increased the length over which the transmission line will travel by 0.6 mile.

2. It stipulated that construction roads were to be "pioneer" style, thus not being as obvious and more environmentally pleasing. What plan of action do you advise for this company?

CASE STUDY:
A LARGE CONTRACT

The following data are determined:

    Manufacturing labor, 40,000 hours
        Manufacturing hourly rate, $18 per hour
        Overhead rate on basis of direct-labor costs, 200%

    Material, $50,000
        Material overhead rate, 15%

    Engineering labor, 1500 hours
        Engineering hourly rate, $40 per hour
        Overhead rate, 150%

    Profit rate as a markup of full cost: 10%

The contract based on the figures above was awarded with a 120% ceiling and a split of 75/25 above estimated costs and 80/20 below estimated costs. (a) If the contractor actually achieved his figures, what is the reimbursement to the contractor for costs and profit? (b) If the incurred costs amounted to an overrun of 10% above the estimated costs, what is the reimbursement? (c) If the incurred costs amounted to 5% under the contract, find the reimbursement.

Appendices

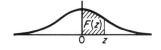

	Areas under the Normal Curve $$F(z) = \int_0^z \frac{1}{\sqrt{2\pi}} e^{-z^2/2}\, dz$$									
z	0.00	0.01	0.02	0.03	0.04	0.05	0.06	0.07	0.08	0.09
0.0	0.0000	0.0040	0.0080	0.0120	0.0159	0.0199	0.0239	0.0279	0.0319	0.0359
0.1	0.0398	0.0438	0.0478	0.0517	0.0557	0.0596	0.0636	0.0675	0.0714	0.0753
0.2	0.0793	0.0832	0.0871	0.0910	0.0948	0.0987	0.1026	0.1064	0.1103	0.1141
0.3	0.1179	0.1217	0.1255	0.1293	0.1331	0.1368	0.1406	0.1443	0.1480	0.1517
0.4	0.1554	0.1591	0.1628	0.1664	0.1700	0.1736	0.1772	0.1808	0.1844	0.1879
0.5	0.1915	0.1950	0.1985	0.2019	0.2054	0.2088	0.2123	0.2157	0.2190	0.2224
0.6	0.2257	0.2291	0.2324	0.2357	0.2389	0.2422	0.2454	0.2486	0.2518	0.2549
0.7	0.2580	0.2611	0.2642	0.2673	0.2704	0.2734	0.2764	0.2794	0.2823	0.2852
0.8	0.2881	0.2910	0.2939	0.2967	0.2995	0.3023	0.3051	0.3078	0.3106	0.3133
0.9	0.3159	0.3186	0.3212	0.3238	0.3264	0.3289	0.3315	0.3340	0.3365	0.3389
1.0	0.3413	0.3438	0.3461	0.3485	0.3508	0.3531	0.3554	0.3577	0.3599	0.3621
1.1	0.3643	0.3665	0.3686	0.3708	0.3729	0.3749	0.3770	0.3790	0.3810	0.3830
1.2	0.3849	0.3869	0.3888	0.3907	0.3925	0.3944	0.3962	0.3980	0.3997	0.4015
1.3	0.4032	0.4049	0.4066	0.4082	0.4099	0.4115	0.4131	0.4147	0.4162	0.4177
1.4	0.4192	0.4207	0.4222	0.4236	0.4251	0.4265	0.4279	0.4292	0.4306	0.4319
1.5	0.4332	0.4345	0.4357	0.4370	0.4382	0.4394	0.4406	0.4418	0.4430	0.4441
1.6	0.4452	0.4463	0.4474	0.4485	0.4495	0.4505	0.4515	0.4525	0.4535	0.4545
1.7	0.4554	0.4564	0.4573	0.4582	0.4591	0.4599	0.4608	0.4616	0.4625	0.4633
1.8	0.4641	0.4649	0.4656	0.4664	0.4671	0.4678	0.4686	0.4693	0.4699	0.4706
1.9	0.4713	0.4719	0.4726	0.4732	0.4738	0.4744	0.4750	0.4756	0.4762	0.4767
2.0	0.4772	0.4778	0.4783	0.4788	0.4793	0.4798	0.4803	0.4808	0.4812	0.4817
2.1	0.4821	0.4826	0.4830	0.4834	0.4838	0.4842	0.4846	0.4850	0.4854	0.4857
2.2	0.4861	0.4865	0.4868	0.4871	0.4875	0.4878	0.4881	0.4884	0.4887	0.4890
2.3	0.4893	0.4896	0.4898	0.4901	0.4904	0.4906	0.4909	0.4911	0.4913	0.4916
2.4	0.4918	0.4920	0.4922	0.4925	0.4727	0.4929	0.4931	0.4932	0.4934	0.4936
2.5	0.4938	0.4940	0.4941	0.4943	0.4945	0.4946	0.4948	0.4949	0.4951	0.4952
2.6	0.4953	0.4955	0.4956	0.4957	0.4959	0.4960	0.4961	0.4962	0.4963	0.4964
2.7	0.4965	0.4966	0.4967	0.4968	0.4969	0.4970	0.4971	0.4972	0.4973	0.4974
2.8	0.4974	0.4975	0.4976	0.4977	0.4977	0.4978	0.4979	0.4980	0.4980	0.4981
2.9	0.4981	0.4982	0.4983	0.4983	0.4984	0.4984	0.4985	0.4985	0.4986	0.4986
3.0	0.4987	0.4987	0.4987	0.4988	0.4988	0.4989	0.4989	0.4989	0.4990	0.4990
3.1	0.4990	0.4991	0.4991	0.4991	0.4992	0.4992	0.4992	0.4992	0.4993	0.4993

*This table gives the probability of a random value of a normal variate falling in the range $z = 0$ to $z = z$ (in the *shaded area in figure*). The probability of the same variate having a deviation greater than z is given by 0.5 − probability from the table for the given z. The table refers to a single tail of the distribution; therefore the probability of a variate falling in the range is $\pm z = 2 \times$ probability from the table for the given z. The probability of a variate falling outside the range $\pm z$ is $1 - 2 \times$ probability from the table for the given z.

The values in this table were obtained by permission of author and publishers from C. E. Weatherburn, *Mathematical Statistics*, Cambridge University Press, London, 1946.

APPENDIX II: VALUES[a] OF THE STUDENT *t* DISTRIBUTION

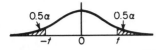

Degrees of Freedom ν	Probability α			
	0.10	0.05	0.01	0.001
1	6.314	12.706	63.657	636.619
2	2.920	4.303	9.925	31.598
3	2.353	3.182	5.841	12.941
4	2.132	2.776	4.604	8.610
5	2.015	2.571	4.032	6.859
6	1.943	2.447	3.707	5.959
7	1.895	2.365	3.499	5.405
8	1.860	2.306	3.355	5.041
9	1.833	2.262	3.250	4.781
10	1.812	2.228	3.169	4.587
11	1.796	2.201	3.106	4.437
12	1.782	2.179	3.055	4.318
13	1.771	2.160	3.012	4.221
14	1.761	2.145	2.977	4.140
15	1.753	2.131	2.947	4.073
16	1.746	2.120	2.921	4.015
17	1.740	2.110	2.898	3.965
18	1.734	2.101	2.878	3.922
19	1.729	2.093	2.861	3.883
20	1.725	2.086	2.845	3.850
21	1.721	2.080	2.831	3.819
22	1.717	2.074	2.819	3.792
23	1.714	2.069	2.807	3.767
24	1.711	2.064	2.797	3.745
25	1.708	2.060	2.787	3.725
26	1.706	2.056	2.779	3.707
27	1.703	2.052	2.771	3.690
28	1.701	2.048	2.763	3.674
29	1.699	2.045	2.756	3.659
30	1.697	2.042	2.750	3.646
40	1.684	2.021	2.704	3.551
60	1.671	2.000	2.660	3.460
120	1.658	1.980	2.617	3.373
∞	1.645	1.960	2.576	3.291

[a]This table gives the values of *t* corresponding to various values of the probability α (level of significance) of a random variable falling inside the shaded area in the figure, for a given number of degrees of freedom ν available for the estimation of error. For a one-sided test the confidence limits are obtained for $\alpha/2$.

This table is taken from Table III of Fisher and Yates, *Statistical Tables for Biological, Agricultural, and Medical Research,* Oliver & Boyd Ltd., Edinburgh, 1963.

APPENDIX III: LEARNING TABLES

N	T_u or T_a'	T_c	T_a	T_c'	T_u'
	Learning Table $\phi = 75\%$				
1	1.0000	1.0000	1.0000	1.0000	1.0000
2	0.7500	1.7500	0.8750	1.5000	0.5000
3	0.6338	2.3838	0.7946	1.9015	0.4015
4	0.5625	2.9463	0.7366	2.2500	0.3485
5	0.5127	3.4591	0.6918	2.5637	0.3137
6	0.4754	3.9345	0.6557	2.8523	0.2885
7	0.4459	4.3804	0.6258	3.1214	0.2691
8	0.4219	4.8022	0.6003	3.3750	0.2536
9	0.4017	5.2040	0.5782	3.6157	0.2407
10	0.3846	5.5886	0.5589	3.8456	0.2299
11	0.3696	5.9582	0.5417	4.0661	0.2205
12	0.3565	6.3147	0.5262	4.2784	0.2123
13	0.3449	6.6596	0.5123	4.4835	0.2051
14	0.3344	6.9941	0.4996	4.6821	0.1986
15	0.3250	7.3190	0.4879	4.8749	0.1928
16	0.3164	7.6355	0.4772	5.0625	0.1876
17	0.3085	7.9440	0.4673	5.2453	0.1828
18	0.3013	8.2453	0.4581	5.4236	0.1783
19	0.2946	8.5399	0.4495	5.5979	0.1743
20	0.2884	8.8284	0.4414	5.7684	0.1705
21	0.2826	9.1110	0.4339	5.9354	0.1670
22	0.2772	9.3882	0.4267	6.0991	0.1637
23	0.2722	9.6604	0.4200	6.2598	0.1607
24	0.2674	9.9278	0.4137	6.4176	0.1578
25	0.2629	10.1907	0.4076	6.5727	0.1551
30	0.2437	11.4458	0.3815	7.3124	0.1436
40	0.2163	13.7232	0.3431	8.6526	0.1272
50	0.1972	15.7761	0.3155	9.8590	0.1158
100	0.1479	24.1786	0.2418	14.7885	0.0867
500	0.0758	63.5897	0.1272	37.9137	0.0444

N	Learning Table $\phi = 80\%$				
	T_u or T_a'	T_c	T_a	T_c'	T_u'
1	1.0000	1.0000	1.0000	1.0000	1.0000
2	0.8000	1.8000	0.9000	1.6000	0.6000
3	0.7021	2.5021	0.8340	2.1063	0.5063
4	0.6400	3.1421	0.7855	2.5600	0.4537
5	0.5956	3.7377	0.7475	2.9782	0.4182
6	0.5617	4.2994	0.7166	3.3701	0.3919
7	0.5345	4.8339	0.6906	3.7414	0.3713
8	0.5120	5.3459	0.6682	4.0960	0.3546
9	0.4929	5.8389	0.6488	4.4365	0.3405
10	0.4765	6.3154	0.6315	4.7651	0.3286
11	0.4621	6.7775	0.6161	5.0832	0.3181
12	0.4493	7.2268	0.6022	5.3922	0.3089
13	0.4379	7.6647	0.5896	5.6929	0.3007
14	0.4276	8.0923	0.5780	5.9863	0.2934
15	0.4182	8.5105	0.5674	6.2730	0.2867
16	0.4096	8.9201	0.5575	6.5536	0.2806
17	0.4017	9.3218	0.5483	6.8286	0.2750
18	0.3944	9.7162	0.5398	7.0985	0.2699
19	0.3876	10.1037	0.5318	7.3635	0.2651
20	0.3812	10.4849	0.5242	7.6242	0.2606
21	0.3753	10.8602	0.5172	5.8806	0.2565
22	0.3697	11.2299	0.5104	8.1332	0.2525
23	0.3644	11.5943	0.5041	8.3820	0.2489
24	0.3595	11.9538	0.4981	8.6274	0.2454
25	0.3548	12.3086	0.4923	8.8696	0.2421
30	0.3346	14.0199	0.4673	10.0368	0.2281
40	0.3050	17.1935	0.4298	12.1986	0.2076
50	0.2838	20.1217	0.4024	14.1913	0.1931
100	0.2271	32.6508	0.3265	22.7062	0.1542
500	0.1352	98.8472	0.1977	67.6232	0.0917

N	Learning Table $\phi = 85\%$ T_u or T_a'	T_c	T_a	T_c'	T_u'
1	1.0000	1.0000	1.0000	1.0000	1.0000
2	0.8500	1.8500	0.9250	1.7000	0.7000
3	0.7729	2.6229	0.8743	2.3187	0.6187
4	0.7225	3.3454	0.8364	2.8900	0.5713
5	0.6857	4.0311	0.8062	3.4284	0.5384
6	0.6570	4.6881	0.7813	3.9419	0.5135
7	0.6337	5.3217	0.7602	4.4356	0.4937
8	0.6141	5.9358	0.7420	4.9130	0.4774
9	0.5974	6.5332	0.7259	5.3766	0.4636
10	0.5828	7.1161	0.7116	5.8282	0.4516
11	0.5699	7.6860	0.6987	6.2693	0.4411
12	0.5584	8.2444	0.6870	6.7012	0.4318
13	0.5480	8.7925	0.6763	7.1246	0.4235
14	0.5386	9.3311	0.6665	7.5405	0.4159
15	0.5300	9.8611	0.6574	7.9495	0.4090
16	0.5220	10.3831	0.6489	8.3521	0.4026
17	0.5146	10.8977	0.6410	8.7489	0.3968
18	0.5078	11.4055	0.6336	9.1402	0.3913
19	0.5014	11.9069	0.6267	9.5264	0.3863
20	0.4954	12.4023	0.6201	9.9079	0.3815
21	0.4898	12.8920	0.6139	10.2850	0.3771
22	0.4844	13.3765	0.6080	10.6579	0.3729
23	0.4794	13.8559	0.6024	11.0268	0.3689
24	0.4747	14.3306	0.5971	11.3920	0.3652
25	0.4701	14.8007	0.5920	11.7536	0.3616
30	0.4505	17.0907	0.5697	13.5141	0.3462
40	0.4211	21.4252	0.5356	16.8435	0.3233
50	0.3996	25.5131	0.5103	19.9811	0.3066
100	0.3397	43.7539	0.4375	33.9680	0.2603
500	0.2329	151.4504	0.3029	116.4542	0.1783

N	T_u or T_a'	T_c	T_a	T_c'	T_u'
		Learning Table $\phi = 90\%$			
1	1.0000	1.0000	1.0000	1.0000	1.0000
2	0.9000	1.9000	0.9500	1.8000	0.8000
3	0.8462	2.7462	0.9154	2.5386	0.7386
4	0.8100	3.5562	0.8891	3.2400	0.7014
5	0.7830	4.3392	0.8678	3.9149	0.6749
6	0.7616	5.1008	0.8501	4.5695	0.6546
7	0.7439	5.8447	0.8350	5.2076	0.6381
8	0.7290	6.5737	0.8217	5.8320	0.6244
9	0.7161	7.2898	0.8100	6.4446	0.6126
10	0.7047	7.9945	0.7994	7.0469	0.6023
11	0.6946	8.6890	0.7899	7.6401	0.5932
12	0.6854	9.3745	0.7812	8.2251	0.5850
13	0.6771	10.0516	0.7732	8.8028	0.5777
14	0.6696	10.7211	0.7658	9.3737	0.5709
15	0.6626	11.3837	0.7589	9.9385	0.5648
16	0.6561	12.0398	0.7525	10.4976	0.5591
17	0.6501	12.6899	0.7465	11.0514	0.5538
18	0.6445	13.3344	0.7408	11.6002	0.5489
19	0.6392	13.9735	0.7354	12.1445	0.5442
20	0.6342	14.6078	0.7304	12.6844	0.5399
21	0.6295	15.2373	0.7256	13.2202	0.5358
22	0.6251	15.8624	0.7210	13.7521	0.5319
23	0.6209	16.4833	0.7167	14.2804	0.5283
24	0.6169	17.1002	0.7125	14.8052	0.5248
25	0.6131	17.7132	0.7085	15.3267	0.5215
30	0.5963	20.7269	0.6909	17.8893	0.5070
40	0.5708	26.5427	0.6636	22.8319	0.4850
50	0.5518	32.1420	0.6438	27.5881	0.4686
100	0.4966	58.1410	0.5814	49.6585	0.4214
500	0.3888	228.7851	0.4576	194.4098	0.3298

N	T_u or T_a'	T_c	T_a	T_c'	T_u'
		Learning Table $\phi = 95\%$			
1	1.0000	1.0000	1.0000	1.0000	1.0000
2	0.9500	1.9500	0.9750	1.9000	0.9000
3	0.9219	2.8719	0.9573	2.7658	0.8658
4	0.9025	3.7744	0.9436	3.6100	0.8442
5	0.8877	4.6621	0.9324	4.4386	0.8286
6	0.8758	5.5380	0.9230	5.2549	0.8163
7	0.8659	6.4039	0.9148	6.0612	0.8063
8	0.8574	7.2610	0.9077	6.8590	0.7978
9	0.8499	8.1112	0.9012	7.6494	0.7904
10	0.8433	8.9545	0.8954	8.4333	0.7839
11	0.8374	9.7919	0.8902	9.2115	0.7781
12	0.8320	10.6239	0.8853	9.9844	0.7729
13	0.8271	11.4511	0.8808	10.7525	0.7682
14	0.8226	12.2736	0.8767	11.5163	0.7638
15	0.8184	13.0921	0.8728	12.2761	0.7598
16	0.8145	13.9066	0.8692	13.0321	0.7560
17	0.8109	14.7174	0.8657	13.7846	0.7525
18	0.8074	15.5249	0.8625	14.5339	0.7493
19	0.8042	16.3291	0.8594	15.2801	0.7462
20	0.8012	17.1302	0.8565	16.0233	0.7433
21	0.7983	17.9285	0.8537	16.7639	0.7405
22	0.7955	18.7241	0.8511	17.5018	0.7379
23	0.7929	19.5170	0.8486	18.2372	0.7354
24	0.7904	20.3074	0.8461	18.9703	0.7331
25	0.7880	21.0955	0.8438	19.7012	0.7308
30	0.7775	25.0032	0.8334	23.3246	0.7208
40	0.7611	32.6838	0.8171	30.4443	0.7054
50	0.7486	40.2339	0.8045	37.4322	0.6938
100	0.7112	76.5864	0.7659	71.1212	0.6588
500	0.6314	340.6472	0.6813	315.6782	0.5847

Selected Answers

CHAPTER 1

1.2. 295.4 MJ, 2.7×10^{13} J = 2.7×10^7 MJ   **1.4. (a)** 5.5 m, 0.61 m; **(b)** 254 mm, 0.25 mm, 2540 mm, 0.0038 mm   **1.6. (a)** 240.29 kg/m^3, **(b)** 11.24 lbm/ft^3 **1.8. (a)** 2732°F, 392°F, 1832°F; **(b)** 93.3°C, 537.8°C   **1.10. (a)** 0.01 m^3, 3.54 m^3, 19.82 m^3; **(b)** 163.8 mm^3, 19,650 mm^3, 2,457,000 mm^3; **(c)** 764.5 m^3; **(d)** 1.5×10^{-2} in.^{3}, 4.88×10^{-3} in.^{3}, 9.16×10^{-2} in.^{3} **1.12. (a)** 34.07 DM/unit   **1.14. (a)** $57.60   **1.16. (a)** $3,150,000; **(b)** 10,546,875 country $\times$ currency; **(c)** $10,775,325 U.S. = 32.3×10^6 country $\times$ currency   **1.18.** $20,353 metal unit cost; billing cost = $142.47

CHAPTER 2

2.2. (a) 90.9 hr/1000 units; **(b)** 3.390 hr/100 units; **(c)** 6.5 units/hr

2.4.

Element	Standard Time
1	0.056 (min)
2	0.0143
3	0.115

Units per hour = 191

2.6. (a) Total standard time = 0.544; **(b)** production per hour = 110, hours per 100 units = 0.907   **2.8. (a)** Standard time = 0.039 min, pieces per hour = 1538; **(b)** standard time = 0.035 min/unit   **2.10. (a)** Total cost = $2770/job, cost per yard = $15.39/yd^3; **(b)** total cost = $3141.50/job, nonproduction cost = $2.064/job

2.12.

	Item			
	1	2	3	4
Observations	92	99	37	11
Percent	23	25	9	3
Hour	46	49.5	18.5	5.5

2.14.

Element	I	Relative Accuracy (%)
A	0.0061	± 18.3
B	0.0118	± 8.8
C	0.0224	± 3.4
D	0.0234	± 2.0

2.16. (a) N_i = 323; (b) N = 900, I = 3.9%; (c) N_i = 2010   **2.18.** (a) H_A = 11.55 hr/A, H_B = 23.2 hr/B, H_C = 46.5 hr/C   **2.19.** Effective gross hourly rate = \$12.91   **2.20.** (a) Effective gross hourly rate = \$23.71   **2.22.** Annual cost = \$32,760, annual excess cost = \$5695 **2.23.** Effective gross hourly cost = \$20.19 at FICA = 6.63%   **2.24.** \$136.00   **2.26.** (b) Dollars per hour = \$16.67; labor efficiency = 133.3%   **2.28.** \$24,675   **2.30** \$0.293/unit, \$0.397/unit, and \$0.19/unit; (c) \$0.352/unit and \$0.235/unit   **2.32.** (a) 25%; (b) \$0.943/unit

CHAPTER 3

3.2. (a) 78.75 BF; (b) 167.2 BF   **3.4.** (a) 0.94 ft^3; (b) 1.06 ft^3; (c) 1.41 ft^3 **3.6.** (a) \$8.97/ unit; (b) approx. yield = 48%   **3.8.** (a) Unit cost of raw material = \$6.89 without salvage; (b) cost of waste = \$4.22; (c) yield = 32%   **3.10.** (a) Finished block = 16.3 in.^{3}, raw block = 22 in.^{3}; (b) yield = 74%   **3.12.** (a) Left design material cost = \$0.063/unit and \$.06/unit, right design \$0.057/unit or considering waste, \$0.055/unit   **3.14.** (d) LTR = \$12.54/unit, Del = \$10.01/unit, MOOP = \$11.14/unit   **3.16.** (a) Original = \$8.95; (b) last = \$9.00; (c) current = \$12.00; (d) LTR = \$10.01; (e) delivery = \$11.84; (f) MOOP = \$9.78   **3.18.** (a) \$2.20/100 units, \$0.1344/100 units, \$2.33/100 units   **Case Study:** A = 6754.4 mm^3 = 7.09 g, B = 8639.3 mm^3 = 9.07 g, C = 40,054 mm^3 = 42.06 g, prorated loss = \$0.53, shape efficiency = 85.3%

CHAPTER 4

4.2. Total assets = \$5350; Total liabilities = \$3560; Capital Stock = \$1790.   **4.4.** Total assets = \$485,000; Total liabilities = \$235,000; Capital Stock = \$250,000.   **4.7.** Net profit (to retained earnings) = \$300,000; Total Assets = \$900,000.   **4.8.** Total assets = \$1,500,000; Total liabilities & net worth = \$1,500,000.   **4.10.** (a) Net profit = \$45,000; Total assets = \$715,000.

4.12.

Year	AC Cost Rec.	Straight Line	Sum of Years Digits
1	\$4300	\$ 4000	\$ 7273
2	7740	4000	6545
3	6880	4000	5818
	\$18,920	\$12,000	\$19,636

4.13.

Year	SL Dep.	Book Value	AC Dep.	Book Value
1	\$47,000	\$203,000	\$50,000	\$200,000
2	47,000	156,000	80,000	120,000

4.15.

Year	ACR Dep	Book Value	SL Dep	Book Value	SOYD Dep	Book Value
0		250		250		250
1	50	200	42	208	71	179
2	80	120	42	167	60	118

4.16. (a) Dep = \$.175/mi, **(b)** Cost = \$5421/yr = \$.542 mi.

4.18.

	80%	100%	125%
Direct costing	.6	.6	.6
Absorption	1.8	1.56	1.37

4.20.

Center	$C_w + C_m$	%	Area OH Rate	Dollars OH Rate	Hours OH Rate
Fab	31,000	76	\$1.726	6.151	25.625
Assm	8,500	18	1.902	5.034	19.531
Fin	6,000	5	3.646	6.346	25.000
Plant	45,500	100	1.869	5.913	24.023

4.22.

Job	Blanket Total OH	Dept.
1	\$59.40	\$18.00
2	59.40	91.60

4.24.

Dept.	Total OH	Mach Rate
Fab	\$55,568	\$34.73
Assm	16,048	25.08
Fin	10,084	31.51
Total	\$81,700	

Plant wide rate on basis of direct labor = \$2.62

4.25 Total variable cost = \$1,217,930

CHAPTER 5

5.4. (a) Mean = 4.9, median = 5, mode = 5, range = 8, std. dev. = 2.4   **5.5.** y = \$2592
5.6. (a) $y = 85 + 7.9x$; **(b)** when $x = 11$, $y = 186.6$ **5.8.** $y = 128.7x + 1020$ **5.10.**
(a) $t_\alpha = 1.812$ **5.11.** $y = 84.875 = 2.389x$; **(b)** $S^2_{y_T} = 1.59$; **(c)** 120.4, 125.8   **5.12. (b)**
$y = 96.6 + 4.74x$ **5.14. (a)** $y = -0.1156 + 0.0608x$; **(b)** $y = 0.0139 + 0.0026x$
5.16. (a) $T = 348.7N^{-0.44}$; **(b)** $\log Y = 2.624 - 0.364 \log Y$, $T = 419N^{-0.364}$ **5.18. (a)**
$y = 59.4(1.74)^x$; **(b)** $y = 101x^{0.289}$ **5.20. (a)** $y = 0.93x^{0.82}$; **(b)** $y = 1.403 \times 10^4 + 0.0581x$
5.22. $y = 1184.5 + 29.8x - 985y$ **5.24.** $y = 12.72 + 0.3517x - 1.6y$

5.26.

Period	Price	Moving Total	Moving Average	$S_t(x)$
1	60.20	——	——	60.20
2	60.50	——	——	60.30
3	68.70	——	——	62.40
4	60.20	249.60	62.40	61.90

5.28.

	Date			
	10	9	8	7
Cost	23.2	24.1	26.3	25.7
Moving total	---	---	73.6	76.1
Moving average	---	---	24.5	25.4

5.30. Bid cost = $101 million   **5.32.** C_{20} = $2.59 × 10^6   **5.34.** French cost = $285, U.S.
= $269

5.36.

Period	1	2	3	4
Index	100	100.1	102.5	103.8

5.38. (a) I_5 = 144; **(b)** C = 231.14   **Case Study:** y = 84.9 + 13.1x; lost to inflation $328.67;
r = 11.4%

CHAPTER 6

6.4. $73/ft^2 **6.6 (a)** 1360 hr; **(b)** s = −0.2009, K = 252.23, T_a' = $114.9 for N = 50, T_a' =
$87 for N = 200; **(c)** T_c' = 3171 hr; **(d)** T_u' = 781 for N = 5, T_u' = 638 for N = 40; **(e)** K = 197.7,
T_a' = 114 for N = 101   **6.8. (a)** s = −0.2615, K = 162.4, T_a' = 108.3 at N = 15, T_c' = 2370
at N = 25; **(b)** s = −0.467, K = 4547, T_a' = 730.5 at N = 50, T_u' = 391 at N = 50, T_a' = 528.4
hr and T_u' = 282 hr at N = 100   **6.10. (a)** T_u' = $3346 for A at N = 15, T_u' = $3975 for B at N
= 15; **(b)** s = −0.2385 at ϕ = 90%, K = 360,579 and T = 164,318 at N = 27

6.14.

N	T_u or T_a'	T_c	T_a	T_c'	T_u'
2	0.7300	1.7300	0.8650	1.4600	0.4600
3	0.6073	2.3373	0.7791	1.8218	0.3618
4	0.5329	2.8702	0.7176	2.1317	0.3099

6.16. $27,731   **6.18.** m = 0.318, $159.10

6.20.

Year	Depreciation	Maintenance	Value	3% Price	Depreciation	Value
2	6,437	400	6,300	13,351	6,437	6,694
3	8,408	800	3,929	13,937	8,408	4,737
10	13,006	2,000	−1,869	17,141	13,006	2,135

(a) Trade in at end of year 8 approx. **(b)** Should not trade in during first 10 years   **6.22.** Average A
= $12.88 × 10^6$, s = $10.01 × 10^6$, cost Y = $−8 \ln[1 − F(y)]$ **6.24. (a)** C total = 57.74,
C_{ave} = $5.77; **(b)** C bar = 7.67   **6.26. (a)** $E(C_T)$ = $28.75, var (C) = $3.007; **(b)** prob. =
94.4%   **6.27. (a)** E_g = 2.1%, E_{ad} = 14.8%, E_{at} = 0.035 min. Using the P values, variable and
constant elements will be the same; **(b)** elements 2 and 5 constant, E_g = 12.6%, E_{ad} = 24%, E_{at} =
0.22 min   **6.28. (a)** 3.65 min, $1.52/unit, $152/.00 units, 16.4 pc/hr   **6.30** Y_1 = 5.85 × 10^{−4} +
2.74 × 10^{−3}X_1, Y_4 = 0.07 + 0.14X_4, Y_2 = 0.031, Y_3 = 0.027

6.32.

Element	Equation	Type
1	2.32 + 0.029 ft^3	Constant
2	−0.208 + 0.048 BF	Variable
3	5.129 + 0.056 lb	Variable
4	14.89 + 0.961 lb	Variable
5	6.686 + 0.006 lb	Constant

6.34. (a) Bench-mark cost = $1,440,329; **(b)** engineering factor = 0.85, erection factor = 1.40, direct materials = 2.75; **(c)** total cost approx. = $13,375,000   **6.36. (a)** Cost for 500 units = $950, cost for 700 units = $1277, marginal total cost = $327, marginal unit cost = $1.635, total profit = $23, min. break-even = $327   **6.38. (a)** $C_T = 10^5 + 200n - 3 \times 10^{-3}n^2 + 10^{-7}n^3$, marginal cost = $200 - 6 \times 10^{-3}n + 3 \times 10^{-7}n^2$; **(b)** $6 \times 10^{-3} + 6 \times 10^{-7}n = 0$, $n = 10,000$, $C_m = \$170$ min., $C_a = \$190$ average cost, $R_m = 250$, total profit = $50n + 3 \times 10^{-3}n^2 - 10^{-7}n^3 - 10^5$, marginal profit = $50 + 6 \times 10^{-3}n - 3 \times 10^{-7}n^2$, at marginal profit = 0, $n = 800$

Case Study:

Cavities per die	Tool Cost	Unit Cost	Total Revenue	Marginal Cost	Marginal Revenue	Marginal Profit
1	$ 5,400	$13,500	0		0	
2	6,200	6,750	$6,750	$800	$6,750	$5,950
3	7,000	4,500	2,250	800	2,250	1,450
16	17,400	843.75	56.25	800	56.25	-744

Full cost is $11,175. Optimum = four cavities per die. Student should note that table is incomplete.

CHAPTER 7

7.2. (a) Handling cost = $1.65; **(b)** 3.19 min.; **(c)** 30.13 min.; **(d)** Tool changing cost = $1.99, T = 30.13 min; **(e)** Tool cost/operation = $.299   **7.4. (a)** L_a = 497 mm, L_d = 750 mm, L_s = 5 mm, L = 1257 mm; **(b)** Rough pass = 16.70 in., finish pass = 15.85 in.; **(c)** L = 21.8 mm.   **7.5. (a)** L = 825 in.; **(b)** L = 11.38 in.; **(c)** Cast iron = .15 in. Stainless steel = .10 in.   **7.6. (a)** L = 11.125 in., t_m = 1.36 min., N = 324 rpm, f_{at} = 8.16 in./min.; **(b)** L = 2.125, Rough t_m = .13 min., N = 325 rpm, finish t_m = 1.55 min., N = 363 rpm, feed = 16.3 in./min., 13.7 in./min.   **7.8. (a)** L = 1.27 in., time to drill = 1.85 min., time to tap = 2.65 min.; **(b)** L = 1.176 in., time to drill = 0.294 min., time to tap = 0.376 min.   **7.10.** n = 0.11, K = 162, tool life for 60 min. = 8300 min. (hardly a useful rpm), N = 286 rpm   **7.12.** T_{max} = 36 min., V_{max} = 120 ft./min., t_m = 8.71 min., T_u = 11.68 min.   **7.14.** V_{max} is about 340 fpm, V_{max} = 347 fpm, T_{max} = 11.3 min.   **7.16.** Unit material cost = $0.41/unit

Operation No.	Setup	Cycle
1	0.1	0.001
2	0.1	0.001
3	0.5	0.038
4	0.3	.043
5	0.1	.001
6	.1	.005
7	.3	.005
8	.3	.005
9	.3	.027
10	.1	.001
11	0.1	0.005
	2.3 hr	.132 hr

7.18.

Tool element	Time
2 dog ears	60 hr.
1 90° bend	30
1 90° bend	30
	120 = $9000

7.20. Tooling cost = $6800; Unit op cost is about $5.90/hr = C_{dlo}; $\Sigma\, C_{dlo}$ = $283.20, C_{dm} = $1446.30, $\Sigma\, C_{ot}$ = $6800; Total operation cost is about $8532; Unit op cost = $0.71

7.22. Approx length = 1.125 m., C_{dm} = $0.0079/unit, C_{ot} = $5875, C_{ot} = $0.1469/unit;

Element	Setup	Cycle
1	0.1	0.001
2	0.4	0.0015
3	0.4	0.0015
4	0.4	0.0015
5	0.1	0.005
	1.4	0.0105

C_{dl} = $0.2107/unit, C_n = $0.016/unit, operation cost = $0.3815/unit

7.24. **(a)**

Direct labor	= $0.0341	
Variable OH	= 0.0256	
Material OH	= 0.0084	
Make value	= 0.0681	
Vendor price	= 0.075,	decision: make

(b)

Full variable cost	= $0.0681	
Fixed OH	= 0.05	
Make value	= 0.1181	
Vendor price	= 0.1180,	decision: buy

7.26.

Takeoff	n_i	Subtotal	Manhour	Unit Cost	Row Total
Excavation	444		0.027	$112.5	$ 180.60
Forms	675	$ 303	0.035		1166.05
Steel	248	223	0.004		257.40
Concrete	11	810			809.92
Backfill	30.7		0.02		92.10
Total		1336			2506.1
Cost/yd³		120.3			$ 225.57

7.28.

Takeoff	Qty	Material	Manhour	Unit Cost	Row Total
Facebrick	960	$ 921.60	38.4	$25.20	$1889.28
Facebrick	640	614.90	25.6	25.20	1259.52
Rein.	588	117.60	3.5	25.20	205.80
Bolts	20	15.20	1.0	25.20	40.40
Sill	80	72.00	6.4	26.80	243.52
Total		1740.80			3638.52
Cost/LF		43.52			90.96
Cost/SF		5.44			11.37

7.30

Description	Qty	Material	Manhour	Man Cost	Total
Grading	10,000		8	$2240	$ 2240
Forms		$ 784	12	3024	3808
Pouring	10,000		16	4736	4736
Rein.	10,000	4900			4900
Concrete	200	12200			12200
Bumpers	39	312			312
Lines	840	84			84
Total		$18280			12280
Cost/SF		$ 1.82			2.82

7.32.

No.	Total Cycle Time	Total Time	Labor Cost
1	4.19	54.69	$ 834.02
2	12.53	12.73	213.23
3	8.36	34.36	575.53
4	2.51	15.41	258.12
5	1.28	26.38	402.30
6	3.75	3.85	55.83
7	1.50	1.60	28.00
			$2367.03

(a) Joint labor cost is approx. $2,637.03; (c) Net labor cost = $1.85/unit

CHAPTER 8

8.1.

Period	0	1	2	3	4	5
Cumulative		−50	−52.5	−47.5	−25	0	20

8.2.

Period	0	1	2	3	4	5
Cumulative	−120	−122.5	−117	−95	−76	60

8.4. $s = -0.1041$ or 93%, $K = 99.3$, $T_c' = 24.677$ hr   **8.6.** Average for lot = 57.9 hr., cost = $85,085   **8.8** (a) For $\phi = 75\%$, $K = 1107.5$, For $\phi = 85\%$, $K = 908$, For $\phi = 75\%$, $T_u = 1107$ (b) Between $\phi = 80\%$ and 75%, 44.54 hr. less; Between $\phi = 80\%$ and 85%, 43.8 hr. more
8.10. Retrofit $K = 271.9$, $T_c = 8739$ for units 1-50; For units 50-100, $K = 150$; $T_c = 6,847.4$; Additional total hours = 15.586 hrs.   **8.12.** Note similarity to case study in Chapter 7

(a)

Operation	Unit Cost of Labor and OH
1	0.00215
2	0.0555
3	0.05551
4	0.00257
5	0.03540
	0.15113
Material	0.0966
Cost total	0.24773
G & A	0.06194
Sales	0.03716

Cost = $0.34684

8.12. (b) Full cost = $868.82 total; (c) Total unit cost = $0.343   **8.14.** (a) Total direct material cost/unit is about $12.90; Total direct labor cost/unit is about $4.784; (b) Cost of material and labor is about $17.68; (c) G & A & S = 35.36, Cost = 53.04, Margin = 13.26, Sales price = $66.30; (d) Sales price = $70.72, profit = $17.68

8.15. Material cost is approx. $3.42; For $N = 500$, approx. cost = $9560; For $N = 1000$, approx. cost = $12,385   **8.16.** (a) Approx. bid price = $27,180, $T = 120$ hr.

8.17.

Cost item	10th unit	10 unit total
Labor	$ 487,782	$ 5,707,989
Material	15,678	168,666
Support	6,420	67,167
Overhead	494,202	5,775,156
Distribution	98,840	115,031
Sales	9,884	115,503
Full	1,112,806	12,989,512
Profit	111,280	1,298,951
Price	1,224,087	14,288,463

8.18. P = \$200, R_m = \$0.25, P = \$228.57, R_m = 42.9%   **8.20.** P = \$33.33/unit
8.22. (a) Full variable cost = \$3.; at price = \$4, contribution = 75%; at price = \$6, contribution
= 50%   **8.24** t = 5.1 yr, margin = \$6.50, t = 10.5 yr   **8.25.** Total cost to importer =
\$2,398   **8.26.** Single plant price = \$3.45, twin plant price = \$2.26

CHAPTER 9

9.2. Cost of one bridge = \$559,787   **9.3.** Cost of bags = \$10,251   **9.6.** Four levels
9.7. Cumulative baseline cost = \$690

9.8.

Period	Commitment	Expenditure
0	650	—
1	1170	520
2	2340	1625
3	1820	2535
4	520	1365
5	—	455
	6500	6500

Approx midpoint = 2 3/4 periods   **9.9.** Project cost total = \$11,350   **9.10.** R_o = 4.74%, R_j
= 2.47%, C_{op} = \$10.815 × 10^6 **9.12.** Job overhead rate = 30.9%, Office overhead rate =
50%, Direct cost = \$256,000   **9.13.** 25% underrun is about \$24 × 10^6, 25% overrun is about
\$26 × 10^6, 50% overrun is about \$27 × 10^6 **9.15.** Contingent present time cost = \$43,000
approx. above real cost of \$100,000. Contingent cash flow is about \$44,075 when indexed. There is
very little to commend this practice.   **9.17.** C_a = \$1,600,000, C_m = \$2,288,000, t_{ai} = 0.7
month, t_{af} = 3.6 month.

Period	CBV %	Profit	Retainage	Net Cash Flow
1	14.3	288,800	1,144,000	(915,200)
2	42.9	686,400	2,402,400	(1,716,000)
3	71.5	1,144,000	2,631,200	(1,487,200)
4	92.9	1,486,400	2,284,000	(797,600)
5	100.0	1,600,000	1,311,200	(288,800)
6	100.0	1,600,000	800,000	800,000
7	100.0	1,600,000	0	1,600,000

9.18.

Period	Net Cash Flow 10^6	Period	Net Cash Flow 10^6
1	(1.3)	9	(8.2)
2	(3.9)	10	(7.4)
3	(6.4)	11	(7.0)
4	(8.6)	12	(6.2)
5	(10.6)	13	(3.5)
6	(10.2)	14	(1.1)
7	(9.4)	15	(5.4)
8	(8.9)	16	7.5
		17	15.0

9.20. Cost to contractor = \$7,272,727; Cost to subcontractor = \$6,060,606; Total cost of labor =
\$3,030,303; Manpower = 101,010 hours; 582.9 man months; Average number of direct labor
employees = 117; Maximum number of direct labor employers = 167   **9.22.** Total interest paid
= \$2,831, Net profit = \$12,169

9.23.

Month	10^5 End of Month Outstanding
1	$1.32
2	3.98
3	6.52
4	8.76

9.24.

Month	Outstanding Loan
1	$ 932,198
2	1,976,260
3	2,202,225
4	1,966,610

9.26. (a) Total budget cost committed = $100 million; (b) Total budget cost expended about $100 million. **9.27.** (a) 10%, 20%; (b) 17.5% **9.28.** (a) % return = 16.7%, payback = 6 years; (b) For process A, capital is recovered between 3rd and 4th year, for process B, capital is recovered between 2nd and 3rd year **9.30.** (a) $90; (b) 4%; (c) $90,000 simple; $107,946 compound; (d) $565; (e) $8572; (f) $422; (g) 22.5 years; (h) 1 year 6.67%, 2 years 3.28%. **9.32.** (a) NPW = $18, NFW = $24, Annual eq. = $426.80, Net annual equivalent = $7.35; (b) NPW = $55, NFW = $71, Net annual eq. = $22
9.40. Approximate solution to project bid summary

Project: Transmission Line	
Direct labor	$3,417,000
Direct material	1,575,000
Subcontract items	440,000
Facilities	198,800
Equipment	600,000
Engineering	42,000
Office overhead at 4%	217,000
Job overhead at 5%	272,000
Subtotal	$6,761,800
Contingency, 1/2%	33,800
Interest with retainage at $i = 1\ 1/4\%$	84,500
Total	$6,880,100
Profit, 8%	550,500
Bid	$7,430,600

9.41. Approximate solution to project bid summary

Direct labor	$9,240,000
Direct material, sub contract	12,133,000
Facilities and equipment	1,315,000
Engineering	84,000
Direct costs	$14,457,000
Office overhead @ 4% direct costs	578,000
Job overhead @ 5% direct costs	722,000
Subtotal	$15,758,000
Contingency @ 1/2%	79,000
Interest with retainage, 1 1/4%	79,000
Total	$16,034,000
Markup @ 8%	1,283,000
Bid	$17,316,000

CHAPTER 10

10.2. (a) Maximum value is given each goal column

$G_1 : A_1$ $E_{11} = 80 > E_{i1}, i = 2,3,4,5$
$G_2 : A_2$ $E_{32} = 70 > E_{i2}, i = 1,2,4,5$
$G_3 : A_5$ $E_{53} = 75 > E_{i3}, i = 1,2,3,4$

(b) $(X E_{11} + E_{12} + E_{13}) > (X E_{i1} + E_{i2} + E_{i3})\ i = 2,3,4,5$

i	E_{i1}	$E_{i2} + E_{i3}$	X_i
1	80	41	—
2	50	83	1.4
3	35	91	1.1
4	39	95	1.3
5	25	100	.9

Thus $X > 1.4$

10.3. The $20,000 is a sunk cost and is irrelevant to the decision, except that it gives a feel for winning of the business. You should be willing to spend $50,000. If you win the business after spending exactly $50,000 more, your prosperity is weakened by $20,000. Obviously, business can't be conducted this way for long.   **10.5. (a)** The new system should include $10,000 for rent of the building since it can be rented and therefore offers an opportunity for return. The meaningful measure = net equivalent annual income − rent. **(b)** If no renter, the answer is yes, as this affects the opportunity. **(c)** If a renter is available for one or two years, and a system is available, then the discounted value is used to choose the most effective choice. **(d)** Yes, once the decision is made, the alternative is given up, and consideration is only useful in a past-tense way, i.e., helpful to future choices.

10.6. Before the decision:
      System cost$_1 = E_1 + P_1 + W_1 + OM_1 + I_1 + R_1 + C_1$
      $SC_2 = E_2 + P_2 + W_2 + OM_2 + I_2 + R_2 + C_2$
      Marginal difference $= E_1 - E_2 + W_1 - W_2 + OM_1 - OM_2 + I_1 - R_2 + C_1 - C_2$
      Nonrecurring = engineering + project + (sometimes product)
      Investment = product + project
      Opportunity cost for selection option 1: I_1
      Opportunity cost for selection option 2: $I_2 = 0, R_1 = 0$
      After the decision: There is no opportunity
10.13. Alternatives:
      I. ABC alone with reconstruction, mandatory
      II. ABC and ADC jointly
            Project costs for plan I = 21.68×10^6
            Project costs for Plan II = 45.22×10^6
            Difference between plans = 23.54×10^6
            Discounted traffic costs for ABC = 125.62×10^6
            Discounted traffic costs for Plan II = 116.75×10^6
            Undiscounted traffic costs for ABC = 201.66×10^6
            B/C = .4   Advise ABC

10.14. Undiscounted B/C = 7.6 = discounted B/C   **10.16.** $B/C_A = 1.26, B/C_B = 1.46, B/C_C$
= 1.19, $B/C_D = 1.32$, Select B.

10.17.

Cost Element	Total Cash Flow
Design	$ 40,000
Product	265,000
Installation	30,000
Manpower	327,040
Preventive	3,900
Corrective	5,840
Power	26,864
Spares	1,326
Undiscounted LCC	699,970
Discounted LCC	476,498

10.18. $C_1 = \$1.39/hr.$, $C_2 = \$2.21/hr.$, $C_3 = \$1.40$; Select contractor 1, but contractor 3 is so close that other factors might be considered. **10.21.** A = $387.50, B = $385.00, C = $325.00

Case Study No. of PM actions = 1/yr
Cost/yr = $104
Corrective maintenance = $41.60/yr.
Power cost = $13.875/yr
Total undiscounted LCC = $202,300
Total discounted LCC = $136,600

CHAPTER 11

11.1.

Element	Cost
Direct labor	$1,906.25
Direct material	1,376.00
Other material	145.00
Overhead	953.13
Profit	1,095.10
Total	$5,475.48

Final profit = $225.50

11.3.

Direct labor at 10th unit =	$570,807
Direct material	16,866
Overhead	570,807
Subtotal	$1,158,480
Profit @ 15%	173,772
Total	$1,332,252

If actual cost = $1,250,000, error = $91,520 in cost
= 7.9% of cost or
= 6.9% of total bid
Net profit = $82,252

For effective profit margin = $82,252 is 6.2% of total bid or 6.6% of actual cost, and 7.1% of estimated cost. **11.5.** Capture rate = 48.7%

11.6.

Quarter	Error %	Capture %	Productivity
1	1.04	51.9	.93
2	−.50	49.8	1.00
3	−6.01	47.1	1.06

11.7. Hours first: Total variance $= -\$0.034$ favorable; Wages first: Total variance $= -\$0.034$ favorable **11.8** Total variance $= \$224$ U **11.10.** Total variance $= \$2.44$ U **11.12.** Net variance $= \$60.7$ U, PF $= 1.06$ approx **11.14.** \$125 variance unfavorable, PF $= 1.045$ **11.16.** Net variance for labor $= \$4.97$. Lot hours estimated $= 5.83$, material net variance $= \$244$ U **11.17 (a)** \$0.207 unfavorable **11.18.** Net variance on constant overhead percentage

	Estimate	Variance	Actual
Direct labor	\$ 5.28	+0.53	\$ 5.81
Material	17.38	−0.45	16.93
Overhead	7.92	0.80	8.72
	\$30.58	0.88 unfavorable	\$31.46

Net variance on constant overhead amount

	Estimate	Variance	Actual
Direct labor	\$ 5.28	+0.53	\$ 5.81
Material	17.38	−0.45	16.93
Overhead	7.92	0	7.92
	\$30.58	+0.08 unfavorable	\$30.66

11.20 (a) Net profit percent of net sales $= 19.8\%$;
(b) Percent of net sales of profit contribution at actual: I, 34.5%, II, 47% (best), III, 8.2%.

11.21 Percent of net sales $= 2.6\%$ final.

11.22

		Variance		Forecast		
Period	Schedule	Cost	BCWP	ACWP	Variance
4	$\approx \frac{3}{4}$ mo.	\$1,500			
5	≈ 1.1	1,200	5800	6800	1000
6	$\approx .5$	1,100	6400	6900	500

11.25.

SV 4			SV 5		Approx.	
\$	Periods	CV 4	\$	Periods	Overrun	Slippage
\$1000	0.75	\$1500	\$750	1	\$1300	1

CHAPTER 12

12.1.

Pile, in.	Contract value
12	\$1,350,000
18	1,875,328
20	550,425
	\$3,775,753

12.2.

Center	Hourly Cost	Job	Markup Hourly Cost	Quote
Light	\$39.16	80	\$ 43.80	\$3446.08
Heavy	90.88	40	109.06	4362.24
Assembly	32.19	20	37.02	740.37
Finishing	42.33	15	44.47	66.70

12.4   Cost plus profit = $952,000

12.6

Weight	$/100 lb
120 lb	$143.45
2000	88.57
6000	82.95

References

ADRIAN, JAMES J., *Construction Estimating,* Reston Publishing Company, Inc., a Prentice-Hall Company, Reston, Va., 1982.

AMSTEAD, B.H., PHILLIP F. OSTWALD and MYRON L. BEGEMAN, *Manufacturing Processes,* 7th ed., John Wiley & Sons, New York, 1977.

ARMSTRONG, J. SCOTT, *Long-Range Forecasting,* Wiley Interscience, New York, 1978.

BLANCHARD, BENJAMIN S., *Design and Manage to Life Cycle Cost,* M/A Press, Portland, Oreg., 1978.

Building Cost File, Construction Publishing Co., Inc., New York, Annual Volume.

CALDER, GRANVILLE, *The Principles and Techniques of Engineering Estimating,* Pergamon Press Ltd., Oxford, 1978.

CLARK, FORREST D., and A. B. LORENZONI, *Applied Cost Engineering,* Marcel Dekker, Inc., New York, 1978.

COLLIER, KEITH, F., *Fundamentals of Construction Estimating For Project Control,* Prentice-Hall, Inc., Englewood Cliffs, N.J., 1974.

GALLAGHER, PAUL F., *Parametric Estimating for Executives and Estimators,* Van Nostrand Reinhold Company, Inc., New York, 1982.

GODFREY, ROBERT STURGES, Ed., *Building Construction Cost Data,* Robert Snow Means Company, Duxbury, Ma., Annual Volume.

HAJEK, VICTOR, *Management of Engineering Projects,* McGraw-Hill Book Company, New York, 1965.

HUMPHREYS, K. and S. KATELL, *Basic Cost Engineering,* Marcel Dekker, Inc., New York, 1982.

JELEN, F. C., and J. BLACK, Eds., *Cost and Optimization Engineering,* 2nd Ed., McGraw-Hill Book Company, New York, 1982.

Machining Data Handbook, 3rd ed., Machinability Data Center, Metcut Research Associates, Inc., Cincinnati, Ohio, 1980.

MALSTROM, ERIC M., *What Every Engineer Should Know About Manufacturing Cost Estimating,* Marcel Dekker, Inc., New York, 1981.

MATHEWS, LAWRENCE M., *Estimating Manufacturing Costs,* McGraw-Hill Book Company, New York, 1983.

O'NEIL, JAMES N., *Construction Cost Estimating for Project Control,* Prentice-Hall, Inc., Englewood Cliffs, N.J., 1982.

OSTWALD, PHILLIP F., Ed., *Manufacturing Cost Estimating,* Society of Manufacturing Engineers, Dearborn, Mich., 1980.

OSTWALD, PHILLIP F., *American Machinist Manufacturing Cost Estimating Guide,* McGraw-Hill Book Company, New York, 1983.

PATRASCU, ANGHEL, *Construction Cost Engineering,* Craftsman Book Co., Solana Beach, Calif., 1978.

PETERS, MAX S. and KLAUS D. TIMMERHAUS, *Plant Design and Economics for Chemical Engineers,* 3rd ed., McGraw-Hill Book Company, New York, 1980.

RIGGS, JAMES L., *Engineering Economics,* 2nd ed., McGraw-Hill Book Company, New York, 1982.

STEWART, RODNEY D., *Cost Estimating,* John Wiley & Sons, New York, 1982.

THEUSEN, H. G., W. J. FABRYCKY, and G. J. THUESON, *Engineering Economy,* 5th Ed., Prentice-Hall, Inc., Englewood Cliffs, N.J., 1977.

Index